A HISTORY OF
INDIAN LITERATURE

MAURICE WINTERNITZ

A HISTORY OF *Indian Literature*

VOLUME ONE

Introduction, Veda, Epics, Purāṇas and Tantras

A NEW AUTHORITATIVE TRANSLATION
FROM ORIGINAL GERMAN BY
V. SRINIVASA SARMA

MOTILAL BANARSIDASS
Delhi Varanasi Patna Madras

First Published in Delhi 1981
Reprinted 1987

MOTILAL BANARSIDASS
Bungalow Road, Jawahar Nagar, Delhi 110 007
Branches
Chowk, Varanasi 221 001
Ashok Rajpath, Patna 800 004
120, Royapettah High Road, Mylapore, Madras 600 004

ISBN: 81-208-0264-0

PRINTED IN INDIA
BY JAINENDRA PRAKASH JAIN AT SHRI JAINENDRA PRESS, A-45 NARAINA INDUSTRIAL AREA, PHASE I, NEW DELHI 110 028 AND PUBLISHED BY NARENDRA PRAKASH JAIN FOR MOTILAL BANARSIDASS, DELHI 110 007.

TRANSLATOR'S NOTE

The present edition of the German work *Geschichte der Indischen Literatur* by Moriz Winternitz published by K.F. Koehler Verlag, Stuttgart has been translated and revised in the light of Mrs. Ketkar's translation.

FOREWORD

As the publishers have announced in their notice, the collection of works in which the present volume devoted to the oldest period of Indian Literature appears is meant not for scholarly circles but for all educated people of the nation. Accordingly, always in the course of my work I was having in mind such readers as know nothing of Indian literature and do not have any special knowledge of the subject of Indology; I however did not think of those people who would also like to know something about Indian literature in the course of one short hour; but I had in view those people who would like to get such a thorough acquaintance with it as is possible without a knowledge of Indian languages. But a history of Indian literature cannot be, like a history of German, English or French literature, a simple presentation of the development process of already known literary works, but it must also give as much information as possible about the contents of literary phenomena through extracts and synopsis in all cases where there are no German translations, and this is so in a majority of cases. In other words—the History of Literature must be at the same time also the description of Literature. Especially in the case of the popular epics and *purāṇas*, with which the second half of the present volume deals, very few have appeared till now in German translations. Comprehensive synopsis and extracts have therefore had to be provided, if the reader should get even a faint idea of the works dealt with.

Consequently the volume grew to a larger extent than was originally planned. One more factor contributed to this. In particular the oldest Indian literature treated in this volume is in a way hanging in the air. Not even one of the many and extensive works which form part of the Veda, of the epics or of the *purāṇas*, can be attributed with any degree of certainty to one century or the other. It is however simply impossible to give information about the age of the Veda, the *Mahābhārata*, the *Rāmāyaṇa* and even the *Purāṇas*. Even the layman will not be satisfied if we say that we do not know anything definite about the time of these works. It is necessary to draw clearly the boundaries within which our ignorance ranges and to state the reasons supporting an approximate fixation of time although this was attained only through presumptions. So it was necessary to devote more extensive chapters to the questions of the age of the Veda, the epics and the *Purāṇas*. I emphasise particularly that these chapters too are written not for the specialist alone but mainly for the layman above described, whom I had in view as my reader. If in spite of this they contain something which is new even for the specialist—perhaps something which could even provoke contradiction—then the reason is that they deal with questions which have been in recent years objects of new investigations, new discoveries and several controversies.

The bibliography furnished in the notes is meant for the specialist whom it shall convince of the correctness of the author's stand on the most important issues under dispute. Of course a book written for the 'Educated people of the Nation' should stand the test of the specialist and should be subjected to it thoroughly. On the other hand, in my notes for the layman I thought it important to draw his attention to all the accessible German translations and where these are not available, to the English and French translations. I have made use of these translations only in a few cases, where they appeared to me to produce the original in an excellent manner. Where no other translator's name is mentioned, the translations are by me.

After these explanations it is not surprising that the original frame of work conceived for one volume was found to be inadequate for this History of Indian Literature. And I am indeed grateful to the publisher that he was convinced of the reasons adduced for enlarging the framework originally planned and gave his approval to a second volume. This enlargement entirely corresponds with the extent and significance of the Indian Literature—for which I may draw my readers' attention to the Introduction (p. 1 ff). While the present volume treats in a certain way the 'Prehistoric' time of the Indian Literature,—at least the beginnings of the Veda as well as the popular epics reach back to a hoary past shrouded in obscurity incapable of being reduced to definite dates—the second volume shall begin with the Buddhistic literature and introduce the reader to the literature of the actual historical time of India.

Information about the works which served as sources to me and to which I am indebted, is found in the Notes to the individual chapters. It was not possible for me to record in every individual case, what I owe to the basic *Academic lectures on the History of Indian Literature* by Albrecht Weber (2nd edition, Berlin 1876) and to the inspiring and valuable lectures on *Indian Literature and Culture in Historical Development* by Leopold Schroeder (Leipzig 1881). I am also indebted to the valuable "Bulletins des Religions de l'Inde" by A. Barth (in the *Revue de l' Histoire des Religions* I, III, V, XI, XIV, XXVIII f, XLI f and XLV, 1880-1902) although I have not made special mention of it each time. The scholarly essays of H. Oldenberg *Die Literatur des alten Indien* (The Literature of Ancient India) (Stuttgart and Berlin 1903) are rather an aesthetic observation and assessment of the Indian literature, which was far from my intention. The works of A. Baumgartner (*History of World-Literature* II, The literatures of India and East Asia, 3rd and 4th edition, Freiburg i. B. 1902), A. A. Macdonell (*A History of Sanskrit Literature*, London 1900) and V. Henry (*Les Litteratures de l'Inde*, Paris 1904) offered me scarcely anything new. Richard Pischel's short but excellent survey of Indian Literature in Part I, section VII ('Oriental literatures') of the collected works *Die Kultur der Gegenwart* (Berlin and Leipzig 1906) appeared only when my manuscript was already completed and was also partly printed. I should also mention the services rendered to me by the *Orientalische Bibliographie* of Lucian Scherman which is so indispensable to every orientalist. In conclusion I would like to thank sincerely all those who have reviewed favourably or criticised objectively the first half-volume which appeared two years ago.

Prag-Kgl. Weinberge
15th October 1907. M. Winternitz

LIST OF ABBREVIATIONS USED IN THE NOTES

ABA = Abhandlungen der Berliner Akademie der Wissenschaften, Philol.-histor. Klasse.

ABayA = Abhandlungen der Bayerischen Akademie der Wissenschaften Phil. Klasse.

AGGW = Abhandlungen der Königl. Gesellschaft der Wissenschaften zu Göttingen, Philol.-histor. Klasse.

AKM = Abhandlungen für die Kunde des Morgenlandes, herausg. von der Deutschen Morgenländischen Gesellschaft.

Album Kern = Album-Kern: Opstellen geschreven ter eere von Dr. H. Kern... op zijn zeventigsten verjaardag. Leiden 1903.

AMG = Annales du Musée Guimet (Paris).

Ann. Bh. Inst. = Annals of the Bhandarkar Institute, Poona.

ĀnSS = Ānandāśrama Sanskrit Series (Poona)

AR = Archiv für Religionsgeschichte.

ASGW = Abhandlungen der philol.-histor. Klasse der Königl. Sächs. Gesellschaft der Wissenschaften.

Aufrecht, Bodl. Cat. = Th. Aufrecht, Catalogus Codicum MSS. Sanscriticorum Bibliothecae Bodleianae, Oxonii 1859-64.

Aufrecht CC = Th. Aufrecht: Catalogus Catalogorum. Leipzig 1891; II, 1896; III, 1903.

Aufrecht, Leipzig = Katalog der Sanskrit-Handschriften der Universitätsbibliothek zu Leipzig, 1901.

BEFEO = Bulletin de l'école française d'Extrême Orient.

BenSS = Benares Sanskrit Series.

Bezz. Beitr. = Beiträge zur Kunde der indogermanischen Sprachen, herausg. von A. Bezzenberger.

Bhandarkar, Report 1882-83 = R. G. Bhandarkar, Report on the Search for Sanskrit Manuscripts in the Bombay Presidency during the year 1882-83, Bombay 1884.

Bhandarkar, Report 1883-84 = R. G. Bhandarkar, Report etc. during the year 1883-84, Bombay 1887.

Bhandarkar Comm. Vol. = Commemorative Essays presented to Sir Ramkrishna Gopal Bhandarkar, Poona 1917.

Bhandarkar, Vaiṣṇavism etc. = R. G. Bhandarkar, Vaiṣṇavism, Śaivism and Minor Religious Systems (Grundriss III, 6, 1913).

Bibl. Ind. = Bibliotheca Indica

BSGW = Berichte über die Verhandlungen der Königl. Sächsischen Gesellschaft der Wissenschaften zu Leipzig, Philol.-histor. Klasse.

BSOS = Bulletin of the School of Oriental Studies, London Institution

BSS = Bombay Sanskrit Series

Bühler, Report = G. Bühler, Detailed Report of a Tour in Search of Sanskrit MSS. made in Kashmir, Rajputana and Central India. (Extra Number of the JBRAS 1877).

Burnell, Tanjore = A. C. Burnell, A Classified Index to the Sanskrit MSS. in the Palace at Tanjore, London 1880.

Cambridge History = The Cambridge History of India, Vol. I, Ancient India, Ed. by E. J. Rapson, Cambridge 1922.

Deussen, AGPh = P. Deussen, Allgemeine Geschichte der Philosophie, I, 1-3. Leipzig 1894 (2nd ed. 1906-1908).

DLZ = Deutsche Literaturzeitung.

Ep. Ind. = Epigraphia Indica.

ERE = Encyclopaedia of Religion and Ethics, edited by James Hastings.

Farquhar, Outline = J. N. Farquhar: An Outline of the Religious Literature of India, London, 1920.

Festschrift Kuhn = Aufsätze zur Kultur—und Sprachgeschichte vornehmlich des Orients Ernst Kuhn...gewidmet... München 1916.

Festschrift Wackernagel = Antidoron, Festschrift Jacob Wackernagel zur Vollendung des 70. Lebensjahres, Göttingen 1924.

Festschrift Windisch = Festschrift Ernst Windisch zum 70. Geburtstag...dargebracht...Leipzig 1914.

GGA = Göttinger Gelehrte Anzeigen.

GOS = Gaekwad's Oriental Series, Baroda.

Grundriss = Grundriss der indo-arischen Philologie und Altertumskunde.

GSAI = Giornale della societa Asiatica Italiana.

Gurupūjākaumudī = Gurupūjākaumudī, Festgabe zum fünfzigjährigen Doctorjubiläum Albrecht Weber dargebracht von seinen Freunden und Schülern, Leipzig 1896.

Haraprasad, Report I, II = Haraprasad Sastri, Report on the Search of Sanskrit MSS, (1895-1900), Calcutta 1901 and (1901-02 to 1905-06), Calcutta 1905.

HOS = Harvard Oriental Series, ed. by Ch. R. Lanmann.

Ind. Hist. Qu. = The Indian Historical Quarterly, edited by Narendra Nath Law.

Ind. Ant. = Indian Antiquary

Ind. Off. Cat. = Catalogue of the Sanskrit Manuscripts in the Library of the India Office, London 1887 ff.

Ind. Stud. = Indische Studien, herausgegeben von A. Weber

JA = Journal Asiatique.

JAOS = Journal of the American Oriental Society.

JASB = Journal of the Asiatic Society of Bengal.

JBRAS = Journal of the Bombay Branch of the Royal Asiatic Society.

JRAS = Journal of the Royal Asiatic Society of Great Britain and Ireland.

LZB = Literarisches Zentralblatt.

Mélanges Lévi = Mélanges d'Indianisme offerts par ses élèves a M. Sylvan Levi...Paris 1911.

NGGW = Nachrichten von der Kgl. Gesellschaft der Wissenschaften, Göttingen, Philolog.-histor. Klasse.

NSP = Nirnaya Sagara Press (Bombay)

OC = Transactions (Verhandlungen, Actes) of Congresses of Orientalists.

OTF = Oriental Translation Fund.

Pischel, KG = R. Pischel, Die indische Literatur, in Kultur der Gegenwart I, 7, 1906.

Proc. I (II, III) OC = Proceedings and Transactions of the First (Second, Third) Oriental Conference.

RHR = Revue de l' histoire des Religions, Paris.

RSO = Rivista degli studi, orientali, Rome.

SBA = Sitzungsberichte der Berliner Akademie der Wissenschaften.

SBayA = Sitzungsberichte der Bayerischen Akademie der Wiss., Phil.-histor. Kl.

SBE = Sacred Books of the East (Oxford)

SBH = Sacred Books of the Hindus, published by the Panini Office, Allahabad.

Schroeder, ILC = L. von Schroeder, Indiens Literatur, und Cultur Leipzig 1887.

SIFI = Studi Italiani di Filologia Indo-Iranica.

Smith, Early History = Vincent A. Smith, The Early History of India, Fourth Edition, revised by S. M. Edwardes, Oxford 1924.

SWA = Sitzungsberichte der Wiener Akademie der Wissenschaften.

TSS = Trivandrum Sanskrit Series.

Weber, HSS. Verz. = A. Weber, Verzeichnis der Sanskrit und Prakrit-Hand schriften der K. Bibliothek zu Berlin.

Weber, HIL = A. Weber, History of Indian Literature, Fourth Edition, 1904, Popular Re-issue, 1914.

Winternitz-Keith, Bodl. Cat. = Catalogue of Sanskrit Manuscripts in the Bodleian Library, vol. II begun by M. Winternitz, continued and completed by A. B. Keith, Oxford, 1905.

WZKM = Wiener Zeitschrift für die Kunde des Morgenlandes.

ZB = Zeitschrift für Buddhismus (Oskar Schloss, München).

ZDMG = Zeitschrift der Deutschen Morgenländischen Gesellschaft.

ZII = Zeitschrift für Indologie und Iranistik, herausg. von der Deutschen Morgenländischen Gesellschaft.

ZVV = Zeitschrift des Vereins für Volkskunde in Berlin.

CONTENTS

INTRODUCTION

Extent and Significance of Indian Literature

The history of Indian literature is the history of the mental activity of at least three millennia expressed in speech and writing. And the place of this mental activity continued uninterrupted through the millennia in a country which extends from the Hindukush to the Cape Comorin and covers an area of one and a half million square miles, equal in extent to the whole of Europe excluding Russia—a country extending from 8°N to 35°N, thus stretching from the hottest equatorial regions right into the temperate zone. The influence that this literature exercised over the intellectual life of other folks even in olden days however is felt far beyond the frontiers of India and (Further India), in Tibet as well as China, Japan and Korea and in the South in Ceylon and the Malayan Peninsula and further beyond in the island groups of the Indian and the Pacific oceans, while in the West we find traces of Indian intellectual life in places reaching deep into Central Asia and East Turkistan, where Indian manuscripts were found buried in the sands of the desert.

In content Indian literature comprises everything which is included in the word 'literature' in the broadest sense of the term : religious and mundane, epic and lyric, dramatic and didactic poetry as well as narrative and scientific prose.

In the forefront we find religious literature. Not only the Brahmins in their Veda and the Buddhists in their Tipiṭaka but also many other numerous religious sects that have appeared in India have on record plenty of literary works—hymns, sacrificial songs, magic songs, myths and legends, sermons, theological treatises and polemic writings, text books of rituals and of religious order. In this literature is found heaped up material of inestimable value which cannot be ignored by any scholar of religion. In addition to this activity in the field of religious literature begun thousands of years ago and being continued even till the present day there have been in India even in ancient times songs of heroes which in the course of centuries got condensed into two great popular epics—the Mahābhārata and the Rāmayāṇa. These sagas were the sources which supplied material for centuries to the poets of India in the Middle Ages and works of epic poetry were thus born which are termed artistic epics in contrast to those popular epics. Although these works of epic poetry with their excessively exaggerated artistry are often not to our taste, still their authors have left us works of lyric and drama which can be compared with the most beautiful creations of modern European literature by virtue of their delicacy and fervour and also of the power of dramatic formation. And in one field Belles Lettres, in the field of aphorisms (epigrammatic poetry) Indians have achieved a mastery which has never been achieved by any other folk. India is also the land of fairy tales and fables. Indian collections of fairy tales, fables and tales in prose have played no small role in the history of world literature. Indeed the research into fairy tales — such an attractive study of fairy tales and of the pursuit of the motifs of fairy tales in their wanderings from folk to folk — has developed into an independent branch of knowledge only after Benfey's fundamental work on *Pañcatantra*, the collection of Indian fairy tales.

It is one of the peculiar features of the Indian mind, that it has never drawn a clear line of demarcation between purely artistic creation and scientific activity, so that a distinction between 'Belles Lettres' and 'Scientific Literature' is indeed impossible in India. What appears to us as a collection of fairy tales and fables, is considered by Indians as a text book of politics and moral. On the other hand history and biography have never been treated in India except by poets and as degenerate epic poetry. Differentiation between the forms of poetry and prose is also not known in India. Every object can be treated equally well in verses as well as in prose form. We find novels which are different from the artistic epics only in this that they do not have a metrical form. There is a special preference for mixing prose and verse from ancient times. And for what we call scientific literature, the prose form was used in India only to a small measure and to a very large extent only the verse form has been used. This is true of the works of philosophy and law as well as those of medicine, astronomy, architecture etc. Indeed even grammars and dictionaries have been written by Indians in metric forms. Perhaps nothing can be more characteristic than the fact that there is a big artistic epic in 22 chapters which serves the express purpose of illustrating and stressing the rules of grammar. Philosophy has been in India even from early times, object of literary work — of course at first as a continuation of religious literature, but later even independent of it. Similarly even in very olden days law and moral — of course as above at first in connection with religion — was made the object of an independent literature of law, composed partly in verse and partly in prose. Even today distinguished jurists and sociologists esteem the significance of this literature of law for research of comparative law and for sociology. Even centuries before Christ's birth grammar was studied as a science in which Indians by far surpassed all other folks of antiquity. Lexicography also attains a ripe old age. Indian poets of artistic poetry of later times have not sung what God gave them, but they studied the rules of grammar and looked up in dictionaries for rare and poetic expressions; they composed according to the teachings and rules that were laid down in scientific works of metre and prosody. The Indian mind had always a special preference for classifying and treating all objects in a pedantic scientific way. Hence we find in India not only a rich and partly ancient literature on medicine, astrology and astronomy, arithmetic and geometry, but also on music, singing, dancing and the art of acting, magic and mantik, indeed even erotics have been reduced to scientific systems and have been treated in separate text books.

In each one of the branches of literature mentioned here a simply unmanageable quantity of literary products got accumulated in the course of the centuries not in the least also due to the fact that in almost all fields of religious literature, that of poetry as well as of science, the Commentators developed a very keen activity. Some of the most significant and extensive works on grammar, philosophy and law are only commentaries to old works. And to these commentaries very often again further commentaries were written. In India it is not seldom that an author has written a commentary to his own work. Thus it is no wonder that the whole mass of Indian literature is almost unmanageable. And although the lists of Indian manuscripts which are available in Indian and European libraries contain many thousands of book titles and authors' names, yet numerous works of Indian literature have been lost and many names of ancient authors are known only through quotations by later authors or have fully disappeared.

All these facts — the age, the large geographical area of usage, the quantity and richness, the aesthetic and cultural historical value of Indian literature — would completely suffice to make our interest for this great, peculiar and ancient literature appear justified. There is however something more that makes Indian literature interesting to us. The Indo-Aryan languages together with the Iranian languages constitute the eastern branch of that great linguistic family to which also German and also most languages of Europe belong and which are called Indo-Germanic. It was precisely Indian literature whose research has led to the discovery of this linguistic relationship — a discovery which was so truly epoch-making, because it threw such a surprisingly new light on the relations of nations to one another in prehistoric times. For, the kinship of languages led necessarily to the conclusion that in earlier times there was unity of languages and this in its turn led to the conclusion that the peoples speaking these Indo-Germanic languages were closely knit together. Even today serious errors are prevalent in the matter of the relationship of the Indo-Germanic peoples. One speaks of an Indo-Germanic 'race' which does not at all exist and has never existed. We still hear that Indians, Persians, Greeks, Romans, Germans and Slavs are of one and the same blood, descendants of one and the same ancient Indo-Germanic Folk. These were however too hasty conclusions. Although it is more than doubtful that the peoples who speak Indo-Germanic languages have all descended from the same forefathers, yet there may not be any doubt that the commonness of the language, of this most important tool of all mental activity, presupposes a mental relationship and a common culture. Although Indians are not flesh of our flesh and blood of our blood, still we can discover in the Indian mental-world mind of our mind. In order to have a knowledge of the 'Indo-Germanic mind' that is of the peculiarity in thinking, viewing and writing which is common to all these folks, it is absolutely necessary that our onesided knowledge of Indo-Germanic character which we have acquired through the study of European literatures should be supplemented by an acquaintance with the Indo-Germanic mind as it has been active in the far-East. Therefore Indian literature constitutes precisely an essential supplement to the classical literature of ancient Greece and Rome for everyone who would like to view Indo-Germanic character in its proper perspective. In the matter of artistic value Indian literature may not stand comparison with Greek literature; it is true that Indian mental world has not exercised, even in the remotest sense of the term such an influence on modern European mental life as Greek and Roman cultures. But if we want to learn to understand the beginnings of our own culture, of the oldest Indo-Germanic culture, then we must go to India, where the oldest literature of an Indo-Germanic folk is preserved. For, in whatever manner the question of the age of Indian literature may be decided, this much might be certain, that the oldest literary monument of Indians is at the same time also the oldest monument of Indo-German literature that we have.

Moreover the direct influence of Indian literature on our own literature is also considerably high. We shall see that the narrative literature of Europe is dependent in no small measure on the fairy tale literature of India. And German literature and German philosophy have been specially influenced manifold by Indian thinking since the beginning of the 19th century; and this influence is no doubt still on the increase and will grow still further in the course of our century.

For, the affinity of mind which is revealed by the Indo-Germanic linguistic unity is clearly recognisable even today and this nowhere so much as between Indians and Germans. The conspicuous concurrences of German and Indian minds have been pointed out quite often.[1] 'Indians', says Leopold v.

1. Refer in particular to G. Brandes (*Hauptstroemungen der Literatur des neunzehnten Jahrhunderts*. Berlin 1872. I, p. 270) and Leopold v. Schroeder (*Indiens Literatur und Cultur*, Leipzig 1887. p. 6 f.)

Schroeder, 'are the folk of romanticism in ancient times; Germans are so in modern times'.

The inclination to perspective observation and to abstract speculation as well as the leanings to pantheism which are common to Germans and Indians have already been pointed out by G. Brandes. In many other respects also German and Indian characters concur conspicuously. Not only German poets have sung about 'World-suffering'. 'World-suffering' is also the basic thought on which Buddha's teachings are built-up; and many Indian poets have lamented the pain and suffering of the world, the transitoriness and futility of all that is earthly in words which remind us remarkably of the verse of our great poet of world-suffering, Nikolaus Lenau. And when Heine says —

"Sweet is sleep, death is better
Best would be, not to have been born"

he expresses thereby the same idea as those Indian philosophers who strive only for that death which is followed by no rebirth. Sentimentality and natural feeling are equally characteristic of German and Indian poetry whereas they are entirely unknown to Hebrew or Greek poetry.

Germans and Indians love nature descriptions; and German as well as Indian poets love to see a relationship between the joys and sorrows of men and those of the nature around them. And in yet another field we come across the similarity between Germans and Indians. Reference has already been made to the inclination of Indians for building up scientific systems; and we can rightly say that Indians were the nation of scholars in olden times as the Germans are today. Just as in the hoary past Indians analysed philologically their holy scriptures, classified linguistic phenomena in a scientific system and developed grammar to such an extent that even today modern linguistics can use their achievements as starting point for further research, similarly Germans are today indisputable leaders in all fields of philology and linguistics.

Even in the field of Indian philology and in conducting research in Indian literature Germans have been leaders and pioneers. Although we owe a lot to Englishmen who as rulers of India were motivated by practical needs to study Indian language and literature, although much has been done also by excellent French, Italian, Dutch, Danish, American, Russian and—last but not least—native Indian scholars for conducting research in Indian literature and culture,—still in the matter of publishing texts, and in investigating and explaining them and in the matter of compiling dictionaries and grammars Germans have indisputably had a lion's share.

THE BEGINNINGS OF THE STUDY OF INDIAN LITERATURE IN EUROPE[1]

The great mass of Indian literary works which can hardly be surveyed by a single research scholar has been made accessible to research only in the course of a little more than a century.

Of course as early as in the 17th century and still more in the 18th century individual travellers and missionaries acquired a certain knowledge of Indian languages and got themselves acquainted with one or the other work of Indian literature. But the inspirations that they gave did not fall on fertile soil. Thus reported in 1651 the Dutch Abraham Roger who had lived as preacher in Paliacatta (Pulicat), north of Madras, in his work *Offene Thür zv dem verborgenen Heidentum*"[2] [Open door to the hidden Heathendom] on ancient Brahmanic literature of Indians and published some of the sayings of Bhartṛhari translated for him into Portuguese by a Brahmin. Later on Herder drew upon them for his book *Stimmen der Völker in Liedern.* In 1699 the Jesuit Father Johann Ernst Hanxleden went to India and worked there for over 30 years in the Malabar Mission. He was using Indian languages and his *Grammatica Granthamia seu Samscrdumica* was the first Sanskrit grammar written by a European. It was never printed, was however used by Fra Paolino de St Bartholomeo. This Fra Paolino—an Austrian Carmelite, whose actual name was J. Ph. Wessdin—is

1. For this chapter see E. Windisch, *Geschichte der Sanskrit-Philologie und indischen Altertumskunde*, I, II (Grundriss I, 1, 1917 and 1920).

2. The work appeared in Dutch in 1651 and in German translation in 1663 in Nuremberg. The Dutch title is *Open-Deure tot het verborgen Heydendom*; a new edition of this work appeared in 1915, edited by W. Caland.

indisputably the most significant of the missionaries who worked at exploring Indian literature in most early days. He was a missionary on the Malabar coast from 1776 to 1789 and died in 1805 in Rome. He wrote two Sanskrit grammars and several scholarly treatises and books. His *Systema Brahmanicum* (Rome 1792) and his *Reise mach Ostindien* (translated into German by J. R. Forster, Berlin 1798) testify to his profound knowledge of India and the Brahminical literature as also an intensive study of Indian languages, especially of Indian religion. But even of his work there are only poor traces left behind.

By about the same time Englishmen also had begun to take interest in the language and literature of Indians. It was no less a person than Warren Hastings, the real founder of British rule in India from whom the first fruitful stimulus for the study of Indian literature emanated and this continued without any interruption since then. He had recognised that England's rule over India would be ensured only if the rulers could protect and nurture the social and religious prejudices of the natives as far as possible. This view was not given up by the English at any time. Warren Hastings was responsible for incorporating in the law for administering India a rule that native scholars should be present during Court proceedings so that the English judges might pay due attention to the paragraphs of Indian books of law while pronouncing judgements. And when Warren Hastings was appointed Governor-General of Bengal in 1773 and entrusted with supreme powers over all English possessions in India, he made a number of Brahmins well-versed in law compile a book based on Indian law books. This book was entitled *Vivādārṇavasetu* (Bridge to cross the Ocean of disputes) and contained everything important on Indian law of succession, family etc. When the book was completed there was nobody who could translate it directly from Sanskrit into English. So it had to be translated first from Sanskrit into Persian from which it was translated into English by Nathaniel Brassey Halhed. This translation was printed with the title *A Code of Gentoo Law*[1]

1. A German translation appeared in Hamburg in 1778. "Gentoo" is the Anglo-Indian form of the Portuguese "gentio", "heathen", and is used to denote the Indian "heathens", i.e. the Hindus in contradistinction to the Mohammedans.

in the year 1770 and the expenses were met by the East India Company. A German translation of this law book appeared in 1778 with the title *Law Book of the Gentoos or Collection of the Laws of the Pandits, as per a Persian translation of the original written in Sanskrit language*, translated from the English translation of Rud. Erich Raspe.

The first Englishman to acquire a knowlege of Sanskrit was Charles Wilkins, who had been encouraged by Warren Hastings to take lessons from the Pandits in Banaras, the centre of Indian scholarship. As the first fruit of his Sanskrit studies he published in 1785 an English translation of the philosophic poem *Bhagavadgitā*. With this, a Sanskrit work was translated for the first time directly from Sanskrit into a European language. This was followed two years later by a translation of *Hitopadeśa*, the Book of Fables and in 1795 by a translation of the *Śākuntala* Episode from the *Mahābhārata*. For his Sanskrit Grammar which appeared in 1808 Sanskrit types were used for the first time in Europe which he himself had cut and cast. He was also the first to study Indian inscriptions and translate some of them into English.

Still more important for exploring larger fields of Indian literature was however the work of the famous English Orientalist William Jones[1] (born in 1746, died in 1794) who came to India in 1783 to take up the post of Superior judge in Fort William. Even in his younger days Jones had made a study of oriental poetry and had translated Arabic and Persian poetry into English. No wonder, that, having arrived in India, he began to study with great interest Sanskrit and Indian literature. Hardly one year had passed after his arrival in India when he founded the Asiatic Society of Bengal which soon turned out extremely useful work by publishing many journals and especially by printing editions of many Indian texts. In 1789 he published his English translation of the famous drama '*Śākuntala*' by Kālidāsa. This English translation was translated

---

1. William Jones was not only a learned and enthusiastic Orientalist, but also the first Anglo-Indian poet. He composed suggestive hymns to Brahman, Nārāyaṇa, Lakṣmi etc.; See E. F. Oaten, *A sketch of Anglo-Indian Literature*, London, 1908, p. 19 ff.

into German by George Forster in 1791 and roused the enthusiasm of people like Herder and Goethe. Another work of the same poet Kālidāsa, the lyrical poem *Ṛtusamhāra* was published in Calcutta in the year 1792 by Jones in its original form and this was the first Sanskrit text that appeared in print. It is of still greater significance that W. Jones translated into English the most famous and the most respected work of Indian legal literature, the *Law Book of Manu*. This translation appeared in Calcutta in 1794 with the title *Institutes of Hindu Law, or the Ordinances of Manu*. A German translation of this work appeared in 1797 in Weimar.[1] Finally, it was also W. Jones who was the first man to pronounce the genealogical connection of Sanskrit with Greek and Latin with absolute certainty and to presume its connection with German, Celtic and Persian. He also pointed out the similarities of ancient Indian and Graeco-Roman mythology.

While the rapturous W. Jones inspired the others by the enthusiasm with which he brought to light many treasures of Indian literature, the sober Henry Thomas Colebrooke who continued the work of W. Jones became the real founder of Indian philology and archaeology. Colebrooke had begun his career by entering Government service in Calcutta as a lad of 17 years in the year 1782 and in the first eleven years of his stay in India he did not take any interest in Sanskrit and its literature. But when W. Jones died in 1794, Colebrooke had learnt Sanskrit and took over the translation of the teachings of Indian law books on the law of succession and contracts, which were compiled by native scholars who worked under the directions of Jones. This translation appeared in 1797 and 1798 under the title *A Digest of Hindu Law on Contracts and Successions* in four folio-volumes. From then onwards he devoted himself with untiring enthusiasm to researches in Indian literature. And of course he was, unlike Jones, not so much interested in

1. Hindu's law-giving, or Menu's Laws as per Culluca's commentary, a concept of Indian system of religious and civil rights. Translated faithfully from the Sanskrit language into English by W. Jones and rendered into German based on the Calcutta edition and with a glossary and notes by Joh. Christ. Hüttner.

the poetic as in the scientific literature. Therefore we owe to him not only further books on Indian law but also pioneering essays on philosophy and religion, on grammar, astronomy and arithmetic of Indians. Moreover it was he who gave exact and reliable information about the ancient holy books of Indians[1] for the first time in his famous essay on the Vedas in the year 1805. He is also the publisher of the *Amarakośa* and other Indian dictionaries, of the famous Grammar of Pāṇini, of *Hitopadeśa*, the collection of fables and of the ornate epic *Kirātārjunīya*. Besides he is the author of a Sanskrit grammar and has adapted and translated a number of inscriptions. He had also an exceedingly voluminous rich collection of Indian manuscripts which are said to have cost him about £ 10,000 and which on his return to England he presented to the East India Company. This collection of manuscripts is one of the most valuable treasures of the India Office library in London.

Among the Englishmen who, like Jones and Colebrooke, learnt Sanskrit in India about the turn of the 18th century was also Alexander Hamilton. He came back to Europe in 1802 and stopped over for a short time in Paris while travelling through France. It was a chance coincidence, unpleasant for him but extremely favourable to the spread of knowledge, that just at that time the animosities between England and France interrupted only for a short time by the Peace of Amiens once again flared up, and Napolean ordered that all Englishmen who were in France at the time the war broke out be prevented from going back to their Motherland and be held back in

1. The alleged translation of the Yajurveda which appeared in 1778 under the title *Ezour-Vedam* in French and in 1779 also in German, is a spurious one, a pious fraud, which probably originates from the missionary Robertus de Nobilibus. But W. Caland, Th. Zachariae (GGA 1921, p. 157), and others deny, that he was the author of the fraud. Voltaire received this supposed translation from the hands of a govt. official coming back from Pondichery and gave it over to the royal library in Paris. Voltaire thought it to be an old commentary on the Veda, translated into French by a respectable, hundred year old Brahmin. And he often quotes the *Ezour-Veda* as the source of Indian antiquity. As early as in the year 1782 Sonnerat declared this work to be a spurious one. (A. W. Schlegel, *Indische Bibliothek* II, p. 50 ff).

Paris. Alexander Hamilton was also one of these Englishmen. In the same year 1802 the German poet Friedrich Schlegel had also come to Paris, to stay there with some interruptions till 1807 — exactly during the period of the forced stay of A. Hemilton. The works of Englishmen had already attracted the attention of the people in Germany. The abovementioned translation of '*Śākuntala*' by W. Jones particularly made interesting news and had also been translated immediately into German in 1791. Also in the years 1795-97 the treatises of William Jones had already appeared in German translation.[1] Further, Jones' Translation of Manu's Law book had already been rendered into German. The works of Fra Paolino de St. Bartholomeo were also not unknown in Germany. It was in particular however the romantic school led by the Schlegel-brothers for which Indian literature had a special attraction. It was a time when people turned to foreign literatures with a great enthusiasm. Herder had already drawn the attention of Germans to the Orient by his *Stimmen der Völker in Liedern* (1778) and "*Ideen zur Geschichte der Menschheit*" (1784-91). However it was the romantics who plunged with the greatest enthusiasm into everything that was foreign, strange and distant and were particularly attracted by India. From India they expected to obtain nothing less than 'information about the history of the primeval world, whose history has not yet been revealed to man' as Friedrich Schlegel put it, "and friends of poetry hoped, especially after the appearance of *Sokuntola* to get from there (India) many more such beautiful pictures of Asian mind as this one which is inspired by charm and love". No wonder therefore, that on meeting Alexander Hamilton in Paris, Friedrich Schlegel immediately seized the opportunity to learn Sanskrit from him. During the years 1803 and 1804 he enjoyed his lessons and the remaining years of his stay in Paris he employed for his studies in the library there which had then already about 200 Indian manuscripts.[2] As the fruit of these

1. W. Jones, *Treatises on the History, Antiquities etc. of Asia*, Riga 1795-97 4 volumes.

2. A catalogue of these was published by Alexander Hamilton (in cooperation with L. Langles, who translated Hamilton's notes into French) Paris 1807.

studies there appeared in the year 1808 that work through which Friedrich Schlegel became the founder of Indian philology in Germany; *On the language and wisdom of Indians. A contribution to the Foundation of Archaeology.* This book was written with enthusiam and was suited to rouse enthusiasm. It contained also translation of a few pieces from the *Rāmāyaṇa*, from Manu's Law book, from the *Bhagavadgītā* and from the *Śākuntala*-episode of the *Mahābhārata*. These were the first direct translations from Sanskrit into German, because what had been available of Indian literature in Germany till then was translated from English.

While Friedrich Schlegel inspired others. by his work, his brother August Wilhelm von Schlegel was the first to develop an extensive activity as Sanskrit scholar in Germany by his text editions, translations and other philological works. He was also the first professor of Sanskrit in Germany and was appointed to this post in 1818 at the newly established University of Bonn. Just like his brother he too had begun in Paris his Sanskrit studies in 1814. But his teacher was a Frenchman, A. L. Chézy, the first French scholar who learnt and taught Sanskrit; he was also the first Sanskrit professor at the College de France and distinguished himself as editor and translator of Indian works. In 1823 appeared the first volume of the periodical *Indische Bibliothek* which was founded and whose articles were almost entirely written by August Wilhelm von Schlegel. It contained numerous essays on Indian philology. In the same year, he also published a good edition of the *Bhagavadgītā* with a Latin translation, while in 1829 there appeared the first part of the most significant work of Schlegel, namely his incomplete edition of the *Rāmāyaṇa*.

A contemporary of August Wilhelm von Schlegel was Franz Bopp (born in 1791) who went to Paris in 1812 in order to study oriental languages and learnt there Sanskrit along with Schlegel from Chézy. But whereas the Schlegel brothers as romantic poets were enamoured of India and considered the study of Indian literature as a kind of 'adventure,'[1] Bopp

1. Thus Friedrich Schlegel writes in a letter to Goethe, that he has set himself the task of "bringing to the light of the day what was forgotten and

approached these studies as a sober investigator and it was he that became the founder of a new science, the science of comparative philology, which was to have such a bright future. His work *On the Conjugation System of Sanskrit Language* in comparison with that of Greek, Latin, Persian and Germanic languages, appeared in 1816.

But even by conducting researches in Indian literature Bopp distinguished himself extraordinarily. In his 'Conjugation system' he already gave as an appendix some episodes from *Rāmāyaṇa* and *Mahābhārata* in metrical translations from the original text as also some samples of the Veda as per Colebrooke's English translation. With rare skill he then took out the wonderful story of King *Nala* and his faithful wife Damayantī from the great epic of *Mahābhārata* and made it accessible to the public through his good critical edition with a good Latin translation.[1] It was precisely this one of the numberless episodes of the *Mahābhārata* which being complete in itself is one of the most beautiful pieces of the great epic; it is also one of the most charming creations of Indian art of poetry which is specially suited to rouse one's enthusiasm for Indian literature and love for Sanskrit studies. It has therefore become almost traditional at all Universities where Sanskrit is taught, to choose the Nala-episode as the first lesson to read for Sanskrit students. The simplicity of the language is another special reason for this choice. Bopp edited for the first time and translated into German for the first time a number of other episodes from the *Mahābhārata*. His Sanskrit grammars (1827, 1832 and 1834) and his *Glossarium Sanscritum* (Berlin 1830) greatly helped the study of Sanskrit in Germany.

---

missed" and therefore has turned from Dante to Shakespeare, to Petrarca and Calderon, to the hero-songs of ancient Germany. So much so that I had exhausted so to say European literature and turned my attention to Asia in order to experience a new adventure. (A. Hillebrandt, *Alt Indien*, Breslau 1899. p. 37). And Aug. Wilh. von Schlegel writes (*Indische Bibliothek* I, p. 8) that with his essay he wants to show the way to a certain extent to such of those of his countrymen "as want to go through the adventure (for it still remains an adventure").

1. *Nalus, carmen Sanscritum e Mahabharato*, edidit, latine vertit et adnotationibus illustravit Franciscus Bopp. London 1819.

It was the good fortune of the young science of philology and of Sanskrit studies closely connected with it that the intellectual and influential Wilhelm von Humboldt with his multifarious interests was attracted by these branches of knowledge. In 1821 he began to learn Sanskrit for he had realised — as he wrote in a letter to August Wilhelm von Schlegel[1] — "that without a thorough study of Sanskrit we cannot achieve anything in the science of language or in the kind of history that is connected with it". And when Schlegel turned his thoughts back to Indian studies, he esteemed it as a matter of particular good fortune for the new science that it "found a warm friend and patron in Wilhelm von Humboldt". Schlegel's edition of the *Bhagavadgītā* had drawn Humboldt's attention to this theosophical poem. He devoted to it some treatises and he wrote to Fr. von Gentz in those days (1827): "It is perhaps the most profound and the most sublime that the world has on record". And later (1828) when he sent to his friend his work on the *Bhagavadgītā* which was in the meanwhile reviewed by Hegel, he wrote that although he was indifferent to the evaluation by Hegel, he esteemed highly the philosophic poem of India. "I read the Indian poem", he writes, 'for the first time on the countryside in Silesia and since then it has been by strong feeling of gratefulness to destiny that it has allowed me to live long enough to get acquainted with this work".[2]

We have to mention the name of one more great hero of German literature who, to the good fortune of our science, was enthused by Indian poetry. It is that of Friedrich Rückert, the incomparable master of the art of translation. Of the most beautiful pearls of Indian epic and lyric literature much

"That rustled millenia ago
In the tops of Indian palms"

became the common property of the German folk through his efforts.[3]

1. *Indische Bibliothek* I, p. 433.
2. *Works of Friedrich von Gentz*. published by Gustav Schlesier. Mannheim 1840. vol. V. p. 291 and 300.
3. Rückert's translations from Indian classical poetry have been re-edited by H. von Glasenapp, *Indische Liebeslyrik*, München, 1921.

Till 1830 it was almost exclusively the so called "classical Sanskrit Literature" to which European researchers turned their attention. The drama *Śākuntala* the philosophic poem Bhagavadgītā, the Law Book of Manu, the sayings of Bhartṛhari, the collection of fables *Hitopadeśa* and isolated works from the great epics — these were about all the major works with which they occupied themselves and which they considered to be the main stock of Indian Literature. The great and most important field of Indian literature — the Veda — was almost totally unknown and of the great mighty Buddhist literature nothing was known as yet.

What little was known of the Veda till 1830 was restricted to meagre and inexact details given by earlier writers on India. The first reliable informations were given by Colebrooke in the aforesaid treatise on the Vedas in the year 1805.[1] Compared to this, much was known of the Upaniṣads the philosophic discussions belonging to the Veda. These Upaniṣads were translated into Persian in the 17th century by the unfortunate prince Mohammed Dara Shakoh,[2] brother of Aurangazeb and son of the Great Moghul Shah Jahan. From Persian it was translated at the beginning of the 19th century into Latin under the title *Oupnekhat*[3]

1. *Miscellaneous Essays*, Madras 1872 pp. 9 ff. A German translation appeard in 1847. H. Th. Colebrooke's Treatise on the holy scriptures of Indians. Translated by Ludwig Poley from English. Together with fragments of the oldest religious poems of Indians. Leipzig. For the beginnings of Vedic research, see W. Caland, *De Ontdekkings a geschiedenis van den Veda*, Amsterdam 1918, and Th. Zachariae, GGA., 1921, 148 ff. (English in the *Journal of Indian History*, May, 1923).

2. The fate of this prince is the theme of a beautiful but unfortunately little known tragedy by L. von Schroeder, *Dara or Shahjahan and his sons* (*Dara oder Schah Dschehan und seine Söhne* Mitau 1891.

3. The complete title is as follows: *Oupnek'hat*, i.e. secretum tegendum, opus ipsa in India rarissimum, continens antiqum et arcanamas theologicam et philosophicam doctrinam equatuor sacris Indorum libris, Rak Beid, Djedir Beid, Sam Beid, Athrban Beid excerptam; ad verbum e persico idiomate, Sanscreticis vocabulis intermixto in latinum conversum. . . studio et opera Anquetil du Perron. . . Parisiis 1801-1802, 4, 2 volumes". Partly translated into German under the title *Attempts to portray ancient India* All-one-Theory: or of the famous collection Twy Oupnekhatwy first part, called Oupnek'hat Tschehandouk. According to the Latin translation from Persian by Mr. Anquetil du Perron, freely rendered into German and provided with notes by Th. A. Rixner, Nuremberg 1808". "Oupnek'hat is a mutilation of "Upanisad" and "Rak Beid" etc. are corruptions of "Rg-Veda", "Yajur-Veda", "Sama-Veda" and "Atharva-veda".

by the French scholar Anquetil Duperron.[1] Although the Latin translation was quite incomplete and full of misinterpretations, still it became important for the history of learning because it roused the enthusiasm of German philosophers like Schelling and in particular Schoperhauer for Indian philosophy. It was not the *Upaniṣads* as we now understand and explain them with all the means of Indian philology and our more precise knowledge of the whole philosophy of Indians at our command today that Schopenhauer declared to be, "the product of the highest human wisdom", but it was the *Oupnekhat* that absolutely incomplete Persian-Latin translation of Anquetil Duperron. And at about the same time when Schopenhauer in Germany was fancying to see his own ideas in the Upaniṣads of the Hindus rather than deduce them from them, there lived in India one of the wisest and noblest men that this country produced—Ram Mohan Roy—the founder of the 'Brahmo Samaj', (a new sect that sought to unite the best in the religions of Europe with the religion of the Hindus), — an Indian who found the purest divine faith in the same Upaniṣads and from the same Upaniṣads tried to prove to his countrymen that although idolatry of the present day Indian religions was to be condemned, yet there was no reason for Indians to accept Christianity; and that they could, if only they understood them, find a pure religion in them. With the intention of proclaiming this new teaching which was however found already in the ancient holy scripture, and to spread it through the *Brahma Samaj* (or the community of God) founded by him, and at the same time with the intention of convincing the christian theologians and missionaries whom he esteemed, that the best of what they taught was already found in the Upaniṣads, he translated into English a large number of the Upaniṣads and edited some of them in original text.[2]

---

1. Anquetil du Perron, too, was among those who were inspired by the Upaniṣads, and was himself a kind of Indian ascetic. See E. Windisch, *Die altindischen Religionsurkunden und die christliche Mission*, Leipzig, 1897, p. 15, and *Geschichte der Sanskrit-Philologie*, pp. 48 ff.

2. Smaller fractions of the Upaniṣads appeared also in Othmar Franks *Chrestomathia Sanscrita* (1820-1821) and in the same "Vyasa, on philosophy, mythology, literature and language of the Hindus" (1826-1830).

The actual philological research into the Veda however began only with the first eighth of the Ṛgveda by Friedrich Rosen in Calcutta in the year 1838. Premature death prevented this Friedrich Rosen from completing his edition. However it was in particular the French orientalist Eugene Burnouf who taught at the College de France in the beginning of the forties and who by collecting around himself a circle of pupils who became later excellent scholars of the Veda laid thereby the foundation to the study of the Veda in Europe. One of these pupils was Rudolph Roth, who laid the foundation to the study of the *Veda* in Germany with his work *On the literature and History of the Veda*. Roth himself and a good number of his pupils devoted themselves in the following years and decades with fiery enthusiasm to researches in the various branches of this oldest literature of India. Another famous pupil of Burnouf was F. Max Mueller, who was introduced by Burnouf into the study of the Veda at the same time as Roth. Inspired by Burnouf, Max Mueller planned to edit the hymns of the Ṛgveda with the great commentary of Sāyana. This edition, indispensable for all further researches, appeared in the years 1849-1875.[1] Even before this was completed, Th. Aufrecht distinguished himself as an extremely good researcher by editing the complete texts of the Hymns of Ṛgveda (1861) 1863[2].

The same Eugene Burnouf, who stood at the cradle of the Veda studies laid the foundation to the study of Pali and to researches in Buddhist literature through his *Essai sur le Pali* which he published in collaboration with Christian Lassen in 1826 and through his *Introduction a l' historie du Buddhisme indien* which appeared in 1844.

With the conquest of the large area of Vedic literature and with the exploration of Buddhistic literature the story of the childhood of Indian philology comes to an end. It grew in strength and became a great branch of knowledge in which the number of workers increases from year to year. There appeared now in rapid succession critical editions of the most

1. A second, improved edition appeared in the years 1890-1892.

2. A second edition of Aufrecht's text of the Hymns of the Rg-veda was published in Bonn in 1877.

important texts and scholars of all countries competed with one another in their laudable efforts to interpret them.[1] But what has been accomplished during the last 60 years in the individual fields of study in Indian literature must be mentioned in the individual chapters of this history of literature. Here only the main stations on the road of Indology and the most important events in its history may be mentioned in short.

Here we must mention the name of a pupil of August-Wilhelm von Schlegel. It is Christian Lassen who tried to summarise all that was known then about India in his work *Indian Archaeology* which was planned on a large scale. It began to appear in 1843 and comprised four thick volumes, the last of which appeared in 1862. That this work has become out of date now is not the fault of its author, but it is only a convincing proof of the mighty progress that has been made by our science in the second half of the 19th century.

The strongest impetus for these advances and perhaps the chief event in the history of Sanskrit research was the appearance of the *Sanskrit Dictionary* compiled by Otto Böhtlingk and Rudolph Roth and published by the Academy of Sciences (Akademic der Wissenschaften) in St. Petersburg. The first part of this work appeared in 1852 and in the year 1875 the work was available, completed in seven folio volumes, a glorious monument to German diligence.

And in the same year, 1852, when the great *Petersburg Dictionary* began to appear, Albrecht Weber made the first attempt to write acomplete history of Indian literature. The book appeared under the title *Academic Lectures on Indian History of Literature.*[2] The book was printed again in 1876, and it indicates not only a milestone in the History of Indology but even today it is, despite its imperfections in style which make it hard to assimilate

1. As early as in 1823 A.W. v. Schlegel had said so beautifully: Should the Englishmen have a monopoly of Indian literature? It is too late now. They may keep their cinnamon and cloves, but these intellectual treasures are the common property of all educated people of the world (*Ind. Bibl.* I, 15).

2. An English translation of Weber's *History of Indian Literature* appeared in Trübner's Oriental Series.

for the layman, the most reliable and complete handbook of Indian literature, that we have.

If one wants to have an idea of the astonishing progress made by the research in Indian literature in the relatively short time of its existence, then one should read the essay 'On the present situation of Indian philology' written in the year 1819 by August. Wilhelm von Schlegel in which little more than a dozen Sanskrit works have been enumerated as having been known through publications or translations. Let us throw a glance at Friedrich Adelung's book *Attempt at a literature of the Sanskrit language*,[1] in which already the titles of over 350 Sanskrit works were enumerated; with this we must compare Weber's *History of Indian Literature* which reviews (as per an approximate estimate) about 500 works of Indian literature in the year 1852. And then we must look at the Catalogus Catalogorum, published by Theodor Aufrecht in the years 1891, 1896 and 1903, containing an alphabetical list of all Sanskrit works and authors based on a thorough investigation of all available literatures of manuscripts. In this monumental work, at which Aufrecht worked for over 40 years the catalogues of Sanskrit manuscripts of all big libraries in India and Europe have been processed and the number of the available Sanskrit works, amounts, as per this Catalogus Catalogorum, to several thousands. In spite of this, this Catalogue does not include the whole of Buddhist literature and all the literary works that are written not in Sanskrit but in other Indian languages.

Researches in Buddhist literature have been greatly promoted by the 'Pali Text Society' founded by T.W. Rhys Davids in the year 1882. And yet another big branch of literature, viz. the literature of the Jaina sect which is as old as Buddhism, was thrown open to knowledge by Albrecht Weber who wrote a big treatise *On the Sacred Scriptures of the Jains* (in 1883 & 1885).[2]

More and more of Indian literature has been gradually discovered to such an extent that today it is hardly possible

1. This is rather a bibliography than a history of literature. About 230 edited texts are mentioned by J. Gildemeister, *Bibliothecae Sanskritae sive recensus librorum Sanskritorum*. . . Specimen Bonnae ad Rh. 1847.

2. *Indische Studien*, vols. 16 and 17.

for one scholar to master all its branches. Consequently, even a few years ago it was found necessary to give an idea in summary-form of all that has been achieved in various branches till then. The plan for this work which has been appearing since 1897[1] under the title "Grundriss (Plan) of Indo-Aryan Philology and Archaeology" was drawn by Georg Bühler the most significant and versatile Sanskrit scholar of recent decades. Thirty scholars from Germany, Austria, England, Holland, India and America have joined together under Bühler's leadership — and after his premature death, under Franz Kielhorn's leadership in order to deal with the various parts of this work. The appearance of this 'Grundriss' is the latest and also the most joyous chief event in the development of Indology. If we compare the knowledge about India and its literature, contained in the fifteen numbers of this 'Grundriss' (=Plan) that have appeared so far and that constitute not even one half of the total number with what Lassen was able to say about India only a few decades ago in his *Indian Archaeology*, then we can view with justifiable pride the progress that our science has made in a comparatively short span of time.

The Chronology of Indian Literature

Although so much has been achieved in the matter of exploring Indian literature, still its actual history is dark and unexplored. Especially, the chronology of Indian literary history is shrouded in a frightening darkness and researches have yet to solve here most of the riddles. It would be indeed fine, convenient and especially for a handbook quite desirable if we could divide Indian literature into three or four periods defined clearly by dates and put the various literary products into one or the other of these periods. But any such attempt is bound to fail in the present state of affairs and any mention of hypothetical dates would be only an eyewash which would do more harm than good. It is much better to be clear about

1. Published by Karl J. Trübner, Strassburg, now Vereinigung Wissenschaftlicher Verleger Walter de Gruyter & Co., Berlin and Leipzig.

this, that regarding the oldest period of Indian literary history, we cannot give any specific data and regarding the later periods we can give only very few particulars. Years ago the famous American Sanskrit research scholar W.D. Whitney[1] said the following sentence which has been often quoted since then: "All the data given in Indian literary history are, like skittles set up for being knocked down". And this is the case to a large extent even today. Even today the most significant researchers differ about the age of the most important Indian literary works not by about a few years or decades, but even by about a few centuries, if not by one to two millennia. What can be ascertained with a certain degree of precision is mostly a sort of relative chronology. We can say often: This or that work, this or that literary form is older than some other; but about its real age we can only make presumptions. Language is still the safest differentiating feature for this relative chronology. Peculiarities of style are less reliable, for it has often happened in India that later works have imitated the style of earlier works in order to create an impression of *antiquity*. Moreover considerable harm is done to relative chronology also by the fact that many works of Indian literature — especially those that were most popular with the masses, hence of special interest to us — have undergone several revisions and have come down to us in several modified forms. If, for example, we find that in a work whose date has been approximately fixed, *Rāmāyaṇa* or *Mahābhārata* is quoted, then the question arises as to whether this quotation refers to the epics as we have them now or to some earlier versions of the same. The uncertainty is all the greater, because in the case of a large majority of the works of the ancient literature the names of the authors are almost unknown to us. They are handed down to us as works of families, schools or monasteries or the author is supposed to be a legendary seer of ancient times. And if we at last come to a period when we deal with works of quite specific individual authors, then we find that as a rule only the family names are mentioned. And it is as vague as when we find in German the

1. In the Introduction to his *Sanskrit Grammar*, Leipzig, 1879 (second edition 1889).

names of Meier, Schultze or Müller when they do not appear with Christian names. If for example a work appears under the name of Kālidāsa, or if the name Kālidāsa is mentioned somewhere, then it is not clear whether thereby the great poet of the same name is meant—it can be another Kālidāsa as well [1]

In this ocean of uncertainty there are only some fixed points, which I would like to mention here in order that the reader may not be frightened.

Firstly, there is the proof of language, which shows that the songs and hymns, prayers and magic formulas of the Vedas are indisputably the oldest that we have of Indian literature. Further, it is also certain that Buddhism was born in India by about 500 B.C.[2] and that it presumes that the whole vedic literature as is found in its chief works has essentially come to a close so that it may be said: "Vedic literature is, except for its last few ramifications, largely pre-Buddhist, that means, it had come to a close before 500 B.C. Moreover the literatures of Buddhism and of Jainism are fortunately not so uncertain as the Brahminic literature. What the Buddhists and the Jains handed down to us regarding the origin or collection of their canonical works has proved to be considerably reliable. And the inscriptions on the ruins of temples and stupas of these religious sects give us hints to the History of their literature for which we must be thankful to them.

But the most certain dates of Indian history are those which we get not from Indians themselves. Thus the attack of Alexander the Great on India in the year 326 B.C. is a certain date which is important for the history of Indian literature also, especially when it is a question of deciding whether Greek influence is to be presumed in any literary work or literary form. From the Greeks we know also that about 315 B.C.

1. The history of Indian literature encounters an additional difficulty in the frequent occurrence of the same name in different forms, and in the circumstances that one and the same author often has two or several different names, as name synonyms and abbreviations of names are very general in India; see R.O. Franke, *Indische Genuslehren*, pp. 57 ff. and GGA, 1892, pp. 482 ff.

2. The year 477 B.C. is looked upon with considerable certainty as the year of Buddha's death.

Chandragupta, the 'Sandrakottos' of Greek writers, led successfully the rebellion of Alexander's Prefects, seized the throne and became the founder of the Mauryan dynasty in Pāṭaliputra (Patibothra of the Greeks, today's Patna). At about the same time or a few years later it was that the Greek Megasthenes was sent by Selukos as Ambassador to the court of Chandragupta. Fragments of his description of India which have come down to us give us a picture of the state of Indian culture at that time and also enable us to draw conclusions regarding the dating of some Indian literary works. A grandson of Chandragupta is the famous King Aśoka, who was crowned about 259 (or 269)[1] B.C. and to whom we owe the oldest datable Indian inscriptions that we have found till now. These inscriptions, written partly on rocks and partly on pillars are the oldest testimonials of Indian script that we possess. They show us this mighty king as a patron and protector of Buddhism, who used his power extending from extreme North to extreme South for spreading the teaching of Buddha everywhere and who in his rock and pillar edicts did not narrate about his victories and famous deeds as other rulers have done, but called upon the people to become virtuous, warned them against the dangers of sin and preached love and tolerance. These unique edicts of King Aśoka are in themselves valuable literary monuments carved in stone and are also of great importance for the history of literature on account of their script and language as well as their references from the point of view of the history of religion. In the year 178 B.C. — 137 years after *Candragupta's* coronation — the last descendant of the *Maurya* dynasty was overthrown by a king called Puṣyamitra. The mention of this Puṣyamitra — for example in a drama of Kālidāsa — is an important clue for fixing the date of several works of Indian literature. The same is true of the Graeco-Bactrian king Menander who ruled about 144 B.C. He appears under the name of Milinda in the famous Buddhistic work *Milindapañha*.

After the Greeks it is to the Chinese that we owe the determination of some of the most important dates in the History

1. See also Fleet, *JRAS* 1912, 239.

of Indian literature. Since the 1st century A.D. we have reports of Buddhist Missionaries who go to China and translate Buddhist notes into Chinese, of Indian Ambassadors in China and of Chinese pilgrims who come to India visiting the places holy for Buddhism. Works of Indian literature are translated into Chinese and the Chinese gave us exact dates, when these translations were made. It is in particular three Chinese pilgrims — Fa-hian who came to India in 399, Hiuen-Tsiang who travelled at length in India from 630 to 645 and I-tsing who lived in India from 671 to 695 — whose travel-reports have been preserved to the present day giving us a lot of instructive information on Indian antiquities and literary works. The chronological data of the Chinese are, as against those of Indians, singularly exact and reliable. What the Arabian traveller Alberuni, who also wrote a very important book on India in 1030, has said of the Indians is only too true. He wrote: 'Indians unfortunately pay very little attention to the historical sequence of things; they are very careless in the enumeration of the chronological order of their kings and if they are pressed for a clarification, and they do not know what to say, they immediately begin to tell tales'.[1]

And yet we should not believe as has been so often said, that Indians did not at all have the historical sense. History has been written in India also, as we shall see; in any case we find in India many inscriptions with exact dates — which would hardly have been the case if the Indians had not had any historical sense. Only this much is true, that while writing their history, Indians freely mixed facts with phantasy, that they always considered events to be more important than their chronological order and that especially in literary matters they did not at all attach any importance to the question whether a particular event was earlier or later than another. Whatever seems to an Indian to be great, true and right, he pushes into as old an age as possible and if he wants to bestow special sanctity on any particular precept or if he desires that his book be spread most widely and enjoy esteem, then he conceals his name in a modest incognito and mentions some

1. See E.C. Sachau, *Alberuni's India*, English Ed. II, pp. 10.

ancient seer as the author of the book. This happens even to this day, it was not much different in the past centuries. Thus it also happens that so many quite modern books go under the time honoured name of 'Upaniṣads' or 'Purāṇas' — new or sour wine poured into 'old bottles'. An intention to cheat thereby can however be ruled out in general. There is only extreme indifference to literary copyright and the claim to the same. It is only in the later centuries that authors give their name, at great length together with the names of their parents, grand parents, teachers and patrons and also give a few scanty particulars of their own biography. Authors of astronomical works then used them also to give the exact date of the day on which they completed their work. From the 5th century A.D. onwards even some inscriptions give us at last information about some authors. And it is to these inscriptions, in the deciphering of which great progress has been made in the last 20 years[1] — a *Corpus Inscriptionum Indicarum* and the journal *Epigraphia Indica* bear testimony to this — that we not only owe the most certain dates of Indian literary history we have till now but it is also in these that we look to for information about its chronological riddles remaining unsolved till today.

The Script and the Tradition of Indian Literature

The inscriptions are of such a great significance to us because they give us information on the question of the age of script in India which is very important for the history of literature. As we shall presently see the history of Indian literature does in no way commence with *written* literature and in the oldest periods of the History of Indian literature we find actually not *written* works, but only texts which were handed down by word of mouth. Nevertheless it is clear that the question as to when literary products were written down and handed down in writing is very important for the history of literature. Now the oldest datable Indian inscriptions which have been discovered till now are, as we have already mentioned, the edicts of King Aśoka

1. In the field of inscription-researches great services have been rendered by G. Bühler, F. Kielhorn, E. Hultzsch and J. F. Fleet.

belonging to the 3rd century B.C. But it would be quite wrong to deduce from this — as Max Mueller also has done — that the use of script in India would not have commenced earlier. Palaeographical facts prove indisputably that at the time of Aśoka the script cannot have been possibly a new invention, but it must have already had a long history of its own. The oldest Indian script, from which the Nāgarī script best known in Europe and all the numerous alphabtes used in Indian manuscripts are to be derived, is called Brāhmī-script, as, according to an Indian legend it is supposed to have been invented by the creator Brahmā himself. According to G. Bühler's thorough investigations[2] this script is to be traced back to a Semetic origin, especially to the oldest North-Semetic characters as are found in Phonecian inscriptions and on the stones of Mesa around 890 B.C. It was probably merchants who — perhaps as early as 800 B.C. — introduced the script into India. For a long time it would have been employed exclusively for commercial purposes, documents, correspondence, bills etc. As they began to use the script in royal courts also for recording messages, orders, documents etc., the kings must have also employed learned grammarians, Brahmins, who adapted the foreign alphabets more and more to the needs of Indian phonetics and worked up a complete alphabet of 44 letters from out of the 22 Semetic characters, as shown by the oldest inscriptions. But since when the script has been employed in India also for recording literary products is a much disputed question which it is difficult to answer.

For we do not have sure proofs of the existence of manuscripts or even authentic information about writing down texts from olden days. It has not been possible till now to find, in the whole Vedic literature any evidence of the knowledge of script. In the Buddhist canon which was completed probably about 400 B.C. there is no mention of manuscripts, although there are numerous proofs for the knowledge of the art of writing and of the widespread use of script in those days. Writing is referred to as an excellent branch of knowledge and

1. Indian Palaeography in *Grundriss* (Outline) 1, 2 and "on the origin of the Indian Brahma Alphabet" 2nd Ed., Strassburg 1898.

Buddhist nuns are expressly permitted to pursue the art of writing; we hear of monks who by praising religious suicide in writing cause the death of others; it is said that a 'registered' thief (i.e. a thief whose name stands written in the king's palace) may not be admitted to the monk's order; we find a game of letters)[1] and also read that parents get writing and reckoning taught to their children. Still there is not even the slightest hint in the holy scriptures of Buddhism that the books were copied or read by themselves. This is all the more noteworthy as we learn from the holy texts of Buddhism even the apparently insignificant features of the life of the monks. 'From morning till evening we can follow the monks in their everyday life, on their wanderings and during rest, in their loneliness and in company with other monks or laymen; we know the furnishings in the rooms occupied by them, their tools, the contents of their store-rooms; but nowhere do we read that they read or copied their sacred texts, or that the monks' houses had such things as writing materials or manuscripts. The memory of the clerical brothers "rich in hearing" — what we call today well-read was called in those days 'rich in hearing' — was a substitute to the libraries of monasteries; and if there was a danger that in a community the knowledge of an indispensable text — e.g. the confession formula that had to be recited in the congregation of the brethren on every newmoon and fullmoon day — would disappear, then the following procedure was adopted, as prescribed in an old Buddhistic community order. Of those monks one shall be immediately sent to the neighbouring community. To him one shall say: 'Go brother, and when you have learnt by heart the confession-formula, the complete or the abridged one, then come back to us."[2] And wherever there is reference to the preservation of the teachings of the master and the value of the sacred texts, there is always a mention of hearing and memorising, nowhere of writing and reading.

From such facts one might conclude that at that time — i.e. in the 5th century B.C. — they did not think of the idea

1. This consists in the guessing of letters which one writes in the air or on the back of a playmate.

2. H. Oldenberg. *Aus Indien und Iran.* Berlin 1899. p. 22 f.

that books can also be written. But that would be a hasty conclusion. For it is an interesting phenomenon that in India from the oldest times upto the present day what mattered for the whole literary and the scientific activity was the spoken word and not the script. Even today when Indians know the art of writing for centuries, when they have innumerable manuscripts and these manuscripts enjoy even a certain holiness and respect, when the most important texts are accessible even in India in cheap print, — even today the whole literary and scientific activity in India is based on the spoken word. Not from manuscripts or books do they learn the texts, but from the mouth of the teacher—today as millennia ago. The written text can at best be used as an aid while learning as a support to memory but it does not command any authority. Only the spoken word of the tea cher enjoys authority. And today if all manuscripts and printed books were lost, still Indian literature would not in any way thereby disappear from the surface of the earth, but a large part of it could be brought to light from the memory of scholars and reciters. For even the works of poets have been meant in India never for readers but always only for listeners. And even modern authors do not wish to be read, but it is their wish, that their poems may become 'an ornament for the throats of the experts'.[1]

Hence the fact that nowhere in older literary works is there any mention of manuscripts is in no way any absolute proof of the non-existence of the same. Perhaps they have not been mentioned for the simple reason that writing and reading them did not play any role at all because all teaching and learning took place orally. Therefore it could be possible, that even in very olden days books were copied and used as aids to teaching as today. That is the opinion of several researchers.[2] Nevertheless it seems remarkable to me that in the later literature — in the later Purāṇas, in Buddhistic Mahāyāna texts and in modern supplements to old epics — the copying and presenting of books

1. G. Bühler, Indische Palaeographie (*Grundriss* I, 2) p. 3 ff.

2. On the age of the art of writing in India, see also Barth, *RHR* 41, 1900, 184 ff. =*Oeuvres* II, 317 ff. The arguments brought forward by Shyamaji Krishnavarma, *OC* VI, Leyden 1883, pp. 305 ff. for the knowledge and use of writing, even at the Vedic period, are well worthy of notice.

is praised as a religiously meritorious deed, whereas there is no trace of it in the whole of the older literature. It is also characteristic that the older works on phonetics and grammar and even the Mahābhāṣya of Patañjali of the 2nd century B.C. do not pay any attention to the script, that they deal always with spoken sounds and never with written words and that the whole grammatical terminology always concerns only the spoken word and never the written text. After considering all this, we may say that in India *probably* there were no written books in olden days.

For this peculiar phenomenon that they knew the script for centuries without using them for literary purposes, several causes may be thought of. Firstly, there was perhaps a lack of suitable writing material. It could have been found if there had been a pressing need for it. Not only such a need was not there, but it was also always in the interest of the priests who were the pillars of the oldest literature that the sacred texts that they taught in their schools were not recorded. Thus they retained firmly in their hands a very lucrative monopoly. Whoever wanted to learn something had to come to them and reward them richly; and it was in their hands to keep those texts away from the people to whom they did not want to impart the sacred knowledge. How important this was to them we learn from the Brahminical law books which repeatedly stress the law that members of the lower castes (the Śūdras and the Caṇḍālas) must not learn the sacred texts; for unclean like a corpse, like a burial ground is a Śūdra, therefore in his vicinity the Veda must not be recited. And in the old law book of Gautama it is said:[1] "If a Śūdra hears the Veda, his ears must be filled with molten tin or lac, if he recites the sacred texts his tongue must be cut off, if he retains them in memory, his body must be cut up in two." How could they have written down their texts and thus expose them to the danger of being read by unworthy people? And in any case the handing down of the texts by the mouth of the teacher was a sure method of preserving them – why should this fashionable invention, the script, take its place? And the

1. XII, 4-6.

main reason[1] for the script not having been used for literary purposes so long is that Indians got acquainted with the art of writing only long after they possessed a rich literature which had been transmitted by word of mouth.

It is certain that the whole ancient literature of Indians, the Brahminic as well as the Buddhistic, originated without the art of writing and was transmitted without it for centuries.[2] Whoever wanted to know a text had to go to a teacher to hear it from him. So we read again and again inan cient literature that a warrior or Brāhmin who wants to acquire any knowledge goes to a famous teacher and undergoes untold pain and sacrifices in order to acquire learning which cannot be acquired in any other way. So the teacher is held as carrier and preserver of the sacred knowledge in very great reverence according to ancient Indian law—as spiritual father he is sometimes considered as equal to the physical father and sometimes even superior to him, he is looked upon as an image of God Brahmā and whoever serves the teacher loyally is assured of Brahmā's heaven. This is also the reason why the conducting of the pupil to the teacher, who shall teach him the sacred texts, one of the most sacred ceremonies which no Aryan Indian should miss if he did not want to lose his caste. A book existed only if and when there were teachers and pupils who taught and learnt it. What we call various branches of literature, various theological and philosophical systems, various editions or recensions of a work were, in ancient India, in reality various schools in which particular texts were taught, heard and learnt from generation to generation. Only when we do not lose sight of this fact can we understand the whole development of the oldest Indian literature.

We must also note that the way of handing down religious texts was different from that of handing down profane ones. Religious texts were held sacred and exactness of learning them was a strict requirement of religion. The pupil had to repeat what the teacher said exactly word for word avoiding carefully

1. Cf. in particular T. W. Rhys Davids, *Buddhist India*, London 1903, p. 112 ff.

2. I-tsing (Transl. Takakusu, pp. 182 f.) mentions that in his time (7th century A.D.) the Vedas were still only handed down orally.

every mistake in pronunciation, intonation and in the manner of recitation, and thus he had to commit to memory. And there can be no doubt that this kind of orally handing down is a better guarantee for the preservation of the original text than the copying down again and again of manuscripts. Indeed we have—as we shall see later—direct proofs, that for example the text of the songs of Ṛgveda as we read them today in our printed editions, has remained since the 5th century B.C. almost unchanged word for word, syllable for syllable, accent for accent. It was of course not so with profane works, especially with the epic poems. There however the texts were subjected to numerous mutilations, there every teacher, every reciter considered himself to be justified to change, to correct, to omit and to add as he liked,—and critics have a difficult and often impossible task when they try to produce such texts in their oldest and most original form.

And yet oral transmission, where it is still possible to have recourse to it—and this is so in the case of the oldest Veda texts with the help of the ancient text books on phonetics (Prātiśākhya) and otherwise often with the help of the commentaries—is the most valuable means of producing our texts. For, manuscripts from which we get most of our texts date back to very old times. The oldest writing material on which Indians have written, are palm leaves,—and it is characteristic of the conservative mind of Indians that in spite of knowing the so much more convenient paper and in spite of the general use of printing, even today manuscripts are written on palm-leaves—and strips of birch barks. Both materials are very fragile and rapidly perishable in the climate of India. Therefore, it is that a great majority of the manuscripts which we possess and according to which almost all our text editions have been prepared, are from the last few centuries. Even manuscripts from the 14th century are extremely rare. Bühler has discovered some manuscripts in India which date back to the 12th century.[1] But the oldest Indian manucripts have been found in Nepal, Japan and

1. Kielhorn discovered the oldest manuscripts of Western India, of the 11th century (*Report on the Search for Sanskrit MSS in the Bombay Presidency during the year* 1880-81, Bombay, 1881).

Eastern Turkistan. Those found in Nepal date back to the 10th century and in Japan some manuscripts on palm leaves were found that originate from the first half of the 6th century. Since the year 1889 manuscripts have been found in Kaṣgar and its surroundings which take us back to the 5th century, and in 1900 M. A. Stein has excavated from desert sands over 500 inscriptions on wooden plaques near Khotan in the Taklmekan – desert which date back to the 4th century and perhaps even to an older date. Also by means of the Prussian Turfan Expedition and the more recent discoveries of M. A. Stein, fragments of manuscripts from the earliest centuries after Christ have been brought to light.[1]

Wood as writing material is mentioned already in Buddhistic texts, and it must have been in use since a very long time. But the use of palm leaves can also be traced back to the first century A.D. Only seldom were cotton materials, leather, metals and stones used as writing materials in India. The Buddhists mention here and there the recording of documents and also of verses and aphorisms on gold plates. A gold plate with a votive inscription has also been preserved till today. Documents and even the smaller manuscripts on silver plates have been found several times in India. However very often copper plates were used for the recordings of documents, especially gift-deeds and these have been preserved to us in a large number. And the Chinese pilgrim Hiuen-Tsiang reports that King Kaniṣka who ascended the throne in 78 A.D. got the sacred scriptures of Buddhists engraved on copper plates. Whether this is based on facts we do not know, but it can be certainly believed. For literary works have indeed been found on copper plates. It would be hard to believe that literary notes have been engraved in rocks, if rock inscriptions had not been found a few years ago in Ajmer containing complete dramatic writings – of course dramas written by a king and his court poet.

A great majority of Indian manuscripts however, on which our texts are based, is written on paper. But paper was

1. See Lüders, *Über die literarischen Funde von Osttürkestan*, SBA, 1914, pp. 90 ff.

introduced into India only by the Mohammedans and the oldest paper inscription is supposed to have been written in 1223/4 A.D.

In spite of the preference of Indians for oral teaching and learning they already began many centuries ago, to collect manuscripts and preserve them in libraries. Such libraries—Indians call them 'treasure-houses of the Goddess of speech'—were found and are often found even today in monasteries and temples, in the palaces of princes and even in the private residences of rich people. It is said of Bāṇa (around 620 A.D.) that he maintained his own reader; he must have therefore possessed a considerably large private library. In the 11th century King Bhoja of Dhārā had a famous library. In the course of centuries these libraries became remarkably big. Thus Bühler found in Khambay over 30,000 manuscripts in two libraries and the palace library of Tanjore in South India contains over 12,000 manuscripts. A systematic investigation of these Indian libraries and a thorough search for manuscripts that spread over the whole of India began in the year 1868. Of course even earlier Colebrooke and other Englishmen had brought considerably large collections of manuscripts to Europe. But in the year 1868 a complete cataloguing of all Sanskrit manuscripts was begun on a suggestion from the meritorious Celtist Whitley Stokes, the then Secretary to the Indian Council in Simla and since then Government of India has allotted in its annual budget a large sum of Rs. 24,000 for the purpose of the search of Sanskrit manuscripts. Thus it is through the devotion of the Anglo-Indian Government and through the tireless efforts of English, German and Indian scholars that we possess today so to say a view of the huge mass of Indian literature as far as it is accessible through manuscripts.

Indian Languages in Their Relationship to Literature[1]

This whole literature that has come down to us, is composed for the most part in Sanskrit. Yet, the two concepts 'Indian Literature' and 'Sanskrit Literature' do not at all coincide with

1. See R.G. Bhandarkar, *JBRAS* 16, 245 ff; 17, 1ff., and G. Grierson, *BSOS* I, 3, 1920 pp. 51 ff.

each other. The history of Indian literature in the most comprehensive sense of the word is the history of a literature that not only extends over long periods of time and over a huge area but which also comprises several languages.

The Indian languages belonging to the Indo-Germanic family have passed through three great development phases, chronologically one after another, but partly also running parallel to one another. They are: I. The ancient Indian. II. The Middle Indian and III. The Modern Indian languages and dialects.

I. *Ancient Indian*

The language of the oldest Indian literary monuments, of the songs, prayers and magic formulas of the Veda is called sometimes 'Ancient Indian' in a narrow sense, sometimes also 'Vedic' (also improperly 'Vedic Sanskrit'), 'Ancient High Indian'[1] would perhaps be the best name for this language which, although is based on a spoken dialect is not any longer an actual peoples' language but is only a literary language bequeathed from generation to generation and intentionally preserved in its antiquity. The dialect which is the basis for this Ancient High Indian as it (the dialect) was spoken by Aryan immigrants in Northwest-India was very closely related to Ancient Persian and Ancient Bactrian and was not much different from the Indo-Iranian basic language.[2] Indeed the language of the Veda and this Indo-Iranian Basic language seem to be closer to each other than the Indian languages Sanskrit and Pali. The vedic language differs from Sanskrit almost not at all in its phonetic content but in its greater antiquity especially by a richer stock of grammatical forms. Thus for example, Ancient Indian has a subjunctive which is lacking in Sanskrit; it has a dozen different infinitive endings of which there is only one left behind in Sanskrit. The aorist forms, plentifully represented in the Vedic language disappear more and more in Sanskrit. The

1. It is called thus by Rhys Davids, *Buddhist India*, p. 153.

2. That is also the basic language to be inferred on a comparison of the language of the Veda with the Ancient Persian of the cuneiform inscriptions and the Ancient Bactrian of the Avesta.

case-endings and personal endings are more perfect in the oldest language than in later Sanskrit.

A later phase of Ancient High Indian appears already in the hymns of the X Book of the Ṛgveda and in some parts of the Atharvaveda and of the collections of the Yajurveda. As against this, the language of the Vedic prose works of the Brāhmaṇas, Āraṇyakas and Upaniṣads has retained only some isolated antiquities of Ancient High Indian; the language of these works is by and large already what is called 'Sanskrit', whereas the language of the Sūtras belonging to Vedāṅgas present Vedic forms only in very exceptional cases, and is essentially pure Sanskrit. Only the numerous Mantras taken from the numerous ancient Vedic hymns, that is only the numerous verses, prayers, epigrams and magic formulas that we find quoted in Vedic prose works and Sūtras belong, as regards language, to Ancient Indian. The Sanskrit of this oldest prose literature — of the Brāhmaṇas, Āraṇyakas, Upaniṣads and the Sūtras -- is little different from the Sanskrit which is taught in the famous grammar of Pāṇini (whose date might be fixed, according to many researchers roughly about 350 B.C.) One can call it best as 'Old Sanskrit'. It is the language which was spoken by the educated in Pāṇini's time and certainly even earlier, especially in the circles of priests and scholars. It is the Sanskrit of which even Patañjali, a grammarian of the 2nd century B.C. says that in order to learn it properly one must learn it from the Śiṣṭas, i.e. from the Brahmins, who were learned and proficient in literature. That the circle of Sanskrit speaking people extended much further — to all 'educated' in fact — is narrated by the same Patañjali in an anecdote in which a grammarian converses with a carriage-driver in Sanskrit and they both debate on etymologies and if in the Indian dramas the languages are distributed in such a way that the King, the Brahmins and respectable persons speak Sanskrit whereas women and all common folk employ the popular languages only with the notable exception that some educated women (nuns and courtesans) now and then speak also Sanskrit, uneducated Brahmins on the other hand are introduced as speaking popular dialects, this reflects certainly the use of languages in real life—and this not only in post-Christian era to which time these dramas belong, but also in earlier centuries. Sanskrit was certainly never actually a language of the masses, but it was a cultivated language spoken in wide circles of the educated and understood in even wider circles. For just as dialogue took place between Sanskrit-speaking and Prakrit-speaking people, so also in real life Sanskrit must have been understood by those who did not speak it themselves.[1] Also the rhapsodies who recited the popular epics in the palaces of kings and in the homes of the rich and the aristocrats must have been understood. And the language of the epics is also Sanskrit. We call it 'Epic Sanskrit and it differs from 'classical Sanskrit' only very little, partly because it has retained much that is ancient, but more because it follows the rules of grammar less strictly and comes closer to the language of the people so that it can be called a more popular form of Sanskrit. Never would there have been popular epics composed in Sanskrit.[2] If it had never been a language understood in large circles — similar to the Modern High German being in general understood nowadays in Germany although it deviates essentially from all spoken dialects.

That Sanskrit was a 'high language' or 'class language' or 'literary language' — in whatever manner we may call it in contrast with the actual peoples' language — is expressed by the

1. The language-relations in ancient India of which we get such a good picture through the dramas, have undergone little change till today. Even today it happens that in an aristocratic household with numerous servants who come from various regions a dozen different languages and dialects are spoken and generally understood. G.A. Grierson describes a case known to him. In this case not less than 13 different languages and dialects are spoken in a house in Bengal. The master of the house speaks with Europeans in the high Bengali language of the elite, whereas in normal life he uses colloquial Bengali which deviates widely from the colloquial language. His wife comes from a place 100 miles away and speaks the particular women's dialect of her region. His secondary wife who usually speaks in Urdu of Lucknow falls into Jargon when she is angry. His estate-manager speaks Dhaki, whereas of the servants some speak Oriya and the others Bhojpuri, Awadhi, Maithili, Ahiri and Chatgaiya. All of them understand one another perfectly well although each speaks only his own dialect. It is only seldom that one uses the dialect of the person whom he addresses. (*Indian Antiquary* XXX 1901, p. 556).

2. It has been presumed that the popular epics were written originally in a dialect and were then translated. This presumption has no factual support, as has been shown by H. Jacobi (*ZDMG* 48, 107 ff).

Indians themselves with the name 'Sanskrit' for, Sanskrit—*Saṃskṛta*, that is 'set right, put in order, prepared, complete, pure, sacred,—means the noble or sacred language, as against '*Prākṛt*'—*Prākṛta*, that is, 'original, natural, usual, common,—which means the 'common popular language'.

And yet one must not speak of Sanskrit as a 'dead language', but rather as a 'confined or bound' language, in as much as it has been fixed at a particular stage by the rules of grammar. For by the rules of Pāṇini a fixed norm was reached in the 4th century B.C. or even earlier and this norm remained the standard for the Sanskrit language for all times to come. What we call 'Classical Sanskrit' means Pāṇinic Sanskrit i.e. that Sanskrit[1] which alone is correct as per the rules of the grammar of Pāṇini. The language however continued to live in these 'fetters' of this grammar. The large volume of poetical and scientific literature has been produced for a thousand years indeed in this language, in 'classical sanskrit'. Even today Sanskrit is not a 'dead language'. Even today there are many Sanskrit journals in India and current affairs are discussed in Sanskrit pamphlets. Also the Mahābhārata is read in public even today and this certainly requires at least partial understanding. Even today poets write and compose in Sanskrit and it is even today the language in which Indian scholars converse with one another on scientific questions. Sanskrit plays in India even today at least the same role as Latin during the Middle Ages in Europe or Hebrew for the Jews.[2]

1. The Indians call "Sanskrit" only this literary language fixed by Indian grammarians. If they speak of "Vedic Sanskrit" as they do so often, then they extend this term "Sanskrit" to Ancient Indian in general.

2. There are epigraphical grounds for assuming that Sanskrit is a modification of a Northern Indian dialect, which was developed by schools of grammar, and which in historical times spread slowly throughout India among the educated classes; see Bühler, *Ep. Ind.*, I, p. 5. Sanskrit is called a sacred language of a certain class of society. Cf. Windisch, Über den sprachlichen Charakter des Pāli (*OC.*, XIV, Paris, 1906), pp. 14.; Thomas *JRAS* 1904. 747 f.; W. Peterson, *JAOS.*, 32, 1912, 414 ff.; T. Michelson, *JAOS.*, 33, 1913, 145 ff. About the wide use of Sanskrit in the India of today, Paul Deussen (*Erinnerungen an Indien*, Kiel, 1904, pp. 2 f) says : "Not only the

1. Summing up I should like to divide Ancient Indian language in relation to its literature as follows :

— Ancient High Indian

(a) Language of the oldest hymns and Mantras, especially those of the Ṛgveda.

(b) Language of the later hymns and Mantras, especially those of the other Vedas as also the Mantras contained in the Brāhmaṇas and Sūtras.

— Sanskrit :

(a) Ancient Sanskrit, the language of the vedic prose works (excluding the Mantras) and of Pāṇini.

(b) Epic Sanskrit, the language of the popular epics.

(c) Classical Sanskrit, the language of classical Sanskrit literature after Pāṇini.

II. *The Middle Indian Languages and Dialects*

1. Simultaneously with the development of Sanskrit and parallel to it the popular dialects spoken by the Aryan Indians

---

professional scholars, as especially the native Sanskrit Professors of the Indian Universities, speak Sanskrit with great elegance, not only their hearers are able to handle it as well as our students of classical philology can handle Latin, but the numerous private scholars, saints, ascetics, and even wider circles can speak and write Sanskrit with facility: I have repeatedly conversed in it for hours with the Mahārājā of Benares: manufacturers, industrials, merchants, partly speak it or understand what is spoken: in every little village my first enquiry was for one who speaks Sanskrit, whereupon immediately one or another came forward, who usually became my guide, indeed often my friend." When he gave lectures in English, he was often invited to repeat in Sanskrit what he had said. "After this had been done, a discussion followed in which some spoke English, others Sanskrit, yet others Hindi, which therefore was also understood, to a certain extent, because pure Hindi differs from Sanskrit in little more than by the loss of inflectional endings. Hence every Hindu understands as much of Sanskrit as an Italian of Latin, especially as, in the real Hindustan, the script has remained the same: and a smattering of Sanskrit can be traced down to the circles of servants and the lower classes wherefore a letter to Benares with only a Sanskrit address will without difficulty reach its destination, through every postal messenger." As to Sanskrit as a "living" language, see also S. Krishnavarma in *OC* V, Berlin, 1831, II b, p. 222; R. G. Bhandarkar, *JBRAS.*, 16, 1885, 268 ff., 327 ff. Windisch, *OC* XIV, Paris, 1897, I. 257, 266; Hertel, *Tantrākhyāyikā*, Transl I., pp. 8 ff., and *HOS.*, Vol. XII, pp. 80 ff.

also developed further in a more natural way. And the languages and dialects which are termed 'Middle Indian' cannot be derived directly so to say from Sanskrit but rather from the Indo-Aryan popular languages which are the basis for Ancient High Indian and Sanskrit or are close to them. When we consider the size of India, it is not surprising that with the gradual spread of the Aryan immigrants from west to east a large number of dialects varying from one another developed. We get an idea of the variety of these dialects from the oldest inscriptions all of which are written in Middle Indian and not in Sanskrit. A number of such popular languages has been raised to the rank of literary languages. Only these will be enumerated here shortly:

The oldest of the Middle Indian literary languages is Pāli, the religious language of the Buddhists of Ceylon, Burma and Siam. It is the language in which the oldest collection of the writings of the Buddhism preserved to our day is composed. The Buddhists themselves tell us that unlike the Brahmins, who preached in the scholarly Sanskrit, the 'Buddha spoke to the people in the language of the folk itself.' And because the Buddha at first preached in *Magadha* (South Bihar) and developed there his excellent efficacy, say the Buddhists, Pāli is the same as *Magadhī*, the language of the province *Magadha.* That cannot be correct, as the dialect of *Māgadha* known to us from a different source, is not the same as *Pāli.* It is more probable that Pāli is a mixed language the foundation of which was *Māgadhi.* Whatever it may be, this much is certain, that the Buddhist canon is the most reliable for our knowledge of the old Buddhism and for the original teachings of the *Buddha.* The word '*Pāli*' means actually 'row', then 'order', direction, rule and therefore also sacred text and finally the language of the sacred texts as against old Sinhalese, a language in which the commentaries to these texts were written.[1]

---

1. This is the view of E. Windisch, "Über den sprachlichen Charakter des Pāli" (*OC.*, XIV., Paris, 1906) and of G. A. Grierson, Bhandarkar Com. Vol., 117 ff. The latter agrees with Sten Konow (*ZDMG* 64, 1910, 114 ff.), that Pāli is similar to Paiśāci-Prākrit. The latter was probably the local dialect of Eastern Gāndhāra and the district of Taxila, a famous seat of learning at the time of Buddha.

2. In addition to the *Pāli* literature there is also a Buddhistic Sanskrit literature. Now in these Buddhistic works often only the prose is Sanskrit whereas the metrical pieces found interspersed in them the so called 'gāthās' (i.e. 'songs' or 'verses') are composed in a Middle Indian dialect. Therefore this dialect has been called 'Gāthā dialect'. This term is however not quite appropriate, as the same dialect is also found in pieces of prose and also some complete works in prose contain the same. It is an old Middle Indian dialect that has been made to approach Sanskrit by adopting in a rather clumsy manner Sanskrit endings and other Sanskritisms. For this reason, Senart has suggested the name "Mixed Sanskrit'[1] for it.

3. Similar to the Buddhists, the Jains also have used for their sacred scriptures not Sanskrit but Middle Indian dialects namely two different Prākrits.[2]

(a) The Jaina-Prākṛt (also called Ardha Māgadhi or Ārṣa), the language of the older works of the Jaina-canons; and

(b) The Jaina-Mahārāṣṭrī the language in which the commentaries to the Jaina canon and the secular poetical works of the Jainas are composed.[3] This dialect is very closely related to that *Prākrit* which has been used most frequently as literary language for secular poetry, viz.

4. The *Mahārāṣtrī*, the language of Mahārāṣṭra, of the land of the Marathas. This is supposed to be the best Prākṛt in general and when Indians speak of *Prākṛt* as such, they mean (the) *Mahārāṣtrī*. It was used mainly for lyrical poetry,

---

1. See S. Lefmann, *ZDMG*, 212 ff.: and E. Senart, *Ind. Ant.*, 21, 1892, 243 ff.

2. Indians use the term "Prākrit" to mean not the popular language as such but only those popular languages which are used in literature. Cf. for this complete chapter R. Pischel, "Grammar of the Prākrit languages" (in *Grundriss* I, 8, Introduction) and H. Jacobi in *A Bay*. A XXIX, 4, 1918, pp. 81 ff.

3. See H. Jacobi, Über das Prākrit in der Erzählungs-litteratur der Jainas, in *RSO*, II, 1909, pp. 231 ff.

especially also for the lyrical portions in dramas. There are also epic poems in *Mahārāṣṭrī*. Other important Prākṛt dialects that are used in drama are:

5. *Śaurasenī*, which is spoken mainly by high-class women in the prose of the dramas. Its basis is the dialect of the *Sūrasena* country whose capital is Mathurā.

6. Low class people speak *Māgadhī*, the dialect of Magadha in the dramas, and

7. *Paiśācī* is spoken in dramas by the people of the lowest classes. Originally the word denoted probably the dialect of a clan of people — of the Paiśācas, although Indians declare it as the language of the demons called Piśācas. In this Paiśācī dialect also a famous work of narrative literature is composed — Guṇāḍhya's — *Bṛhatkathā*.

8. Finally, a number of Prākṛt dialects which are found now and then in dramas, are all included under the name 'Apabhraṁśa'.[1] The word 'Apabhraṁśa' denoted originally everything that deviates from Sanskrit, then the living popular languages in particular and lastly certain Prākrit dialects.

III. *The Modern Indian Languages and Dialects*[2]

We can notice from the 10th century onwards the third stage of development of the Indian, that is, of the Modern Indian languages. And from the 12th century onwards these languages can show their own literature that is partly independent and partly dependant on Sanskrit literature. The most important of the living modern Indian languages which have developed from the Middle Indian Dialects are the following:

Sindhi, Gujarati, Panjabi and West Hindi in Western India, Garhwali (spoken between the Sutlej and the Ganges), Kumaonī (between the Ganges and the Gogra), Kashmiri

1. On the Apabhraṁśas see H. Jacobi in *A Bay A* XXIX, 4. 1918, pp. 53 ff.; XXXI, 2, 1921, pp. xviii ff., and in *Festschrift für Wackernagel*, pp. 124 ff. Jacobi is of opinion, that the Apabhraṁśa was first used by the poets of the Ābhīras and Gūrjaras.

2. Based on the excellent survey of the Indo-Aryan Vernaculars given by Sir George Grierson in *BSOS* I., 1. 1918, pp. 47 ff. Compare also E. J. Rapson, *Cambridge History* I, 37 ff.

and Naipali (language of Nepal) in North India; Marathi in South India and Bihari, Bengali, Oriya and Asami in Eastern India. Besides there is also Urdu or Hindustani, which is Hindi with a strong mixture, of Persian and Arabic elements.[1] It was born in the 12th century in the region around Delhi, the Centre of Mohammedan power, in the camps (Urdu) of the soldiers, and hence the name 'Urdu' i.e. 'camp-language'. In the 16th century it also began to produce literature. Today it is the general language of communication in India.

Lastly, Sinhalese, the language of Ceylon (Sri Lanka) is also an Indo-Germanic dialect derived from the Middle Indian. By the introduction of Buddhism and of Buddhistic Pāli literature into Ceylon (Sri Lanka) a literary activity began here which first restricted itself to explaining religious texts. In the centuries after this, we find also a secular literature influenced by Sanskrit poetry.[2]

All the Indian languages mentioned till now belong to the family of Indo-Germanic languages. But we have, in addition to these, also a number of non-Indo-Germanic languages in South India.[3] These languages are termed as 'Dravidian Languages' and they form a group of languages in themselves. These "Dravidian Languages" must at one time have been common in the North as well, for the Indo-Aryan languages show strong Dravidian influence.[4] The most important of these languages are: Tamil, Telugu, Malayalam and Kannada. Although these languages are not Indo-Germanic, yet numerous Sanskritisms have entered into them, and even the literature of these languages, which is by no means insignificant, is dependent on Sanskrit literature to a very large extent.

In this book we will have to restrict ourselves essentially to Sanskrit, Pāli and Prākrit literatures. It may be possible to treat Modern Indian Literature at best only in the appendix.

---

1. Also the script is Persian-Arabic.
2. Cf: Wilhelm Geiger, Literatur und Sprache der Singhalesen in *Grundriss* I, 10.
3. Even in the Ganges valley and in the extreme north-west of India (i.e. in Baluchistan) some Dravidian dialects, like Brahui, have been preserved.
4. See Grierson, *BSOS.*, I, 3, 1920, pp. 71 f.

SECTION I

THE VEDA OR THE VEDIC LITERATURE

What is the Veda ?

As the oldest Indian and also the oldest Indo-Germanic literary monument the Veda deserves an outstanding place in the history of world literature. It deserves it also, if we bear in mind that at least for 3000 years millions of Hindus considered the word of the Veda as the word of God and that the *Veda* controlled their thinking and feeling. Just as the Veda is, on account of its age, foremost in Indian literature, so also no one can understand the spiritual life and the culture of the Indians without acquiring an insight into the Vedic literature. Besides, Buddhism, whose place of birth is India, remains for ever un-understandable to one who does not know the Veda. For, the teachings of the Buddha are related to the Veda as the New Testament to the Old. No one can understand the new faith without getting acquainted with the old faith of which the Veda gives us information.

Now, what is actually the Veda ?

The word 'Veda' means KNOWLEDGE' and then the knowledge par excellence' i.e. the sacred, the religious knowledge', and it does not denote any one single literary work like perhaps the word 'Koran', or any compact collection of a definite number of books, completed at any particular time, like the word 'Bible' (the 'book par excellence') or like the word 'Tipiṭaka' the 'Bible' of the Buddhists, but a large extent of literature that came into being in the course of many millennia and was transmitted centuries long from generation to generation by word of mouth, until at last by a later generation—of course in the hoary past—it was declared as 'sacred knowledge' as 'divine revelation' on account of its age as well as its content. Here it is not a question of a 'canon' that was established at the time of any church-council. But the faith in the 'sacredness' of this literature followed in a way from itself and was only seldom seriously disputed.

But what is called 'Veda' or 'Vedic literature' consists of three different classes of literary works; and to each of these three classes belongs also a large or small number of individual works, of which some have been preserved but many have been also lost today. These three classes are :

I. SAṂHITĀS i.e. 'Collections' namely collections of hymns, prayers, magic songs, benedictory words, sacrificial formulas and litanies.

II. BRĀHMAṆAS, extensive prose texts which contain theological discussions, especially observations on the sacrifice and the practical or mystical significance of the individual sacrificial rites and ceremonies.

III. ĀRAṆYAKAS (Forest Texts) and Upaniṣads (secret teachings) which are partly included in or appended to the Brāhmaṇas themselves and partly are supposed to be independent works. They contain the meditations of hermits in forests and ascetics on God, world and man. And in them a good amount of Indian philosophy is contained.

There must have been once upon a time a fairly large number of Saṃhitās which originated in several schools of priests and singers and have been handed down further by them. Many of these 'collections' were however nothing but slightly different recensions—Śākhās, 'branches', as the Indians say—of one and the same Saṃhitā. But there are four Saṃhitās which differ sharply from one another and which are preserved to us in one or more recensions. They are :

1. The Ṛgveda - Saṃhitā, the collection of the Ṛgveda. The Ṛgveda is 'the veda or the knowledge of the praise—songs (ṛc, plural ṛcas).
2. The Atharvaveda-Saṃhitā, the collection of the Atharva-veda, i.e. of the knowledge of the magic formulas (*atharvan*).
3. The Sāmaveda-Saṃhitā, the collection of the Sāma veda. i.e. 'of the knowledge of the melodies' (Sāman).
4. The Yajurveda-Saṃhitā, the collection of the Yajurveda, i.e. 'of the knowledge of the sacrificial formulas (Yajus, plural Yajūṃṣi) of which there are two recensions which differ from each other rather sharply, namely:

(a) The Saṃhitā of the Kṛṣṇa (Black) Yajurveda which is preserved in various recensions of which the Taittirīya-Saṃhitā and the Maitrāyaṇī-Saṃhitā are most important; and

(b) The Saṃhitā of the Śukla (White) Yajurveda, which is preserved in the Vājasaneyi-Saṃhitā.

Based on these four different Śaṃhitās, the Indians distinguish four different Vedas—and therefore one also speaks often of the 'Vedas' in plural, namely : Ṛgveda, Atharvaveda, Sāmaveda and (Black and White) Yajurveda. And each one of the works of the class of the Brāhmaṇas, the Āraṇyakas or the Upaniṣads is attached to one or the other of the Saṃhitās enumerated above and 'belongs' as one usually says to one of the four Vedas. We have therefore not only Saṃhitās, but also Brāhmaṇas, Āraṇyakas and Upaniṣads of the Ṛgveda as well as of the Atharvaveda, of the Sāmaveda and of the Yajurveda. Thus the Aitareya Brāhmaṇa for e.g. belongs to the Ṛgveda, the Śatapatha Brāhmaṇa to the White Yajurveda, the Chāndogya Upaniṣad to the Sāmaveda etc.

Every work that belongs to one of the three abovementioned classes and to one of the four Vedas, must be described as 'Vedic'; and thus the whole vedic literature presents itself to us therefore as a large number of works of religious content—collections of songs, prayer-books, theological and theosophical treatises—which belong to several successive epoques, which however form one unit in this that altogether they constitute the basis for the Brahminical religious system and have for Brahminism the same significance as the Old Testament for Judaism and the New Testament for Christianity. And as the Jews and the Christians their 'Holy Scripture', so the Brahminical Indians, hold their Veda in its full extent to be divine revelation. It is however characteristic that corresponding to the expression 'Holy Scripture' the Indians have the word 'Śruti', 'hearing' because the revealed texts were not written and read but only spoken and heard. However, that not only the ancient hymns of the Ṛgveda were supposed to have been 'breathed out' by Brahman and 'seen' by the ancient seers, but also that every word in the Upaniṣads, the latest products of the vedic literature were considered as indisputable truth coming from God Brahman, is testified by the whole history of Indian philosophy. Although the various systems of Indian philosophy differ widely from one another, they all agree on this that they hold the Veda as revealed and that they all quote the Veda, especially the Upaniṣads, as authority. There is certainly a high degree of freedom and arbitrariness as regards explaining these texts, and every philosopher reads out of them whatever he wants to find. It is highly characteristic that even the Buddhists who reject the authority of the Veda admit that it was originally proclaimed (or 'created') by God Brahmā; only, they add, that it was falsified by the Brahmins and therefore it contains so many mistakes.

The expression 'Veda' is justified only for this literature considered as revealed. There is however one more class of works which most closely follow the vedic literature but cannot be described as belonging to the Veda. They are the so called Kalpasūtras (sometimes also called shortly 'sūtras') or text books of rituals, which are written in a peculiar, aphoristic prose style. Among them we find

1. The Śrautasūtras, which contain the rules for the execution of the great sacrifices often lasting for many days, during which several sacrificial fires burn and a large number of priests must be employed.
2. The Gṛhyasūtras, which contain rules for the simple ceremonies and sacrificial acts of every day life (at birth, wedding, death etc.) and
3. The Dharmasūtras, the text books of spiritual and worldly law—the oldest law books of the Indians.

Just like the Brāhmaṇas, Āraṇyakas and Upaniṣads these works are appended to one of the four Vedas; and there are Śrauta, Gṛhya and Dharmasūtras which belong to the Ṛgveda, others which belong to the Sāmaveda, to the Yajurveda or to the Atharvaveda. They have originated evidently from particular vedic schools which have set to themselves the task of the study of any one particular Veda. But these text books are considered as man's work and not as divine revelation any more. They do not belong to the Veda but to the 'Vedāṅgas', the 'parts' i.e., 'the auxiliary sciences of the Veda.'

To these 'Vedāṅgas' belong, in addition to the works on rituals also a number of works on phonetics, grammar, etymology, prosody and astronomy. We shall treat these at the end of this chapter.

After this general survey of the Vedic literature and its connected literature, we shall apply ourselves to discussing the most important works belonging to the Veda, above all the Saṃhitās.

The Ṛgveda Saṃhitā

Indisputably the oldest and the most important of all the works of the vedic literature is the Ṛgveda-Saṃhitā, usually called simply 'the Ṛgveda'. Of the various recensions of this Saṃhitā, which have once existed, only one has been preserved till our present day. This[1] consists of the text handed down to us in a collection of 1,028 hymns (sūktas) which are divided into ten books (Maṇḍalas, i.e. 'circles').[2]

That this collection of hymns is the oldest or at least contains the oldest that we have of Indian literature is proved indisputably by the language of the hymns.[3] But the language proves also that the collection is not a unitary work but consists of older and younger pieces. As in the Hebrew Book of Psalms so here also songs which were composed in times wide apart from one another were, at some time, united in one collection and were attributed to famous personalities of an earlier time, most preferably to the forefathers of those families in which the concerned songs were handed down. The majority of the oldest hymns is found in the books II to VII which are usually called the 'family books' because by tradition they are attributed, each one, to a family of reciters. The names of the reciters or Ṛṣis (i.e. 'seers, prophets'), who have, as the Indians say, 'seen' these hymns, are mentioned partly in the Brāhmaṇas and partly

---

1. It is the recension of the Śākalaka-school. On the publication of the texts see supra p. 18 ff.

2. Besides this there is one more purely external division, which pays due regard to the extent, i.e. in 8 Aṣṭakas or "Eights" each one of which is divided into eight Adhyāyas or "Lessons", which in their turn are again divided into smaller Vargas or "chapters" consisting, usually, of five stanzas each.

3. See J. Wackernagel. *Altindische Grammatik* I, pp. xiii ff, on the language of the Ṛgveda.

in independent lists of Authors (Anukramaṇīs) which follow the Vedāṅga-literature. They are called: Gṛtsamada, Viśvāmitra, Vāmadeva, Atri, Bharadvāja and Vasiṣṭha. They and their successors were considered by the Indians as the Ṛṣis or seers—we would say 'Authors'—of the hymns of Maṇḍalas II to VII. The VIII book contains hymns that are attributed to the reciter-family of the Kaṇvas and that of the Aṅgiras. But the Anukramaṇīs give us also the names of the Ṛṣis or 'Authors' of every single hymn of the remaining books (I, IX, X) and it is noteworthy that among them there are also women's names. Unfortunately all these lists of names are almost worthless and in reality the authors of the vedic hymns are quite unknown to us.[1] For, as has been proved long ago, even the tradition that names Gṛtsamada, Viśvāmitra etc. and individuals among their descendants as the Ṛṣis of the hymns contradicts the particulars furnished by the hymns. In those (the hymns) only the descendants of those Ṛṣis are mentioned as the authors of the hymns; but the Ṛṣis Gṛtsamada, Viśvāmitra, Vasiṣṭha or whatever be their names—their names are well known in the whole of Indian literature as the heroes of innumerable myths and legends—are, even in the hymns of the Ṛgveda the seers of an ancient age long forgotten and they are mentioned as the founder-fathers of the reciting-families in which the hymns were handed down. The IX book acquires a unitary character by the fact that it contains exclusively hymns which glorify the Soma-drink and are dedicated to the Soma-god. Soma is the name of a plant out of which an intoxicating juice is extracted which even in the Indo-Iranian period of antiquity was considered as a drink welcome to the Gods and therefore played a prominent role in the sacrifices of the Indians as well as the ancient Iranians—they call it Haoma. In ancient Indian mythology, however, the Soma drink is equated with the drink of immortality of the Gods and the abode of this drink

1. Oldenberg, "Über die Liedverfasser of the Rigveda" in *ZDMG* vol. 42, p. 199 ff.
Even earlier; A. Ludwig, *Der Rigveda*, vol. III, p. XIII and 100 ff.

of the Gods is the moon, the drop[1] shining like gold in the sky. Therefore in the IX book of the Ṛgveda-saṃhitā Soma is celebrated not only as the sacrificial drink dear to the Gods but also as the moon, the king of the sky. As the Soma cult dates back to the Indo-Iranian age, we may presume that also the songs of the IX book most closely connected with the Soma-Sacrifice belong to a considerably early epoque. The latest constituents of our collection of hymns are found however in Books I and X composed of pieces which differ greatly from one another in their character.[2] This does not mean that some very old pieces are also not found in these books. Likewise some younger hymns are also found strewn in the 'family-books'. After all, the question, which hymns are 'earlier' and which are 'later' is not easy to decide. For, the language, on which this differentiation is mainly based, differs not only with the age of the hymns but also with their origin and purpose, depending on whether they stand in relation more to the priestly cult or to the popular religion. A magic-song for example can be differentiated in language from a hymn praising Soma or Indra, but need not, for this reason, be later[3] than that.

The so-called '*Khilas*' which are found in a few manuscripts, represent, on the whole, a later stratum of Ṛgvedic hymn poetry. The word *Khila* means "supplement", and this name in itself indicates that they are texts which were collected and added to the *Saṃhitā* only after the latter had already been concluded. This does not exclude the possibility that *some* of these *Khilas* are of no less antiquity than the hymns of the Ṛgveda-Saṃhitā, but for some reason unknown to us were

---

1. Sanskrit "Indu" means "drop" and "moon". A. Hillebrandt has the distinction of having proved in his *Vedische Mythologie* (Breslau 1891 ff.) that already in the Ṛgveda, *Soma* did not mean only the plant, but also the moon. In the whole of the later literature *Soma* is the moon.

2. See A. Bergaigne, *JA*, 1886-87, on the arrangement of the hymns in Books II-VII, and A. Barth, *RHR* 19, 1889, 134 ff. = *Oeuvres* II, 8 ff on those in Books I, VIII-X. See also Bloomfield, *JAOS*, 31, 1910, pp. 49 ff., for criteria for distinguishing between earlier and later hymns in the Ṛgveda.

3. See M. Bloomfield, "On the Relative Chronology of the Vedic Hymns", (*JAOS*, 21, 1900, pp. 42-49).

not included in the collection. The eleven Vālakhilya-hymns, which in all mansucripts are found at the end of Book VIII, without being included in it, are probably of this kind. Of comparatively high antiquity are probably also the eleven Suparṇa-hymns, as well as the Praiṣasūktāni and the prose Nividas, small collections of sacrificial litanies.[1]

The question as to what is to be understood as "earlier" and what is to be understood as "later" hymns of the Ṛgveda can be dealt with only at the end of this chapter where we have to deal with the question of the age of the Veda as such. Here it must be sufficient to say that the general view regarding the antiquity of the Veda, of even the later constituents is fully justified even by the fact that —as Alfred Ludwig says[2]— that the 'Ṛgveda presupposes nothing that is known to us in Indian literature whereas on the other hand, the whole of Indian literature, the whole of Indian life takes the Veda for granted.'

Next to the language, the system of metres in particular proves the antiquity of the Vedic hymnal poetry. For whereas on the one hand the Vedic system of metres is separated from that of the classical Sanskrit poetry by a big gulf due to the fact that in the Vedic poetry there are numerous metres of which no trace is found in the later poetry while vice versa many metres of classical Sanskrit poetry do not have any parallels in the Veda, on the other hand although some metres

1. The Khilas have been published by I. Scheftelowitz, "Die Apokryphen des Ṛgveda" (*Indische Forschungen*, I), Breslau 1906. See also Scheftelowitz, *ZDMG* 73, 1919, 30 ff.; 74, 1920, 192 ff.; 75, 1921, 37 ff.; *ZTT*, 1, 1922, 50 ff.; 58 ff. Oldenberg, *Die Hymnen des Ṛgveda*, I, Berlin, 1858, 504 ff., and GGA, 1907, 210 ff.; A.B. Keith *JRAS*, 1907, 224 ff. The Khila *Śiva-samkalpa* (edited, translated and explained by Scheftelowitz, *ZDMG*, 75, 1921, 201 ff.), is a regular Upaniṣad, the first part of which (1-13) is old, the rest late sectarian.

2. *Der Rigveda*, III, p. 183. Cf. also ibid, P. 3: "The claim to a hoary past is proved not only internally by the content as well as the form of the language, but also externally by the fact that the Veda was the basis for the literature, for the spiritual and religious life and that within the Veda the pieces of poetry are the prerequisite for the rest, but they themselves do not have anything which forms the basis for them."

of the vedic poetry appear again in the later poetry they do so with a more strongly pronounced hymn than in the Ṛgveda.

In ancient Indian metres only the number of syllables is fixed, whereas the quantity of the syllables is fixed only partly. The vedic verses consist of 8, 11 or 12 lines, more rarely of 5 syllables. These lines, called *Pādas*,[1] are the units of ancient Indian metres, and only the four (or five) last syllables are fixed with reference to rhythm while the last syllable is again a *syllaba anceps*. The regular form of the eight-syllabic pāda is therefore:

o o o o ∪ — ∪ ⊻

Three such lines make the *Gāyatri* and four such lines the stanza called the Anuṣṭubh. In ancient poetry the *Anuṣṭubh* is by far less popular than the *Gāyatri*. Later it is the other way about: the *Anuṣṭubh* becomes the usual verse and from it is developed the *śloka*, the actual metre of epic poetry. The metres *paṅkti* consisting of five eight-syllabic lines and the *Mahā-paṅkti* consisting of six such pādas occur more rarely.

The eleven-syllabic line has a Caesura after the fourth or fifth syllable and its regular form is as follows:

o o o o || o o o — ∪ — ⊻

or o o o o o || o o — ∪ — ⊻

Four such *pādas* form the stanza called *Triṣṭubh*.

The 12 syllabic line differs from the 11-syllabic only in this that it has one more syllable; for the rest the two metres are formed exactly alike. The regular form of the 12-syllabic *pāda* is therefore:

o o o o || o o o — ∪ — ∪ ⊻

or o o o o o || o o — ∪ — ∪ ∪

Four such 12-syllabic *pādas* form a stanza which is called *Jagatī*.

1. Pāda means "foot" and also "quarter". The latter meaning is to be taken here, as in general four Pādas make one stanza. With the "foot" of the Greek metre the word Pāda has nothing to do. A return to such small units as the Greek "verse-feet" is impossible in the ancient Indian system of metres.

The regular form of the 5-syllabic line, of which four or eight together form the stanza called the Dvipāda Virāj is:

⏓ — ⏓ — ⏓

By the combinations of different *Pādas* to a stanza a number of artistic metres are formed like the Uṣṇiḥ-stanzas and the Bṛhatī-stanzas which are composed of 8- and 12-syllabic lines.

What a great importance the ancient Indian metres attach to the number of syllables[1] and what a little importance to rhythm is also proved by the repeated speculations in the *Brāhmaṇas* and the *Upaniṣads* on the mystic significance of the metres where the mysticism of number is also involved, when for example, it is said with a strange logic: 'The words *bhūmi* (earth) *antarikṣa* (air-space) and *dyu* (heaven) form 8 syllables. Therefore he that knows the Gāyatrī gains the three worlds.[2] However, that the metres play such a terrible role in the mysticism of the rituals that they are thought of as divine beings and even receive offerings[3] that mythology is concerned with them, thus more particularly with the Gāyatrī, which in a bird's form fetches the Soma from the heaven, that they are created by Prajāpati like other beings,[4] all this points to the great antiquity of these metres, which were thought to have originated in prehistoric times. Thus the age of the metres is also a proof for the age of the hymns themselves.[5]

We get the clearest idea of the antiquity of these hymns when we look into the geographical and cultural conditions of the time of which they speak to us. Then we see above all that at the time when the hymns of the Ṛgveda originated, the Āryan Indians had not yet spread over the whole of India. We find them settled still in the region of the River Indus (Sindhu)

---

1. See Weber, *Ind. Stud.* 8, 178 f., and H. Weller. *ZTT*, 1, 1922, 115ff.
2. *Bṛhdāraṇyaka-Upaniṣad* V, 15. Dyu is to be pronounced as diu.
3. Vasiṣṭha-Dharmasūtra XIII, 3 among others.
4. For example Śatapatha-Brāhmaṇa VIII, 1, 1-2. How great a role the metres play in the symbolism and mysticism of the ritual, may be seen from numerous passages in the liturgical Saṃhitās and in the Brāhmaṇas: See A. Weber, *Ind. Stud.* 8, pp. 8 ff., 28 ff.
5. See E. V. Arnold, *Vedic Metre*, Cambridge 1905, and A.B. Keith and Arnold, *JRAS*, 1906, 484 ff., 716 ff., 997 ff., on the metre of the Ṛgveda as a criterion of its age.

in today's Panjab.[1] Coming from the West through the passes of the Hindukush, the Aryan clans penetrated into the land of the five rivers and in the songs of the Ṛgveda we still hear of the battles that the Aryans[2] had to fight out with the *Dasyu* or the 'black skin', as the dark-complexioned original inhabitants were called. Only slowly do they press forward from the west to the east upto the Ganges, all the while fighting against the detested '*Anāryas*' (Non-*Āryans*), against the *Dasyus* or *Dāsas* who know no gods, no laws and no sacrifices. And it is characteristic that this river, without which we can hardly imagine to ourselves the India of all later times and which till the present day plays such a prominent role in the poetry as well as in the popular belief of the Indians, is scarcely mentioned in the Ṛgveda. The impressionistic picture of poet Heine

"The fragrance on the Ganges and the splendour
Where mighty trees blossom
And beautiful, quiet people
Kneel before Lotus-flowers."

which brings before us as if by magic the figures and pictures of Kālidāsa's times does not at all match with the time of the Ṛgveda. Even the lotus flower, that is in a way an integral part of later Indian poetry, does not induce the Vedic reciters to any comparisons. The flora and fauna of the *Ṛgveda* are entirely different from those of later times. The Indian fig tree (the Nyagrodha *Ficus indica*) is not found in the *Ṛgveda*. The most terrifying beast of prey in the present day India, the tiger, is not yet mentioned in the hymns—its home is Bengal, where

1. According to E.W. Hopkins (The Punjab and the Ṛgveda, in the *Journal of the American Oriental Society*, XIX, 19-28) the Aryan Indians would have lived in the region around the present day Ambala between the rivers. *Sarasvati* and *Ghuggar*, at the time when most of the hymns were composed' The rivers of the Panjab are praised in the famous "Praise of the Rivers' (nadīstuti), Rv. X, 75 Cf. A. Stein, *JRAS*. 1917, 91 ff. Hertel has not yet convinced me that the Oldest parts of the Ṛgveda were composed in Iran and not in India (*Indo-German Forschungen*, 41, 1923, p 188).

2. Sanskrit Ārya = ancient Bactr. Airya = ancient Persian. Ariya, "the loyal ones", people of one's own clan. Herodotus (VII, 62) says that the Medes were called Arioi, "Arier" is *therefore* the common term used for Indians and Iranians. On the close relationship of the language of Veda with ancient Iranian, see p. 35 above.

the Āryan Indians had not yet penetrated by them. Rice—later on the main fruit of agriculture and the main food of the Indian —is completely unknown to Ṛgveda. Only barley is grown and agriculture played only a very minor role at the time of the hymns. The main occupation was cattle breeding and the main breeding animal was the ox. They also valued very highly the horse, which, harnessed to the war-chariot, carried the warrior to the battle-field and during the popular horse-races brought prize and fame to the winner. We find requests for cattle and horses occurring again and again in the songs and invocations to the gods. The battles with the aboriginal enemies were also fought for the possession of cattle. Therefore the old word for 'war' or 'battle' is called originally 'Demand for oxen' (*gaviṣṭi*). Oxen are praised in the most extravagant expressions as the most exquisite possession.[1] The bellowing of the cows which hurried to their calves is, for the ancient Indians, the dearest music. 'The reciters shouted with joy to God Indra', says a poet, 'as mother-cows bellow to the calf'. Gods are gladly compared with oxen, goddesses with cows. Not only was milk a main article of food, but milk and butter also formed an essential constituent of the offerings to the gods. Milk was gladly drunk warm as it came from the cow, and Vedic poets are surprised at the wonder that the cow in the nature yields boiled milk. And as in the German nursery rhyme,

"O tell me, how come,
Gives white milk the red cow—"

so a Vedic singer praises the god Indra on account of the wonder that he has placed shining white milk in the red and black cows. That cattle were highly esteemed did not however prevent the killing of cows and particularly bullocks at the time of sacrifices; their flesh was also eaten. The killing of cows was not forbidden in the most ancient times. The word "aghnyā"[2] (meaning she who is not to be killed) for cow, indicates that

1. Exactly similar to this is the case with the Dinka and Kaffers in Africa, whose present economic set up could rather be the same as that of the Vedic Aryans.

2. See A. A. Macdonell and A. B. Keith, *Vedic Index of Names and Subjects*, London 1912, II, 145 ff.

cows were killed only under exceptional circumstances. The skin of the cattle was also used. The tanner processed it into leather-tubes, bow-strings and straps. There were also some other kinds of occupations. Firstly there was the wood worker — carpenter, carriage-maker and cabinet-maker all in one — who made carriages in particular. There were metal workers, smiths who used a bird's wing as bellows. Sea-faring was still in its beginnings. A canoe provided with oars, perhaps consisting of only a hollowed-out tree-trunk served for going on rivers. The sea was perhaps known to the vedic Indians, but whether there was already extensive trade by the sea is, to say the least, highly doubtful.[1] As against this, it is certain that there were traders and extensive trade was carried on, during which cattle and gold ornaments took the place of money. Besides cattle and horses it is mainly gold that the vedic reciters begged of the gods and hoped to get as gifts from rich sacrificers.

While we hear of cattle-breeding and agriculture, of trade and occupation, as of valorous deeds in war and of sacrifices in the *Ṛgveda*, there is no proof yet for that division into castes which gives a peculiar shape to the whole social life of the Indian of later times and which to the present day has remained the curse of the Indians. The four castes—*Brāhmaṇa, Kṣatriya, Vaiśya and Śūdra*—are mentioned only in one hymn which can be proved to be of a later date. Of course there were warriors and priests but there is in the Ṛgveda so little talk of a compact warrior-caste as of one or more lower castes of agriculturists (peasants), cattle-breeders, merchants, artisans and workers. As in later times, so it was even in the Ṛgveda time customary that the King was assisted by a family priest (Purohita) who did the sacrifices for him. But we hear often enough—even in the later vedic time—of sacrifices and ceremonies which the householder himself performs without priestly assistance. The

1. It is certainly no chance coincidence that in the songs of the Ṛgveda innumerable metaphors and similes have been taken from cattle-breeding, whereas only seldom does a metaphor refer to sea-faring. One shall compare, as against this, the wealth of Homer in similes and metaphors which refer to sea-faring.

house-wife takes part in these sacrifices; it is indeed considered as very essential that husband and wife perform the holy ceremonies united. This participation of the wife in the sacrifices proves however that the position of the wife in the earliest time of the Ṛgveda was not yet so low as later when the law books specially forbid the women from performing sacrifices and from uttering sacred formulas. In the Ṛgveda (VIII, 31) we read of the couple (dampatī, householder and housewife) that "extracts the soma with their minds united in harmony cleans it and mixes it with milk" and makes worship to the gods. But Manu explains in his law book that it is unpleasant to the gods when women perform sacrifices (IV, 206) and that women who perform the fire-sacrifice (Agnihotra) sink into the hell (XI,37). And if we hear from the Upaniṣads that women also take lively part in the discussions of philosophers, we should not be surprised that in the hymns of the Ṛgveda women could appear in public without any restriction in festivals, dances etc. And it is in no way necessary, as some scholars do, to think of courtesans when it is said that beautiful women hurry to the festive gatherings. With this we do not deny that already at the time of the Ṛgveda some lonely, unprotected women—one poet calls them 'brotherless girls'—gave themselves up to prostitution; but that even at that time 'a splendid institution of courtesans' existed, as in Vesali at the time of the Buddha or in Athens at the time of Pericles, has not been proved by Pischel and Geldner[1] in spite of all the trouble they have taken in this respect.

Yet we must not imagine a too positive or idyllic picture of the moral conditions in ancient India as perhaps Max Mueller has done sometimes. In the hymns of the Ṛgveda we hear of incest, kidnapping, adultery, procuring abortion as well as of deceit, theft and robbery. But all this proves nothing against the antiquity of the Ṛgveda. Modern etymology knows nothing like 'unspoilt primitive races' just as it does not recognise the view point that all primitive races are rude, wild, cannibalistic monsters. The ethnologist knows that

1. *Vedic Studies* I, p. XXV.

a ladder of endless rungs of intermediary gradations of the most diverse cultural conditions leads one from the primitive races to the semi-cultured races and further on to the cultured-races. We therefore need not think that the folk of the Ṛgveda was an innocent folk of herdsmen or one of rude wild men or even a folk of refined culture. The cultural image which flows towards us out of these songs and which Heinrich Zimmer has described in his masterly way in his *Altindisches Leben*[1] which is a valuable book even today, shows us the Aryan Indians as an active, vivacious and pugnacious race of simple and partly still of rude customs. The Vedic reciters pray to the gods for help against the enemy, for victory in battle, for fame and rich booty. They pray for wealth, heaps of gold and numberless herds of cattle, for rain for their fields, for progeny and long life. In the songs of the Rgveda we do not find yet that soft secluded and pessimistic feature of the Indian character which we will come across again and again in the later Indian literature.

Now there have been researchers who held the hymns of the Ṛgveda to be of such enormous antiquity that they imagined to see in them not so much of Indian spiritual life as of Aryan or Indo-germanic, they thought that the epoque of these hymns was still so close to the Indo-germanic "prehistoric time" that they were more 'Aryan' than actually 'Indian'. As against this, other researchers have claimed that the Ṛgveda is above all a product of the Indian mind and for explaining it we should not apply any other principles than what would be applied for explaining any other text of Indian literature. This is one of the many points in which the commentators of the Ṛgveda differ[2] fairly widely from one another.

Indeed we must not forget here the important fact that the Ṛgveda has in no way been explained completely. There is a large number of hymns whose explanation is as clear as of any other Indian text. But, there are on the other hand many hymns and a large number of verses and individual texts of the

1. Berlin 1879.

2. See Barth, *Oeuvres* II, 237 ff., H. Oldenberg, *Vedaforschung* Stuttgart, 1905; Winternitz *WZKM*, 19, 1905, 419 ff.

Ṛgveda whose proper meaning is still highly doubtful. This is also important for a proper estimate of these old poems. The layman, who takes into his hand a translation of the Ṛgveda often wonders as to how so much in these hymns is unpoetical, even ununderstandable and nonsense. The reason is that the translators do not content themselves with translating what is understandable, but that they believe that they have to translate everything, even that which has not been interpreted till now.

It is however not entirely our fault that we do not yet understand the Ṛgveda rightly and that a complete translation of the same must necessarily contain things that are incorrect. The reason is exactly the great antiquity of these hymns which have become ununderstandable to the Indians themselves even in a very early age. Within the Vedic literature we already find some verses of the Ṛgveda misunderstood and misinterpreted. And in even very early times Indian scholars were concerned with interpreting the Ṛgveda. They compiled collections of rare and obscure words, the so called Nighaṇṭus or 'Glossaries'. And the first commentator whose work is preserved till today, was Yāska, who in his work *Nirukta* (i.e. etymology) explains a large number of Vedic verses on the basis of Nighaṇṭus. This Yāska, who in any case is anterior to Pāṇini[1] quotes already not less than 17 predecessors whose views often differ from one another. Indeed one of the scholars quoted by Yāska maintained in particular that the whole commentary to the Veda was useless

1. The great age of the Nirukta is proved by its language, which is more archaic than that of the remaining non-Vedic Sanskrit literature. See Bhandarkar, *JBRAS* 16, 1885, 265 f., Lakshman Sarup, *The Nighaṇtu and the Nirukta the oldest Indian Treatise on Etymology, Philosophy and Semantics*, Introduction, Oxford 1920, p. 54, merely reflects the universal opinion (without offering any new proofs) that Yāska lived between 700 and 500 B.C. Yāska was acquainted with all the Vedic Saṃhitās and the most important Brāhmaṇas, including the latest Gopatha-Brāhmaṇa, the Prātisākhyas and a few of the Upaniṣads; See Sarup, ibid, pp. 54 f., and P. D. Gune, in Bhandarkar Com. Vol., pp. 43 ff. Yāska already considered the Veda (See Sarup, ibid, pp. 71 ff.). Satyavrata Samasramin in an appendix to his edition of the Nirukta has an interesting treatise in Sanskrit on the age of Yāska (about 1900 B.C.!) and the purpose of the Nirukta: see Barth, *RHR*. 27, 1893, 184 ff., *Oeuvres* II, 94 ff. On Yāska, see also Liebich, "Zur Einfuhrung in die indische einheim". *Sprachwiss.*, II, 22 ff.

because the hymns were obscure, meaningless and mutually contradictory,—upon which Yâska however remarks that 'the beam is not to blame if the blindman does not see it'.

While explaining difficult words Yāska himself relies very often on etymology (which of course does not correspond to the rules of the modern science of philology) and gives two or three different interpretations to one and the same word. From this, it follows that even as early as in Yāska's time the meaning of many words and texts of the Ṛgveda was fixed by means of unbroken tradition. Nothing is preserved to us of the many successors who followed Yâska nor of his predecessors. We have only an exhaustive commentary from the 14th century A.D. which explains the text of the Ṛgveda word for word. This is the famous commentary of Sâyaṇa. Some of the older European interpreters of the Ṛgveda—like the English scholar H.H. Wilson, who has published a complete English translation of the Ṛgveda, which completely follows the Indian commentary —relied completely on Sāyaṇa's commentary, because they proceeded from the assumption that it (Sâyaṇa's commentary) was based on a reliable tradition. Other Veda-researchers on the contrary did not at all care for the native interpretation. They denied that a commentator who lived more than 2000 years after the birth of the work explained by him, could know something which we Europeans could not investigate and understand better with our philological criticism and with our modern means of linguistics. To these researchers belonged Rudolf Roth in particular. One of his pupils and followers was H. Grassmann, who published a complete metrical translation of the hymn,[1] in two volumes. Today most researchers assume a mediatory role. No doubt they admit that we should not follow blindly the native commentators, but they believe that they (the native commentators) drew at least partly from an uninterrupted tradition and should be therefore

1. Leipzig 1876 and 1877. Much more than this translation we recommend the selection "*Seventy songs of the Ṛgveda* translated by Karl Geldner and Adolf Kaegi. With contributions by R. Roth" (Siebenzig Lieder des Rigveda übersetzt von Karl Geldner und Adolf Kaegi mit Beiträgen von R. Roth" Tübingen 1875). This selection also proceeded from Roth's school.

respected and further that because they are Indians they have in a certain way a better knowledge of the Indian atmosphere than we Europeans and hence often see things rightly. One of these commentators is Alfred Ludwig, who in his complete German translation of the Ṛgveda to which an exhaustive and highly valuable commentary[1] is added, has, for the first time, made a thorough use of Sâyaṇa's interpretations without thereby renouncing other aids to interpretations. He is a forerunner of R. Pischel and K.F. Geldner who rendered meritorious services by their 'Vedic studies'[2] (*Vedische Studien*) by clarifying many obscure places of the Ṛgveda. They have also adhered most vehemently—of course not without exaggeration—to the principle that the Ṛgveda must be interpreted as a product of the Indian mind for the right understanding of which the Indian literature of later periods provides the best key.

To all this we must add one more much disputed question, that is of no minor importance to the interpretation of Vedic hymns: namely, whether these hymns originated independent of all sacrificial rituals, as the naive expressions of a pious belief in gods, as the pouring out of the hearts of reciters enthused by God or whether they have been composed by priests with the simple intention of using them as tools at the time of certain sacrifices and ceremonies.

---

1. Prag 1876-1888 in six volumes. In spite of its terrifying form, the prose translation of Ludwig is certainly to be preferred to Grassmann's pleasant verse translation in the matter of accuracy and reliability. We recommend also the English translations of selected hymns of the Rigveda of F. Max Mueller and H. Oldenberg in the *Sacred Books of the East* vols. 32 and 46, into German by K. F. Geldner, in A. Bertholet, *Religionsgeschichtliches Lesebuch* (Tübingen, 1908), p. 71 ff; A. Hillebrandt *Lieder des Ṛgveda*, Göttingen 1913: into English by A. A. Macdonell, *Hymns from the Ṛgveda*, (Heritage of India Series); and by E. J. Thomas *Vedic Hymns* (Wisdom of the East Series), London, 1923. The first part of a new and complete translation of the Ṛgveda by K. F. Geldner has been published in the series *Quellen der Religionsgeschichte* Göttingen, 1923.

2. Stuttgart, 1889-1901, 3 vols. Other important contributions to the interpretation of the Ṛgveda are: Oldenberg, "Ṛgveda, Textkritische und exegitische Noten", *AGGW*, N. F., Vol XI, No. 5, and Vol. XIII, No. 3, 1909 and 1912; Geldner, *Der Ṛgveda in Auswahl* I. Glossar, II, Kommentar, Stuttgart 1907-1909, and *ZDMG* 71, 1917, 315 ff. M. Bloomfield, *JAOS*, 27, 1906, 72 ff.; E. W. Fay, ibid, 403 ff.; A.B. Keith, *JRAS*, 1910. 921 ff.

How largely at variance with one another the different estimates of the values of these songs can be, depending on the points of view assumed by the interpreter can be seen by contrasting the opinions of two important researchers. In his beautiful book *the Ṛgveda, the Oldest Literature of the Indians,*[1] which can be recommended even today, Ad. Kaegi says about the hymns of the Ṛgveda: 'A great majority of the songs are invocations and glorifications of the godhoods addressed; their fundamental tone is a simple pouring out of the heart, a prayer to the Eternal, an invitation to accept favourably the gift consecrated with piety... What a god placed in his soul and made him feel: the singer wants to give eloquent expression to the urge of his heart'. He admits that inferior pieces may also find a place in the collections, 'but in all of them there blows a fresh breeze of most powerful, natural poetry: whoever takes the trouble of entering into the religious and moral thinking and acting, composing and creating of a folk and an age which present to us in the best possible manner the first mental development of our own race, will feel himself attracted in many ways by many of these songs by virtue of the child-like simplicity of some of them, or the freshness and gentleness of some others or the boldness of imagination or the swing of phantasy of yet others".

And now let us hear what H. Oldenberg the gifted and sensitive connoisseur of Indian literature says about these songs in his *Religion of the Veda.*[2] He finds, even in this 'oldest document of Indian literature and religion', "clear traces of a mental lethargy which was gaining more and more the upper hand". He speaks of the 'sacrificial songs and litanies with which the priests of the Vedic Aryans invoked their gods on sacrificial places without temples, at the sacrificial fires surrounded by the meadows—barbarian priests invoking barbarian gods, who on horse and carriage came riding through sky and air, in order to eat the sacrificial cake, butter and flesh and to drink

1. 2nd edition, Leipzig 1881. An English translation (*The Ṛig-veda, the Oldest Literature of the Indians*) with additions by R. Arrowsmith, appeared in 1886.

2. Berlin 1894, p. 3.

courage and divine power from the intoxicating Soma-juice. The singers of the Ṛgveda, composing in the old hereditary manner for the great and splendid Soma-sacrifice, do not wish to narrate about the god whom they extol, but they wish to praise him. ... So they shower on him all glorifying attributes which were at the command of the flattering plump oratory of phantasy loving the bright and the gaudy. "Only in the closed circles of priestly sacrificial technicians", thinks Oldenberg, "could such a poetry have been born".

Both of these opinions appear to me exaggerated and the truth lies in my opinion in the middle, as in the case of all disputes regarding the Ṛgveda-interpretation. Let us not forget that the collection of the hymns of the Ṛgveda is composed of earlier and later pieces. And so, as there are hymns in the Saṃhitā that belong to various epoques there are also hymns whose contents vary from one another in their value and origin. No doubt, that a large number of them have come into existence independent of all sacrificial rituals and that in them a breeze of genuine, primeval religious poetry blows.[1] Although many of these hymns were used later on for sacrificial purposes that does not in any way prove that they have been composed for this purpose to start with. On the other hand, it is equally certain, that many pieces of the Ṛgveda-Saṃhitā were supposed to be, even to start with, sacrificial songs and litanies and have been put together as tools by priestly singers. It is certainly exaggerated when W. D. Whitney says[2] : 'The Vedas seem to be not an Indian but an Indo-Germanic work'. It is however certainly equally exaggerated when Pischel and Geldner (along with H. H. Wilson) maintain that the Indians had already reached at the time of the Ṛgveda a stage in culture

1. Only, one must not come forward with such exaggerations as H. Brunnhofer (*On the mind of the Indian lyric*, Leipzig 1882) who makes the author of one of the later philosophical hymns of the Ṛgveda "a prince among poets who shoots up from the mists of ancient times" (p. 15) and is driven by emotion to say: "The Veda is like the chirping of the lark in the morning of humanity waking up into the consciousness of its greatness" (p. 41). This the Veda is certainly not.

2. *Language and its study*, London, 1876, p. 227.

that was little different from that which Alexander the Great found before himself when he attacked India.[1]

Although the gulf which separates the hymns of the Ṛgveda from the remaining Indian literature may not be so great, as some older researchers have assumed,—still a gulf is certainly there.[2] This is proved by the language, the cultural conditions hinted at above and especially also the stage of the religious development that we come across in the hymns. And this much is certain: whatever may be the poetic content of the songs of the Ṛgveda, there is no more important source for investigating into the earliest stages of the development of the Indian religion, no more important literary source for investigating into the mythology of the Indo-Germanic peoples, indeed, of the peoples themselves, than these songs of the Ṛgveda.

To put it in a nutshell: What makes these hymns valuable, is the circumstance that we see in them before us a mythology in the making.[3] We see the gods rising up so to say before our eyes. Many of the hymns are addressed not to a Sun-god, not to a Moon-god, not to a Fire-god, not to a Sky-god, not to Storm-gods and Water-godhoods, not to a goddess of the Dawn and to an Earth-goddess, but the shining Sun, the beaming moon at the nocturnal firmament, the fire in flames on the hearth or on the altar or the lightning striking from the cloud, the bright sky of the day or the stormy night-sky, the lashing storms, the rushing waters of the clouds and of the rivers, the glowing crimson of the morning and the fertile soil expanding

1. *Vedic Studies* (*Vedische Studien*) I, p. XXVI.
2. Similarly also A. Hillebrandt: *Vedic Mythology* II, 8.
3. L. de la Vallée Poussin, (*Le-Védisme*, Paris 1909, pp. 61 ff., 68) contests this view that the Veda presents "a mythology in the making" and A. B. Keith, *JRAS.*, 1909, p. 469 agrees with him. But I did not mean to say that all mythology first arose at the time of the Ṛgveda-Saṃhitā. The beginnings of the Vedic system of mythology and religion doubtless belong to a far earlier period than the compilation of the Saṃhitā. Those hymns, however, in which the natural phenomena and the deities embodied in them are as yet scarcely distinguished from one another, hark back to the time of the beginnings of Vedic mythology. This, of course, does not assume that the same thing is true of the whole Saṃhitā, or of the whole of Vedic religion.

in its extent—all these natural phenomena are as such glorified, prayed to and invoked. And only gradually does a change take place in the songs of the Ṛgveda itself of these natural phenomena into mythological figures, into gods and goddesses, like *Sūrya* (Sun), *Soma* (Moon), *Agni* (Fire), *Dyaus* (Sky), *Maruts* (Storms), *Vāyu* (Wind), *Āpas* (Waters), *Uṣas* (dawn) and *Pṛthvī* (Earth), whose names also indicate still without any doubt, what they have been originally. Thus the songs of the Ṛgveda prove indisputably that the most excellent mythological figures have originated from personifications of the most conspicuous natural phenomena. Mythological researchers have succeeded however in proving that also the other godhoods, whose names are not so clear, were originally not different from similar natural phenomena like the sun, the moon etc. Such mythological figures, whose original nature has been forgotten in parts already in the hymns and who were therefore celebrated only as powerful, noble beings distinguished by all sorts of the miracles to their credit are *Indra*, *Varuṇa*, *Mitra*, *Aditi*, *Viṣṇu*, *Pūṣan*, both the *Aśvins*, *Rudra* and *Parjanya*. The names of these gods also meant originally natural phenomena and natural beings. Epithets which primarily emphasised one particular aspect of a natural being, became the names of their own gods and then new gods themselves. Thus, *Savitar*, the 'inspirer' the 'animator' and *Vivasvat* 'the shining' were at first epithets, then names of the Sun and became finally independent sun-gods in addition to '*Sūrya*'. The gods of different clans and of different times are also represented in many ways in the polytheism of the Vedic Indians.[1] Thus it happens that *Mitra*, *Viṣṇu* and *Pūṣan* appear as sun-gods in the Ṛgveda. Presumably *Pūṣan* was originally the sun-god of a small clan of herdsmen before he was admitted to the Vedic pantheon as the 'lord of the ways', the protector of the travellers, the God who knows all paths and also brings the cattle that has gone astray back to the right path. *Mitra*, who is identical with the Mithra of the Avesta can thus be recognised as an old *Aryan* sun-god whose origin can be traced back to those times when the Indians and the Iranians formed one race. It is not so easy in the case of all the gods, to find to

1. cf: A. Hillebrandt, *Vedic Mythology* (*Vedische Mythologie*), II, 14 ff.

which natural phenomena their origin can be traced back. Researchers have differences of opinion while interpreting gods like *Indra, Varuṇa, Pūṣan, Aditi* and *Aśvins* — to name only the most important ones. Thus *Indra* is, to some, a storm-god, to the others an old sun-god. *Varuṇa* is considered by some as a god of the sky whereas others consider him as a moon-god. *Rudra*, who is usually considered as a storm-god, because he is the father of the storm-gods (the *Maruts*) would be, according to Oldenberg a mountain and forest-god, and according to Hillebrandt 'a God of fear of the tropical climate'.[1] *Aditi* is, according to one view, the wide heavenly space, according to another view the endlessly expanding earth. Both the *Aśvins*, a pair of gods who are doubtless related to the Greek Dioscures and are also found in the Germanic and Lettic mythology, were even before Yāska, a riddle to the Indian commentators: some considered them as sky and earth and the others as day and night and even today some researchers take them to be the two twilights, others sun and moon, some others the stars of dawn and dusk and yet others the constellation Gemini.[2] But what is most important is — and in this point most of the mythologists are in agreement today — that the largest majority of the Vedic gods have resulted from natural

1. See the learned dissertation by E. Arbman, *Rudra Untersuchungen zum attindischen Glauben* and *Kultus*, Uppsala, 1922. He sees in Rudra a primitive popular deity, the prototype of Śiva.

2. This is not the place to express an opinion on all the questions under dispute regarding Vedic Mythology. The facts of Vedic Mythology are best summarised in A. A. Macdonell's Vedic Mythology (in *Grundriss* III, 1A). Whoever wants to be informed of the interpretations of the myths and beliefs in gods of ancient India must necessarily consult H. Oldenberg's *Religion of the Veda* (*Religion des Veda*) Berlin, 1894 as well as A. Hillebrandt's *Vedic Mythology* (*Vedische Mythologie*) (3 volumes, Breslau 1891-1902). However-different from each other they may be to which these two researchers come, they have contributed a great deal to the widening and deepening of our knowledge of the vedic religion. However, that in the case of the questions considered in this context absolute certainty can never be reached, and that one can only more or less approach the truth, must be clear even to the layman. Meritorious services to the cause of researches in the Vedic religion and even more to the interpretation of the hymns of the Ṛgveda have been rendered by the French scholar Abel Bergaigne (*La religion Védique d' aprés hymnes du Rig-Veda*, 3 Vols, Paris 1878-1883).

phenomena or natural beings.[1] Of course there have been certain godhoods which were initially abstractions and have then become divine beings, but they all appear only in the latest hymns of the tenth book; like *Viśvakarman,* the 'world-architect', *Prajāpati,* 'the Lord of the creatures', or *Śraddhā* 'faith', *Manyu* 'wrath' and some similar personifications. More important are the individual gods of the so called 'lower' mythology, who appear also in the Ṛgveda: the *Ṛbhus* corresponding to the elves, the *Apsaras* who correspond to the nymphs and the *Gandharvas* who are a kind of forest and field-spirits. Numerous demons and evil spirits appear in the hymns as enemies of gods and the *Devas* or the gods hate and fight against them. But the name '*Asura*' with which these enemies of Gods are called in the later Vedic works appears still in the old meaning "possessed of wonderful power" or "god"[2] that has its corresponding word 'Ahura' in the Avesta. And it has the meaning of demons only in very few places. In the Ṛgveda *Dāsa* or *Dasyu* – that was the name given also to the Non-Aryan original inhabitants — was the usual name for the evil demons and in addition, also *Rakṣas* or *Rākṣasas* which is the name used for all kinds of pernicious and ghostly beings in the *Ṛgveda* as well as the whole of the later Indian literature. Also the *Pitaras,* the 'fathers' or the ancestor-spirits are given divine reverence even in the Ṛgveda. And the king of these ancestor-spirits, who reigns in the kingdom of the dead is Yama, a God who belongs to the Indo-Aryan primitive time, for he is identical with Yima who is in the Avesta, the first man, the founder of the race of human beings. As the first (foremost) dead — originally perhaps the sun who sets every day or the moon who vanishes every month — he became the king in the land of the dead. But this land of the dead is in the heaven and the dying one is consoled by the belief that after death he will remain with King *Yama* in the highest heaven. In the

1. Sten Konow, *The Aryan Gods of the Mitaṇi People,* Kristiania, 1921, p. 5, has not convinced me, "that the conception of Vedic religion as a worship of nature and natural phenomena is fundamentally wrong."

2. Cf. Oldenberg, *Religion des Veda,* pp. 162ff.; V. K. Rajwade, *Proc. IOC.,* II pp. 1ff.

Ṛgveda there is as yet no talk of the gloomy belief in a transmigration of the soul and an eternal rebirth — of the belief that governs the whole philosophic thinking of the Indians in the later centuries. Thus we see here also how even in these hymns a quite different spirit is dominant than in the whole of the later Indian literature.

It is exactly these significant differences between the religious views coming to light in the songs of the Ṛgveda and those of the subsequent period which prove that these songs actually reflect the faith of the race of the Aryan Indians. And even if it is correct that the songs of the Ṛgveda are actually not to be called 'popular poetry', that they came into being — at least for a great part — in certain families of singers, in narrow priestly circles, still we should not believe that these priests and singers have created mythology and religion without any consideration for popular belief. Perhaps much of what is reported to us of the Gods is based only "on momentary inspirations of individual poets", but we must assume by and large that these priests and singers have taken up elements that were already existing in the masses, that they stood — as Hillebrandt aptly says — 'above and not outside the folk.[1]

Thus these songs are of inestimable value to us as testimonials of the oldest religious faith of the Aryan Indians. But even as products of the art of poetry they deserve a prominent place in world literature. It is certain that the poets of these hymns reach the sublime swing and the profound fervour of the religious poetry of the Hebrews for instance only extremely seldom. The vedic singer looks up to the God whose glory he sings not with that trembling reverence and not with that unshakable faith as the Psalmist to Jehovah. And not like in the case of these do the prayers of the priestly singers of ancient India rise from the innermost depth of the soul to the heavenly beings. These poets stand on a more familiar footing with the gods whom they praise. When they sing the praise of a god they expect from him that he rewards them richly in

1. cf. Oldenberg *Aus Indien und Iran,* p. 19, *Religion des Veda* p. 13., Hillebrandt: *Vedische Mythologie,* II, 4.

the form of cows and heroic sons and they do not also feel shy to say this to him. 'Do, ut des' is their attitude. Thus a Vedic singer says to God Indra (VIII 14, 1.2)

> "If I, O Indra, like you,
> Lord of all the goods that be,
> My worshipper should never lack
> For herds to call his own.
>
> Gifts would I bestow on him,
> On that wise singer blessings shower,
> If I, as thou, O Lord of power,
> The Master of the cattle were."

And another singer turns to God Agni with the words (RV III, 19, 25, 26):

> "If thou wert mortal, Agni, and I the immortal one,
> Thou son of strength, like Mitra, to whom we sacrifice,
> Thee would I not expose to curse, good God !
> My worshipper should not suffer poverty, neglect or harm."

But the character of the hymns—and I speak firstly of those which contain invocations and praises of gods, without having been composed for any particular sacrificial purposes – varies very much, depending on the godhoods to which they are dedicated. The songs to Varuṇa are indisputably among the sublimest and loftiest poetry. There are however, not many of them. Varuṇa is nevertheless the only one among the Vedic gods, who stands high above the mortals and whom the singer dares approach only with shudder and terror and in humble reverence. It is also Varuṇa, who, more than any other god of the Vedic pantheon takes care of the moral transformation of men and punishes the sinners. The singer approaches him therefore remorsefully and requests that his sins be forgiven. Therefore it is also the songs addressed to Varuṇa the only ones which can be in a way compared with the poetry of the psalms. As a specimen I give here the hymns RV V 85 as translated by R.T.H. Griffith:

"Sing forth a hymn sublime and solemn, grateful to glorious Varuṇa, imperial Ruler,
Who hath struck out, like one who slays the victim, earth as a
Skin to spread in front of Sūrya.
In the tree tops the air he hath extended, put milk in kine and
Vigorous speed in horses,
Set intellect in hearts, fire in the waters,[1] Sūrya in heaven and
Soma on the mountain.
Varuṇa lets the big cask, opening downward, flow through the
Heaven and earth and air's mid-region.
Therewith the universes' Sovran waters earth as the shower of
Rain bedews the barley.
When Varuṇa is fain for milk he moistens the sky, the land, and
Earth to her foundation.
Then straight the mountains clothe them in the rain-cloud: the
Heroes, putting forth their vigour, loose them[2]
I will declare this mighty deed of magic, of glorious Varuṇa the Lord Immortal,
Who standing in the firmament hath meted the earth out with
The Sun as with a measure.
None, verily, hath ever let or hindered this the most wise God's

---

1. Namely, the lightning in the cloud.
2. The milk is the water of the clouds which are compared with cows. The "strong men" are the storm-gods (Maruts) who, in the storm, cause the "milk" of the clouds to flow.

Mighty deed of magic,
Whereby with all their flood, the lucid rivers fill not one sea
Wherein they pour their waters.
If we have sinned against the man who loves us, have ever wronged
A brother, friend, comrade,
The neighbour ever with us, or a stranger, O Varuṇa remove
From us the tresspass.
If we, as gamesters cheat at play, have cheated, done wrong
Unwittingly or sinned of purpose,
Cast all these sins away like loosened fetters, and, Varuṇa, let us
Be thine own beloved."

Varuṇa is also already in the Ṛgveda as he is the god of the sea in the later mythology, a god of the waters and therefore he punishes the people who have sinned, especially by dropsy. A simple prayer of one suffering from dropsy in RV VII 89. I give in the (prose)translation of R. T. H. Griffith:

"Let me not yet, King Varuṇa, enter into the house of clay[1]
Have mercy, spare me, Mighty Lord
When, Thunderer ! I move along tumultuous like a wind-blown skin,
Have mercy, spare me, Mighty Lord.
O Bright and powerful God, through want of strength I erred
And went astray:
Have mercy, spare me Mighty Lord.

---

1. The grave, or the earthern urn in which the ashes of the cremated corpse are preserved, may be meant. On the methods of burial of the ancient Indians, see below pp. 88 ff.

Thirst found thy worshipper though he stood in the midst of Waterfloods:
Have mercy, spare me, Mighty Lord.
O Varuṇa, whatever the offence may be which we as men commit against the heavenly host,
When through our want of strength we violate thy laws, punish
us not, O God, for that iniquity."

A quite different note is struck in the songs to God Indra. We can call Indra actually the national God of the Vedic Indians. As the Indians were at the time of the Ṛgveda still a fighting and struggling race, therefore Indra is also absolutely a fighting god. His mighty power and love of fighting is always described and Vedic singers love to dwell upon Indra's battles with the demons whom he destroyed with his thunderbolt. In particular Indra's battle with Vṛtra is sung in numerous hymns. Attention is drawn again and again to the splendid victory that the god scored over the demon; numberless times is Indra praised jubilantly, that he killed Vṛtra with this thunderbolt. Vṛtra (probably the obstructor, or retarder) is a demon in the form of a snake or a dragon, who holds the waters enclosed or locked up in a mountain. Indra wants to set the waters free. He gets drunk with Soma which gives him courage, rushes to the battle and kills the monster;—now the released waters flow out rushing on the corpse of Vṛtra. This great deed of Indra is vividly described to us in the song RV I, 32, which begins with the verse:[1]

"I will proclaim the many deeds of Indra
The first that he performed, the Lightning-Wielder.
He slew the serpent, then discharged the waters,
And cleft the cavern of the lofty mountains.

He slew the serpent lying on the mountain:
For him the wizzing bolt has Tvaṣṭar fashioned.
Like lowing cows, with rapid current flowing,
The waters to the ocean down have glided."

1. Translated by A. M. Macdonell, *Hymns from the Rigveda*, p.47.

The songs make it absolutely clear that this myth of a fight with the dragon is about a mighty natural phenomenon. Heaven and earth tremble when Indra kills Vṛtra. He kills him not only once but again and again, and he is exhorted to kill him and set the waters always free in future also. Even the old Indian Veda commentators tell us that Indra is a storm-god, that we have to take the mountains in which the waters are imprisoned to be the clouds in which Vṛtra,—the demon of drought—holds the waters imprisoned. And most European mythologists followed them and saw in the Indra armed with thunderbolt a counterpart to the Germanic Thunar, who swings the thunder hammer Mjoelnir, a thunder-god of the prehistoric Indo-Germanic age and in the fight with the dragon they see a mythological representation of the storm. But recently Hillebrandt has tried to prove that Vṛtra is not a cloud-demon and not a drought-demon but is a winter-giant whose might is broken by the sun-god Indra; the 'rivers' which are held imprisoned by Vṛtra and set free by Indra are, according to him, not the downpour of rain, but the rivers of the north-west of India which dry up in winter and are full only when the sun causes the snow masses of Himalayan mountains melt.

Whatever it be, it is certain, that the Vedic reciters themselves had no more clear consciousness of the original natural significance of Indra or of Vṛtra. For them Indra was a champion, a giant of colossal strength, Vṛtra however, the most terrible of the demons who were thought to be personified in the black aboriginals of the country. Indra fights not only with Vṛtra, but also with numerous other demons, and his fights with demons are only illustrations of the battles that the Āryan immigrants had to fight out. Hence Indra is also above all a god of the warriors. And of no other god of the Vedic pantheon do we have information on so many individual features, no other god is in such *life-like* manner portrayed—if we can use this expression for a godhood—in the 250 hymns as this god Indra. Great and strong are his arms. With beautiful lips he sips the Soma drink, and when he has drunk, he moves pleased his jaws and shakes his blond beard. Blond as gold is also his hair and his whole appearance. He is a giant of figure—Heaven and earth would not suffice to serve him as a belt. In strength and power neither a god nor a man can equal him. When he caught the two endless worlds they were only a handful for him. They prefer to call him an ox. Limitless as his strength is also his capacity to drink which is described in the songs often not without humour. Before he killed Vṛtra, he drank off three ponds full of Soma; and once, it is said that, he drank 30 ponds of Soma in one gulp, scarcely was he born—and his was not an ordinary birth, for even when he was still in his mother's womb he said: Here I do not want to go out; this is a bad way; right across the side I want to go out (RV IV, 18,2)"—then he drank also beakerfuls of Soma. Sometimes he did also too much of the good. In the song RV X 119 a singer shows us the intoxicated Indra, as he holds a monologue and ponders what he should do 'I do not want to do it so, no, so', "I want to put the earth here, no, I want to put it there" etc.—whereby every stanza ends with the same expressive burden, "Have I then drunk of the *Soma*?"

This war-like national God was suited more than anyone else as the prince of the gods. And although in the Ṛgveda almost every one of the gods is sometimes praised as the first and the highest of all gods—this is a sort of flattery through which one wished to gain the goodwill of the god, just as later on some court-poets praised one small prince or the other as the ruler of the world—, still Indra is, in the earliest times, doubtless a king among the gods, just similar to Zeus of the Greek Olympia.

As the prince among gods he is praised in the song RV II 12, which is given here as a specimen in the translation : of A. A. Macdonell:[1]

"He who first born as chief god full of spirit
Went far beyond the other gods in wisdom:
Before whose majesty and mighty manhood
The two worlds trembled: he, O men, is Indra.

He made the wide spread earth when quaking steadfast
Who set at rest the agitated mountains,

1. *Hymns from the Rigveda*, pp. 48 ff.

Who measured out air's middle space more widely,
Who gave the sky support: he, men, is Indra.

Who slew the serpent, freed the seven rivers,
Who drove the cattle out from Valas cavern,[1]
Who fire between the two rocks has generated,
A conqueror in fights; he, men, is Indra.

He who has made all earthly things unstable,
Who humbled and dispersed the Dasa colour,
Who, as the player's stake the winning gambler,
The foeman's fortune gains: he, men, is Indra.

Of whom, the terrible, they ask, "Where is he?"
Of him, indeed, they also say, "he is not".
The foeman's wealth, like player's stakes, he lessens.
Believe in him: for he, O men, is Indra.

He furthers worshippers, both rich and needy,
And priests that supplicate his aid and praise him.
Who, fair-lipped, helps the man that presses Soma,
That sets the stones at work: he, men, is Indra.

In whose control are horses and all chariots,
In whose control are villages and cattle;
He who has generated sun and morning,
Who leads the waters: he, O men, is Indra.

Whom two contending armies vie in calling,
On both sides foes, the farther and the nearer;
Two fighters mounted on the self-same chariot[2]
Invoke him variously: he, men, is Indra.

Without whose aid men conquer not in battle,
Whom fighting ever they invoke for succour,

1. Next to the Vṛtra-killing this deliverance of the cows is the greatest heroic deed of Indra. It has been compared, I think rightly, with the deed of Hercules, who kills the three-headed Geryoneus and leads away the herds of oxen stolen by him. In the same way Hercules and Cacus. Cf. Oldenberg *Rel. des Veda* p. 143 f. Hillebrandt : *Ved Myth.*, III 260 ff.

2. Namely the warrior and the charioteer.

Who shows himself a match for every foeman,
Who moves what is unmoved: he, men, is Indra.

Who with his arrow slays the unexpecting
Unnumbered crew of gravely guilty sinners:
Who yields not to the boasting foe in boldness,
Who slays the demons: he, O men, is Indra.

He who detected in the fortieth autumn
Śambara[1] dwelling far among the mountains;
Who slew the serpent that put forth his vigour,
The demon as he lay: he, men, is Indra.

Who with his seven rays, the bull, the mighty,[2]
Let loose the seven streams to flow in torrents:
Who, both in arms, spurned in Rauhiṇa, the demon,
On scaling heaven bent; he, men, is Indra.

Both Heaven and Earth, themselves, bow down before
him;
Before his might the very mountains tremble,
Who, famed as Soma-drinker, armed with lightning,
Is wielder of the bolt: he, men, is Indra.

Who with his aid helps him that presses Soma,
That bakes and lauds and ever sacrifices;[3]
Whom swelling prayer, whom Soma pressings strengthen,
And now this offering: he, O men, is Indra.

Who, fierce, on him that bakes and him that presses
Bestowest booty: thou indeed are trusted,
May we, for ever dear to thee, O Indra,
Endowed with hero sons address the Synod."

---

1. Name of a demon.
2. Indra has a chariot provided with seven reins. (RV II, 18, I; VI, 44, 24) i.e. many horses — "seven" in the Ṛgveda often means "many" — are harnessed to his chariot.
3. These are the four sacrificial priests of the older period.

If the hymns to Varuṇa and Indra show to us that the Vedic poets were not wanting in pathos, power and primeval strength, the songs to Agni, fire or the fire-god show that these poets could also find often the simple, warm tone of the heart. Agni — as the sacrificial fire and the fire burning on the hearth — is considered as a friend of men; he is the mediator between them and the gods and to him the poet speaks as to a dear friend. He prays to him that he bless him, 'as the father the son', and he assumes that his song makes the god happy who then fulfills the singer's wish. If Indra is the god of war, Agni is the god of the householder protecting his wife and children and makes his house and property flourish. He is himself called often 'Lord of the House' (*Gṛhaspati*). He is the 'guest of every house, 'the foremost of all guests'. Being himself immortal, he has taken his abode among mortals; and under his protection is the prosperity of the family. Since times immemorial the bride, who entered the new house, was led round the fire, and therefore Agni is also called the 'lover of girls,' the husband of women, (RV I, 66, 8) and in a marriage text it is said that Agni is the husband of the girls and that the bridegroom receives the bride from Agni. Simple prayers were addressed to him at the time of wedding, at the birth of children and similar family events. During wedding sacrifice they prayed to Agni for the bride: 'May Agni the Lord of the House protect her. May he lead her offsprings to a ripe age; may she be of blessed womb, mother of living childern. May she witness the joy of her sons !" As sacrificial fire Agni is the 'messenger' between gods and men; and it is said sometimes that in this capacity he carries upward the sacrificial offerings to the gods and sometimes it is also said that he brings the gods downward to the sacrifice. He is, therefore, called the priest, the wise one, the Brahmin, the purohita (family-priest) and is given the beloved title of 'Hotar' — this is how the most prominent among the priests is called. In the songs to Agni we can hardly distinguish mythology and poetry from each other in their development. By profusely pouring molten butter the sacrificial fire was maintained glowing brightly, and the poet says: "Agni's face is glowing or his back is glowing, molten butter is trickling down his hair". And when he is described as flame-haired and red-haired, red-bearded having sharp jaws and teeth glittering like gold, when they speak of the flames of fire as Agni's tongues; when the poet while thinking of the bright fire radiating on all sides speaks of Agni as four-eyed or thousand-eyed, then one can call all that poetry as well as mythology. Thus the crackling and the rustling of the fire can be compared with the roaring of the bull[1] — and Agni is described as the bull. The flames shooting up sharply are imagined to be the horns and a reciter mentions Agni as 'having a thousand horns'; while another says that he whets his horns and shakes in anger. Equally often Agni is also compared to a horse neighing with joy, to a 'fiery runner' — in mythology as in cult Agni stands in close relationship to the horse. Even when Agni is described as the bird, the heavenly eagle, which in its rapid flight rushes between heaven and earth, then we have to think of the lightning flames striking down from the sky. The poet thinks again of another phenomenon of fire when he says (RV I, 143, 5): "Agni eats the forests with his sharp jaws; he masticates them, he rases them to the ground as the warrior does his enemies." And similarly another poet (RV I, 65, 8) "When Agni, fanned by the wind, spreads through the forests, he shears the hair of the earth (i.e. grass and plants).

Even the actual Agni myths have their origin in the poetical metaphoric and enigmatic language. Agni has three births — three places of birth: In the sky he shines as fire of the sun, on the earth he is produced by men out of the two pieces of tinder wood and as lightning he is born in water. And as he is produced from two pieces of tinder wood (*Araṇis*), it is said that he has two mothers, — and hardly is the child born when it consumes both the mothers" (RV X, 79, 4). An older poet says however: "Ten indefatigable virgins have brought forth this child of Tvaṣṭṛ (i.e. the Agni)" (RV I, 95, 2) whereby the ten fingers are meant which had to be used for churning the fire; and as it was possible to produce fire from the pieces of wood only by applying a great force, Agni is called in the whole of the Ṛgveda 'the son of force'.

1. In English also we speak of the "roaring fire."

When we consider the extensive role the fire-cult played in the life of the ancient Indians it is not astonishing that of the numerous songs in the Ṛgveda which are devoted to Agni — there are about 200 of them — the majority is used as sacrificial songs, and many have even been composed only for the purpose of sacrifice. But in spite of this we find among these songs many simple and modest prayers which are the works of priests or in any case that of poets. As an example I give below the opening hymns of our Ṛgveda-Saṃhitā in the translation of A.A. Macdonell, which reflects the character of the original very well.[1]

"Agni I praise the household priest,
God, minister of sacrifice,
Invoker, best bestowing wealth.

Agni is worthy to be praised,
By present as by seers of old:
May he to us conduct the gods.

Through Agni may we riches gain,
And day by day prosperity
Replete with fame and manly sons.

The worship and the sacrifice
Guarded by thee on every side
Go straight, O Agni, to the gods.

May Agni, the invoker, wise
And true, of most resplendent fame,
The God, come hither with the gods.

Whatever good thou will bestow
O Agni, on the pious man,
That gift comes true, O Aṅgiras.

To thee, O Agni, day by day,
O thou illuminer of gloom,
With thought we, bearing homage, come:

1. *Hymns from the Ṛgveda*. pp. 72 ff.

To thee the lord of Sacrifice,
The radiant guardian of the Law,
That growest in thine own abode.

So, like a father to his son,
Be easy of approach to us;
Agni, for weal abide with us."

Some pearls of lyrical poetry, which are charming by virtue of a fine comprehension of the beauties of nature as also of their metaphoric language are found among the songs to Sūrya (the Sun), to Parjanya (the rain god), to the Maruts (the storm-gods) and above all to Uṣas (the dawn). In the hymns addressed to *Uṣas* the singers excel one another in splendid metaphors that are supposed to describe the magnificence of the resplendent dawn. Radiating like a virgin ornamented by her mother she approaches proud of the beauty of her body. She wears a superb attire like a danceuse and reveals her bosom to the mortals. Clad in light the virgin appears in the east and discloses her charms. Opening the gates of the heaven she steps out of it radiantly. Her charms are compared again and again to those of a woman tempting to love. Thus we read (RV V, 80, 5. 6)[1]

"As conscious that her limbs are bright with bathing, she stands, as 'twere, erect that we may see her.
Driving away malignity and darkness, Dawn, child of Heaven, hath come to us with lustre.
The daughter of the sky, like some chaste woman, bends, opposite to men, her forehead down.
The Maid, disclosing boons to him who worships, hath brought again the daylight as aforetime."

The following hymn to dawn (RV VI, 64) I am giving in the translation of Griffith:

"The radiant Dawns have risen up for glory, in their white splendour like the waves of waters.

1. Translated by Griffith.

She maketh paths all easy, fair to travel, and, rich, hath shown herself benign and friendly.

We see that thou art good: far shines thy lustre; thy beams, thy splendours have flown up to heaven.

Decking thyself, thou makest bare thy bosom, shining in majesty, thou Goddess Morning.

Red are the kine and luminous that bear her the Blessed one who spreadeth through the distance.

The foes she chaseth like a valiant archer, like a shift warrior she repelleth darkness.

Thy ways are easy on the hills: thou passest Invincible! Self-luminous! through waters.

So lofty Goddess with thine ample pathway, Daughter of Heaven, being wealth to give us comfort.

Dawn, bring me wealth: untroubled, with thine oxen thou bearest riches at thy will and pleasure;

Thou who, a Goddess, child of Heaven, hast shown thee lovely through bounty when we called thee early.

As the birds fly forth from their resting-places, so men with store of food rise at thy dawning.

Yea, to the liberal mortal who remaineth at home, O Goddess Dawn, much good thou bringest."

The following hymn (RV X 168), which I give in the translation of Macdonell[1] is addressed to Vāta, the leader of the Maruts, the storm-gods:

"Of Vāta's car I now will praise the greatness!
Rending it speeds along; its noise is thunder.
Touching the sky it flies, creating lightnings;
Scattering dust it traverses earth's ridges.

The hosts of Vāta onward speed together!
They haste to him as women to a concourse.
The god with them upon the same car mounted,
The king of all this universe speeds onward.

1. *Hymns from the Rigveda*, p. 62.

In air, along his pathways speeding onwards
Never on any day he tarries resting.
The first-born, order-loving friend of waters:
Where was he born, and whence has he arisen ?

Of gods the breadth, and of the world the offspring,
This god according to his liking wanders,
His sound is heard, his form is never looked on:
That Vāta let us worship with oblation."

In addition to these songs, which deserve to be valued as works of the poetic art, there are however a second class of hymns in the Ṛgveda which have been composed only as sacrificial, songs and litanies for very specific ritual purposes. It is however not possible to make a clear distinction here. Whether we view a song as the spontaneous expression of a pious belief, as the work of a poet inspired by God or as the sacrificial prayer composed in an artisan-like manner, is a matter of taste. But characteristic of these prayers and sacrificial songs is the extreme monotony attached to them. There are always the same expressions with which one god as the other is praised as great and powerful; always the same formulas with which the sacrificing priest prays to the gods for treasures of cattle and riches. Many of these sacrificial songs can be easily recognised by this that in one and the same hymn many gods and sometimes even all the gods of the Vedic pantheon are invoked one after another. For during the great Soma-sacrifice every god must obtain his share and every offering must be accompanied by a verse. We may compare for example a sacrificial litany as the following (RV VII 35) with the above mentioned songs to Varuṇa, Indra and Agni:

May Indra and Agni give us prosperity with their grace, Indra and Varuṇa to whom sacrificial offerings are made, may Indra and Soma give us prosperity, welfare, prosperity and blessings ! May Indra and Pūṣan favour us while winning the booty.

May Bhaga favour us, may our song of praise give us prosperity, may Purandhi give us prosperity, may the riches make us happy.

> May Dhātar and Dhartā make us happy, may the far-extended one[1] with her comforts make us happy; may the two great spaces[2] make us happy; may the mountain make us happy, may the favourable invocations of the gods.
>
> May the light-faced Agni make us prosper; may Mitra and Varuṇa and the two Aśvins make us happy; may the good works of the pious ones make us happy! May the strong wind-god blow us into prosperity.

And so on it goes through 15 long stanzas.

To these sacrificial songs belong also, among others, the so called *Apri-sūktas,* ("appeasing hymns") (i.e. hymns for appeasing or appeasement-hymns), pacifying certain deities, demons and certain personified objects connected with the sacrifice. These hymns, of which there are ten in the Ṛgveda-saṃhitā, have a very specific application at the time of animal-sacrifices. They all have 11 or 12 verses and Agni is invoked in them under different names, so that he may bring the gods down to the sacrifice. In the 4th or 5th verse the priests are asked to strew the sacred grass on which the gods should sit in order to accept the sacrificial offerings. With these hymns certain goddesses also are invoked regularly and the penultimate verse contains usually an invocation to the post which serves to tie the sacrificial animal; for example, 'O divine tree, let the sacrificial food go to the gods'.

The above mentioned hymns of the IX book are out and out sacrificial songs which are all addressed to Soma and are used at the time of the Great Soma-sacrifice. In sheer endless monotony they praise again and again the same processes, the pressing of the Soma, the mixing and purification of the same and pouring into the barrels etc., again and again Indra is invited to Soma-drinking, Soma and Indra are together praised and are prayed for riches or for rain of which the Soma juice trickling down the sieve is a symbol. Only very rarely in these

1. that is, the Earth.
2. Heaven and Earth.

monotonous *litanies* do we come upon a beautiful picture, as instance, when it is said of *Soma* (RV IX, 16,6) :

Purified in the sheep hair-sieve
He rises to full glory
And stands there as after the battle
The hero by the robbed cows.

That verses can be composed for ritual purposes and can still be of poetic beauty is proved by the funeral song of which some are preserved to us in the X book of the Ṛgveda. Corpses were burnt as a rule in ancient India, but in the prehistoric times the Indians like the other Indo-Germanic tribes probably buried the dead. The beautiful verses (ṚV X, 18, 10-13) refer to a burial :[1]

"Approach the bosom of the earth, the mother,
This earth, the far-extending, most propitious;
Young, soft as wool to bounteous givers, may she
Preserve thee from the lap of dissolution.

Wide open, earth, O press not heavily on him;
Be easy of approach to him, a refuge safe;
As with a robe a mother hides
Her son, so shroud this man, O earth.

Now opening wide may here the earth stand steadfast.
May here a thousand columns rise to prop her;
May here those mansions ever drip with butter,
And here be always shelter to protect him.

For thee I now prop up the earth around thee here;
In lowering this clod may I receive no harm.
May the fathers hold up for thee this column,
And Yama here provide for thee fit mansions."

It is quite possible—as Oldenberg[2] means—to include these verses in the cremation ceremonies of dead bodies. As the

1. Translated by A. A. Macdonell, *Hymns from the Rigveda*, p. 88.
2. "*Religion des Veda*", p. 571.

ritual books tell us, in ancient India the bones were gathered after the cremation and were placed in an urn and this was buried then. Accordingly these verses could have been spoken while burying this bone-urn. I do not consider it probable. The words "Open yourself O earth, do not wound him" etc. appear to make sense, in my opinion, only while erecting a grave-mound over the actual corpse. The custom of burying the bones is, in my view, a remnant of an older custom of burying the corpses, to which our verses refer.[1]

As against this, the song RV X. 16, 1-6 taking its origin presumably at a later date, is meant for the ceremony of the cremation of dead bodies. When the pyre is arranged, the dead body is placed on it and fire is lit. And while the flames rise up and unite over it, the priests pray:

Burn him not, scorch him not, O Agni,
Crush not his skin and his limbs;
When you have prepared him well, O Jātavedas,
May you send him on to our forefathers.

Yes, when you have prepared him, O Jātavedas,
May you hand him over to our forefathers;
If he has joined them
He will serve the gods faithfully.

May your eye go to the sun, to the wind your soul
As befits you go to heaven, go to earth
Go to the waters if it pleases you;
The parts of the body rest in the plants.

The eternal parts — warm it with your warmth
Warm it with your light, with your fires

1. At the time, when burning of dead bodies was already the general custom, children and ascetics were still buried. But nothing in the above verses indicates that it is about the burial of a child or ascetic. W. Caland, *Die altindischen Toten—und Bestattungsgebräuche,*" Amsterdam, 1896, pp. 163 ff. as against R. Roth (*ZDMG* 8, 1854, 467 ff.), has proved that the hymn in Ṛgveda X, 18 is not one uniform production. Only the verses 10 to 13 form a separate poem. See also W. D. Whitney, *Oriental and Linguistic Studies,* New York, 1873, 51 ff., and L. v. Schroeder, *WZKM* 9, 1895, 112 f.

O god of fire, take a gentle form
And carry him softly away to the world of the pious.

Here there are already philosophical views on the life after death and on the fate of the soul entering into the mythological notions of Agni and the forefathers. These allusions do not stand isolated, but there are about a dozen hymns in the Ṛgveda which we can call philosophical hymns, in which besides speculations on the universe and the creation of the world, for the first time that great pantheistic idea of the world-soul crops up which is one with the cosmos—an idea which from that time onwards dominated the whole Indian philosophy.

Even from early times doubts rose in the minds of the Indians regarding the might, indeed even the existence of the gods. Even in the song RV II 12 translated above, which so confidently praises the might and the powerful deeds of Indra and whose individual stanzas end with the devoutly pronounced burden: 'That, you people, is Indra', even there, we already hear, that there were people who did not have faith in Indra': "Of whom, the people ask, where is he"? and of whom they say "he is not at all there" ... ... have faith in him—that, you people, is Indra"? We come across similar doubts in the peculiar hymn RV VIII, 100 where the priests are exhorted to sing a song of praise to Indra, "a veritable one, if he is in reality; for so many say: "There is no Indra, who has ever seen him? To whom should we address the song of praise?" Whereupon Indra personally appears then, in order to ensure his existence and his greatness; "Here I am, singers, look at me, I excel all beings in greatness" etc.

When one had begun to doubt even Indra, who was of course the highest and mightiest of all gods, doubts began to arise in the minds of the people so much more about the plurality of the gods as such and as to whether there was any use in offering sacrifices to the gods. Thus in the hymns RV X, 121, in which Prajāpati is praised as the creator and preserver of the world and in the burden of the song, "which god should we honour by sacrifice?" The thought lies hidden that there is nothing in the plurality of gods and that only the one and the only one, the Creator Prajāpati, deserves respect. Finally, this scepticism has found its most powerful expression in the profound poem of creation (RV X, 129).[1] It begins with the description of the time before the creation:

"Nor aught existed then, nor naught existed,
There was no air, nor heaven beyond.
What covered all ? Wherein ? In whose shelter was it ?
Was it the water, deep and fathomless ?

No death was then, nor was there life immortal.
Of day and night there was then no distinction.
That one above breathed windless by itself.
Than that, forsooth, no other thing existed."

Only very timidly does the poet attempt to give an answer to the question of the origin of the world. He imagines to himself the situation before the creation as darkness", shrouded by darkness", far and wide nothing but an impenetrable flood of water, until by the power of tapas,[2] i.e. heat (perhaps a kind of brooding-heat) "the one" was born. This "one" was already an intellectual being; and as the first product of his intellect"--"the first fruit of the intellect" as the poet says—was born *Kāma,* i.e. "sexual desire, Love"[3] and in this Kāma "have the wise ones, investigating the heart, found the connection of the being with the non-being". However, the poet dares give only gentle hints, soon doubts arise again and he concludes with the timid questions:

"Yet, who is succeeded in finding out
Wherefrom the world has come, who has seen it ?

1. Translation by R. T. H. Griffith.

2. Tapas, may here have its original meaning of "heat" (some "creative heat" analogous to the heat by which the broodhen produces life from the egg) or it may mean the 'fervour' of austerity; or, as Deussen thinks, both meanings may be implied in the word.

3. Not the Schopenhaueric "will" as Deussen and the others presume. As the sexual desire leads to creation and birth of the beings, so also did these old thinkers imagine the sexual desire to be the primary origin of all beings. Tapas can also mean "asceticism".

The gods are born this side of the world
Who says that wherefrom it (the world) has come ?[1]

He who has created the world
He who looks down at it in supreme heavenly light
He who has created it or not created it
He knows it or does not he too know it ?[2]

Indeed in most of the philosophical hymns of the Ṛgveda the thought of a world-creator comes up, who is called sometimes Prajāpati, sometimes Brahmaṇaspati or Bṛhaspati and sometimes Viśvakarman, but who is still imagined as a personal god. But even in the verse quoted above it seems doubtful to the poet whether the creation is 'made' or has come into being in any other way, and the creative principle does not receive any name in the poem, but it is called "the one". Thus even in the hymns the great thought of the All-one-ness is prepared, namely the thought that all that we see in the nature and that the popular belief calls "gods" is in reality only the emanation of the One and the only One existing, that all plurality is only an illusion—a thought that is already pronounced clearly and simply in the verses RV I, 164, 46 :

They call it Indra, Varuṇa and Mitra
Agni, the beautiful-winged bird of Heaven
Many names to the only one give the poets;
They call it Agni, Yama, Mātariśvan.

While these philosophical hymns build a sort of a bridge to the philosophical speculation of the Upaṇiṣads, there are also

1. That means the gods being themselves created (by someone else) cannot tell us wherefrom the world has come.

2. The verses of this famous hymn have been often translated and discussed, thus by H. T. Colebrooke, *Miscellaneous Essays* (2nd Ed., Madras, 1872), I, pp. 33 f.; Max Mueller: *History of Ancient Sanskrit Literature*, 2nd Ed. London, 1860, p. 564; J. Muir : *Original Sanskrit Texts*, V, p. 356; H. W. Wallis, *Cosmology of the Rigveda*, London, 1887, pp. 89 ff.; W. D. Whitney, *JAOS*, XI, p. cix; P. Deussen, *Allgemeine Geschichte der Philosophie I* (where all the philosophical hymns of the Ṛgveda are discussed); L. Scherman, *Philosophische Hymnen aus der Rig-und Atharvaveda-Saṃhita*, Strassburg, 1887, pp. 1 ff. It has also been translated by Macdonell, E. J. Thomas, etc.

a number of poems in the Ṛgveda-Saṁhitā—there might be about 20 of them—which take us on to epic poetry. These are fragments of narratives in the form of dialogues which we call now Ākhyāna-hymns as Oldenberg who was the first to make a thorough study of this class of Vedic hymns, always calls them.[1] Oldenberg has shown that the oldest form of epic poetry in India[2] consists of a mixture of prose and verse in the following way—the verses contained mostly[3] only the portions spoken by the characters whereas the incidents that caused these speeches were told in prose. Originally however, only the verses were committed to memory and handed down while the prose could be told by every narrator as he liked in his own words. Now in the Ākhyāna hymns of the Ṛgveda only the poetical dialogues of the persons appearing in the story are preserved to us, while the prose parts have been lost. Only some of these stories we can now complete at least partly with the help of the Brāhmaṇas or of the later epic literature or also from commentaries. This is the theory of Oldenberg, which for a long time was almost generally accepted by scholars.

Of late, however, the theory has also met with a great deal of opposition. Many years back Max Mueller and Sylvain Levi had already suggested that the dialogue poems of the

1. "Das altindische-Ākhyāna", in *ZDMG* 37 (1883), 54 ff and "Ākhyāna-hymnen in Rigveda" in *ZDMG* 39 (1885), 52 ff. Ākhyāna means tale.

2. At the 33rd meeting of German philologists and pedagogues Ernst Windisch had indicated the significance of very similar phenomena in ancient Irish saga poetry and thereby he had also pointed to the related phenomena in Indian literature.

3. Besides these dialogues, the chief events of a story were also recited in verses sometimes. Very short speeches were, on the other hand, delivered in prose form. "As it is probably from the outset, that in the old narratives short and minor dialogues were composed in prose and only the most exciting part, the main dialogue in which the whole as it were culminated, was composed in poetry, so also it appears on the other hand, that the most uninteresting and monotonous narrative has swung to pathetic heights of metrical diction at certain important and concluding stages".

— Geldner in *Vedische Studien*, I, p. 291 f.

4. *Le Theatre-Indien*, Paris, 1890, pp. 301 ff.

Ṛgveda might be a kind of dramas. This idea has been taken up by Joh. Hertel[1] and L. von Schroeder,[2] who tried to prove that these Samvâda-hymns are really speeches belonging to some dramatic performances connected with the religious cult. We have only, they say, to supply dramatic action, and the difficulties which these hymns offer to interpretation will disappear. What kind of action has to be supplied can of course only be guessed from the dialogues themselves.

The fact is, that poems like the dialogue-hymns of the Ṛgveda are of frequent occurrence in Indian literature. We shall find similar semi-epic and semi-dramatic poems, consisting chiefly or entirely of dialogues or conversations, in the Mahābhārata, in the Purāṇas, and especially in Buddhist literature. All these poems are nothing else but ancient ballads of the same kind as are found also in the literatures of many other peoples.[3] This ancient ballad poetry is the source both of the epic and of the drama, for these ballads consist of a narrative and of a dramatic element. The epic developed from the narrative, the drama arose from the dramatic elements of the ancient ballad. These ancient Ākhyānas or ballads were not always composed entirely in verse, but sometimes an introductory or a concluding story was told in prose, and occasionally the verses were linked together by short explanations in prose. Thus it may

1. *WZKM* 18, 1904, 59 ff., 137 ff.; 23, 1909, 273 ff.; *Indische Marchen,* Jena, 1921, pp. 344, 367 f.

2. *Mysterium und Mimus im Rigveda,* Leipzig, 1908.

3. A. Barth (*RHR* 19, 1889, 130 f.....*Oeuvres,* II, 5 f.) has already compared the Ākhyāna of Purūravas and Urvaśī in the Śatapatha-Brāhmaṇa with the ballad of King Rasalu in Temple's *Legends of the Panjab.* On the whole question, see Pischel, *GGA* 1891, 355 ff.; Oldenberg, *GGA* 1909, 66 ff.; *NGGW* 1911, 459 ff.; Bloomfield, *American Journal of Philology,* 30, 1909, 78 ff.; A. B. Keith, *JRAS,* 1909, 200 ff.; 1911, 979 ff.; 1912, 429 ff.; *ZDMG* 64, 1910, 534 ff.; J. Charpentier, *WZKM* 23, 1909, 151 f.; 25, 1911, 307 ff.; *Die Suparnasage,* Uppsala 1920, p. 13 ff. W. Caland, *AR* 14, 1911, 499 ff.; Hillebrandt, *Lieder des Ṛgveda,* passim; K. F. Geldner, *Die indische Balladendichtung, Festschrift der Universität Marburg,* 1913, pp. 93ff.; E. Windisch, *Geschichte der Sanskrit Philologie,* pp. 404 ff.; M. Winternitz, *WZKM* 23, 1909, 102 ff.; *Oesterreichische Monats-schrift fur den Orient* 41, 1915, 173 ff., and the Lecture on "Ancient Indian Ballad Poetry" in the *Calcutta Review,* December, 1923.

be that in some cases there might have been a connecting prose story (as Oldenberg assumed), which, if we knew it, would make the conversations of the hymns clear. But most of these hymns are simply ballads of the half-epic, half-dramatic type, though not real dramas, as some scholars have thought them to be.

The most famous of these Vedic ballads or Samvāda-hymns is RV X, 95. This is a poem of 18 stanzas, consisting of the dialogue between Purūravas and Urvaśi. Purūravas is a mortal and Urvaśī a nymph (Apsaras). For four years the divine beauty stayed on the earth as the wife of Purūravas, until she became pregnant. Then she disappeared "as the first of the dawns". Thereupon he went out in search of her; at last he finds her, as she is sporting on a lake together with other water-nymphs. That is about all that we can gather from the obscure, often wholly un-understandable verses—the dialogue between the deserted one and goddess romping about with her playmates in the pond. Luckily for us this ancient story of the love of a mortal king for a daughter of the gods is also preserved elsewhere in Indian literature and we can therefore in a way complete the poem of the Ṛgveda. Even in a Brāhmaṇa[1] the Saga of Purūravas and Urvaśī is told. And the verses of the Ṛgveda are woven into the narrative. There it is said that the nymph, while agreeing to become the wife of Purūravas put forth three conditions, one of which was that she should not see him naked. The Gandharvas—demi-gods of the same region to which the Apsaras belong—want to win back Urvaśi. Therefore they rob in the night two lambkins which she loves like children and which are tied at her bedside. And as Urvaśi bitterly complains that she was being robbed as if there were no man there, Purūravas jumps up—naked as he was, for he thought it would be too late, if he should put on his dress—to pursue the thieves. But at this moment the Gandharvas let a lightning appear so that it becomes as bright as at day time and Urvaśi finds the king naked. Then she disappeared, and as Purūrvas came back, she was gone. Mad with grief the king thereupon wandered about in his country until one day he came to a pond, in which

1. Śatapatha-Brāhmaṇa XI, 5, 1.

nymphs were swimming about in the form of swans. And here ensues the dialogue that is preserved in the Ṛgveda and that is reproduced in the Brāhmaṇa[1] with explanatory adjuncts. But in vain are all requests of Purūravas, that she might return to him. Even when he desparately talks of suicide—he wants to plunge down from the rock, to be eaten up by the fierce wolves—she has only the following reply :

"Die not, Purūravas, do not jump down
From the rock, as food for the wild wolves—
There is no friendship with women,
They have hearts like hyaenas."

Whether and how Purūravas is reunited with his beloved is not very clear either from the Ṛgveda or from the Śatapatha-Brāhmaṇa. It appears that he changes into a Gandharva and reaches heaven where he experiences the happiness of reunion. The story of Purūravas and Urvaśi has been often retold in India; it is shortly hinted at in the Kāṭhaka belonging to the Black Yajurveda, it is again narrated in the exegetic works attached to the Veda,[2] in the Harivaṃśa, an appendix to the Mahābhārata, in the Viṣṇu Purāṇa and in the Kathāsaritsāgara, the book of fairy tales. And no less a person than Kālidāsa has created from it one of his immortal dramas. How far the Ṛgveda is chronologically anterior to all that we possess of the Indian literature, is proved by the fact that in spite of all our efforts to harmonise the verses of the Ṛgveda with the later narratives and to employ these later narratives[3] for explaining Ṛgvedic poems, much still remains obscure and unclarified in these texts.

Another valuable fragment of the ancient art of narration is preserved in the dialogue between Yama and Yamī (RV X 10).

1. The-Śatapatha-Brāhmaṇa has only 15 of the 18 verses of the Ṛgveda.

2. Baudhāyana-Śrautasūtra (see Caland, in the *Album Kern*, pp. 57 ff.) Bṛhaddevatā, Ṣaḍguruśiṣya's commentary on the Sarvānukramaṇi of the Ṛgveda.

3. See especially Geldner in the *Vedische Studien* I, 243-295. Also Oldenberg, *ZDMG* 39, 72 ff., and *Die Literature des alten Indien*, pp. 53 ff. The Purūravas-Urvaśi dialogue has also been translated by Hertel, *Indogerm. Forschungen* 31, 1912, 143 ff., and Hillebrandt, *Lieder des Rgveda*, pp. 142 ff.

An old myth on the origin of the human beings from the first pair of twins forms the basis for this dialogue.[1] Yami seeks to seduce her brother to incest, in order that the human race may not go extinct. In passionate words glowing with love the sister tempts the brother to love—in calm, quiet words Yama rejects, pointing to the eternal laws of the gods that forbid the union of blood-relatives. These speeches, in which unfortunately so much is still unclear, are full of dramatic power. Yamī speaks first :

> "For friendship I draw my friend to me
> And though he went across the wide sea
> Of him may place a child in me
> The Creator, thinking of the earth's future !"
>
> (RV X 10, 1)

Yama replies thereupon:

> "Thy friend loves not the friendship which considers her who is near in kindred as a stranger.
> Sons of the mighty Asura, the Heroes, supporters of the heavens,
> see far around them." (2)

But Yamī seeks to persuade her brother, that the gods themselves wish that he should unite her to continue the species. As he will not listen, she becomes more and more energetic and passionate:

> "I, Yamī, am possessed by love of Yama, that I may rest on the same
> couch beside him.
> I as a wife would yield myself to my husband. Like car-wheels let us
> speed to meet each other." (7)

3. See A. Weber, *SBA.* 1895, 822 ff. "Yama " means "twin", and "Yami" is a feminine form of "Yama". · A. Winter has attempted a mythological interpretation of the myth in the essay : "Mein Bruder freit um mich" (*ZVV.* VII, 1897, pp. 172 ff.), where he compares Rv. X, 10 with a Lettic popular song, in which a brother attempts to seduce his sister to incest. Schroeder (*Mysterium und Mimus*, pp. 275 ff.), explains the hymn as a drama connected with some rite of fertility. This is certainly wrong. See Winternitz, *WZKM* 23, 1909, 118 f. and Charpentier, *Die Suparṇasage*, p. 99.

Yama nevertheless turns down with the words:

"They stand not still, they never close their eyelids, those sentinels
of God who wander round us.
Not me—go quickly, wanton, with another, and hasten like a chariot-
wheel to meet him." (8)

But the sister becomes more and more impetuous, more and more vehemently does she covet Yama's embraces until she bursts out upon his repeated refusals—in the words:

"Alas thou art indeed a weakling, Yama, we find in thee no trace
of heart or spirit
As round the tree the woodbine clings, another will cling about thee
girt as with a girdle." (13)

Whereupon Yama closes the dialogue with the words:

"Embrace another, Yamī; let another, even as the woodbine rings the tree, enfold thee.
Win thou his heart and let him win thy fancy, and he shall form with thee a blest alliance"[1] (14)

How the story of Yama and Yamī ended, we do not know. No later source gives any information about it. So the poem of the Ṛgveda is only a torso, but a torso which shows signs of an excellent work of art.

I should like to count the Sūryāsūkta (RV X 85)[2] also among the Ākhyāna-hymns. This hymn describes the wedding of Sūryā (sun's daughter, as the dawn is called here) with Soma (the moon), whereby the two Aśvins were the bride-suitors. This hymn consists of 47 verses which are all rather loosely connected with one another. These verses refer almost all to

1. Verses 2, 7, 8, 13, 14 translated by R. T. H. Griffith, the first verse by the author.

2. Translated into German by A. Weber, *Ind. Stud.* 5, 177 ff. See also J. Ebni, *ZDMG*, 23, 1879, 166 ff.; Pischel, *Vedische Studien*, I. 14 ff.; Oldenberg, *GGA*, 1869, p. 7.

the wedding ritual and most of them were also used during the wedding of ordinary mortals, as we know from the Gṛhyasūtras the textbooks of household rituals. Still I do not think that these verses — as it is also partly true of the burial hymns — were simply collected from the rituals; so that they might perhaps be considered like passages to be used at wedding ceremonies collected all in one chapter of a prayerbook. I would rather think that we have here an epic piece that narrated the marriage of Sūryā. As in the case of other Ākhyāna hymns here also the prose of the actual narrative has been lost and we are left only with the speeches of the priests, the passages and the prayer formulas as they occur in a marriage, together with some verses in which the main instants of the narrative are summarised shortly.[1] But among the wedding passages, which are found in this Sūryāsūkta, there are many which by virtue of the simple and warm tone of the heart in which they speak, remind us of the burial songs we have discussed above. Thus the bridal pair is felicitated with the nice words.

"Happy be thou and prosper with thy children here: be vigilant to rule thy household in this home.
Closely unite thy body with this man, thy lord. So shall ye, full of years, address your company". (27)

And the spectators, past whom the wedding procession goes, are acclaimed thus:

"Signs of good fortune mark the bride: Come all of you and look at her
Wish her prosperity, and then return unto your homes again". (33)

And when the bridegroom, following the ancient Indo-Germanic marriage-custom holds the bride's hand, then he says the text

"I take thy hand in mine for happy fortune that thou mayst reach old age with me thy husband.
Gods, Aryaman, Bhaga, Savitar, Purandhi, have given thee to be my household's mistress". (36)

1. See above p. 92.

When at last the bridal couple enters the new home, it is received with the words

"Be ye not parted; dwell ye here; reach the full time of human life.
With sons and grandsons sport and play, rejoicing in your own abode". (42)

And the bride is blessed with

"O bounteous Indra, make this bride blest in her sons and fortunate.
Vouchsafe to her ten sons, and make her husband the 11th man ! (45)[1]

Some of these marriage texts have however, more the character of magic formulas. Among them we find exorcisms against the evil eye and other disastrous magic by which the bride could harm her future husband, as well as magic spells by which the demons who follow the bride are supposed to be scared away. And these magic spells stand in no way in isolation, but there are in the Ṛgveda also about thirty magic songs. And indeed we find texts and formulas for healing various diseases, for protecting the foetus, for warding off wicked dreams and inauspicious symptoms, for scaring away malevolent demons, for destroying enemies and ill-disposed magicians, magic formulas against poison and vermin, spells for the removal of rivals in love; we find also a field-benediction, a cattle-benediction, a battle-benediction, a spell to narcotize and many more similar ones. The funny "frog song" (RV VII, 103) is also one of them. Here the frogs are compared to the Brahmins. In the dry season they will be lying about like the Brahmins who have taken the vow of silence. When the rain comes, then they greet one another with joyous croaking "as the son the father". And one repeats the croaking of the other, as in a Brahmin-school, while learning the Veda the pupils repeat the words of the teachers. In manifold ways they modulate their voices. As the priests sit during the Soma-sacrifice singing around the barrel filled with the soma-juice, so also do the frogs celebrate the commencement of the rainy season with their song. At the close there is a prayer for wealth:

1. The five verses translated by R. T. H. Griffith.

"Both lowing cow and bleating goat have given
Spotty and Tawny, too, have given us riches.
The frogs give kine by hundreds: they for pressings
Of Soma thousandfold, prolong existence".[1]

All this sounds very funny and almost in general the song is looked upon as a parody on the sacrificial songs and a wicked satire against the Brahmins.[2]

But Bloomfield has conclusively proved that[3] it is a magic-song that was used for conjuring rain and that the frogs which according to ancient Indian popular belief could bring about water are praised and invoked as rainbringers. The comparison with the Brahmins should not be any satire on the Brahmins but only a flattery — a *captatio-benevolantiae* — for the frogs. It could be however, that a poem which was originally meant as a satire was later on worked up into a magic song here. Similarly the song RV VI 75 might have been also a battle-song which was later on transformed into a battle-benediction. While individual verses of this song are distinguished by a great poetic beauty and in particular by daring metaphors, the other verses move completely within the range of the dry artless language of magic songs. The first three verses sound not like a magic song, but like a battle song:

"The warrior's look is like a thunderous rain-cloud's
when, armed with mail, he seeks the lap of battle.

---

1. Translated by A. A. Macdonell, *Hymns from the Rgveda,* p. 96. A free poetical translation of the hymn is to be found in J. Muir, *Metrical Translations from Sanskrit Writers* pp. 194 f.

2. Even Paul Deussen is of this view. *Allgemeine Geschichte der Philosophie* I, 1, p. 100-f.

3. *Journal of the American Oriental Society,* Vol. XVII 1896, p. 173 ff. Previously M. Hung (*Brahma und die Brahmanen,* Munich 1871, p. 12) had also held the same view and added in this context the following interesting information : The song together with the previous one addressed to the rain God (Parjanya), is still used at the time of a great drought when the much needed rain fails. Twenty to thirty Brahmins go to a river and recite both these hymns to induce the rain to come down. See also L. v. Schroeder, *Mysterium und Mimus im Rgveda,* pp. 396 ff. and-J. W. Hauer, *Die Anfänge der yogapraxis,* Berlin 1922, pp. 68 ff.

Be thou victorious with unwounded body so let the thickness of thy
mail protect thee.
With bow let us win kine, with bow the battle, with bow the victors in our hot encounters.
The bow brings grief and sorrow to the foeman: armed with the bow
may we subdue all regions.
Close to his ear, as fain to speak, she presses, holding her well-loved
friend in her embraces.
Strained on the bow, she whispers like a woman—this bow-string that preserves us in the combat."[1]

By and large however the magic songs of the Ṛgveda do not differ in any way from those of the Atharvaveda, of which we will speak soon.[2] But it is significant that besides the hymns to the great gods and the sacrificial songs, such magic songs have been included in the Ṛgveda-Saṃhitā and not simply in the X book of the same.

And it is still more significant that some absolutely secular poems got mixed with the sacred songs and sacrificial songs of the Ṛgveda. Thus we find for example in RV IX, 112 in the midst of the Soma-songs a satirical poem that mocks at the manifold wishes of men. This has been possibly included in the Ṛgveda-Saṃhitā only for the reason that a witty interpolator has hit upon the idea of appending to each verse the most inappropriate burden: "May Soma flow to the Indra."

This is probably an old popular song of the "labour song" type. It could be sung as an accompaniment to any kind of work, and here the refrain "Flow, Indu,[3] flow, for Indra's sake[4] indicates that it was adapted for the work of pressing

1. Translated by R. T. H. Griffith.
2. See p. 110 ff. below.
3. Indu=Soma.
4. There is no justification for omitting this refrain, as some translators have done, for instance, Muir, *Metrical Translations from Sanskrit writers*, p. 190; Macdonell, *Hymns from the Rgveda*, p. 90. But see Pischel, *Vedische Studien*, I, 107.

Soma.[1] I give the remarkable poem in the translation of R.T.H. Griffith:

"We all have various thoughts and plans, and diverse are the ways of men.

The Brahman seeks the worshipper, wright seeks the cracked, and leech the maimed. Flow, Indu, flow for Indra's sake.

The smith with ripe and seasoned plants, with feathers of the birds of air,

With stones, and with enkindled flames seeks him who hath a store of gold. Flow, Indu, flow for Indra's sake.

A bard am I, my dad's a leech, mummy lays corn upon the stones.

Striving for wealth, with varied plans, we follow our desires like kine. Flow, Indu, flow for Indra's sake.

The horse would draw an easy car, gay hosts attract the laugh and jest.

The male desires his mate's approach,[2] the frog is eager for the flood. Flow, Indu, flow for Indra's sake."

But the most beautiful among the non-religious poems of the Ṛgveda-Saṁhitā is the song of the gambler, RV, X, 34. It is the monologue of a repentant sinner who has destroyed his happy life by his irresistible love for gambling. In verses composed in a language that moves the listeners the gambler describes how the dice have robbed him of his domestic happiness:

---

1. Some of the Soma hymns (e.g. Rv. I, 28; IX, 2; 6; 8 etc.) are "Labour songs" in which the whole process of preparing the Soma juice is described. See K. Būcher, *Arbeit und Rhythnus*, 5. Aufl., Leipzig, 1919, pp. 412 f. L. v. Schroder (*Mysterium und Mimus im Rigveda*, pp. 408 ff) has with bold imagination tried to show that the hymn was used at a popular procession during a Soma festival. But there are no facts on which this hypothesis could be founded. Oldenberg (*GGA*, 1909, 80 f.) thinks that the hymn was intended as a prayer at some Soma sacrifice offered for attaining special wishes. So also Charpentier, *Die Suparnasage*, pp. 80 f.

2. Expressed much more coarsely in the original.

"She wrangles not with me, nor is she angry:
To me and comrades she was ever kindly.
For dice that only luckless throws effected
I have driven away from home a wife devoted. (2)

Her mother hates me, she herself rejects me !
For one in such distress there is no pity.
I find a gambling man is no more useful
Than is an aged horse that's in the market. (3)

Others embrace the wife of him whose chattels
The eager dice have striven hard to capture;
And father, mother, brothers say about him:
We know him not; lead him away a captive". (4)

But the awful power of the dice is also painted in powerful words thus:

"When to myself I think, I'll not go with them,
I'll stay behind my friends that go to gamble,
And those brown nuts, thrown down, have raised their voices,
I go, like wench, straight to the place of meeting. (5)

And of the dice it is said:

"The dice attract the gambler, but declare and wound,
Both paining men at play and causing them to pain.
Like boys they offer first and then take back their gifts:
With honey sweet to gamblers by their magic charm (7)

Downward they roll, then swiftly springing upward,
They overcome the man with hands, though handless.
Cast on the board like magic bits of charcoal,
Though cold themselves, they burn heart to ashes". (9)

And however much he may lament his fate, he still falls a victim to the power of the dice:

"Grieved is the gambler's wife by him abandoned,
Grieved, too, his mother as he aimless wanders.

Indebted, fearing, he desiring money
At night approaches other people's houses. (10)

It pains the gambler when he sees a woman
Another's wife, and their well-ordered household;
He yokes those brown steeds early in the morning[1]
And when the fire is low sinks down a beggar."[2]

In the end better thoughts prevail: he begs of the dice to release him as he, following the commandment of Savitar, wants to give up gambling, to cultivate his land and live for his family.

Finally a kind of intermediary role between religious and secular poetry is played by such of those hymns which, are connected with the so-called "Dānastutis", "songs praising generosity" (namely of princes and lords of sacrifices for whom the poems were composed). There are about forty such hymns.[3] Some of them are victory-songs in which god Indra is praised, because he has helped some king or the other to defeat his enemy. With the praise of God is the glorification of the king connected. In the end the singer praises his lord who has presented him with cattle, horses and beautiful women as slaves from the spoils of war, and thereby some crude, obscene pleasures are also mentioned which the female slaves provide for the singer. Others are very extensive sacrificial songs[4] also mostly addressed to Indra which were obviously composed for some specific occasions on the orders of a prince or a rich man and

1. i.e. he begins to play with the brown-dice.

2. Translated by A. A. Macdonell, *Hymns from the Rgveda*, pp. 88 ff. The hymn has also been translated by J. Muir, *Metrical Translations from Sanskrit Writers*, pp. 190 ff. L. v. Schroeder (*Mysterium und Mimus im Rgveda*, pp. 377 ff.) explains the poem as a drama in form of a monologue. Charpentier (*Die Suparṇasage*, pp. 83 ff.) thinks that it was composed for "didactic purposes". It seems to me more probable that this soliloquy of a gambler is part of a ballad, in which some epic story was told like that of Yudhiṣṭhira, or Nala.

3. Only one hymn (RV I, 126) is wholly a Dānastuti. In all other cases it is usually only 3 to 5 verses at the end of the hymn which contain the Dānastuti.

4. One has the impression that the longer the poem, the greater was the reward.

were sung at the time of a sacrifice; in the end there are however again some verses, in which the lord of the sacrifice is praised for having given to the singer rich priestly rewards. But the full name of the pious donor is mentioned again and again in the Dānastutis and they undoubtedly refer to historical events or in any case to real happenings. Therefore they are also not unimportant. As poetry of course they are quite worthless. They are produced by artisan-like working verse-makers with their eye fixed on the reward that they might expect. Indeed many hymns of the Ṛgveda, even if they are not connected with any Dānastuti, have been "hammered together" in an artisan-like manner for a good reward. The Vedic singers themselves compare their work with that of the carpenter.[1] Still it is noteworthy that among these hymns which somehow excel as works of the art of poetry there is not a single one that ends in a Dānastuti. When therefore H. Oldenberg[2] says about the Ṛgveda-poetry in general, "This poetry does not serve beauty as this religion does not serve the task of purifying the souls and to uplift them; but both serve the interest of classes, personal interest, the interest of the reward", then he certainly forgets that among the 1028 hymns of the Ṛgveda there are only 40 which end in Dānastutis. In my opinion, there have been among the authors of Vedic hymns certainly artisans, but there have been equally certainly also poets.

There is one hymn in the Ṛgveda which is in a higher sense a Dānastuti, a "praise of generosity". It is the hymn RV X 117 which also deserves to be mentioned because in it a quite strange and moralising note is struck that is not found anywhere else. The Ṛgveda is anything but a textbook of morals. And the hymn, which is translated literally as follows by A. A. Macdonell,[3] stands completely isolated in the *Ṛgveda*:

---

1. RV I, 130, 6. "This speech was made for you by men, who want riches, as a skilled master makes a carriage". RV I, 61, 4. "To him (Indra) I send this song of praise, as the carpenter sends a carriage to the man who ordered it.

2. *Die Literatur des alten Indien*, p. 20.

3. *Hymns from the Rigveda*, pp. 92 f. Freely translated by J. Muir, *Metrical Translations from Sanskrit Writers*, pp. 193 -f. See also Deussen, *AG Ph.* I, I, pp. 93 ˙.

"The gods inflict not hunger as a means to kill:
Death frequently befalls even satiated men.
The charitable giver's wealth melts not away;
The niggard never finds a man to pity him.

Who, of abundant food possessed, makes hard his heart
Towards a needy and decrepit suppliant
Whom once he courted, come to pray to him for bread:
A man like this as well finds none to pity him.

He is the liberal man who helps the beggar
That, craving food, emaciated wanders,
And coming to his aid, when asked to succour,
Immediately makes him a friend hereafter.

He is no friend who gives not of his substance
To his devoted, intimate companion:
This friend should turn from him—here is no haven
And seek a stranger elsewhere as a helper.

The wealthier man should give unto the needy,
Considering the course of life hereafter;
For riches are like chariot wheels revolving !
Now to one man they come, now to another.[1]

The foolish man from food has no advantage;
In truth I say: it is but his undoing;
No friend he ever fosters, no companion:
He eats alone, and he alone is guilty.

The plough that cleaves the soil produces nurture;
He that bestirs his feet completes his journey.
The speaking Brahmin earns more than the silent;
A friend who gives is better than the niggard.

The one-foot strides more than the biped;
The biped goes beyond him who has three feet.

---

1. Geldner (*Siebenzig Lieder*, p. 156) translates beautifully thus: He who can, shall give alms to the needy/ponder well the long way of life ! Fortune turns up and down like carriage-wheels/ Now it calls on this one, now on that one.

The quadruped comes at the call of bipeds,
And watches near where groups of five are gathered—[1]

Two hands though equal make not what is equal;
No sister cows yield milk in equal measure,
Unequal is the strength even of twin children;
The gifts of even kinsmen are unequal."[2]

The penultimate stanza is an example for the riddle-poetry that was very popular with the ancient Indians as with other ancient folks. A large number of such riddles, unfortunately ununderstandable to us, are found in the hymn RV I, 164. There it is said for example :

"Seven harness a one-wheeled carriage; it is drawn by a horse with seven names; three hubs has the eternal impetuous wheel on which all these beings stand."

That can mean: The seven sacrificial priests harness (by means of sacrifice) the chariot of the sun that is drawn by seven horses or by a horse that has seven forms; this eternal wheel of the Sun has three hubs, namely the three seasons (summer, rainy and winter) in which the life of all men pass. However, other solutions of the riddle are also possible.

It may perhaps be not worth the trouble of wanting to go deep into the meaning of the following riddle.

"Carrying three mothers and three fathers the one stands there and they do not tire them; on the back of the sky there they consult the Omniscient but not All-pervading Vāc (Goddess of Speech).

He who has made him, knows nothing of him; he who has seen him, from him is he hidden; he lies rolled up in the

1. The translation is scarcely doubtful, so much the more the meaning. One presumes, that with the "one-footed ram", a storm-God is meant and that the "three-foot" is the old man supported by the ram and the "four-foot" is the dog. It is by no means certain.

2. Cf. Deussen—*Allgemeine Geschichte der Philosophie* I, 1, p. 93f.

womb of the mother; many children has he and yet gone to Nirṛti.[1]

The sky is my father and my creator, there is the navel; my mother, related to me is this great earth. Between the two spread out Soma vessels is the womb; therein laid the father the seed in the daughter."

As against this, it is clear that the sun is meant when it is said:

"A herdsman I saw, who does not fall down, who wanders about again and again on his paths; covering himself with the converging and the diverging,[2] he goes round and round in the worlds."

Equally clear is the interpretation of the riddle:

"Twelve wheel-rims, one wheel, three hubs: Who knows that?

Fixed in it there are altogether about 360 movable stakes."

What is meant is the year with the 12 months, 3 seasons and about 360 days.[3]

Such riddle-questions and riddle-games were among the most popular means of entertainment in ancient India; during some sacrifices they formed especially a part of the ritual. And we come across the same again in the Atharvaveda as well as in the Yajurveda.

If we now survey the colourful contents of Ṛgveda-Saṃhitā of which I tried here to give an idea, we gain the conviction that in this collection we have to see on the whole the fragments of the oldest Indian poetry, that the songs, hymns and poems of the Ṛgveda are only a fraction of a much more extensive

---

1. Nirṛti is the Goddess of death and ruin. "Going to Nirṛti" means to be ruined completely; to vanish into nothingness.

2. The rays are meant.

3. The riddles of RV I, 164 have been thoroughly treated by Martin Haug in his *Vedische Rätselfragen und Rätselsprüche* (Sitzungsberichte der philos-philol Klasse der bayern. Akademi der Wissenschaften, München 1875) and by P. Deussen in his *Allgemeine Geschichte der Philosophie*, I, 1, p. 105-119.

See also R. Roth, *ZDMG* 46, 1892, 759 f.; E. Windisch, *ZDMG* 48, 1894, 353 f.; H. Stumme, *ZDMG* 64, 1910, 485 f. and V. Henry, *Revue Critique*, 1905, p. 403.

poetry—religious and secular—most of which has been perhaps irrecoverably lost. But as these hymns are in a large majority, there are either sacrificial psalms or were used as prayers or as sacrificial songs or could be used as such, so we may presume that it was just on account of these hymns that it was all actually collected and compiled in a "book". But the collectors who will have had in addition to the religious interest also a purely literary interest in the collection have not hesitated, to include in this collection, also non-sacral poems, which have proved to be, by virtue of their language and metre, just as old and time-honoured as the sacrificial psalms. Only by being included in a "book", i.e. in a school-text meant for being learnt by heart—could they be saved from being forgotten. Of course, there has been also much, that has appeared to them as too unholy to be included in the Ṛgveda-Saṃhitā. Of this much has been in its turn rescued for us by the fact that they have been included later in another collection—in the Atharvaveda-Saṃhitā.

The Atharvaveda-Saṃhitā[1]

"Atharvaveda" means so to say "the Veda of the Atharvans" or "the knowledge of the magic spells". Originally however the word meant a fire-priest and it is perhaps the

1. There is no complete German translation of the Atharva Veda; of course we have translations of individual books and of selected hymns. A large selection of hymns is translated by Alfred Ludwig in the 3rd Vol. of his *ṚgVeda* (Prag 1878) p. 428-551. A selection of metrical translations is given by Julius Grill, *Hundert Lieder des Atharva-Veda.* (2nd edition, Stuttgart 1888). A. Weber has translated : the books I to V & XIV in the 4th, 13th, 17th & 18th and 5th volumes of the *Indische Studien* "respectively; and Book XVIII in the "Sitzungsberichten der Berliner Akademie der Wissenchaften 1895 and 1896". The XV Book has been translated into German by Th. Aufrecht in the I vol of "*Indische Studien*" and the first 50 hymns of the VI Book by C. H. Florenz (Göttingen 1887, Thesis for Doctorate). Victor Henry translated the books VII to XIII into French (Paris 1891-96). A complete English translation by R. T. H. Griffith is available (Varanasi 1895-6). The best selection in excellent English translation is that of M. Bloomfield (*SBE*, Vol. 42). The same scholar has also treated the Atharva-veda very thoroughly in the *Grundriss* (vol. II, No. 1 B). The author (M. Winternitz) is indebted to this excellent work for the following

oldest Indian name for "priest" as such, for the word can be traced back to the Indo-Iranian times. Corresponding to the Indian Atharvans there are the Atharvans or "Firemen" of the Avesta.[1] Fire-cult played in the everyday life of the ancient Indians no less a role than in the case of the ancient Persians who were so often termed as "Fireworshippers" the priests of this aboriginal fire cult were also — like the Shamans of North Asia and the Medicine men of the Red Indians — "magic-priests", i.e. priests and magicians in one, as also in the word "magician" — as the Atharvans were called in Medea — the concepts "magician" and "priest" overlap each other. Thus it is clear that the word "atharvan" was used also to mean the "spells of the Atharvans or of the magic-priests" i.e. the "magic spells and the magic-formulas themselves. The oldest name however by which this Veda is known in Indian Literature, is known as Atharvāṅgirasaḥ, i.e, "the Atharvans and the Aṅgiras". The Aṅgiras are similarly a class of fire-priests of prehistorical times and the word acquired, just like the atharvan, the meaning of "magic-formulas and magic-spells". But the two words Atharvan and Aṅgiras describe two different kinds of magic-formulas; Atharvan is "sacred, auspicious magic" whereas Aṅgiras means "hostile, black magic" The magic-formulas that serve to cure diseases for example belong to the Atharvans while the curses on enemies, on rivals in love and on wicked magicians etc. belong to the Aṅgiras. The old name Atharvāṅgirasaḥ denotes therefore both these kinds of magic-formulas which form the main theme of the Atharva-veda. The later name Atharva-veda is only an abbreviation for "Veda of the Atharvans and Aṅgiras".[2]

description, especially for the classification of the hymns. For the contents and interpretation of the Atharvaveda see also V. Henry, *La magie dans l'Inde Antique,* Paris 1904; Oldenberg, *AR* 7, 1904, 217 ff; F. Edgerton, *American Journal of Philology,* 35,1914, 435 ff.

1. Even in ancient Rome the Flamines who were to perform the fire-sacrifice were among the oldest priests. (Th. Mommsen, *Römische Geschichte,* 4th edition. I, p. 170 f.).

2. In later literature we meet also with the terms bhṛgvaṅgirasaḥ and bhṛguvistara (Cūlikā-Upaniṣad II) for the Atharvaveda. The Bhṛgus also were ancient fire-priests.

Now the Atharvaveda-Saṃhitā — usually called just "the Atharvaveda" — is, in the recension which is preserved to us in the best condition,[1] a collection of 731 hymns which contain approximately 6000 verses. It is divided into 20 books.[2] Of these, the X book has been added only later on, and also the XIX book did not originally belong to the Saṃhitā. The XX book consists almost entirely of hymns that are literally taken out of the Ṛgveda-Saṃhitā. Moreover, in addition to this approximately one seventh of the Atharvaveda is also taken from the Ṛgveda; and this is as follows — more than half the verses which the Atharvaveda has in common with the Ṛgveda, are found in the X book and most of the remaining verses are found in the I and VIII book of the Ṛgveda. The order of the hymns in the 18 genuine books follows a particular plan and exhibits rather carefully executed editorial work. The first seven books consist of numerous short hymns as follows — the hymns in book I have generally 4, those in book II five, those in books III 6, those in book IV seven verses. The hymns of the V book have a minimum of 8 and a maximum of 18 verses. The VI book consists of 142 hymns of mostly 3 verses each and the VII book consists of 118 hymns most of which have only 1 or 2 verses. The books VIII-XIV, XVII and XVIII consist generally of very long hymns and here the shortest hymn (with 21 verses.) heads the list (VIII, 1) and the longest (with 89 verses) closes the same

1. It is the Śaunaka recension or the Saṃhitā-text belonging to the Śaunaka-school. The Paippalāda-recension is known to us only through a single, inexact manuscript. The text of the Śaunaka-Recension has been published by R. Roth and W. D. Whitney, Berlin 1856. The Atharvaveda-Saṃhitā with the commentary of Sāyaṇa, has been published by Shankar P. Pandit, 4 vols., Bombay 1895-1898. The manuscript of the Paippalāda recension has been published in facsimile by M. Bloomfield and R. Garbe (The Kashmirian Atharvaveda, Stuttgart 1901). Books I, II, IV-X of the Kashmirian recension have been published with critical notes on the text by Le Roy carr Barret and F. Edgerton in *JAOS*, vols. 26, 30, 32, 34, 35, 37, 40-43, 1906-1923.

2. We can distinguish three main divisions of the Saṃhitā, Cf. Lanman, *HOS*, vol. 7, pp. CXXVII ff.) 1. Books I—VI, an appendix to which is contained in Book VII; 2. Books VIII—XII and 3. Books XIII—XVIII, an appendix to which is contained in Book XIX.

(XVIII, 4). Book XV and the greatest part of Book XVI which interrupt this series, are composed in prose and are similar to the Brāhmaṇas in style and language. Although while arranging this order only the purely external aspect like the number of verses was given special consideration, still some attention has also been paid to the contents. Two, three, four and even more hymns having the same theme often stand together. Sometimes the first hymn of a book is placed at the beginning, paying regard to its content; thus the Books II, IV, V and VII begin with theosophical hymns, which is certainly intentional. On the whole we can say thus:[1] Books I to VII contain the short hymns of misc. content and Books VIII to XII the long hymns; the Books XIII-XVIII are, in their contents, almost unitary; thus Book XIV contains only marriage-texts and Book XVIII only funeral hymns.

The Language and metre of the hymns of the Atharvaveda are essentially the same as those of the Ṛgveda-Saṃhitā. Still we find in the language of the Atharvaveda to some extent decidedly later forms and to some extent more popular ones; and also the metre is not used as strictly as in the Ṛgveda. Apart from Book X which is composed wholly and Book XVI which is composed mostly in prose, we find also now and then prose pieces among the verses; and it is often not easy to decide, whether a piece is composed in high prose or in ill-formed verses. It also happens that an originally correct metre is destroyed by an interpolation or corruption of the text.[2] In individual cases the language and metrical factors indicate that they are later pieces. However, we cannot draw any conclusions from the language and metre about the time of composition of the hymns, still less about the age of our Saṃhitā edition. For the question will remain always open, whether the peculiarities of the language and the liberties in metre by which the magic-texts of the Atharvaveda distinguish themselves from the

---

1. On the divisions of the Atharvaveda-Saṃhitā see Whitney and Lanman, *HOS*, vol. 7, pp. cxxvii ff.

2. On the metre of the Atharvaveda see Whitney, *HOS*, vol. 7, pp. cxxvi f. Irregularities of metre are equally peculiar to the Atharvaveda as to all metrical Vedic texts other than the Ṛgveda. To correct the metre everywhere, would mean changing the text arbitrarily.

hymnal poetry of the Ṛgveda are based on a difference in the time of origin or on a difference between popular and priestly poetry. (Compare page 51 ff above).

As against this there are other facts which prove irrefutably that our edition of the Atharvaveda-Saṃhitā is younger than the Ṛgveda – Saṃhitā. First of all, the geographical and cultural conditions as they are reflected in the Atharvaveda take us to a later date. The Vedic Aryans have already advanced further into the south-east and had already settled in the land of the Gaṅga. The tiger, which is a native of the swampy woods of Bengal and hence not known to the Ṛgveda appears in the Atharvaveda already as the mightiest and the most terrible of all animals of prey, and at the time of royal consecration the king treads on the skin of a tiger, the symbol of royal power. The Atharvaveda knows not only the four castes — Brahmins, Kṣatriyas, Vaiśyas and Śūdras — but in a series of hymns tallest claims are already made by the priestly caste (as it is later on more and more the case) and the Brahmins are already termed the gods[1] of this earth. The magic songs of the Atharvaveda which by virtue of their chief constituents are certainly popular and ancient, do not have in the Saṃhitā their original form any more, but they are Brahminised. These old spells and formulas, whose authors are as unknown as those of the magic spells and magic songs of other peoples, and which were originally "popular poetry" just as the "magic poetry" is everywhere, have already partly lost their popular character in the Atharvaveda-Saṃhitā. We see at each step that the collection is compiled by priests and that many of the hymns also have been composed by them. This priestly horizon of the editors and partly also of the authors of the hymns of the Atharvaveda is betrayed in occasional similes and metaphors as, for instance, when it is said in a spell against the vermin of the fields, that they should leave the grain untouched "as the Brahmin the sacrificial food that is not yet ready". A whole class of hymns of the Atharvaveda — of which we will speak later on — is concerned only with the

---

1. Once the expression "god" is used for "priest" in the Ṛgveda also. (RV I, 128, 8). cf. Zimmer, *Altindisches Leben*, p. 205 ff.

interests of the Brahmins, of the feeding of the Brahmins, of the sacrificial rewards and similar things, and they are evidently the work of priests.

Just as the brahminising of the ancient magic-poetry denotes a later time of editing, similarly the role that the Vedic gods play in the Atharvaveda proves the later origin of the Saṃhitā. Here we come across the same gods as in the Ṛgveda —Agni, Indra etc., but they are completely faded in their character, they scarcely distinguish themselves from one another, their original significance as natural beings is almost entirely forgotten; and as the magic songs are mainly concerned with exorcism and destruction of demons, so the gods are also invoked only for this purpose. They have all been made demon-killers. Finally, also those hymns of the Atharvaveda which contain theosophical and cosmological speculations indicate a later time. In these hymns we find already a considerably well developed philosophical terminology and a pantheism of the same stage of development as the philosophy of the Upaniṣads. But that even these philosophical hymns are used for purposes of magic, that for example a philosophical concept like Asat, "the not-being" is used as a means for destroying enemies, demons and magicians[1] shows that we have here already a very modern development of ancient magic.

It is no sign of a later date that the sacredness of the Atharvaveda was not recognised for a long time even by the Indians themselves and is disputed in many ways even today. The reason for this is to be sought in the character of this Veda. The purpose of the Atharvaveda is, as the Indians say, "to appease, to bless and to curse".[2] Those numerous magic-formulas however, which contain curses and exorcisms, belong to the field of "unholy magic", from which the priesthood and the priestly religion were endeavouring more and more to free themselves. Basically there is evidently no essential difference between cult and magic : through both man seeks to exercise influence on the supernatural world. Also priests and magicians are originally one and the same. But in the history of all races there begins

1. Ath IV, 19, 6.
2. i.e. to appease the demons, to bless the friends and to curse the enemies.

an epoque when the cult of gods and that of magic make efforts to go asunder (in which they never completely succeed), when the priest who is friendly with the gods severs his connections with the magician associated with the sinister world of the demons and looks down upon him from above. This opposition between the magician and the priest has developed in India also. Not only are the Buddhist and Jain monks forbidden from concerning themselves with the exorcisms of the Atharvaveda and with magic but even the Brahminical law books declare magic as a sin, place magicians and cheats and rascals in one class and exhort the king to proceed against them with penalties.[1] Of course at other places of law books the Brahmins are given express permission, to employ the exorcisms of the Atharvaveda against their enemies[2] and the ritual texts which describe great sacrifices contain unenumerable formulas of exorcism and descriptions of magic-rites through which the priest can annihilate—"him, who hates us and him, whom we hate"—as the standing formula says. Yet there arose in priestly circles a certain dislike against the Veda of the magic spells; it was not considered to be orthodox enough and was in many ways excluded from the canon of the sacred texts. A peculiar position was given to it in the sacred literature from the beginnings. Wherever in the older works there is a reference to sacred knowledge, mention is first made always of the *trayi Vidyā*, "of the threefold knowledge", i.e. *Ṛgveda*, *Yajurveda* and *Sāmaveda* : The Atharvaveda follows always only after the trayī vidyā and is also often ignored. It even happens that the Vedāṅgas and the epic narratives (Itihāsapurāṇas) are mentioned as sacred texts whereas there is no mention of the Atharvaveda. Thus in a Gṛhyasūtra[3] a ceremony is described, by which the Vedas shall be "laid" in the newborn child. This happens by means of a text in which it is said : "The Ṛgveda I lay in you, the Yajurveda I lay in you, the Sāmaveda I lay in you, the dialogues (Vākovākya)

1. *SBE* X. II p. 176-XLV p. 105, 133, 363 Manu IX, 258, 290. XI 64. Viṣṇu-smṛti 54, 25.
2. Manu XI, 33; See also page 137 below.
3. Sānkhāyana-Gṛhyasūtra I, 24, 8.

I lay in you, the sagas and legends (Itihāsapurāṇas) I lay in you, all Vedas I lay in you". Here also the Atharvaveda has been ignored intentionally. Even in Old Buddhistic texts it is said of learned Brahmins that they are proficient in the three Vedas.[1] That however the non-mentioning of the Atharvaveda is no proof of the late origin of the Saṃhitā follows even from the fact that already in a Saṃhitā of the Black Yajurveda[2] and also occasionally in some other places of old Brāhmaṇas and Upaniṣads the Atharvaveda is mentioned along with the three other Vedas.

Although it is a fact that our edition of the Atharvaveda-Saṃhitā is younger than that of the Ṛgveda-Saṃhitā, it does not at all follow from this that the hymns are themselves younger than the Ṛgveda hymns. Only this much follows that the youngest hymns of the Atharvaveda are younger than the youngest hymns of the Ṛgveda. Just as certain as that there are among the hymns of the Atharvaveda many which are younger than the great majority of the Ṛgveda hymns, it is also certain that the magic-poetry of the Atharvaveda as such is as old if not older than the sacrificial poetry of Ṛgveda and that numerous pieces of the Atharvaveda can be traced back to the same hoary past as the oldest songs of Ṛgveda. For it is not at all possible to speak for example of a "Period of the Atharvaveda". Like the Ṛgveda-Saṃhitā the collection of the Atharvaveda also contains pieces which are separated from one another by many centuries. And only in the case of the later constituents of the Atharvaveda-Saṃhitā one can say that some of them have been composed according to the model of the Ṛgveda-hymns. I consider as wrong the view of Oldenberg[3] that the oldest form of the magic formulas in India have been the prose ones and that the whole literature of magic verses and magic songs has

1. Particularly peculiar is Suttanipāta, Selasutta, where of the Brahmin Sela it is said that he is proficient in the three Vedas, in the Vedāṅgas and fifthly in the Itihāsa. (Ed. Fausböll, p. 101). Also in Suttanipāta 1019 it is said of Bhāravi that he has mastered the three Vedas. *SBE*, vol. X,II, p. 98 & 189).

2. Taittirīya-Saṃhitā VII, 5.11, 2. where the plural of Aṅgiras is in the meaning of "Atharvaveda". See above p. 110 f.

3. *Literatur des alten Indien*, p. 41.

been produced only following the "model of its elder sister, the poetry of the sacrificial hymns".

The magic songs of the Atharvaveda reveal to us a mind that is entirely different from what we find in the hymns of the Ṛgveda. Here we move in an entirely different world. There (in the Ṛgveda) the great gods of the heaven, who personify the mighty natural phenomena which the singer glorifies and praises, to whom he performs sacrifices and to whom he prays, strong, obliging, partly sublime beings, mostly kind and shining deities—here (in the Atharvaveda) the dark demonic powers which bring upon human beings disease and misfortune, ghostly beings against which the magician hurls his wild curses or which he wants to appease and banish with flattering speeches. Many of these magic songs belong evidently, along with their magic rites, to a circle of notions and ideas, which, spread over the whole earth, reappear again and again in the most different peoples with astonishing similarity. We find exactly the same views, exactly the same peculiar springs of thought of the magic songs and magic-rites as the Atharvaveda of the ancient Indians has preserved, also in the Red Indians of North America, in the Negroes of Africa, in the Malays and Mongols, in the ancient Greeks and Romans and in many respects even in the countryfolk in modern Europe. There are also many verses in the Atharvaveda, which in their character and often even in their content, are so little different from the magic spells of the Red Indian medicine men and the Tartar Shamans as from the magic spells of Merseburg, which belong to the scanty remnants of the oldest German poetry. Thus we read for example, in one of the Merseburg magic spells that "Wodan who understood it well" spoke the charm over Balder's foalen with the words:

> "Bone to bone,
> Blood to blood,
> Limb to limbs,
> As though they were glued."

And very similar to this is in the Atharvaveda IV, 12 in a spell against bone-fracture:

"With marrow be the marrow joined, thy limb united with the limb
Let what hath fallen of thy flesh, and the bone also grow again. (3)
Let marrow close with marrow, let skin grow united with the skin,
Let blood and bone grow strong in thee, flesh grow together with the flesh (4)
Join thou together hair with hair[1] join thou together skin with skin
Let blood and bone grow strong in thee. Unite the broken-part, O Plant"[2] (5)

The great significance of the Atharvaveda-Saṃhitā lies in this that it is for us an inestimable source of knowledge of the actual popular religion which is not yet influenced by the priestly religion, of the belief in numberless spirits, goblins, ghosts and demons of all kinds and of the practice of magic that is of such great importance to ethnology and the history of religion. How important the Atharvaveda is exactly to the ethnologist will be shown by the following survey of the various classes of hymns that the collection contains.

The songs and the charms for healing diseases which belong to the magic-healing-rites (bhaiṣajyāni) form the main constituent of the Atharvaveda-Saṃhitā. They are addressed either to the diseases themselves[3] which are thought of as personal beings and as demons or to whole classes of demons which are supposed to be the causes of diseases. And as in other peoples, there is also in India, the belief, that these demons either afflict and torture their victim from outside or that he is possessed from within. Some of these charms are also invocations and

1. The healing herb is addressed.
2. Translated by R. T. H. Griffith.
3. The name of the disease is at the same time also the name of the demon. It is exactly so for example in the Malayas as well; they have as many names of the spirits of diseases as they know diseases.

praises of the medicinal plant that shall serve to cure the disease; others are prayers to water, to which special healing power is attributed, or to fire, whom the Indians suppose to be a powerful frightener of demons. These magic songs together with their magic-rites, of which we know from the Kauśikasūtra which we will mention later, constitute the oldest system of the Indian Medical Science. With great clarity the symptoms of the various diseases are often described in the songs, and they are therefore not uninteresting for the history of medicine. This is specially true of the spells against fever. On account of its frequency and vehemence fever is called "the king of diseases" even in the later textbooks of medicine. And to the Takman[1]—this is the name of the fever imagined as a demon in the Atharvaveda—numerous charms are addressed. Thus for example I may quote here a few verses of the hymn Ath. V, 22:

"And thou thyself who makest all men yellow, consuming them with burning heat like Agni,
Thou, Fever! then be weak and ineffective. Pass hence into the realms below or vanish (2)
Endowed with universal power! send Fever downward, far away,
The spotty, like red-coloured dust, sprung from a spotty ancestor (3)
Go, Fever, to the Mūjavans, or farther, to the Bāhlikas,[2]
Seek a lascivious Śūdra-girl and seem to shake her through and through (7)
Since thou now cold, now burning hot, with cough besides, hast made us shake,
Terrible, Fever, are thy darts; forbear to injure us with these (10)
Fever, with consumption, thy brother, and with thy sister cough,

1. On the hymn to Takman, see J. V. Grohmann, *Ind. Stud.* 9, 1865, 381 ff.

2. Names of tribes.

And with thy nephew Hespes, go away unto that alien folk[1] (12)

This pious wish, that the disease may go to other folks, may befall other countries, appears again and again in the songs of the Atharvaveda. In a similar way the cough is sent away from the patient to a distant place with the charm (Ath. VI, 105):

"As the soul with the soul's desires swiftly to a distance flies, thus do
Thou, O cough, fly forth along the soul's course of flight! (1)
As a well-sharpened arrow swiftly to a distance flees, thus do
Thou, O cough, fly forth along the expanse of the earth! (2)
As the rays of the sun swiftly to a distance fly, thus do thou, O cough, fly forth along the flood of the sea!"[2] (3)

On account of their metaphoric, spirited language these magic songs deserve to be esteemed also as products of lyrical poetry. Of course too high demands must not be made of this poetry, one must be contented with being surprised by a beautiful image here and there, as when in a charm against bleeding the magician addresses the veins as girls clad in red (Ath I, 17)

"Those maidens there, the veins, who run their course in robes of ruddy hue,
Must now stand quiet, reft of power, like sisters who are brotherless (1)
Stay still, thou upper vein, stay still, thou lower, stay, thou midmost one,
The smallest one of all stand still: let the great vessel e'en be still. (2)
Among a thousand vessels charged with blood, among a thousand veins,
Even these the middlemost stand still and their extremities have rest. (3)

---

1. Translated by R. T. H. Griffith.
2. Translated by M. Bloomfield, *SBE*, 42 p. 8.

A mighty rampart built of sand hath circled and encompassed you.
Be still, and quietly take rest".[1]

But these charms are not always so poetical. Even quite often they are very monotonous, and many of them have this in common with the poetries or primitive races, that it is the monotonous repetition of the same words and sentences which constitutes the poetical form for them.[2] It is also not seldom as is usually the case with the magic-spells of all races, that their meaning is intentionally mysterious and obscure. One such monotonous and at the same time obscure charm is for example the one against scrofulous ulcers (Ath. VI, 25)

"The five and fifty (sores) that gathes together upon the nape of the neck, from here they all shall pass away, as the pustules of the (disease called) apakit ! (1)

The seven and seventy (sores) that gather together upon the neck, from here they all shall pass away, as the pustules of the (disease called) apakit ! (2)

The nine and ninety (sores) that gather together upon the shoulders from here they all shall pass away, as the pustules of the (disease called) apakit!"[3] (3)

There is a remarkable agreement here also between Indian and German magic-charms. Just as the Atharvaveda speaks of 55, 77, 99 diseases, so also we find in German magic-charms 77 or 99 diseases mentioned. Thus a German charm against fever runs:

"This water and Christ's blood
Is for the 77 kinds of fever good."

A belief that the ancient Indians have in common not only with the Germans but with many other races is that many diseases are caused by worms. There are therefore a series of

1. Translated by R. T. H. Griffith.

2. Regarding repetition as the crudest initial form of poetry, cf. H. Schurtz, *Urgeschichte der Kultur*, Leipzig and Wien 1900, p. 523 ff.

3. Translated by M. Bloomfield, *SBE*. 42, p. 19.

magic songs, which are supposed to serve for conjuring, and expelling all kinds of worms. Thus we read in Ath II 31:

> The worm that is in the intestines, that which is in the head and that which is in the ribs...these worms we crush with this spell. (4)

The worms that have settled in the mountains, in the forests, in the plants, in the cattle, in the waters and those which have settled in our bodies, the whole of this worm-race I smash. (5)

One imagines these worms as demonic beings, speaks of their king and viceroy, of male and female, of worms in many colours and shapes and similar ones; thus for instance in the spell against worms in children (Ath V, 23) :

> Slay the worms in this boy. O Indra, lord of treasures! Slain are all the evil pavers by my fierce imprecation! (2)
>
> Him that moves about in the eyes, that moves about in the nose, that gets to the middle of the teeth, that worm do we crash. (3)
>
> The two of like colour, the two of different colour: the two black ones, and the two red ones; the brown one; and the brown eared one; the (one like a) vulture, and the (one like a) cuckoo, are slain. (4)
>
> The worms with white shoulders, the black ones with white arms, and all those that are variegated, these worms do we crush. (5)
>
> Slain is the king of the worms and their viceroy also is slain, Slain is the worm, with him his mother slain, his brother slain, his sister slain. (11)
>
> Slain are they who are inmates with him, slain are his neighbours; moreover all the quite tiny worms are slain. (12)
>
> Of all the male worms and of all the female worms do I split the head with the stone, I burn their faces with fire.[1]

Quite similar to these are German magic-spells directed against 'male and female worm' and mention is also made of

1. Translated by M. Bloomfield, *SBE*. 42, p. 24.,

worms of many colours in the German magic spell against tooth-ache:

"Pear tree, I complain to you,
Three worms are stinging me,
One is grey,
Another is blue,
The third is red—
I would wish they were all the three dead:[1]

Quite numerous are also the magic-songs which are directed against whole classes of demons, who are supposed to be the causes of diseases, thus in particular again Piśācas (goblins) and Rākṣasas (devils). The purpose of these spells is the expelling or exorcising of these demonic beings. An example of this is the song Ath IV, 36 against the Pisācas. The following verses translated taken from this song show the unlimited self-consciousness of the magician:

"A pest I am to the Piśācas, like the tiger to the owners of cattle
Like the dogs when they have caught sight of the lion, they have no hiding place. (6)
Should I not finish the Piśācas and thieves and robbers?
From the village where I set foot vanish the Piśācas. (7)

From the village where my furious power enters,
Vanish the Piśācas; incapable of any more evil" (8)

In addition to this belief in diabolical beings who bring diseases upon men, we find in India also the worldwide belief in male and female demons (Incubi and Succubi) which visit mortal men and women in the night. These are the Apsaras and

1. The belief that tooth-ache is caused by worms is wide spread not only in India, Germany, England and France. In Madagascar also they say when some body is suffering from tooth-ache, "he is sick by the worm" and the Cherokees have a charm against tooth-ache in which it is said "the intruder into the tooth has spoken, and it is only the worm. (James Mooney in the 7th *Annual Report of the Bureau of Ethnology* 1885-86, Washington 1891, p. 357 f.)

Gandharvas of the popular belief in ancient India. These correspond in every respect and surprisingly to the elves and mares of popular belief in Germany. Rivers and trees are their resorts which they leave only to tempt the mortals and to harm them by unnatural cohabitation. To drive away these spirits the ancient Indian magicians used a sweet-smelling plant called Ajaśṛṅgi (Bockshorn, Odina Pinnata) and spoke thereby the song Ath IV, 37 from which I have taken the following verses:

> "With thee do we scatter the Apsaras and Gandharvas.
>
> O Ajaśṛṅgi (Odina Pinnata), goad (aga) the Rākṣasas drive them all away with thy smell (2)
>
> The Apsaras, Guggulū, Pīlā, Nalādī, Aukshagandhī, and Pramandanī (by name), shall go to the river, to the ford of the waters, as if blown away! Thither do ye, O Apsaras, pass away, (since) ye have been recognised ![1]
>
> Where grow the aśvattha (Ficus religiosa) and the banyan-trees, the great trees with crowns, thither do ye, O Apsaras pass away, (since) ye have been recognised!
>
> Of the crested Gandharva, the husband of the Apsaras, who comes dancing hither, I crush the two mushkas and cut off the sepas. (7)
>
> One is like a dog, one like an ape. As a youth with luxuriant locks, pleasant to look upon, the Gandharva hangs about the woman. Him do we drive out from here with our powerful charm. (11)
>
> The Apsaras, you know, are your wives; ye, the Gandharvas are their husbands. Speed away, ye immortals, do not go after mortals."[2]

---

1. According to the Indian belief in magic-practices, as in that of other races, spirits and ghosts become powerless when they are recognised and called by name. Guggulu etc. are names of particular Apsaras.

2. Translated by M. Bloomfield, *SBE.*, Vol. 42, pp. 33 f.

Just as in this song of the Atharvaveda, so also in German magic-spells the mare is exhorted to leave the houses of the mortals and go to rivers and trees. And like the Apsaras and Gandharvas the Germanic nymphs and elves also love music and dancing, with which they tempt mortal men and women. As in the magic songs of ancient India the Gandharva appears sometimes as a dog, sometimes as a monkey and sometimes as a beautifully dressed youth, so also in the German sagas the mare usually appears in all sorts of forms. And as the Apsaras of the Indians have their swings in the branches of banyan and fig trees, so also in the popular belief of Germans the nymphs swing in the branches and tops of trees. And just as here in the Atharvaveda a sweet smelling plant serves to drive away the demons, so also in the German belief in spirits sweet-smelling herbs (like the thyme) serve as excellent means to scare away elves and other ghostly spirits. These concurrences are hardly accidental and we may presume as Adalbert Kuhn has done, who has compared Indian and Germanic magic-spells forty years ago,[1] that not simply certain phenomena of the belief in magic but also certain conspicuous forms of magic songs and magic spells can be traced back to the prehistoric Indo-Germanic times and that therefore we can deduce from the German and Indian magic songs a sort of prehistoric poetry of the Indo-Germanic race.

Little different from the healing magic spells are the prayers for health and long life, called by the Indians "Āyuṣyāṇi Sūktāni" i.e. "hymns causing long life" which constitute the second class of the hymns of the Atharvaveda. These are prayers which were used mainly at family celebrations like the first hair-cutting of the boy, the beard-cutting of the youth, the initiation of the pupil. In a rather monotonous way the request is again and again repeated here for long life, for a life of 100 autumns or 100 winters, for liberation from 100 or 101 kinds of death and for protection from all sorts of diseases. The XVII book consisting of 30 stanzas is also of this nature. Just as in the magic spells of health the herb used by the magic doctor is

1. In the XIII vol. of the journal *Zeitschrift für vergleichende-Sprachwissenschaft* (1864) p. 49 ff, 113 ff.

often invoked, so also many of these prayers for long life are addressed to amulets which are supposed to ensure health and longevity to those who wear them.

And mostly closely connected with these prayers are the extraordinarily numerous benedictory-spells (pauṣṭikāni) by which the peasant, the herdsman, and the merchant hope to attain fortune and prosperity in their undertakings. In them we find a prayer that is used while building a house, benedictory spells while ploughing, while sowing, for the growth of corn, and exorcisms against field vermin, spells against danger due to fire, prayers for rain used at the time of conjuring up rain, numerous benedictory spells for the prosperity of herds of cattle, exorcisms of a herdsman against animals and robbers, prayers of a merchant for good business and good luck while travelling, of a gambler for luck with the dice, charming spells and conjuring formulas against snakes and many more of this sort. Only few of these songs and spells have any significance as pieces of poetry. However it often happens that we find some individual verses of great beauty in a rather lengthy poem of only average poetic beauty. Most beautiful is perhaps the rain song Ath IV, 151. Driven by the wind — it is said there — may the clouds come and while the big cloud-covered bull bellows,[1] may the rustling waters refresh the earth". Parjanya himself is invoked with the words

> "Roar, thunder, set the sea in agitation, bedew the
> ground with thy sweet rain, Parjanya!
> Send plenteous showers on him who seeketh shelter,
> and let the owner of lean kine go homeward".[2]

The least poetic content have those benedictory spells which contain only very general requests for luck and benediction or for protection from danger and misfortune. The so-called "Mṛgāra-sūktāni (Ath. IV, 23-29), a litany consisting of

1. The rain-god Parjanya.

2. Ath. IV, 15, 6, translated by R. T. H. Griffith. In the time of drought the cows have become lean on account of scanty fodder. Now the herdsman must flee from rain, and for the cattle better times will come. (Weber — *Indische Studien*, vol. 18, p. 62).

seven hymns of seven verses each belong to the last group. They are addressed respectively to Agni (1), Indra (2), Vāyu and Savitar (3), Heaven and Earth (4) the Maruts (5), Bhava and Śarva[1] (6), Mitra and Varuṇa (7) and every verse ends with the burden-like request for liberation from distress.

But the word "ambas" which we have translated as "distress" combines in itself the meanings of "trouble, misfortune" on the one hand and "fault, sin" on the other hand. Hence the above-mentioned litany can be also included in that of the hymns of the Atharvaveda which are associated with the expiatory ceremonies (prāyaścittāni). These expiatory formulas and spells for purification from guilt and sin are less different from the healing magic spells than one would believe. For, according to Indian concepts an expiation a "prāyaścitta" is necessary not only for "sins" in our sense (as understood by us) i.e. violation of the moral law or offences against religion but in addition to expiatory formulas for imperfectly performed sacrifices and ceremonies, for crimes committed knowingly and unknowingly, for thought-sins, for not paying debts, espcially debts incurred while gambling, for the marrying of the younger brother before the elder one (which is forbidden by law) and in addition to prayers generaliy held for liberation from guilt and sin and their consequences, we find also expiatory-formulas and songs and spells associated with expiatory ceremonies by means of which mental and bodily infirmity, omens foreboding ill-luck, (for example by means of the flight of birds or the birth of twins or the birth of a child under an inauspicious star), wicked dreams, and sudden "misfortunes" are supposed to be "expiated" i.e., warded off or weakened in their effect. The concept "guilt", "sin", "disaster", and "misfortune" run incessantly into one another. Everything bad — disease and misfortune as well as guilt and sin — is supposed to be caused by ill-meaning demons by wicked spirits. Just as the patient and the madman, so also the evil-doer and the sinner are possessed by a wicked demon. And

1. Names or forms of Rudra, a god who plays an important role in magic and the magic-songs of the Atharvaveda, whereas he is of secondary importance in the hymns of the Rgveda.

the same beings, inimical to man, which bring diseases, send also the evil symptoms and the misfortunes themselves. Thus for example in Ath X, 3 an amulet that one ties around is praised exuberantly and glorified as a powerful protection from enemies and rivals in love, against dangers and evil of all kinds, against black magic, wicked dreams and bad omens, against "the sins which my mother, my father, my brothers and my sister and we ourselves have committed" and at the same time also as a panacea for all diseases.

Through the influence of demons or wicked magicians family quarrels are also caused. Therefore we find in the Atharvaveda also a number of magic spells for establishing harmony, which are between expiatory formulas and benedictory spells. For to these belong not only the texts by which peace and harmony shall be restored in the family but also formulas by which the anger of a great lord shall be appeased or an assembly shall be influenced or the art of oration shall be attained in front of a court of justice or similar things shall be achieved. One of the most appealing among the songs is Ath III. 30 that begins with the words:

"Of one heart, one mind
Free from hatred I make you
Be happy with each other
As the cow with the newborn calf

May the son obey the father
Be in harmony with the mother

Be the speech sweet and peaceful
That the wife says to husband

May the brother not hate the brother
And the sister not the sister :
Of one mind and one leaning
Speak words full of love!"

It is understandable that some of these reconciliatory texts could be employed for establishing harmony between spouses. Indeed the magic-songs referring to marriage and love constitute.

a big class of hymns of the Atharvaveda as such; and from the Kauśikasūtra we get to know the manifold varieties of love-magic and all the magic-rites, which the Indians call "Strīkarmāṇi" or "Women's rites" and for which these songs and spells can be employed. There are also two kinds of spells of this class. Some of them have a pleasant and peaceful character and refer to marriage and procreation. They are pious texts connected with harmless magic rites by means of which a young girl seeks to get a husband or a young man a bride, benedictory texts on the bride and bridegroom and the newly married couple, magic songs and texts through which conception can be promoted and the birth of a male child achieved, prayers for protection for the pregnant woman as well as for the unborn and the newborn child and similar things. Of this kind is the whole XIV book which contains a collection of marriage texts and is essentially a second, greatly enlarged edition of the marriage texts of the Ṛgveda.[1] But the second kind of these texts consisting of exorcisms and curses is more numerous. They refer to rivalry in love and disturbances in married life. Quite harmless are the magic spells by which a woman wants to pacify the jealousy of her husband or the verses which are supposed to bring back to a husband his faithless wife or the soporific magic (Ath. IV, 5) in which the verse[2] "May the mother sleep, may the father sleep, may the dog sleep, the eldest of the house sleep, may her relatives sleep, may all people around sleep", proves that the song is employed by a lover who sneaks to his beloved. Less harmless and partly of primeval wildness are the magic spells through which a person is supposed to be forced to love against his own will. The belief spread in the whole world, that through the medium of a picture one can harm a person or exercise power over him is found in ancient India also. If a man wanted to secure the love of a

---

1. See above p. 98 f. The marriage texts of the Ṛgveda as well as of the Atharvaveda and the magic songs of love of the Atharvaveda have been translated and explained by A. Weber in the V vol. of "*Indische Studien*".

2. Bloomfield (*SBE*, vol. 42, p. 105) calls this verse a "charm at an assignation," Whitney (*HOS*, vol. 7, p. 151) "an incantation to put to sleep." See also Th. Aufrecht, *Ind. Stud.* 4, 337 ff. on the two sleeping-spells, Ṛv VII, 55 and Ath. IV, 5.

woman, he made a picture of mud (earth), took a bow with a string of hemp, an arrow whose barb was a thorn, whose quill was taken from an owl, whose stock was made of black wood and began to bore through the picture with the arrow—a symbolic piercing of the heart of the beloved with the arrow of love-god *Kāma*—during which he recited the verses of the magic song Ath. III, 25:

"May (love) the disquieter, disquiet thee; do not hold upon thy bed: with the terrible arrow of Kāma (love) do I pierce thee in the heart.

The arrow, winged with longing, barbed with love, whose shaft is undeviating desire, with that, well-aimed, Kāma shall pierce thee in the heart !

With that well aimed arrow of Kāma which parches the spleen, whose plume flies forward, which burns up, do I pierce thee in the heart.

Consumed by burning ardour, with parched mouth, do thou (woman) come to me, plaint (thy) pride laid aside, mine alone, speaking sweetly and to me devoted !

I drive thee with a goad from thy mother and thy father, so that thou shalt be in my power, shalt come up to my wish.

All her thought do ye, O Mitra and Varuṇa, drive out of her !

Then having deprived her of her will, put her into my power alone ![1]

In a similar way a woman also proceeds when she wants to win the love of a man. She makes a picture of the man, places it in front of herself and hurls heated arrow-heads against it while uttering the songs of Ath. VI, 130 and 131 with the burden: "Send gods, love-sickness ! He shall be infatuated with love for me ?" where it is said for example :

"Madden him, Maruts, madden him, Madden him,
Madden him, O Air.

---

1. Translated by M. Bloomfield, *SBE.*, vol. 42, p. 102.

Madden him, Agni, madden him. Let him consume with love of me. (130, 4).

Down upon thee, from head to foot, I draw the pangs of longing love.

Send forth the charm, ye Deities ! Let him consume with love of me. (131, 1.)

If thou shouldst run three leagues away, five leagues, a horse's daily stage,

Thence thou shalt come to me again and be the father of our sons" (131, 3).[1]

The wildest magic songs scintillating with downright hatred are those with which women seek to oust their rivals in love. An example is Ath. I, 14:

"I have taken unto myself her fortune and her glory, as a wreath of a tree. Like a mountain with broad foundation may she sit a long time with her parents !

This woman shall be subjected to thee as thy wife, O King Yama[2] (till then) let her be fixed to the house of her mother, or her brother, or her father !

This woman shall be the keeper of thy house, O King (Yama), and her do we make over to thee ! May she long sit with her relatives, until (her hair) drops from her head !

With the incantation of Asita, of Kasyapa, and of Gaya[3] do I cover up thy fortune, as women cover (something) within a chest"[4]

An unequivocal language of unbridled wildness is spoken by the songs, by which a woman is supposed to be made barren (Ath. VII, 35) or a man robbed of his power of procreation (Ath. VI, 138; VII 90).

---

1. Translated by R. T. H. Griffith.
2. The god of death.
3. Probably names of famous wizards.
4. Translated by M. Bloomfield. (*SBE*. vol. 42, p. 107) who was the first to give a correct interpretation of this difficult charm (ib. pp. 252 ff). Whitney (*HOS*, vol. 7 p. 15) describes it as an imprecation of spinsterhood on a woman.

These magic love songs indeed belong to that class of hymns which are called by the name "Angiras"[1] to the class of curses and exorcisms against demons, magicians and enemies (Ābhicārikāni). Some of the magic spells of healing can be included in this class as well, as far as they contain exorcisms against the demons of diseases. To this class belongs along with the others also the second half of the XVI book, which contains an exorcism against the mare or incubus in which the demon is asked to visit the enemies. In these exorcisms no difference is made between demons and malevolent wizards and witches and Agni (fire)—as destroyer of the demons—is specially called for help. Numerous popular names of demons (which are otherwise quite unknown) are found in these hymns, in which on the whole we find at every step really popular notions. Thus here we come across the notion that is deeply rooted in popular belief —of all peoples—that disease and misfortune can be caused not only by demons but also by wicked men endowed with the power of magic. The magic, by which these wicked men cause evil is often personified in the songs and an anti-dote to counteract it—a herb, an amulet, or a talisman. Spells and songs associated with this inimical magic and counter-magic often distinguish themselves by a primeval power and wildness, which is not devoid of a certain charm. Anyhow, in some of these curses and exorcisms of the Atharvaveda there is more good popular poetry than in most of the sacrificial songs and prayers of the Ṛgveda. An example is the song, Ath. V, 14 used for defending against a wicked magician and of which some verses are quoted below:

"An eagle found thee: with his snout a wild boar dug thee from the earth,
Harm thou, O Plant, the mischievous, and drive the sorcerer away. (1)
Beat thou, the Yātudhānas back, drive thou away the sorcerer;
And chase afar, O Plant, the man who fain would do us injury. (2)

1. See page 110 f. above.

As 'twere a strip cut round from skin of a white-footed
antelope,
Bind, like a golden chain, O God, his witchcraft on the
sorcerer. (3)
Take thou his sorcery by the hand, and to the sorcerer
lead it back.
Lay it before him, face to face, that it may kill the
sorcerer. (4)
Back on the wizard fall his craft, upon the curser light
his curse.
Let witchcraft, like a well-naved car, roll back upon the
sorcerer. (5)
Whose, for other's harm hath dealt—woman or man—
in magic arts,
To him we lead the sorcery back, even as a courser with
a rope (6)
Go as a son goes to his sire: bite as a trampled viper
bites,
As one who flies from bonds, go back, O Witchcraft
to the sorcerer".[1] (10)

Similarly in the song Ath. 37 the curse is personified and is sent back to the curse-maker with the powerful verses:

Hitherward, having yoked his steeds, came
Imprecation, thousand-eyed,
Seeking my curser, as a wolf the home of one who
owneth sheep. (1)
Avoid us, Imprecation ! as consuming fire avoids the
lake.
Smite thou the man who curses us, as the sky's lightning
strikes the tree. (2)
Who curses us, himself uncursed, or, cursed, who curses
us again,
Him cast I as a sop to Death, as to a dog one throws a
bone.[2]

1. Translated by R. T. H. Griffith.
2. Translated by R. T. H. Griffith.

To these belongs also the splendid hymn to Varuṇa (Ath. IV, 16) the first half of which extols the omnipotence and omniscience of god in a language such as the one we find in the psalms, but which is heard in India very rarely, whereas the second half is nothing but a powerful exorcism-formula against liars and slanderers as we find them often in the Atharvaveda. A translation of this peculiar poem is given below:[1]

"The mighty lord on high our deeds, as if at hand espies;
The gods know all men do, though men would fain their acts disguise, (1)
Whoever stands, whoever moves, or steals from place to place,
Or hides him in his secret cell, the gods his movements trace.
Wherever two together plot, and deem they are alone,
King Varuṇa is there, a third and all their schemes are known (2)
This earth is his, to him belong those vast and boundless skies;
Both seas within him rest, and yet in that small pool he lies. (3)
Whoever far beyond the sky should think his way to wing,
He could not there elude the grasp of Varuṇa the king,
His spies, descending from the skies, glide all this world around;
Their thousand eyes all scanning sweep to earth's remotest bound. (4)
Whate'er exists in heaven and earth, whatever beyond the skies,
Before the eyes of Varuṇa, the king, unfolded lies.
The ceaseless winkings all he counts of every mortal's eyes,
He wields this universal frame as gamester throws his dice (5)

1. Translated by Muir, *Metrical translations from Sanskrit Writers*, p. 163.

May all thy fateful toils which seven by seven, threefold, lies spread out, ensnare him that speaks falsehood: him that speaks the truth they shall let go! (6)

With a hundred snares, O Varuṇa, surround him, let the liar not go free from thee, O thou that observest men! The rogue shall sit his belly hanging loose, like a cask without hoops, bursting all about! (7)

With (the snare of) Varuṇa which is fastened lengthwise and that which (is fastened) broadwise, with the indigenous and the foreign, with the divine and the human,[1]— (8)

With all these snares do I fetter thee, O. N. N., descended from N. N., the son of the woman N. N. : all these do I design for thee.[2]

Roth[3] makes the following remark about this song: "In the whole of the Vedic literature there is no other song which pronounces divine omniscience in such forceful terms, and yet this beautiful piece has been degraded into the exodium of an exorcism. And yet, here as in the case of many other texts of this Veda, it can be easily presumed that available fragments of other hymns were used for embellishing magic-formulas. The first five or even six verses of our song could be viewed as a fragment of this kind." I can only concur with this view; Bloomfield's presumption[4] that the whole poem, in the form in which it is now found, has been composed even at the beginning, for purposes of magic, appears improbable to me.

There is a fairly large class of magic-songs consisting partly of exorcisms against enemies, partly of benedictory texts meant

1. The translation of this verse is very doubtful. It is one of the many verses in the Atharvaveda, whose language is a sort of non-sense, as is found in the magic-spells of all peoples of the world.

2. *SBE.*, vol. 42, pp. 88 f. — Verses 6-9, translated into prose by M. Bloomfield.

3. *Abhandlungen über den Atharvaveda,* Tübingen 1856, pp. 29 f. where the hymn is translated into German. For other translations of the hymn see Whitney, *HOS.*, vol. 7, p. 176

4. *SBE*, 42 p. 389.

for the requirements of the king. In ancient India every kind had to maintain a Purohita or house-priest (or family-priest) and this house (=family) priest had to be well versed in the magic rites having a bearing to the king (rājakarmāṇi = king's rites) and had to be very well skilled in the songs and spells belonging to these rites. Hence the Atharvaveda is most intimately connected with the warrior caste. Thus we find here the songs referring to the king's election, whereby holy consecrated water is sprinkled on the king who treads on a tiger-skin; we find magic spells, which are supposed to ensure him mastery over other princes, power and fame in general, prayers for the king when he puts on his armour, when he mounts the war-chariot and similar things. Of special interest to us is a prayer (Ath. III, 4) at the time of the election of a king during which the heavenly king Varuṇa appears as one who elects the king and here the name of the god Varuṇa is connected ethnologically with the verb *var* (= to elect). Another magic spell (Ath. III, 3) for the restoration of a banished king is also peculiar. Among the most beautiful hymns of this class are also the battle songs and the magic songs of war, in particular the two songs addressed to the war-drum which shall call the warriors to battle and to victory (Ath. V, 20, 121)

As an example some verses of V, 20 are given below:

Formed out of wood, compact with straps of leather, loud is the war-drum as he plays the hero.

Whetting thy voice and vanquishing opponents, roar at them like a lion fain to conquer ![1] (1)

Like a lion thunders the drum made of wood, with the hide stretched on it

Like a bull bellowing to a voluptuous cow. A bull, O drum, you are

1. Translated by R. T. H. Griffith. In Southern India, even in much later times, the Battle Drum was an object of worship, and "was regarded with the same veneration that regiments used to bestow upon the regimental flag in the armies of Europe." H. A. Popley, *The Music of India*, London, 1921, p. 11.

And the enemies are killed. Yours is Indra's fire forcing the enemies[1] (2)
Like a bull marked by strength among the cattle, roar seeking kine and gathering up the booty.
Pierce through our adversaries' heart with sorrow, and let our routed foes desert their hamlets.[2] (3)
Hearing the Drum's far-reaching voice resounding, let the foe's dame, waked by the roar, afflicted,
Grasping her son, run forward in her terror amid the conflict of the deadly weapons.[2] (5)

The Brahmins were, from the beginning, too practical a people to use the magic spells always only in the interest of kings or other people and not also for themselves. Even in the class of the magic songs of the "king's rites", are some which are concerned more with the purohita, the indispensable family priest of the king than with the king himself. And although there is no want of attacks on the magic and exorcism in Brahminical literature,[3] still the law book of Manu XI, 33 says clearly and plainly: "Without any hesitation shall the Brahmin use the sacred texts of the Atharvaveda; the word is indeed the weapon of the Brahmin; with it he shall kill his enemies". So we find also in the Atharvaveda a number of magic songs and exorcisms in the interests of the Brahmins. In these hymns it is enjoined in the strongest terms that the Brahmins are inviolable and their possessions inassailable and hardest curses are pronounced against those who attack the life and property of Brahmins. Besides, the mystical significance of the Dakṣiṇā i.e. the sacrificial reward, is stressed in the most extravagant terms. To suppress Brahmins is the most serious of all sins, to give them rich sacrificial rewards is the highest peak of piousness: these are the basic ideas which run through all these songs, which belong to the most unedifying in the

1. Translated by R. T. H. Griffith. In Southern India, even in much later times, the Battle Drum was an object of worship, and "was regarded with the same veneration that regiments used to bestow upon the regimental flag in the armies of Europe." H. A. Poley, *The Music of India*, London, 1921, p, 11.

2. Translated by the author.

3. See page 115 above.

whole of the Atharvaveda. Only a few of the better ones among these hymns contain prayers for realisation, wisdom, honour and theological knowledge. All songs belonging to this class may be classified unhesitatingly with the latest texts of the Saṃhitā.

In the class of the later parts of the Saṃhitā we may also include the songs and texts meant for sacrificial purposes which have been included in the Atharvaveda only in order that this Veda may be associated with sacrifice and thus may be recognised as real "Veda". Thus for example we find two Āpri hymns[1] and other songs corresponding to the sacrificial songs of the Ṛgveda. We find also prose formulas for example in the XVI book which correspond to those of the Yajurveda. The whole first half of this book consists of formulas in which water is glorified and which are connected with any ritual to purify by sacrifice. The XVIII book containing texts for funeral ritual and ancestral worship also belongs to this class. The cremation songs of the X book of the Ṛgveda[2] are found here again literally repeated and enlarged with many additions. The whole of the XX book which has been added very late and whose hymns are with very few exceptions, all borrowed from the Ṛgveda, is related to the Soma-sacrifice. Only the remarkable "Kuntapa hymns"[3] (Ath. XX, 127-136) are new in this book. They are suited as liturgies in the sacrificial ritual, but with regard to their contents they coincide partly with the Dānastutis of the Ṛgveda[4] by praising the generosity of certain princes; they are partly riddles and their solutions[5] and partly also obscene songs and dirty jokes. During certain sacrifices lasting for many days these hymns formed the prescribed entertainment for the priests which — to use the appropriate expression of M. Bloomfield — degenerated into a sort of "filthy drinking party of liturgy".[6]

1. See page 86 f. above.
2. See page 87 ff. above.
3. What the name "Kuntapa" signifies is not known.
4. See page 104 ff. above.
5. Like those of the Ṛgveda—See page 106 f. above.
6. A detailed account of the Kuntapa hymns has been given by M. Bloomfield. The Atharvaveda (*Grundriss*, II, 1B), pp. 96 ff. They were

Also of ritual origin is probably the XV book composed in prose. This is a mystically confused glorification of the Vrâtya, i.e. of the Non-Aryans who have been admitted to the Brahmin caste and the texts were perhaps used at a ceremony by means of which this admission was made.

But on account of its mystical and partly philosophic content we can also include this book in the last class of the hymns of the Atharvaveda which are yet to be mentioned, namely the hymns of theosophical and cosmological contents, which certainly are among the latest parts of the Atharvaveda. Nothing appears to be farther from magic than philosophy and one could wonder that the Atharvaveda-Saṃhitā contains, in addition to magic-songs, curses and benedictory texts also hymns of philosophical content. But if we look at these hymns more closely, we will soon find that they too serve to a large extent like the magic songs, only practical purposes.[1] What is expressed in them is not the seeking and yearning for truth, for the obscure riddle of the world, but here also there are only magicians who behave as though they were philosophers by abusing the prevalent philosophical expressions to weave them into an artistic or rather artificial fabric of foolish and crazy phantasmagoria, in order to create an impression of the mystic, of the mysterious. What appears to us at first sight as a profound meaning is in reality, often nothing but empty secretiveness behind which more nonsense than profound sense lies hidden, and a wizard needs as his tool, the concealing of the real behind a veil of mysticism. But these philosophical hymns presuppose a highly developed metaphysical thinking. The main thoughts of the Upaniṣads, the idea of a supreme God as creator and preserver of the world (Prajāpati) and even that of the impersonal creative principle as well as a series of cultivated philosophical expressions like Brahman, tapas, asat, prāṇa, manas must have been already widely known and become common

probably part of the jollification on the occasion of the bestowal of the dakṣiṇā, which "in many instances must have led to gormandizing and drunkenness,... followed by shallow witticisms, by obscene talk, and worse" (ibid p. 100).

1. Cf. F. Edgerton, *The Philosophical Materials of the Atharva Veda* (Studies in Honor of Maurice Bloomfield, New Haven, 1920, pp. 117 ff.).

thought content of large circles of people at the time when these hymns were composed. Therefore in the theosophical and cosmological hymns of the Atharvaveda we must not see a stage of development of the Indian philosophy. The fruitful thoughts of the true philosophical hymns of the Ṛgveda have been improved further only in the Upaniṣads, and the philosophical hymns of the Atharvaveda cannot at all be viewed as a transitory stage from the oldest philosophy to that of the Upaniṣads. "They are" as Deussen says, "not so much within the great process of development as by its side".[1]

Many a deeper and truly philosophical thought flashes out sometimes from the mystical fog of these hymns, but in most cases one may be able to say, that the originator of these thoughts was not the Atharvaveda — poet, but that he has made others' mind serve his purposes. Thus it is a thought worthy of a philosopher that Kāla, the time, is the foundation of all being. But it is the language of the mystic and not the philosopher, when we read Ath. XIX, 53:[2]

> "Time, the steed, runs with seven reins (rays), thousand-eyed, ageless, rich in seed. The seers, thinking holy thoughts, mount him, all the beings (worlds) are his wheels.
>
> With the seven wheels does this Time ride, seven naves has he, immortality is his axle. He carries hither all these beings (worlds). Time, the first god, now hastens onward.
>
> A full jar has been placed upon Time; him, verily, we see existing in many forms. He carries away all these beings (worlds); they call him Time in the highest heaven;" and so on.
>
> The idea that Kāla, the time, has produced everything, certainly finds apt expression in the two verses 5 and 6.
>
> "Time begot yonder heaven, Time also (begot) these earths, That which was, and that which shall be, urged forth by Time, spreads out.

1. Deussen, *Allgemeine Geschichte der Philosophie* I, 1, p. 209.
2. On this hymn see F. O. Schrader *Über den Stand der indischen Philosophie zur Zeit Mahaviras und Buddhas*, 1902, pp. 20 f.

Time created the earth, in Time the sun burns. In Time are all beings, in Time the eye looks abroad".[1]

But in the verses immediately following and in the following hymn (Ath. XIX, 54), everything possible is enumerated, in a quite mechanical way, as originating from the time. And the various names of divine things known to those times are declared one after another, to have been created by Kāla — thus Prajāpati, the Brahman, the Tapas (asceticism), the Prāṇa (life-breath) etc.

More secretiveness than true philosophy is found also in the long Rohita-hymns, of which the XIII book of the Atharvaveda consists and in which moreover all sorts of things not connected with one another appear to have been thrown together. There is for instance in the first hymn Rohita "the red one" i.e. the sun or a spirit of the sun, praised as the creative principle — "he created the heaven and the earth", "he has fortified the earth and the heaven" — simultaneously however an earthly king is glorified and the heavenly king Rohita is associated with the earthly king in an intentionally confused manner: In the midst of all this we find also curses against enemies and rivals in love and against the one who kicks a cow with his foot or passes urine against the sun. And again in the hymn XIII 3 Rohita is praised as the supreme being in some verses whose pathos reminds us of the Varuṇa hymn quoted above, but a burden of the song is added on to these verses in which the same Rohita is exhorted to crush in his wrath the one who tortures a Brahmin. It is said for example:

He who engendered these, the earth and heaven,
Who made the worlds the mantle that he weareth,

In whom abide the six wide-spreading regions
through which the bird's keen vision penetrateth,

1. Translated by Bloomfield, *SBE.*, col. 42, p. 224.

This God is wrath offended by the sinner who wrongs
the Brahman who has gained this knowledge.
Agitate him O Rohita; destroy him: entangle in thy
snares the Brahman's tyrant. (1)
He from whom winds blow pure in ordered season,
from whom the seas flow forth in all directions,
This God, etc. etc. etc. (2)
He who takes life away, he who bestows it; from
whom comes breath to every living creature,
This God, etc. etc. etc. (3)
Who with the breath he draws sates earth and
heaven, with expiration fills the ocean's belly,
This God, etc. etc. etc.[1]

By the side of such spirited glorifications of Rohita there are also mystical thought-gymnastics, as when it is said that the two sacrificial melodies Bṛhat and Rathantara have produced Rohita, or when the metre of the Gāyatrī verse is termed as "the womb of immortality". It would be perhaps in vain to want to throw light on the mystical penumbra that surrounds such and similar verses. Similarly I do not also believe that we may presume that there are great philosophical truths in a hymn like Ath. IV, 11, where the ox is praised as the creator and preserver of the world:

"The Ox bears the earth and the heaven
The Ox bears the great atmosphere
The Ox bears the six great heavenly spaces
The Ox permeates the whole universe.

We do not find it imposing, when it is said that this ox is equal to Indra and other supreme gods, still less when it is said that he gives milk — "his milk is the sacrifice, the sacrificial reward is his milking" — and we would believe that "he who knows the seven inexhaustible milkings of the ox, will have progeny and will obtain heaven". With this ox it is not much different than with the bull which in Ath. IX, 4 is praised

1. Translated by R. T. H. Griffith.

very specially — he bears all forms in his belly-sides, he was at the commencement an image of the aboriginal water and similar things, — and of whom it is finally found out that he is only an ordinary sacrificial animal, that shall be slaughtered. But that this pseudophilosophy and secretiveness basically has a very practical aim, is proved by a hymn like Ath. X, 10. Here the great mystery of the cow is proclaimed: Heaven and earth and waters are protected by the cow. A hundred buckets, a hundred milkmen, a hundred protectors are on her back. The gods that breathe in the cow, they also know the cow. ... The cow is the mother of the warrior, the sacrifice is the weapon of the cow, from her originated the thought. In this manner it continues until the secret teaching attains its climax in the words: "The cow alone is called immortality, the cow alone is honoured as the death, the cow became this universe, gods, men, asuras, manes and seers, (all of them are the cow)." But now follows the practical application: Only he who knows this great secret may accept a cow as present; and he who makes a gift of a cow to a Brahmin, gains all worlds, for in the cow is all that is supreme — Ṛta (the world-order), Brahman (the world-soul) and the tapas (the asceticism) included, and:

> "Gods live on the cow and the men live on the cow;
> The cow is this whole world, as far as the sun looks down."

Just as the Rohita, the Ox, and the Cow are praised as the Highest Being, so there is one hymn (XI, 5) in which the Brahmacārin, the Vedic student, is celebrated in a similar way. And again in the still more mysterious cycle of hymns forming Book XV of the Saṃhitā, the Highest Brahman is conceived and exalted as the Vrātya, — both as the heavenly Vrātya, identified with the Great God (mahādeva), the Lord (īśāna) Rudra, and as his prototype, the earthly Vrātya. The Vrātyas were certain, probable Eastern, tribes, whether Aryan or Non-Aryan, but certainly living outside the pale of Brahmanism, roving about in bands — on rough wagons covered with boards in a rather war-like fashion, owners of cattle, having their own peculiar customs and religious cults, whose members however could be received into brahminical society by means of certain sacrificial rites and ceremonies. Such a Vrātya who has already been converted to Brāhmanism, seems to be glorified in the Vrātya-book of the Atharvaveda.[1]

Deussen[2] took immense trouble to discover reason and sense in the "philosophical" hymns of the Atharvaveda and to establish a certain relevance to one another. He finds for example, in Ath. X, 2 and XI, 8, the thought which treats the "realisation of the Brahman in man" in X, 2 "more from the physical, teleological" and in XI 8, "more from the psychical side."[3] I cannot discover so much of philosophy in these hymns; I think rather, that here too it is only a case of pseudo-philosophers, who did not proclaim any new theory of the world-soul in man, but who already found this theory before them and gave it out in a mystically confounded irrelevance. Whereas in a famous hymn of the Ṛgveda (X, 121) a profound thinker and a true poet points in a bold language to the splendour of the cosmos and asks in doubt about the Creator, in the Atharvaveda X, 2 a verse-maker enumerates all the limbs of man one after another and asks who has made them:

"By whom are man's heels made ? By whom the flesh, by whom the ankles, by whom the well shaped fingers ? By whom the holes ? Why have they made the ankles of the feet below and why the knee-caps above ? Why did they put down the knees apart from each other and where are the joints of the knees ? Who has planned all that ? etc. etc."

---

1. See A. Weber and Th. F. Aufrecht in *Ind. Stud.* I, 1850; A. Hillebrandt, Ritual-Literatur (*Grundriss* III, 2), pp. 139 f.; M. Bloomfield, The Atharvaveda (*Grundriss*, II, 1 B) pp. 96 ff.; Chas. Lanman, *HOS.*, Vol. 8, pp. 769 ff. Macdonell and Keith, *Vedic Index*, II, pp. 341 ff. Rajaram Ramkrishna Bhagavat, *JBRAS.*, 19, 1896, 357 ff. considers the Vrātyas to be non-Aryans. J. Charpentier (*WZKM.* 23, 151 ff.; 25, 355 ff.) considers the Vrātyas to be early worshippers of Rudra Śiva, see Keith, *JRAS.* 1913, 155 ff. According to J. W. Hauer, *Die Anfänge der Yogapraxis*, Berlin 1922, pp. 11 ff., 172 ff. they were ecstatics of the Kṣatriya class and fore-runners of the Yogins. Cf. Winternitz in *Festschrift für L. Scherman.*

2. Deussen, *AGPh.* I, 1, pp. 209 ff.

Compare also Lucian Sherman : *Philosophische Hymnen aus der Ṛg-und Atharvaveda-Samhitā, verglichen mit den Philosophemen der älteren Upanishads,* Strassburg, 1887.

3. Deussen, ibid, pp. 264 ff.

Thus it continues through eight verses. Then follow nine verses in which questions are put about everything that belongs to human organism and to human life in general: "Wherefrom do likes and dislikes come, wherefrom sleep, fear, lethargy, wherefrom all joys and delights of man ? Wherefrom trouble and misery ?" etc. In the same tone the following questions are also put helter-skelter: "Who has placed water in the body and blood in the veins, wherefrom has man obtained form, stature and name, who has lent him gait, intelligence, breath, truth and untruth, immortality and death, clothing, long life, strength and swiftness ... etc ?" It is further questioned as to wherefrom man gets mastery over nature and all these questions are answered away simply by saying that man as Brahman (world-soul) has become that what he is, and has attained his power. Thus far the hymn is not particularly beautiful, but at least to a certain extent clear. But now follows the usual mystical swindle in the concluding verses 26-33, where it is said:

> "When the *Atharvan* had stitched together his heart and his head, then he inspired him as purifier from his head above his brain.

To the *Atharvan* belongs this head, a tightly closed box of the gods, and this head is protected by the breath, food and intelligence.

I think one does these verses too great an honour when one seeks a profound wisdom in them. Therefore I cannot also find so much profound sense in the hymn Ath. XI 8, which according to Deussen is supposed to describe "the origin of man from psychical and physical collision of factors which are on the whole dependent on Brahman". Just as the liar must speak the truth sometimes, in order that his lies may be believed, similarly the mystic must also include in his patchwork here and there a really philosophic idea which he has picked up somewhere, in order that his nonsense also may be held to be high wisdom. Thus the thought of Brahman is, as the prime source of all being and of the unity of man and world-soul, the basis of the hymn XI, 8. But I do not believe that the author thought anything when he said:

"Of what was Indra born, of what Soma, of what Agni? Wherefrom did Tvaṣṭar (=the sculptor; the moulder) come into being? Wherefrom is Dhātar (=the Creator) born? Of Indra was Indra born, of Soma Soma, and of Agni Agni. Tvaṣṭar was born of Tvaṣṭar and of Dhātar Dhātar".

By far above all this verse-making which is neither philosophy nor poetry, stands one hymn of the Atharvaveda which on account of some verses which refer to the origin of the earth, usually classifies with the cosmogonical hymns, which is however free from every trace of mysticism and contains also very little of philosophy, but so much the more true poetry. It is the splendid hymn to the Earth, Ath. XII, 1. In 63 verses Mother Earth is here praised as the bearer and reserver of all that is earthly and is invoked for fortune, grace and protections from all evil. A few verses (in the translation of R. T. H. Griffith) must suffice to give an idea of one of the most beautiful products of religious poetry in ancient India:

"Truth, high and potent Law, the consecrating rite,
Fervour, Brahma, and Sacrifice uphold the Earth.
May she, the Queen of all that is and is to be, may
Prithvī make ample space and room for us. (1)
She who at first was water in the ocean, whom with their wondrous powers the sages followed,
May she whose heart is in the highest heaven, compassed about with truth and everlasting,
May she, this Earth, bestow upon us lustre, and grant us power in loftiest dominion. (8)
She whom the Aśvins measured out, o'er whom the foot of Viṣṇu strode,
Whom Indra, Lord of Power and Might, freed from all foemen for himself,
May Earth pour out her milk for us, a mother unto me her son. (10)
O Prithvi, auspicious be thy woodlands, auspicious be thy hills and snow-clad mountains.

Unslain, unwounded, unsubdued, I have set foot upon the Earth,

On Earth, brown, black, ruddy and every-coloured, on the firm earth that Indra guards from danger. (11)

Produced from thee, on thee move mortal creatures: thou bearest them, both quadruped and biped.

Thine, Pṛthvi, are these five human Races, for whom, though mortals, Sūrya as he rises spreads with his rays the light that is immortal. (15)

On Earth they offer sacrifice and dressed oblation to the gods, men, mortals, live upon the earth by food in their accustomed way.

May that Earth grant us breath and vital power,

Pṛthvi give me life of long duration! (22)

Let what I dig from thee, O Earth, rapidly spring and grow again,

O Purifier, let me not pierce through thy vitals or thy heart. (35)

May she, the Earth, whereon men sing and dance with varied shout and noise,

Whereon men meet in battle, and the war-cry and the drum resound,

May she drive off our foemen, may Pṛthvi rid me of my foes (41)

Supporting both the foolish and the weighty she bears the death both of the good and evil.

In friendly concord with the boar, Earth opens herself for the wild swine that roams the forest. (48)

O Earth, my Mother, set thou me happily in a place secure

Of one accord with Heaven, O Sage, set me in glory and in wealth". (63)

This hymn, which could be found as well in the Ṛgveda-Saṃhitā proves that although the Atharvaveda-Saṃhitā pursues a homogeneous object more than the Ṛgveda, still it is strewn with variegated fragments of ancient poetry. In this collection also, as in that of the Ṛgveda, we find precious pearls of the oldest poetic art of India by the side of some inferior and even completely worthless verses. And only both these works put together give us a correct idea of the oldest poetry of the Aryan Indians.

Sacrifice in Ancient India and the Vedic Saṃhitās

Both the Saṃhitās discussed till now have also this common, that they have not been compiled for any special liturgical purposes. Although most of the hymns of the Ṛgveda could be used for purposes of sacrifice and were even actually used so, and similarly even though the songs and spells of the Atharvaveda were also used almost completely for ritual and magic purposes, still the compilation and arrangement of the hymns has nothing to do with the various liturgical and ritual purposes. The hymns were collected for their own sake and were put in order and compiled in these two collections paying regard to the alleged authors or the schools of reciters to whom they belonged and partly also paying regard to their contents and still more to their external form—number of verses and similar things. They are, we can say, collections of songs that pursue a literary object.

It is a quite different matter with the Saṃhitās of the two remaining Vedas—the Sāmaveda and the Yajurveda. In these collections we find songs, verses and spells arranged with regard to their practical purposes, exactly in the order in which they were used in the sacrifice. Therefore they are in practice nothing but prayer and hymn-books of practical use to particular sacrificial priests—of course not written books but texts which existed only in the heads of teachers and priests and were preserved in priestly schools through oral teaching and learning.[1] But in order to explain the origin of these Saṃhitās it is now necessary to say a few words on the cult of the Aryan Indians. This is all the more desirable as it is hardly possible to understand Vedic literature completely without a certain insight into the institution of sacrifice in ancient India.

1. Cf. page 29 above.

As far as we can trace back the Vedic-Brahminic religion, there have been always two kinds of cult. We have seen[1] that individual hymns of the Ṛgveda and a large number of songs and spells of the Atharvaveda were used as benedictory texts and prayers at the time of birth and marriage and other occasions of everyday life, at the time of funeral and ancestor worship as well as during various ceremonies which the herdsman had to perform for the prosperity of cattle and the peasant for the growth of the produce of his land. Indians call these ceremonies which are also mostly connected with sacrifices, gṛhyakarmāṇi, i.e. "homely (domestic) ceremonies". Detailed information about these is found in the gṛhyasūtras which will be mentioned later. During the sacrifices which this domestic cult required, the master of the house himself, aided by an individual priest, officiated as the sacrificial priest.[2] And as far as these sacrifices were fire-sacrifices, the fire of domestic hearth served as altar for offering the same. In addition to these sacrifices, which every pious Āryan, whether poor or rich, whether great or small, performed according to ancient tradition, there were also big sacrificial festivals (ceremonies)—especially in connection with the Soma cult associated with Indra, the warrior-god, which could be performed only by the great and the rich, above all by the kings. On a broad place of sacrifice altars were erected for the three sacred fires which were necessary for every such sacrifice and a host of priests headed by four chief priests were occupied with the performance of the numberless extremely complicated rites and ceremonies which were necessary for such a sacrifice. The Yajamāna or "sacrificer" the prince or lord who made the sacrifice—had very little to do then; his main duty was to give a rich reward (daksiṇā) to the priests. No wonder that the Brahmins made these sacrificial ceremonies which brought them plenty of money the object of a zealous study, that they developed a formal science of sacrifice

1. See above p. 87 ff, 98 ff, 125 ff.

2. Āśvalāyana Gṛhyasūtra I, 3, 6. The employment of a Brahmin is optional in the case of domestic sacrifices. Gobhila-Gṛhyasūtra I, 98 f: The Brahmin is the only priest during *Pākayajñas* (i.e. the "simple sacrifices" of the domestic cult); the sacrificer himself is the Hotar (the priest, who recites the Verses).

that is laid down in those texts which we will shortly get to know as Brāhmaṇas and which form an essential part of the Śruti, of the "revelation", i.e. of that literature to which in the course of time divine origin was attributed. These sacrifices were therefore called "Śrautakarmāṇi" "ceremonies based on the śruti" in contrast to the domestic (gṛhya) ceremonies, which are based only on smṛti, on "remembrance", i.e. on tradition and possess no divine authority.

Now the four chief priests who were occupied with the śrauta sacrifices are: 1. Hotar or "Caller; Invoker" who recites the verses (ṛcas) of the hymns in order to praise the gods and invite them to the sacrifice; 2. The Udgātar or "singer" who accompanies with songs (Sāman) the preparation and performance of the sacrifices, especially of the soma libations; 3. the Adhvaryu or "sacrifice-executor" who executes all sacrificial acts and mutters thereby the prose prayers and sacrificial formulas (*Yajus*) and 4. The Brahman or "Highpriest" whose office it is, to protect the sacrifice from harm. For every sacred act, therefore also every sacrifice, is according to Indian view, connected with a certain amount of danger; if an act is not performed exactly as per the ritual prescription, a spell or prayer-formula is not pronounced correctly or a melody wrongly sung, then that brings about the ruin of the performer of the sacrifice. Therefore to the south of the place of sacrifice—south is the direction of the god of death and the direction from where the demons inimical to the sacrifice threaten men—the Brahman sits, in order to protect the sacrifice. He follows mentally the course of the whole sacrifice and as soon as he notices the smallest mistake in a sacrificial act, in a recitation or in a song, he must make amends for the harm by pronouncing sacred words. Therefore the Brahman is called in an ancient text "the best doctor among the sacrificial priests".[1] However in order to occupy this office the Brahman must be "full of the Veda"; he discharges his duties as sacrificial priest "with the threefold knowledge", i.e. by virtue of

1. Śatapatha-Brāhmaṇa XIV, 2, 2, 19 of Chāndogya-Upaniṣad IV, 17, 8f.

his knowledge of all the three Vedas, which enables him to discover any mistake at once.[1]

As against this, the three other priests need know only one Veda each. The verses with which the **Hotar** invokes the gods to the sacrifice, the so-called "Verses of invitation" (Anuvākyas) and the verses with which he accompanies the offerings, the so-called "sacrificial verses" he takes from the Ṛgveda. He must be also conversant with the Ṛgveda-Saṃhitā, i.e. he must have learnt them by heart, in order to compile from the same, the so-called Śāstras or "praise-songs", which he had to recite during the Soma-sacrifice. Thus the Ṛgveda-Saṃhitā bears a certain relationship to the Hotar although it has in no way been collected or ordered for the purposes of the priest.

But to the Soma-sacrifice belong not only the praise-songs recited by the Hotar, but also the so-called stotras or "laudatory hymns" which were sung by the Udgātar and his assistants.[2] Such stotras consist of hymn-stanzas, i.e. of verses (ṛcas) which had been made the bearers of some definite melodies (sāman). These melodies as well as the hymn-stanzas with which they were connected, the Udgātar-priests learnt in the schools of the Sāmaveda, and the Sāmaveda texts are nothing but collections of texts which have been compiled for the purposes of the Udgātar not simply for their own sake, but for the sake of the tunes which they carried.

---

1. Aitareya-Āraṇyaka III, 2, 3, 6 Śatapatha Brāhmaṇa XI, 5, 8, 7. Only at a later date the Brahman was connected to the Atharvaveda, so that "Brahmaveda" or "the veda of the Brahman was exactly a term used for the Atharvaveda; and the followers of the Atharvaveda explained that the Brahma must be knowing the Atharvaveda Saṃhitā. In reality the office of the Brahman of a Śrauta-sacrifice has nothing to do with the Atharvaveda. It is however understandable that one could connect the two with each other. For when the Brahman, as remarked above, officiates as the only priest during domestic sacrifices (gṛhya-sacrifices), he must be conversant with the benedictory spells occurring for the most part in the Atharvaveda.

2. The Hotar recites the hymn, i.e. he repeats it from memory in a sort of sing-song manner, the Udgātar sings the praise-songs according to particular melodies, the Adhvaryu mutters the prayers. Only the so-called "Nigadas" a variety of the *Yajus*-formula, whose function it is, to exort the other priests to do their various duties, had of course to be said loudly by the Adhvaryu.

The Adhvaryu-priest, finally, has to say continuously in a gentle voice partly short prose-formulas and partly long prayers in prose and verse — the prose-formulas and prayers are called Yajus (plural. Yajūṃṣi), the verses ṛc (plural ṛcas). In the Saṃhitās of the Yajurveda all these prose-formulas and prayers compiled just in the order in which they were used during sacrifices, by the Adhvaryu-priests, mostly also together with the rules and debates on the sacrificial acts during which they are to be muttered.

We will now turn our attention to the discussion of the liturgical Saṃhitās as in accordance with the above exposition, we can call the Saṃhitās of the Sāmaveda and of the Yajurveda, (as contrasted with those of the Ṛgveda and the Atharvaveda).

The Sāmaveda-Saṃhitā

Of all the numerous Saṃhitās of the Sāmaveda, which are said to have existed once, — the Purāṇas speak of even a thousand Saṃhitās[1] — only three have come down to us.[2] The best known of these, the Sāmaveda-Saṃhitā of the Kauthumas[3] consists of two parts, the Ārcika or the "collection of stanzas" and the "Uttarārcika" the "second collection of stanzas". Both parts consist of verses all of which recur in the Ṛgveda. Of the 1810 — or if we subtract the repetitions, 1549 — verses, which both parts contain altogether, all except 75 are also found in the Ṛgveda-Saṃhitā and that largely in the VIII and IX books. Most of these verses are composed in the Gāyatrī metre or in the Pragātha-stanzas made up of Gāyatrī- and Jagatī-lines. And the stanzas and songs composed in these metres were doubtless meant even from the beginning for

1. Later authors also speak of a thousand schools of the Sāmaveda. cf. R. Simon, *Beiträge zur Kenntnis der vedischen Schulen* (Kiel 1889) p. 27, 30 f.

2. The Saṃhitā of the Rāṇāyanīyas has been edited and translated by J. Stevenson, London, 1842; that of the Kauthumas by Th. Benfey, Leipzig, 1848, and by Satyavrata Sāmaśramin, *Bibl. Ind.*, 1871 ff. The Jaiminīya-Saṃhitā has been edited by W. Caland (*Indische Forschungen*, 2, Breslau 1907).

3. About this and the other two Saṃhitās see Caland, ibid. Introduction. See also Oldenberg, *GGA*, 1908, 711 ff.

singing[1]. The 75 verses which do not occur in the Ṛgveda are found partly in other Saṃhitās and partly in various works on rituals; some may originate from recensions unknown to us, but some have been patched together from various verses of the Ṛgveda, without making any proper sense. We come across the verses of the Ṛgveda in the Sāmaveda partly also with divergent readings and it was believed that they may be an archaic text. But Theodor Aufrecht[2] has already proved that the divergent readings of the Sāmaveda were based only on arbitrary, intentional or accidental changes, — changes, as would occur even otherwise when words are set to music. In the Sāmaveda, the text is — both in the Ārcika as well as in the Uttarārcika — only a means to an end. What is essential is the melody, and the purpose of both parts is to teach the melodies. The pupil who wanted to be trained as Udgātar-priest in the schools of the Sāmaveda had to learn the hymn-melodies: this was done with the help of the Ārcika; only then could he learn by heart the stotras as they were sung in the sacrifice, and the Uttarārcika served this purpose.

The first part of our Sāmaveda-Saṃhitā, the Ārcika consists of 585 individual stanzas (ṛc), to which the various hymn-melodies (sāman) belong, which were used during the sacrifice. The word sāman although used for denoting the text made and meant for singing, means originally only "hymn-tune" or "melody". Just as we say that a stanza is sung "according to a particular melody", similarly the Indians say the other way about, "This or that melody (sāman) is sung "on a particular stanza". Vedic theologians view the relationship of melody and stanza in this way that they say, the melody is born of the stanza. The stanza (ṛc) is therefore termed "yoni" i.e. "womb"

1. This is already proved by the names "Gāyatrī" and "Pragātha" which are derived from the verb ga or praga respectively which mean to sing. Cf. H. Oldenberg "*Ṛgveda Saṃhitā und Sāmavedārcika*" in *ZDMG* XXXVIII, 1884, p. 439 ff., 464 ff.

2. In the foreword to his edition of the *Hymns of the Ṛgveda* (2nd impression, Bonn 1877) II, p. XXXVIII ff. See also J. Brune, *Zur Textkritik der dem Sāmaveda mit dem achten Maṇḍala des Ṛgveda gemeinsamen Stellen,* Diss. Kiel, 1909, who comes to the same conclusion as Aufrecht, ibid. and Oldenberg, *Hymnen des Rigveda* I, pp. 289 f.

out of which the hymn-melody has come. And although of course one stanza can be sung according to various melodies and one melody to various stanzas, still there are certain stanzas which in general can be looked upon as texts for certain melodies — as "yonis", as the Indian expression is called. It is like our associating particular melodies with the German texts *Stimmt an mit hellem, hohem Klang* or, *Es steht ein Baum im Odenwald* etc. The Ārcika is therefore nothing but a collection of 585 "yonis" or individual stanzas, which are sung according to just as many different melodies.[1] We may imagine to ourselves a textbook of songs in which of each song only the text of the first stanza would be given as aide memoire for the melody.

The Uttarārcika, the second part of the Sāmaveda-Saṃhitā consists of 400 songs, mostly of three stanzas each,[2] from which the stotras sung at the main sacrifices are formed. Whereas in the *ārcika* the stanzas appear arranged partly accor ding to the metres and partly according to the gods — and that in the order Agni, Indra, Soma — the songs in the Uttarārcika are arranged in the order of the chief sacrifices.[3] A stotra therefore consists of more than one stanza, usually three stanzas, all of them will be sung according to the same melody and this melody is taught by the Ārcika. We can compare the Uttarārcika with a textbook of songs in which the text of the songs is given completely whereas the melodies are assumed to be known. It is usually presumed that the Uttarārcika is of a later origin than the Ārcika.[4] This presumption is supported by the fact that the Ārcika knows many "yonis", i.e. many hymn-melodies, which do not at all occur in the Uttarārcika and that the Uttarārcika also contains many hymns for which the Ārcika

1. See Oldenberg, GGA.

2. 287 songs consist of 3 verses each, 66 of 2, 13 of 1, 10 of 6, 9 of 4, 4 of 5, 3 of 9, 3 of 10, 2 of 7, 2 of 12 and 1 of 8 verses.

3. On the Stotras of the Sāmaveda and their use in a sacrifice, cf. A. Hillebrandt, Ritualliteratur, p. 99ff. in *Grundriss* III. 2.

4. Caland (*De wording van den Sāmaveda*, Amsterdam (Akad.), 1907; *Die Jaiminīya-Saṃhitā*, pp. 4f. and *WZKM*, 22, 1908, 436 ff.) endeavours to prove that the Uttarārcika is older. Oldenberg, *GGA*, 1908, 713, 722, disputes this on good grounds. For the question of the origin of the Sāmaveda, see Caland, *Eene unbekende Recencie van den Sāmaveda*, Amsterdam (Akad.), 1905.

does not teach the melody. On the other hand we must also say that the Uttarārcika is an essential supplement to the Ārcika; the latter is like the first and the former the second course in the education of the Udgātar.

Both parts of the Saṃhitā give us only the texts as they are spoken. However the melodies themselves were taught in the earliest days only by oral repetition or by playing them on instruments. Only from a later date do we have so-called Gānas or actul "song-books" (from *ga* = to sing), which describe the melodies by notes and in which the texts are recorded in the form which they have while singing, i.e. with all syllable-expansions, repetitions and insertions of syllables and even of complete words — of the so-called "*Stobhas*" like hoyi, huva, hoi etc. which are not unlike our joyous shouts and yodeless. The oldest note-marking is probably the one by means of syllables like ta, co, no etc. But more common is the making of the seven notes with the figures 1, 2, 3, 4, 5, 6 & 7, to which F, E, D, C, B, A, G of our scale correspond. While singing the priests mark these different notes by the movements of their hand and fingers.[1] It appears that the hymn-melodies for the Soma-sacrifices performed in the village were different from those for the sacrifices of the hermits living in the forest, for an *ārcika* has a Grāmageyagāna (= "Village song-book") and an Āraṇyagāna (= "Forest song-book"). The latter contained melodies which were considered as dangerous (taboo) and hence had to be learnt only in the forest.[2] There are also two other books of songs, the Ūhāgāna and the Ūhyagāna. These were composed for the purpose of giving the Sāmans in the order in which they were employed at the ritual, the Ūhāgāna being connected with Grāmageyagāna, the Ūhyagāna with the Āraṇyagāna.[3]

The number of the known melodies must have been very large[4] and even in very olden times each melody had a special name.

1. More about this oldest music of the Indians is found in A. C. Burnell, *The Aitareya-Brāhmaṇa*...of the Sāma-Veda (Mangalore 1876) Introd. p. XXVIII, XLI-XLVIII.
2. See W. Caland, *Die Jaiminīya-Saṃhitā*, p. 10; H. Oldenberg, *GGA*, 1908, pp. 722 f.
3. See Caland, *Die Jaiminīya-Saṃhitā*, pp. 2 ff.
4. A later writer gives the no. of Sāmans as 8000. (R. Simon, ibid, p. 31).

Not only are they known in the ritual books under these names, but several symbolic meanings are also ascribed to them, and they play no small role in the symbolism and mysticism of the Brāhmaṇas, Āraṇyakas and Upaniṣads, some of them in particular, like the two melodies "Bṛhat" and "Rathantara" which occur in the Ṛgveda. Of course the priests and theologians have not themselves invented all these melodies. The oldest of them were presumably popular tunes according to which in primeval times half-religious songs were sung on the occasions of solistices and other popular festivals, and yet others may be traced back to that noisy music with which the pre-brahminic magicians (magic-priests)—not unlike the magicians, sharmans and medicinemen of primitive races—accompanied their wild songs and rites.[1] Traces of this popular origin of the Sāman-melodies are already seen in the above-mentioned stobhas or joyous shouts and especially in this, that the melodies of the Sāmaveda were considered as having magical powers even in the brahminic age.[2] And there is a ritual-book of the Sāmaveda—it is called Sāmavidhāna-Brāhmaṇa—, whose second part is a special hand-book of magic, in which the use of various Sāmans for purposes of magic is taught. In this also we can see traces of the connection of the Sāman-melodies with the pre-brāhminic primitive religion and magic-practices taught by the brahminic law books, that the recitation of the Ṛgveda and the Yajurveda must be interrupted as soon as the sound of a Śāman is heard.

---

1. Cf. A. Hillebrandt, *The solstices-festivals in ancient India* (Sep. from the felicitation-volume for Konrad Hofmann), Erlangen 1889, p. 22 ff., 34 ff. M. Bloomfield, the God Indra and the Sāma-Veda, in *WZKM*, XVII 1903, p. 156 ff.

2. Probably the primary meaning of *sāman* is "appeasement song", "a means for pacifying gods and demons". The word *sāman* occurs also in the meaning of "mildness, kind help". When the *Sāma-Veda* is quoted in the literature of olden times, it is usually done with the words : "The *chandogas* say", "*Chandoga*" means "*chandas*-singers" and *chandas* combines in itself the meanings : "Sacred text" and "Metre". Therefore the basic meaning of the word must be "rhythmically moved speech". It may be connected with the root *chand* (to please, to satisfy or to favour" (Cf. *Chanda*, "pleasing, tempting, inviting").

Particularly clear is Āpastamba's lawbook[1] where the barking of dogs, the braying of donkeys, the howling of wolves and jackals, the hooting of owls, the sound of music-instruments, weeping and the sound of Sāmans are all enumerated as sounds on hearing which one must interrupt the study of the Veda.

Thus the Sāmaveda-Saṃhitā is certainly valuable to the history of the Indian concept of sacrifice and magic and its gānas are certainly very important for the history or music,[2] although not yet completely exploited for this purpose. As a literary product however this Saṃhitā is as good as worthless for us.

The Saṃhitās of the Yajurveda

Just as the Sāmaveda-Saṃhitā is the textbook of songs for the Udgātar, so also the Yajurveda-Saṃhitās are the prayer-books for the Adhvaryu-priest. The grammarian Patañjali[3] speaks of "101 schools of the Veda of the Adhvaryu" and it is understandable that there are many schools of just this particular Veda; because with respect to the individual sacrificial acts as the Adhvaryu had to perform them and to accompany them with his prayers, easily differences of opinion and sectarian variations were caused which led to the creation of their own handbooks and prayer-books. The slightest divergence in ceremony or liturgy was enough for the foundation of a new Vedic school. We know till today the following five Saṃhitās and schools of the Yajurveda:

---

1. I, 3, 10, 19.

2. Oldenberg concludes his investigations of the Sāmaveda (*GGA*, 1908, 734) with the remark that these literary investigations "after all only touch upon the problems lying on the surface of the Sāmaveda"; for, in order to penetrate to greater depths, the philologist would have to be a student of the history of music as well. Since then we have gained an idea of the present-day mode of reciting the Sāmans in E. Felber (*Die indische Musik der vedischen und der klassischen Zeit, mit Texten und Übersetzungen von* B. Geiger, SWA, 1912), based on the records of the Phonogramm-Archiv of the Vienna Academy. It is still doubtful, however, whether this necessarily teaches us how the ancient Udgātars sang 3,000 years ago. See also R. Simon, Die Notationen der vedischen Lieder-bücher (*WZKM*, 27, 1913,305 ff.).

3. In the introduction to his "Mahābhāṣya".

1. The Kāṭhaka, the Yajurveda-Saṃhitā in the recension of the Kaṭha-school, which was known for a long time only as a manuscript in the Berlin library, but is now published by L. von Schroeder.[1]

2. The Kapiṣṭhala-Kaṭha-Saṃhitā which is preserved in only few fragments of manuscripts.[2]

3. The Maitrāyaṇī-Saṃhitā, the Yajurveda-Saṃhitā in the recension of the Maitrāyaṇīya-school, which L. von Schroeder has edited.[3]

4. The Taittirīya-Saṃhitā, i.e. the Yajurveda-Saṃhitā in the recension of the Taittirīya-school, according to the Āpastamba-school, one of the main schools in which this text was taught, also called "Āpastamba-Saṃhitā". The same was edited by A. Weber.[4]

These four recensions are closely related to one another and are described as belonging to the "black Yajurveda". Different from these is—

5. The Vājasaneyī-Saṃhitā or the Saṃhitā of the "white Yajurveda" which derives its name from Yājñavalkya Vājasaneya, the principal teacher of this Veda. Of this Vājasaneyī-Saṃhitā there are two recensions, that of the Kāṇva school and that of the Mādhyandina school, which however differ from each other in minor aspects. This Saṃhitā also was edited by A. Weber.[5]

---

1. Edited by L. v. Schroeder, Leipzig, 1900-1910, *Index Verborum* by R. Simon, 1912. For the contents of the Kāṭhaka see A. Weber, *Ind. Stud.* 3,451 ff.; for the text and its interpretation see Keith, *JRAS*, 1910, 517 ff; 1912, 1095 ff.; Caland, *ZDMG*, 72, 1918, 12 ff.

2. See L. v. Schroeder, *WZKM*, 12, 362 f.

3. Leipzig 1881-1886. Numerous quotations from this Saṃhitā in German translation are found in L. von Schroeder : *Indiens Literatur und Kunst.* (Leipzig, 1887) p. 110-162. See also Schroeder, *ZDMG* 33, 1879, 177 ff; Caland, *ZDMG*, 72, 1918, 6 ff.

4. Ed. by A. Weber in the 11th and 12th volumes of his *Indische Studien*, 1871 and 1872; with Sāyaṇa's commentary in *Bibl. Ind.*, 1860-1899, and in *Ān. SS* Nr. 42; translated into English by A. B. Keith, *HOS*, vols. 18, 19, 1914.

5. The White Yajurveda, Part I, The Vājasaneyī-Saṃhitā...with the commentary of Mahīdhara, Berlin-London 1852. An English translation of the same is available by R. T. H. Griffith (*The texts of the White Yajurveda*, translated with a popular commentary, Benaras 1899).

The main difference between the Saṃhitās of the "black" and the "white" Yajurveda lies in this that the Vājasaneyī-Saṃhitā contains only the mantras, i.e. the prayers and sacrificial formulas which the Adhvaryu priest has to say, while the Saṃhitās of the black Yajurveda contain, in addition to the Mantras, also a description of the sacrificial rites together with discussions on them. Thus there is, in the Saṃhitās of the black Yajurveda that which is called "Brāhmaṇa" or "theological discussion" and which constitutes the contents of the Brāhmaṇas to be discussed in the next chapter, mixed with the Mantras. It is therefore easy to understand that in the prayerbooks meant for the use of the Adhvaryus the sacrificial performances were also discussed because these priests had to perform especially the individual sacrificial acts, and the murmuring of prayers and formulas in intimate relationship with these acts constituted only a small part of their duties. It can therefore be scarcely doubted that the Saṃhitās of the black Yajurveda are older than the Vājasaneyī Saṃhitā. Only later systematisers among the Yajurveda theologians perhaps felt the need to have analogous to the other Vedas, a Saṃhitā consisting of only Mantras by the side of a Brāhmaṇa devoid of them.[1]

However significant the differences between the individual Saṃhitās of the Yajurveda might be for the priests and theologians of ancient India, for us they are quite insignificant; and even chronologically the various Saṃhitās of the black and white

---

1. It is usually presumed that the name "white" Yajurveda means "clear, (ordered) arranged" Yajurveda and indicates the pure distinction between sacrificial text and ritual commentary in the same, whereas "black" Yajurveda signifies "unarranged" Yajurveda. This explanation which can be traced back even to Indian commentators, appears to me, to be highly improbable. But even Śatap. Br. XIV, 9, 4, 33 (of IV, 4, 5, 19) are called "the white sacrificial texts" (Śuklāni yajūṃṣi) as Ādityāni, "revealed by the sun"; and also the *Purāṇas* narrate that Yajñavalkya received new sacrificial texts from the sun (Viṣṇu-Purāṇa, III, 5) I believe that "white Yajurveda" owes its name to this connection with the sun. As against this the older Yajurveda was called "black". It is most probable "that the Saṃhitā of the white Yajurveda is most closely related to the original form of the Veda of the Adhvaryu," as Pischel thinks, *KG*, 172. Cf. Keith, *HOS*, Vol. 18, pp. lxxxv ff, on the mutual relationship of the Saṃhitās of the Yajurveda.

Yajurveda might not be wide apart from each other. If I now give hereunder a short description of the contents of the Vājasaneyī-Saṃhitā, it is entirely sufficient to give to the reader an idea of the content and character of the Saṃhitās of the Yajuraveda in general.

The Vājasaneyī-Saṃhitā consists of 40 chapters, of which however the last 15 (perhaps even the last 25) chapters are of a later date. The first 25 chapters contain the prayers for the most important big sacrifices. And the first two chapters give the prayers for the New-moon and Fullmoon-sacrifices (Darśa-pūrṇamāsa) with their connected sacrifices for the manes (piṇḍapitṛyajña). Then follow in the third chapter the prayers for the daily fire-cult, for the inception of fire and for the fire-offerings (Agnihotra) to be made every morning and evening and for the seasonal-sacrifices (Cāturmāsya) performed once every four months. The prayers for the Soma-sacrifice[1] in general including the animal sacrifice connected with it are found in chapters IV to VIII. Among the Soma-sacrifices there are some which last for one day and some which last for many days. Among the one-day sacrifices is the Vājapeya or "contest drink", a sacrifice which was performed originally perhaps only by warriors and kings which was connected with a chariot-race and in the course of which, apart from the Soma, brandy (surā)[2] which was normally forbidden according to brahminical law, was drunk. The sacrifice at a king's coronation or "Rājasūya" a sacrificial festival connected with some sorts of popular customs—with a symbolic battle march, with the play at dice and with all sorts of magic rites. The prayers for these two kinds of Soma sacrifices are found in the chapters IX and

---

1. The sacrifices of ancient Indians fall into two broad categories : Food-sacrifices (during which chiefly milk, butter, cakes, stewed fruit, and corns are sacrificed) and Soma-sacrifices (whose main constituents are the Soma-libations). The individual sacrifices fall into one or the other of these two categories. The animal sacrifice is connected with sacrifices of the first category as well as with those of the second. Connected with all these kinds of sacrifices is the fire-cult, which is, in a certain way, the pre-requisite for every kind of worship of gods.

2. According to the law books the drinking of brandy is a sin as great as the murder of a Brahmin.

X. Then follow in chapters XI to XVIII numerous prayers and sacrificial formulas for the Agnicayana or the "Fire-altar-laying", a ceremony which extends over one whole year and to which a profound mystic symbolic significance is attributed in the Brāhmaṇas. The fire altar is nothing but "Agni" and is considered as identical with the god of fire. It is built with 10800 bricks in the shape of a big bird with its wings stretched out. In the lowest layer of the altar the heads of five sacrificial animals are immured and the bodies of the animals are thrown into the water out of which the mud is taken for making the bricks and the fire-bowl. The shaping and baking of the fire-bowl and of the individual bricks, of which many have special names and their own special significance, takes place with great ceremony and under incessant chanting of charms and prayer-formulas. The chapters XIX to XXI following that give the prayers for the Sautrāmaṇī ceremony, a peculiar sacrificial ceremony during which brandy is used instead of the Soma drink and is offered to the Aśvins and to goddess Sarasvatī and to Indra. The ceremony is recommended to one who has drunk too much Soma or who cannot endure it—and this might be the original purpose of it—but also for a Brahmin who desires success, for a banished king who wants to regain his throne, for a warrior who wants to gain victory and a Vaiśya who wants to attain great wealth. The texts connected with this sacrifice make many references to the saga of Indra who had qualms of conscience due to excessive enjoyment of Soma and who had to be cured by the Aśvins and Sarasvatī.[1] Finally chapters XXII to XXV with which the old part of the Vājasaneyī-Saṃhitā ends, contain the prayers for the great horse sacrifice (Aśvamedha), which only a powerful king, a mighty conqueror or "world-ruler" was permitted to perform. Old sagas and epic poems give reports of kings of prehistoric times who performed this sacrifice and it is considered as the highest fame for a ruler if it can be said of him: "He has performed the horse-sacrifice". The purpose of this great sacrifice is given out very beautifully in the prayer Vāj. Saṃh. XXII, 22:

---

1. Cf. page 72 above.

"O Brahman! May in this kingdom the Brahmin be born who shines by holy knowledge! May the warrior who is a hero, an excellent archer, of perfect aim and a great chariot-fighter! Also the cow that yields good milk, the ox that pulls well, the swift horse, the honourable housewife! May to this sacrificer a heroic son be born, who is victorious, an excellent chariot-fighter and eloquent in assembly. May Parjanya send us rain as we desire! May our fruit-bearing plants ripen! May we have luck and prosperity!"

That the last 15 chapters are of later origin is not doubtful. The chapters XXVI to XXXV are termed even by Indian tradition as "khilas" i.e. "additions", "supplements". Actually XXVI to XXIX contain only additions to the prayers of the preceding chapters. The XXX chapter proves itself to be a supplement even by the fact that it does not contain any prayers but only an enumeration of people who shall be sacrificed at the Puruṣamedha or human sacrifice to the most diverse divine beings and powers or to those that have been elevated to the status of deities for the moment. Not less than 184 persons should be butchered during this puruṣamedha; and that as follows—for example: a Brahmin is sacrificed to priestly honour, a warrior to royal honour, a Vaiśya to the Maruts, a Śūdra to an ascetic, a thief to darkness, a murderer to hell, a eunuch to evil, a whore to pleasure, a singer to noise, a bard to dance, an actor to song, a hunter to death, a gambler to the dice, a blindman to sleep, a deafman to injustice, an incendiary to lustre, a washerwoman to the sacrifice, a dyer-woman to greed, a barren woman to Yama, a Vīnā-player to the joy of ceremony, a flute-player to shouting, a cripple to the earth, a bald-headed man to the heaven etc. It is certainly not likely that all these kinds of people were brought together and should have been killed. This is perhaps only a symbolic act which represents a sort of "human sacrifice" by which the great horse sacrifice must be surpassed which however existed only as a constituent of the sacrificial-mystic and sacrificial theory, but which in reality hardly ever happened.[1] Moreover it is also true that the XXXI

1. So also Oldenberg, *Religion des Veda*, 2nd Ed., pp. 362 f. and Keith, *HOS*., Vol. 18, pp. cxxxvii, who says: "There can be no doubt that the ritual

chapter contains a version of the Puruṣasūkta known to us from the Ṛgveda—i.e. of the hymn RV, X 90 in which the birth of the world is explained as by sacrificing the Puruṣa and the identification of the world with the Puruṣa, and thereby Puruṣa, "the man" is at the same time considered as the highest being—and this that chapter which the Brahman should recite at the Puruṣamedha is also described as Upaniṣad i.e. secret teaching. The XXXII chapter is also, in form and content, nothing but an Upaniṣad: The Creator Prajāpati is equated here with the Puruṣa and the Brahman. The first six verses of the XXXIV chapter are similarly classified as Upaniṣads—and are given the title Śivasaṃkalpa-Upaniṣad.[1] The texts of chapters XXXII to XXXIV are to be used during the so-called Sarvamedha or "All-sacrifice". This is the highest sacrifice that exists and it ends with the sacrificer giving away all his movable and immovable property as sacrifical reward to priests and then retiring as a hermit to the forest to spend the rest of his life there. The XXXV chapter contains some verses for funeral ceremonies which are taken from the Ṛgveda. Chapters XXXVI to XXXIX contain the prayers for a ceremony called Pravargya in which a drum is heated to glow on the sacrificial fire to represent the sun symbolically; in this drum milk is then boiled and offered to the Aśvins. The whole ceremony is considered as a great mystery. At the end the sacrificial implements are put up in such a way that they represent a man: The milk pots are the head, on which a bundle of holy grass represents the locks of hair; two milking tubs represent the ears, two small gold leaves the eyes, two shells the ankles, the flour strewn all over

---

is a mere priestly invention to fill up the apparent gap in the sacrificial system which provided no place for man." Hillebrandt (Ritualliteratur, *Grundirss* III, 2, pp. 153), however, considers the Puruṣamedha to be a real human sacrifice. There can be no doubt that human sacrifices occurred in ancient India, though not in the Brahmanical cult — only survivals of it can be traced in the rite of building the brick-altar for the fire, and in the Śunaḥsepa legend — , just as cruel-human sacrifices occurred even in modern times among certain sects. But this does not prove that the Puruṣamedha was such a sacrifice.

1. Vāj. Saṃh. 34, 1-6, is found as an Upaniṣad in the *Oupnekhat* of Duperron, and translated by Deussen, *Sechzig Upanishads des Veda,* p. 837. See above pp. 16-17.

the body the marrow, a mixture of milk and honey the blood etc. To the mysterious ceremonies correspond naturally also the prayers and formulas.[1] The XL and the last chapter of the Vājasaneyī Saṃhitā contains once again an Upaniṣad, and indeed one that is found in all collections of Upaniṣads, very important Īśa-Upaniṣad, about which we have to speak once again in the chapter on the Upaniṣads.

If it is clear even from the contents of the last chapters that they are of a later origin, it is still further testified by the fact that the prayers contained in the Saṃhitās of the Black Yajurveda correspond only to those of the first half of the Vājasaneyī-Saṃhitā.[2]

As regards the prayers and sacrificial formulas themselves, which form the main content of the Yajurveda-Saṃhitā, they consist partly of verses (ṛc) and partly of prose texts. It is the latter that are termed as "Yajus" and from which the Yajurveda gets its name. The prose of these texts is sometimes also a measured one and is even elevated here and there to a rhythmic swing.[3] The verses that occur here are also found for the most part in the Ṛgveda-Saṃhitā. The divergent readings however, which the Yajurveda often offers, are not in any way older than the text found in the Ṛgveda, but they are mostly changes intentionally made in order to connect the verses more closely with the sacrificial acts. Only rarely have whole hymns of the Ṛgveda been included in the Yajurveda-Saṃhitās; mostly they are simply individual verses, isolated from the context which appeared to be suitable for some sacrificial ceremony and were hence included in the Veda of prayers. Therefore we have less

1. More about all these sacrifices and festivals is found in A. Hillebrandt's "Ritual Literatur, Vedische Opfer und Zauber" (Grundriss III, 2) p. 97-166, H. Oldenberg, *Religion des Veda* (*2nd-Ed. p.* 437-474), É. Hardy, *Die Vedisch-brahmanische Periode der Religion des alten Indiens,* Münster i.W. 1893, p. 154 ff. and Keith, HOS, Vol. 18, pp. ciii ff.

2. Only the first 18 Adhyāyas of the Vājasaneyī Saṃhitā are completely presented word for word and explained in the Śatapatha Brāhmaṇa belonging to the White Yajurveda.

3. See Keith, *HOS.*, Vol. 18, pp. cxl ff., and H. Oldenberg, Zur Geschichte der altindischen Prosa-(*AGGW.* N. F. Bd. 16, Berlin, 1917), pp. 2 ff. On the language of the Yajus.

interest in these verses as well. What is characteristic of the Yajurveda are the prose formulas and prayers.[1]

The simplest prayer that we can imagine, is the dedication of an offering with just mentioning the name of the deity to whom it is offered. Formulas of this kind are very numerous in the Yajurveda. "you for Agni", "you for Indra" or "this for Agni", or even simply "Hail Agni" or "Hail Indra" etc.—with such words the offerings were placed or thrown in the sacred fire. And we can hardly imagine a shorter and simpler hymn of praise to god than the words with which every morning and evening the fire-offering (Agnihotra) consisting of milk is offered : "Agni is light, light is Agni, hail ! (in the evening) and "Sūrya is light, light is Sūrya, hail !" (in the morning). In just as short words the purpose of a sacred act is also often hinted at, when for example the sacrificial priest cuts the branch with which the calves are driven from the cows and says then: "you to sap, you to power !" Or the object serving a holy act is shortly named and a wish is added, when for example the wooden splinter with which the sacrificial fire is to be lit, is consecrated with the words: "This, Agni, is your igniter; through this you shall grow and prosper. May we too grow and prosper !" If there is fear of evil or of a harmful spell, then a short text is used for protection against the same. Thus to the halter with which the sacrificial animal is tied to the post the following words are addressed : "Do not become a snake, do not become a viper !" To the razor with which the sacrificer is shaved of his beard when he is consecrated for the sacrifice, the priest says : "O razor, do not wound him !" During the coronation the king looks down to earth and prays : "Mother earth, may you not wound me, nor I you !"[2]

The deities are not always invoked or praised in these sacrificial formulas, but sacrificial implements and sacrificial acts are made to associate with deities in the most diverse ways. Thus for instance the priest ties a string round the girdle of

1. Also the Brāhmaṇa-like theological discussions which the Saṃhitās of the Black Yajurveda contain in addition to the prayers and formulas, are here left out of consideration. For, what will be said in the following chapter about the Brāhmaṇas applies to them as well.

2. Vāj. IV, 1; VI, 12; II, 14; I, 1; III, 9; X, 23.

the sacrificer's wife participating in the sacrifice with the words : "A girdle you are for Aditi". At the consecration to the Soma-sacrifice the sacrificer ties round his girdle a belt made of hemp and reed-grass with the words : "You are the power of Aṅgiras,[1] soft like wool; lend me power !" Then he binds a knot in his underclothing and says : "you are the knot of Soma". Thereupon he covers his head with a turban (or with his upper cloth) while murmuring the words : "You are Viṣṇu's umbrella, the umbrella of the sacrificer". And to the horn of a black antilope which he wraps in the hem of his garment he says : "You are Indra's womb". He takes the sacrificial food from the carriage with the words : "You are the body of Agni, you to Agni. You are the body of Soma, you to Viṣṇu". When the priest takes any sacrificial implement in his hand he does it with the oft repeated formula: "Induced by God Savitar I take you up with the arms of the Aśvins, with the arms of Pūṣan."[2]

The holy sacrificial fire must be churned according to the primitive method with a fire-borer;[3] and the production of fire is compared, even in Ṛgveda with the process of reproduction, by considering the lower plank as the mother, the upper churn-staff as the father of the child Agni (fire).[4] Thus the formulas are explained with which the fire-churning at a Soma-sacrifice is done, in which the two rubbing pieces of wood as the pair of lovers Purūravas and Urvaśī producing Āyu are addressed.[5] The priest takes the lower piece of wood with the

1. The old fire and magic priests thought of as semi-divine beings.

2. Vāj. I, 30; IV, 10; V, 1; VI, 30.

3. It consists of two "Araṇis" or rubbing pieces of wood, of which one is a plank and the other a staff with a sharp pointed tip, which is turned round until a flame ensues. This fire producing device still in use with many primitive races like the Eskimos, is certainly one of the most primitive implements of mankind.

4. The Malays in Indonesia even today call the wooden board in which the firestaff is turned round, the "mother" or "woman" while they call the churning staff itself "man". Ancient Arabs also had two pieces of wood for producing fire and of these two they considered one as feminine and the other as masculine.

5. See above p. 87 f.

words : "You are Agni's birth-place", lays two stalks of sacred grass on it and says : "You are the two semen-pourers (testicles)". Then he lays the plank with the words : "You are Urvaśī", touches the frying pan with the churning staff while saying : "You are Āyu", and with the words, "You are Purūravas" inserts the churning staff into the lower piece of wood. Then he churns with the texts : "I churn you with the Gāyatrī metre, I churn you with the Triṣṭubh-meter, I churn you with the Jagatī metre".[1]

We should not seek any profound symbolical significance in the mention of the above metres. They are words, nothing but words, which fulfil their purpose just like any other words would do. And formal usages of the kind which have little or no sense are quite numerous in the Yajurveda. Only relatively seldom do we come across long prose texts in which the sacrificer announces his wishes to the deity as in the prayer already mentioned above which has been spoken at the horse-sacrifice. More frequent are of course the formal prayers like the following ones which nevertheless convey a good sense.

> "You, Agni, are the protector of the bodies; protect my body ! you Agni, are the giver of life, give me life ! You, Agni, are the giver of power; give me power ! You Agni, make perfect, what is imperfect in my body". (Vāj. III, 17)
> "May life flourish through sacrifice ! May the breath flourish through sacrifice ! May the eye flourish through sacrifice. May the ear flourish through sacrifice ! May the back flourish through sacrifice ! May sacrifice flourish through sacrifice !" (Vāj. IX, 21)

But even more frequently do we find endless texts in which the meaning is of more secondary importance, for example :

"Agni has won the breath with the monosyllabic (word); may I win him ! The Aśvins have won the two-footed man with the two syllabic (word) ! Viṣṇu has won the three worlds with the three-syllabic (word), may I win them! Soma has won the four-footed cattle with the four-syllabic; may I win it!

1. Vāj V, 2. Śatapatha-Brāhmaṇa III, 4, 1, 20 ff. Cf. Śatapatha Br. VIII, 5, 2, 1; Weber, *Ind. Stud.*, 8, 1863, pp. 8 ff., 28 ff., and above p. 59 f.

Pūṣan has won the five parts of the world with the five-syllabic; may I win them! Savitar has won the six seasons with the six-syllabic; may I win them ! The Maruts have won the seven tame animals with the seven-syllabic; may I win them! Bṛhaspati has won the Gāyatrī with the eight syllabic; may I win it. Aditi has won the sixteen-fold Stoma with the sixteen syllabic; may I win it ! Prajāpati has won the seventeenfold Stoma with the seventeen-syllabic; may I win it !" (Vāj. IX, 31-34).

But what specially contributes to the fact that these prayers and sacrificial formulas appear to us only as a senseless heaping up of words, is the favourite equating and combining of things in the Yajurveda which have nothing to do with one another. A cooking pot for example is placed on fire with the following words:

"You are the heaven, you are the earth, you are the drum of the Mātariśvan".[1] (Vāj. I, 2).

Or the cow, with which the *Soma* is brought, the priest addresses with the following words:

"You are the thought, you are the mind, you are the intellect, you are the sacrificial reward, you are suitable for mastery, you are suitable for sacrifice, you are the double-headed Aditi". (Vāj. IV, 19).

To the fire that is taken round in the pan at the time of laying the fire altar the following prayer is addressed: You are the beautifully-winged bird, the hymn of praise Trivṛt is your head, the Gāyatrī-melody is your eye, the two melodies Bṛhat and Rathantara are your wings, the hymn of praise is your soul, the metres are your limbs, the Yajus-formulas your name, the Vāmadevya-melody your body, the Yajñayagñīya-melody your tail, the fire-places are your hoofs, you are the beautifully-winged bird, go to heaven, fly to light!" (Vāj XII, 4).

Then the priest takes three steps with the fire pan and speaks :

1. Mātariśvan is here the wind-god; therefore "the drum of Mātariśvan means "space".

"You are Viṣṇu's step destroying the rivals in love; mount the Gāyatrī metre, march along the earth! You are Viṣṇu's step destroying persecutors; mount the Triṣṭubh-metre march along the air ! You are Viṣṇu's step destroying the malicious ones; mount the *Jagatī* metre, march along the heaven! You are Viṣṇu's step destroying the inimical ones; mount the Anuṣṭubh metre, march along the parts of the world!" (Vāj. XII, 5).

Referring to this kind of prayers, Leopold von Schroeder says: "One should often even doubt that one finds here people who are still intelligent, and it is in this respect quite interesting to observe, that in the written records of persons in the stage of imbecility the tedious and monotonous variations of one and the same idea are especially characteristic". He then gives some of the recordings preserved by psychiatrists about lunatics and these recordings show a striking similarity to many of the prayers of the Yajurveda.[1] We must not however forget that we do not have here very ancient popular magic formulas as in the Atharvaveda or partly also in the Yajurveda, but we have here only very clumsy works of priests, who had to provide the innumerable sacrificial rites ingeniously thought out by them with similarly innumerable texts and formulas.

Many a prayer formula of the Yajurveda is however nothing but magic charms in prose. Even exorcisms and curses quite similar to those which we have come across in the Atharvaveda, we find also in the prayers of the Yajurveda. For there are also sacrificial acts through which one can do harm to an enemy. Thus the priest says to the yoke of the chariot carrying the sacrificial implements : "A yoke you are, subjugate the subjugator, subjugate him who subjugates us, subjugate him whom we subjugate". (Vāj. I, 8).[2] The following examples of such sacrificial prayers are given by L. von Schroeder[3] from the Maitrāyaṇī Saṃhitā :

---

1. L. von Schroeder, *Indiens Literatur und Kultur*, p. 113 f.

2. Also an example for the alliteration so fondly used in the Yajus-formulas. The text runs : dhūr asi, dhūrva dhūrvantam, dhūrva tam yo 'smān dhūrvati, tam dhūrva yam dhūrvāmaḥ.

3. *Indiens Literatur und Kultur*, p. 122.

"Which man is hostile to us and which one hates us, which one wants to abuse and harm us, all of them you shall crush into dust!"

"O Agni with your incandescence glow off against him who hates us and whom we hate! O Agni with your flame burn off against him who hates us and whom we hate! O Agni, with your radiance radiate against him who hates us and whom we hate! O Agni, with your pouncing power pounce him who hates us and whom we hate"!

"The god of death, devastation shall seize the rivals in love".

Just as these exorcisms have in themselves something primeval and popular, we find also among the riddles that are preserved in the Yajurveda in addition to truly theological riddles, which certainly deserve the technical name "Brahmodya"[1], because they presuppose an acquaintance with the Brahman or the holy knowledge, also some old popular riddles. We have already got acquainted with this very old kind of literature in the Ṛgveda and the Atharvaveda. In the Yajurveda we also get to know the occasions when the games of riddles were common and indeed even formed a part of the cult. Thus we find in the Vājasaneyī-Saṃhitā in the XXIII chapter[2] a number of riddles with which the priests entertained themselves during the famous horse-sacrifice. Some of them remind us of our children's riddles, whereas the others refer to the sacrificial mysticism of the Brāhmaṇas and the philosophy of the Upaniṣads. As example the riddles of Vāj. XXIII — 45-48, 51 ff may be quoted :

The Hotar: "Who wanders lonely on his way?
Who is born always anew ?
What is the cure for cold?
What is the great corn-container called?"

1. On the Brahmodyas see Ludwig, *Der Rigveda.* Koegel, III, 390 ff. Rud Koegel, *Geschichte der deutschen Litteratur,* I, 1, 1894, pp. 5, 64 ff. includes the Brahmodyas, with which he compares the Old Germanic riddle poetry in the poetic heritage of the Indo-European period.

2. Similarly also in Taittirīya-Saṃhitā, VII, 4, 18.

The Adhvaryu: "The Sun wanders lonely on his way
The moon is always born anew
The fire is the cure for cold
The earth is the great corn-container".

The Adhvaryu: "What is the light equal to the sun?
What the name of the flood equal to the sea?
And what is greater than the earth?
What is that which is immeasurable?"

The Hotar: "The Brahman[1] is the light equal to the sun
The heaven is the flood equal to the sea,
And greater than the earth is god Indra
And it is the cow of which no one knows the measure".

The Udgātar: "In what things is the Puruṣa permeated?
And what things are in Puruṣa contained?
The riddle, Brahman, I give you to solve;
What have you to say now in reply?

The Brahman: "The five it is in which the Puruṣa is permeated,
And these too are in Puruṣa contained[2]
That is it, what I have thought out as reply
In the miraculous power of knowledge you can't excel me".

These games with riddles are as important constituents of the veneration of gods as the prayers and sacrificial formulas. Of course the words "veneration of gods" express only inadequately the purpose of the prayers and formulas and even of

1. This word with multifarious meanings signifies here probably "the priesthood", perhaps "the sacred knowledge".

2. Puruṣa means "man", "person" and also "spirit", "world-spirit". "The five" are the five senses, which are contained in the Puruṣa, i.e. "in the man" and permeated by the Puruṣa i.e. by "the world-spirit".

the sacrifices themselves. The majority of the sacrificial ceremonies like the Yajus-formulas do not have the object of "venerating" the gods but of influencing them, of forcing them, in order that they may fulfil the desires of the sacrificer. And even the gods love *panem et circenses,* they too do not want merely to be fed but also to be entertained; that however the gods find a peculiar pleasure in what is mysterious, obscure, and only hinted at, is made clear to us very often by the Vedic texts.[1]

In the Yajurveda we also find already a sort of influencing the gods which later on gained the upper hand to a very great extent. This consists in showering on a god as many names and attributes as possible and to show reverence to him under all his names in this way in order to win some favour from him. Thus we find in later literature texts, which enumerate a thousand names of Viṣṇu, of thousand names of Śiva, and whose recitation is considered as a very effective and meritorious act of worship. The earliest beginnings of this kind of prayers are found in the Śatarudrīya, the enumeration of the hundred names of the god Rudra, in the XVI chapter of the Vājasaneyī-Saṃhitā and in the Taittirīya-Saṃhitā IV, 5.

Finally—there is another sort of "prayers"—as we must of course call them—which we come across even in the Yajurveda and with which in later times a lot of mischief was played. These are the individual syllables or words which do not have any sense or whose sense has been lost, which are pronounced in the most ceremonious way at particular occasions of the sacrificial performance and which are held to be extremely holy. There is firstly the sacrificial invocation "svāhā',, which we usually translate with "hail", with which every offering for the gods is thrown into the fire whereas the invocation "svadhā" is used in the case of sacrificial offerings for the manes. Other quite ununderstandable exclamations of this kind are vaṣat, vet, vat and above all the most sacred syllable om. This syllable,

1. "The gods love what is hinted at, what is mysterious," is a sentence, again and again repeated in the *Brāhmaṇas,* for example in the Śatapatha Brāhmaṇa VI, 1, 1, 2; 11; 2, 3, 7, 1, 23; VII, 4, 1, 10 etc. Bṛhadāraṇyaka Upaniṣad IV, 2, 2 : "The gods love what is secretively hinted at and hate what is directly said".

originally nothing but a consent,[1] was considered by the Hindus over many thousands of years and is considered even to the present day as extremely holy and full of mystical significance. In the Upaniṣads it is equated with the Brahman the world-soul and recommended to the wise as the highest object of meditation, the Kaṭha-Upaniṣad (II, 16) says about it: "This syllable is indeed the Brahman, this syllable is the highest, for he who knows this syllable, for him, all the desires will be fulfilled." And this syllable om is joined by the three "great words" (mahāvyāhṛti), namely bhūr, bhuvaḥ, svar (explained by the Indians as "earth, air, heaven, which however is doubtful) of which it is said in a text :[2] "This indeed is the Brahman, this the truth, this the law; without this there is no sacrifice !".

Centuries later, in the Tantras, the religious books of later Indian sects, the use of such mystic syllables and words gained the upper hand in such a manner that often for pages at a stretch we find nothing but unarticulated sounds like "um, am, hrīm, um, em, krom, phaṭ, aḥ etc. It is also characteristic that the word "mantra" which originally meant the verses and prayers (ṛc and yajus) of the vedic saṃhitās, later on had only the meaning of a magic formula". Even in the Yajurveda we can very well follow this transition from prayer to magic formula these were both never strictly separate from each other.

And however tedious, uninteresting and unedifying the Yajurveda-Saṃhitās may be, if one wants to read them as literary works, still they are of very great importance and indeed of interest for the investigator of religion who studies them as source-books not only for the Indian but also for general theology. Whoever wants to delve deep into the origin, development and theological significance of prayer—and this is one of the most interesting chapters of theology—should in no case fail to get acquainted with the prayers of the Yajurveda.

---

1. According to the Aitareya-Brāhmaṇa VII, 18 Om means in the language used for the gods the same thing as what is expressed among men by "tathā" (so may it be), "yes". Similarly it is said in the Chāndogya-Upaniṣad I, 1, 8 : "This syllable Om expresses consent for when one consents to something he says : "Om". With the Hebrew "amen" the syllable *om* coincides only purely accidentally somewhat in its meaning and in its pronunciation.

2. Maitrāyaṇī-Saṃhitā I, 8, 5.

Further, these Saṃhitās are also indispensable for understanding the whole religious and philosophic literature of the Indians in later times. Without the Yajurveda we cannot understand the Brāhmaṇas and without these, the Upaniṣads.

THE BRĀHMAṆAS[1]

Max Müller said once of the Brāhmaṇas, the second great class of works that belong to the Vedas, "However interesting the Brāhmaṇas may be for the researcher in the field of Indian Literature, they are of little interest for the general educated public. Their chief content is prattle and—what is worse—theological prattle. Nobody who does not know the role that the Brāhmaṇas play in the history of the Indian mind could read more than ten pages without closing the book."[2] Indeed it is even more true than of the Yajurveda that it is not enjoyable reading but is indispensable for the whole subsequent religious and philosophical literature of Indians and of utmost interest for theology in general. As the Saṃhitās of the Yajurveda for the history of prayer so are the Brāhmaṇas inestimable sources for the researcher of the history of the institution of sacrifice and of priesthood.

The word "Brāhmaṇa"[3] (neutral) means primarily an "explanation or expression of a learned priest, a doctor of Sacrificial science on some point of the ritual". Used collectively

1. Cf. L. von Schroeder, *I.L.C.*, pp. 127-167, 179-190. Sylvain Lévi, *La doctrine du sacrifice dans les Brāhmaṇas* (Bibliotheque de l'école des hautes études), Paris, 1898. H. Oldenberg, *Vorwissenschftlkiche Wissenschaft, die Weltanschauung der Brāhmaṇa-Texte*, Göttingen, 1919, endeavours to do justice to the thoughts contained in the Brāhmaṇas. What Oldenberg calls "prescientific knowledge," should, however, be more correctly called "priestly pseudo-science." For the prose of the Brāhmaṇas, see Oldenberg, *Zur Geschichte der altindischen Prosa*, pp. 13 ff., 20 ff.

2. Max Müller : *Essays* (Leipzig 1869) p. 105; (*Chips from a German Workshop*, vol. I).

3. The etymology of the word is doubtful. It can be derived from either bráhman (neuter) meaning "holy speech, prayer, holy knowledge" or from brahmán (masc.) meaning "priest" in general or "Brahmin priest" or also from brāhmaṇa (masc.) "the Brahmin", the member of the priestly caste, "the theologian".

this word denotes then a collection of such pronouncements and discussions of the priests on the science of sacrifice. For although the Brāhmaṇas fortunately contain somethings which have only a distant relationship with sacrificial services like cosmogonical myths, old legends and tales, still sacrifice is the sole theme, it is sacrifice which is the starting point of all discussions and around which everything revolves. And the Brāhmaṇas treat one after another the great sacrifices which we have found in the contents of the Vājasaneyī-Saṃhitā,[1] give rules for the individual rites and ceremonies, add to them observations on the relationships of the individual sacrificial acts to one another and to the texts and prayers given sometimes in full and sometimes abridged[2]. Symbolic explanations and speculative reasons for the ceremonies and for the connection with the prayer-formulas follow them. When the views of the scholars on the details of the ritual differ, as it so often happens, one view will be defended and the other rejected. Sometimes there is also the talk of the differences in the ceremonies in different parts of the country as well as of the modifications of certain sacrificial rites under special circumstances. They never fail to mention in the case of every sacrifice, what the reward for the priests, the Dakṣiṇā should consist in. Similarly the sacrificer is told clearly what all advantages he can obtain through the various sacrificial rites in this life or after death. In short, if we may be permitted to apply the word "science" to theological knowledge, we can describe the Brāhmaṇas at best as texts, which deal with the "science of sacrifice".

There must have been many such texts. This is assured by the Indians themselves and this is borne out by the numerous quotations from the lost Brāhmaṇas which we find in our texts. Even the number of the Brāhmaṇas that have been preserved

1. P. 150-154.

2. The oldest name for "Brāhmaṇa" is bandhu, "connection", which indicates that the main purpose of the discussions of the Brāhmaṇas was originally to explain the deeper connection between the sacrificial act and prayer. In later passages the word "Brāhmaṇa" is used in the same sense. Cf. Weber, *HIL*, p. 11; *Ind. Stud.*, 5, 60; 9, 351; Oldenberg, *Vorwissenschaftl. Wissenschaft*, p. 4.

is not at all small, and they all belong to the extensive works of the Indian literature. The four Vedas were divided, as we know, according to the four Vedic Saṃhitās with which we got acquainted and to each of them belong usually many Brāhmaṇas which have originated from various schools (śākhās). We have seen that even the Saṃhitās of the Black Yajurveda considered, in addition to the mantras or prayers, also utterances and discussions on the sense and purpose of sacrifice. In these Brāhmaṇa-like parts of the Yajurveda-Saṃhitā we will have to find the beginnings of the Brāhmaṇa-literature. It was exactly these instructions for the performance of sacrificial ceremonies and the discussions on the sense and purpose of the ritual which were directly connected to the Saṃhitās of the Black Yajurveda that were the theme of the original works of one school after another. And soon it was considered as a rule that every Vedic school must also possess a Brāhmaṇa. Thus it is clear there is such a large number of Brāhmaṇas and also that some works are called Brāhmaṇas which do not at all deserve this name either by virtue of their content or of their extent and which belong to the latest products of the vedic literature. Such are the numerous so-called 'Brāhmaṇas' of the Sāma-Veda which are nothing but vedāṅgas[1] and also the Gopatha-Brāhmaṇa belonging to the Atharvaveda. This Gopatha-Brāhmaṇa is one of the latest works of the whole Vedic literature. In olden days there was evidently no Brāhmaṇa to the Atharvaveda. Only a later time which could not imagine a Veda without a Brāhmaṇa has then tried to fill this gap.[2]

We may now enumerate the most important of the ancient Brāhmaṇas.

The Aitareya Brāhmaṇa belongs to the Ṛgveda. It consists of 40 adhyāyas or 'lessons' which are divided into eight pañcakas or 'fifths'. Tradition has it that Mahīdāsa Aitareya is the

1. See *Chapter* on the Vedāṅgas.

2. The Gopatha-Brāhmaṇa is elaborately dealt with by M. Bloomfield. The Atharva Veda (*Grundriss* II, IB) pp. 101-124. The Gopatha-Brāhmaṇa has been edited by D. Gaastra, Leyden, 1919. While Bloomfield considers the Gopatha-Brāhmaṇa later than the Vaitānasūtra (*Der Atharvaveda*, 101 ff., *GGA*, 1912, No. 1), Caland (*WZKM* 18, 1904, 191 ff.) and Keith (*JRAS* 1910, 934 ff) consider it earlier.

author of this work. In reality he was only the compiler or publisher of the same. This Brāhmaṇa deals mainly with the Soma-sacrifice and in addition only the fire-sacrifice (Agnihotra) and the festival of the King's consecration (Rājasūya). It is presumed that the last ten chapters are of later origin.[1]

In the closest relationship with this Brāhmaṇa is the Kauṣītakī or Sāṅkhāyana-Brāhmaṇa, also belonging to the Ṛgveda, and consisting of thirty Adhyāyas or "lessons". The first six Adhyāyas deal with the food-sacrifice (fire-laying, fire-sacrifice, new- and full-moon sacrifices and the sacrifices of the seasons), while Adhyāyas VII to XXX deal with the Soma-sacrifice fairly agreeing with the Aitareya-Brāhmaṇa.[2] The Kauṣītakī-Brāhmaṇa is later than the Aitareya-Brāhmaṇa. However, while the latter is not the work of one hand and of one period, the Kauṣītakī-Brāhmaṇa is a uniform work.

To the Sāmaveda belongs the Tāṇḍya-Mahā-Brāhmaṇa,[3] also called Pañcaviṃśa, i.e. "Brāhmaṇa consisting of twenty-five books." This is one of the oldest Brāhmaṇas and contains some important old legends. Of special interest are the Vrātya-

1. Edited and translated into English by Martin Haug, Bombay, 1863. A much better edition with extracts from Sāyaṇa's commentary by Th. Aufrecht, Bonn, 1879. Edited with Sāyaṇa's commentary in *AnSS* No. 32. Translated into English by A. B. Keith, *HOS*, Vol. 25, 1920. According to Keith (ibid pp. 44 ff.) the Aitareya-Brāhmaṇa is probably older than the Brāhmaṇa parts of the Taittirīya-Saṃhitā, and certainly older than the Jaiminīya — and Śatapatha-Brāhmaṇa. On the language of the Ait. Br. see Liebich, *Pāṇini*, pp. 23 ff. On Mahīdāsa Aitareya see Keith, *Aitareya-Āraṇyaka*, Introd. pp. 16 f.

2. The Kauṣītaki-Brāhmaṇa is edited by B. Lindner, Jena, 1887, also in *ĀnSS* No. 65, translated into English by A. B. Keith, *HOS* vol. 25, 1920; chapter X translated into German by R. Löbbecke, *Ueber das Verhältnis von Brāhmaṇas und Śrautasūtren*, Leipzig, 1908. Āpastamba mentions the Kauṣītakins, but his quotations from a "Bahvṛca-Brāhmaṇa," that is a Brāhmaṇa of the Ṛgvedins" do not occur either in the Aitareya or in the Kauṣītaki-Brāhmaṇa; they must, therefore, refer to another Ṛgveda-Brāhmaṇa which has not come down to us (Keith, ibid p. 48). For critical and exegetical notes on Ait. Br. and Kaus. Br. see W. Caland, *ZDMG* 72, 1918, 23 ff.

3. Edited in *Bibl. Ind.* 1870-1874. An analysis of it has been given by E. W. Hopkins, "Gods and Saints of the great Brāhmaṇa" (*Transactions of the Connecticut Academy of Arts and Sciences*, vol. 15, 1909, pp. 20-69). Critical notes on it by Caland, *ZDMG* 72, 1918, 19 ff.

stomas, and the description of sacrificial ceremonies by means of which the Vrâtyas were received into the community of the Brāhmaṇas.[1] The Ṣaḍviṃśa-Brāhmaṇa, i.e. the "Twenty-sixth Brāhmaṇa,"[2] is only a completion of the Tāṇḍya which consists of twenty-five books. The last part of the Ṣaḍviṃśa is the so-called "Adbhuta-Brāhmaṇa," a Vedāṅga-text on miracles and omens.[3] The Jaiminīya-Brāhmaṇa of the Sāmaveda is even older than the Tāṇḍya-Mahā-Brāhmaṇa. This work is of special interest for the history both of religion and legend, but unfortunately the manuscript material is so fragmentary that it cannot be edited. Hitherto only portions of it have been made known.[4]

The Taittirīya-Brāhmaṇa of the Black Yajurveda is nothing but a continuation of the Taittirīya-Saṃhitā[5] for the Brāhmaṇas were already included in the Saṃhitās of the Black Yajurveda. The Taittirīya-Brāhmaṇa, therefore, contains only later additions to the Saṃhitā. We find here only a description of the Puruṣa-medha, the symbolical "human sacrifice";[6] and that this sacrifice

1. See above p. 143, and Weber, *HIL*, pp. 67f.

2. Edited by H. F. Eelsingh, Leyden, 1908, and the first Prapāṭhaka by Kurt Klemm, with extracts from Sāyana's commentary, and a German translation (Güterslöh 1894). Liebich (*Indogermanische Forschungen*, Anzeiger, 1895, pp. 30 f) has shown that the language of the Ṣaḍviṃśa is pre-Pāṇinean.

3. Edited and translated into German by A. Weber, "Zwei vedische Texte über Omina und Portenta," *ABA* 1858.

4. A selection from the Jaiminiya-Brāhmaṇa, texts with German translations, has been edited by W. Caland (Verhandeligen der kon. Akad. van Wetenschappen te Amsterdam, Afd. Lett. Deel I, *N.R.D. XIX*, No. 4) 1919. Legends from the Jaim. Br. have been made known before by A. C. Burnell and W. D. Whitney, *Ind. Ant.* 13, 1884, 16 ff., 21 ff., and by H. Oertel in *JAOS*, vols 14, 15, 18, 19, 23, 26, 28 in *OC* XI, Paris 1897, I, 225 ff. and in *Transactions of the Connecticut Academy of Arts and Sciences*, vol. 15, 1909. See also Caland, *WZKM* 28, 1914, 61 ff. and "Over en uit het Jaiminiya-Brāhmaṇa" (*Verslagen ei Mededeclingen der kon. Akademie van Wetensch.*, Afd-Lett, 5, 1) Amsterdam, 1914. The Śāṭyāyana-Brāhmaṇa of the Sāmaveda is only known by quotations (especially in Sāyana's *Ṛgvedabhāṣya*), see H. Oertel, *JAOS* 18, 1897, pp. 15 ff.

5. Editions in *Bibl. Ind.* 1855-1890, and *ĀnSS* No. 37. For the contents of the Taitt. Br. see Keith, *HOS*, vol. 18, pp. lxxvi ff.

6. See above p. 162 f.

is missing in the Saṃhitā is one of the many proofs of the fact that the same is only a considerably late product of the science of sacrifice.

To the white Yajurveda belongs the Śatapatha-Brāhmaṇa, "the Brāhmaṇa of the hundred paths", so called because it consists of a hundred adhyāyas or "lessons". This is the most famous, extensive and doubtless also by virtue of its content most insignificant of all the Brāhmaṇas.[1] As of the Vājasaneyī-Saṃhitā we have also of this Brāhmaṇa two recensions, that of the Kaṇva and that of the Mādhyandinas. In the latter the hundred Adhyāyas are divided into fourteen books (Kāṇḍas). The first nine books are exactly a continuous commentary to the first eighteen chapters of the Vājasaneyī-Saṃhitā. They are decidedly older than the five last books. Probably the books I to V are connected with each other more closely. In them Yājñavalkya who is described at the end of the 14th book as the proclaimer of the whole of the Śatapatha-Brāhmaṇa is named as the teacher, whose authority is decisive. As against this, in the books VI to IX which deal with the laying of the fire-altar (Agnicayana), Yājñavalkya is not at all mentioned. Instead, another teacher, Śāṇḍilya, is mentioned as authority; and the same Śāṇḍilya is also considered to be the proclaimer of the Agni-Rahasya, i.e. the "fire-altar-mystery" which constitutes the content of the XX book. The books XI to XIV contain besides supplements to the preceding books also some interesting chapters on objects which are otherwise not treated in the Brāhmaṇas, for example, on the Upanayana, the initiation of the pupil or the introduction of the pupil to the teacher, who shall teach him the sacred texts (XI : 5, 4), on the everyday veda-study (Svādhyāya)[2] which is viewed as an offering to God Brahman (XI : 5, 6-8), and on the funeral ceremonies and the erection of a grave-mound (XIII, 8). The horse-sacrifice (Aśvamedha), the "human sacrifice" (Puruṣamedha) and the total sacrifice" (Sarvamedha) are treated in

1. The text was published by A. Weber (*The White Yajurveda Part* II. The Śatapatha-Brāhmaṇa, Berlin and London 1855). An excellent English translation with important introductions and notes has been given by Julius Eggeling in 5 volumes (*Sacred Books of the East*, Vols. 12, 26, 41, 43 and 44).

2. The 'learning' or reciting of the veda as a religious duty for the Indians has an exact parallel in the Thora-reading or "learning" of the Jews.

the XIII and the Pravargya-ceremony is treated in the XIV book. The old and important Bṛhadāraṇyaka-Upaniṣad, which we shall get to know in the next chapter, forms the close of this old and extensive work.

The difference between the Brāhmaṇas which belong to the individual Vedas lies mainly in the fact that while describing the ritual, the Brāhmaṇas of the Ṛgveda stress that which is of importance to the Hotar — priest who has to recite the verses and hymns of the Ṛgveda, whereas the Brāhmaṇas of the Sāmaveda are concerned with the duties of the Udgātar and those of the Yajurveda are concerned with duties of the Adhvaryu. In their essential contents all the Brāhmaṇas almost concur with one another. Fundamentally they all deal with the same objects, and they all have the same characteristic features. This becomes much more conspicuous as we are forced to presume a period of many thousands of years for the origin and spread of this literature. If we might believe the tradition which enumerates in the so-called Vaṃśas[1] or "genealogies", tables of genealogies of teachers with 50 to 60 names, then not even a thousand years would be enough to accommodate all the generations of teachers whose names are mentioned. Although the purpose of these genealogies is to trace back the origin of the sacrificial theory to some deity — Brahma, Prajāpati or the Sun—yet they also contain so many names which appear to be real family-names that it is difficult to consider them as having been fully invented. But even apart from these teachers' lists, there are the numerous other teachers who are

1. The Sāmaveda has a so-called Brāhmaṇa, the Vaṃśa-Brāhmaṇa of its own, which contains only such a list of 53 teachers, the last of whom, Kaśyapa, is supposed to have received the tradition from Agni. In the Śatapatha-Brāhmaṇa there are four different vaṃśas. The one that is given at the end of the work begins with the words "We have received this from the son of Bharadvāji, the son of Bharadvāja from the son of Vatsimandari" etc. Then follow 40 more teachers, all with their mothers' names. Only as the 45th in the list appears Yājñavalkya, as whose teacher Uddālaka is mentioned who is known to us from the Upaniṣads. The last (55th) human teacher is Kaśyapa Naidhruvi, to whom the Brāhmaṇa is supposed to have been revealed by Vac — (the goddess of speech). This Vac is supposed to have received it from Ambhṛṇi (the thunder voice) and this again from Āditya, the Sun.

mentioned in the Brāhmaṇas themselves as authorities, and the fact remains that the collectors and compilers of the Brāhmaṇas place the beginnings of the sacrificial science recorded in them in the hoary past. Even this sacrificial science however needs thousands of years for its development.

But if we now ask in which period we have to place these centuries of the development of the Brāhmaṇa-literature, we can think of so little of any definite dates as in the case of fixing the date of the Saṃhitās, only this much is certain, that the Saṃhitā of the Ṛgveda was already completed and the hymn-composing was already a thing of hoary antiquity when one began to make the prayers and sacrifices the object of a special 'science'. It is perhaps also certain that a great majority of the magic-songs, charms and formulas of the Atharvaveda and of the Yajurveda as also the melodies of the Sāmaveda are by far older than the speculations of the Brāhmaṇas. As against this it is probable that the final compilation of the Saṃhitā of the Atharvaveda and the liturgical Saṃhitās were somewhat simultaneous with the beginnings of the Brāhmaṇa literature, so that the latest constituents of these Saṃhitās might have originated at the same time as the oldest constituents of the Brāhmaṇas. This is at least indicated by the geographical and cultural conditions as they are represented in the Saṃhitās of the Atharvaveda, the Sāmaveda and the Yajurveda on the one hand and in the Brāhmaṇas on the other hand in comparison with those of the Ṛgveda. We have seen how even in the period of the Atharvaveda-Saṃhitā the Aryan clans had spread from the Indus-land, the homeland of the Ṛgveda, eastward to the land of the Gaṅgā and the Jamunā. The region to which the Saṃhitās of the Yajurveda as well as all the Brāhmaṇas point, is the land of the Kurus and Pāñcālas, of those two big clans whose great battles form the nucleus of the great Indian epic, the Mahābhārata. In particular, Kurukṣetra, "the land of the Kurus is considered to be a sacred land in which—as is often said—the gods themselves performed their sacrificial ceremonies. This land, Kurukṣetra, lay between the two small rivers Sarasvatī and Dṛṣadvatī in the plains to the west of the Ganges and the Jamunā, and the neighbouring region of the Pāñcālas extended from the northwest to the southwest between the Ganges and the Jamunā. This part of India, the Doab between the Ganges and the Jamunā, from around Delhi to Mathura is considered, even in later times, as the actual "Brahman-country" (Brahmāvarta), whose customs and manners shall be binding on the whole of India according to the Brahminic law books. It is this region that is not only the birth-place of the Saṃhitās of the Yajurveda and of the Brāhmaṇas, but is also the native land of the whole Brahminic culture that has spread from here to the whole of India.

The religious and social conditions have undergone many changes since the times of the Ṛgveda. As in the Atharvaveda, so also in the Yajurveda-Brāhmaṇas, the old gods of the Ṛgveda appear. But their significance is faded and all the power that they possess, they owe to the sacrifice alone. Also some gods, who play only a subordinate role in the Ṛgveda appear in a much stronger role in the liturgical Saṃhitās and in the Brāhmaṇas; thus Viṣṇu and especially Rudra or Śiva. Most significant is now also Prajāpati, "the Lord of the Creation" who is considered as the father of the gods (Devas) as well as of the demons (Asuras). The word Asura,[1] which has in the Ṛgveda still the meaning of "god" corresponding to the "Ahura" of the Avesta, and which occurs often as an attribute of god Varuṇa, has now the meaning of "demon", which it has always in later Sanskrit and in the Brāhmaṇas there is again and again the talk of battles between Devas and Asuras. Yet these battles have nothing Titanen-like in them as for instance the battle between Indra and Vṛtra in the Ṛgveda but the gods and Asuras strive to excel each other by means of sacrifice. For in these Brāhmaṇas the gods themselves have actually to sacrifice if they want to attain something Sacrifice is here no more a means to an end but it is an end in itself, indeed the highest purpose of life. Sacrifice is also an all-conquering power, indeed a creative natural power. That is why sacrifice is identical with Prajāpati, the Creator. "Prajāpati is sacrifice", is an oft-quoted sentence of the Brāhmaṇas. "The soul of all beings, all gods is this, sacrifice." "Truly, he who dedicates himself to sacrifice, dedicates himself to the

1. See above p. 70.

universe, for only after sacrifice comes the universe; by making preparations for the sacrifice to which he dedicates himself, he creates the universe out of himself.[1] And equally miraculous in power and significance is everything that is connected with sacrifice, the implements of sacrifice no less than the prayers and formulas, the verses and their metres, the songs and their melodies. Every single sacrificial act is treated with greatest circumspection; enormous importance is attached to the most trifling circumstances, to the most immaterial details. Whether an act has to be performed towards the left or right side, whether a pot is placed at this or that point of the sacrificial place, whether a stalk of grass shall be placed with its tip pointing to the north or north-east, whether the priest goes to the front or to the back of the fire, to which direction he must have his face turned, in how many parts the sacrificial cake is to be cut, whether the butter shall be poured in the northern or in the southern half or in the middle of the fire, in which moment the recitation of some text, the singing of some song has to take place[2]— these are questions on which generations of the masters of the sacrificial art have pondered and which are most thoroughly treated in the Brāhmaṇas. And on the proper knowledge of all these details depends the weal and woe of the sacrificer : "These, yes these, are the forests and deserts of sacrifice which require hundreds and hundreds of days of cart-journey, and those ignorant people who enter them will meet the same fate as the foolish people, who, wandering about in jungles, are tortured by hunger and thirst, are persecuted by wicked men and monsters. But learned men go from one safe place to another, from one deity to another as if from one river to

1. Śat. XIV, 3, 2, 1. III, 6, 3, 1.

2. Eggeling (*Sacred Books of the East*, Vol. XII p. x) reminds that in the case of ancient Romans also, the Pontifics attained power and influence exactly by virtue of the fact that they alone understood all the details of the sacrificial ceremonial which although small, were declared to be extremely important. It happened in Rome that a sacrifice had to be repeated 30 times because some small mistake was committed in the course of a small ceremony; and in ancient Rome also a ceremony was considered null and void if a word was pronounced wrongly or an act was not performed quite right or if the playing of the music was not stopped just at the right moment. cf. Marquar and Mommsen, *Handbuch der römischen Altertürmer*, VI, p. 172, 174, 213.

another; they attain salvation, the Kingdom of Heaven.[1] But, "the learned men" the guides through the jungle of the sacrificial art, are the priests and it is no wonder that the claims of the priestly caste—for we must now speak of such a caste, because the caste system has been completely built up — exceed all limits in the Brāhmaṇas. Now the Brahmins are often declared to be gods. "Indeed, gods in person are they, the Brāhmins."[2] And clearly enough does the Brāhmaṇa express himself in the following words :

> "There are two kinds of gods forsooth, namely the gods are the gods and the learned and learning Brahmins[3] are the human gods. Between these two is the sacrifice divided : the sacrificial offerings are for the gods, the gifts (Dakṣiṇās) for the human gods, for the learned and learning Brahmins; by sacrificial offerings the gods are pleased, by presents the human gods, the learned and learning; these two kinds of gods transport him (the sacrificer), when they are satisfied, into the happiness of the heaven."[4]

Four duties has the Brahmin: Brahmanic heritage, conduct corresponding to it, fame (through scholarship) and "ripening the men." (i.e. offering sacrifices by which human beings are made ripe for the other world.) But the "ripened men" also have four duties towards the Brahmins: They must show respect towards them, give them presents, must not cause hardship to them and must not kill them. Under no circumstances shall the King lay his hand on a Brahmin's property; and if a king gifts to the priests the whole of his kingdom with all that is in it as sacrificial reward, then the property of the Brahmins is *eo ipso* excepted. Of course the king can also oppress a Brahmin, but if he does so, evil will befall him. At the royal consecration the priest says: "This man, ye people, is your King; Soma is the king of us, the Brahmins," on which there is a remark in the

1. Śat. XII : 2, 3, 12.
2. Taittirīya-Saṃhitā I : 7, 3, 1.
3. Literally : "Those who have heard and who repeat (recite) (what they have heard).
4. Śat. II : 2, 2, 6; IV : 3, 4, 4.

Śataptha-Brāhmaṇa: "By this incantation he makes the whole folk food for the king."[1]; only the Brahmins he excepts; therefore the Brahmin should not be exploited for food; because he has Soma for his king."[2] Only the murder of a Brahmin is a real murder. In a dispute between a Brahmin and a non-Brahmin the judge must always admit the case of the Brahmin as right, for the Brahmin must not be contradicted.[3] All that is due to some reason or other taboo, what one must not touch or cannot use in any other manner, for example, the stone and earthen vessels of a dead man or a cow meant for Agnihotra milk that has become stubborn or ill, must be given to the Brahmin, especially sacrificial remnants and foods that are taboo for the others, because "nothing harms a Brahmin's stomach."[4]

Thus it is driven finally to such an extent that the Brahmin is not any more a "human god" in addition to the heavenly gods, but that he raises himself above the gods themselves. Even in the Śatapatha-Brāhmaṇa it is said: "The Brahmin descending from a Ṛṣi is indeed all deities."[5] i.e. in him are all deities personified. This presumptuousness of the priests which we find in the Brāhmaṇas at the time of their beginnings, is of interest not only as an example of priestly presumptuousness in its beginnings, is of great interest not only as an example of priestly exaltation, but it is also the early stage of a phenomenon that we can follow through the whole Indian antiquity and which, in my view, is deeply rooted in the essence of the Indo-German mind. While the Hebrew poet says for instance! "What is man that you think of him and what is man's son that you care so much for him? and adds: "Man is equal to nothing", the Greek poet uttered the great words: "Many

1. i.e. the king lives on the folk who must pay him taxes.
2. Śat. XI : 5, 7, 1; XIII : 5, 4, 24; XIII : 1, 5, 4; V : 4, 2, 3.
3. Śat X III : 3, 5, 3; Taittirīya-Saṃhitā II, 5, 11, 9.
4. Taittirīya-Saṃhitā II : 6, 8, 7. Cf. Goethe's *Faust* :

   "The Church has a good belly
   Has eaten whole countries
   And has still never become satiate."

5. XII : 4, 4, 6. Later on it is said in Manu's Law book : "A Brahmin is, whether learned or not, is a great deity," and immediately thereafter, "the Brahmin is the highest god." (Manu IX. 317, 319).

powers there are, but the most powerful is man." And a German poet—the same one that has created the superman[1] Faust, that knocks furiously at the door of the world of Spirits —he had sung the song of Prometheus, who shouts to the gods:

"I know nothing more pitiable
Under the sun than you —O gods !"

And in India we see that even in the Brāhmaṇas the priest is exalted through sacrifices even above the gods; in the epics we read numerous stories of ascetics who, through their asceticism, attain such superior strength that even gods trembled on their thrones. And in Buddhism even the heavenly ones along with Indra, the prince of gods, have faded into mere insignificant beings who distinguish themselves from ordinary mortals only by their being situated in a better position,—but this also only as long as they are pious Buddhists; and by far above the gods is not only the Buddha himself but also every man who through love towards all beings and renouncement of the world has become Arhat or holy.[2]

Thus even in the Brāhmaṇas that great movement is prepared, to which Buddhism owes its origin. For there is no doubt that the old or genuine Brāhmaṇas belong to a pre-Buddhist time. Whereas not the least trace is found of an acquaintance with Buddhism[3] the Buddhist texts presuppose the existence of a Brāhmaṇa literature. Therefore we are justified in saying that the centuries in which the liturgical Saṃhitās and the Brāhmaṇas have originated must be in a time that is after the completion of the hymn-composing and the Ṛgveda-Saṃhitā and before the appearance of Buddhism.

As regards the actual contents of these works, a few examples will give the reader the best idea of the same. Indians

1. "What a wretched horror seizes you, oh superman !"
2. See A. Weber, *S.B.A.* 1897, I, 594, ff.
3. It is significant that in the list of human sacrifices in the Vājasaneyi-Saṃhitā XXX (cf. p. 162 above) there is no mention of either monks or nuns or even of Buddhists. And yet this list is probably later than the oldest Brāhmaṇas.

themselves usually put the contents of the Brāhmaṇas under two main categories which they call Vidhi and Arthavāda. Vidhi means "rule, regulation", Arthavada "sense-explanation". The Brāhmaṇas give at first rules for performing the individual ceremonies and to them are then appended the explanations and discussions on the purpose and significance of the sacrificial acts and prayers. Thus begins for example the Śatapatha-Brāhmaṇa with the rules for the oath of abstinence which the sacrificer has to take on the day before the Newmoon and Fullmoon sacrifice. There it is said (Śat. I, 1, 1, 1.):

> "He who is about to take a vow, dips his hand in water by standing between the sacrificial fire and the family-fire, his face turned towards east. The reason why he dips his hand in water is as follows: Impure is man because he speaks untruth; so he performs an inner purification; pure for sacrifice is water. He thinks: 'After I have become pure for sacrifice, I will take the vow. 'A means of purification is water. 'Purified with the means of purification, I will take the vow; he thinks: and that is why he dips his hand in water." (Śat. I, 1, 1, 1)

Such explanations are often followed by discussions of the views of several teachers on some question of ritual or the other. Thus the question raised here is as to whether one should or should not fast at the time of taking the vow in question, and it is said (Śat, I: 1, 1, 7-9):

> "Now, with respect to eating or fasting, Āṣāḍha Sāvayasa is of the opinion that the vow consists just in fasting. For, says he, gods evidently know the intention of men. They know that he who takes this vow, will offer sacrifice to them on the next morning. So all gods come to his house then; they live with him (*upavasanti*) in his house; therefore is this day an *upavasatha* (i.e. 'fast day'). Now it would be certainly inappropriate if one would eat before the men (who have come to his house as guests) have eaten, how much more would it be so if he would eat before gods (who live as

guests in his house)[1] have eaten. Therefore he shall not eat in any case. But Yājñavalkya says on the other hand: "If he does not eat he behaves as a worshipper of the manes;[2] but if he eats then he insults the gods by eating before they have eaten; therefore he shall eat something, which when it is eaten, is considered as not having been eaten. That however, from which no sacrificial food is taken, is considered, even when it is eaten, as not having been eaten. Through such a food he does not become a worshipper of manes on the one hand and on the other hand, when he eats something from which no sacrificial food is taken, he does not insult the gods by eating before they have eaten. Therefore he shall eat only that which grows in the forest, be it forest herbs or fruits of trees." (Śat. I, I, 1, 1, 7-10)

Etymologies as that of 'upavasatha' in the above-mentioned text are very frequent in the Brāhmaṇas. Neverthless it is considered as specially good if the etymology is not exactly correct because "gods love the concealed." Thus for example the name of god Indra is derived from Indh, "ignite" and it is said, "He is therefore actually called Indho, and one calls him 'Indra' for the simple reason that the gods love what is concealed. Or, the word ulūkhala which means "mortar" is drived from uru kavat, "may he make broad", and ulūkhala is explained as a mystical term for urukara:[3] Just like etymologising so also identifying and symbolising plays an important role in the Brāhmaṇas even more than in the Yajurveda-Saṃhitā[4], and thereby the most dissimilar things are put together and brought in relationship to one another. On each page of the Brāhmaṇas we find discussions like the following:

1. The sentences within the brackets are added from the context to complete the meaning. It is impossible to give an exact translation of the original without adding such complements. Evidently the Brāhmaṇas are not *written for readers* but *spoken for listeners* and therefore much has been omitted that the speaker can express through intonation of individual words, through movements of his hands and similar things.

2. Because fasting is prescribed at the time of worshipping the manes.

3. Śat. VI, 1, 1, 2. VII, 5, 1, 2, 2. Cf. p. 161 above.

4. See p. 168 above. On identifications in the Brāhmaṇas see Oldenberg, *Vorwissenschafiliche Wissenschaft,* pp. 110 ff.

"In pairs he fetches the sacrificial tools, namely, sieve and the fire-sacrifice-spoon, wooden-knife and bowl, wedge and antelope-skin, mortar and pestle, big and small grinding stone. They are ten. For the Virāj-metre consists of ten syllables; virāj (i.e. 'shining') is however also the sacrifice; precisely by this he makes sacrifice similar to Virāj. In pairs does he bring them for the reason that a pair signifies evidently power; where to undertake something there is naturally power there. But a pair represents also mating and reproduction; thus (through the fetching of the sacrificial tools in pairs) therefore (mating and reproduction is encouraged."

(Śat. I: 1, 1, 22)

Sacrifice is indeed man. And sacrifice is indeed man because man spreads it (on the sacrificial place); and by being spread it is precisely made so big as man.[1] Therefore sacrifice is man. To this manlike sacrifice belongs the Juhu;[2] (as the right arm) and the upabhṛt[2] (as the left arm) ; but the Dhruva is the trunk. But now all limbs originate from the trunk, therefore the whole sacrifice originates from the *Dhruva*. The ghee-spoon[3] however is the breath. The breath of man goes through all limbs and therefore the ghee-spoon goes from one sacrificial spoon to the other. Of this (man)[4] is the Juhu that heaven there and the upabhṛt is the space here; but the Dhruva is this (here) (i.e. the earth). But in reality, from this (the earth) originate all words; therefore the whole sacrifice originates from the Dhruva. This ghee-spoon here is however that one which blows there (i.e. the wind)—it is that which blows through all the worlds —, and therefore the ghee-spoon goes from one sacrificial spoon to the other." (Śat. I, 3, 2, 1-5).

1. Because while measuring out the sacrificial place such measures like "man's length", "arm-length", "span" etc. are employed.

2. Names of various sacrificial spoons.

3. With this spoon (sruva) the melted butter is taken out of the ghee pot and poured into the sacrificial spoons with which offerings are made.

4. "Man" means Puruṣa. But Puruṣa means also "Spirit" and denotes also the "Great Spirit" which is one with Prajāpati, the creator of the world. Sacrifice is, therefore, identified not only with man (the sacrificer) but also with the world-spirit and Prajāpati. (cf. above p. 171, fn. 2).

At numerous places in the Brāhmaṇas sacrifice is equated with god Viṣṇu and equally frequently with the creator Prajāpati. But the year also is identified with Prajāpati innumerable times, whereas on the other hand Agni as the fire-altar, is considered as equal to the year because the construction of the fire-altar takes one year. Thus we read: "Agni is the year, and the year is these worlds," and immediately thereafter, "Agni is Prajāpati and Prajāpati is the year." Or, "Prajāpati is indeed the sacrifice and the year, the new-moon—night is his gate and moon is the bolt of the gate."[1] A great role is played here by the symbolism of numbers. Thus we read for example—

"With four (verses) he takes (some ash) away; by this he covers him with that which is available of quadruped cattle. But now cattle is food; therefore he covers him with food. With three (verses) he brings (the ash to water). That makes seven, because of seven layers consists the fire-altar (Agni). Seven seasons are one year, and the year is Agni; as great as Agni is the measure of the year, as great will this (universe) become." (Śat. VI, 8.2.7.)

Now and then these futile discussions acquire some interest by the fact that they throw some light on the moral notions and social conditions of that time, to which the Brāhmaṇas belong. Thus for example when Soma is offered one of the offerings is consecrated to "Agni Patnīvat, i.e. to Agni who has wives."[2] This libation is different in some details from the other Soma-offerings and these deviations in their performances are explained by indicating the weakness of the feminine sex and women's lack of claim to any rights :

"With the remnants of ghee left in the sacrificial spoon he mixes (the soma). Other Soma libations he makes strong by mixing them; but these he weakens; because ghee is indeed a thunderbolt and with the thunderbolt, the ghee, have gods beaten their wives and weakened them; and thus beaten and weakened they had no claim either to their own body or to any heir. And just in the same way he beats and weakens now the women with the thunderbolt, with the ghee; and thus

1. Śat. VIII. 2, 1, 17, 18. XI. 1, 1, 1.
2. Cf. above. p. 74.

beaten and weakened, they have no claim to their own body or to a heir." Śat. IV. 4, 2, 13.)

This would, therefore, be a ritual basis for the bondage of woman.[1]

At another place the relation of the woman to her husband appears in a somewhat more friendly light. During the Vājapeya-sacrifice the following ceremony occurs : A ladder is placed leaning against the sacrificial post and the sacrificer climbs it with his wife :

"When he is about to climb up, he addresses his wife with the following words : 'Wife, we will climb up to the heaven.' The reason for his addressing his wife thus is as follows—She, the wife, that is indeed his own half; therefore as long as he has no wife, he does not procreate himself; he is not a complete man; but when he has a wife he procreates himself, then he is complete. 'As a complete man I will go this way (to the heaven)' he thinks; therefore he addresses his wife thus."

(Śat. V. 2, 1, 10.)

The sacrificial place on the altar (Vedī, fem.) is represented as a woman in the symbolism of the Brāhmaṇas. And the following rule regarding the erection of the altar gives us information on the ancient Indian ideal of feminine beauty.

"It[2] shall be too much broad towards the west, notched in the middle and again broad in the east. In this way one admires a woman. 'Broad about the hips, a little narrower between the shoulders and in the middle to hold'. Just in this way he makes it pleasant to the gods." (Śat. I, 2, 5, 16).

A sharp light is thrown on the sexual moral of those times by a brutal sacrificial custom that occurs in one of the seasonal sacrifices and described in the following manner :

"Then the Pratiprasthātar[3] gets back (to the place where the

1. We also read in the Brāhmaṇas such sentences as : "Verily, the sacrifice is right and truth, woman is something wrong" (Maitrāyaṇīya-Saṃhitā, I, 10, 11), "Nirṛti (i.e. Evil personified) is woman." (Maitr. I, 10, 16), "Woman, the Śūdra, the dog, and the black-bird (the crow) are something wrong". (Śat. 14, 1, 1, 31), etc. See Lévi, *La doctrine du sacrifice dans les Brāhmaṇas*, pp. 156 ff.; Oldenberg, *Vorwissenschaftliche Wissenschaften*, pp. 44 f; and Winternitz, *Die Frau in den indischen Religionen*, I, pp. 4 f., 10 ff., 43.

2. That is, the *Vedī* or sacrificial place.

3. One of the priests, an assistant of the Adhvaryu.

sacrificer's wife is sitting); and when he is about to lead his wife up[1] he asks her: 'With whom do you sleep?" For really, a woman commits a sin against Varuṇa if she, while belonging to one, sleeps with another. Because he thinks: "That she may not sacrifice with a thorn in her heart; therefore he questions her. When one confesses a sin, it becomes indeed smaller; for it becomes truth. Just because of this he questions her. But what she does not confess, is enough to bring disaster to her relatives." (Śat. II. 5, 2, 20)

Besides, this is one of those few texts in the Brāhmaṇas, where moral is thought of. Otherwise it is a strong characteristic of these texts that there is practically no talk of moral in them. The Brāhmaṇas are a brilliant proof of the fact that immense religion can be combined with, not the least traces of moral. Religious acts, sacrifices and ceremonies are the one and only one theme of all these voluminous works,—but with moral these acts have nothing to do.[2] The contrary is the fact. Sacrificial acts are performed not only in order that the gods fulfil the very material desires of the sacrificer, but quite often also in order to do harm to an enemy. Yes, the Brāhmaṇas even give directions to the priests as to how they can do harm by means of the sacrifice to the sacrificer himself by whom they are employed, if they do not give sufficient gifts to them. They need only to perform the prescribed ceremonies in the reverse order or to apply the charms at a wrong place,—and the fate of the sacrificer is sealed.

Now, enough of this intricate science of sacrifice which forms the main contents of the Brāhmaṇas. Fortunately a part of the

1. That is, to the altar, where she shall make an offering to Varuṇa.

2. "La morale n'a pas trouvez de place dans ce systeme : le sacrifice qui regle les rapports de l'homme avec les divinités est une operation mécanique qui agit par son energie intime; caché au sein de la nature, il ne s'en degagé que sous l'action magique du pretre"....."En fait il est difficile de concevoir rien de plus brutal et de plus materiel que la theologie des Brāhmaṇas; les notions que l'usage a lentement affinées et qu'il a revetues d'un aspect moral, surprennent par leur réalisme sauvage." (Sylvain Lévi, *La doctrine du Sacrifice*, V. 9 (cf. 164 ff).

Moreover Oldenberg (*Vorwissenschaftliche Wissenschaft*, pp. 19 ff., 124 ff., 184 ff.) has taken great pains to collect all that can be found on ethical ideas in the Brāhmaṇas. It does not amount to much.

Arthavāda or of the "sense-explanation" is also constituted by the so-called Itihāsas, Ākhyānas and Purāṇas, i.e. stories, tales and legends, which are told in order to establish some ritual act or the other. As in the Talmud to which the Brāhmaṇas bear a similarity in some respects, the flourishing garden of the Hagada, so beautifully praised by Heine stands by the side of the theological shadow-boxing of the Halacha, so also in the Brāhmaṇas, the wilderness of desertlike theological speculation is now and then pleasantly interrupted by an oasis in which the flower of poetry blossoms—a poetical story or a legend on creation which is profound in thought.

Such an oasis in the desert is the fairy tale of a hoary past narrated in the Śatapatha-Brāhmaṇa,[1] that of Purūravas and Urvaśī, that was already known to the singers of the Ṛgveda. It tells us how the nymph (Apsaras) Urvaśī loved King Purūravas, how she stipulated her conditions when she became his wife and how the Gandharvas contrived that he had to break one of these conditions. Then she vanishes from him and Purūravas combs lamenting and bemoaning the whole of Kurukṣetra, until he comes to a lotus-pond where nymphs are swimming around in the form of swans. Among them is Urvaśī and there ensues the dialogue that is known to us from the Ākhyāna-stanzas of the Ṛgveda.

"Then she was sincerely sorry for him. And she spoke : 'In a year from today you shall come; then you may stay with me for a night; by then your son whom I am now carrying in my womb[2] would have been born.' And in the night when the year was over he came again. Ay! there stood a golden palace ! Then they spoke to him alone : 'Enter here!' Thereupon they sent Urvaśī to him. But she spoke : 'The Gandharvas will grant you a boon tomorrow, choose one!' 'You choose for me!' 'I want to become one of you, shall you say.' The next morning the Gandharvas granted him a boon. But he spoke, "I want to become one of you."

1. XI, 5, 1. A good German translation of the piece is given by K. Geldner (in the 'Vedic Studies' I, 244 ff.) Cf. above p. 90 f.

2. Literally : "This your son here". One of the many expressions which can be made clear only by oral delivery. Similarly in the Brāhmaṇas often "this here" means "earth", "that there" means "heaven" and so on.

Thereupon the Gandharvas taught him a special form of the fire-sacrifice by which a mortal will be transformed into a Gandharva. To the description of this sacrifice we owe the adaption to the Brāhmaṇas of the fairy tale of antiquity from which not even the scholars of the sacrificial art are able to expel all the magic of poetry.

In the Śatapatha-Brāhmaṇa[1] we also find in its oldest form the Indian legend of the deluge which in all probability can be traced back to a Semitic source :

"To Manu they brought in the morning water for washing, just as even today one usually brings water to a man for washing his hands. As he washed himself, a fish came into his hands. And it spoke to him the following words : 'Preserve my life, and I will save you.' 'From what will you save me ?' 'A flood will carry off all these beings. From that I will save you.' 'How shall I preserve your life ?' It spoke, 'As long as we are small, many dangers threaten our life; one fish devours the other. You shall preserve me at first in a pot, and when I have outgrown it, you shall dig a pit and preserve me in it, and when I have outgrown it you shall bring me to the sea, for then I will be out of all danger (to my life).' And soon it was a jhaṣa-fish; a jhaṣa-fish grows biggest. Then he spoke, "In such and such a year a flood will come. Therefore make a ship for yourself and wait for me. And when the flood has risen, then you shall go on board the ship and I will save you.' After he had preserved its life in this manner he brought it to the sea. And in the year which the fish had indicated to him, he made a ship for himself and waited. When the flood rose he went on board the ship and the fish came swimming to him. But he tied the rope to the horn of the fish; and with it he sailed quickly across to the northern mountain over there. Then the fish spoke : "I have saved you. Tie the ship to a tree. Let not the water cut you off from the earth when you are on the

1. I, 8, 1. Translated into German by A. Weber, *Indische Streifen* I, Berlin, 1868, p. 9 f. In the same volume Weber has also translated some other legends (Legend of the further wandering of the Aryans towards the East, Legend of the Fountain of Youth, Legend of Purūravas and Urvaśī and a legend on the penal retaliation after death) as well as the whole first Adhyāya of the Śatapatha Brāhmaṇa.

mountain! Therefore descend gradually, as the water drains away." Quite gradually he descended. And precisely this point of the northern mountain is called even today "Manu's Descent. The flood, however, carried away all beings; Manu alone was left behind." (Śat. I, 8,1)

So far does the old legend go, which must have continued the narration, as the human race was again preserved through Manu. But the Brāhmaṇa tells, that Manu performed a sacrifice in order to obtain successors; out of this sacrifice a female being was born and through her the human race was regenerated. This daughter of Manu is called Iḍā—and the tale is adapted only to explain the significance of the offering called by the name Iḍā.

These narratives are of significance to us also as the oldest examples of a narrative prose that we have of the Indians. That this prose of the oldest epic literature is often interspersed with verses has been already stated above.[1] But whereas in the story of Purūravas and Urvaśī the verses appear not only in the Ṛgveda collection but also belong to the oldest Vedic poetry in the matter of their language and metre, we find in the Aitareya-Brāhmaṇa an Ākhyāna, in which the Gāthās or stanzas strewn in prose approach the epic in the matter of language as well as in meter. This is the legend of Śunaḥśepa[2] interesting to us in more than one respect. It begins as follows :

"Hariścandra, son of Vedhas, a king of the race of the Ikṣvākus, was childless. He had a hundred wives, but got no son from any of them. Once Parvata and Nārada[3] came to him, and he asked Nārada:

'As all people wish for a son, the wise ones as well as the fools,

1. See p. 85.

2. Aitareya-Brāhmaṇa, VII, 13-18, English translation by Max Müller, *History of Ancient Sanskrit Literature*, 2nd ed., London, 1860, pp. 408 ff., by M. Haug, and by A. B. Keith in their respective translations of the Aitareya-Brāhmaṇa. German translation by R. Roth, *Ind. Stud.*, 2. 112 ff.; A. Weber, *SBA.*, 1891, pp. 776 ff.; Keith, *HOS.*, Vol. 25, pp. 61 ff.; Charpentier, *Die Suparṇasage*, pp. 58 f. The story is called an "Ākhyāna" in the text itself.

3. Two Ṛṣis or holy men who live sometimes in heaven, sometimes on earth and often serve the gods as messengers.

So tell me, O Nārada, what one then attains through a son.'
Questioned thus with one stanza, he replies to him with ten:

'The father who the face of his son sees, born to him alive,
pays off his debt in him, attains through him immortality.[1]

Of all joys, which are there for the creatures on the earth,
In fire and in water, is the father's joy over the son the greatest.
Always have the fathers through the son all darkness conquered.
He himself is again produced anew, the son is for him a boat of rescue.
Why the dirt, why the antilope-skin, why the beard, why the asceticism[2]
Brahmins, desire for yourselves a son ! in him you have the world of heaven
Food is life, shelter is protection and gold jewellery is beauty;
Marriage brings cattle;[3] a friend,[4] is the wife, a misery the daughter[5]

1. The best explanation to this verse is given by the two Brāhmaṇa-texts Taittirīya-Saṃhitā VI.3, 10, 5 : "From the moment of his birth the Brāhmin is burdened with three debts : To the ṛṣis he owes the vow of the learning of the Vedas, to the gods the sacrifice, and to the manes succession; he is freed from his debts who begets a son, performs sacrifices and keeps the vow of learning the Veda." And Taittirīya-Brāhmaṇa I. 5, 5, 6 : "In your successors you regenerate yourself; that, O mortal, is your immortality." Even in the Ṛgveda V. 4, 10 it is said : "May I, O Agni, through successors attain immortality !"

2. This verse is against the hermits and ascetics in the forest.

3. Because the price for the daughter was paid by the ancient Indians as well as the ancient Greeks in the form of cows—compare the 'virgins who bring cows' in Homer.

4. During marriage in ancient India the bride and bridegroom took seven steps with each other, whereupon the bridegroom said, "Be my friend with the seventh step."

5. Only under the rule of the English has it become possible, to abolish the custom of killing female children, a custom deeply rooted in India as well as in the whole world just as the widely spread notion that the daughter is "a misery". "When a daughter is born, all the four walls weep." See also Winternitz, *Die Frau in den indischen Religionen,* I pp. 21 ff.

Light in the highest world of heaven is the son for the father.
The husband enters his wife and becomes a germ in her womb;
Is brought by her into the world as a new man in the tenth month."

.......................[1]. After he spoke these words he said to him: 'Turn to Varuṇa and speak: May a son be born to me; him I will sacrifice to you.' 'Yes, I will' said he and ran to King Varuṇa, praying: 'May a son be born to me; him I shall sacrifice to you.' 'So may it be' (spoke Varuṇa). Then was a son born to him, by name Rohita. And Varuṇa said to him: 'Now a son has been born to you; sacrifice him to me.' But he said, "When an animal is more than ten days old, only then he is suitable for sacrifice. Let him become over ten days old, then I will sacrifice him to you." 'Let it be so'. And he became over ten days old. Then he spoke to him, "Now he has become over ten days old; sacrifice him to me." But he said, 'when an animal has got teeth, only then is it suitable for sacrifice. Let him get teeth; then I will sacrifice him to you'. 'Let it be so'!

In a similar way Hariścandra keeps god Varuṇa off until Rohita has attained manhood. Then he wants to sacrifice him at last, but Rohita runs away into the forest where he wanders about for one year. Thereupon Hariścandra is seized with dropsy which is sent upon him by Varuṇa as a punishment. Rohita hears of it and wants to go back, but Indra accosts him in the form of a Brahmin, praises the good fortune of the wanderer and asks him to wander further. And a second, a third, a fourth, a fifth year the youth wanders about in the forest; again and again he wants to go back, and again and again Indra accosts him and implores him to wander further. Now when he was wandering about the forest in the sixth year, he met the ṛṣi Ajīgarta, who, tortured by hunger, was roaming about the forest. He had three sons called Śunaḥpuccha, Śunaḥśepa, Śunolāṅgūla.[2]

1. There follow four more verses in which the same thoughts are varied.

2. These peculiar names, which mean "dog's hind part," "dog's pizzle" "dog's tail" are chosen perhaps intentionally, in order to make the Ṛṣi

Rohita offers him a hundred cows for one of his sons whose life he could then offer instead of his own life and he receives—as the father does not want to give the eldest and the mother the youngest son—the middle one, Śunaḥśepa. With this one Rohita goes to his father. And as Varuṇa agrees that Śunaḥśepa will be sacrificed to him instead of Rohita – for "a Brahmin is more valuable than a warrior, said Varuṇa"—shall the same be offered in the place of the sacrificial animal during the sacrifice of the King's consecration (Rājasūya). Everything is got ready for the sacrifice but there is nobody who is ready to tie the victim. Then Ajīgarta says: "Give me a second hundred, and I will tie him." And for a second hundred cows he ties his son Śunaḥśepa to the sacrificial post; for a third hundred, however, he offers to kill him. He is given a further hundred cows and he comes upon his son with his knife sharpened. Then this one thought: "They want to kill me as if I were not a human being; well I will seek refuge in the gods." And he praised one after another all the excellent gods of the Vedic pantheon in a number of hymns which are all found in our Ṛgveda-Saṃhitā. But as he at last praised Uṣas, the dawn, in three verses, then the fetters dropped down from him one after another and Hariścandra's water-stomach became smaller, and with the last verse he was free from the fetters and Hariścandra healthy. Thereupon the priests admitted him to the sacrificial gathering and Śunaḥśepa saw a special kind of Soma-sacrifice. But Viśvāmitra, the legendary ṛṣi, who occupied the office of the Hotar during Hariścandra's sacrifice, took Śunaḥśepa as his son and ceremoniously made him his successor disregarding his own hundred sons. In the end it is said......

"This is the story (Ākhyāna) of Śunaḥśepa, which contains over hundred Ṛgveda verses and in addition to them also stanzas.[1] These *the Hotar* tells the king after he has been provided with consecrated water in the Rājasūya. Seated on a golden cushion he narrates. Seated on a golden cushion (the Adhvaryu) shouts the replies. Gold means indeed fame. He makes him thus prosper

---

Ajigarta— the name means 'he who has nothing to eat' — appear in as bad a light as possible. Anyhow these names also prove the more popular than priestly character of the narrative.

1. "Gāthās", epic stanzas like those marked above.

in fame. "Om" is the reply cry for a Ṛg verse, "Yes" that for a Gāthā.[1] "Om" is evidently divine and "yes" is human. In this way he frees him from misfortune and sin by divine and human word. Therefore a king who wants to be victorious may have the Śunaḥśepa legend narrated to him even if he is not a sacrificer; then not even the smallest sin remains attached to him. Thousand cows he shall give to the narrator, hundred to the priest who calls out the replies and each one of them the golden cushion on which he has been sitting: moreover a mule-drawn silver carriage is due to the Hotar. Also those who desire a son shall have this legend narrated to them: then they will certainly obtain a son."

If, however, this Śunaḥśepa legend was even for the author or the compiler of the Aitareya Brāhmaṇa already a venerable old legend, whose narration formed a special constituent of the ritual during the sacrifice of the king's consecration,[2] how old must the legend itself be! It must be very old also for this reason that in it is preserved the memory of human sacrifice which must have been offered during the Rājasūya in prehistoric times, although otherwise there is no talk of human sacrifices at the time of king's consecration anywhere in the Brāhmaṇas or in the ritual books (Śrauta-sūtras). And yet the Śunaḥśepa legend is young compared to the Ṛgveda. For the hymns[3] which, according to the Aitareya-Brāhmaṇa, Śunaḥśepa is said to have "seen", are partly such as might have been composed by a Ṛṣi Śunaḥśepa as well as any other Ṛṣi, although in them not even the least is contained that could have any relation to our legend; partly, however, are they hymns which do not at all

1. That means, always when the Hotar recites a Ṛg verse, the Adhvaryu cries at the end of the same "Om"; when he has recited an epic stanza, he cries : ". . . . Yes". cf. above p. 173, fn. 1.

2. As an ākhyāna belonging to the Rājasūya it is also related in the Sānkhyāyana-Śrautasūtra, 15, 17 ff. In the same Śrautasūtra, 16, 11, 1-3, it is mentioned as one of the ākhyānas to be told at the Puruṣamedha. It is also referred to in the Śrautasūtras of Kātyāyana, Āpastamba, and Baudhāyana. See Keith, *HOS.*, Vol. 25, pp. 29 f., 40 f., 61 f., 67.

3. Namely Ṛv I, 24-30 and IX, 3. The Gāthās of the Śunaḥśepa-Ākhyāna are, of course, much later than the verses of the Ṛgveda. Yet from the metre, it seems that they are older than the metrical portions of the Upaniṣads; see Keith, *HOS.*, vol. 25, p. 50.

agree with the character of Śunaḥśepa of the legend, as for example the song of Ṛgveda I, 29 with the refrain, "Let us hope O generously gifting Indra, for a thousand shining cows and horses," or which like RV I, 24 contain verses which cannot have been possibly composed by Śunaḥśepa of the Aitareya-Brāhmaṇa. For it is said here, "He whom Śunaḥśepa called when he was caught, King Varuṇa, may he redeem us !" and Śunaḥśepa called really, as he was caught and tied to the three posts, the Āditya." These are verses, which must refer to another much older Śunaḥśepa legend. If the Aitareya Brāhmaṇa ascribes these hymns to Śunaḥśepa, the reason for this may be that the same absolutely unreliable tradition which is found in our Anukramaṇis[1] attributed those hymns to a Ṛṣi Śunaḥśepa even at the time of the Aitareya Brāhmaṇa. Here we have again a proof of the fact, how far behind chronologically the Ṛgveda hymns are to all others which belong to the Veda.

Unfortunately only few stories have been preserved to us so completely in the Brāhmaṇas as that of Śunaḥśepa. Mostly the stories are adjusted to suit the purpose which they are supposed to serve, namely the explanation or substantiation of a sacrificial ceremony, and sometimes it is not easy to get out of them the pith of an old legend or an old myth. Also, not all tales which we find in the Brāhmaṇas can be traced back to old myths and legends, but they have been often invented only for explaining some sacrificial ceremony or the other. But sometimes these invented stories are also not uninteresting. In order to explain, for example, why during the sacrificial offerings which are dedicated to Prajāpati, the prayers shall be said only gently the following beautiful allegory is told:

"There broke out once a quarrel between the mind and the speech, as to who of the two was better. "I am the better one," said both of them, the mind and the speech. The mind said, 'Indeed I am better than you, for you speak nothing that I have not thought first; and as you are only an imitator of my deeds, only a follower of mine, so I am in any case better than you.' But then spoke the speech, 'Of course I am better than you, for what you know, that only I make known, that I communi-

1. See above p. 52 f. and below p. 235.

cate.' They went to Prajāpati so that he might settle the quarrel. But Prajāpati decided in favour of the mind by saying to the speech, "The mind is better than you, for indeed you are only an imitator of his deeds, only his follower, and inferior is certainly he that is only an imitator of the deeds of a better one, only his follower.' Now the speech was very much dismayed that the decision went against her. (As a result of the excitement) she had a miscarriage. However she, the speech, spoke thus to Prajāpati, "Never shall I be your sacrifice-carrier, because you have decided against me.' Hence during the sacrifice every ceremony dedicated to Prajāpati, is performed gently, for the speech refused to carry the offerings to *Prajāpati*." (Śat. I, 4, 5, 8-12.)

Vāc, the speech, forms also the object of many stories in which it is put up as the primitive symbol of the woman. Thus we come across her for instance, in the legend of the Soma-theft occurring frequently in the Brāhmaṇas. The Soma was in the heaven, and Gāyatrī in the form of a bird brought it down. As she carried it away, she was robbed by a Gandharva. Now the gods counselled as to how they could get back the stolen Soma.

"The gods spoke, 'The Gandharvas are fond of women, we will send the Vāc to them, and she will come back to us with the Soma.' And they sent the Vāc to them, and she came back with the Soma. The Gandharvas however followed her and said, 'The Soma belongs to you, but the Vāc shall belong to us.' 'Well,' said the gods; but if she would perfer coming to us, then you shall not lead her away by force; we will compete with you in courting her.' Thus they competed in courting her. The Gandharvas recited the Vedas to her and said, "So, yes, so we know.'[1] The gods however made the lute and set themselves playing and singing, to Vāc, saying, 'Thus we will sing before you, thus we will make you happy.' Then she turned to the gods; yes, so she turned towards what is vain, by turning away from the praising and admiring ones to dance and song. This is the reason why even to this day women yield only to vain gewgaw. So *Vāc* evidently turned to that and other women

1. Because the *Veda* is knowledge *par excellence*. See also p. 43.

followed suit. It is, therefore, that women are most fond of following him who sings and him who dances.[1]

Just as this little story is invented, in order to explain a quality of women, so also there are numerous stories in the Brāhmaṇas which are concerned with the origin of something or of some usage. Such legends of origins, to which also the legends of creation belong, are termed by the Indians as Purāṇas[2] as distinguished from the Itihāsas (or Ākhyānas) as the stories of gods and men are called. Further, among these stories there are some which have been simply invented by the Brāhmaṇa-theologians, whereas the others can be traced back to old and popular myths and legends or at least are based on tradition that is independent of the sacrificial science. Thus in the Brāhmaṇa the birth of the four castes is often narrated. Even in one of the philosophical hymns of the Ṛgveda, the Puruṣa-sūkta[3] is told, how the Brahmin is born out of the mouth, the warrior from the arms, the Vaiśya from the thighs and the Śūdra from the feet of the Puruṣa sacrificed by the gods. In the Brāhmaṇas it is Prajāpati who made the Brahmin together with the god Agni originate in his mouth, the warrior together with Indra originate in his breast and both arms, the Vaiśya and the universal gods originate in the centre of his body, but the Śūdra takes birth in his feet. Along with the Śūdra no deity was created; he is therefore unfit for sacrifice. As a consequence of this kind of creation, the Brahmin performs his work with the mouth, the warrior with the arms; the Vaiśya does not perish however much he may be 'consumed', i.e. exploited by priests and warriors, because he is created from the centre of the body, where the productive power lies; but of all religious ceremonies the Śūdra can perform only the feet-washing of the members of the higher castes, because he is born of the feet.[4] More appeal-

1. Śat. III : 2, 4, 2-6. Cf. also Śat. III : 2, 1, 19 ff.

2. Purāṇa means 'old', then 'old legend', 'old story', especially cosmogonical and cosmological myths. In later times one termed as Purāṇa a whole class of works about which we may have to speak in a later chapter.

3. X.90, 12. Cf. above p. 144 Deussen, *Allgemeine Geschichte der Philosophie* I, 1, p. 150 ff.

4. Taittirīya-Saṃhitā VII : 1, 1, 4-6. Tāṇḍya Brāhmaṇa VI : 1, 6-11 cf. Weber, *Indische Studien* X 7-10.

ing are the two ingenious stories of the creation of night and of the winged mountains which L. Von Schroeder[1] has picked out of the Maitrāyaṇi Saṃhitā:

"Yama had died. The gods tried to make Yamī[2] forget Yama. When they asked her, she said. "Only today he has died.' Then the gods said, "So indeed she will never forget him; we will create night!" At that time there was only day and no night. The gods created night; then day was born with morning; thereupon she forgot him. Therefore it is said: 'Day and night indeed make one forget suffering.' (Maitr. I, 5, 12.)

The oldest children of Prajāpati were the mountains and they had wings. They flew away and sat wherever they just wanted. But in those times the earth was still shaking up and down. Then Indra cut off the wings of the mountains and fixed them to the earth. The wings, however, became the storm-clouds; therefore these hover always towards mountains" (Maitr. I, 10, 13).[3]

Very many are in the Brāhmaṇas the creation legends. How metaphysical thinking unites here with playful explanations of sacrificial rules can be shown by an example. To the most important sacrifices belong the fire-sacrifice, (Agnihotra)[4] consisting in this that every morning and every evening a milk-offering is made to the fire. On the origin and significance of this sacrifice a Brāhmaṇa[5] expresses its view as follows:

"In the beginning there was only *Prajāpati* alone here. He thought to himself, 'How can I propagate myself?' He tortured himself, he mortified himself.[6] He produced Agni from his

1. *Indiens Literatur und Kunst*, p. 142.
2. Twin-sister of *Yama*, cf. above p. 97.
3. The legend of the winged mountains is already known to the reciters of the Ṛgveda and is also a popular theme of the later poets. cf. Pischel, *Vedische Studien* I, 174.
4. See above p. 160.
5. Śat. II, 2, 4.
6. Almost all creation legends begin in the same way. As the magician for his feats of magic and the priest for the sacrifice must prepare themselves by self-torture and mortification, so also Prajāpati must prepare himself in the same manner for the great work of creation. From the root 'śram',

mouth. And because he produced him from his mouth, Agni is a consumer of food. And truly he who knows that Agni is consumer of food, becomes himself a consumer of food. Of the gods he thus produced him at first (agre) and therefore he is called Agni, for the name Agni is called actually Agri.[1] Now Prajāpati thought for himself, 'This Agni, I have produced him as a food-consumer for me. But here there is no other food than I myself, — let him not eat up me myself!' In those days this earth was evidently quite barren; there were neither plants nor trees. Prajāpati was worried about this. Now Agni turned to him with open (mouth) and from Prajāpati disappeared his own greatness because he feared. His own greatness, but that was his speech, and this speech of his left him." (It is then said further, that Prajāpati desires for himself an offering and obtains an offering of butter or milk by rubbing his hands, whereupon plants are born. As a result of a second offering of butter or milk the Sūrya, the Sun and Vāyu the wind are born). "And by making an offering Prajāpati propagated himself on the one hand and on the other hand he also saved himself from Agni, the death, as this Agni was about to consume him. And he who, knowing this, performs fire-sacrifice, that one propagates himself on the one hand through his descendants and on the other hand saves himself from death when he is about to consume him. And when he dies, when he is laid on fire, he is born again from fire, the fire consumes only his body.[2] And as though he were born of his father and his mother, just in the same way is he born

---

'to exert oneself' 'to torture oneself' is the later word Śramaṇa, 'the ascetic' derived, which occurs often especially in the Buddhist literature. The word 'tapas' means actually "heat", and then the heating for the purpose of asceticism and then the asceticism itself. 'Indeed even if the most varied forms of mortification are understood by the term '*tapas*' yet in the olden days in particular the special reference was to heat as the vehicle of mortification". Cf. the excellent expositions on the tapas by Oldenberg, (Religion of the Veda) — *Religion des Veda* p. 402 ff. According to the Śat. X. 4, 4, 1 f. Prajāpati once mortified himself a thousand years, until as a result of the 'heat' of the mortification, lights shot out of his pores, — stars evolved from them.

1. cf. above p. 190.

2. One of the few texts in the Brāhmaṇas where there is talk of life after death.

of fire. But whoever does not perform the fire-sacrifice, does not arise to new life again. Therefore one must perform the fire sacrifice without fail. " (Then it is narrated at great length how the gods Agni, Vāyu and Sūrya themselves who have been produced by Prajāpati again perform sacrifices and how the cow was created.) "But Agni desired this cow while he thought, "I would like to mate with her. He united with her and poured his semen into her. This became then milk. Therefore it is boiled whereas the cow itself is raw, because milk is Agni's semen; and therefore it is also that milk, whether in a black or red cow, is always white and shining like fire, as it is Agni's semen. And therefore it is also warm even while milking, for it is Agni's semen."[1]

Just as these creation-legends begin thus, that Prajāpati "tortures and mortifies himself", we read also often, that after creation was completed, he was tired, exhausted and weary, whereupon some sacrifice is then described, by which he had to be strengthened anew. Once it is the gods who make this sacrifice, another time Agni does this favour to Prajāpati alone and on another occasion he regains his strength by creating the sacrificial animals and sacrificing them.[2]—"after he has sung the hymns and exerted himself." It is indeed peculiar that this world-creator Prajāpati, who is actually the greatest god in the Brāhmaṇas has got nothing noble about himself and often plays a rather wretched role. He is himself even offered as sacrificial offering by the gods ![3] In an oftquoted legend he is accused of incest with his daughter Dyaus (heaven) or Uṣas (dawn). In order to punish him for this sin, the gods created, from their most terrifying forms, the god Rudra. This Rudra with his arrow pierced through Prajāpati and thus were born Orion and other constellations.[4] It is also very important to note that in the Brāhmaṇas (and in the Veda in general) there is not a single story of creation, which — like the Biblical story in Europe — would more or less be accepted throughout

1. Cf. above p. 58.
2. Sat. IV, 6, 4, 1 VII, 4, 1, 16 and more often VI, 1, 2,-12 ff.-III, 9, 1.
3. Śat. X, 2, 2.
4. Aitareya Brāhmaṇa III, 33. cf. Śat. I, 7, 4, 1. II, 1, 2, 8 VI, 1, 3, 8.

India, but we have a large number of stories of creation which contain most diverse notions and speculations, which are not comparable with one another. Thus we find for instance in the Śatapatha-Brāhmaṇa, shortly after the above-mentioned legend an entirely different story of creation. Prajāpati, it is said here also,[1] tortured and mortified himself in order to create beings. He produced creatures, at first the birds, then the small reptiles, then the snakes — but hardly were they produced when they all again disappeared, and Prajāpati was again alone. He cogitated keenly over this as to how it happened and at last it occurred to him that the creatures died for want of food. Then he created new beings, from whose breasts he made milk to spring out and these remained alive. At some other place in the same work[2] we find that Prajāpati creates the animals out of his own organs of life as follows — the human beings from his mind, the horse out of his eye, the cow out of his breath, the sheep out of his ear, the goat out of his voice. As man is created from Prajāpati's mind and as the mind is the first of the living organs, therefore man is, the first and strongest of all animals.[3]

In a majority of the legends however is Prajāpati the only creator, from whom the world and the beings are born. But even in the Brāhmaṇas there are texts where Prajāpati himself is considered as created and the creation begins with the primeval water or with the non-being or with the Brahman. Thus the story of creation goes. (Śat. XI, I, 6.) :—

"In the beginning there was nothing but water here, a sea of water. These waters desired to propagate themselves. They tortured themselves, they mortified themselves. And as they had mortified themselves[4] a golden egg was born in them.

1. Śat. II, 5, 1, 1-3.
2. Śat. VII, 5, 2, 6.
3. Here the sacrificial animals are meant in particular.
4. As the expression Tapas means not only mortification but also heat, it is possible that when we hear "as they mortified themselves" which also can mean "as they got heated" we think of the hatching heat and it is quite possible that there is an intentional ambiguity in the Sanskrit words. cf. above p. 81 and 203. Deussen, *Allgemeine Geschichte der Philosophie* I, 1, p. 182, 2, p. 60 ff.

There was no year then as yet; but this golden egg was swimming about so long as a year lasts. After a year a man was born out of it, that was Prajāpati. Therefore a woman or a cow or a mare bears within a year; because Prajāpati was born after one year. He broke the golden egg open. At that time there was no fixed place. So this egg which bore him was swimming about for the duration of one year. After one year he tried to speak and he spoke: "bhūḥ", and this (word) became the earth here; (he spoke): "bhuvaḥ", and this (word) became the atmosphere, then "suvar"[1] and this became the heaven there. Therefore a child tries to speak after one year because Prajāpati spoke after one year. When Prajāpati spoke first he spoke mono and by-syllabic words. Those (three words) form five syllables. Out of these he made the five seasons, — thus there are five seasons here.[2] This Prajāpati got up on the worlds thus created after one year; therefore a child tries to stand after one year, because Prajāpati stood up after one year. He was born with a life of a thousand years. As one sees the other bank of a river, from a distance, he saw the other bank of his life.[3] And singing the glory and torturing himself he lived thus until he desired to propagate himself. He placed the power of reproduction in himself and with his mouth he created the gods. . . . After he had created them it was as bright as day (diva) to him and that is the godhood of the gods (deva) so that after he had created them it was for him, as bright as day. Now with the breath that is below he created the Asuras (demons). ... And after they had been created, it was dark for him. He knew 'Indeed, I have brought disaster to me myself, as it is dark for me after they have been created'. And even then he struck them with disaster, and it was all up with them. Therefore it is said, 'It is not true, what is said partly in the tales (Anvākhyāna) and partly in legends (Itihāsas) about the battles between gods and asuras,[4] for even then it was all up with them'. ... What was bright like the day for him as he created the gods out of it he made

1. cf. above p. 173 on the 3 holy words bhūḥ, bhuvaḥ, suvar (or svar).
2. namely : spring, summer, rainy season, autumn and winter.
3. Because Prajāpati is born, he must be also mortal.
4. With this all the other numerous legends of the Brāhmaṇas that speak about the battles between gods and asuras are declared as lies.

the day; and what was dark like the night for him as he created the Asuras, out of it he made the night. Thus there were now day and night". (Śat. XI: 1, 6, 1-11.)

Still more peculiar, certainly also more unclear is another creation-legend (Śat. VI: 1, 1) which begins with the words: "In the beginning there was only the non-being (Asat) here." But it is added that this non-being were actually the Ṛṣis, for these produced everything by their self-torture and mortification. These Ṛṣis were however the Prāṇas or Life-spirits, and they created — how they go about it is not at all clear — first seven Puruṣas or "human beings" and united them into a single Puruṣa, the Prajāpati.

"This *Puruṣa* (human being) desired to multiply himself, to propagate himself. He tortured himself, he mortified himself. After he tortured and mortified himself he created first the Brahman, i.e. the threefold knowledge (trayī vidyā). This was the basis for him. Therefore it is said, 'Brahman is the basis for all'. Therefore one stands firm when one has learnt the Vedas; for this the Brāhmaṇa (i.e. the Veda) is the basis."

Then it is further narrated, how Prajāpati, standing firmly on this basis, "mortified himself and then only created water". With the help of the Veda he produced an egg; from the egg was born fire and the egg-shell became the earth etc. It is a very verbose and confusing report. But it is important to see that the Brahman, meaning prayer or magic-charm originally, later sacred knowledge or Veda, is made here already to be the foundation of all being. From here it was only one step to the theory of the Brāhmaṇa himself as a creative principle. This theory also is already found in the Śatapatha-Brāhmaṇas (XI: 2, 3, 1), where it is said:

"In the beginning there was only the Brahman here. He created the gods, and after he created the gods, he gave them these worlds as abodes[1] that is, this earthly world here to Agni, the atmosphere to Vāyu and the sky to Sūrya."

Thus we see how in the Brāhmaṇas — and here lies their great significance for the History of the Indian thinking —

1. Literally: "made them mount these worlds."

already all those ideas are prepared which have reached their full development only in the Āraṇyakas and the Upaniṣads, as proclaimed by Śāṇḍilya already in the Śatapatha Brāhmaṇa.[1]

Āraṇyakas and Upaniṣads

When R. Garbe[2] terms the sacrificial science of the Brāhmaṇas as "the only literary evidence of these intellectually poor centuries prior to the awakening of philosophical speculation" he gives thereby expression to a generally prevalent, but in my view, erroneous opinion. It would be terrible to think that in the case of Indians who must have been such a talented people as has been testified even by the Ṛgveda hymns, the futile musings on the sense and purpose of sacrificial ceremonies should have filled even the entire thinking of the priests, not to speak of the warriors and the other classes of people. In reality we find in the Brāhmaṇas themselves clearly, as Sāyaṇa has already stressed, and as we ourselves have seen above, in addition to the rules for the rituals (kalpa) and their explanations, also the tales and legends (itihāsa), cosmogonic myths (purāṇa), epic poetry — stanzas and songs in praise of heroes (Nārāśaṃsi).[3] In other words, the beginnings of epic poetry go as far back as to the time of the Brāhmaṇas. Of course the great and expensive sacrifices treated in the Brāhmaṇas were possible only in the circumstances in which an active and busy people lived; and it is unthinkable that the warriors and the merchants, the peasants and the cattle-owners, the artisans and the workers of those times did not sing any songs and did not tell any tales. But that which was sung and told in those days (for example, the legend of Śunaḥśepa) is partly contained in the Vedic texts themselves, much of it however is contained in the later epics and purāṇas. The Brāhmaṇas also presuppose the beginnings of

1. X. 6, 3 cf. p. 230 infra.
2. *Beiträge zur indischen Kulturgeschichte*, Berlin 1903, p. 6.
3. Max Müller : *History of Ancient Sanskrit Literature*, 2nd ed. London, 1860. p. 344 cf. Śat. XI 5, 6, 8, 7, 9. "Knowers of the Tales" (Ākhyānavidas) are called as a special class of literateurs in the Sāṅkhyāyana-Śrauta-sūtra *Indische Studien*. II. s. p. 313.

grammar, phonetics, astronomy, that is of those sciences which later on were pursued more independently.[1] But even the "Awakening of the philosophical speculations" is not posterior to the time of the Brāhmaṇas, but anterior to this. We have already seen how in some hymns of the Ṛgveda doubt and concern are expressed with respect to the popular belief in gods and the priestly cult. These sceptics and thinkers, these first philosophers of ancient India certainly did not remain isolated. That they also "established a school", that their teachings also spread is proved clearly by the "philosophical hymns of the Atharvaveda and the individual pieces of the Yajurveda-Saṃhitā in which of course the teachings of the philosophers often occur only in a mutilated form.[2] But these mutilated forms themselves prove that philosophical speculation was continued to be fostered even during those centuries during which the sacrificial science of the Brāhmaṇas prospered.

Of course it is not probable that these oldest philosophers of ancient India belonged to the priestly class. For, their teachings, which were against the plurality of the gods, were in open conflict with the interests of the life of the priests. We cannot easily imagine that the Brāhmaṇas who lived on sacrifices had among themselves people who were most hated by the priests among the "greedy ones" who believed in nothing, i.e. those who offered no sacrifices and gave no gifts to the priests.

That the warrior-caste was not far from the intellectual life and the literary activity of the ancient times is borne out by numerous texts of the Upaniṣads and also of the Brāhmaṇas. In the Kauṣītakī-Brāhmaṇa (XXVI, 5) a king has a talk with the priests on the subject of the sacrificial science. And in the XI book of the Śatapatha-Brāhmaṇa there is repeated mention of the king *Janaka* of *Videha*, who, by virtue of his knowledge puts all priests to shame. Especially instructive is the text where Janaka asks the priests Śvetaketu, Somaśuṣma and Yājñavalkya as to how

1. On the beginning of the Vedāṅgas in the Brāhmaṇas cf. Max Müller, *History of Ancient Sanskrit Literature* p. 110 ff.

2. cf. above p. 83 ff, 123 ff, 153 f.

to perform the fire-sacrifice (Agnihotra). None gives a satisfactory reply. But Yājñavalkya obtains a gift of a hundred cows because he has investigated most the meaning and purpose of sacrifice, although, as King Janaka remarks, even to him the meaning and purpose of Agnihotra is not clear. After the king has gone away, the priests say to one another; "Indeed this warrior has put us to shame by his speech. Well, we will challenge him to a theological debate (Brahmodya). But Yājñavalkya advises them against that, saying, "we are Brahmins, but he is only a warrior. If we defeat him, whom, shall we say, have we defeated ? If however he should defeat us, then people would say of us, 'A warrior has defeated the Brahmins', so don't think of that !" The other two priests agreed with him; Yājñavalkya however goes to King Janaka and learns from him[1] — Also Ayasthūṇa, the sacrifice-organiser who teaches his priests[2] is hardly a Brahmin, although Sāyaṇa declares him to be a ṛṣi. The ṛṣis or authors of the hymns of the Ṛgveda were according to tradition not always members of the priestly caste. Thus it is said of a ṛṣi Kavaṣa, that he was a non-Brahmin, the son of a slave. As he wanted to take part in a big sacrifice the priests drove him away, in order that he might die of hunger and thirst. The waters and the goddess Sarasvatī take care of him kindly and he "sees" a hymn, whereupon the priests recognize him as a ṛṣi and admit him again to their midst.[3]

In the Upaniṣads, however, we find not only kings but also women and even people of low birth who take active part in the philosophical efforts and are often in possession of the highest knowledge. Thus in the Bṛhadāraṇyka Upaniṣad Gārgī, the daughter of Vacaknu interrogates Yājñavalkya on the prime cause of all being so long that the latter says, "Don't ask too much, Gārgi ! so that your head may not burst. Indeed about godhood one must not put too many questions. You ask too much, Gārgi — do not ask too much.' And at another place the same Gārgī opposes the famous teacher Yājñavalkya in the midst of an assembly with the words: "I rise against you,

1. Śat. XI. 6, 2 cf. XI. 3, 1, 2-4. XI. 6, 3.
2. Śat. XI. 4, 2, 17-20.
3. Aitareya-Brāhmaṇa II, 19.

Yājñavalkya! Like a hero's son from Banaras or Videha who makes the slackened bow taut with the string and two sharply piercing arrows in his hand, just like that I rise against you with two questions — you reply to me! "In the same Upaniṣad Yājñavalkya enlightens his wife Maitreyī on the highest knowledge of the Ātman.[1] How little this highest knowledge was a privilege of the Brahmins is proved by the interesting story of Raikva with the go-cart,[2] who sits under his cart and scratches at his leprous wounds, but possessing the highest wisdom, is proud like a king. The rich donor Jānaśruti approaches him humbly in order to be taught by him. Raikva calls him a Śūdra[3] and laughs over the presents that the rich man offers him. Only when he offers him his daughter in marriage does he condescend to teach him.[4] Charmingly naive is also the following story:

"Satyakāma Jābāla spoke to his mother Jabālā, 'I want to enter as a Brahmin pupil, O respected mother! Tell me, of which family I am.' She spoke to him: "That I do not know, my son, of which family you are; in my youth I wandered very much as a servant; then I got you; I do not know it myself, of which family you are; my name is Jābāla and your name is Satyakāma; So I name you (instead of after your father) Satyakāma, son of Jābalā." Then he went to Haridrumata, the Gautami and said: "I would like to be admitted as Brahmacārin by your Reverence. Revered Sir, admit me." He said to him, "Of which family are you, my dear?" — He said, "That I do not know, respected master, of which family I am, I have asked my mother and she has replied, 'in my youth I wandered very much as a servant, then I got you; I do not know myself of which family you are; my name is Jabālā and your name is Satyakāma.' So I call myself Satyakāma, the son of Jabālā, O master!" — He spoke to him, "Only a Brahman can speak so plainly. Fetch the firewood (that is required for the ceremony),

1. Bṛhadāraṇyaka Upaniṣad II, 6; III, 8; II, 4 and IV, 5.

2. Raikva is called a "Brāhmaṇa" in the sense of "one who knows the Brahman", not in the sense of "a member of the priestly class."

3. The word is here used as a term of abuse.

4. Chāndogya-Upaniṣad, IV, 1-3.

my dear; I will admit you, for you have not gone away from the path of Truth."[1]

This text shows what little importance was given in those ancient times to Brahminical origin whereas later on—in the law books—it is again and again stressed that only the Brahmin may teach and only a member of the three highest castes may be taught the Veda. In the Upaniṣads we are told repeatedly the kings or warriors are in possession of the highest knowledge and that Brahmins go to learn from them. Thus the Brahmin Gautama, Śvetaketu's father, goes to King Pravāhaṇa, in order to be taught by him, about the other world. And it is said that the king felt very embarrassed by Gautama's demand. For, what he had to teach had not been accessible to the Brahmins ever before, "and that is exactly why in all the worlds the warrior-caste is ruling." At last however the king teaches him,—and of course this is the doctrine of the transmigration of the soul, which, appearing for the first time, clearly proves to be a doctrine initially foreign to the Brāhmanic theology, born out of the warrior caste.[2] That the chief doctrine of the Upaniṣads the doctrine of the Ātman, the only one, is born of non-Brahminical castes, is proved by another text, where five highly learned Brahmins go to the wise Uddāla Āruni in order to learn from him the doctrine of the Ātman. He reflects in himself, "These great men and great scholars will question me and I will not be able to reply to all their questions. Well, I will direct them to another one." And he directs them to King Aśvapati Kaikeya, to whom they go for learning.[3]

---

1. Chāndogya Upaniṣad IV, 4. translated by Max Müller, *SBE,* Vol. I, p. 60. In the Vaṃśas or teachers' lists of the Śatapatha Brāhmaṇa numerous teachers are named after their mothers. Cf. above p. 162.

Note. Satyakāma means 'truth-loving'. The passage has also been translated into German and explained by H. Lüders, *SBA.*, 1922, pp. 227 ff.

2. Chāndogya-Upaniṣad. V, 3. Bṛhadāraṇyaka Upaniṣad VI, 2. In the Kauṣitakī-Upaniṣad I, 1 the Kṣatriya Citra teaches the 'first of the priests' Āruṇi about the Other World.

3. Chāndogya-Upaniṣad V, 11 ff, (One version of this story is found already in Śat. X, 6, 1. Cf. Deussen, *System des Vedanta* , (Leipzig, 1883), p. 18 f. *Allgemeine Geschichte der Philosophie* I, 1, p. 166. I, 2, p. 17 ff. R. Garbe, *Beiträge zur indischen Kulturgeschichte* (Berlin, 1903), p. 1 ff.; *Die Weisheit des Brahmanen oder des Kriegers* ?

Thus even while the Brahmins were indulging in their futile sacrificial science, other circles were concerning themselves with such most important questions, which have been treated in such an admirable way in the Upaniṣads. From these circles far from the priestly caste, were born the hermits and wandering ascetics who not only renounced the world and its pleasures but also did not associate themselves with the sacrifices and ceremonies of the Brahmins. From the same circles were then formed several sects which were more or less antagonistic to Brahminism, of which that of the Buddhists attained such a great significance. That these sects, particularly Buddhism were so widely spread, shows however on how fertile a soil the teachings of the ancient philosophers must have fallen and how much resonance the teaching opposed to the sacrificial system must have found among the common folk.

We should not, however, presume that the Brahmins took no part in philosophical speculations; for warriors and members of the higher castes in general were educated in the Brahmins' schools, and there must have been a brisk exchange of philosophical ideas between the Brahmins and the other educated classes at all times.[1] Moreover, not every Brahmin

1. Cf. A. Hillebrandt, *Aus Brahmanas und Upanisaden*, pp. 10 ff., with whom I quite agree when he says that the philosophy of the Upaniṣads should be called neither a "Brahmanical" nor a "Kṣatriya philosophy". But it should not be doubted that non-Brahmins, especially Kṣatriyas, had a considerable share in the spiritual and intellectual life of ancient India. See P. Deussen, *System des Vedanta*, Leipzig, 1883, pp. 18 f., *AGPh.* I, 1, 166, 1, 2, 17 ff.; R. Garbe, *Beiträge zur Indischen Kulturgeschichte*, Berlin, 1903, pp. 1 ff.; R. Pick, *The Social Organisation in North-East India in Buddha's Time,* transl. by S. Maitra, Calcutta, 1920, pp. 90 ff. The view that the Kṣatriyas had an essential share in the development of the Upaniṣad ideas, has been contested by H. Oldenberg, *Die Lehre der Upanisaden und die Anfänge des Buddhismus*, Göttingen, 1915, pp. 166 f.; P. Oltramare, *L'histoire des idées théosophiques dans l'Inde*, 1, 96 f.; A B. Keith, *Aitareya Āraṇyaka*, p. 50 and *JRAS*, 1915, p. 550; also by S. Dasgupta, *A History of Indian Philosophy,* I, Cambridge, 1922, pp. 33 ff., though he admits (p. 31) "that among the Kṣatriyas in general there existed earnest philosophic enquiries which must be regarded as having exerted an important influence in the formation of the Upaniṣad doctrines." The fact is that the ancient Upaniṣads as literary compositions were arranged in the Brahmanic schools and were "Brahmanical" in this sense. But it does not follow from this that all or even the most essential *ideas* contained in these

was a priest or an adept in the art of the sacrifice. There were Brahmins, both rich and poor, who pursued worldly professions,[1] and there must have been many of these who sympathised with the sceptics and the exponents of new doctrines. Lastly, as has so often been the case in the history of Indian thought, the Brahmins had the knack of bringing into line with their own priestly wisdom and orthodoxy even such ideas as were in opposition to them. They succeeded in doing this by means of the doctrine of the four Āśramas (stages of life), whereby the ascetic and hermit life was made an essential part of the brahmanical religious system. This doctrine consists of the principle that every "Aryan", i.e., every man belonging to one of the three highest castes, who wishes to lead an ideal life, must pass through four stages of life. First, as a pupil (Brahmacārin), he must live with a tẹacher and learn the Veda; when his period of training is accomplished, he must found a household, and as a house-holder (Gṛhastha) beget children and offer the prescribed sacrifices to the gods or cause such sacrifices to be offered. When ripe old age approaches however, he may leave his house and as a forest-dweller (vānaprastha) he may now perform sacrificial service only in a limited manner, but to that extent meditate on the mystic and symbolic significance of sacrifice. But only when he feels his end approach shall he give up even this sacrifice and meditations, renounce all action-based piety and as a recluse ascetic (Saṃyāṣin) meditate only on Brahman, the highest world-principle and strive for union with the same.[2]

With this doctrine of the Brahminic ideal in life are also connected the chapters of the Brāhmaṇas which as Āraṇyakas or

---

texts were first *conceived* in priestly circles. It is worth mentioning that even the Āpastambīya-Dharmasūtra (II, 2, 4, 25) permits a Brahmin to learn under a Kṣatriya or a Vaiśya teacher "in time of need" (āpadi).

1. Cf. Oldenberg, *Die Lehre der Upanishadẹn*, etc., p. 5.

2. In the oldest Upaniṣads (Chāndogya-Up. II, 23; VIII, 1) three branches of an ideal life are spoken of, but there is no mention yet of three or four successive stages of life. Only in later Upaniṣads (Maitr. IV, 3; Āśrama-Up). in the Mahābhārata and in the Dharmaśāstras the Āśrama theory is fully developed. See Deussen, *Sechzig Upaniṣads* pp. 96 f.; *ERE.*, II, 128 ff.; and Jacobi, *ERE.*, II, 802.

"forest-books" i.e. texts to be studied by hermits (Vānaprasthas) in the forest, were separate from the other texts to be studied in the Brahminic schools and were partly even added to them.[1] The main contents of these Āraṇyakas are no longer the rules on the performance of sacrifices and the explanation of ceremonies but the sacrificial mysticism, sacrificial symbolism and the priestly philosophy. With this priestly philosophy which we can pursue in the Brāhmaṇas and the Āraṇyakas belonging to them and which raised partly the sacrifice and partly the holy word (Brahma) inseparably united with it to the highest principle and made it the origin of all being, the doctrine of the inner-self (Ātman) as that of the only being, which doctrine was born outside the priestly circles and which actually runs contrary to the priestly religion was amalgamated. The result of this unnatural and violent amalgamation are the Upaniṣads. The doctrine of the four stages of life it was also, however, which enabled these Upaniṣads to be made a constituent of the Veda. We find the oldest Upaniṣads evidently partly embedded the Āraṇyakas, partly appended to them, as those texts which shall be studied by the ascetics (Saṃnyāsins) who are in the last Āśrama. They constituted in more than one sense the Vedānta, i.e. "the end of the Veda."[2] Firstly, most of these texts are of later origin and synchronise with the end of the Vedic period. Further we must never forget that this whole Vedic literature

1. Thus it is said in the Āruṇeya Upaniṣad 2 (Deussen : *Sixty Upaniṣads of the Veda*, p. 693), that the forest-hermit shall recite of all the Vedas only the *Āraṇyaka* and the *Upaniṣad*. Also Rāmānuja (*SBE* Vol. 48 p. 645) explains the mention of the sacrificial ceremonies in the Āraṇyaka — like beginnings of the Upaniṣads by saying that they had to be studied in the forest. Cf. also Max Müller : *History of Ancient Sanskrit Literature*, p. 313 ff. According to H. Oldenberg (*Die Hymnen des Rigveda*, I, Berlin 1888, p. 291) the Āraṇyakas were called so certainly because they were communicated "in the forest instead of in the village on account of their highly mystical sacredness." It is possible that even the teaching of these texts took place in the forest. (which may perhaps be deduced from the Sāṅkhyāyana Gṛhyasūtra II, 12, 11 ff). Manu, VI, 29, says that the hermit should learn "the Upaniṣad texts" (aupaniṣadīḥ śrutīḥ). Strict rules of austerity are prescribed at the reading of the Upaniṣads, see Baudhāyana-Dharmasūtra, II, 10, 18, 15 ff.

2. "Vedānta" means originally only the Upaniṣads. Only later was the word used for the system of philosophy based on the Upaniṣads.

did not consist of written books but was only handed down orally. What we find in the individual Brāhmaṇas and usually call "works" or "books" is therefore nothing but the subject-matter taught by different schools of priests. This subject-matter was taught to the pupils within a certain period of time. And this period comprised a number of years during which the pupil had to live with the teacher and serve him. It was natural that the teaching of what was most difficult to understand—i.e. the mysteries, the mystic and philosophic teachings as they are contained in the Āraṇyakas and Upaniṣads—took place at the end of this course. Also while reciting the Veda as a holy act and religious duty these texts constituted the end. At last the later philosophers saw in the teachings of the Upaniṣads not the end but the aim of the Veda.[1]

As Vedānta or "veda-end" the Āraṇyakas as well as the older Upaniṣads belong to various Vedic schools; indeed they actually form only constituents of the Brāhmaṇas. Thus Aitareya-Brāhmaṇa belonging to the Ṛgveda is followed by an Aitareya-Āraṇyaka in which the Aitareya-Upaniṣad is included. Similarly Kauṣītakī-Brāhmaṇa belonging to the Ṛgveda ends with the Kauṣītakī-Āraṇyaka, of which the Kauṣītakī-Upaniṣad[2] forms only a part. In the Black-Yajurveda the Taittirīya-Āraṇyaka[3] is only a continuation of the Taittirīya-Brāhmaṇa, and the conclusion of the Āraṇyaka is formed by the Taittirīya-Upaniṣad and the Mahā-Nārāyaṇa-Upaniṣad. In the great Śatapatha-Brāhmaṇa of the White-Yajurveda, the first third of Book XIV is an Āraṇyaka, while the end of the book is formed by the greatest and most

---

1. Cf. P. Deussen : *System des Vedanta,* p. 3 f. *Allgemeine Geschichte der Philosophie.* I, 2, p. 5.

2. The Aitareya-Āraṇyaka has been published and translated into English by A. B. Keith (*Anecdota Oxoniensia, Aryan Series,* Part IX, Oxford 1919) and as an appendix to it a portion of the Sāṅkhyāyana-Āraṇyaka (VII-XV). Adhyāyas I and II of this Āraṇyaka are published and translated by W. Friedlander, *Der mahāvrata Abschnitt des Cāṅkhāyana-Āraṇyaka,* Berlin 1900, Adhyāyas III to VI, by Cowell, Calcutta 1901. On the title, antiquity and contents of the Sāṅkhyāyana — or Kauṣitaki-Āraṇyaka, see Keith, *JRAS,* 1908, 363 ff. The Sāṅkhyāyana-Āraṇyaka with an Appendix on the Mahāvrata, (transl.) by A. B. Keith, *O.T.F.* London, 1908.

3. Ed. with Sāyaṇa's Comm. in Bibl. Ind. and in An. SS. No. 36.

important of all Upaniṣads, the Bṛhadāraṇyaka-Upaniṣad. The Chāndogya-Upaniṣad, the first section of which is nothing but an Āraṇyaka, belongs to a Brāhmaṇa of the Sāmaveda—probably the Tāṇḍya-Mahā-Brāhmaṇa[1] is an Āraṇyaka of the Jaiminīya- or Talavakāra-school of the Sāmaveda, and the Kena-Upaniṣad, also called Talavakāra-Upaniṣad, forms a part of it.

With the exception of the Mahā-Nārāyaṇa-Upaniṣad, which was only added to the Taittirīya-Āraṇyaka at a later period, all the above-mentioned Upaniṣads belong to the oldest works of this kind. In language and style they resemble the Brāhmaṇas, component parts of which they are, or to which they are immediately attached. It is the same simple, slightly clumsy prose, but—especially in the narrative portions—by no means lacking in beauty. Only half of the Kena-Upaniṣad is metrical, and it is the latest of the Upaniṣads enumerated. Although each one of the great Upaniṣads contains, as Deussen says,[2] "earlier and later texts side by side, hence the age of each individual piece must be determined separately," yet even the later portions of the above-mentioned Upaniṣads may claim great antiquity, if only on linguistic grounds.[3] We may take it that the greater Upaniṣads, like the Bṛhadāraṇyaka- and the Chāndogya-Upaniṣad, originated in the *fusion* of several longer or shorter texts which had originally been regarded as separate Upaniṣads. This would also explain the fact that the same texts are sometimes to be found in several Upaniṣads. The individual texts of which the greater Upaniṣads are composed, all belong to a period which cannot be very far removed from that of the Brāhmaṇas and the Āraṇyakas, and is before Buddha and before Pāṇini. For this reason the six above-mentioned Upaniṣads—Aitareya,

1. The Jaiminīya or Talavakāra Upaniṣad Brāhmaṇa, Text, Translation and Notes by Hanns Oertel, in *JAOS*, Vol. XVI, 1896.

2. *AGPh.*, 1, 2, p. 22.

3. On the language of the Upaniṣads see B. Liebich, Pāṇini, Leipzig, 1891, p. 62 ff; Otto Wecker, *Der Gebrauch der Kasus in der Upanisadliteratur*, Göttingen, 1905 (Bezz. Beitr.); W. Kirfel, *Beiträge zur Geschichte der Nominalkomposition in den Upanisads und im Epos*, Diss, Bonn, 1908; A. Furst, *Der Sprachgebrauch der alteren Upanisads verglichen mit dem der früheren vedischen Perioden und des klassischen Sanskrit*, Diss. (Tubingen), Göttingen, 1915; also Oldenberg, *Zur Geschichte der altindischen Prosa*, pp. 28 ff.

Bṛhadāraṇyaka, Chāndogya, Taittirīya, Kauṣītakī and Kena—undoubtedly represent the earliest stage of development in the literature of the Upaniṣads. They contain the so-called Vedānta doctrine in its pure, original form.

A few Upaniṣads which are written entirely or for the most part in *verse*, belong to a period which is somewhat later, though still early, and probably pre-Buddhistic. These, too, are assigned to certain Vedic schools, though they have not always come down to us as portions of an Āraṇyaka. In this category we may include the Kaṭha- or Kāṭhaka-Upaniṣad,[1] the very name of which points to its connection with a school of the Black-Yajurveda (see above p. 158). The Śvetāśvatara-Upaniṣad,[2] and the Mahā-Nārāyaṇa-Upaniṣad which has come down to us as an appendix to the Taittirīya-Āraṇyaka, are also counted among the texts of the Black-Yajurveda. The short, but most valuable Īśa-Upaniṣad[3] which forms the last section of the Vājasaneyī-Saṃhitā, belongs to the White-Yajurveda. The Muṇḍaka-Upaniṣad,[4] and the Praśna-Upaniṣad,[5] half of which is in prose, half in verse, belong to the Atharvaveda. Though these six Upaniṣads,

1. Edited with Śaṅkara's commentary by Śrīdhara-Śāstri Pāṭhaka, Poona, 1919; transl. by W. D. Whitney, *Transactions of the American Philological Association*, Vol. 21. On text-criticism see R. Fritsche, *ZDMG.*, 66, 1912, 727 f.; Hillebrandt, *ZDMG.*, 68, 1914, 579 ff.; and Hertel, *Die Weisheit der Upanishaden*, pp. 42 ff.

2. On this Up. see Weber, Ind. Stud. I, 420 ff. and R. G. Bhandarkar, *Vaiṣṇavism, Śaivism and Minor Religious Systems* (Grundriss III, 6, 1913), pp. 106 ff.

3. Transl. (with text) and analysis by Aurobindo Ghose, Calcutta (*Ideal and Progress Series*, No. 5). Metrical transl. by H. Baynes, *Ind. Ant.*, 26. 1897, 213 ff. On text criticism see Baynes, ibid, and Hertel, *Die Weisheit der Upanischaden*, pp. 25 ff.

4. J. Hertel (Muṇḍaka-Upaniṣad, *kritische Ausgabe*, Leipzig, 1924) has tried to restore the original text of this Upaniṣad. Its connection with the Atharvaveda (X, 7 and 8) has been pointed out by Hertel, ibid, pp. 45 ff. The title probably means, "the Upaniṣad of the bald-headed, "that is, of some sect of ascetics with shaven heads. Hertel (ibid pp. 64 ff.) suggests some connection between the Muṇḍ.-Up., and the Jainas.

5. In this Upaniṣad the sage Pippalāda, the founder of the Paippalāda school of the Atharvaveda, appears as teacher. On text criticism, see Hillebrandt, *ZDMG.*, 68, 1914, 581 f.

too, contain Vedânta the doctrine, we here find it interwoven to a great extent with Sâṃkhya and Yoga doctrines and with monotheistic views. We must, however, leave it to future scholars to decide to what degree the various philosophical doctrines mingled, and to what degree this mingling was consequent upon retouched versions of the text; for all these texts show distinct signs of having been touched up. There are for instance, as many as three separate recensions of the Mahâ-Nârâyaṇa-Upaniṣad, and this shows how uncertain the text is.[1]

The Maitrâyaṇîya-Upaniṣad,[2] which, by reason of its title, is attributed to a school of the Black Yajurveda,[3] belongs to a considerably later period which must have been post-Buddhistic. It is again written in prose, like the earliest Upaniṣads. This prose, however, no longer shows any Vedic traces. On the grounds of language, style and contents, we may place the work in the period of classical Sanskrit literature. The Mâṇḍûkya-Upaniṣad[4] of the Atharvaveda probably also belongs to

1. Cf. R. Zimmermann, *Die Quellen der Mahā-nārāyana-Upaniṣad und das Verhältnis der verschiedenen Rezensionen zueinander*, Diss., Berlin, 1913, and *Ind. Ant.*, 44, 1915, 130 ff., 177 ff.; Barth, *RHR.* 19, 1889, 150 f.=*Oeuvres*, II, 23. Edition by G. A. Jacob, *BSS* Nr. 35, 1888.

2. Other titles are : Maitrâyaṇa-Brâhmaṇa-Up., Maitrâyaṇa-Up., Maitrâyaṇîya-Up., and Maitrî. Up. See Max Müller, *SBE*, Vol. 15, pp. xliii ff. There are several recensions of the text. The text (ed., with the commentary of Râmatîrtha, by E. B. Cowell, 2nd. ed. revised by Satischandra Vidyâbhûṣan, *Bib. Ind.* 1913 ff.) which has hitherto been translated consists of 7 Prapâṭhakas. But the two last Prapâṭhakas (declared to be supplementary by Deussen, *Sechzig Upaniṣads*, p. 330) are missing in the edition of Mahâdeva Śâstri (*Sāmānya Vedānta Upaniṣads*, pp. 388 ff.), where Prap., IV, 5 corresponds to the 5th Prapâṭhaka of the older editions. A different work is the metrical Maitreya-Upaniṣad (*Minor Upaniṣads*, ed. Schrader, 1, pp. 105 ff.), which only in the prose introduction partly agrees with our Maitrây.-Up.

3. In some MSS. it is given as part of the Maitrâyaṇîya-Saṃhitâ.

4. On this Upaniṣad see H. Baynes, *Ind. Ant.*, 26, 1897, 169 ff. The Gauḍapâdîya-Kârikâ, one of the most important works of Indian Philosophy is based on the Mâṅḍ. Up. Pandit Vidhusekhara Bhattacharya (*Sir Asutosh Mukherjee Silver Jubilee Volume*, pp. 103 ff.) has proved that Śaṅkara is not the author of the commentary ascribed to him on this Up. The same learned Pandit thinks, and intends to prove, that the Mâṇḍûkya Up. is later than Gauḍapâda's Kârikâ, and was even unknown to Śaṅkara.

this same later period. Śaṅkara, who quotes the twelve Upaniṣads previously enumerated as sacred and authoritative texts in his commentary on the Brahmasūtras mentions neither the Maitrāyaṇīya- nor the Māṇḍūkya-Upaniṣad.[1]

Though the remaining Upaniṣads—and there are over 200 texts which have come down to us either independently as Upaniṣads or in larger collections—are also attributed by tradition to one or other of the Vedic schools, only a few of them have any real connection with the Veda. Most of them are religious rather than philosophical works, and contain the doctrines and views of schools of philosophers and religious sects of a much later period. Many of them are much more nearly related to the Purāṇas and Tantras chronologically as well as in content, than to the Veda. This latest Upaniṣad literature may be classified as follows, according to its purpose and contents : (1) those works which present Vedānta doctrines,[2] (2) those which teach Yoga,[3] (3) those which extol the ascetic life

1. Cf. Deussen, *System des Vedānta*, pp. 32 f., on the Upaniṣads quoted by Śaṅkara. As regards the chronological order of the fourteen Vedic Upaniṣads, absolute certainty cannot be obtained. Keith (*The Aitareya Āraṇyaka*, pp. 45 ff.) has tried to prove that the Aitareya-Upaniṣad is the oldest, dating back to about 700-600 B.C. Others consider the Bṛhadāraṇyaka-Up. to be the oldest. S. Radhakrishnan, *Indian Philosophy*, I, pp. 141 f., says "that the accepted dates for the early Upaniṣads are 1000 B.C. to 3000 B.C." By whom are these dates "accepted" ? Cf. Deussen in *Transactions of the 3rd International Congress for the History of Religion*, Oxford, 1908, II, pp. 19 ff.; Oldenberg, *Die Lehre der Upanishaden*, pp. 288 f., 341; Hillebrandt, *Aus Brahmanas und Upanisaden*, p. 170. Benimadhab Barua (*A History of Pre-Buddhistic Indian Philosophy*, Calcutta, 1921) has made a remarkable and creditable, though not always successful, attempt from the chronology of the literary works. But this designation of the philosophy of the Upaniṣads as "post-Vedic" (pp. 39 ff.) is very confusing.

2. *The Sāmānya Vedānta Upanisads* with the commentary of Upaniṣad-Brahma-Yogin, ed. by Pandit A. Mahadeva Sastri, Adyar Library (Theosophical Society), 1921.

3. *The Yoga Upaniṣads* with the Commentary of Upaniṣad-Brahma-Yogin, ed. by A. Mahadeva Sastri, Adyar, 1920. The Cūlikā-Up., and Amṛtanāda-Up. have been edited and translated into German by A. Weber, *Ind. Stud.*, 9, pp. 10 ff., 23 ff.

(saṃnyāsa),[1] (4) those which glorify Viṣṇu,[2] and (5) those which glorify Śiva as the highest divinity, and (6) Upaniṣads of the Śāktas and of other more insignificant sects.[3] These Upaniṣads are written partly in prose, partly in a mixture of prose and verse, and partly in epic Ślokas. Whilst the latter are on the same chronological level as the latest Purāṇas and Tantras, there are some works among the former which may be of greater antiquity, and which might consequently still be associated with the Veda. The following are probably examples of such earlier Upaniṣads : the Jābāla-Upaniṣad[4] which is quoted by Śaṅkara as an authority, and which closes with a beautiful description of the ascetic named Paramahaṃsa the Paramahaṃsa-Upaniṣad,[5] describing the path of the Paramahaṃsa still more vividly; the very extensive Subāla-Upaniṣad,[6] often quoted by Rāmānuja, and dealing with cosmology, physiology, psychology and metaphysics; the Garbha-Upaniṣad[7] part of which reads like

---

1. *The Minor Upaniṣads* critically edited by F. Otto Schrader, Vol. I : *Saṃnyāsa-Upaniṣads*. The Adyar Library, Madras, S. 1912. The Mṛtyulāṃgala Up. (ed. by A. C. Burnell, *Ind. Ant.*, 2, 1873, pp. 266 f.) is a purely Tantric work.

2. *The Vaishnava-Upaniṣads* with the Commentary of Upaniṣad-Brahma Yogin, ed. by A. Mahadeva Sastri, Adyar 1923. The Rāma-Tāpanīya-Upaniṣad, text and German translation by A. Weber, *ABA.*, 1864, pp. 271 ff.; the Nṛsiṁha-Tāpanīya-Up. by the same scholar, *Ind. Stud.*, 9, 53-173. On Nirālamba-Up. and Garuḍa-Up. see Weber, *Ind. Stud.*, 3, 324 ff.; 17, 136 ff., 161 ff.

3. Edition of the Śaiva and Śākta Upaniṣads by Pandit Mahadeva Sastri of the Adyar Library are in preparation. This classification of the non-Vedic Upaniṣads was first proposed by Deussen, *Sechzig Upaniṣads*, pp. 542 f. and then adopted by F. O. Schrader. *Minor Upaniṣads*, pp. ii-f. in an amplified form. It is useful for practical purposes, though not always strictly applicable. For some Upaniṣads teach *brahmavidyā* by means of Yoga, and might be classified as well with the Vedānta as with the Yoga Upaniṣads; and some Yoga Upaniṣads might as well be classified as Vaiṣṇava, etc.

4. Minor Upaniṣads, ed. F. O. Schrader, I, pp. 57 ff. Deussen, *Sechzig Upaniṣads*, pp. 706 ff.

5. *The Minor Upaniṣads*, I, pp. 43 ff.; Deussen, ibid, pp. 703 ff.

6. *Sāmānya Vedānta Upaniṣads*, ed. Mahadeva Sastri, pp. 460 ff.

7. *Sāmānya Vedānta Upaṇisads*, pp. 168 ff; Deussen, *Sechzig Upaniṣads*, pp. 605 ff.

a treatise on embryology, but which is obviously a meditation on the embryo with the aim of preventing rebirth in a new womb; and the Śaivite Atharvaśiras-Upaniṣad,[1] which is already mentioned in the Dharmasūtras[2] as a sacred text, and by virtue of which sins can be washed away. The Vajrasūcika-Upaniṣad,[3] which teaches that only he who knows the Brahman as the One without a second, is a Brahman, is not of very late origin. Another factor which makes it difficult to determine the date of these Upaniṣads is the fact that they are often to be found in various recensions of very uneven bulk.[4]

These non-Vedic Upaniṣads, as we may call them, have come down in large collections[5] which are not ancient as such.

---

1. Deussen, ibid. pp. 716 ff. See also Bhandarkar, *Vaiṣṇavism, Śaivism,* etc. pp. 111 f.

2. *Sāmānya Vedānta Upaniṣads,* p. 416 ff. In some MSS. this Upaniṣad is ascribed to Śaṅkara. One version of it, expanded into an attack on the caste system, is ascribed to the Buddhist poet Aśvaghoṣa. Cf. A. Weber, *ABA,* 1859, 259 ff.

3. Thus Deussen, *Sechzig Upaniṣads,* pp. 743 ff., translates a Mahā-Upaniṣad which is so short, that it does not deserve its name, the "Great Upaniṣad" at all, while in the South Indian recension (*Sāmānya Vedānta Upaniṣads,* pp. 234 ff.) it is indeed one of the longest Upaniṣads.

4. Gautama XIX, 12; Baudhāyana, III, 10, 10; Vasiṣṭha, XXII, 9; XXVIII, 14, Viṣṇu, 56, 22.

5. The collection translated into Persian in 1656, called *Oupnek'hat* (See above, p. 16) contains 50 Upaniṣads. An analysis of these Upaniṣads from Duperron's Latin translation has been given by A. Weber, *Ind. Stud.* Vols. 1,2 and 9. On a list of 52 Upaniṣads of the Atharvaveda, see Colebrooke, *Misc. Essays,* I, pp. 93 ff., and Bhandarkar, *Report,* 1883-84, pp. 24 f. For another list, see Weber, *HSS.,* Verz., p. 95. Editions : *Eleven Atharvana-Upaniṣads,* ed. by G. A. Jacob, BSS., Nr. 40, 1891. At the *NSP.,* Bombay, a collection of 108 Upaniṣads has been published in 1913, one of 112 Upaniṣads in 1917, one of 28 Upaniṣads in 1918, the eleven (principal) Upaniṣads (Ekādaśopaniṣadaḥ), with commentaries, by Swami Achintya Bhagawan, ib. 1910. The most important Upaniṣads have been edited, with Śaṅkara's commentaries, in the Bibl. Ind. and in *AnSS.* Nos. 5-17, 29-31, 62-64. Bṛhadāraṇyaka-Up. and Chāndogya-Up. have been critically edited and translated into German by O. Böhtlingk, St. Petersburg and Leipzig, 1889, the Kaṭha-, Aitareya-, and Praśna-Up. by the same scholar in *BSWG.,* 1890, and critical notes on these Upaniṣads by the same scholar in *BSWG.,* 1891. Kena-Up. with comm. ed. by Śrīdhara-śāstri Pāṭhaka, Poona, 1919. Translations : (*Twelve principal*) *Upaniṣads*

For the philosopher Śaṅkara (about 800 A.D.) still quotes the Upaniṣads as parts of the Veda texts to which they belong: and even Rāmānuja (about 1100 A.D.) speaks of the "Chandogas," the "Vājasaneyins" or the "Kauṣītakins" when quoting the Upaniṣads of the schools in question; the Subāla-Upaniṣad is the only one which he quotes by this title. In the Muktikā-Upaniṣad, which is certainly one of the latest, we read that salvation may be attained by the study of the 108 Upaniṣads, and a list of 108 Upaniṣads is set forth, classified according to the four Vedas: 10 Upaniṣads coming under the Ṛgveda, 19 under the White-Yajurveda, 32 under the Black-Yajurveda, 16 under the Sāmaveda and 31 under the Atharvaveda. This classification, however, can scarcely be based on an ancient tradition.[1] All these Upaniṣads which are, properly speaking non-Vedic, are generally called "Upaniṣads of the Atharvaveda." They were associated with the Atharvaveda, because the authority of this Veda as sacred tradition was always dubious and it was therefore no difficult matter to associate all kinds of apocryphal texts with the literature belonging to the Atharvaveda. Furthermore, the Atharvaveda, as we have seen, was above

---

translated by Max Müller, *SBE*, Vols. I and XV. *The Thirteen Principal Upaniṣads* translated by R. E. Hume, Oxford, 1921. *Sechzig Upanishads des Veda übersetzt von P. Deussen*, Leipzig, 1897. Selections in German translation by A. Hillebrandt, *Aus Brahmanas und Upanisaden*, Jena, 1921, and J. Hertel, *Die Weisheit der Upanısaden*, München, 1921. Translations of Īśa-, Kena-, and Muṇḍaka-, and of Kaṭha-, and Praśna-Up. with Śaṅkara's commentary by S. Sitaram Sastri, Madras, 1898; the Chāndogya-Up. with Śaṅkara's comm. translated by Ganganath Jha, Madras, 1899; Aitareya-Up. with Śaṅkara's Comm. transl. by H. M. Bhadkamkar, Bombay, 1899. Amṛtabindu and Kaivalya-Upaniṣads with Comm. transl. by A. Mahadeva Sastri; 2nd ed., Madras, 1921. The principal Upaniṣads with Madhva's commentary transl. by Rai Bahadur Srisa Chandra Vidyarnava, Īśa and Kena according to Śaṅkara by the same, and Śvetāśvatara transl. by Siddhesvari Prasad Varma Sastri appeared in the *Sacred Books of the Hindus*, Pāṇinī Office, Allahabad. A useful help for the study of the Upaniṣads is G. A. Jacob's *Concordance*, *BSS.*, 1891. A selected and classified bibliography of the Upaniṣads is given by R. E. Hume, ibid., p. 459 ff.

1. Rāmānuja quotes the Garbha-Up. and the Mantrika-(Cūlikā-) Up. as Atharvaveda-Upaniṣads, although the list in the Muktikā-Up. counts the one as belonging to the Black, and the other to the White Yajurveda.

all the Veda of magic and the secretiveness connected with it.[1] The real meaning of "Upaniṣad"—and this meaning has never been forgotten—was "secret doctrine." What was more natural than that a large class of works which were regarded as Upaniṣads or secret doctrines, should be joined to the Atharvaveda, which itself was indeed nothing but a collection of sercet doctrines !

The word "Upaniṣad" is, in fact, derived from the verb "upa-niṣad," "to sit down near some one," and it originally meant the sitting down of the pupil near the teacher for the purpose of a confidential communication, there a "confidential" or "secret session." Out of this idea of the "secret session," the meaning "*secret doctrine*" that which is communicated at such a confidential session—was developed.[2] The Indians generally give as a synonym of the word "upaniṣad" the word "*rahasyam,*" which means "mystery, secret." In the Upaniṣad texts themselves the expressions "*iti rahasyam*" and "iti Upaniṣad" are frequently used side by side in the sense of "thus says the secret doctrine." Often enough we find in the Upaniṣads themselves the warning against communicating some doctrine to an

1. See above, p. 139 f.

2. See Deussen, *AGPh.*, 1, 2, pp. 14 ff., who is right in rejecting Oldenberg's explanation of Upaniṣad (*ZDMG*, 50, 1896, 458 ff.; 54, 1900, 70 ff.; Die Lehre der Upanishaden, etc., pp. 36 f., 155 ff., 348 f.) as "a form of worship." Upaniṣad is used frequently enough as a synonym of rahasyam, but never synonymous with upāsanā. Besides E. Senart (Florilegium Melchior de Vogua, Paris, 1909, pp. 575 ff.) has shown that even the verb *upas* in the Upaniṣads does not mean "to worship", but "to have a profound knowledge, belief" ("connaisance, croyance") does not hit the meaning of the word as well as "secret doctrine." M. R. Bodas (*JBRAS.*, 22, pp. 69 f.) takes the original meaning of *upaniṣad* to be "sitting down near the sacrificial fire," as the conversations contained in the Upaniṣads are said to have taken place at the great sacrifices. This is not more probable than the explanation of J. V. Hauer (*Anfänge der Yoga-praxis*, p. 27), who gives "mysterious wisdom obtained by Tapas and meditation" as the original meaning of *upaniṣad*, connecting it with the quiet sitting as part of the Yoga practice. Nārāyaṇa in his commentary on Manu, VI, 29 defines upaniṣad as "that which is recited seated near, "i.e. (a text) which is recited (while the pupils are) seated near (the teacher)"; see Bühler, *SBE.*, Vol., 25, pp. 203 n. Cf also Macdonell and Keith, *Vedic Index*, I, pp. 91 f.

unworthy one. "This doctrine of Brahman," it is said for example,[1] "may a father impart to his eldest son or to a trusted pupil, but not to another, whoever he may be, even if the latter should give him the whole earth, surrounded by the waters and filled with treasures." Very frequently it is also related in the Upaniṣads how a teacher is entreated to communicate some knowledge or other, but only after repeated entreaty and urging of the pupil, gives way and reveals his doctrine to him.[2]

According to this original meaning of the word "Upaniṣad," the oldest Upaniṣads already contain very heterogeneous matters. An Upaniṣad was, above all, a "mystery," and every doctrine which was not intended for the masses, but was only communicated within a narrow circle of privileged persons—be it a profound philosophical doctrine or some futile symbolism or allegory, a symbolical sacrifice serving as magic, puzzled out by a Brahmin, or some would-be wisdom serving as a magic formula—was called Upaniṣad. All this we actually find already in the *old* Upaniṣads side by side and jumbled up, but particularly so in the so-called "Atharvaveda-Upaniṣads."[3]

Thus the Kauṣītakī-Upaniṣad contains, besides psychological

---

1. Chāndogya-Upaniṣad, III, 11,5 f. Cf. Deussen, ibid., pp. 12 f.

2. The word *upaniṣad* occurs in the Upaniṣads themselves in three senses; it means:—(1) "mystic sense," e.g., the secret significance of the syllable Om; (2) "secret word," certain expressions and formulas which are intelligible only to the initiated, as tajjalān, "in him growing, passing away, breathing," or satyasya satyam, "the truth of truth," as designation of the highest being; (3' "secret text," i.e., "esoteric doctrine" and "secret knowledge," cf. Deussen, ibid., pp. 16 f.

3. According to Āśvalāyana-Gṛhyasūtra, I, 13, 1, certain rites connected with conception, procreation of male children, etc., are taught in an "Upaniṣad". The charm in Rv. 1, 191 is called an "Upaniṣad" by Kātyāyana in his Sarvānukramaṇikā. In the manual of politics (Kauṭilya-Arthaśāstra, XIV) all kinds of magic rites of the purpose of arson, assassinations, blinding, etc., and in the manuals of erotics all sorts of secret prescription relating to sexual intercourse and to cosmetics are taught in an "Upaniṣadic chapter" (see Kauṭilya-Arthaśāstra, XIV; Vātsyāyana's Kāmasūtra, VII; and R. Schmidt, *Beiträge zur indischen Erotic,* Leipzig 1902, pp. 817 ff.). Rāmānuja (on Brahmasūtra II, 2, 43, see *SBE.*; Vol. 48, p. 528) calls the Pancarātraśāstra "a great Upaniṣad."

and metaphysical expositions and a detailed eschatology,[1] also descriptions of sacrificial rites, by which one can attain some good or other, or effect a love-charm, ceremonies for the prevention of the death of children, and even an "Upaniṣad," i.e., a secret doctrine, the knowledge of which serves as magic for the annihilation of enemies. Similarly the Chāndogya-Upaniṣad contains deep philosophical thoughts upon the creation, the universe and the soul, but among these also mystical speculations upon the syllable Om, secret rites for the healing of diseases and so on. In the Atharvaveda-Upaniṣads, indeed we find for instance a whole Upaniṣad—"the Garuḍa-Upaniṣad,"[2] —which is nothing but a snake charm that might just as well be included in the Atharvaveda-Saṃhitā.

This should be borne in mind when a "philosophy of the Upaniṣads" or even a "system of the Upaniṣads" is spoken of. A philosophy of the Upaniṣads exists only in so far as, in these collections of all sorts of mysteries, the teachings of the philosophers were also included. A system of the Upaniṣad philosophy can only be said to exist in a very restricted sense.[3] For it is not the thought of one single philosopher or of one uniform *school* of philosophers, that might be traced back to one single teacher, which are before us in the Upaniṣads, but it is the teachings of various men,[4] even of various periods, which are presented in the single sections of the Upaniṣads.

1. On this chapter of the Kauṣītakī-Up. compared with another version of it in the Jaiminīya-Brāhmaṇa, see E. Windisch, *BSGW.*, 1907, 111 ff.

2. Deussen, *Sechzig Upanishads des Veda*, pp. 627 f.

3. "That the Upaniṣads teach not one but various systems, must follow from the fact that they are compilations just as the Ṛgveda-Saṃhitā is," *R. G. Bhandarkar, Vaiṣṇavism, Śaivism*, etc., p. 1, Cf. G. Thibaut, *SBE*, Vol. 34, pp. ci ff.

4. How far the persons mentioned by name in the Upaniṣads, such as Yājñavalkya, Śāṇḍilya, Bālāki, Śvetaketu and others, were really the teachers of the doctrines ascribed to them (as Barua in his "Pre-Buddhistic Indian Philosophy" takes them to be), is not quite certain. Yājñavalkya is said to be the author of the Bṛhadāraṇyaka-Up., as of the whole White Yajurveda (see Bṛh.-Up., VI, 5, 3, and Yājñavalkya-Smṛti III, 110); but in the Bṛh-Up. itself other teachers also are mentioned. Besides, so many

There are, it is true, a few fundamental doctrines, which lend an appearance of uniformity to the philosophical thoughts which stand out in the genuine Upaniṣads, and it is only of these that we wish to speak here: with respect to these fundamental doctrines alone is it possible to speak (as Deussen does) —though always with reserve—of a "system of the Upaniṣads." We must therefore not seek deep wisdom in every chapter of the Upaniṣads, or expect a Platonic dialogue in every Upaniṣad. It is indeed remarkable enough that in the very oldest and most beautiful portions of the Upaniṣads we find the same form of the *dialogue* as in the works of the great Greek philosopher.[1] And just as Plato's dialogues reveal to us a wonderfully life-like picture of the life and doings of the Ancient Greeks, so the dialogues of the older Upaniṣads frequently afford us a surprising insight into the life at the ancient Indian princely courts, where priests and famous wandering teachers, including learned women, flocked together, in order to hold their disputations before the king, who not infrequently entered into the theological and philosophical conversations and confounded the learned Brahmins by his knowledge; as well as insight into the school-life of those ancient times, when travelling scholars undertook long journeys in order to "hear" some famous teacher, to whom pupils came from all sides "as waters precipitate themselves into the abyss and months sink into the year."[2] But besides sections of deep philosophical content, and portions which very well bear comparison with Plato's dialogues we also find in the Upaniṣads much that is inferior as philosophy or literature.

The Fundamental Doctrines of the Upaniṣads[3]

But the most precious in the Upaniṣads are those fundamental ideas, for whose sake we can speak of a "philosophy of the

---

different doctrines both ritual and metaphysical are ascribed to Yājñavalkya, that it seems difficult to credit him with all of them. On the other hand it is quite possible that Śāṇḍilya for instance was really the teacher of the famous doctrine ascribed to him.

1. On the dialogues of the Upaniṣads, cf. Oldenberg, *Die Lehre der Upanishaden*, pp. 160 ff.

2. Taittirīya-Upaniṣad, I, 3.

3. See A.E, Gough, *The Philosophy of the Upanishads*, London, 1882; P. Deussen, *The Philosophy of the Upanishads*. Authorised English Translation

Upaniṣads", above all the fundamental teachings which are found through all genuine Upaniṣads and which can be summarised in the sentence. "The universe is Brahman, but the Brahman is the Ātman," which would mean in our philosophical way of expression: "The world is God, and God is my soul."

The whole thinking of the upaniṣad-philosophers revolves round the two concepts Brahman and Ātman, and it is necessary to be clear about these concepts, in order to be able to understand the philosophy of the Upaniṣads. The etymology of the world Brahman[1] is doubtful. If we refer to the Petersburg Sanskrit dictionary, we find Brahman explained as "the devotion which appears as the craving and fulness of the soul and strives for the gods" while according to Deussen[2] the Brahman is supposed to be "the will of man striving upwards to that which is sacred and divine." These explanations may correspond to the Jewish-Christian ideas of divinity, they are diametrically opposite to the Indian view of the relation between the gods

---

by A. S. Geden, Edinburgh, 1919 (from *AGPh.*, I, 2); G. Thibaut, *SBE*, Vol. 34, pp. cxv ff.; P. Oltramare, *L'histoire des idées théosophiques dans l'Inde*, t. I, Paris, 1906, pp. 63 ff.; H. Jacobi, *ERE.*, II, p. 801; H. Oldenberg, *Die Lehre der Upanishaden und die Anfänge des Buddhismus*, Göttingen 1915; B. Barua, *A History of Pre-Buddhistic Indian Philosophy*, Calcutta, 1921; R. E. Hume, *The Thirteen Principal Upanishads*, Introduction; S. Dasgupta, *A History of Indian Philosophy*, I, Cambridge, 1922, pp. 28 ff.; S. Radhakrishnan, *Indian Philosophy*, I, London, 1923, pp. 137 ff.

1. The most probable etymology is that suggested by H. Osthoff (*Bezz. Bettr.*, 24, 1899, 113 ff.) who connects brahman with Old Irish *bricht*, "magic, magic formula." Oldenburg (Lehre der Upanishaden, pp. 44 ff., and "Zur Geschichte des Worts *brahman*," *NGGW.*, 1916, pp. 715 ff.) and Hillebrandt (*ERE*, 11, pp. 796 ff.) have also accepted this etymology. An older etymology is that from the root *bṛh* "to grow" (M. Haug). Hillebrandt and Dasgupta (ibid. p. 36) follow M. Haug in explaining *brahman* as "the magical force which is derived from the orderly co-operation of the hymns, the chants, and the sacrificial gifts." J. Hertel (*Das* Brahman" in *Indogerman. Forschungen*, 41, 1923, pp. 185 ff.) connects *brahman* etymologically with Greek Latin flagro, and tries to prove that the original meaning of *brahman* was "fire," viz., both the internal fire in man and the cosmic fire.

2. *System des Vedanta*, p. 128, *Allgemeine Geschichte der Philosophie*, I, 1, p. 241 f.

and men as known to us from the Saṃhitās and Brāhmaṇas.[1] What the word means etymologically we simply do not know. But in the Veda itself Brahman appears many times with the meaning of "prayer" or "charm", although there is nowhere the talk of a prayer or turning to the divine, but only charms and verses are meant through which man wants to influence the divine beings and obtain and even extort something from them. As at a later time the charms and prayers were combined into "books" or "school-books", they were called trayī vidyā or "threefold knowledge" and also simply Brahman. But as they attributed to this Veda or Brahman (both words were used quite synonymously) divine origin and as the sacrifice, which as we have seen, was in itself viewed as a divine power, originated according to the Indian view from the Veda or was contained in the Veda.[2] So they finally went to such an extent as to term this Brahman—the "word of God", the holy knowledge—as the first created (*brahma prathamajam*) and to make it at last even the creative principle, the foundation of all being (brahmā svayaṁbhū). Thus the Brahman is as divine principle a concept of the priestly philosophy and can be easily understood with the Brāhminic views on prayer and sacrifice.[3]

The history of the word Ātman is more simple. The etymology of this word is also uncertain. Some derive it from the root "breathe" and explain it as a breeze, breath, soul, self. "Others like Deussen[4] like to derive it from two pronominal

---

1. Cf. above p. 67 f. 167 f. 183.

2. Śat. V, 5, 5, 10 : "The whole sacrifice is as great as the three-fold Veda". According to Chāndogya Upaniṣad VII, 4, 1, "the sacrificial acts are contained in the Mantras" (i.e. in the Veda).

3. Cf. above, pp. 211 f. A. Weber already has compared Brahman with the logos-idea in Neo-Platonism and in Christianity. Thus also Deussen, *System des Vedanta,* p. 51 and Max F. Hecker, *Schopenhauer und die indische Philosophie* (Cologne, 1897), p. 3. Deussen desires to bring Brahman into accord with the "will" of Schopenhauer, but, as Hecker (p. 82) mildly expresses it, is forced "to offer some violence to the conception of Brahman." A comparison which is more justifiable is that with the "*mana*" of the Melanesians, which has been emphasised by N. Söderblom, in his *Das Werden des Götterglaubens,* 1916, pp. 270 ff.

4. *AGPh,* I, 1, p. 285.

roots, so that it would originally mean "This I". Whatever it be, Ātman is not simply a philosophical concept but a word frequently occurring in Sanskrit whose meaning is fully clear. It means "self", is used often as a reflexive pronoun and means as a noun one's own person, one's own body as against the eternal world, sometimes the trunk as against the limbs, but most frequently it means the soul, the actual soul as against the body.[1]

In the philosophy of the Upaniṣads both the concepts of Brahman and Ātman have got fused with each other. Thus the famous teaching of Śāṇḍilya beginnings with the words: "Indeed this whole is Brahman" and ends after a description of the Ātman with the explanation, that Brahman and Ātman are one.

This my Ātman in the interior of my heart is smaller than a grain of rice, or a grain of barley or a grain of mustard or a grain of millet. This my Ātman in the interior of my heart is bigger than the sky, bigger than all these spaces. In it are all actions, all desires, all odours, all tastes; he holds this whole contained in himself; he does not speak, he does not care for anything;—this my Ātman in the interior of the heart is that Brahman. With that I shall be united when I depart from life. Whoever knows this, for him indeed there is no doubt. Thus spoke Śāṇḍilya-Śāṇḍilya."[2]

Precisely and aptly does Deussen express this fundamental idea of the Upaniṣads in the following words: "Brahman, the power which stands before us incarnated in all beings, which creates all worlds, supports, preserves and withdraws again into itself, this eternal, endless, divine power is identical with the Ātman, with that, which after the removal of everything that is external, we find as our innermost and true essence, as our

---

1. On the term Ātman see Deussen, *ERE.* III, 195 ff.; Jacobi, *ERE.* II, 801; Dasgupta, *History of Indian Philosophy*, I, 25 f. According to Deussen, Ātman is "the most abstract, and therefore the best name which philosophy has found for its sole and eternal theme." Schopenhauer named his white poodle "Ātman", whereby, following the Vedantic doctrine, he desired to acknowledge the inner being as equal in man and beast." (Hecker, ibid. p. 8).

2. Chāndogya-Upaniṣad III 14. cf. above p. 208.

actual self, as the soul in us."[1] This teaching has found its strongest and boldest expression in the Upaniṣad-words which have subsequently become the faith of millions of Indians, in the words *tat tvam asi*, "that you are", i.e. the universe and the Brahman, that you yourself are, or in other words: "The world is only to the extent it makes its appearance in your own interior. Let us hear how the poet-philosophers of the Upaniṣads endeavour to make clear this theory of the essential unity of the world with the Brahman and of the Brahman with the Ātman.[2]

"Śvetaketu was the son of the Uddālaka Āruṇi. To him spoke his father: "Śvetaketu, go as a Veda pupil to a teacher. For, in our family it is not usual that one is a Brahmin only in name, without having learnt the Veda." So he, twelve years old, took the pupil's initiation. And after he had learnt all the Vedas, now 24 years old, he came home—haughty, vain, considering himself a scholar: Then his father spoke to him: Now my dear Śvetaketu, as you are so haughty and vain and consider yourself a scholar, tell me, have you also inquired into that doctrine, through which the unheard becomes heard, the unthought becomes thought, the unknown becomes known ?' 'Revered one, what then is this doctrine?' 'Just as, my dear, through a lump of earth everything earthen is recognized and the difference lies only in the name, is only a name—in reality it is only earth —; and just as, my dear, by a copper ornament everything made of copper is recognized and the difference lies only in the word, is only a name—but in reality it is only copper—and just as, my dear, by scissors everything made of iron is recognized and the difference lies only in the word, is only a name—but in reality it is iron: so, my dear, it is with this doctrine'. 'Certainly my revered teachers have not known this; for if they had known this, why would they not have communicated it to me ? So may you, oh revered one, explain it to me.' 'Well, my dear', said the father.

1. *AGPh.* I, 2, p. 37; See also Deussen, *The Philosophy of the Upaniṣads*, translated by A. S. Geden, Edinburgh, 1906, p. 39.

2. Chāndogya Upaniṣad, VI, 1, ff.

'Only the being my dear, was here in the beginning, and that only as one without a second. Some have perhaps said: "Only the not-being was here in the beginning, and that only as one without a second, and out of this not-being is the being born. How, my dear, could this be so? How should the being be born out of the not-being? Only the being, my dear, was here in the beginning, and that only as one without a second." (He then elaborates how this being created fire, this then created water and this created the food; and how the being, by permeating those three elements, developed out of itself the world of the senses. With the phenomena of sleep, hunger and thirst, he explains then, how everything follows from the three elements: fire, water, food, or as we would say: fire, water, earth, whereas these three elements are again based on the being. As however this being with the Ātman, his soul, permeates all beings, so it is also the soul in us. Therefore if a man dies, he becomes again that which he was originally; he unites again with the being out of which he was born. Now follow a series of metaphors all of which are supposed to explain the theory of the unity of the world with the only being and the human soul. "Just as, my dear, the bees, while preparing honey, collect the juices of most diverse trees and then make them into one single juice;—just as in this unity those juices retain no difference, so that they could say: I am the juice of this tree, I am the juice of that tree,—thus, my dear, all these creatures here also when they have merged in the being, are not conscious that they have merged in the being. Whatever they may be here, whether tiger or lion, wolf or boar, horsefly or fly—they become this; i.e. the being. And this subtle one is it that constitutes the essence of the whole, that is the real one, that is the Ātman, that you are, O Śvetaketu !" 'O revered one, teach me still further.' 'Well, my dear...

'Fetch me a fruit of the fig tree there'. 'Here it is, revered one.' 'Split it open.' 'It is split open, O revered one.' 'What do you see in it ?' 'Quite minute grains, revered one.' 'Split one of these open'. 'It is split open'. 'What do you see in it ?' 'Nothing, revered one'. Then he spoke to him: 'My dear, that very subtle one that you do not perceive in it, as a result of which this great fig tree stands there. Believe me, my dear, it is just this subtle one which constitutes the essence of the universe, that is the real one, that is the Ātman, that you are, O Śvetaketu. 'O revered one, teach me still further.' 'Well my dear.'

'Put this piece of salt in water and come again to me tomorrow morning. He did so. Then spoke the father to him: "Bring me the salt that you have put in the water yesterday evening." He put his hand and searched for it, but did not find it; it was as if it had vanished. 'Just taste the water on one side. How does it taste?' 'Salty' 'Taste the water in the middle. How does it taste ? 'Salty'. 'Taste on the other side. How does it taste ? 'Salty'. 'Eat something now and come again to me'. He did so, but the saltiness still remained. Then the father said to him, 'Indeed, my dear, even here (in the body) you do not take cognizance of the being, and yet it is there. And it is this subtle thing that constitutes the essence of the universe, that is the real one, that is the Ātman, that you are, O Śvetaketu."

What should instil in us the greatest respect for these ancient thinkers of India is the earnestness and the interest, with which they sought to investigate into the divine principle or what Kant would call the thing, in itself—whether they called it 'the one' or 'the being' or 'the Brahman' or 'the 'Ātman'. Thus we read in a dialogue which recurs in two Upaniṣads in two different versions,[1] how Gārgya Bālāki, a proud and scholarly Brahmin comes to the king of Banaras and undertakes to explain the Brahman to him. He declares one after another the Puruṣa, i.e. the personal spirit in the sun, in the moon, in the lightning, in ether, in wind, fire and water and then the spirit which appears as a reflection or shadow, which appears in the echo, in tone, in dream and human body or eye, to be the Brahman. But Ajātaśatru is not satisfied by any of these explanations, so that finally the learned Brahmin himself becomes a pupil of the king who then explains to him that the real Brahman is to be sought only in the recognizing spirit (Puruṣa) in man i.e. in the Ātman, in self. "As a spider with its web goes out of itself, as from a fire the small sparks fly out in all directions, so are born from this Ātman all life-spirits, all worlds, all gods and all beings."

---

1. Kauṣītakī Upaniṣad IV and Bṛhadāraṇyaka Upaniṣad II, I.

Similarly in a famous Upaniṣad-text the difference between the real and the false Ātman is demonstrated. There we read :

"The Ātman, which is free of all evil, age, death and sorrow, which is without hunger and without thirst, whose desires and whose decisions are truthful, that should be investigated, that should be sought to be recognized; he attains all worlds and the fulfilment of all desires, who has found and recognized this Ātman. 'Thus spoke Prajāpati. That was heard by the gods as well as the demons too and they spoke : "Well, let us investigate this Ātman— the Ātman, by inquiring into which one attains all the worlds and the fulfilment of all desires. And from the gods Indra set out and from the demons Virocana and both came to Prajāpati with firewood in their hand[1] without having previously fixed an appointment. They stayed with him as pupils for 32 years. Then Prajāpati spoke to them : "What do you wish, that you have lived here as pupils ?" And they spoke : The Ātman which is free of all evil, age...found and recognised this Ātman... This speech of yours, O revered one, we have heard. One yearning is for this (Ātman) ; so we have lived with you as pupils.' (Prajāpati now explains to them at first that the Puruṣa is in the eye or in the shadow of the Ātman. Virocana is satisfied with this, goes back to the demons and proclaims to them the doctrine that the body is the Ātman and that one need only please the body and nurse it in order to attain all the worlds. Indra however soon realises that the explanation given by Prajāpati could not have been meant seriously. He returns dissatisfied and stays once again for 32 years as a pupil with Prajāpati. Then he spoke to him : The (spirit) which in dream[2] joyously wanders about, that is the

1. The pupil must live with the teacher and serve him, especially mind the holy fire. "To come with firewood in the hand" therefore amounts to saying "to go as a pupil to someone for learning."

2. Just as in the Upaniṣads the development of the Ātman concept is followed through the earlier stages of the Puruṣa in the eye, in the reflection, in the shadow and in the dream-image (to which often the Prāṇa or the life-breath is added) upto the real Ātman, so also we find a remarkable concurrence of this with the ideas of the primitive people whose faith in the soul

Ātman, that is the immortal, the secure, that is the Brahman.' Then Indra went away satisfied. (But before he reached the gods, he understood that even the dream-image could not be the real Ātman. Once again he comes back to Prajāpati and stays with him as his pupil for 32 years. Now Prajāpati declares the soul in dreamless deep sleep to be the real Ātman. Even with this Indra is not yet satisfied, he returns and Prajāpati lets him live with him for 5 years more, whereupon he at last reveals to him the doctrine of the real Ātman. "O Indra, mortal indeed is this body, taken possession of by death. It is the abode of that immortal, bodiless Ātman. In the possession of love and aversion is the Ātman bound with the body, for as long as it is bound with the body, there is no protection for it from love and aversion. But when it is bodiless then it is certainly not affected by love and aversion. ... If now the eye is fixed on the ether there, then it is the spirit (Puruṣa) in the eye, but the eye serves only to see. And the Ātman it is which knows, "This I like to smell." The organ of smell serves only to smell. And the Ātman it is which knows, "This I like to speak," the voice serves only to speak. And the Ātman it is which knows, "This I like to hear", the organ of hearing serves only to hear. And the Ātman it is which knows, "This I want to think"; the organ of thinking is his divine eye. But it is he, who feels happy when he sees with the thinking organ, this divine eye, the objects of his desires. The gods of the Brahman world venerate indeed him, this Ātman; therefore all the worlds are possessed by them and all their desires fulfilled. And whoever has found this Ātman and recognised it attains all the worlds, and the fulfilment of all desires.' Thus spoke Prajāpati, so spoke Prajāpti."[1]

Thus here also the real Ātman is again declared to be the knowing and recognising spirit in man : However, that this Ātman is the same as the universe and everything exists only to

---

considers the breath, the apple of the eye, the reflection, the shadow and the dream images as earlier stages. (cf. E.B. Tylor, *The Beginnings of Culture*, Leipzig, 1873, I. p. 422 ff. Fritz Schulze, *Psychology of primitive folks*, Leipzig, 1900 p. 247 ff.

1. Chāndogya-Upaniṣad VIII, 7-12. A very free poetic treatment of this piece is found under the title "The teaching of the gods" with Luise Hitz, *Ganga-Wellen*, Munich, 1893.

the extent it is in the recognising self, is taught by the beautiful conversation between Yājñavalkya and Maitreyī. Yājñavalkya is about to leave his house in order to spend the last days of his life as a hermit in the forest. So he wants to divide his property between his two wives and tells it to his wife Maitreyī.

"Then spoke Maitreyī, 'If, my lord, this entire earth with all its wealth would belong to me, would I be on that score immortal?' 'Not at all!' spoke Yājñavalkya, 'but like the life of the well-to-do would therefore your life be; but there is no hope of immortality through wealth.'—Then spoke Maitreyī, 'What shall I do with that, through which I do not become immortal? Give me that knowledge, O Lord, which you possess.'—Yājñavalkya spoke, 'Dear, indeed, you are to us and lovingly do you speak; come, sit down, I will explain to you; but you take note of what I tell you.' And he spoke, 'Forsooth, not for the sake of the husband is the husband dear, but for the sake of the self is the husband dear; forsooth not for the sake of the wife is the wife dear, but for the sake of the self is the wife dear; forsooth not for the sake of the sons are the sons dear, but for the sake of the self are the sons dear; forsooth not for the sake of the gods are the gods dear, but for the sake of the self are the gods dear; forsooth not for the sake of the beings are the beings dear, but for the sake of the self are the beings dear; forsooth not for the sake of the universe is the universe dear, but for the sake of the self is the universe dear. The self forsooth, shall one see, shall one hear, shall one understand, shall one contemplate, O Maitreyi; forsooth, he who has seen, heard, understood and recognized, this whole world will be known by him.[1]

One of the most frequent names of the Ātman in the Upaniṣads is the word Prāṇa, i.e. "life-breath, life, life-principle". And numerous texts of the Upaniṣads are concerned with this Prāṇa, which is identified with the recognising self; or also with the relation of the same to the organs of the soul, to the so-called Prāṇas (prāṇāh, plural of prāṇa). To these organs — speech, breath, light, hearing, and thinking organ —

1. Bṛhadāraṇyaka-Upaniṣad II, 4. German Translation by P. Deussen, *Sechzig Upanishads*, p. 416 ff.

correspond in the universe five nature-powers : the fire, the wind, the sun, the quarters of heaven and the moon. And to the mutual action between the organs and the nature-powers references are made often in the Upanișads. It is the psychology of the Upanișad that is in a certain way not to be separated from metaphysics. Very popular is the oft narrated "psychological fairy-tale" of the fight for importance of the organs of life. There it is said how the Prāṇas or the life-organs once fought for the first place. They went to Father Prajāpati, so that he might settle their dispute :

He however spoke to them: 'That one is the best of you, after whose departure the body is in the worst condition.' Then the speech departed and after staying abroad for one year, it came back and spoke: 'How could you live without me ?' 'Just like dumb ones', they said, 'who do not speak, but breathe with the breath, see with sight, hear with ear, and think with the thinking organ.' And speech entered (the body) again. Then sight departed and after staying abroad for one year, it came back and spoke, 'How could you live without me? 'Just like blind ones,' they said, who do not see, but breathe with the breath, speak with the speech, hear with the ear and think with the thinking organ.' And the sight went inside again. Then the sense of hearing departed and after staying abroad for one year, it came back and spoke, 'How could you live without me ?' 'Just like the deaf ones,' they said, 'who do not hear, but breathe with the breath, speak with the speech, see with the sight and think with the thinking organ.' And the sense of hearing went inside again. Then the thinking organ departed, and after staying abroad for one year he came back and spoke, 'How could you live without me ?' 'Just like fools,' they said 'who do not think, but breathe with the breath, speak with the speech, see with the sight and hear with the ear.' And the thinking-organ went in again. But now, as the breath (Prāṇa) wanted to depart, he pulled the other life-organs along with himself, just as a noble horse pulls off the pegs to which its feet are chained. Then they all came to him and spoke, 'Revered one, come, you are the best of us. Do not depart !'...........Therefore they are called not the speeches, not the sights, not the senses of hearing, not the thinking organs, but they are called the Prāṇas, because just the Prāṇa are they all.[1]

Just as the doctrine of the Prāṇa and the Prāṇas is connected with the basic doctrine of the Ātman, the same doctrine also provides the poet-philosophers of the Upaniṣads with opportunities for splendid philosophical poetical compositions, as they can perhaps be termed best, on the destinies of the individual Ātman, i.e. of the human soul, in the waking and dreaming states, in the deep-sleep and the dying states and in their wanderings to the beyond up to their final 'salvation', i.e. their complete merger with the Brahman. Bṛhadāraṇyaka Upaniṣad in particular draws up (IV, 3-4) a picture of the destinies of the soul, which picture, as Deussen[2] rightly remarks, "stands out with respect to richness and warmth of description, certainly unique in Indian literature and perhaps even in the literature of all folks." Here we find also clearly and vividly developed for the first time, the doctrine of the transmigration of the soul and the ethical doctrine of Karma or deed which is most intimately connected with it, which must have its consequences with the certainty of a law of nature. This great doctrine of deed, later (especially in Buddhism) preached in all streets and bye-lanes is in the Upaniṣads still a great mystery. Ārtabhāga asks Yājñavalkya:

"Yājñavalkya,' said he, if after the death of this man his voice enters the fire, his breath the wind, his sights the sun, his thinking organ the moon, his sense of the hearing the quarters of heaven, his body the earth, his soul (Ātman) enters the ether, the hair on his body enters the herbs, the hair of his head enters the trees and his blood and semen are put down in water,—where then is this man?' 'Take me by the hand, my dear!' spoke Yājñavalkya: 'Ārtabhāga, both of us want to know that; this matter of ours is not to be be discussed amidst the people!' and they both went out and discussed with each other; and it was the deed, of which they spoke; the deed

1. Chāndogya Upaniṣad V: 1, Cf. Bṛhadāraṇyaka Upaniṣad VI, 1, 7-14.
2. *Sechzig Upaniṣads* (Sixty Upaniṣads) p. 463.

it was, which they praised. Good, forsooth, does he become through good deed, bad through bad deed."[1]

More exhaustively is this doctrine treated then following the splendid description of the departure of the soul from the body. There it is said:

"The peak of his heart begins to glow and in this light the Ātman departs, be it from the eye or from the head or from other parts of the body. And while he departs the life-breath (Prāṇa) follows him; and following the departure of life-breath all the life organs depart, and also the consciousness follows them. He however, the cognising Ātman is equipped with cognition. To him remain attached knowledge and deeds, the experiences of earlier lives. Just as a caterpillar[2] on reaching the tip of a stalk of grass withdraws into itself, similarly does man withdraw into his own self (Ātman) when he discarded the body and freed himself from ignorance. Just as an embroiderer takes out a small piece separately and makes out of it another, a quite new and more beautiful form, similarly man creates for himself here, after he has discarded this body and has freed himself from ignorance, another, a quite new and more beautiful form, that of the spirit of a maṇe or of a Gandharva, of a Brahmin or of a Prajāpati, of a god or of a man or of any other being... what he becomes will depend on what he has done and how he has lived, whoever has done good will have a good birth once again and whoever has done evil will be reborn as an evil being. Through good deeds he will become good and through evil deeds evil. Therefore it is said indeed, "Man is composed here fully of desire, and his determination is guided by his desire, and he acts as per his determination and his destiny and is dependent on his deed.[3]

As a consequence of this doctrine of Karman themoral element plays a much more important role in the Upaniṣads than in the Brāhmaṇas. Moreover, we should not ignore the fact that the metaphysical doctrine of the Ātman, for whose sake we love

1. Bṛhadāraṇyaka Upaniṣad, III, 2, 13 f.
2. See Barua, *Pre-Buddhistic Indian Philosophy* p. 175.
3. Bṛhadāraṇyaka Upaniṣad, IV, 4, 2-5.

our fellow-creatures[1] involves a deep ethical idea: as it is in reality the universal soul which we love in each individual, love for all creatures wells up from the recognition of the Ātman.[2] However, in the Upaniṣad too, there is not much scope for actual moral doctrine. We come across moral prescriptions only rather seldom, as for example, in the Taittirīya Upaniṣad (I, 11) where the teacher gives parting pupil advice for his life:

"Speak the truth, do your duty, do not neglect the study of the Veda. After you have given to your teacher (on completing discipleship) your present with love, take care that the thread of your family does not snap...do not neglect the ceremonies for gods and manes. Let your mother be a god to you, your father a god your teacher a god your guest a god' "etc.

More interesting and much more Upaniṣad-like than these moral-prescriptions is another text on the ethics that we find in the Bṛhadāraṇyaka Upaniṣad (V, 2.).

"Three kinds of sons of Prajāpati, the gods, the men and the demons, were staying as pupils with their father Prajāpati. After the gods had spent their time as pupils they said: "Tell us something O Lord!" And he told them the syllable 'da' and said: "Have you understood that ?" 'We have understood that' said they: 'you have told us: 'damyata' (control yourselves) 'Yes' said he; 'you have understood it.'—Then the men said to him, 'Tell us something O, Lord !' And he spoke to them just the same syllable 'da' and said, 'Have you understood that ?' 'We have understood that', said they, 'you have told us, datta (give)', 'Yes' said he 'you have understood it'—Then the demons spoke to him, Tell us something, O Lord'. And he spoke to them just the same syllable 'da', and said, 'Have you understood that?' We have understood it said they; 'you have told us, dayadhvam (have sympathy)', "Yes," said he 'you have understood it'—And it is just this, what is proclaimed by that divine voice, the thunder: da, —da, —da that means: damyata datta, dayadhvam. Therefore may he learn these three things: Self-discipline, generosity and sympathy."

1. See above, pp. 231 ff.

2. On the ethics of the Upaniṣads, see Hume, *The Thirteen Principal Upaniṣads*, pp. 58 ff. John Mackenzie, *Hindu Ethics*, London, 1922, pp. 67 ff. S. Radhakrishnan, *Indian Philosophy*, I, pp. 207 ff.

That we come across such ethical teachings in the Upaniṣads only rarely is easy to understand. According to the teachings of the Upaniṣads the highest goal worthy of attaining is the union with the Brahman and this union is to be attained only by giving up ignorance, by means of knowledge. Only he who has recognised the unity of the Ātman with the Brahman, the unity of the soul with god obtains salvation, i.e. complete unity with the Brahman. But in order to attain this highest aim it is necessary to give up all work, good as well as bad. Sacrifice and pious deeds lead evidently only to new re-births, knowledge alone leads beyond this labyrinth to the absolute and eternal one. Just as water does not stick to the lotus leaf, so also no evil deed attaches to him who knows this."[1] Even in the Brāhmaṇas and Āraṇyakas are very often references made to the advantages which are obtained by one who knows some secret doctrine of the sacrificial science,—"he who knows this,"—"who knows this." For the Upaniṣads however, nothing is more characteristic than the numerously repeated promises and of happiness bliss, of earthly possessions and heavenly happiness as reward for him "who knows this." The idea that knowledge is not simply power, but the highest aim worthy of attaining runs through all the Upaniṣads. Not only does Indra serve Prajāpati as a pupil for 101 years, but it is said also of human beings, that they serve a teacher for years together, in order to receive handed down from him some knowledge. Kings are prepared to gift thousands of cows and heaps of gold to the Brahmins, who can proclaim to them the doctrine of the real Ātman or Brahman. But even Brahmins submit humbly to Kings, rich people to beggars if these are, as is not seldom the case, in possessesion of higher wisdom.[2] However this yearning for knowledge has found its most effective expression in the magnificent poem on Naciketas which is handed down to us by the Kāṭhaka-Upaniṣad.

The youth Naciketas has descended to the nether world and the Death-god has granted him three wishes. Naciketas wishes firstly that he might go back to his father alive, secondly, he

---

1. Chāndogya Upaniṣad, IV. 14,3. cf. Kauṣitaki Up.-I, 4, III, 8.
2. Cf. above p. 210 ff.

wishes heavenly bliss for himself. As he has to spell out his third wish, he says:

> "A doubt rules, when men is dead:
> 'He is' says one; 'he is not' says another.
> That I should like to investigate with your help
> Let that be the third wish, that I choose!"

Thereupon Yama replies that this question, as to what may happen to man after death, is so difficult to investigate, that even the gods were once in doubt; and he requests the youth to give up this wish of his:

> "Choose hundred-year old children and grand-children,
> Many herds of cattle, elephants, gold and horses,
> Choose for yourself possession of vast fields,
> And live yourself, as many autumns as you want!
>
> If you prize this as wish in value
> Then choose for yourself wealth and long life
> A great man may you be on the earth
> I shall make you enjoy all pleasures.
>
> What can be got of pleasure only with hardships
> Ask for yourself all that as you like—
> Look here on the chariot pretty women with harps,
> As such are not to be attained by men.
> I gift them to you, that they serve you,—
> Only, don't ask Naciketas about dying!"

But Naciketas does not let himself be diverted from his wish by these promises of earthly riches:

> "What of the power of senses, O Death, is granted to us—
> Fear of the next day makes it fade.
> Even fully lived is the life indeed only short
> Keep your chariots, dance and games.
>
> Through wealth is man not to be made happy!
> Whom tempted ever wealth, who confronted you?

Let us live as long as you please!
But as gift I choose only that....

About which there is doubt prevailing here,
What happens at the great departure, that tell us;
The desire, that inquiring pierces into this secret,
That chooses, and nothing else, Naciketas."

Then Yama, the Death-god praises Naciketas, that he has chosen knowledge and not the pleasures, and gives him at last the doctrine of immortality of the soul.[1]

But how this esteem of knowledge leads not only to dislike of earthly pleasures but also to a contempt for the world[2] is shown to us by another Upaniṣad in which for the first time that pessimistic basic feature of Indian thinking becomes visible which we come across again and again in later Indian literature. There we read:[3]

"It happened that a king named Bṛhadratha, after appointing his son to rule the country, knowing that this body is ephemeral, turned to renunciation and went out into the forest. There he subjected himself to extreme mortification by standing, looking into the sun and with his arms stretched upward. After a thousand days had passed, the Ātman knowing, venerable Śākāyanya approached him. 'Get up, Get up and choose for yourself a wish !' so he spoke to the king. He paid his respect to him and spoke: 'O venerable one ! I do not have the knowledge of the Ātman. You know its essence, as we have heard; this you will explain to us !" (The Brahmin wants to persuade him to give up this wish and exorts him to wish

1. The above verses are a translation of P. Deussen's German translation (*Sixty Upaniṣads*, p. 27 ff). A very free poetic treatment of the poem is given by Luise Hitz, *Ganga-Wellen*, München, 1893. Without violating the spirit of the Upaniṣad the poetess has condensed and rounded off as a whole the description which is, in the original, somewhat fragmentary and unclear. A fine poetical, but very free translation of the legend is given by J. Muir, Metrical Translations from Sanskrit writers, pp. 54 ff.

2. Cf. P. Regnaud, *Le Pessimisme Brahmanique* (Annales du Musée Guimet, t. I, pp. 101 ff.)

3. Maitrāyaṇa Upaniṣad I 2-4 in the translation of Deussen, *Sixty Upaniṣads*, p. 315 ff.

for something else. Then the king bursts out in the words: "O venerable one ! In this stinking body composed by pouring together bones, skin, sinews, marrow, flesh, semen, blood, mucous, tears, gum of the eyes filth, urine, bile and phlegm, which is without any essence,—how can one enjoy happiness ! In this body to which are attached passion, wrath, greed, illusion, fear, shyness, jealousy, separation from the dear ones, bonds with the unlovable, hunger, thirst, age, death, disease, worry and similar things,—how may one enjoy happiness ? Besides we see that this whole world is transitory, like those horseflies, flies and similar ones, these herbs and trees which are born and again decay." (There follows then an enumeration of kings and heroes of pre-historic times who all had to perish, as well as of gods and demi-gods all of whom fell a victim to destruction.) "But why should I talk of all this ? There are indeed other things—drying up of great oceans, crumbling of mountains, wavering of the pole-star . . . sinking of the earth, fall of the gods from their positions—in the course of the world where such things occur how may one ever enjoy happiness ! In particular, whoever is satisfied with it, must return again and again ! Therefore save me ! For in this worldly race I feel myself like a frog in a blind (waterless) hole of a well. You, O venerable one, are our refuge."

It is however noteworthy, that this text to which there are numerous parallels found in the Buddhistic as well as in the later Sanskrit literature belongs to one of the later Upaniṣads. For by virtue of its language and style the Maitrāyaṇa-Upaniṣad stands closer to the classical Sanskrit literature than to the Veda and is decidedly post-Buddhistic.[1] In the ancient Vedic Upaniṣads only the germs of pessimism are found in the doctrine of the non-reality of the world. Real is indeed only the Brahman and this is the Ātman, the soul, "which is beyond hunger and thirst, pain and illusion, age and death." "What is different from it, that is full of suffering"—a to 'nyad ārtam.[2]

1. Maitrāyaṇa Upaniṣad VII, 8 f. contains clear allusions to the Buddhists as heretics. On the style of the Maitrāyaṇīya-Upaniṣad, see Oldenberg, *Zur Geschichte der altindischen Prosa*, p. 33.

2. Bṛhadāraṇyaka Upaniṣad III, 5.

But what is different from it, that indeed does not simply exist in reality and therefore the suffering and pain of the world is not real. The knowing one, who has understood the doctrine of unity, knows no fear, no pain. "He who knows the bliss of the Brahman, for him there is no fear." "Where would be illusion, where worry for him who knows the unity ?" "Bliss" (ānanda) is a name of the Brahman "consisting of bliss" (ānandamaya) is the Ātman. And like a triumphal song of optimism sound the words of an Upaniṣad: "Bliss is Brahman. For indeed out of bliss are born all those beings, through bliss do they live after they are born and with bliss do they again merge, when they depart from life."[1]

Thus the teaching of the upaniṣads is basically not pessimistic. Of course it is just one small step from the belief in the non-reality of the world to world-contempt. The more rapturously the bliss of the Brahman is praised, the more void and worthless did the earthly existence appear.[2] Therefore the pessimism of later Indian philosophy had its roots really in the Upaniṣads.

Indeed the entire later philosophy of the Indians is rooted in the Upaniṣads. Their teachings constituted the basis for the Vedānta-sūtras of Bādarāyaṇa, a work of which a later writer[3] says: "The text-book is the most important of all text-books. All other text books serve only to supplement it. Therefore it should be esteemed by all who endeavour to attain salvation." This text book is the foundation on which are built the theological-philosophical systems of Śaṅkara and of Rāmānuja whose followers even today are found in millions. But all other philosophic systems and religious faiths also, which have developed in India in the course of centuries, the heretic Buddhism no less than the Orthodox-Brahmanic religion of the post-Buddhistic era, have grown up on the soil of the Upaniṣadic teachings.

However, what has lent to this philosophic poetry (they can be hardly described in a better manner) such a mighty

---

1. Taittirīya Upaniṣad II, 9. III, 6 Īśa-up. 7.
2. Cf. M. F. Hecker, *Schopenhauer und die indische Philosophie*, pp. 116-120.
3. *Madhusūdana Sarasvatī* (in Weber's *Indische Studien* I p. 9 and 20) in his Prasthānabheda.

power over the mind, was not the belief in their divine revelation—indeed the simplest hymns and the most senseless Brāhmaṇa-texts were considered as proclaimed by Godhood—but rather the fact that clothed in the language of poetry they appealed as much to the heart as to the mind. And the Upaniṣads have so much to say even to us over a period of many thousands of years not because, as Schopenhauer maintains, they represent the "fruit of the highest human knowledge and wisdom" and contain "almost superhuman conceptions, whose authors cannot be imagined as mere human beings"[1] not because, as Deussen thinks, these thinkers "had if not the most scientific, still the most intimate and direct revelation of the ultimate secret of existence," and because—with which Deussen tries to justify the revelation-faith of the Indians—in the Upaniṣads "such philosophical conceptions are found as do not have their equals either in India or anywhere else in the world"[2]; but for this reason, that these old thinkers fight so earnestly for truth, that in their philosophical poetry the perpetually unfulfilled yearning of man for knowledge has found such fervent expression. The Upaniṣads contain no "superhuman conceptions", but—and this is exactly what makes them so valuable to us—may contain human, entirely human attempts, to come closer to reality.

However, for the history-researcher, who pursues the history of human thinking, the Upaniṣads have another much greater significance. Starting from the mystic teachings of the Upaniṣads a thought current reaches the mysticism of the Persian Sufism, and the mystic-theosophic logos-doctrine of Neo-Platonists and the Alexandrian Christians right up to the teachings of Christian mystics Eckhart and Tauber and finally to the philosophy of the great German mystics of the 19th century—Schopenhauer.[3] What Schopenhauer owed to the Indians he himself has told us often enough. Plato, Kant and the "Vedas" (by which Schopenhauer always meant the

1. Hecker, Ibid p. 7.
2. Deussen : *System des Vedānta* p. 50, 99 f. what exaggerations.
3. On Schopenhauer as a mystic cf. Hecker ibid. p. 85 f.

Upaniṣads) he himself calls his teachers. In the manuscript meant to be read out as an academic lecture by him he wrote, "The results of what I propose to deliver before you are in agreement with the oldest of all world-views, namely, the Vedas." The exploration of the Sanskrit literature he termed as the "greatest gifts of our century" and he prophesies that the Indian pantheism might develop into a sort of mass-religion even in the occident. The coincidence of his own system with that of the Upaniṣads appears to him to be specially marvellous and he tells us that "every one of the individual and disconnected sentences which form the Upaniṣads could be derived as the conclusion from the thoughts conveyed by him (Schopenhauer) although it cannot at all be said that vice-versa these thoughts are also found there." It is well-known that on his table the Oupnek'hat was lying open and that before going to bed he "worshipped" it. And about this book he said, "There is no other book (the original text excepted) in the whole world, the reading of which is as rewarding and solemn as that of this book; it has comforted me in my life and it will also comfort me while dying.[1] The basic teaching of the Upaniṣads however is the same, which according to Schopenhauer was "at all times the mockery of fools and the endless meditation of the wise people," namely the doctrine of unity, i.e. the doctrine "that all diversity is only apparent, that in all the individuals of this world, in however many endless numbers they might appear alongside one another or one following another, in all of them the same present, identical, truly being essence manifests itself."[2] And if Ludwig Stein is right who has said not long ago, "The philosophy of the present is monism, i.e. the unitary signification of all world-happening,[3] —then this 'philosophy of the present" has been the philosophy of the ancient Indians already thousands of years ago.

---

1. *Parerga and Paralipomena* published by J. Frauenstadt II p. 427 (§ 185) Hecker ibid p. 6 ff.

2. Schopenhauer, *Grundlage der Moral* 22 (Works, published by J. Frauenstadt, IV, p. 268 ff.).

3. Supplement of *Neue Freie Presse*, 10 July 1904.

The Vedāṅgas

In one of the Upaniṣads we are told that there are two kinds of knowledge, a higher and a lower one. The higher one is that in which the immortal Brāhmaṇa is realised, the lower one however consists of "Ṛgveda, Yajurveda, Sāmaveda, Atharvaveda, Phonetics, Rituals, Grammar, Etymology, Metres and Astronomy".[1] This is the earliest enumeration of the so-called six Vedāṅgas, i.e. the six "limbs" or auxiliary sciences of the Veda.[2] Originally they did not mean either any independent books or schools, but only subjects of study which had to be learnt in the Vedic schools in order to understand the Vedic texts. We, therefore, find the beginnings of the Vedāṅgas already in the Brāhmaṇas and Āraṇyakas where in addition to the explanations of sacrificial rituals we also find already incidentally phonetic, grammatical, etymological, metrical and astronomical discussions. But in the course of time these subjects were treated more systematically and there arose—still within the framework of the Vedic schools—special schools of study for every one of the six auxiliary sciences of the Veda. Out of these were then born independent texts of "text-books", the Sūtras, composed in a peculiar style of prose that could be learnt by heart.

The word 'sūtra' means originally "thread", and then a "short rule", a theorem condensed into a few words—just as out of many threads—this might be the explanation for the transition of the meaning—a texture is made, so also a system of theory[3] is woven by putting together such short theorems. A bigger work, which is produced by putting together a number of such sūtras is also called Sūtra[4] then. The purpose of these

1. Muṇḍaka Upaniṣad I, 1,5. *ṛgveda yajurveda sāmavedo'tharvavedaḥśikṣā kalpovyākaraṇam niruktam chando jyotiṣam.*

2. cf. above 50-51 and Ludwig, *Der Ṛgveda* III, p. 74 ff.

3. Similarly the word tantra means originally "web" than a system of theory, a literary work, a book. In Chinese too, the word; "king" means originally "the warp of a texture", then "standard, canon", and finally, in a metaphorical sense, "any book which is considered as a rule or canon," see W. Grube, *Geschichte der chinesischen Literature,* Leipzig. 1902, p. 31.

4. We may compare the word brāhmaṇa which originally means "utterance of a theologician", then used collectively for the collections of such utterances and the word upaniṣad which means at first a secret teaching, but then a bigger work, a collection of secret teachings. (above p. 157 and 225.

works is a purely practical one. In them some knowledge is supposed to be systematically presented in a precisely condensed form, so that the pupil can learn by heart easily. Perhaps in the entire literature of the world there is nothing similar to these sūtras of the Indians. The author of such a work is keen on saying as much as possible in as few words as possible—even at the cost of clarity and understandability. Patañjali, the grammarian, is the author of the oft-quoted saying, that a sūtra-author is just as happy when he can save half a short syllable as when a son is born to him. Only through examples is it possible to give an idea of the very peculiar aphoristic prose of these works, of the Sūtra-style. In the following two texts of our translation we must supply the words in brackets in order to make the meaning of the detached sentences understandable:

Āpastambīya - *Dharmasūtra* I, 1, 1, 4-8:

Sūtra 4: (There are) four castes; Brahmins, Kṣatriyas, Vaiśyas and Śūdras.

Sūtra 5: Of these (is) the preceding by birth better (than every succeeding one)

Sūtra 6: For (those who) (are) not Śūdras and have not committed evil acts, (is prescribed) initiation as pupils, Veda-study, Fire-inception; and (these holy) acts (are) fruit-bearing (in this world and in the next.)

Sūtra 7: Obedience to the other castes (is the duty) of the Śūdras.

Sūtra 8: In the case of every previous caste (is) the welfare greater (i.e. the higher the caste which the Śūdra serves the greater is the welfare that accords to him on that account in the next world).

Gobhila-*Gṛhyasūtra*—I, 5, 1-5; 8-9:

Sūtra 1: Now on New- and full-moon (i.e. on new-moon day and full-moon day the following ceremonies are to be performed)

Sūtra 2: On the full-moon day (when the moon) at (the time of the evening) dusk (rises) he shall fast.

Sūtra 3: Some (teachers say): On the next (day, i.e. when the moon rises shortly after sunset) (he shall fast).

Sūtra 4: Further (he shall fast) on the day on which the moon is not seen (by) (considering) this as the new-moon day.

Sūtra 5: At the end of the month-halves one shall fast, at the beginning of the month-halves one shall sacrifice (i.e. the sacrifices on the new-moon day or full-moon day shall be always preceded by a day of fasting.)

Sūtra 8: But (the day on which the moon is not seen), that shall be made the new-moon day (i.e. that shall be celebrated as the new-moon day.

Sūtra 9: Even if (the moon) is seen once (in the day just a little bit) (can this day be celebrated as new-moon day, then one says evidently), that (the moon) has already covered its way.

Thus the Sanskrit text contains only the words outside the brackets. The pupil learnt only these aphoristical sentences by heart; the necessary explanations he received from the teacher. In later times these explanations of the teachers were also written down and they are preserved to us in the extensive commentaries, which there are for all Sūtra texts and without which the Sūtra texts would not be understandable for us. This peculiar Sūtra-style is born out of the prose of the Brāhmaṇas. This prose of the Brāhmaṇas consisting almost entirely of short sentences which is lacking in indirect speech in which the series of main clauses are only seldom interrupted by a relative clause or a conditional clause and whose monotony gets a certain change only by participle-constructions; in which further —in spite of a certain verbosity which is seen particularly in awkward repetitions—much remains unsaid which is self-evident during oral delivery and instruction, while we have to supplement it in our translations,[1] by means of a more and more

1. Cf. above p. 169 note 1.

simplification this prose could be easily modified into such lapidary, abrupt sentences set up only by putting together the absolutely indispensable particles, as we find them in the Sūtras. For the purpose of larger saving in syllables and a still more scanty summarising now one more new element was added: the formation of long composites, which we come across for the first time in the Sūtras, and which have then become especially characteristic for classical Sanskrit literature, and has gained more and more upper hand in later times. That the Sūtra-style has developed from the prose of the Brāhmaṇas can be seen clearly even today from the fact that in the oldest Sūtra-texts frequently quotations are found from the Brāhmaṇas and even more frequently that even without being quoted Brāhamaṇa-like texts are found in the midst of the Sūtras.[1]

The Ritual Literature

The oldest Sūtra works are then indeed also those which, in the matter of content, immediately follow the Brāhmaṇas and Āraṇyakas. Obviously in the Aitareya Āraṇyaka there are texts, which are nothing but Sūtras and are even traditionally ascribed to the Sūtra-authors Āśvalāyana and Śaunaka and are termed as not having been revealed.[2] To the Sāmaveda also belong some texts which are wrongly termed as "Brāhmaṇas", which are in reality Sūtras and must be classified, as per their contents, with the Vedāṅga-literature. The ritual (kalpa), which really forms the main contents of the Brāhmaṇas is also the particular Vedāṅga which is the first to undergo a systematic treatment in independent text-books, in the so-called kalpasūtras. They were born out of the necessity to compile the rules for the sacrificial ritual in a shorter and more perspicuous and

1. Thus certain sections of the Sāṅkhyāyana-Śrautasūtra are similar in style and character to the Brāhmaṇas (Weber, *HIL.*, p. 54. Hillebrandt in the preface to his edition of the Sāṅkhyāyana-Śrautasūtra). In the Baudhāyana-Kalpasūtra too, three are numerous passages which read just like Brāhmaṇas. The Śrautasūtras were not however, written on the basis of the Brāhmaṇas, but on that of a long oral tradition: see R. Löbbecke *Über das Verhältnis der Brāhmaṇas und Śrautasūtren*" Diss., Leipzig, 1908.

2. Cf. Max Müller *History of Ancient Sanskrit Literature*, pp. 314 f., 339.

connected manner for the practical purposes of the priests. According as these kalpasūtras treated the Śrauta-sacrifices taught in the Brāhmaṇas or the domestic ceremonies and sacrifices of the daily life, the Gṛhya-rites, they are called Śrautasūtras and Gṛhyasūtras.[1]

Accordingly the Śrautasūtras contain the rules for the inception of the three sacrificial fires—for the fire-sacrifice (Agnihotra), for the new-moon and full-moon sacrifices, for the seasonal offerings, for the animal sacrifice and in particular for the Soma-sacrifice with its numerous deviations.[2] They are for us the most important source for understanding the Indian sacrificial cult and their significance as sources for the history of religion cannot be appreciated adequately.[3]

Still more diverse and in some respects more interesting is the content of the Gṛhyasūtras.[4] They contain the rules for all customs, ceremonies and sacrifices through which the life of an Indian, starting with the moment when he is received in his

---

1. Cf. above, p. 49 f. and 130 f.

2. cf. above p. 141 ff.

3. There is, till now, no translation of a Śrautasūtra. But the content of these works has been treated partly in the works of A. Hillebrandt *Das altindische Neu-und Vollamondopfer*, Jena 1879 and Julius Schwab, *Das altindische Tieropfer*", Erlangen, 1886. The entire ritual literature and the main features of the ritual itself as well as the Śrauta- and the Gṛhya ceremonies, have been treated exhaustively by A. Hillebrandt in "*Grundriss*. Vol. III Number 2 *Ritual Literatur—Vedische Opfer und Zauber*, Strassburg 1897.) The significance of the Śrautasūtras for the general science of Religion has been fully appreciated at first by H. Hubert and M. Mauss in their *Essai sur la nature et la function du sacrifice* (Année Sociologique, Paris 1897-1898, pp 29—138.)

4. The Gṛhyasūtras are easily accessible in the following editions: Indische Hausregeln, Sanskrit and German, published by A.F. Stenzler—I-Āśvalāyana Leipzig 1864-65. II Pāraskara—Leipzig 1876 and 1878. *Abhandlungen für die Kunde des Morgenlandes* III, IV, VI) *Das Cankkhyayana-grhyam* (Sanskrit and German) by H. Oldenberg (in vol. XV of the *Indische Studien*. In the Gobhilīya Gṛhyasūtra, published and translated by Friedrich Knauer—Dorpart 1884 cf. also M. Bloomfield, Das Grhyasangrahapariśishta des Gobhilaputra (in *ZDMG* vol. XXXV), and P. V. Bradke, Über das Mānava-Gṛhya-Sūtra (in *ZDMG* vol. XXXVI). An English translation of the most important Gṛhyasūtras has been published by H. Oldenberg in *The Sacred Books of the East*, vols. 29 and 30.

mother's womb up to the hour of his death and even beyond this by means of the funeral rites and the soul-cult, receives a higher "initiation" which the Indians call "saṃskāra". Accordingly we find in these works exhaustively treated a large number of really popular customs and manners connected with conception, birth, mother in child-bed and the new born child, name-giving, the first outing, the first eating by the child, we find exact rules for the hair-cutting of the boy, conducting the pupil to the teacher (upanayanam or 'pupil-initiation'), for the way of life of the Brahmacārin or Veda-pupil, for the relation between pupil and teacher and the parting of the pupil from the teacher. Then the customs of courting, engagement and marriage are described in an exhaustive manner. Here in the Gṛhyasūtras also the "five great sacrifices" mentioned already in the Śatapatha-Brāhmaṇa (XI. 5, 6) are also described at length. "They are indeed great sacrificial festivals" says the Brāhmaṇa and they are called "great sacrifices" because the performance of the same is a part of the most important religious duties of each house-holder, although in reality they consist only in small offerings and a few, simple ceremonies. These are the daily offerings to gods, demons and manes, which need consist only in the fervent placing of a stick of wood on the holy fire of the hearth, some food offerings and a water offering, and in entertaining a guest (described as "offering to men) and fifthly the daily reading of a Veda-chapter considered as "the offering to the Brāhmaṇa or the Ṛṣis. The simple evening and morning offerings, New-moon and Full-moon-offerings and the annual festivals connected with sacrifices (out of which the Agnihotra, Darśapūrṇamāsa and Cāturmāsya offerings of the Śrauta-sacrifices might have been born) are found likewise described in the Gṛhyasūtras. Moreover the customs and ceremonies are described which are connected with the house constructions, cattle breeding and agriculture. Similarly the magic rites which are supposed to serve for warding off diseases, and omens signifying misfortune, as well as exorcisms and rites for love-charms etc. To conclude, the Gṛhyasūtras also deal with the funeral customs and offerings to manes (Śrāddhas) which were however considered so important that they have been treated at great length in some texts (Śrāddhakalpas).[1]

Thus, however insignificant these Gṛhyasūtras may be as literary works, they give us a deep insight into the life of ancient Indians. They are indeed a veritable treasure for researchers of culture. One need only think with what great difficulty researchers into antiquity must gather information about the daily life of ancient Greeks and Romans from the most diverse books. Here in India we have now in these unpretentious texts in the form of rules and regulations the most reliable information—we may say: from eye-witnesses—on the daily life of ancient Indi^ns. They are like the "folklore journals" of ancient India. Of course they describe the life of the Indian householder only from the religious side. But because for ancient Indians, religion penetrated the whole existence so much that nothing could happen without there being at the same time a religious ceremony, so these Gṛhyasūtras are, for folklore research inestimable sources for the popular manners and customs of those ancient times. They are so much the more important as, according to discoveries made long ago, numerous parallels are found in the manners and customs of the Indo-Germanic folks to those described in the Gṛhyasūtras. A comparison of the Greek, Roman, Germanic and Slavic marriage customs with those of the rules contained in the Gṛhyasūtras has shown that the relation of the Indo-German folks is not restricted to the language alone, but that these linguistically connected folks have also preserved in their manners and customs many common features of prehistoric times.[2]

---

1. By his researches into the funeral customs and the mane-cult on the basis Indian ritual literature W. Caland has particularly distinguished himself by the works: On the veneration of the dead by some of the Indo-German folks, Amsterdam, 1888. *Ancient Indian Mane-cult,* Leiden, 1893. *Ancient Indian Obsequies and Funeral Customs,* Amsterdam, 1896. Cf. Winternitz, Notes on Śrāddhas, *WZKM*, 4, 1890, pp. 199ff.

2. Cf. E. Hāns and A. Weber, Die Heiratsgebräuche der alten Inder, nach den Grihyasūtra (in the fifth volume of (*Indische Studien*). L.V. Schroeder, *Die Hochzeitsgebräuche der Esten und einiger anderer finnisch-ugrischer Völkerschaften in Vergleichung mit denen der indogermanischen Völker*, Berlin, 1888. B.W. Leist,

No less important is a third class of text-books, which immediately follow the Gṛhyasūtras and which have perhaps come into being as their continuation viz., the Dharmasūtras i.e. text-books which deal with the Dharma. Dharma means "justice, duty, law," as well as "religion, moral custom." These works, therefore, deal with the mundane as well as religious laws, which in India cannot be separated from each other. They give us rules and regulations on the duties of the castes and the stages of life (Āśramas). Through these works the Brahmins succeeded in modifying the customary law of ancient India in their favour and in making their influence recognized in all directions. We will speak in greater detail about these Dharmasūtras in the chapter on the literature of law. Here they must simply be mentioned because they have come into being, like the Śrauta and the Gṛhyasūtras, in the vedic schools and form with them a constituent of the Kalpasūtras or text-books of ritual.

Finally, to these Kalpasūtras belong also the Śulvasūtras which directly follow the Śrautasūtras. They contain precise rules for the measuring—Śulva means "measuring-string"—and for the erection of the place of sacrifice and the fire-altar and they are, as the oldest works on Indian geometry, of no mean significance to the history of science.

Of great importance are the Śrauta and Gṛhyasūtras also for the explanation of the Veda. They contain not only the rules for the ritual, but also for the use (viniyoga) of the Mantras, i.e. the prayers and formulas. They are, for the most part, verses or Yajus-sentences, which occur in the vedic

---

Altarisches Jus gentium, Jena 1889. M. Winternitz, Das Altindische Hochzeitsrituell nach dem Āpastambīya-Gṛhyasūtra und einigen anderen verwandten Werken, Mit Vergleichung der Hochzeitsgebräuche bei den übrigen indogermanischen Völkern. (*Denkschriften der kais. Akademie der Wissenschaften in Wien* phil-hist. Kl. Bd. XL. Wien 1891). M. Winternitz, on a comparative study of Indo-European customs, with special reference to the Marriage customs (*the International Folke-lore Congress* 1891, *Papers and Transactions,* London 1892, pp. 267-291). O. Schrader, *Reallexikon der indogermanischen Altertumskunde,* Strassburg 1901, p. 353 ff. Th. Zachariae, Zum altindischen Hochzeitsritual (in the *Wiener Zeitschrift für die Kunde des Morgenlandes,* Bd. XVII, p. 135 ff, 211 ff.

Saṃhitās; and for their proper explanation their use in sacrificial rites is not at all unimportant. Of course, the Mantras have, often enough, nothing to do with the sacrificial acts for which they are prescribed—and from the point of view of the history of religion it is extremely interesting to see how prayers are often used for purposes for which they are not at all suited and how they have been often misundertsood, wrongly construed and also arbitrarily changed[1]—, but sometimes their ritual use does certainly give the key for explaining a difficult Veda-text. In general the Mantras are included in the Sūtras and are quoted sometimes completely and sometimes only with the initial words of the verses which are supposed to be known.

It is also the Mantras by means of which the Kalpasūtras give expression most clearly that they belong to particular vedic schools. Thus for example the Śrauta and Gṛhyasūtras belonging to the Black Yajurveda give the prayers in the form which they have in the Saṃhitās of the Black Yajurveda; and they give the verses of the yajus-sentences which are taken from the saṃhitās to which they belong, only with the initial words, i.e. they suppose them as known, whereas they give the other Mantras, for example, those of the Ṛgveda and Atharvaveda, completely. Moreover, there are, in all sūtras, a number of mantras which do not occur in the Saṃhitās. And there are two Gṛahyasūtras in which the Mantras have been clearly separated from the Sūtra-text and combined in independent prayer-books; these are the mantra-brāhmaṇa,[2] which contains the prayers for the Gobhila-Gṛhyasūtra and the mantrapāṭha[3] belonging to the Āpastaṃba-Gṛhyasūtra.

Only in the case of the Baudhāyana and Āpastamba schools belonging to the Black Yajurveda do we find kalpasūtras which

1. See Winternitz. *The Mantrapāṭha*, pp. xxix f and Edwin W. Fay, *The Rig Veda Mantras in the Gṛhya Sūtras*, Diss. Roanoke, Va, 1899.

2. *The Mantra Brāhmaṇa* I Prapāṭhaka (Sanskrit and German)by Heinrich Stönner. Halle. S. 1901 (Inaugural dissertation); *The Mantra-Brāhmaṇa* II Prapāṭhaka, with Sāyaṇas commentary and German translation, by Hans Jörgensen, Darmstadt 1911 (Diss. Kiel); The Mantra Brāhmaṇa, Ed. with Comm. by Satyavrata Sāmaśrami in the *Uṣā* Calcutta 1890.

3. The Mantrapāṭha or the Prayer Book of-the Āpastambins. Edited by M. Winternitz, Oxford (Anecdota Oxoniensia) 1897.

contain all the four kinds of sūtra-texts—Śrauta-Gṛhya; Dharma- and Śulvasūtras—whereby it can be also proved that these works are really as much connected with one another that they can be in a certain way looked upon as the four volumes of a unitary work. If Baudhāyana and Āpastamba were not really the authors of the complete kalpasūtras embracing all the four kinds of texts—which is also possible—then in any case the Śrauta, Gṛhya, Dharma and Śulvasūtras belonging to the Baudhāyana, or the Āpastamba school as the case may be, are certainly in each case, works of those two schools[1] of the Black Yajurveda which have been composed as per a unitary plan.

Closely related to the sūtras of the Āpastamba school are those of the schools of the Bharadvāja and of Satyāṣāḍha Hiraṇyakeśin. The Śrautasūtra of the Bharadvājas is only known in manuscripts, whereas the Gṛhyasūtra has been published.[2] Both the Śrauta- and the Gṛhyasūtras[3] of the Hiraṇyakeśins have been published, while the Hiraṇyakeśī-Dharmasūtra hardly differs from the Āpastambīya-Dharmasūtra.

All these sūtras, to which we may add those of the hitherto

1. The Baudhāyana-Śrautasūtra has been edited by W. Caland, *Bibl. Ind.*, 1904-1924, the Baudhāyana-Gṛhyasūtra by L. Śrīnivāsācharya, Mysore 1904 (*Bibliotheca Sanscrita No.* 32); selections from the Gṛhyasūtra translated by P. Harting, Amersfoort 1922; the Baudhāyana-Śulvasūtra has been edited and translated by G. Thibaut in the *Pandit*, Vols. IX ff. 'On the Baudhāyana-Sūtras, see Caland, *Das rituelle Sūtra des Baudhāyana*, Leipzig, 190 3 (AKM., XII, 1),—The Āpastambīya-Śrautasūtra has been edited by, R. Garbe, *Bibl. Ind.* 1882-1903 and Books 1-7 translated into German by W. Caland, Göttingen 1921, The *Āpastambīya-Gṛhyasūtra* ed. by M. Winternitz, Vienna 1887, and translated, with the Āpastamba-Paribhāṣāsūtras, by Oldenberg, *SBE.*, Vol. 30; the Āpastambīya-Śulvasūtr. ed. and translated into German by Albert Burk, *ZDMG.*, Vols. 55, 56, 1901-2. Critical and explanatory notes on the Āpast.-Śraut. by Caland, *ZDMG.* 72, 1918, pp. 27 ff. On the Śrautasūtras of the Black Yajurveda see also A.B. Keith, *HOS.*, Vol. 18, pp. xlii ff.

2. By Henriette J. W. Salomons, Leyden 1913.

3. Hiraṇyakeśī-Śrautasūtra ed. with Comm. in *AnSS* No. 53; Hiraṇyakeśī-Gṛhyasūtra ed. by J. Kirste, Vienna 1889, and translated by Oldenberg in *SBE.*, Vol. 30.

less known schools of the Vādhūlas[1] and Vaikhānasas,[2] are closely associated with the Tāittirīya-Saṃhitā. There can be no doubt that Baudhāyana is the earliest of these sūtra-writers,[3] his successors being Bharadvāja, Āpastamba and Hiraṇyakeśin in chronological order. The Śrauta- Gṛhya- and Śulvasūtras of the Mānava school,[4] and the Kāṭhaka-Gṛhyasūtra,[5] which is related to the Mānava-Gṛhyasūtra, come under the Maitrāyaṇī-Saṃhitā.

Whether a Kalpasūtra embracing all four kinds of sūtras has always existed in every other Vedic school, as in the cases of the schools of Baudhāyana and Āpastamba, cannot be determined. Of those schools which do not belong to the Black Yajurveda we actually only possess here a Śrautasūtra, and there a Gṛhyasūtra, connection of a few Dharmasūtras with schools of the Ṛgveda or of the White Yajurveda is but a very loose one. To the White Yajurveda belong: a Kātyāyana-Śrautasūtra,[6] a Pāraskara-Gṛhyasūtra[7] and a Kātyāyana-Śulvasūtra,[8] to the

1. On some fragments of the Vādhūla- Sūtras, which are related to those of Baudhāyana, see Caland, *Acta Orientalia* I, pp. 3 ff.; II, pp. 142 ff.

2. On the Vaikhānasa-Sūtras see Th. Bloch, *Über das Gṛhya- und Dharmasūtra der Vaikhānasa*, Leipzig, 1896. The Vaikhānasadharmapraśna has been published by Gaṇapati-Śāstri in *TSS.* No. 28, 1913.

3. This is also confirmed by Baudhāyana's style, which is sometimes intermediate between Brāhmaṇa and Sūtra style. Baudhāyana is sometimes called a pravacanakāra, and it seems that pravacana is a term for a literary type which forms a transitory stage between Brāhmaṇas and Sūtras; see Winternitz *WZKM*, 17, 1903, pp. 289 ff.

4. Mānava-Śrautasūtra, Books I-V, edited by F. Knauer, St. Petersburg 1900 ff-; the Cayana of the Mānava-Śrautasūtra, by J. M. van Gelder, Leyden 1921 (Diss.); the Mānava-Gṛhyasūtra by F. Knauer, St. Petersburg 1897. The Mānava-Śrautasūtra is perhaps the oldest Śrautasūtra. Garbe (Āpastamba Śrautasūtra Ed. Vol. III, pp. xxii f.) has shown that it is certainly older than Āpastamba who refers to it. On the Mānava-Gṛhyasūtra, see also P.van Bradke, *ZDMG* Vol.36. The Varāhagṛhyasūtra (ed. by R. Sama-Sastry, *Gaekwad's Oriental Series*, No. 18, Baroda 1921), belonging to a school of the Maitrāyaṇīya, is a late work.

5. An edition of the Kāṭhaka- Gṛhyasūtra by W. Caland is announced as being in the press by the D.A.V. College, Lahore.

6. Ed. by A. Weber, *The White Yajurveda*, Vol. III.

7. Ed. with a German translation by A.F. Stenzler, Indische Hausregeln, *AKM*. VI. 2 and 4, 1876-78; with Harihara's comm. by Ladharam Sarman, Bombay 1890; translated by H. Oldenberg, *SBE.*, Vol. 29.

8. A Pariśiṣṭa to this (Kātīyam Śulbapariśiṣṭam) ed. by G. Thibaut in *Pandit*, N.S. Vol. 4.

Ṛgveda an Āśvalāyana-Śrautasūtra,[1] and Āśvalāyana-Gṛhyasūtra[2] and a Gṛhyasūtra of Sāṅkhyāyana;[3] to the Sāmaveda the closely related Śrautasūtras of Lāṭyāyana[4] and Drāhyāyana,[5] a Śrautasūtra and a Gṛhyasūtra of the Jaiminīya school,[6] and the Gṛhyasūtras of Gobhila[7] and Khādira.[8] Sāmaveda literature also includes the Ārṣeyakalpa, also known as the Maśakakalpasūtra,[9] which teaches which melodies are to be sung to the various stanzas at the soma festivals. This sūtra is intimately connected with the Pañcaviṃśa-Brāhmaṇa and is earlier than the Lāṭyāyana-Śrautasūtra. Lastly, among Atharvaveda literature we have a Vaitāna-Śrautasūtra,[10] a work which originated very late

1. Edition in *Bibl. Ind.* Cf. Keith, *HOS.*, Vol. 25, pp. 51 ff.; P. Sabbathier, L'Agnistoma d'après le Crauta-sutra d'Acvalayana, *JA.* 15, 1890,1 ff., 186 ff.

2. Ed. with commentary of Gārgya Nārāyaṇa., in *Bibl. Ind.* 1869; with commentary of Haradattācārya, by Gaṇapati Śāstri in *TSS.* No. 78, 1923; with German translation by A.F. Stenzler, Indische Hausregeln, *AKM.* III, 4, 1864 and IV, 1,1865; translated into English by H. Oldenberg, *SBE.*, Vol. 29.

3. Sāṅkhyāyana-Śrautasūtra ed. by A. Hillebrandt in *Bibl. Ind.* 1818 ff. Cf. Keith, *JRAS.* 1907, pp. 410 ff. and *HOS.*, Vol. 25, pp. 50 f. Sāṅkhyāyana-Gṛhyasūtra, Sanskrit and German by H. Oldenberg, *Ind. Stud.*, Vol. 15; English translation by the same scholar, *SBE.*, Vol. 29, *Sāṅkhyāyana-gṛhyasaṃgraha* by Pandita Vasudeva ed. by Somanāthopādhyāya, Nyāyopādhyāya and Kāvyatīrtha, and Kauṣītakigṛhyasūtras ed. by Ratna Gopala Bhatta, *Ben SS* 1908.

4. Edition in *Bibli. Ind.* A few chapters translated into German by R. Simon *ZII.*, Vol. 2. 1923, pp. 1 ff.

5. Ed. by J.N. Reuter, Part I, London 1904.

6. D. Gaastra, *Bijdrage tot de Kennis van het vedische ritueel, Jaiminiya-Srautasutra*, Leyden 1906, being text and translation of the Agniṣṭoma chapter; text of the *Śrautakārikā* ib. pp. 36-60. The Jaiminīyagṛhyasūtra ed. and translated by W. Caland, Lahore 1922 (*Punjab Sanskrit Series*, No. 2).

7. Ed. with Comm. by Chandrakānta Tarkālankar, 2nd ed., in *Bibl. Ind.* 1906-1908. Critically edited, with German translation, by F. Knauer, Dorpat 1884, 1886. Translated into English by H. Oldenberg *SBE.*, Vol. 30.

8. Text and English translation by H. Oldenberg in *SBE.*, Vol. 29.

9. Ed. by W. Caland, *AKM.* XII. 3, Leipzig, 1908. Maśaka is the name of the author.

10. Edited and translated into German by R. Garbe. London and Strassburg 1878; the translation is superseded by that of W. Caland, Amsterdam (Akad.) 1910. On the position of the Vaitānasūtra in the Atharvaveda literature see Caland, *WZKM.* 18, 1904, 185 ff.; Keith, *JRAS.* 1910, 934 ff.; Bloomfield, *GGA.* 1912, No. 1.

and which was added to the Atharvaveda in order to make it of equal value with the remaining three Vedas, and the much older and more important Kauśikasūtra.[1] This is only partly a Gṛhyasūtra, which like the other Gṛhyasūtras, treats of domestic ritual; but it is much more extensive and also contains the most minute directions for the performance of those magic rites for which the songs and spells of the Atharvaveda were used. This Kauśikasūtra is thus a most valuable complement to the Atharvaveda-Saṃhitā and an inestimable source for our knowledge of ancient Indian magic. The Sāmavidhāna-Brāhmaṇa,[2] too, attached to the Sāmaveda, is an interesting book of magic, belonging, in spite of its titles, to the Sūtra literature.

The Gṛhyasūtras are followed up by the Śrāddhakalpas and Pitṛmedhasūtras, which contain rules for the Śrāddhas and the ancestral sacrifices. Some of these texts may be classed in the categories of the ritual texts of the Vedic schools after which they are named, while others are later productions.[3] The Sūtra texts, however, do not exhaust the literature on ritual by any means. Just as the Upaniṣads of the Veda are followed up by the post-Vedic Upaniṣad literature, so the Vedic ritual literature is followed up by literary activity in the realm of ritual, which has continued down to the most recent times.

---

1. Edited by M. Bloomfield, New Haven 1890. Numerous extracts from this Sūtra have been given by the same scholar in the Notes to his English translation of selected hymns of the Atharvaveda (*SBE.*, Vol. 42). The most important sections of the Kauśikasūtra referring to magic, have also been translated into German by W. Caland in his work: *Alt-indisches Zauberritual*, Amsterdam, 1900.

2. Edited by A.C. Burnell, London 1873. Translated into German by Sten Konow, Das Sāmavidhānabrāhmaṇa, *ein altindisches Handbuch der Zauberei* Halle a.S. 1893.

3. Mānavaśrāddhakalpa ed. by W. Caland, *Altindischer Ahnencult*, pp. 228 ff., Śrāddhakalpa of the Śaunakins, ibid. pp. 240 ff., Fragments of a Paippalāda-śrāddhakalpa, ibid. pp. 243 ff., Kātyāyanaśrāddhakalpa, ibid. pp. 245 ff. On the Gautamaśrāddhakalpa, see Caland in *Bijdragen tot de taal, land en volkenkunde van Ned. Indie*, 6e Volg. deel I, 1894. The Pitṛmedhasūtras of Baudhāyana. Hiraṇyakeśin, *Gautama* ed. W. Caland *AKM*. X, 3, 1896; the 2nd and 3rd Praśnas of Baudh.—Pitṛmedhasūtra, by C.H. Raabe, *Bijdrage tot de kennis van het hindoesche toodenritueel*. Leyden 1911.

Next after the Śrauta- and Gṛhyasūtras follow the Pariśiṣṭas or "addenda," in which certain things are treated in greater detail, which have merely been briefly indicated in the Sūtras. The Pariśiṣṭas appended to the Gobhilagṛhyasūtra are of importance, namely the Gṛhyasaṃgrahapariśiṣṭa of Gobhilaputra,[1] and the Karmapradīpa.[2] The Pariśiṣṭas of the Atharvaveda,[3] which throw light more especially on all kinds of magical practices, omens and portents and the like, are of great value from the point of view of the history of religion. One of the oldest Pariśiṣṭas is the Prāyaścittasūtra,[4] which has come down as part of the *Vaitānasūtra*, and treats of the expiatory rites. Later ritual works are the Prayogas, "practical handbooks," the Paddhatis, "outlines," and the Kārikās, versified presentations of the ritual. All these works deal either with the complete ritual of some Vedic school or, which is more often the case, with some special rites. The special works on marriage customs, burial of the dead and ancestral sacrifices (Śrāddhas), are of particular importance, though most of these works are known only through manuscripts and Indian prints.

The Exegetic Vedāṅgas

At least as old as the Kalpasūtras are those sūtra-texts which deal with the śikṣā or phonetics. Whereas the kalpasūtras are

---

1. See M. Bloomfield in *ZDMG.*, Vol. 35. Edited by Ch. Tarkalankar, *Bibl. Ind.* 1910. Other Gobhilīya-Pariśiṣṭas (Sandhyāsūtra, Snānasūtra, Śrāddhakalpa, etc.), ed. by the same scholar, *Bibl. Ind.* 1909.

2. The first part of the Karmapradīpa, ed. and translated into German by F. Schrader Halle a.S, 1889, the second part by A. v. Stael-Holstein, Halle a.S. 1900 (Diss) Cf. Hillebrandt, *Ritualliteratur*, pp. 37 f., and Caland, *Altindischer Ahnencult*, pp. 112 ff.

3. Ed. by G.M. Bolling and J. von Negelein, Leipzig 1909-10. See also J.v. Negelein, *Orientalistische Literaturzeitung* 1908, 447 ff., Winternitz, *WZKM* 23, 1909, 401 ff., and Keith, *JRAS.* 1912, 757 ff. The Śāntikalpa of the Atharvaveda (ed. by G.M. Bolling, *Transactions of the American Philological Association*, Vol. 35, 1904, 77 ff.: *JAOS*, 33, 1913, 265ff.) treats of rites for driving away the evil consequences of portents. The Ath. Pariśiṣṭas sometimes give a clue to the explanation of the hymns of the Atharvaveda where the Kauśikasūtra fails; see F. Edgerton, *Studies in Honor of M. Bloomfield*, p. 118.

4. The Atharvaprāyascittāni have been edited by J. v. Negelein, New Haven 1915 (reprinted from *JAOS*, 1913-14). See also Caland, *WZKM* 18, 1904, 197 ff.

auxiliary to the Brāhmaṇa portions of the Veda, the sūtras belonging to the Vedāṅga śikṣā are closely connected with the Saṃhitās of the Vedas.

Śikṣā means actually "instruction", then in particular 'instruction in reciting' i.e. in the correct pronunciation, intonation etc. of the Saṃhitā texts. The earliest mention of these Vedāṅgas is found in the Taittirīya-Upaniṣad (I, 2) where the lessons on letters and their intonation, syllabic measure (quantity) and volume, melody and word-combination are enumerated as the six chapters of Śikṣā. Just like the lesson on ritual so also the śikṣā has come into being out of religious necessity. For in order to rightly perform a sacrificial act it was not only necessary to know the ritual, but one had to also pronounce the holy texts accurately and without mistakes—and that in such a manner as was handed down in the Saṃhitās. This presupposes that at a time when the textbooks of Śikṣā came into being, the Vedic Saṃhitās were already fixed as holy texts, that they had received a definite form in the hands of phonetically trained editors. Indeed it can be proved that for example the Ṛgveda-Saṃhitā does not give the hymns in the form in which they have been composed by the old singers. Of course the editors have not changed anything of the texts, but in the matter of pronunciation of initial and final sounds of the words, avoiding the hiatus and similar things by phonetic theories, they allowed themselves to be influenced to deviate from the original manner of recitation. So we read for example in our Saṃhitā *tvam hyagne*, but (on the basis of metre) we can prove that the ancient singers had pronounced *tuam hi agne*. Therefore the Vedic Saṃhitās themselves are already the work of phoneticians. But in addition to the Saṃhitā-pāṭhas, i.e. the Saṃhitā-texts as they had to be recited according to the teachings of the śikṣā, there are also the so-called Pada-pāṭhas or words-texts in which the single words of the phonetic combination in which the Saṃhitā-text offers them, appear separated from one another. One example will suffice to show the difference between the Saṃhitā-pāṭha and Pada-pāṭha clearly. A verse of the Ṛgveda-Saṃhitā is as follows:

agniḥ pūrvebhirṛṣibhiriḍyonirtanairuta sa devam eha vakṣati.

In the *Pada-pāṭha* this verse reads :

agniḥ/pūrvebhiḥ/ṛṣibhiḥ/īḍyaḥ/nirtaniḥ/uta/sa/devam/ā/iha/vakṣati./

These Pada-pāṭhas are naturally the work of phonetically trained theologians, indeed of grammarians; for they offer the text of the verses in a completely grammatical analysis. Yet they must be quite old. The Pada-pāṭha of the Ṛgveda is attributed to Śākalya, a teacher who is mentioned already in the Aitareya Āraṇyaka.[1]

Saṃhitā-pāṭhas and Pada-pāṭhas are therefore the oldest products of the Śikṣā schools. The oldest textbooks preserved to us belonging to this Vedāṅga are however the Prātiśakhyās, which contain the rules with whose help one can reconstruct the Saṃhitā-pāṭha from the Pada-pāṭha. Hence they contain instructions on pronunciation, intonation, euphonic changes of sounds in word combinations as well as in the initial and final sounds of words in a sentence, on elongation of vowels, in short: on the whole manner of recitation of the Saṃhitā. For every Śākhā or version of a Saṃhitā there was one such textbook —hence the name Prāti-śākhyas i.e. "textbooks meant for each śākhā". First of all one Ṛgveda-Prātiśākhya[2] has been preserved till the present day. This is attributed to Śaunaka who is supposed to have been a teacher of Āśvalāyana. This work is composed in verse and is probably a later modification of an older sūtra-text; in manuscripts and quotations it is even termed as 'Śūtra'. To the *Taittiriya-Saṃhitā* belongs the Taittirīya-Prātiśākhya-sūtra;[3] to the Vājasaneyī-saṃhitā a Vājasaneyī-

1. On the Padapāṭha of Śākalya, see B. Liebich *Zur Einführung in die indische einheimische Sprachwissenschaft* II, Heidelberg 1919, pp. 20 ff. On the Padapāṭha of the Taittirīya-Saṃhitā, see A. Weber, *Ind. Stud.* 13,1-128, and A.B. Keith *HOS.*, Vol. 18. pp. xxx ff.

2. *Rigveda-Prātiśākhya, the oldest textbook of Vedic phonetics.* Samskrit text with translation and notes published by Max Müller, Leipzig, 1856-69. On the metrics of the Ṛgveda-Prātiśākhya, see H. Oldenberg *NGGW*, 1919, pp. 170 ff.

3. *The Taittirīya-Prātiśākhya.* Text, Translation and Notes by W.D. Whitney New Haven, 1871 (*Journal of the American Oriental Society*, Vol. IX). On the re lation of the Taittirīya-Prātiśākhya to the Taitt. Saṃhitā, see Keith, *HOS*, Vol. 18. pp. xxxi ff. It is certainly older than Pāṇini.

Prātiśākhya[1] sūtra attributed to Kātyāyana and to the Atharvaveda-saṃhitā an Atharvaveda *Prātiśākhya-sūtra*[2] which is supposed to be of the school of the *Śaunakas*. There is also a Sāmaprātiśākhya[3] and the Puṣpasūtra[4] is a kind of Prātiśākhya to the Uttaragāna of the Sāmaveda. A further work dealing with the manner of singing the Sāmans at the sacrifice, is the Pañcavidhasūtra.[5]

These works are of importance to us in two different ways. Firstly, for the history of the study of grammar in India, which begins for us with these Prātiśākhyas. Although they are not themselves actual works of grammar, still they deal with subjects which belong to grammar. By the fact that they also quote many grammarians, they also prove that in their times the study of grammar was already flourishing well. Secondly they are still more important by the fact that they bear testimony to the fact that the texts of the saṃhitās have been preserved without any change throughout all these centuries since the time of the Prātiśākhyas. Thus the rules of the Ṛgveda-Prātiśākhya presuppose that at that time the Ṛgveda Saṃhitā was already in its final form with its division into ten Maṇḍalas but also that the order of the hymns in every Maṇḍala was the same as now. The minute rules of the Śaunaka do not leave any doubt that during its time the text of the Ṛgveda-Saṃhitā was almost word for word and syllable for

1. *Kātyāyana's Prātiśākhya of the White Yajurveda*, ed. by P.T. Pathaka, Benaras, 1883-88; text with German transln. by A. Weber, *Ind. Stud.* 4, 65-160, 177-331. The Pratijñāsūtra (ed. and explained by Weber in *ABA*. 1871. pp. 69 ff.) is an appendix to this Prātiśākhya.

2. Critically edited by Vishva Bandhu Vidyarthi Sastri, Part I, Punjab University 1923. This is different from the Śaunakīya Caturādhyāyikā which has been edited and translated as an Atharvaveda-Prātiśākhya by W.D. Whitney, New Haven 1862 (*JAOS*) vol. 7).

3. Ed. by Satyavrata Sāmaśramī in *Uṣā*, Calcutta 1890.

4. Ed. and translated into German by R. Simon, *A Bay A*, 1909, pp. 481-780. On the mutual relation between Puṣpasūtra, Ārṣeyakalpa and Uttaragāna, see Simon, ibid. 499 ff., *ZDMG*, 63, 1909, 730 ff. and Caland, 64, 1910, 347f.

5. Ed. and translated into German by R. Simon, Breslau 1913 (*Indische Forschungen*, Nr. 5).

syllable exactly the same as we find it today in our printed editions.

These Prātiśākhyas are the oldest representatives of the Vedāṅga Śikṣā. There are, in addition to this, more modern works, small treatises on phonetics which are called Śikṣā and give out as their authors famous names like Bharadvāja, Vyāsa, Vasiṣṭha, Yājñavalkya etc. They follow the Prātiśākhyas almost in the same way as versified law books followed the ancient Vedic Dharmasūtras in later times, which law books also named similarly famous names as their authors. Some of these Śikṣās are comparatively old and follow more directly some Prātiśākhya—for example the Vyāsa-Śikṣā[1] follows the Taittirīya Prātiśākhya,—whereas others are of much later origin and are of importance neither for the grammar nor for the history of the Vedic texts.[2]

Śaunaka and Kātyāyana, who are named as authors of Prātiśākhyas are also considered to be the authors of works which are very close to the Vedāṅga-literature because they are also concerned with the texts of the Vedic Saṃhitās which one, of course, does not call Vedāṅgas. It is the Anukramaṇīs, i.e. "lists, indices," which give the contents of the Vedic Saṃhitās according to different subjects.[3] Thus Śaunaka composed an Anukramaṇī or a list of the Ṛṣis of the Ṛgveda-hymns, a list of the metres, one of the deities and one of the hymns. Of Kātyāyana we possess a Sarvānukramaṇī,[4] i.e. "a list of all things" for

1. Cf. H. Lüders, *Die Vyāsa-Śikṣā besonders in ihrem Verhältnis zum Taittirīya-Prātiśākhya*, Kiel, 1895.

2. On the Śikṣās, see F. Kielhorn, *Ind. Ant.* 5, 1876, 141 ff, 193 ff. On the Pāṇinīya-Śikṣā, see A. Weber, *Ind. Stud.* 4, 435 ff. and B. Liebich, *Zur Einfuhrüng in die indische einheimische Sprachwissenschaft* II, p. 20, who says that though late in form, it is old in contents. The Nāradiya-Śikṣā is edited in Satyavrata Sāmaśramī *Uṣā*, I, 4, Calcutta 1890; the Bharadvāja-Śikṣā (*cum versione latina, excerptis excommentario* etc.) by E. Sieg, Berlin 1892. A collection of Śikṣās (*Śikṣāsaṃgraha*) has been published in *Ben SS*, 1893.

3. *The Atharvavedīyapañcapaṭalika* (ed. by Bhagavaddatta, Lahore 1920) is an Anukramāṇī of the Atharvaveda-Saṃhitā. The so-called *Ārṣeya-Brāhmaṇa of the Sāmaveda* (ed. by A.C. Burnell, Mangalore 1876, and with commentary by Satyavrata Sāmaśramī in *Uṣā*, II, 1, Calcutta 1892) is also an Anukramaṇī.

4. Edited by A.A. Macdonell, Oxford (*Anecdota Oxoniensia*) 1886. On a Kashmirian recension of the Sarvānukramaṇī, see Scheftelowitz, *ZII*, 1, 1922, 89 ff.

the Ṛgveda. This work gives in the form of Sūtras the initial words of each hymn, then the number of the verse, the name and the generation of the Ṛṣi to whom it is attributed, of the deities to whom the individual verses are addressed and of the metre or metres in which the hymn is composed. To Śaunaka are also attributed the two metrical works—Bṛhaddevatā and Ṛgvidhāna. The Bṛhaddevatā[1] is an enlarged catalogue of the gods worshipped in the individual hymns of the Ṛgveda; for it contains also myths and legends referring to these deities, and is therefore at the same time an important work from the point of view of Indian narrative literature. The Bṛhaddevatā is obviously one of the earliest Indian narrative works, for its metres the triṣṭubh as well as the Śloka, occupy a middle position in point of time between Vedic and epic metre; and furthermore, those legends which are common to the Bṛhaddevatā and the Mahābhārata, appear in a later form in the epic.[2] The Ṛgvidhāna,[3] also in the form of a catalogue following the division of our Ṛgvedasaṃhitā, states the magic power which can be obtained by the recitation of each hymn or even single verses. It is somewhat similar to the above-mentioned Sāmavidhāna-Brāhmaṇa.

The importance of the Anukramaṇīs and of the connected works lies in the fact that they too prove that even in very ancient times the texts of the Vedic Saṃhitās were available almost exactly in the same form, in the same division, with the same number of verses etc. as they are found today.

The same is true also of Nirukta[4] of Yāska mentioned already. This work also, the only one which we possess as the remnant

---

1. Ed. by Rajendralala Mitra in *Bibl. Ind.* 1892; critically edited and translated into English by A.A. Macdonell, *HOS.*, Vols. 5 and 6, 1904.

2. See A. Kuhn, *Ind. Stud.* I, 101 ff.; Keith, *JRAS.* 1906, pp. 1 ff.; 1912, pp. 769 ff. Winternitz, *WZKM.* 20, 1906, pp. 1 ff.; *Liebich Zur Einführung in die ind. einh. Spachwiss.* II, 30 ff.

3. Ṛgvidhānam edidit cum praefatione Rudolf Meyer, Berolini 1878.

4. See above p. 62. The Nirukta was first edited by R. Roth, Göttingen, 1852; with commentaries and useful indexes by Satyavrata Sāmaśrami in *Bibl. Ind.*, 1882-91; with commentary of Durgācārya, Vol. 1, Adhy. 1-6, edited by V.K. Rajavade, *AnSS.*, No. 88, 1921. On S. Sarup's edition see above.

of the Vedāṅga Nirukta, presupposes the Ṛgveda-Saṃhitā in essentially the same state in which we know it today. Tradition wrongly ascribes also the Nighaṇṭus or "Word-lists" to Yāska. In reality however the work of Yāska is only a commentary to these "Word-lists", of which Yāska himself says, that they, have been compiled by the descendants of the ancient sages for more easy understanding of the texts handed down by tradition. The Nighaṇṭus are, as is well known, five lists of words, that are divided into three parts. The first part (Naighaṇṭuka-kāṇḍa) consists of three lists, in which Vedic words are compiled under certain main headings. For example, 21 names are enumerated for "earth", 15 for "gold", 16 for "air", 101 for "water", 122 verbs for "go", 26 adjectives and adverbs for "fast" or "fastly", 12 for "much" etc. The second part (Naigama-kāṇḍa or Aikapādika) contains a list of individual words with many meanings and of specially difficult words of the Veda, while the third part (Daivata-kāṇḍa) gives a classification of the deities according to the three regions—earth, sky and heaven.[1] With the compilation of such glossaries the Veda-exegesis has probably begun and it was only one more stage of development, as they composed to these glossaries commentaries in the manner of our Nirukta in which commentaries, explanations of difficult Veda verses were interspersed, until in still later times exhaustive and continuous commentaries have been written to the Vedic texts. It is certain that Yāska had many predecessors and that his work, although it is certainly very old and for us simply the oldest Veda-exegetic work, can be still considered only as the last, perhaps also the most complete product of the literature belonging to the Vedāṅga Nirukta.

Of the Vedāṅgas of metrics and astronomy, too, it is only the latest offshoots of an earlier scientific literature that remain.

---

1 On these Nighaṇṭus as the beginnings of Indian lexicography see Th. Zachariae, *Die indischen Wörterbücher* (Grundriss, I, 3 B), Strassburg, 1897, pp. 2f. S.K. Belvalkar (*Proc.*, *SOC.*, pp. 11 ff.) has shown that it is possible, with the help of the Nighaṇṭus, especially the Aikapadika list, to distinguish literary strata in the Ṛgveda. Belvalkar dates Yāska's Nirukta from the 7th century B.C. This is likely enough, though not certain. But we have no idea how much earlier the Nighaṇṭus may be.

For the Sāmaveda there is the Nidānasūtra, containing not only metrical but other investigations into the various component parts of the Sāmaveda (Uktha, Stoma, Gāna). It is also important from the grammatical point of view, and some of the ancient teachers ascribe it to Patañjali.[1] The text book of Piṅgala on prosody, although it is considered by the Indians as a Vedāṅga belonging to the Ṛgveda or Yajurveda respectively—it is handed down to us in two recensions — is still the work of a later period; because it treats also verse-feet (verse-metres), which belong only to the later poetry in Sanskrit.[2] The Jyotiṣa-Vedāṅga is a small text-book on astronomy composed in verse —it contains in the recension of the Yajurveda 43 and in that of the Ṛgveda 36 verses—which mainly states the positions of the moon and the sun at the solstices as well as the new and full moons in the circle of the 27 Nakṣatras or stars of the zodiac, propounds rules for calculating them.[3] Even the fact that it is not composed in Sūtras, assigns to this small work, which moreover has not yet been sufficiently explained, a later date.

We have completely lost the ancient Vedāṅga texts on grammar. This science also has certainly come into being in connection with the Veda-exegesis and it has originated in the Veda-school. We certainly find even in the Āraṇyakas, individual grammatical artistic expressions. But the oldest and the most significant text-book of grammar that has come down to us, that of Pāṇini, treats the vedic language more in a casual manner; it is not in any close relationship with any vedic school and belongs to a period in which the science of grammar was already treated in special schools, independent of theology.

---

1. Cf. Weber *HIL.*, pp. 81 f., E. Sieg, Die Sagenstoffe des Ṛgveda, Stuttgart, 1902, pp. 29, 35, 65; and Caland, Ārṣeyakalpa, pp. xvii ff. A Nidāna of the Sāmaveda is quoted in the Bṛhaddevatā, V, 23. But the quotation is not found in the Nidānasūtra, printed in the *Uṣā*, Calcutta, 1896.

2. The Sūtra of Piṅgala was edited and explained by A. Weber in Vol. 8 of *Ind. Stud.* Cf. also A. Weber, *HIL.*, p. 60.

3. Cf. A. Weber, "Über den Vedakalender namens jyotisam (*Abhandlungen der Academie der Wissenschaften zu Berlin* 1862) and G Thibaut, Astronomie (in the *Grundriss*, III, 9, p 17, 20 and 28. Ātharvaṇa Jyotiṣam edited by Bhagavad Datta, Lahore, 1924 (*Punjab Sanskrit Series*, No. 6)

For even in India, as we shall see later in the chapter on scientific literature, science has made itself more and more free from theology in which originally it was almost wholly included.

The Age of the Veda

We have pursued the whole Vedic literature up to its final offshoots and addenda and cannot avoid any more the question of the age of this great literature. If it were possible to state—even to within a few centuries—how far back into the past the oldest hymns of the Ṛgveda and of the Atharvaveda would reach, then it would be unnecessary to devote a special chapter to this question. It would suffice to give the approximate date in a few words. But unfortunately it is a fact, —and it is particularly regrettable to have to admit this fact—, that the opinions of the best researchers in the matter of the age of the Ṛgveda differ not by a few centuries, but by a few thousands of years, that some put the lower limit for the Ṛgvedic hymns at the year 1000 B.C., whereas others put it somewhere between 3000 and 2500 B.C. Where the opinions of experts are at such great divergence from one another, it is not enough, even in a handbook meant for laymen, to give some approximate date, but even the layman must have an idea as to what is the basis for the divergent opinions on the age of the Veda. It is so much the more necessary as the question of the age of the oldest Indian literature is linked with the question of the beginnings of the Indo-Aryan culture, a question which is of great importance for every historian, researcher of archaeology and philologist. For, only when we can fix chronologically the oldest testimonies of Aryan culture in India can we draw conclusions about the period of the development of Indo-Iranian and further of the Indo-Germanic culture. But even for the historian who is concerned with the history of the ancient world and wants to pursue the multifarious relations among the cultured peoples of the ancient world, it is of importance to know what was the relationship of India with reference to the beginnings of its oldest cultural epoch to the three other great cultural centres of the orient—Babylon, Egypt and China.

Under such circumstances it seems to be unavoidably necessary to tender even to the layman an account of the question and, as far as it is possible, to show the limits and to substantiate our ignorance or our knowledge.

When Indian literature became known to the world for the first time, one was inclined to attribute an exceedingly old age to all works of Indian literature. Friedrich Schlegel expected from India, as we all know, nothing less than "information about the history of the ancient world that is so dark till now.[1] As late as in 1852 A. Weber wrote in his *History of Indian Literature*, "The Indian Literature is generally considered as the oldest literature, of which we possess written documents, and this justly so," and added only in 1876 in the second edition, "as long as there are no objections raised against this by the monumental writings and papyrus-rolls of Egypt or perhaps even by the Assyrian literature discovered most recently." The grounds on which, according to Weber, "The Indian literature has to be considered as the oldest literature of which extensive written documents are handed down to us," would be partly geographical ones and partly based on the history of religion. In the older parts of the Ṛgveda the Indian folk appears to us as settled in the Punjab. The gradual spread from there to the east over Hindustan towards the Ganges can be pursued in the later parts of the Vedic literature. Then the epic literature shows us further the spread of Brahminism towards the south. It must have taken some centuries before such a vast stretch of lands "inhabited by wild, mighty tribes of men" could be Brahminised. It must have also taken many centuries for the development in the history of religion from the simple nature-worship of the Ṛgveda hymns upto the theosophical-philosophical speculations of the Upaniṣads and again to those phases of belief in gods and cults as was found by Megasthenes about 300 B.C. in India. A more exact determination of the age of the Veda was not at all attempted by Weber; he even declares expressly every such attempt to be entirely futile.[2]

---

1. Cf. above p. 12
2. Weber: *Indische Literaturgeschichte*, p. 2, ff, 7.

The first one who made this attempt and tried to put up a sort of chronology of the oldest Indian literature was Max Müller in his *History of Ancient Sanskrit Literature* which appeared in 1859. Starting from the less reliable clues which we possess for the Indian chronology, the attack of Alexander and the appearance of Buddhism[1] he drew further conclusions in the following manner : Buddhism is nothing but a reaction against Brahminism and it presupposes the existence of the whole Veda, i.e. of the literature consisting of the hymns, the Brāhmaṇas, Āraṇyakas and Upaniṣads. This entire literature must have originated before Buddhism i.e. before 500 B.C. The Vedāṅga or Sūtra literature might be almost simultaneous with the birth and the early propagation of Buddhism. These Sūtra-works, whose origin falls into the period between 600 and 200 B.C.—with the propounding of these purely arbitrary dates begins the untenable element of the Max Müller calculations—are so conceived that the Brāhmaṇa-literature must have necessarily preceded them. But the Brāhmaṇas of which there are older and younger ones, in which are contained long lists of teachers, which older Brāhmaṇas handed down, cannot be possibly accommodated in less than 200 years. Hence in the opinion of Max Müller, one will have to accept as the period of birth of these prose works the period between 800 and 600 B.C. But the Brāhmaṇas in their turn again presuppose the existence of the Vedic Saṃhitās. But at least 200 years were necessary to compile these collections of songs and prayers, hence the space of approximately 1000 to 800 B.C. might have to be considered as the period on which these collections were made. But prior to the origin of these compilations, which were already considered as sacred sacrificial poetry and authorised prayer books, there must have been a period in which the songs and prayers contained in them have originated as popular or religious poetry. This period, Max Müller concluded, must be anterior to 1000 B.C. And as he had already presumed 200 years once for the "Brāhmaṇa period" and another 200 years for the "Mantra period" so named by him, therefore he presumed also—however not laying much emphasis

1. Cf. above, p. 23 f.

on this number 200 years for the birth of this poetry and arrived thus at 1200 to 1000 B.C. as the initial period of Vedic poetry.

Now it is clear that the presumption of 200 years for each of the various literary epoques in the birth of the Veda is purely arbitrary. And Max Müller himself did not want to say anything more than this, that at *least* such an interval must be presumed and that at *least* by 1000 B.C. our Ṛgveda-Saṃhitā must have been already completed. He has looked upon his dating of 1200 to 1000 B.C. always only as *terminus ad quem*, and in his lectures on "Physical Religion" which appeared in 1890 he said expressly, that we must not hope to propose a *terminus a quo*. "No power on earth will be able to determine"[1] he says, "whether the Vedic hymns were composed in 1000 or 1500 or 2000 or 3000 before Christ." But it is remarkable, how strong the power of suggestion is even in science. The purely hypothetical and actually quite arbitrary chronological fixation of the Vedic epoques by Max Müller received, without the addition of any new arguments or actual proofs, in course of time more and more the recognition and character of a scientifically proved fact. One formed the habit — and even W. D. Whitney[2] reprimanded this habit — of saying, Max Müller has proved 1200 to 1000 B.C. to be the date of the Ṛgveda. Only with hesitation did some researchers like L. von Schroeder[3] dare to go beyond, upto 1500 or even upto 2000 B.C. And when a few years ago, by reason of astronomical calculatioms H. Jacobi tried to push back the Vedic literature into the 3rd millenium before Christ, a hue and cry was raised by the scholars against such a heretic step, and even today most researchers cannot comprehend that Jacobi could put forth such a crazy view on the age of the Veda. It was strangely forgotten, on how weak a footing "the prevailing view" actually stood which they tried to defend so vigorously.

The idea of drawing conclusions about the chronology of the oldest Indian literature from the history of the starry sky

---

1 *Physische Religion*, Gifford-Lectures delivered by F. Max Müller. Translated from English by R.O. Franke Leipzig, 1892 p. 86 f. English original (*Physical Religion*) pub. London, 1901, p. 91.

2. *Oriental and Linguistic Studies* : First series, New York, 1872, p. 78.

3. *Indiens Literatur und Kultur* p. 291 f.

with the help of astronomical data is nothing new. Even A. Ludwig has made such an attempt[1] based on solar eclipses. The priests of ancient India who had to determine the times of sacrifices were, just like the pontifices in ancient Rome, at the same time also calendar-makers. They had to observe the starry sky to regulate and determine in advance the times of the sacrifices. And so we find also numerous data on astronomy and calendars in the Brāhmaṇas and the Sūtras. In them the so-called Nakṣatras or "Moonhouses" play an important role. The ancient Indians have naturally noticed, that the moon needs for sidereal revolution approximately 27 daynights and spends every night of the sidereal month in a different constellation. These stars or constellations, all of which lie not far from the ecliptic, were combined into a kind of zodiac, a series of 27 Nakṣatras encircling the sphere; and this lunar zodiac was used for the purpose of giving out the position of the moon at a particular time.[2] So there are many texts in the Vedic literature which say that a particular sacrificial act must take place "under such and such Nakṣatra" i.e. "when the moon is in conjunction with that Nakṣatra." Still more numerous are the texts in which the Nakṣatras are brought in relation to full moon and new moon. And even in the more early literature very often only 12 of the 27 Nakṣatras appear connected with the full moon, by which we can explain the names of the months derived from the 12 Nakṣatras. These names of the months were originally applied only to lunar months but were extended

1. Refer "Über die Erwähnung von Sonnenfinsternissen im Ṛgveda". (*Sitzungsberichte der Königl. böhmischen Gesellschaft der Wissenschaften*, Prag 1885).

2. The lunar zodiac has remained in vogue in India till the present day beside the solar zodiac which has probably entered India only with the teachings of the Greek astronomers in the first century A.D. The question of the origin of this lunar zodiac and the relationship between the Indian Nakṣatras, the Manāzil of the Arabs and the Sieou of the Chinese is still undecided. See especially A. Weber, Die vedischen Nachrichten von den Naxatra, 1,2, *ABA* 1860, 1862; G. Thibaut, Astronomie (*Grundriss* III, 9), pp, 12 ff; H. Oldenberg, Nakṣatra und sieou, *NGGW* 1909, 544 ff. Macdonell and Keith *Vedic Index*, I, 427 ff., plead for Babylonian origin, which F. Hommel (*ZDMG* 45, 1891, 592 ff) has tried to prove; but see B.V. Kamesvara Aiyar, *Ind. Ant.* 48, 1919, 95 ff.

later also to the twelfth part of the solar year. As even in the Vedic times the solar and lunar years were somehow tried to be made to correspond to each other, the question arises, whether from the combination of particular full-moon Nakṣatras with the seasons and the beginning of the year it is not possible to draw inferences about the time from which the concerned calendar-data originate. Such inferences, which led to surprising results, have been sought to be made in 1899 simultaneously and independent of each other by H. Jacobi in Bonn and the Indian Bal Gangadhar Tilak in Bombay.[1] Following different ways, both researchers have come to the opinion that during the time of the Brāhmaṇas the Pleiades (Kṛttikās) which formed in those days the starting point of the Nakṣatra-series, coincided with the spring-equinox, but also in the Vedic texts there are also traces of an older calendar in which the spring-equinox fell in the Orion (Mṛgaśira). From a calculation of the value of the precision it follows however that by about 2500 B.C. the spring-equinox lay in the Pleiades and by about 4500 in the Orion. But whereas Tilak goes so far as to trace back some Vedic texts upto the year 6000 B.C. Jacobi is contented with pushing back to about 4500 B.C. "the beginning of the cultural-period, as whose ripe, perhaps even late product the songs of the Ṛgveda have come down to us." This period of culture stretched according to him approximately from 4500 to 2500 B.C. and he is inclined to ascribe "the collection of

1. A. Ludwig, *Der Rigveda* III, Prag, 1878, pp. 183 ff. and R.G. Bhandarkar, Report, 1883-1884, p. 39, have already pointed out the chronological significance of the Kṛttikās heading the list of the Nakṣatras in the Brāhmaṇas. But Bhandarkar places the Brāhmaṇas between 1200 and 900 B.C. Violent discussions were aroused by H. Jacobi's papers in *Festgruss an Rudolf von Roth*, Stuttgart, 1893, pp. 68-73, in *NGGW*, 1894, pp. 105-116, and in *OC*, X, Geneva, 1894, I, pp. 103-08, and the book of B.G. Tilak. *The Orion or Researches into the Antiquity of the Vedas*, Bombay, 1893. Cf. G. Bühler, *Ind. Ant.* 23, 1894, pp. 238 ff.; W.D. Whitney in *JAOS*, *Proceedings*. March 1894, (reprinted in *Ind. Ant.* 24, 1895, p. 361 ff.) ; G. Thibaut, *Ind. Ant.* 24, pp. 85 ff.; and Astronomie (*Grundriss* III, 9) pp. 18 f. A Barth, *JA* 1894, pp. 156 ff.; *Oeuvres* II, 248 ff.; A. Weber, *SBA* 1894, pp. 775 ff.; H. Oldenberg in *ZDMG* 48, 1894, pp. 629 ff.; 49, pp. 470 ff.; 50 pp. 450 ff.; Jacobi in *ZDMG* 49, pp. 218 ff.; 50, pp. 69 ff,; S.B. Dikshit in the *Ind. Ant.*, Vol. 24, p. 245 f., E.W. Hopkins, *The Religions of India*, Boston and London, 1895, pp. 4 ff.; A.A. Macdonell, *History of Sanskrit Literature*, London, 1900, p. 12.

hymns preserved to our present day to the second half of this period.[1] In this view Jacobi was strengthened further by a second astronomical observation. The Gṛhya-sūtras tell us about a marriage-custom in ancient India which consisted in the following — After arriving in the new house the bridegroom and the bride had to sit still on an ox-skin, until the stars became visible, whereupon the bridegroom showed to his bride the Pole star—called "Dhruva" "the firm"—and said a sentence then as for example, "Be firm, flourishing with me", whereupon she replied: "Firm you, firm I may be in the house of my husband". Of great importance is the name 'Dhruva' "the firm" under which this star appears in the marriage-rite, and the whole ceremony during which the star appears especially as a symbol of firmness, of unchangeable loyalty, is based on this that the pole star was considered to be immovable or one did not notice its movement. This description as well as the ceremony can therefore originate at a time in which a bright star was so close to the celestial pole that it appeared to stand still to the observer of that time. Now it is again a result of the precesion that along with the gradual change of the celestial equator its north pole also moves and it evidently describes in approximately 26000 years a circle of $23\frac{1}{2}°$ radius around the fixed pole of the ecliptic. By this slowly one star after another moves nearer and becomes Northern star or Pole Star, but only sometimes does a bright star approach the pole so much that for all practical purposes it can be considered as "a firm one" "Dhruva". At present the star of 2nd magnitude in the Little Bear is the Polestar on the northern hemisphere. Obviously this star cannot be meant when the Polestar of the Vedic times is referred to, because it was, 2000 years ago still so far away from the pole that it could not have been possibly called "firm". But only in 2780 B.C. do we come across another Polestar that deserves this name. At that time Alpha Draconis stood for over half a millenium so close to the pole that it had to appear as immovable when observed with the naked eye. Therefore we must put the origin of the name Dhruva as well as of the custom of showing the 'fixed' star to the bride as a symbol of firmness in

1. *Festgruss an Roth*, p. 71 f.

the wedding night, in a period in which Alpha Draconis was the Polestar, i.e., in the first half of the third millenium B.C. In the marriage texts of the Ṛgveda there is no mention of this custom yet, and this is the reason why Jacobi considers it probable "that the use of Dhruva in the marriage ceremonies belongs not to the time of the Ṛgveda but to the following period, and that therefore the Ṛgvedic period of culture lies anterior to the third pre-Christian millenium."[1]

As has been said, the assertions of Jacobi and Tilak met with violent opposition. The most serious objection to the argument about the Pleiades was that the Indians of the most ancient times were concerned only with the position of the Nakṣatras in relation to the moon and not to the sun, and that there is not a single trace of any observation of the equinoxes to be found in the most ancient times. The passage[2] in which we read that the Pleiades "do not swerve from the East" should probably not be interpreted as meaning that they rose "due east" (which would have been the case in the third millenary B.C., and would point to a knowledge of the vernal equinox): the correct interpretation is more likely that they remain visible in the eastern region which was the case about 1100 B.C.[3] Coming to the argument of the New Year in various

1. *ZDMG.*, Vol. 50, p. 71.

2. Śat. Br. II, 1,2,3. See Oldenberg and Jacobi, *ZDMG.* 48, p. 631, note; 50, pp. 72 and 452. Sankar B. Dikshit (*Ind. Ant.* 24, 1895, pp. 245 f.), B. V. Kamesvara Aiyar (The Age of the Brāhmaṇas, in the *Quarterly Journal of the Mythis Society* 1922, and previously in *Proc. FOC* I, pp. 1 ff. and Dhirendranath Mukhopadhyaya, The Hindu Nakṣatras, pp. 41 f. (Reprint from Vol. VI of the *Journal of the Department of Science*, Calcutta University, 1923), have concluded from this passage, that the Śatapatha-Brāhmaṇa was written about 3000 B.C.

3. This explanation is given by Professor A. Prey, the astronomer of the University of Calcutta, who informs that, in about 1100 B.C. the Pleiades rose approximately 13° to the north of the east point, approaching nearer and nearer the east line, and crossing it as late as 2 h 11 m after their rise, at a height of 29°, when seen from a place situated at 25° North latitude. They thus remain almost due east long enough to serve as a convenient basis for orientation. This interpretation of the passage is proved to be the correct one, by Baudhāyana-Śrautasūtra 27,5 (cf. W. Caland, *Über das rituelle Sūtra des Baudhāyana*, Leipzig, 1903, pp. 37 ff.), where it is prescribed that the

millenia, it is most difficult to decide these questions, primarily because in our texts the year sometimes begins with spring, sometimes with winter, and sometimes with the rainy season, and moreover the number of seasons varies between three, five and six.[1] The argument of the Pole Star, too, provoked serious objections. We cannot deny the possibility of one of the lesser stars in the Little Bear having been visible (about 1250 B.C. and even later still) as the Pole Star in the clear Indian firmament.[2] At any rate it is not permissible to draw any conclusion from the non-mention of this custom in the Ṛgveda: for by no means all of the marriage-customs are mentioned in the marriage-hymn of the Ṛgveda, So there is no reason why this custom should have been singled out for mention in preference to another.

Though the astronomical arguments of Tilak and Jacobi did not succeed in proving what was to be proved, they have stimulated the enquiry whether there are no other grounds for assuming a greater antiquity of Vedic culture. From the point of view of Indian history there is no argument against the presumption that the Vedic literature reached as far back as the third millenium and ancient Indian culture upto the fourth millenium, whereas the suggestion of 1200 or even 1500 made by Max Müller for the beginning of the Vedic period is not compatible any more with the present state of our knowledge about the political history as well as the literary and religious history of ancient India. This has been convincingly proved in my opinion by G. Bühler[3] in particular.

Inscriptions show that in the third century B.C. South India was conquered by Aryan Indians and overrun by Brahminic

porting beams of a hut on the place of sacrifice shall face the east, and that this direction shall be fixed after the Pleiades appear, as the latter "do not depart from the eastern region." It is true that, about 2100 B.C., or about 3100 B.C., the Pleiades touched the east line earlier, but they proceeded southwards so rapidly that they were not suitable for orientation.

1. In the Śat. Br. XII, 8,2,35, it is said: "All seasons are the first, all are the intermediate, all are the last."

2. Professor Prey believes that Groombridge 2001 and 2029, stars of the fifth to the sixth magnitude in Little Bear, the first of which approached the pole as far as 17′ in about 1250 B.C., and the second of which approached the pole as far as 8′ in 1500 B.C., are easily visible in view of the favourable atmospheric conditions of India.

3. *Indian Antiquary*, XXIII, 1894, p. 245 ff.

culture. But the fact that some Vedic schools as those of the Baudhāyana and Āpastamba have originated in the south, makes it probable that the conquest of the south by the Aryans has taken place already much earlier — perhaps already in the 7th or 8th century B.C. For immediately after the conquest the whole country cannot have been so completely colonised and Brahmanised, that Vedic schools could come into being in the distant south. But we cannot at all reconcile with the conquest of southern India about 700 or 600 B.C.[1] the presumption that the Indo-Aryans were still settled in the north western corner of India or in eastern Afghanistan around 1200 or even around 1500 B.C. Bühler says, "the idea that the Indo-Aryan race of the Vedic age with its numerous divisions into clans and the continuous battles should have conquered the 1,23,000 sq. miles of actual India (excluding Punjab, Assam and Burma), within 5, 6 or even 8 centuries, should have founded states and should have organised as per one and the same pattern, appears simply ridiculous; especially when one considers that this area was inhabited not by forest tribes but partly by races which possessed a culture which was not much inferior to those of the conquerors.

Now, one could say, — and it has been said by Oldenberg— : 700 years are a good span of time in which much can happen. "one need only to consider," says Oldenberg,[2] "what 400 years have meant for the vast areas of northern and southern America." This is however a wrong comparison. The races and cultures which came into collision in America, were quite different from those, with which we are concerned in India. As regards the political conditions of ancient India, we learn from some songs of the Ṛgveda and from the epics that just exactly as the later history of India shows us, in early and in the earliest times the individual Aryan clans were continuously fighting among themselves. Under such circumstances the conquest of India could take place only very slowly, only step by step. In fact we also see, when we compare the two oldest layers of the Indian literature with each other, that the

1. Bühler, *Ind. Ant.* 23, 1894, p. 247.
2. *ZDMG*, Vol. 49, p. 479.

advancement of the Aryans towards east and south progressed only very slowly. In the hymns of the Ṛgveda we find the Indo-Aryan folk still settled exclusively in the extreme north-west of India and in eastern Afghanistan. And yet the periods in which the hymns of the Ṛgveda have originated must have extended over centuries. This is proved by the numerous different layers of earlier and later components which we find in these hymns. This is proved by the fact that the Ṛṣis who are wrongly termed not only in the Anukramaṇis but also in the Brāhmaṇas as "Seers" or authors of hymns, are considered in the hymns themselves as seers of a preceding age.[1] And the authors of the hymns speak also rather too often of "old songs", of "songs composed as per old melody" as if this poetry had been practised since times immemorial.[2] M. Bloomfield[3] has shown that, of the approximately 40,000 lines of the Ṛgveda, nearly 5,000 lines are repetitions. This proves that, at the time when the Ṛgveda was composed, the more modern poets would frequently borrow lines and expressions from older ones, and that there was actually in existence a large number of floating lines of verse, which any singer could incorporate in his song if he so fancied. But in this chapter we have seen repeatedly how backward the Ṛgveda is behind all other literary works belonging to the Veda. Even the language of the hymns is much older than that of the Vedic prose works. The religious views and the cultural conditions are quite different. The Brāhmaṇas, Āraṇyakas, and the Upaniṣads presuppose not only the hymns of the Ṛgveda but also the sentences and prayers of the remaining Saṃhitās as primeval holy texts. Indeed these old hymns and sentences were mostly not understood any more. The old legends had fallen into oblivion. Let us remember only the gap that separates the Śunaḥśepa-legend of the Aitareya-Brāhmaṇa from the hymns of the Ṛgveda.[4]

The oral tradition presupposes still longer intervals, than when these texts would have been written down. Generations

---

1. Cf. above, p. 52 f.
2. Cf. Ludwig, *Der Rigveda*, III, p. 180 f.
3. The Vedic Concordance, *HOS*, Vol. 10, 1906; Rig-Veda Repetitions, *HOS*, Vols. 20 and 24, 1916; *JAOS* 29, 1908, p. 287 f.; 31,1910, 49 ff.
4. Cf. above pp. 52, 54, 56 ff, 61 f, 67, 70 f, 95, 181 ff., 199.

of pupils and teachers must have passed, before all the existing and the numerous lost texts had acquired a fixed form in the Vedic schools.[1] On linguistic, literary and cultural-historical grounds we must therefore presume that between the time of the oldest hymns and the final combination of the hymns to a Saṃhitā or "collection"—for the Ṛgveda Saṃhitā describes evidently only the close of a long preceding period.[2]—and many centuries have again lapsed between Ṛgveda Saṃhitā and the Brāhmaṇas. But the Brāhmaṇas themselves with their numerous schools and ramifications of schools, with their endless lists of teachers and the numerous indications regarding teachers of the earlier times require a period of many centuries for their formation.[3] Both these literature and the propagation of Brahmanic culture, of theological knowledge and last but not least important of priestly supremacy which goes hand in hand with it, must have taken centuries. And when we come to the Upaniṣads, we see that they too belong to different periods of time, that they too presuppose generations of teachers and a long tradition.[4] And yet we see that during the whole of this period, which has lasted from the first beginnings up to the last offshoots of the Vedic literature, the Indo-Aryan race has conquered only the relatively small stretch of land from the Indus to the Ganges, the actual Hindostan. If even this advancement from the extreme north-west upto the eastern Gangetic land has taken such a long time, how many centuries must the conquest of the whole Central and South India have taken ! When we consider this, 700 years will not appear to us as a long period any more.

There are other considerations besides this. It is indisputably to the credit of Max Müller to have shown that

1. That the texts have been written down, when one did not fully understand them any more and a break in the tradition had come, is explained to us also by the fact that such diverse pieces of varied content and of different times occur in all Vedic texts, that for example some Upaniṣads are found in the Saṃhitās and Brāhmaṇas. Cf. above p. 114, 139 ff., 210.

2. Even the Aitareya Āraṇyaka presupposes the Ṛgveda-Saṃhitā with its division into ten books (Max Müller, *History of Sanskrit Literature*, p. 340 f.)

3. Cf. above p. 181.

4. Cf. above p. 218 ff.

Buddhism at about 500 B.C. absolutely presupposes the existence of the whole of Vedic literature. In refutation of the view, held by some scholars,[1] that the earliest Upaniṣads should not be placed prior to the 6th century B.C., Oldenberg[2] has shown that centuries must have elapsed between the earliest Upaniṣads and the earliest Buddhist literature. Buddhist literature, however, presupposes not only the Veda, but the Vedāṅgas also,[3] and indeed brahmanical literature and science in a highly developed state. Today, too, more light has been thrown on the religious conditions of ancient India than was the case in Max Müller's day, when it was thought possible to squeeze the whole development of the religious history of India up to the appearance of Buddhism within the limit of 700 years. Even before the appearance of Buddhism, there were sects in India, as Bühler has pointed out, which denied the sanctity of the Veda. The tradition of one of these sects, the Jainas, has in other respects proved so reliable as to chronology, that we may regard with some confidence a report which places the life of the first founder of this sect about 750 B.C. Bühler also thought he could prove that other sects antagonistic to the Veda and to Brahmanism went back to a much more hoary antiquity than had hitherto been supposed.[4] Unfortunately he did not live to demonstrate this proof.

The discoveries made by Hugo Winckler in Boghazköi in Asia Minor in the year 1907, gave an impetus to more recent discussions on the question of the age of the Ṛgveda and of Vedic culture.[5] The clay tablets from the archives of the

1. Cf. Hopkins, *JAOS* 22, 336 n.; Rapson, *Ancient India*, p. 181.

2. *Die Lehre der Upanishaden und die Anfänge des Buddhismus*, pp. 288, 357.

3. It is noteworthy that the Buddhists, too, call their didactic texts "Sūtras", although these are by no means composed in the "Sūtra" style indicated above. They took "Sūtra" to mean "didactic text."

4. R. Garbe, too (*Beiträge zur indischen Kulturgeschichte*, pp. 27 ff.), is inclined to date the origin of the sect of the Bhāgavatas or Pañcarātras back to pre-Buddhist times.

5. Cf. Ed. Meyer, *SBA* 1908, pp. 14 ff.; *Zeitschrift für vergleichende Sprachwissenschaft*, 42, 1909, pp. 1ff.; *Geschichte des Altertums*, 2. Auflage, 1,2, (1909) § 551,574; H. Jacobi, *JRAS* 1909, 721 ff., 1910, 456 ff.; *Internat. Wochenschrift*, 5, 1911, 387; A.B. Keith, *JRAS* 1909, 1100 ff.; 1910, 464 ff.; *Bhandarkar, Com, Vol.*, pp. 81 ff. and *HOS*., Vol. 18 Introd. (where the whole

capital of the ancient Hittite kingdom, which were found in Boghazköi, included records of treaties concluded by the king of the Hittites and the king of Mitani at the beginning of the 14th century B.C. The gods of both kingdoms are invoked as guardians of the treaties, and in the list of gods there appear, beside numerous Babylonian and Hittite deities, the names of Mitra, Varuṇa, Indra and Nāsatyau among the gods of Mitani.[1] How did the names of these deities reach the Mitanis in Asia Minor? Scholars diverge greatly in their reply to this question. The historian Ed. Meyer ascribes these gods to the Aryan period, i.e., the period when the Indians and Iranians as yet formed an undivided nation in language and religion[2]; and assumes that, at the same time as these "Aryans" appeared in western Mesopotamia and Syria, the separate development of the Aryans in the north-western India had already begun: the Vedic hymns, the earliest of which arose "probably not later than about 1500 B.C." bearing witness to this development. A similar opinion has been expressed by P. Giles. Oldenberg[3] thinks it more likely "that these are the gods of some western Aryan tribe akin to the Indians, inherited from some common past, as the Indians on their part had inherited

development of Vedic literature is crammed in between 1200 and 350 B.C., see esp. pp. clxv f.); A.A. Macdonell in *Vedic Index* I, pp. viii f. and *ERE* 7, 1914, pp. 49 ff.; H. Oldenberg, *JRAS* 1909, 1095 ff.; 1910, pp. 846 ff.; L. de la Valleé Poussin, *Le Vedisme,* 3 ième ed. Paris, 1909, pp. 29 f.; Winternitz, *Oesterreichische Monatschrift für den Orient*, 41, 1915 pp. 168 ff.; *Calcutta Review*, Nov., 1923. pp. 119 ff.; Sten Konow, *The Āryan Gods of the Mitani People* (Royal Frederik University Publications of the Indian Institute, Kristiania, 1921); F. E. Pargiter, *Ancient Indian Historical Tradition*, London, 1922, pp. 300 ff.; R. Giles, *Cambridge History of India*, I. pp. 72 f.

1. At least, nearly all scholars agree with Winckler (*Mitteilungen der Deutschen Orient-Gesellschaft* No. 35, 1907, p. 51, *s. Boghazköi-Studien* VIII, Leipzig 1923, pp. 32 f., 54 f.) that these names of gods have to be recognised in the following cuneiform text: ilani Mi-it-ra as-si-il ilfani U-ru-wa-na-as-si-el (in another text: A-ru-na-as-si-il) In-dar (other text: In-da-ra) ilani Na-sa-at-ti-ya-as-na. Doubts against this identification have only been raised by J. Halevy in *Revue Semitique*, 16, 1908, pp. 247 ff.

2. H. Winckler (*Orinetalist. Literaturzeitung*, 13, 1910, 289 ff.; *Mitteilungen der Vorderasiatischen Gesellschaft* 18, 1913, H. 4, pp. 75 ff.) even thinks that the Harri who in the inscriptions are mentioned as the ruling class in Mitani are identical with these very "Āryans." But this is quite uncertain. Cf. A. H. Sayce, *JRAS* 1909, pp. 1106 f.

3. *NGGW*, Geschäftliche Mitteilungen, 1918, p. 91.

them from the same source." He leaves the question open whether these were Iranians before Zoroaster's time, or whether a third branch of the Aryans is meant, and takes the view that this discovery does not justify us in assuming greater antiquity for the Veda.

It is a fact, however, that this particular grouping of the gods Varuṇa and Mitra, Indra and Nāsatyau, with these forms of their names, can be traced *only in the Veda*. For this reason I agree with Jacobi, Konow and Hillebrandt in considering these gods to be Indian, Vedic deities and that there is no possible justification for any other view. We shall have to assume that, just as there were Aryan immigrations into India from the west, there must have been isolated migrations back to the west. We may think either of warlike adventurers or of connections by marriage. Nor should we forget that, at the time of the Ṛgveda, the Aryan Indians were as yet much nearer the west from the geographical point of view.[1] As regards chronology, however, all that we can glean from the inscriptions at Boghazköi is that, about the middle of the second millenium B.C., Aryan tribes which worshipped Vedic gods must already have been established in north-western India for a very considerable time, as several of these tribes had migrated far back to the west as early as about 1400 B.C.[2] This small but important

1. See A. Hillebrandt, *Aus Alt- und Neuindien*, Breslau, 1922, pp. 1ff and *ZII* 3, 1924, pp. 1ff who points out traces of relations to Western countries especially in the eighth Book of the Ṛgveda. For other views about the Aryan Indians in Asia Minor see R. G. Bhandarkar, *JBRAS* 25, 1918, pp. 76 ff., and E. Forster, Die Acht Sprachen der Boghazköi-Inschriften, *SBA* 1919, pp. 1036 f.

2. Konow suggests that the Nāsatyas are mentioned in the Mitani treaty on account of their playing a role in the ancient marriage-rites, because the treaty, following upon a war between the Hittite king Subbiluliuma and the Mitani king Mattiuza, was confirmed by a marriage of the latter with the Hittite king's daughter. As this connection of the Aśvins with the marriage-ritual, however, occurs only in the late Sūrya sūkta, Konow concludes "that the extension of Indo-Āryan civilisation into Mesopotamia took place after the bulk of the Ṛgveda had come into existence" so that the oldest portions of the collection would "have to be considered as considerably older than the Mitani treaty." There is no force in this argument, as Indra and the Nāsatyau (Indranāsatyā) are invoked together in Rv. VIII, 26,8, where they

fact would be supported still further, if it should prove to be true that also traces of Indian numerals are to be found in the Boghazköi texts.[1]

The idea of so early a date as the third millenium B.C. for the Veda would certainly be out of the question, if it were proved that the individual Indo-European peoples had not yet separated from the primitive Indo-Europeans in the third millenium.[2] This view which is very unlikely and has not been satisfactorily proved, is welcomed by those who wish to assign as low a date as possible to the Ṛgveda and to the beginnings of Indian culture. Thus J. Hertel[3] promises to demonstrate that the Ṛgveda originated, not in north-western India but in Iran, and at a time not far distant from that of Zoroaster, who, according to Hertel, lived about 550 B.C. G. Hüsling[4] goes still further, and turns and twists certain of

have nothing to do with marriage. K. Chattopadhyaya (*Calcutta Review*, May 1924, pp. 287 ff.) concludes from the mention of Vedic gods in the Boghazkōi treaties that between 2000 and 1500 B.C. there were several arrivals of Aryan peoples in Asia Minor at the same time when other Aryan tribes entered India from Central Asia and became known as Vrātyas. This chronological combination of the Vrātyas with the Indians in Asia Minor has no foundation in fact whatsoever, hence Mr. Chattopadhyaya's chronological conclusion (Brāhmaṇa period from 2000 B.C. to 1400 B.C., Yajurveda and Atharvaveda about 2000 B.C. and Ṛgveda before 3000 B.C.) are quite unfounded.

1. Cf. P. Jensen Indische Zahlwōrter in Keilschrithittitischen Texten, *SBA* 1919, pp. 367 ff.

2. Gunther Ipsen (*Indogerman. Forschungen* 41, 1923, pp. 174 ff.; Stand und Aufgaben der Sprachwissenschaft, *Festschrift für W. Streitberg*, Heidelberg 1924, pp. 200 ff.), endeavours to prove that the Indo-European words for "copper", "cow", and "star" were borrowed from the Sumerian, and not earlier than between 3000 and 2100 B.C. However, when we consider that the domestic cow and copper are among the most ancient of prehistoric finds, we shall hesitate to accept Ipsen's theory.

3. *Indogerman. Forschungen*, 41, 1923, p. 188; *Die Zeit Zoroasters*, Leipzig, 1924; *Die Himmelstore im Veda und im Avesta*, Leipzig, 1924, pp. 7. f. A book by Hertel on the age and home of the Ṛgveda is announced, but has not yet been published. Zoroaster's date is still uncertain, but there are good reasons for placing him about 1000 B.C. See C. Clemen, *Die griechischen und lateinischen Nachrichten über die perisisiche Religion*, Giessen, 1920, pp. 11 ff.; H. Reichelt in *Festschrift für W. Streitberg*, pp. 282 f.

4. *Die Inder in Boghazköi, in Prace linguistycyzne ofiarowane Janowi Baudouinowi de Courtenay*. . . Krakow 1921, pp. 151 ff.

the names of kings occurring in the cuneiform inscriptions so long that they are metamorphosed into those of Indian kings. On the basis of these "facts," he then concludes that from about 1000 B.C. the Indians wandered from Armenia to Afghanistan, which was the scene of the Ṛgvedic period, and that it was only later that they were driven further towards India. Following a suggestion of H. Brunnhofer, he even assumes that the king Kānita Pṛthuśravas[1] who is mentioned in the Ṛgveda is identical with a Scythian king Kānitas who is mentioned in a Greek inscription and on a coin, and who lived in the 2nd century B.C. This would mean that "the collection of these songs was not yet completed in the 2nd century B.C." This must surely be the very latest date ever yet assumed as that of the Ṛgveda!

The strongest argument for a later dating of the Veda is undoubtedly the close relationship between the Veda and the Avesta with regard to language and religious views.[2] There are, however, very great differences to counteract the points of agreement in religion. Moreover the points of agreement can easily be explained, considering firstly that Indians and Iranians once formed one Aryan cultural unit at a pre-Vedic and pre-Avestic period, and secondly that they remained neighbours even after the separation. As regards the kinship of the languages, it is quite impossible to state definite chronological limits within which languages change. Some languages change very rapidly, others remain more or less unaltered for a long period.[3] It is true that hieratic languages, like those of the Vedic hymns and the Avesta, can remain unaltered much longer than spoken vernaculars.

---

1. Rv. VIII, 46, 21; 24. The story of this King Pṛthuśravas is one of the old tales which, like the Ākhyāna of Śunaḥśepa, were recited at the Puruṣamedha, see Sānkhāyana-Śrautasūtra XVI, 11,23.

2. Thus A. A. Macdonell (*ERE*. Vol. 7, 1914, pp. 49 ff.) says, that "it seems impossible to avoid the conclusion that the Indians cannot have separated from the Iranians much earlier than about 1300 B.C."

3. Cf. A. C. Woolner (*Proc. FOC* I, pp. xvii.; II, p. 20 ff.) who rightly says "that as far as any philological estimates go, 2000 B.C. remains quite as possible as 1200 B.C. for the earliest Mantra." See also B. V. Kamesvara Aiyar, *Quarterly Journal of the Mythic Society* XII, 1, p. 4.

Nevertheless, all that we know of the history of other languages and branches of languages compels us to say that languages do not remain unchanged for an indefinite number of millenia, let alone tens of thousands of years. For this reason, the fantastic figures of 16000 or even 25000 B.C.[1] as the date of the Veda, built up on the basis of astronomical or geological speculations, are absolutely impossible. Figures like this imply, too, that scarcely any cultural progress worthy of the name was made in the whole course of that overwhelmingly long aeon, which would be most surprising in the case of so talented a race as the Indians. These figures are impossible, too, because the continuity between the Vedic and the later brahmanical culture, which cannot be explained away especially as regards religion would then become utterly inexplicable. Moreover, classical Sanskrit, as fixed by Pāṇini in his Grammar more especially on the basis of the language of the Brāhmaṇas which still formed part of the Veda proper, and again the language of the inscriptions of King Aśoka in the third century B.C., show too close a relationship with the language of the Veda for it to be feasible that a stretch of so very many thousands of years lay between.

In summing up, we may say:

1. Attempts to determine the period of the Veda by the aid of *astronomy* come to grief owing to the fact that there are certain passages in the Vedic texts which admit of various interpretations. However correct the astronomical calculations may be, they prove nothing unless the texts in question admit of an unambiguous interpretation.

2. The *historical* facts and hypotheses, such as the mention of Vedic gods in the cuneiform inscriptions, and the relationship of Vedic antiquity to the Āryan (Indo-Iranian) and Indo-European period, are so uncertain in themselves that the most divergent and contradictory conclusions have been drawn from them. Nevertheless, we have now such likely evidence of relations between ancient India and western Asia penetrating as far west as Asia Minor in the second millenium B.C., that

1. Refer also Abinas Chandra Das, *Rig-Vedic India*, I, Calcutta 1921 (see also *Calcutta Review*, March 1924, pp. 540 ff.) and D. N. Mukhopadhyaya, The Hindu Nakṣatras (reprinted from Vol. VI of *Journal of the Department of Science*, Calcutta University, 1923).

Vedic-culture can be traced back *at least* to the second millenium B.C.

3. The linguistic facts, the near relationship between the language of the Veda and that of the Avesta on the one hand, and between the Vedic language and classical Sanskrit on the other, do not yield any positive results;

4. they serve as a warning to us, however, to refrain from dating the Veda back to an inconceivable distant period on the strength of astronomical or *geological* speculations.

5. As all the external evidence fails, we are compelled to rely on *the evidence arising out of the history of Indian literature itself*, for the age of the Veda. The surest evidence in this respect is still the fact that Pārśva, Mahāvīra and Buddha pre-suppose the entire Veda as a literature to all intents and purposes completed, and this is a limit which we must not exceed. We cannot, however, explain the development of the whole of this great literature, if we assume as late a date as round about 1200 B.C. or 1500 B.C. as its starting-point. We shall probably have to date the beginning of this development about 2000 or 2500 B.C., and the end of it between 750 and 500 B.C. The more prudent course, however, is to steer clear of any fixed dates, and to guard against the extremes of a stupendously ancient period or a ludicrously modern epoch.

SECTION II

THE POPULAR EPICS AND THE PURĀṆAS

The Beginnings of Epic Poetry in India

The earliest traces of epic poetry in India could already be found in the Vedic literature—in the Ākhyāna hymns of the Ṛgveda, as well as in the Ākhyānas, Itihāsas and Purāṇas of the Brāhmaṇas.[1] From the Brāhmaṇas and the ritual literature we also know that reciting such narrative poems constituted a part of the religious ceremonies during sacrificial ceremonies and domestic festivals.

Thus a part of the year-long preparatory celebrations to the great horse-sacrifice is the daily discourse of sagas of gods and heroes. In a series repeated once in ten days stories of certain gods and heroes were told; and also two lute-players were present, a Brahmin and a warrior, of whom one extolled in self-composed verses (gāthās) the generosity and the other similarly the battledeeds of the prince who performed the sacrifice. The lute-players who sang the glory of a real king or the Soma as the king of the Brahmins were not to be missing at the hair-parting ceremony also, which was performed for the prospective mother in the fourth month of pregnancy with an offering for the prosperity of the embryo. After a funeral it was an old custom (and this is testified even by Bāṇa in the 7th century A.D.) that the mourners sat down at a shady place outside the house and found diversion and consolation by hearing discourses on ancient Itihāsas or Purāṇas. And when after a death or any other calamity in the family the old hearth-fire was taken out for warding off further misfortune and a new fire was lighted in the house by rubbing pieces of wood, then the members of the family sat down, keeping the fire burning in flames till late in the quiet night, while hearing stories of

1. Cf. above p. 92 ff, 193. ff, 209. Indians are not consistent in the use of the expressions Ākhyāna, Itihāsa and Purāṇa, as they use them sometimes as synonyms, and sometimes to denote different kinds of tales. The epic 'Mahābhārata' is called even in the introduction sometimes as Itihāsa, sometimes as Purāṇa or Ākhyāna. Cf. also Emil Sieg on these terms in *Die Sagenstoffe des Ṛgveda und die indische Itihasatradition* I. Stuttgart, 1902. Introd.

people who attained a ripe old age and of auspicious Itihāsas and Purāṇas that were narrated to them.[1]

There were not only single ballads (Ākhyānas, Itihāsas) but also cycles of ballads. At least one cycle of this kind has come down to us in the Suparṇākhyāna, also called Suparṇādhyāya or Suparṇa.[2] This is an apocryphal work belonging to the later Vedic literature, the author trying his utmost to imitate the hymns of the Ṛgveda in language, accentuation and external form, so that his work should appear to belong to the Ṛgveda. The date of this work is quite uncertain, but on metrical grounds we may place it approximately in the period of the metrical Upaniṣads, such as the Kaṭha-Upaniṣad.[3] It is a cycle of ballads dealing with the legend of Kadru, the snake-mother, and Vinata, the bird-mother, and the enmity between Garuḍa and the snakes, a legend which dates far back into Vedic times,[4] and which appears in epic form in the Āstīkaparvan of the Mahābhārata.

Not infrequently in the ancient texts Itihāsa and Purāṇa are also enumerated in addition to the Vedas and other branches

---

1. Śatapatha-Brāhmaṇa XIII, 4, 3. Sāṅkhāyana-Gṛhyasūtra, I, 22,11 f.; Āśvalāyana-Gṛhyasūtra I. 14, 6 f.; IV, 6,6. Pāraskara-Gṛhyasūtra, I, 15,7 f. Āpastambiya-Gṛhyasūtra 14, 4 f. Cf. also A. Weber, Episches im Vedischen Ritual (*SBA* 1891) and H. Lüders in *ZDMG*, Vol. 58, pp. 707 ff. At the Puruṣamedha, too, the recitation of Ākhyānas forms part of the ritual, s. Sāṅkhāyana-Śrautasūtra, 16, 11.

2. The text, which has come down in very bad condition, was first edited by E. Grube, Berlin, 1875 (reprinted in *Ind. Stud.*, Vol. 14); newly edited, translated into German and annotated by J. Charpentier, *Die Suparnasage*, Uppsala 1920, pp. 190 ff.; Cf. J. v. Negelein in *GGA*, 1924, pp. 65 ff., 87 ff. J. Hertel considers this work to be a dramatic poem after the style of the Swang described by R. Temple (*WZKM* 23, 1909, 273 ff.; 24, 1910, 117 ff.; *Indische Märchen*, pp. 314 f., Jena 1919); and he has translated it into German as a drama (*Indische Märchen*, Jena, 1919, pp. 344 ff.). Cf. Winternitz, *Oesterreichische Monatsschrift fur den Orient* 41, 1915, pp. 176 f., Oldenberg, *Zur Geschichte der altindischen Prosa*, pp. 61 ff. and *NGGW* 1919, pp. 79 ff. This Suparṇādhyāya has no connection with the Suparṇa songs belonging to the Khilas of the Ṛgveda, which are also called "Suparṇādhyāya" (see above p. 54 and Scheftelowitz, *ZDMG* 74, 1920, p. 203).

3. Charpentier, ibid. pp. 196 f. J. v. Negelein (ibid. pp. 196, f.) doubts the justification of Charpentier's conclusions.

4. Charpentier, ibid. pp. 288 ff.; Śatapatha-Br. III, 6,2.

of knowledge, their study is considered as an act pleasing the gods and indeed the Itihāsapurāṇa is even termed as the fifth Veda.[1] That they gain a rather popular character is proved by the close relationship to which they are brought with the Atharvaveda.[2] Sagas of gods and tales of demons, serpent-goddesses, ancient sages (Ṛṣis) and kings of the past formed mainly the contents of these Itihāsas and Purāṇas. Sometimes however, as texts by means of whose recitation the gods are pleased, in addition to Itihāsas and Purāṇas also the "praise songs of men" (Gāthā-nārāśaṁsī) are mentioned,[3] and these we may consider to be the actual fore-runners of a hero-epic. But if one would like to, as some scholars do,[4] conclude from the abovementioned texts that already in the Vedic times there was a collection in the book form of narrative poetry under the title "Itihāsas" or "Itihāsa-purāṇa", then one would have to suppose that similarly under the title "Gāthā-nārāśaṁsī" there has been a collection of hero-songs as a book.

Similarly the existence of such collected works or 'books' for the Vedic period has not been proved.[5] That there have

1. Chāndogya-Up. VII, 1 f. and 7. In the Buddhist Suttanipāta III, 7, (Selasutta), Itihāsa is called "the fifth" after the three Vedas and the Vedāṅgas. Cf. A. Weber, ibid. and J. Dhalmann, *Das Mahābhārata als Epos and Rechtsbuch*, Berlin 1895, pp. 281 ff.

2. According to Chāndogya-Up. III, 3,4 the magic songs of the Atharvaveda stand in the same relationship to the Itihāsapurāṇa as the hymns (ṛc) to the Ṛgveda, the prayer formulas (Yajus) to the Yajurveda and the melodies (sāman) to the Sāmaveda. According to the Kauṭilya-Arthaśāstra, p. 7, the Atharvaveda and the "Itihāsaveda" together with the trayi, "the threefold knowledge", form the Vedas. Cf. above, p. 115, and Bloomfield, *SBE.*, Vol. 42, pp. xxxvi f.

3. Śatapatha-Br. XI, 5,6,8; Āśvalāyana-Gṛhyas. III, 3. The fact that, in these songs, panegyrics were more important than historical truth, is evident from the Vedic texts themselves, for they declare these Gāthās to be "lies" (Maitrāyaṇī-Saṃhitā 1,11,5: Kāṭhaka 14,5).

4. K. F. Geldner: *Vedische Studien* I, 5, 290 f.; E. Sieg, *Die Sagenstoffe des Ṛgveda und die indische Itihāsatradition* I, p. 33. Against this, H. Oldenberg in *GGA* 1890, p. 419.

5. The theory that there was a book called "Itihāsaveda" or "Itihāsa-purāṇa" is advanced by K. F. Geldner, *Vedische Studien* I, pp. 290 f.; E. Sieg, *Die Sagenstoffe des Ṛgveda und die indische Itihāsatradition* I. p. 33 and *ERE* VII, 1914, 461 ff.; J. Hertel, *WZKM* 23, 1909, p. 295; 24, p. 420, R. Pischel *KG*

been professional story-tellers (Aitihāsikas, Paurāṇikas) even in very olden times, may not have to be doubted. It is also certain that as early as at about the time of the Buddha (i.e. in the fifth century B.C.) there must have been already an inexhaustible stock of stories in prose and verse—Ākhyānas, Itihāsas, Purāṇas and Gāthās—as a sort of common literary property from which the Buddhists and Jainas as well as the epic poets drew their material.

Besides this Itihāsa literature as we can shortly term the common literary possession of narrative poetry whose existence in the Vedic period has been proved, there must have been already actual epic poems, hero-songs and perhaps even cycles of epic songs in ancient times. For, the two epics, the Mahābhārata and the Rāmāyaṇa which are the only two epics preserved till our present day represent certainly only the outcome of a long preceding period of epic poetry. Long before there have been these two epics as such, the songs of the great battle of races which is the subject-matter of the Mahābhārata and of the deeds of Rāma, the hero of the Rāmāyaṇa, must have been sung. It is not also easy to imagine that the battles of Kauravas and Pāṇḍavas and the adventures of Rāma were the only subject-matter of poetry. Many other heroes and great events in many other royal families have also been the themes of poetry. Not all of this ancient hero-poetry whose existence we must presume has entirely vanished; in ruins and remnants some of them have been preserved in our two epics.[1]

The authors, reciters and preservers of this hero-poetry were the bards usually called Sūtas who lived at the courts of the kings and recited or sang their songs during great festivals to

---

168; H. Oertel, *WZKM* 24, p. 121; H. Jacobi, *SBA* 1911, p. 969. But the very passage in Kauṭilya I, 5, p. 10, which is quoted by these scholars proves that "Itihāsa" should be interpreted, not as a single work, but as a class of literary productions: for "Veda" only means a certain kind of learning, not a book: Āyurveda is "medical science", Gāndharvaveda is "music", Ṛgveda, Sāmaveda, etc., are classes of texts, and not single books. Thus, "Itihāsa-veda" is not any particular book, but that branch of learning which consists of legends, stories, etc.

1. Cf. H. Jacobi, Über ein verlorenes Heldengedicht der Sindhu-Sauvira in *Mélanges Kern*, Leiden 1903, pp. 53 ff.

proclaim the fame of the princes. They accompanied them to the battle-field in order to be able to sing the heroic deeds of the warriors by witnessing them. Thus in the Mahābhārata itself there is the Sūta, Sañjaya, who describes to the king Dhṛtarāṣṭra the happenings on the battle-field. These court-singers formed a special caste[1] in which the epic songs were inherited from generation to generation. The epic poetry would have originated in the circles of such bards who were in any case close to the warrior-caste. The propagation of the hero-songs among the masses was then taken over also by the wandering singers, called Kuśīlavas who learnt the songs by heart and sang in public to the accompaniment of the lute.[2] Thus it is said in the Rāmāyaṇa—of course in a song inserted later[3] how the two sons of Rāma, Kuśa and Lava, roamed about as wandering singers and recited in a public gathering the poem that they had learnt from Vālmīki.

But what we know as the popular epics of the Indians—the Mahābhārata and the Rāmāyaṇa—are not the old hero-songs as those court-bards and those wandering musicians of ancient India have sung, processed by great poets or at least by shrewed poetically talented compilers into unitary poetry but they are collections of many diverse poems of varying values, which have come into existence as a result of continuous interpolations and changes in the course of many centuries. No doubt

---

1. According to the law-book of Manu (X, 11 and 17), the Sūtas are a mixed caste descended from the intermarriage of warriors with Brahmin women, while the Māgadhas, who, as well as the Sūtas, are usually called singers, are said to be descended from the intermarriage of Vaiśyas with Kṣatriya women. In war, the Sūtas are also the charioteers of the princes. Originally the Māgadhas were undoubtedly bards from the land of Magadha, and the Sūtas, too, were probably inhabitants of a country situated to the east of Magadha. Cf. F. E. Pargiter. *Ancient Indian Historical Tradition*, London 1922, p. 16. J. J. Meyer. *Das Weib im altindischen Epos*, Leipzig, 1915, p. 62 note, compares the modern Bhats of the Rājpūts to the Sūtas. On the Bhats and other kinds of singers in the India of today, cf. R. C. Temple, *The Legends of the Panjab*, Vol. I. (1884), p. viii; and A. Baines, Ethnography (*Grundriss* II, 5, 1912), pp. 85 ff.

2. Cf. A. Holtzmann, *Das Mahābhārata* I, p. 54 f., 65 f., H. Jacobi, *Das Rāmāyaṇa*, pp. 67.

3. I, 4.

old hero songs form the nucleus of both the works, but the more religious Itihāsa literature has also been included in them to a large extent and by the addition of extensive, religious didactic pieces the Mahābhārata in particular has almost completely lost the character of an epic.

What is the Mahābhārata[1]

In reality one can speak of the Mahābhārata as an epic and as a "poem" only in a very restricted sense. Indeed, in a certain sense the Mahābhārata is not at all a poetic product, but rather, an entire literature.

---

1. For orientation about the contents of the epic one may best refer to H. Jacobi, *Mahābhārata, Inhaltsangabe, Index und Konkordanz der Kalkuttaer und Bombayer Ausgaben.* Bonn 1903. On the problems of the Mahābhārata the best book that can be consulted is: E. W. Hopkins, *The Great Epic of India, Its Character and Origin.* New York 1901. A rich collection of material unfortunately far too little lucid—is contained in A. Holtzmann, *Das Mahābhārata und seine Teile.* In 4 volumes. Kiel 1892-1895. The value of this great work is largely impaired by the untenable theories of the author on the revised versions of the Mahābhārata. Untenable are also the contrary theories on the unitary origin of the epic which Joseph Dahlmann has presented in the books *Das Mahābhārata als Epos und Rechtbuch,* Berlin 1895, *Genesis des Mahābhārata* Berlin, 1899 and *Die Samkhya-Philosophie als Naturlehre und Erlösungslehre, nach dem Mahābhārata,* Berlin 1902. The first of these books has the special distinction of having fostered anew the study of epics; it has given rise to formal "Dahlmann-literature". Cf. H. Jacobi in *GGA* 1896 No. 1 and 1899 No. 11; A. Ludwig in *Sitzungsber. der kgl böhmischen Ges. der Wiss., Cl. f. Phil.,* Prag 1896; A. Barth in *Journal des savants,* avril, juin, juillet 1897 and *Revue de l' histoire des religions,* 45, 1902, p. 191 ff; M. Winternitz in *JRAS* 1897, p. 713 ff and *WZKM* XIV, 1900, p. 53 ff; E. W. Hopkins in *American Journal of Philology,* 1898, XIX, no. 1; W. Cartellieri in *WZKM* XIII, 1899, p. 57 ff. J. Kirste in *Ind. Ant* XXXI, 1902, p. 5 ff. Of still older literature on the Mahābhārata the following works compiled by Holtzmann, ibid IV, p. 165 ff. deserve special mention: Monier Williams, *Indian Wisdom,* 4th. edition, London, 1893; Sören Sörensen, *Om Mahābhārata's stilling i den Indiske literatur* (with a "Summarium" in the latin language), Copenhagen 1893; A. Ludwig, Über das Rāmāyaṇa und die Beziehungen desselben zum Mahābhārata (*II. Annual Report of the Wissens. Verein für Volkskunde und Linguistik in Prague* 1894). See also Hopkins. *ERE* VIII, 1915, 325 ff. and H. Oldenberg, *Das Mahābhārata, seine Entstehung, sein Inhalt, seine Form.* Göttingen, 1922.

Mahābhārata[1] means "the story of the great battle of the Bharatas". The Bharatas are mentioned in the Ṛgveda already as a warlike race and Bharata the son of Duṣyanta and Śakuntalā, who is considered as the forefather of the royal house of the Bharatas, confronts us already in the Brāhmaṇas. The seats of these Bhāratas or Bharatas were the land on the upper Ganges and on the Jumna. Among the descendants of Bharata one ruler named Kuru was particularly famous and his descendants, the Kauravas (derived from Kuru) were the ruling house of the Bharatas that the name Kuru or Kaurava has, in course of time, also established itself as the name for the race of the Bharatas and their country is the Kuruksetra or "Kuru-land",[2] known to us already from the Yajurveda and the Brāhmaṇas. A family-feud in the royal house of the Kauravas leads to a bloody battle, a really annihilating battle in which the old Kuru-house and with it the family of the Bharatas is almost completely ruined. The story of this bloody battle—in which we may find a historical event, although we learn of it only from the Mahābhārata—was sung in songs and some great poet whose name has disappeared, has combined these songs to a hero-poem of the great battle in the Kuru-field. Thus as in the Ilias and as in the Nibelungenlied, the tragedy of a terrible annihilating forms the actual topic of the hero-poetry. This old hero-poetry forms the nucleus of the Mahābhārata.

Around this nucleus a great mass of the most diverse forms of poetry has gathered. At first numerous sagas which are more or less loosely knit with the ancient hero-poetry—sagas which refer to the earlier history of the heroes or narrate all kinds of adventures of the same without having any connection with the great battle—were included in the poem. Also fragments of other sagas of heroes and saga-cycles which refer to some famous kings and heroes of pre-historic times found entry into the poem, although they had absolutely nothing to do

1. Bhārata means "battle of the Bharatas" (bharatāḥ saṅgrāmaḥ; Pāṇini IV, 2, 56). In the Mahābhārata itself we find Mahābhāratayuddha (XIV, 81, 8) "the great Bhārata battle", and "Mahābhāratākhyānam (I, 62, 39), "the story of the great Bhārata battle", of which the title "Mahābhārata" is an abbreviation.

2. See page 181 above.

with the song of the great Kuru-battle. What of this old bard-poetry already belonged to the original poem as episodes and what was added only later, can be hardly ever determined. But in ancient times many of these episodes must have been recited by the minstrels as independent poems.[1] In any case our Mahābhārata is not merely the hero-poem of the battle of the Bharatas but at the same time also a repertoire of ancient bard-poetry as such.

But it is still much, very much more. We know that the literary activity in ancient India lay mostly in the hands of the priests, the Brahmins; and we have seen indeed how they have Brahminised the popular magic-songs of the Atharvaveda and how they diluted the philosophy of the Upaniṣads which was actually foreign to the priesthood and even antagonistic philosophy of the Upaniṣads with their priestly wisdom.[2] But now the more popular and likeable the hero-songs became, the more must the Brahmins have got interested in wanting to attain mastery over this epic poetry also and they knew how best they could dilute the poetry which was in its full essence purely of mundane character, with their own religious poetry and theological-priestly bits of knowledge. Thus it happens that also sagas of gods, mythological stories of Brahminic origin, and even didactic pieces of greater content connected with Brahminic philosophy and ethics and Brahminic law were included in the Mahābhārata. For this priestly caste the popular epic was precisely a welcome medium to spread their own teachings and thus strengthen and fortify their power and influence. It was they who inserted all the numerous sagas and legends[3] (Itihāsas) into the epic in which

1. It seems that individual bards made a speciality of the recitation of certain poems; for Patañjali (Pāṇini IV, 2, 60) teaches the formation of words like Yavakritika, "one who knows the story of Yavakrita", "Yayātika", "one who knows the story of Yayāti etc. Cf. F. Lacote, *Essai sur Guṇaḍhya et la Bṛhatkathā*, Paris, 1908, pp. 138 f.

2. Cf. above, p. 113 and 213 ff.

3. Some of these legends can still be traced. In Brahminic texts, for instance, the story of Bhaṅgāsvana who was changed into a woman, in Mahābh. XIII, 12, is found in the Baudhāyana-Śrautasūtra; see Winternitz and Caland in *WZKM* 17, 1903, 292 f. 351 ff.

(sagas and legends) miracles are told about the famous seers of prehistoric times, of the ṛṣis, the forefathers of the Brahmins —how by means of sacrifice and asceticism they attain mighty powers not only over men but also over gods themselves and how, when displeased, they cause by their curse the downfall of princes and great people and indeed even kings of gods.

But the Mahābhārata was too much of a chap-book, too much the property of vast circles of people, especially the warrior caste that it would ever have become an actual Brahminical work or the property of any Vedic school. It was also not so much the scholarly Brahmins well-versed in the Vedas that took part in the shaping of the Mahābhārata—hence the conspicuously poor knowledge of the actual Brahminic theology and sacrificial science that we find even in those parts of the epic in which Brahminic influence is unmistakably strong—as Purohitas, priests who just like the Sūtas (bards) were in the service of the kings and even on this ground came into contact more with the epic poetry. It was also this less learned priestly class which later served as temple priests in famous places of worship dedicated mostly to the gods Viṣṇu or Śiva and took literary interest in the cultivation of the local sagas connected with such holy places and also of the legends connected with the gods Viṣṇu and Śiva. This happened, as we shall see, mainly in the Purāṇas, and also into the Mahābhārata into which numerous local sagas, Viṣṇu and Śiva myths all composed in the style of the Purāṇas as well as purāṇa-like cosmologies, geographical lists and genealogies have found their way.

However, as the epic-poetry was cultivated more in those regions of India where the worship of Viṣṇu as the supreme god was prevalent, it is easy to explain that in the religious didactic-parts of the Mahābhārata this god stands out so prominent that the work sometimes creates the impression of a book of worship dedicated to Viṣṇu. Apart from this there is no lack of Śiva-legends and interludes dedicated to the Śiva-cult, which can be recognised everywhere as later additions. They were inserted as the epic also spread over regions where the Śiva-cult was at home.[1]

1. H. Jacobi in *GGA*, 1892, p. 629 f.

But there were also other intellectual circles which developed a literary activity already in the olden days and partly even tried to win over the great mass of the people to their own side even more than the Brahmins. These were the ascetics, forest-hermits and mendicant-monks, the founders of sects and monastic orders which were already quite numerous in India at the time of the Buddha. They too had their own poetry: holy legends, sayings of wisdom, in which they preached their doctrines of abstinence and contempt of the world, self-sacrifice and love to all beings, and also fables, parables, fairy-tales and moral stories which were meant to explain the sayings of wisdom and moral teachings of the ascetics by means of examples. This ascetic poetry also has been included in the Mahābhārata to a great extent.

To such an extent had the Mahābhārata become a compendium of narratives of all descriptions rather than an epic, that even prose pieces, brahminical legends and moral tales, some entirely in prose form and others partly in verse and partly in prose, were interpolated into the epic.[1]

Thus we find in this most remarkable of all products of literature war-like hero-songs with colourful descriptions of bloody battle-scenes, pious priestly poetry with frequent interesting discussions on philosophy, religion and law and gentle ascetic poetry full of serene wisdom and overflowing love towards man and beast, all these by the side of one another and intermixed with one another to a confusing degree.

Therefore the Indians themselves consider the Mahābhārata doubtless as an epic, as a work of the art of poetry (Kāvya), but at the same time they consider it also as a text book of morals (śāstra), of law and philosophy based on ancient tradition (smṛti) and hence endowed with indisputable authority; and since more than 1500 years it has served the Indians as much for entertainment as for instruction and sublime edification.

1. In the Pauṣyaparvan (Mahābh. I, 3), in the Mārkaṇḍeya-section of the Vanaparvan, and in the sectarian Nārāyaṇīya. All these are pieces which are really outside the scope of the epic proper. Oldenberg (*Zur Geschichte der altindischen Prosa*, pp. 65 ff.; *Das Mahābhārata*, pp. 21 ff.) may not be right in seeing an earlier stage of the epic in these very pieces. Cf. Hopkins, *The Great Epic of India*. pp, 266 ff,; Winternitz, *DLZ* 1919, No. 44.

At least 1500 years ago[1] this Mahābhārata was already as or at least similar to—what it is today in our manuscripts and editions, a work that had at least the same volume as our epic of today. Just as this it contained even then a long introduction with a framework narrative, a story of the legendary origin, of the poem and a glorification of the same as a didactic and religious book, was divided into 18 books called Parvans to which also a 19th book, Harivaṃśa was added as a supplement (khila); and reached a volume of approximately 1,00,000 stanzas (ślokas). And in spite of the diverse elements of which it consists, this mighty work is considered by the Indians as a unitary compact work[2] which has for its author, the age old ṛṣi Krishna-Dvaipāyana also called Vyāsa. This same ṛṣi is supposed to be the compiler of the four Vedas[3] and the author of the Purāṇas. He was, according to the legend, not only a contemporary but also a close relative of the heroes of the Mahābhārata and sometimes intervenes also in the happenings of the poem. His story is told to us at great length in the Mahābhārata.

He is the son of the famous ascetic, the ṛṣi Parāśara. This great holy man chances to see one day Satyavatī, born of a fish and brought up by fishermen and is enchanted by her beauty so much that he desires her love. She, however, will accept him only under the condition that she regains her virginity after she has borne him a son. The great holy man grants her this wish as also that she might lose her fish-smell and radiate a wonderful fragrance. Immediately after he cohabits with her, she bears him a son on an island in the Jumna and this son is called Dvaipāyana, the "Island-born". The boy grows up and devotes himself to asceticism. While parting from his mother, he tells her that he would appear whenever she needed him, as soon as she thought of him. But Satyavatī, regaining her

1. See further below the chapter on the Age and History of the Mahābhārata.

2. Therefore it is also termed a Saṃhitā, i.e. "a (complete) compilation", "a closely knit text", thus Mahābhārata I, 1, 21.

3. Hence his name Vyāsa or Vedavyāsa, i.e. "Classifier", "Classifier of the Veda". This is the explanation of the name given in the Mahābhārata itself (1,63,88: Viyāsa Vedān yasmat sa tasmād Vyāsa iti smṛtaḥ, of I, 60,5; 105,13).

virginity, became later the wife of the Kuru-king Śāntanu and bore him two sons, Citrāṅgada and Vicitra Vīrya. After Śāntanu and Citrāṅgada died Vicitra Vīrya was made the successor to the throne. He died young and without children, but leaving behind two wives. In order that the family may not disappear for want of progeny, Satyavatī decides to summon her illegitimate son Dvaipāyana in order that he—by virtue of the legal custom of levirat—might produce descendants in his sisters-in-law. Now this Dvaipāyana is no doubt a great penitent and holyman but a very ugly man with stubby hair and gloomy rolling eyes and of dark face (hence perhaps also his name Kṛṣṇa, "the black" and a bad smell emanates from him. Therefore as he approaches one of the two princesses she cannot bear his sight and shuts her eyes; the result is that her son is born blind. It is the subsequent Kuru-Dhṛtarāṣṭra. Thereupon the holyman approaches the second wife and she becomes pale at his sight. As a result of this she delivers a son who is pale and is therefore called Pāṇḍu "the pale". He is the father of the five main heroes of the epic. Dvaipāyana shall approach the first wife once again; but having become wiser she sends, to the holy man, who does not notice the deceit, her servant maid and with this woman he produces Vidura to whose lot in the epic the role of a wise and well-meaning friend of Dhṛtarāṣṭra as well as of the sons of Pāṇḍu falls.[1]

This ugly, stinking holyman, Kṛṣṇa Dvaipāyana Vyāsa, whom legend has made a kind of grandfather[2] of the heroes of the epic, is considered by the Indians upto the present day as the author of the whole Mahābhārata. Only after his three sons had died—tells us the introduction to the Mahābhārata[3]—has Vyāsa made publicly known to men the poem composed by him. And this he made known to his pupil Vaiśaṁpāyana and this Vaiśaṁpāyana recited the whole poem in the intervals of the great serpent sacrifice of king Janamejaya. On this occasion the sūta Ugraśravas, Lomaharṣana's son heard it, and our Mahābhārata begins with

1. Mahābhārata I, 63; 100 ff.

2. According to the Law of Levirats, Vyāsa is only the producer not the father of Dhṛtarāṣṭra and Pāṇḍu. The deceased husband of the two widows is looked upon as their father.

3. I. i, 95 ff.

this that the Ṛṣis who have assembled in the Naimiṣa forest on the occasion of the twelve-year sacrifice of Śaunaka request the Sūta Ugraśravas to narrate to them the story of the Mahābhārata as he had heard it from Vaiśaṁpāyana. The Sūta is ready to do this and narrates the story of the serpent-sacrifice of Janamejaya to proceed then to the narration of the story of Vaiśaṁpāyana.

It is certainly an archaic feature of the Mahābhārata that it contains almost entirely only speeches.[1] Ugraśravas is the reciter of the famed work narrative, and in the poem itself is Vaiśaṁpāyana the speaker. Within the story of Vaiśaṁpāyana again numerous inter-woven stories—and this interweaving of stories in stories is very much liked in Indian literature—are made to be told by different persons. In most cases the stories as well as the speeches of the persons appearing are introduced only with the prose-forms—'Vaiśaṁpāyana spoke', 'Draupadī spoke' etc.

However fanciful all may be, what the introduction to the Mahābhārata tells us about its supposed author, still we find in it some noteworthy particulars. Thus it is said that Ṛṣi Vyāsa has narrated his work in the form of a short summary as well as in the form of an exhaustive description; further, that different reciters begin the poem at three different places and that its volume was not always the same. Ugraśravas says, he knows the poem as having 8800 stanzas, whereas Vyāsa explains that he composed the Saṃhitā of the Bhārata-poem in 24000 stanzas, "and without the sub-stories the Bhārata is recited in this volume by the understanding people". Equally fanciful is the immediately following statement that Vyāsa also composed an epic of 60,00,000 stanzas, namely 30,00,000 for the gods, 15 for the manes, 14 for the Gandharvas and 1,00,000 for the men.[2] This should of

1. "That the old epics of all countries contain speeches and replies, can be seen in the Ilias also; only in the later epics this dramatic element recedes to the background . . . . The completion of the epic poem lies in the fact that for the speeches there is also a framework-narration composed in metrical form. A final stage is, when the speeches recede to the background and only the events are narrated in verse-form." Ernst Windisch, Māra and Buddha (*Abhandl. der philolog-histor-klasse der K. Sächsischen Ges der Wiss* Leipzig 1895). p. 222 ff. The Mahābhārata is still far from that final age."

2. Mahābhārata I, 1, 51 ff; 81; 101 ff.

course indicate only the present volume, which brought to it the name "Śata Sahasra-Saṃhitā", "collection of hundred thousand verses." It is clear from these details that the Indians in spite of their strong belief in the unitary nature of the work have certainly at least remembered that the Mahābhārata has gradually grown up into its present volume starting from an originally small poem.

What the Mahābhārata is to the Indians, is told in the most pompous way in the introduction to the work. There it is said for example

"As the butter among all kinds of sour milk, as the Brahmin among the Aryans, as the Āraṇyakas among the Vedas, as the drink of immortality among medicines, the ocean among all waters and the cow among the quadrupeds is the best, so is of all narrative works (Itihāsas) the Mahābārata the best."

Whoever has once heard this story, he will not like anything else worth hearing; like to him, who has heard the song of the male kokilā[1] the crow's rough voice does not appeal."

From this most excellent of all narrative works originate the thoughts of the poets, as the three world-regions from the five elements."

"He who presents a hundred cows with gold-crated horns to a scholarly Brahmin well versed in the Vedas and he who hears daily the sacred tales of the Bhārata-poem, both earn the same (religious) merit."

"A triumphal charm is this narrative work: a king who desires victory shall hear it, and he will conquer the world and defeat the enemies."

This is a sacred textbook of moral (Dharma); this is the best text book of practical life (artha) and also as a textbook of salvation (mokṣa)[2] it has been recited by the immeasurably wise Vyāsa."

1. The kokilā, the Indian cuckoo is for the Indian poets, the same as what the nightingale is to the German poets.

2. Dharma, "Law and ethics" or "moral", artha "utility", "advantages" "the practical life" and kāma "sensual enjoyment" are the three aims of life, in a way the be-all and end-all of human existence, according to Indian ethics. The aim of all endeavour is however mokṣa, "the salvation", for which the various texts and philosophical systems show various ways.

Every kind of sin committed whether in deeds, thoughts or words, is removed immediately from the man who hears this poem."

"The ascetic Kṛṣṇa Dvaipāyana, getting up everyday (for performing his devotional and penitence-exercises) has composed this wonderful story in three years. What is found in this book regarding moral, practical life, sensual pleasure and salvation[1] is also found elsewhere; what is not here is nowhere in the world."[2]

For us, however, who observe the Mahābhārata not as pious Hindus but as critical literary historians it is nothing less than a work of art; and in no case can we see in it the work of one author, indeed not even that of shrewd collector and compiler. The Mahābhārata as a whole is a literary nonsense. Never has an artist's hand tried—and it would have been also really impossible,—to unite the conflicting elements to a unitary poem. Only theologians and commentators without poetic leanings and unskilled copyists have at last welded together into a disorderly mass the actually non-combinable parts coming down from different centuries. But in this jungle of poetry which science has just begun to clear, much of real and genuine poetry is blooming and flourishing hidden under wild shrubs. Out of the clumsy mass of litter the most charming blossoms of immortal poetic art and profound wisdom are born. And just because the Mahābhārata represents more of an entire literature than a single and unitary work and contains so much and so many kinds of things, is it suited more than any other book, to give us an insight into the most profound depths of the soul of the Indian folk.

This may be shown by the following survey of the summary of the contents of the Mahābhārata and its various components.[3]

1. Ibid., Foot Note 2 on previous page.

2. I, 1. 261 f.; 2, 382 f. 393; 62, 20 f., 23, 25, 52 f. To the last verse compare the Bengali saying, "Whatever is not in the Mahābhārata is not to be found in Bhāratavarṣa", (i.e. in India).

3. There is no complete German translation of the Mahābhārata; translations and treatments of individual pieces of it are mentioned in the notes to the following *abstract* (summary) of contents: The French translation by H. Fauche (Paris 1863-1870) goes only till the end of the 10th book. There are English prose translations of the whole Mahābhārata by Pratap

The main Story of the Mahābhārata

Years ago, Adolf Holtzmann (the senior) made an attempt to explore for the benefit of German friends of poetry, "the basic material of the Mahābhārata[1] the ancient Indian national epic." He proceeded from the undoubtedly correct view that the Mahābhārata is "not the Indian epic" but that "the remnants, the fragments of the ancient Indian hero-songs are contained in the Mahābhārata. ... after manifold modifications, expansions and mutilations." But with enviable self-consciousness he was confident that he possessed the capacity to be able to reconstruct the ancient, original hero-song out of these modified and mutilated "fragments". He thought, that by omissions, abbreviations and changes he wrote an Indian hero-poem in German verse which gave a better idea of the actual Mahābhārata as sung by the ancient Indian bards than a somewhat literal translation of the original text before us would give. Now Holtzmann, with this eye of a genius and profound poetic feeling struck often the right note; but he also strayed from the Sanskrit text with such limitless arbitrariness that his work can be considered only as a very free modification of the ancient

---

Chandra Roy (Calcutta 1884-1896) and Manmatha Nath Dutt (Calcutta, 1895-1905). A beautiful poetic reproduction, partly in metrical translations and partly in prose-synopses is *Mahā-Bhārata, the Epic of Ancient India condensed into English verse* by Romesh Dutt, London, 1899. Bigger and smaller extracts from the Mahābhārata are also found in John Muir's *Original Sanskrit Texts* 5 vols., 1858-1872, Vol. I, 3rd edition 1890 and in the same *Metrical Translations from Sanskrit Writers,* London, 1879 and in Monier Williams' *Indian Wisdom* 4th edition, London, 1893. Ph. E. Faucause gave a collection of bigger pieces from the Mahābhārata in French translation in *Mahabharata onze episode tires de la poeme Epique*, Paris, 1862. P.E. Pavolini gives individual episodes in Italian translation in *Mahabharata, Episodi seeltie li adoth coll col racconto dell 'interno poema* (*Bibliotheca dei pipoli I*) 1902. Some fragments of the last books of the Mahābhārata, translated by Friedrich Rückert, are published in the *Ruckert-Studien* by Robert Boxberger Gotha, 1878, p. 84-122. The following is a collection of the most important philosophical texts of the Mahābhārata in good German translation :

"*Vier philosophische texte des Mahabharata Sanatsujāta-Parvan,—Bhagvadgītā. Mokṣadharma-Aṇugītā* translated from Sanskrit by Paul Deussen (Leipzig, 1906) in collaboration with Dr. Otto Stramp.

1. *Indische Sagen* 2. Teil : *Die Kuruinge*, Karlsruhe 1846.

Mahābhārata and by no means as a faithful reproduction of the same. In reality what Holtzmann has tried is a thing which is impossible. Any attempt to reconstruct "the ancient Indian national epic" is bound to be fraught with so much that is arbitrary that it can have only a purely subjective value.

As against this it is comparatively easy, to obtain by a process of justifying the monstrous mass of the songs of the Mahābhārata a pure nucleus which is the story of the battle between the Kauravas and the Pāṇḍavas, which constituted the motif of the actual epic. This will be done in the following extract which has to be necessarily short. We shall follow the story of the great battle, paying due regard to the most important tributary stories connected with the main heroes as far as is possible. In doing so, we do not want to go into the doubtful hypotheses on the "original" epic, but we shall faithfully follow the Mahābhārata text available to us now by leaving out of our consideration, for the time being, everything that is not connected with the main events of the epic.

THE ORIGIN OF THE KAURAVAS AND THE PĀṆḌAVAS

In the land of the Bharatas there ruled once upon a time a king of the Kuru family Śāntanu by name. He had a son called Bhīṣma by Gaṅgā who assumed the form of a woman[1] and this Bhīṣma he named as his successor to the throne. One day as this Bhīṣma had already grown up into an excellent hero possessing all the virtues of a warrior, Śāntanu met Satyavatī, the fisherman's beautiful daughter, fell in love with her and desired her for wife. But her father, the king of the fishermen wanted to give her to him only under the condition that the son born to his daughter should inherit the throne. Śāntanu did not want to concede this although it was difficult for him to give up his beloved. Bhīṣma however noticed the depressed mood of his father and when he knew the reason for it, he himself went to the fishermen's king to ask him for the hand of his daughter on behalf of his father. He tells not only that

1. Goddess of the River Gaṅgā.

he is ready to renounce the throne, but even takes a vow of celibacy in order that there may not be even the question of a son of his as claimant to the throne. Then Śāntanu marries Satyavatī and produces with her two sons - Citrāṅgada and Vicitravīrya. When Śāntanu died soon thereafter and a Gandharva killed Citrāṅgada in a battle, Bhīṣma as the patriarch of the family initiated Vicitravīrya as king. This Vicitravīrya died young and childless although he had two wives. In order that the family may not die out Satyavatī requests Bhiṣma to follow the ancient legal practice of Levirat and produce descendants with the surviving widows of Vicitravīrya. But Bhīṣma points to his oath of celibacy and declares that the sun may give up its shine, fire its heat, the moon the coolness of its rays, God Indra his bravery, God Dharma[1] his justice, but he can never break the word once given. Then Satyavatī remembers her illegitimate son Vyāsa and with the consent of Bhīṣma she calls upon him to provide for the preservation of the family. And the holy Vyāsa produces, as we have already seen [2] Dhṛtarāṣṭra, Pāṇḍu and Vidura. As Dhṛtarāṣṭra was born blind, the younger brother Pāṇḍu was installed as King. Dhṛtarāṣṭra married Gāndhārī, the daughter of the Gāndhāra-king, and she bore him a hundred sons of whom the eldest was called Duryodhana. But Pāṇḍu had two wives, Pṛthā or Kuntī, the daughter of a king of the Yādavas and Mādrī, the sister of Śalya, the king of the Madras. Kuntī bore him three sons: Yudhiṣṭhira the eldest, Arjuna and Bhīma, who was born on the same day as Duryodhana, while Mādrī became the mother of the twins Nakula and Sahadeva. There is a very fanciful story (not belonging to the old poem) told according to which these five chief heroes of the epic were supposed to be born not of Pāṇḍu but produced for Pāṇḍu. Pāṇḍu, it is said, killed while hunting a pair of antelopes in cohabitation. But in reality it is a ṛṣi who had assumed the form of an antelope, for the purpose of love making. This ṛṣi now curses Pāṇḍu that he shall die while enjoying love. Therefore Pāṇḍu decides to lead an ascetic life and to renounce sexual pleasure. But in order that he might obtain progeny, the gods were evoked to produce

1. The god of death and at the same time the god of justice.
2. P. 302 above.

children through her. Dharma, the god of justice produces with her Yudhiṣṭhira, the wind-god Vāyu the strong Bhīma and Indra the king of the gods Arjuna. On Kuntī's request the two Aśvins cohabit with Mādrī and produce the twins Nakula and Sahadeva.

The Pāṇḍavas and the Kauravas at the Court of Dhṛtarāṣṭra

On Pāṇḍu's death thereafter the blind Dhṛtarāṣṭra took over the government. The five sons of Pāṇḍu with their mother Kuntī (Pāṇḍu's second wife got herself cremated with him as widow) moved to the Court of King Dhṛtarāṣṭra at Hastināpura and were brought up there together with the princes, their cousins.

Even during the sports of childhood the sons of Pāṇḍu distinguished themselves from those of Dhṛtarāṣṭra and roused the jealousy of the latter. Bhīma in particular was extremely arrogant and gave some specimens of his boundless strength, which was quite irksome to the children of Dhṛtarāṣṭra. When the children had climbed on a tree for example, he shook it in such a way that the cousins fell down tumbling along with the fruits. Hence Duryodhana was very spiteful of Bhīma and also made many attacks on his life, without being able to do any harm to him. The boys grew up and received as teachers in the art of using arms two famous Brahmins Kṛpa and Droṇa well-versed in the use of arms. To their pupils belonged in addition to the sons of Dhṛtarāṣṭra and Pāṇḍu, also Aśvatthāman, a son of Droṇa and Karṇa, the son of Sūta or Chariot-driver. Soon-Duryodhana and Bhīma became the best pupils of Droṇa in club-fight, Aśvatthāman in magic-arts, Nakula and Sahadeva in sword fighting and Yudhiṣṭhira in chariot-fighting. But Arjuna was not only the most efficient archer, but also surpassed all the others in every respect. Hence the sons of Dhṛtarāṣṭra were especially jealous of him.

As the princes completed their apprenticeship, Droṇa organised a competition in the course of which his pupils had to show their skills. It is a splendid celebration; the king, the queens and numerous heroes are present. There is a club-fight between Bhīma and Duryodhana which threatens to become so serious that the opponents have to be separated. Arjuna earns general applause for his skill in archery. But Karṇa also enters the arena and performs the same skillful acts as Arjuna. Thereupon Arjuna is enraged while Duryodhana joyously embraces Karṇa and assures him his permanent friendship. Karṇa challenges Arjuna to a duel, but is mocked at by the Pāṇḍavas as the descendant of a chariot driver.

Yudhiṣṭhira Becomes Successor to the Throne—Conspiracy against him and his Brothers (the lac-house)

A year after that Dhṛtarāṣṭra installed as successor (having been the first-born of the Kuru-family) to the throne Yudhiṣṭhira who distinguished himself equally by his bravery and all other virtues. The remaining Pāṇḍavas combined their training in arms and undertook of their own accord also victorious campaigns of conquest. When Dhṛtarāṣṭra heard of these war-deeds of the Pāṇḍavas who were becoming more and more powerful, he began to be somewhat worried about the future of his own sons. Hence when Duryodhana, his younger brother Duśśāsana, his friend Karṇa and his maternal uncle Śakunī hatched a conspiracy against the Pāṇḍavas, they found ready support from the old king. They pursuaded Dhṛtarāṣṭra to remove the Pāṇḍavas to Vāraṇāvata under some pretext. There Duryodhana had a home built by a clever architect out of lac and other easily inflammable materials and the Pāṇḍavas had to live in that house. At the time of sleep in the night fire was to be set to the house in order that the Pāṇḍavas might be destroyed. But Vidura secretly informs Yudhiṣṭhira—he thereby makes use of a mleccha-language, i.e. a language of a non-Indian race, not understood by the others—of the treacherous plan. But in order not to rouse suspicion for they were afraid that Duryodhana would get them killed by assassins in some other manner, they apparently agree to the plan, move to Vāraṇāvata and occupy the lac-house. But by means of an underground path which they got secretly laid, they escape into the forest after they have themselves set fire to the house in which apart from the architect there is only one unknown woman of a low caste with five sons sleeping. While all people believe that the Pāṇḍavas along with their mother Kuntī have been burnt to death, and obsequies are performed at the court of Dhṛtarāṣṭra, the five brothers are wandering with their mother in the forest on the other side of the Ganges. In a dark night they find themselves in the midst of a dense forest—tired, hungry and thirsty. Kuntī complains of thirst and Bhīma brings his mother and four brothers to a banyan tree where they shall take rest while he wants to go in search of water. Following the aquatic birds he comes to a pond where he bathes and drinks and dips his upper cloth in water, in order to fetch water for the others. He returns very quickly and finds all his people asleep under the tree. As he sees his mother and brothers sleeping in this manner he laments bitterly their sad fate.

Hiḍimba, the Giant and His Sister

Near this banyan tree lives a terrible man-eating giant, the Rākṣasa Hiḍimba. He smells human flesh and from the top of a tree he sees the sleeping ones. His mouth waters, and attracted by the prospect of eating human flesh which he had not got for a long time he asks his sister to go and find out what sort of people they were; then they wanted to enjoy the fresh human flesh and blood and merrily dance and sing after that. The giantess goes there but hardly has she seen Bhīma, when she is struck by strong love for the mighty youth of the hero. She assumes the form of a pretty human female and, approaching Bhīma smilingly, she tells him that this forest is haunted by the man-eating Rākṣasa, her brother, who has sent her there; that she loves him and would not have anyone else for husband; he might enjoy her and she would save him. Bhīma replies that he does not want to indulge in pleasure and abandon his mother and brothers. Hiḍimbā says, he might awaken his people, she would save them all. But Bhīma says, he would never agree to awaken his mother and brothers from sweet slumber, of Rākṣasas, Yakṣas (elves), Gandharvas and other spirits he has no fear; he would also manage the man-eater. Now comes actually the giant Hiḍimba as his sister was away from him too long, and in his anger he wants to kill his love-stricken sister. But Bhīma confronts him and challenges him to a fight. After a terrible fight during which the brothers wake up, he kills the giant. Now he wants to dispose Hiḍimbā also in the same way, but Yudhisṭhira warns him not to kill a woman. Upon her fervent entreaties he at last agrees to the union with her until she becomes pregnant and bears a son. Yudhiṣṭhira directs him to spend the daytime with the giantess and return to them before sunset. So Hiḍimbā flies with Bhīma in the air on to mountain tops where they indulge in sports of love-making until she becomes pregnant and bears a son who is also a mighty Rākṣasa. They name him Ghaṭotkaca. This Ghaṭotkaca renders good service to the Pāṇḍavas later in the great battle.[1]

The Giant Baka and the Brahmin Family

The Pāṇḍavas wander about now through many kinds of adventures disguised as penitents from one forest to another and reach at last a town called Ekacakra where without being recognised they find lodgings in a Brahmin's house. During the day they beg their food and bring it home in the evening when Kunti divides the whole food into two halves—one for Bhīma and the other for the rest. One day Kuntī is alone at home with Bhīma. Then they hear from the rooms of the Brahmin whose hospitality they enjoy, loud weeping and lamenting. And they hear how at first the Brahmin in bitter lamentation complains human destiny and says it would be best to die with his whole family, for he could never suffer to sacrifice his faithful wife, his dear daughter or even his little son, but on the other hand he would have to leave the family to certain misery if he would die alone. Thereupon the Brahmin's wife says, he must be alive and take care of his children and preserve his family. But she has fulfilled the purpose of her existence after she has borne him a son and a daughter and she could therefore die in peace. If he would die, then she could never afford food and protection to the children; she could neither protect her daughter from unworthy men nor give to her son an education worthy of a Brahmin. He could take a second wife whereas she as a widow would have only a lamentable fate. "Like birds

1. A very free treatment of the Hiḍimba episode has been given by Friedrich Rückert (*Works* pub. by C. Beyer, vol. 6, p. 426 ff.).

greedily rush to a piece of flesh thrown away, so also men to a woman robbed of her husband". Therefore, she said, she would sacrifice her life. Now begins her daughter to speak, who has heard the speeches of her parents, and she tries to prove that she alone should die for the family. "Is it not said, that one's own self is the son, a friend the wife, a misery the daughter ? Get rid of this misery and let me fulfil my duty". While these three are talking thus to one another and finally all break in tears, the little son comes with eyes wide open to each of them and speaks smilingly in a sweet, childish voice, "Don't weep, father! Don't weep, mother! Don't weep, sister!" And merrily takes the little one a stalk of grass in his hand and says, "With this I kill the man-eating Rākṣasa!" And however deeply sad they all were, when they heard the boy's sweet voice, their hearts were filled with joy. Kuntī the mother of the Pāṇḍavas takes this opportunity to go in and enquire what the matter is. Then she learns that near the town there lives a Rākṣasa, the giant Baka, to whom the inhabitants must send at regular intervals a tribute of a cartload of rice, two buffaloes and a human being. All the families have to dot his by turns and just now it is their turn. Kuntī then comforts the Brahmin and suggests that one of her five sons may take the tribute to the Rākṣasa. But the Brahmin vehemently opposes that a Brahmin and that too a guest should sacrifice his life for him. Kuntī thereupon explains to him that her son is a great hero—which of course he should not reveal to any one—, who will certainly kill the Rākṣasa. Bhīma is at once ready to obey the directive of his mother and on the next day he drives the cart laden with the food for the Rākṣasa into the forest, where the monster lives. As soon as he comes to the forest he begins to eat the food himself—and this is described with great humour —and is not disturbed in this even by the enraged giant who approaches him. Even when the infuriated Rākṣasa thrashes him with both hands he continues to eat calmly. Only after eating up everything does he get ready for a fight. They both uproot the strongest trees of the forest and hurl at each other. But then begins a mighty wrestling at the end of which Bhīma breaks the giant into two upon his knee. He then forces the remaining Rākṣasas, the relatives and subordinates of Baka, to promise never more to kill men and goes back to his brothers. There is great rejoicing in the town. But the disguise of the Pāṇḍavas is continued.

Husband's Choice and Draupadī's Marriage

After some time the Pāṇḍavas decide to leave the town of Ekacakra and move into the Pāñcāla-country. On the way they learn that Drupada, the king of the Pāñcālas, is about to arrange the husband's choice[1] of his daughter. The brothers decide to take part in it and, disguised as Brahmins, they go to the town where Drupada is residing, and they live there in the house of a potter eking their livelihood by begging. But Drupada has a very strong bow made, gets a target fixed high up in the air by means of an artificial contrivance and announces that in the svayaṁvara only that hero would be able to win his daughter Kṛṣṇā who would set arrow to the bow and shoot the target set up. Princes of all countries, including the Kauravas, Duryodhana and his brothers, together with Karṇa, respond to the king's invitation and meet in the ceremoniously decorated hall in which the husband's selection is to take place. Also numberless Brahmins rush to witness the function, and among them are also the five Pāṇḍavas. Splendid festivities take place for a number of days and the kings and Brahmins are treated as guests with great magnificence. At last on the 16th day, in the midst of the usual ceremonies, the beautiful Kṛṣṇā appears in the hall, splendidly dressed and bejewelled, with a garland of flowers in her hand. Her brother Dhṛṣṭadyumna proclaims in a loud voice: "Listen Oh all of you people! Here is the bow, here are the arrows, there is the target. Shoot it through the hole in the contrivance with the five sharp arrows darting through the air.

1. Svayaṁvara, i.e. self-selection is a form of marriage or betrothal which takes place in the following manner: The king's daughter herself selects from among the princes and heroes gathered (after the father has sent a ceremonious invitation) her husband by putting around the neck of the selected one a garland whereupon the wedding takes place. Whereas the Svayaṁvara is frequently described in the epic poetry, the Brahminical law books which treat exhaustively the other different kinds of marriages do not mention this practice at all. Cf. J. J. Meyer, *Das Weib im attindischen Epos*, pp. 60 ff.

He who, endowed with noble birth, beauty and strength, accomplishes this great deed, shall obtain my sister Kṛṣṇā today as his wife—not in vain is my speech". Thereupon he mentions to his sister the names of all the kings present, beginning with Duryodhana. All fall in love with the charming Kṛṣṇā immediately, one is jealous of the other, and each individual hopes to win her. One after the other they try to draw the bow, but none succeeds. Then Karṇa comes forward, he has just drawn the bow and is ready to shoot the target when Kṛṣṇā cries in a loud voice: "A chariot-driver I will not choose!" With a bitter laugh and a look at the sun Karṇa throws down the bow. In vain do the other mighty kings, Śiśupāla, Jarāsandha and Śalya try to draw the bow. Then Arjuna rises from the midst of the Brahmins. Under a loud murmur of approbation of those who admire the imposing youth and of the protests of those who are angry that a Brahmin dare enter the arena against the warriors, he goes up to the bow, draws it immediately and shoots down the target. As Kṛṣṇā sees the youth resembling the gods she offers him the garland gladly and Arjuna, followed by the king's daughter, leaves the hall.

But as the kings gathered there notice that Drupada really wants to give his daughter to the Brahmin they consider it an insult; for a husband's selection is meant only for warriors, not for Brahmins. They want to kill Drupada. But Bhīma and Arjuna rush to his help. Bhīma uproots a mighty tree and stands as the god of death there. Arjuna stands next to him with his bow drawn. Karṇa fights with Arjuna, Śalya with Bhīma. After a hard fight Karṇa and Śalya surrender. The kings give up their fight and go back to their respective countries. But the Pāṇḍavas leave with Kṛṣṇā and go to the potter's house where Kuntī is already worried and waiting for them. Now Arjuna explains here before his mother and brothers, that he will not marry alone, Drupada's daughter Kṛṣṇā whom he has won, but that she must become the common wife of all the five brothers following an old custom in the family.

Among those present at the self-selection of the husband was also Kṛṣṇa, the chieftain of a clan of the Yādavas and the cousin of the Pāṇḍavas (Because Vasudeva, Kṛṣṇa's father was Kuntī's brother). He was the only one who had recognised the

Pāṇḍavas in spite of their disguise. Hence, accompanied by his brother Baladeva, he followed the Pāṇḍavas, visited them in the potter's house and revealed himself to them as their relative. The Pāṇḍavas were very happy over this. In order that they might not be identified by the people, Kṛṣṇa and Baladeva go away soon.

Also Prince Dhṛṣṭadyumna had followed the Pāṇḍavas secretly in order to find out who actually the hero was who had won his sister as his wife. He hides himself in the potter's house and observes how the brothers return home and greet their mother with reverence, how Kuntī instruct Draupadī[1] in the matter of preparing and distributing the food, how they then go to rest after supper when the youngest of the brothers spreads a bed of the Kuśa-grass on which the five brothers then lie down, each on his antilope-skin, in the order of their ages, while their mother makes her bed at their head and Draupadī at their feet; and he hears, how, before falling asleep, the brothers have all sorts of conversations with one another on weapons and war-deeds. Thereupon Dhṛṣṭadyumna goes back to his father to report to him that the supposed Brahmins, as inferred from their conversations, should be warriors, which makes the king mighty pleased. On the next morning Drupada sends an invitation to the Pāṇḍavas to come to the palace in order that the marriage of his daughter might be performed ceremoniously. Only now Yudhiṣṭhira tells him that they are the sons of Pāṇḍu, believed to be dead; and Drupada is very happy over this, because it had been always his desire to get Arjuna as his son-in-law. As he proposes to have the marriage of his daughter with Arjuna performed ceremoniously he is somewhat surprised and little pleased when Yudhiṣṭhira tells him that Kṛṣṇā must become the common wife of all the five brothers. However his misgivings are set aside when they pointed to the ancient custom in the family of the Pāṇḍavas; and Draupadī is married in the presence of the holy fire at first to Yudhiṣṭhira as the eldest, then also to the other brothers in the order of their

1. Kṛṣṇā, "the black one" is usually called "Draupadī", i.e. "daughter of Drupada".

ages.[1] Kuntī blesses her daughter-in-law. To the new couple Kṛṣṇa sends rich and very valuable presents.

---

1. In this five-husbands-marriage the epic has faithfully retained undoubtedly an old feature of the saga. For, although polyandry or rather group-marriage, of which the marriage of the Pāṇḍavas affords an example, is found even today in some isolated parts of India, still it has not been testified to be the legal form of marriage in ancient India and is even quite contrary to the Brahminical views. When Drupada says (I, 197, 27): "The law instructs that one man has many wives; but we have never heard that one woman has many husbands", then with this he gives expression to the general Indian view. If in spite of this the five chief heroes in the epic have only one wife then this is a proof of the fact that this feature was so intimately entwined with the whole legend and the ancient epic that even in later times when the Mahābhārata received a more and more Brahminical character and became a textbook of religion nobody could think of removing this feature. One simply strove to justify this marriage with five men by means of many rather unskilfully inserted stories. Once Vyāsa tells the foolish story of a virgin who could not get a husband and implored Lord Śiva to procure a husband for her. Now because she had cried out five times, "Give me a husband", Śiva promises her five husbands—in a later birth. This virgin is reborn as Kṛṣṇā, Drupada's daughter and obtains therefore the five Pāṇḍavas as husbands. A second story is also not in any way shrewd. The Pāṇḍavas who live in the potter's house as begging Brahmins come home with Draupadī and tell their mother that they have brought home "the alms" that they have collected on their begging rounds. Without looking up says Kuntī as usual, "Enjoy it all together". Only then she notices that the "alms" is a woman and is taken aback; but the word of a mother must not be rendered false and it should be settled that the five brothers enjoy Draupadī in common. A third story that Vyāsa again tells to Drupada is the Śaivite "Five-Indra-Story" (Pañchendropākhyānam), a highly fanciful and confused report as to how Indra, as a penalty for having insulted Śiva, is divided into five parts and is born on the earth, and an incarnation of Lakṣmī or Śrī (Goddess of fortune and beauty) is determined to be his wife. The five Pāṇḍavas are incarnations of one Indra, Draupadī is an incarnation of Lakṣmī; so Draupadī has actually only one husband! There is not even an attempt made to reconcile these three stories of justification with one another or with the main story. On the contrary it is repeatedly expressed that we are concerned here with an old family-custom not for instance with a general Indian but with a particular family-custom of the Pāṇḍavas. In the stories of the Buddhists and the Jains the husband-self-selection of Draupadī is described in this way that she chooses not Arjuna but all the five Pāṇḍavas at the same time. It is funny that some European researchers also have tried to interpret and justify the five-husbands-marriage mythologically, allegorically and symbolically instead of accepting it as an ethnological fact. (cf. M. Winternitz, "Notes on the Mahābhārata" in *JRAS*, 1897, p. 733 ff.)

The Pāṇḍavas get back their Kingdom

Soon the news spreads that the Pāṇḍavas are still alive and that it was Arjuna who won Draupadī at the time of the husband-selection. Duryodhana and his comrades return depressed to Hastināpura and they are very much worried now that by their marriage the Pāṇḍavas have gained too powerful allies—Drupada and the Pāñcālas, Kṛṣṇa and the Yādavas. Duryodhana thinks, they must beware of the Pāṇḍavas now and suggests to defeat them treacherously. Karṇa on the contrary advises open fight. But Bhīṣma, with whom also Vidura and Droṇa agree, counsels Dhṛtarāṣṭra to give to the Pāṇḍavas half the kingdom and to live in peace with them. Dhṛtarāṣṭra considers this suggestion and cedes to the Pāṇḍavas half of his kingdom asking them to settle in the desert of Khāṇḍavaprastha. Yudhiṣṭhira accepts the offer willingly and, accompanied by Kṛṣṇā, the Pāṇḍavas go to Khāṇḍavaprastha. There they found (near the present day Delhi) the big town and fortress Indraprastha as their residence.

Arjuna's Exile and Adventure

Happy and contented the Pāṇḍavas lived with their common wife in the Indraprastha. In order that any jealousy may not crop up its head among themselves, they had agreed (on the advice of the celestial sage Nārada) that whoever of the brothers takes another one by surprise when he is in the intimate company of Draupadī must go into exile for 12 years and must lead a life of celibacy. As a result of this agreement they always live in peace with one another.

One day robbers lift the cattle of a Brahmin and he comes running to the palace with strong reproaches that the king is not protecting his subjects adequately. Arjuna immediately wants to rush to his help. But it so happens that the weapons are hanging in a room in which Yudhiṣṭhira is together with Draupadī. Arjuna is in a dilemma. Should he fulfil the warrior's duty towards the Brahmin and violate the rule with respect to the common wife or should he violate the former in order to observe the latter ? He decides in favour of going into the room to get the weapons, pursues the robbers and gives the cattle back to the Brahmin. Then he goes home and explains to

Yudhiṣṭhira that as per the agreement he will go into exile for 12 years. Although Yudhiṣṭhira tries to hold him back, because he does not feel insulted, Arjuna, following the principle that rule is rule, withdraws into the forest.

Here he has many kinds of experiences. Once for instance he bathes in the Ganges and wants to get up just after making offerings to the manes, when Ulūpī, the daughter of a Nāga king drags him into the kingdom of the Nāgas (snake-demons). She tells him that she has fallen in love with him and requests him to enjoy her. Arjuna replies that he cannot, as he has taken an oath of celibacy. But the snake-virgin counters him saying that this oath was valid only with respect to Draupadī; moreover it is the duty of a warrior to help people in distress—if he will not help her, she will commit suicide—he must therefore save her life. Against these arguments Arjuna has nothing more to say and "in view of his duty" he fulfills the wish of the beautiful Ulūpī and spends a night with her.

On another occasion; in the course of his wanderings he comes to Citravāhana, the king of Maṇipura and falls in love with his beautiful daughter Citrāṅgadā. But she is a son's daughter[1] and the king gives her to him only on condition that a son born to her should be considered as his (Citravāhana's) son. Arjuna agrees to this and lives with her for three years in Maṇipura.[2] After she has borne him a son he takes leave of them all and continues his wanderings.

After visiting several holy places and experiencing more adventures he meets Kṛṣṇa and visits him in his town Dvārakā where he is received with extreme ceremony. A few days later a great festivity of the Vṛṣṇis and Andhakas—two clans of the Yādavas—took place on the Raivataka mountain. With music, singing and dancing noblemen and commoners go out in a procession and it is all very merry. Baladeva, Kṛṣṇa's brother is drunk with his wife Revatī, Ugrasena, the king of the Vṛṣṇis

1. A "putrikā" or son's daughter is a daughter whose son belongs not to her husband but to her father. When for instance a man has no son, he can use his daughter as putrikā, by which a son born to her continues the line of her father, i.e. he is obliged to perform the offerings to the dead and is entitled to inherit.

2. Now there is no talk of celibacy any more.

comes with his thousand wives and numerous other princes also with their wives. On this occasion Arjuna sees Subhadrā, the beautiful sister of Kṛṣṇa and falls in love with her. He asks Kṛṣṇa how he can win her and Kṛṣṇa advises him to forcibly kidnap her in the manner of warriors, because a husband-selection is always an uncertain affair.[1] Then Arjuna sends an emissary to Yudhiṣṭhira to get his permission for kidnapping Subhadrā. Yudhiṣṭhira gives his approval and Arjuna, fully armed like a warrior, goes out in his war-chariot as if he went out to hunt. Subhadrā goes to the Raivataka and as she is just about to return to Dvārakā, Arjuna seizes her, takes her on his chariot and drives off with her towards Indraprastha. Dvārakā is greatly excited; the drunken Baladeva is enraged that Arjuna has exceeded the limits of a guest. But Kṛṣṇa pacifies his relatives saying that Arjuna has not insulted them. On the contrary he (Arjuna) considered the Yādavas to be not so greedy as to want to sell a bride like a head of cattle and he did not want to try the husband-selection and therefore he had no alternative to kidnapping Subhadrā. There is nothing to be said against the marriage. They should only bring back Arjuna and compromise with him. This is done and Subhadrā is married to Arjuna. He remains for one more year in Dvārakā, enjoying Subhadrā. The balance of the 12 years he spends in the holy place of Puṣkara, after which he returns to Indraprastha. Draupadī reproaches him for his marriage with Subhadrā, is however calmed down when Subhadrā subjugates herself to her as a servant. And Draupadī, Subhadrā and Kuntī live from then on happily with one another. Subhadrā bore a son to Arjuna, Abhimanyu by name, and this son became the favourite of his father and uncles. But Draupadī bore a son to each one of the five Pāṇḍavas.

Yudhiṣṭhira becomes Ruler of the World

King Yudhiṣṭhira ruled justly and piously and his subjects who loved him lived happily and contented. The brothers of

1. Evidently the Yādavas were a wild clan of herdsmen among whom marriage by robbing was accepted as legal.

the king too led a happy life. Arjuna's friendship with Kṛṣṇa grew to be strong now. When the friends were amusing themselves in the groves on the banks of the Jumnā (indulging in orgies with many beautiful women, even Draupadī and Subhadrā participating in them), god Agni approached them in the form of a Brahmin and requested them to help him in burning down the Khāṇḍava forest. The god had of course got indigestion as a result of consuming too many sacrificial offerings at a great sacrifice and Brahman had told him, he must burn down the Khāṇḍava-forest, to regain his health. However often he might try to burn the forest, the animals of the forest put out the fire again and again. Arjuna and Kṛṣṇa should prevent that, and for this purpose Agni procures heavenly weapons for them, the powerful bow Gāṇḍīva with two inexhaustible quivers and a magnificent war-chariot drawn by two silver-white horses recognisable from a distance by a monkey-banner for Arjuna; a discus that never misses its target and an irresistible mace to Kṛṣṇa. With these weapons they aid Agni and kill all beings that try to flee from the burning forest. Only the demon Maya, who is a great artist among the celestial beings is spared by them.[1]

Grateful that his life was spared, the demon Maya builds for Yudhiṣṭhira a wonderful palace with extremely artistic contrivances. After some time Yudhiṣṭhira, with consent of Kṛṣṇa resolves to perform the sacrifice of Royal Initiation (Rājasūya). But only a world-ruler, a great conqueror is entitled to perform this sacrifice. Because at this time Jarāsandha the king of Magadha is the most powerful ruler he must therefore be defeated at first. In a dual with Bhīma he is killed. Only then are victorious campaigns undertaken by Arjuna in the north, Bhīma in the east, Sahadeva in the south and Nakula in the west; and thus the whole world belongs to Yudhiṣṭhira now. Now the sacrifice for the royal initiation can be performed and it is actually performed with great pomp. Numerous kings, including the Kauravas are invited for this. At the close of the sacrifice gifts of honour are distributed. On Bhiṣma's suggestion Kṛṣṇa should receive the first gift. Śiśupāla, the king of Cedi, protests

1. Here ends the Ādiparvan or the first book of the Mahābhārata.

against this. As a result a quarrel ensues which ends with Kṛṣṇa killing Śiśupāla.

After the sacrifice is completed the royal invitees go away. Kṛṣṇa also returns to his country. Only Duryodhana and his uncle Śakuni remain for some more time in the palace of the Pāṇḍavas. While going about the wonderful building, all kinds of mishaps befall Duryodhana. He considers a crystal-surface to be a water-surface and removes his clothes to bathe while he considers an artificial lake to be firm land and has a bath against his will, whereupon Bhīma and Arjuna cannot suppress their laughter.[1] This mockery deeply angered Duryodhana who was already filled with envy. Taking leave of his cousins with the bitterest feelings of envy and hatred he goes back to Hastināpura.

The Game of Dice

Duryodhana complains bitterly of his anguish to his uncle Śakuni. He says he cannot bear the humiliation of having to see his enemies celebrate such victories; and he does not see any way of equalling the Pāṇḍavas, he will end his life by means of fire, poison or water. Then Śakuni proposes that a game of dice must be organised and Yudhiṣṭhira invited to participate; he, Śakuni who is a skilful gambler, will easily win from Yudhiṣṭhira his whole kingdom. Immediately they go to the old king Dhṛtarāṣṭra, in order to obtain his approval for the plan. He however does not at all like the idea at first and wants in any case to consult his wise brother Vidura. But as Duryodhana makes the charge that Vidura always favours the Pāṇḍavas, the old weak king finally allows himself to be persuaded and gives orders for the game of dice. Vidura warns the king and does not conceal his fear that this game of dice

1. Duryodhana's adventures in the marvellous palace of Yudhiṣṭhira remind us of the story of the Queen of Sheba, who mistakes a glass floor in Solomon's palace for a sheet of water, and bares her legs. Cf. Quran, 27,38; W. Hertz, *Gesammelte Abhandlungen*, (1905), p. 427; Grierson, *JRAS* 1913, 684 f. There is also a similar story in the legend of the wonders of the new Babylon, built by Nebuchadnezzar; see A. Wesselofsky in *Archiv für slavische Philologie* II, 310 ff. 321.

will give rise to a great misfortune. Dhṛtarāṣṭra too has this fear, but he believes that he must allow fate to take its course. So Vidura goes to the court of King Yudhiṣṭhira to hand over the invitation for the game of dice. He too, being forced by the indisputable power of fate, accepts the invitation, although unwillingly. And, accompanied by his brothers and Draupadī and the other women of the household, he sets out to Hastinā-pura. In the palace of Dhṛtarāṣṭra the guests are received by the relatives with great kindness and honour.

On the next morning Yudhiṣṭhira and his brothers go to the gambling hall, where the Kauravas are already assembled. Śakuni challenges Yudhiṣṭhira to a game, he stakes and loses. And one after another he stakes all his treasures and his riches in gold and precious stones, his splendid chariot, his slaves — men and women, elephants, chariots and horses — and each time he loses. Then Vidura approaches Dhṛtarāṣṭra and advises him to withdraw from his son Duryodhana who will bring about the ruin of the whole family and to forbid the continuation of the game. Now Duryodhana attacks Vidura with the most violent insults, calling him a traitor — a snake which the Kauravas are nourishing in their breast — for he always speaks in favour of their enemies. Vidura turns in vain to Dhṛtarāṣṭra. But Śakuni asks Yudhiṣṭhira mockingly whether he has still something to stake. Yudhiṣṭhira is now seized with a wild passion to gamble and stakes all his possessions, his oxen and cows, his town, his land and his entire kingdom — and loses them all. Also the princes, then the brothers Nakula and Sahadeva he stakes and loses them. Provoked by Śakuni he lets himself be misguided to stake Arjuna and Bhīma and loses them too. At last he stakes himself and again Śakuni wins. Mockingly Śakuni remarks that Yudhiṣ-ṭhira was ill-advised in staking himself, he has yet another treasure – which he can stake – Draupadī. And to the amazement of all elders[1] of Bhīṣma, Droṇa, Kṛpa and Vidura — Yudhiṣ-ṭhira declares his desire to play staking the beautiful Draupadī.

1. It is very remarkable that these impartial and well-meaning people calmly accept that Yudhiṣṭhira loses his brothers and himself in the game, whereas it appears to them as something terrific that he stakes the common wife.

The dice fall under general excitement — and once again Śakuni has won.

With a loud laughter Duryodhana calls upon Vidura to fetch Draupadī so that she might sweep the rooms and join the maids. Vidura reprimands him and warns that by his conduct he will only cause the ruin of the Kauravas. Further, Draupadī has not become a slave, because Yudhiṣṭhira has staked her when Yudhiṣṭhira was not master of himself any more. Then Duryodhana sends a Sūta as messenger to Draupadī to fetch her. She asks him to find out whether Yudhiṣṭhira has lost himself first in the game or her. Duryodhana replies saying that she may come to the gambling hall and put the question herself. As she refuses and sends the messenger back Duryodhana asks his brother Duśśāsana to fetch her by force. He goes to the lady's chamber and soon he fetches the resisting Draupadī – who is unwell and therefore scantily clad – dragging her by the hair into the assembly. She laments bitterly that nobody – not even Bhīṣma and Droṇa – takes pity on her and she throws a desperate look at the Pāṇḍavas. These Pāṇḍavas are afflicted more by the look of Draupadī full of shame and anger than by the loss of their wealth and prowess. Bhīma cannot control himself any more and reproaches Yudhiṣṭhira violently for staking Draupadī and he wants to assault him.[1] But Arjuna rebukes him: Yudhiṣṭhira must be always recognised and respected as the eldest. Now Vikarṇa, one of the youngest brothers of Duryodhana asks the assembly to answer Draupadī's question whether she has been properly staked and lost or not. And as all people keep quiet he himself answers the question in the negative. Karṇa on the other hand declares that the Kauravas have won everything and so the wife of the Pāṇḍavas

1. Bhīma says he will burn both of Yudhiṣṭhira's arms, and asks Sahadeva to bring fire for this purpose (II, 68, 6;10). J. J Meyer (*Das Weib im altindischen Epos*," p. 226) translates differently interpreting the passage as meaning that Bhima wishes to burn his own hands, and Meyer calls this "a typically Indian method of revenge and branding," similar to the "prâyopaveśa" (threat of suicide by hunger, in order to force a right). Nīlakaṇṭha's commentary (*te tava pura iti śeṣaḥ*) would confirm this interpretation. Even if the usual translation be accepted, Bhīma's threat sounds very strange.

also belongs to them. Even the clothes of the Pāṇḍavas and of Draupadī must be removed because these too have been won by the Kauravas. And the Pāṇḍavas remove their upper garments while Duśśāsana, following Karṇa's sign, begins to remove Draupadī's garments off her body.[1] She however prays to god Viṣṇu who contrives that she always remains clad however often Duśśāsana may rip her clothing. But Bhīma utters the terrible oath:

"Hear this word of mine, Oh you warriors of the entire world, a word which has never till now been spoken by men, as will never be spoken by them. Never may I join my forefathers if I do not fulfil what I speak,—if I do not in the battle rip open the breast and drink the blood of this wicked obstinate excretion of the Bhāratas (that is Duśśāsana)."

On hearing these terrible words all the warriors and heroes are seized with horror. Vidura tries to remind those present of their duty to decide the legal question whether Draupadī has been won by the Kauravas or not. But no body heeds to his words. In vain does Draupadī lament and weep and ask her relatives to answer her question. Even the pious Bhīṣma well-versed in law cannot say anything more than that justice is a complicated thing and in this world power suppresses justice. Yudhiṣṭhira is exemplary in matters of justice, so he himself may decide. Duryodhana sarcastically exhorts Yudhiṣṭhira to tell his opinion, whether he considers that they have won Draupadī or not. And as Yudhiṣṭhira merely sits there as if absentminded and does not reply to Duryodhana, the latter hurls most scandalous abuses at the Pāṇḍavas, he shows his left thigh to Draupadī. Then Bhīma speaks these terrible words, "Never shall Bhīma be united with his forefathers if I do not shatter into pieces with my club this thigh in the battle".

While more speeches are exchanged, one hears jackals loudly cry in the house of Dhṛtarāṣṭra, and other bad omens also

1. Not only the Southern Indian manuscripts, but also the play "Dūtavākya" ascribed to Bhāsa, make it seem probable that this miracle of the garments is a very late interpolation; see Winternitz in *Festschrift Kuhn*, pp. 299 ff. Oldenberg (*Das Mahābhārata*, pp. 45 ff.) makes an attempt to distinguish generally between the earlier and later parts in the present narrative of the gambling scene.

appear. Horrified by these the old king Dhṛtarâṣṭra feels that he must intervene. In rude words he blames Duryodhana. Then he pacifies Draupadī and grants her a boon. She chooses the freedom of her husband Yudhiṣṭhira. He grants her a second boon and she chooses the freedom of the remaining Pāṇḍavas. When he grants her a third boon, she says she has no more desire now because as soon as the Pāṇḍavas have become free they would themselves achieve what they needed. But now Karṇa mocks saying, that Draupadī has been the boat by means of which the Pāṇḍavas have saved themselves from danger. Bhīma is burning with rage and thinks that he should perhaps kill the Kauravas on the spot. But Arjuna pacifies him and Yudhiṣṭhira forbids any quarrel whatsoever. King Dhṛtarâṣṭra however gives back to Yudhiṣṭhira his kingdom and exhorts him to forget all that has happened in the past. So they go back pacified to Indraprastha.

The Second Game of Dice and the Banishment of the Pāṇḍavas

But scarcely have the Pāṇḍavas gone away when Duryodhana, Duśśāsana and Śakuni again assail the old king, reproach, what a danger the Kauravas are threatened with from the side of the insulted Pāṇḍavas and they persuade him to give his consent for another game of dice. This time the one who loses shall go into exile for 12 years and stay somewhere incognito in the midst of people in the 13th year and may come back only in the 14th year. If he is recognised in the thirteenth year he must once again go into exile for 12 years. In vain does Gāndhārī the wife of the king try to persuade the latter to withdraw from his wicked son Duryodhana so that he may not be guilty of the ruin of the Kauravas. But the king blindly gives his consent, and a messenger is despatched who overtakes the Pāṇḍavas even before they reach home. Confused by fate, Yudhiṣṭhira accepts the invitation to the game of dice once again. They all go back, the game begins afresh and Yudhiṣṭhira loses again. Now they must go into exile for thirteen years.

Dressed in antilope-hides the Pāṇḍavas get ready to go to the forest. Duryodhana and Duśśāsana triumph and mock at them

But Bhīma hurls horrible words of threat at them. As Duryodhana is poking at their hearts with sharp words, so will he (Bhīma) poke his (Duryodhana's) heart in the battle. And once again he swears to drink Duśśāsana's blood. Arjuna vows to kill Karṇa, Sahadeva vows to kill Śakuni and Nakula to kill the remaining sons of Dhṛtarāṣṭra. But Yudhiṣṭhira takes leave of Dhṛtarāṣṭra, Bhīṣma and other Kauravas and most heartily of the wise and good Vidura. But Draupadī follows her husbands into exile, and her parting from her mother-in-law is a very touching scene. Lamenting with tearful eyes Kuntī sees her children go into exile. All of them however, with the exception of the gentle Yudhiṣṭhira, swear to take bloody vengeance on the Kauravas in the fourteenth year. Evil omens and the prophetic words of the celestial messenger Nārada indicate to King Dhṛtarāṣṭra the destruction of his family and he feels bitter remorse for having given his consent to the game of dice and to the banishment.[1]

THE TWELVE YEARS FOREST-LIFE OF THE PĀṆḌAVAS[2]

Numerous citizens of Hastināpura accompanied the Pāṇḍavas into the forest and Yudhiṣṭhira could send them back only with great difficulty. Many Brahmins however stayed with him for a long time. In order to be able to feed them he practised asceticism and prayed to the sun-god. Then he obtained from him a copper cooking-vessel which filled itself automatically when desired. With this he fed the Brahmins and then went further into the Kāmyaka-forest. The man-eating Kirmira, a brother of Baka and friend of Hiḍimba was killed by Bhīma.

In the meanwhile Dhṛtarāṣṭra has an interview with Vidura who advises the king to call the Pāṇḍavas back from banishment and to compromise with them. Dhṛtarāṣṭra is enraged that Vidura always pleads for the Pāṇḍavas and dismisses him

1. Here ends the Sabhāparvan, the second book.

2. This forms the content of the voluminous third book, called Vanaparvan (="Forest-section").

unkindly with the words, he may go wherever he likes. Vidura goes to the Pāṇḍavas in the Kāmyaka-forest and narrates to them what has happened. Very soon however the old king repents his impetuosity and he sends the chariot-driver Sañjaya to call his brother back. He too comes back and a complete reconciliation takes place between the brothers once again.

When the friends and relatives of the Pāṇḍavas heard of their banishment they came to the forest to visit them. One of the earliest who came was naturally Kṛṣṇa. When the game of dice was taking place he was actually involved in a battle which was the reason for his inability to help his friends. If he had been with them, he could have certainly prevented the game. When Kṛṣṇa suggests to fight Duryodhana and instal Yudhiṣṭhira again in power, Yudhiṣṭhira does not even consider the suggestion, although in bitter words Draupadī laments the humiliation that she received at the hands of the Kauravas. Again Draupadī and also Bhīma assail Yudhiṣṭhira and tell that he might pick up courage and seize his throne by force. But Yudhiṣṭhira declares again and again that he should keep the word he gave and must spend 12 years in the forest. Bhīma reproaches him of being not manly, and says that the warrior's first duty is to fight. Thirteen months have already passed. Yudhiṣṭhira may consider them as thirteen years, or he could compensate by means of a penitent-sacrifice. Then Yudhiṣṭhira also objects saying that Duryodhana too has powerful and unconquerable allies in Bhīṣma, Droṇa, Kṛpa and Karṇa. At this moment appears once again the old Ṛṣi Vyāsa and gives to Yudhiṣṭhira a charm with the help of which Arjuna will obtain divine weapons from gods which would help them for victory over the Kauravas. So soon after that Yudhiṣṭhira sends Arjuna to Indra to make him procure the divine weapons. Arjuna wanders in the Himālayas where Indra accosts him in the form of an ascetic. This ascetic sends him to Śiva who must give the permission for the delivery of the weapons to Arjuna. So Arjuna practises great asceticism whereupon Śiva appears to him in the form of a Kirāta, a wild mountaineer. Arjuna gets involved in a violent fight with the disguised Kirāta until the latter reveals himself as god Śiva and presents him with irresistible weapons. Also the world-protectors Yama, Varuṇa and Kubera appear soon and give him their weapons. But Mātali, Indra's charioteer, takes him to Indra's heavenly city where he obtains many more weapons. In Indra's heaven he lives for five years with great pleasure. On Indra's orders a Gandharva teaches him music and dancing.

In the meanwhile the other Pāṇḍavas live on hunting in the forest and feed miserably on wild animals, roots and fruits. As Arjuna is absent so long, they are much worried about him. Although Ṛṣi Lomaśa who has by chance visited Indra's heaven comes to them and tries to comfort them that Arjuna is well looked after by Indra, they are not consoled and set out to search for Arjuna. They wander in the Gandhamādana-mountains where they are horrified by a terrific gale and a mighty storm. Draupadī loses consciousness due to fear and exhaustion. Then Bhīma thinks of his son Ghaṭotkaca, born to him of the giantess Hiḍimbā; and this Rākṣasa appears at once and takes Draupadī on his back; he calls also other Rākṣasas who take the Pāṇḍavas on their back and in this way they are all carried to a hermitage on the Ganges near the divine mountain of Kailāsa where they stop under a mighty Badari-tree.

As Draupadī desires celestial lotus-flowers, Bhīma combs the mountain-forest to the terror of the wild animals. For he kills one wild elephant with another, one lion with another, when he does not kill them with a mere blow of his fist. Here he meets also the monkey-king Hanumat who blocks his way and warns him not to go farther where only immortals could go. But Bhīma tells him with whom he is dealing and asks him to clear the way. The monkey does not move, pretends to be ill and says, Bhīma may push his tail aside in order to pass by. In vain does Bhīma try to lift the monkey's tail. Then the latter reveals himself smilingly as Hanumat[1] most famous from the Rāmāyaṇa". Bhīma is now very happy to see his brother — both are evidently sons of the wind-god — and begins to converse with him. Finally Hanumat shows to Bhīma the way to Kubera's garden but warns him

1. Thus Bhīma in Mahābh. III, 147, 11 speaks of him. Hanumat gives here a short extract from the Rāmāyaṇa.

from plucking flowers there and they take leave of each other heartily. Soon after Bhīma comes to the lotus-pond and garden of Kubera where the celestial lotuses grow. Rākṣasas oppose him and forbid him from plucking flowers and say that he must first take Kubera's permission. Bhīma replies, "A warrior does not request but takes what he wants". He fights with the Rākṣasas, drives them away and plucks the flowers.

In the midst of various adventures and fights with Rākṣasas the fifth year comes in which Arjuna should come back from heaven. In order to meet him the brothers go to the "white mountain" (Kailāsa, mountain of the gods). Again Bhīma gets involved in a fight with Yakṣas and Rākṣasas, guards of Kubera's garden and kills many of them, among them also Maṇimat who had once spitten on the holy Ṛṣi Agastya's head for which Kubera was cursed by the Ṛṣi. Through Bhīma's deed Kubera is now freed from the curse. Therefore he is not at all angry with Bhīma on account of the blood-bath caused among the demons, but he welcomes him and his brothers warmly.

On the magnificent mountain they meet at last Arjuna again who comes down in Indra's chariot driven by Mātali. After most cordial greetings Arjuna narrates to them all his experiences and adventures, in particular also how he fought and defeated the Nivātakavaca-demons living at the sea-coast and the inhabitants of the city of Hiraṇyapura flying in the air.

Now the Pāṇḍavas live happily in the pleasure-gardens of Kubera and spend four years like a single night. But not to be distracted from their earthly problems and battles, they decide to leave the heavenly regions. Getting down the Kailāsa they go to the mountains and forests on the Jumnā.

Here Bhīma experienced an unpleasant adventure, whereby Yudhiṣṭhira saved his life. Going about the forest he sees a horrifying snake which angrily rushes on him and winds itself strongly round him so that he cannot free himself. Thus Yudhiṣṭhira finds him. But the snake is none else than the famous king of yore, Nahuṣa, who, as a result of a curse of Agastya, has been thrown out of heaven and has been transformed into a serpent. He is supposed to be freed from the curse only when he finds someone who answers all the questions put by him.

Yudhiṣṭhira answers satisfactorily all his philosophical questions, whereupon he lets Bhīma go and himself, freed from his curse, goes back to heaven again.

Soon after the Pāṇḍavas go again to the Kāmyaka-forest. Here they once again receive Kṛṣṇa. He brings to Draupadī news of her children and exhorts Yudhiṣṭhira to ensure allies for the war with the Kauravas and make other preparations for the war. Yudhiṣṭhira assures as always that he wants to remain true to the word he has given and does not want to think of war before the thirteenth year is over.

Often the Pāṇḍavas are visited in the forest also by pious Brahmins. One of these Brahmins goes from the Pāṇḍavas to the court of Dhṛtarāṣṭra and narrates there how ill the Pāṇḍavas and especially Draupadī are doing in their war with wind and weather in the forest. Whereas the old king laments it remorsefully, his son Duryodhana is most heartily happy about it. And, induced by Śakuni and Karṇa he decides to visit the Pāṇḍavas in the forest to enjoy the sight of their misery. To Dhṛtarāṣṭra they give the lame-excuse that they have to visit the cattle-farms near the forest, in order to inspect the herds of cattle, to count them and to inspect the young calves. With great pomp they go out, inspect the cattle and indulge in hunting. As they want to reach the resort of the Pāṇḍavas they are stopped by the Gandharvas. There follows a battle in which Duryodhana is disgracefully taken prisoner. The Kauravas rush to the Pāṇḍavas for help which the noble Yudhiṣṭhira does not refuse to give. After a terrific fight Duryodhana is set free from the captivity of the Gandharva-king by the Pāṇḍavas. Filled with shame and grief due to this humiliation Duryodhana wants to commit suicide. Only with great difficulty do his friends succeed in persuading him to give up the idea of suicide.

Karṇa has now a new plan to irritate the Pāṇḍavas. He undertakes a campaign in all the four world-regions to obtain lordship over the world for Duryodhana, in order that he too might perform a royal sacrifice. After the campaign has been completed victoriously, a great sacrifice is actually performed; But a "royal sacrifice" can be performed only once in one and the same family and Yudhiṣṭhira has already performed one such, so what Duryodhana performs now is a different sacrifice, called Vaiṣṇava, which only god Viṣṇu is supposed to have performed. To irritate the Pāṇḍavas Duryodhana invites them to this sacrifice. Yudhiṣṭhira politely declines while Bhīma sends a message through the messenger that the Pāṇḍavas would pour out the sacrificial butter of their anger on the Kauravas in the sacrifice of the battle.

In the last year of their forest-life the Pāṇḍavas were threatened by a great loss. One day, as all the brothers were out hunting, their wife Draupadī who was left behind at home was robbed by Jayadratha, the king of the Sindhus who happened to come that way. The Pāṇḍavas follow him immediately, he is defeated, chastised and humiliated by Arjuna and Bhīma. Bhīma would certainly have killed him, but Yudhiṣṭhira spares his life as he is a son-in-law of Dhṛtarāṣṭra.

On account of the kidnapping of Draupadī the Pāṇḍavas are very sad. Although Jayadratha has been punished, still they feel themselves disgraced. Yudhiṣṭhira in particular is often depressed and reproaches himself for the mishap for which he himself was responsible and bemoans in particular the lot of Draupadī. Of the Kauravas however Yudhiṣṭhira fears none so much as Karṇa who is born with a natural armour and ear-rings which make him invulnerable. In order to free Yudhiṣṭhira from his fear of Karṇa Indra appears in the guise of a Brahmin before Karṇa and receives from him the armour and ear-rings by begging. Karṇa, who cannot refuse anything to a Brahmin gives him the armour and ear-rings which he cuts off from his own body without turning a hair. In return for this Indra gives him an infallible spear which however can be used against only one enemy and that too only in the moment of greatest danger.

Sullen due to the kidnapping of Draupadī the Pāṇḍavas left the Kāmyaka-forest and went to the Dvaitavana. There they experienced their last forest-adventure. An antelope wandering in the forest catches in its horns by chance the fire-making wooden-pieces of a Brahmin and runs away. The Brahmin who needs them for his sacrifice requests the Pāṇḍavas to procure them for him; and the Pāṇḍavas pursue the animal, giving it a hot chase, but cannot hunt it down and in the end it disappears. They lament over their bad luck. Exhausted from the fruitless hunt and tortured by thirst they look round for water. Nakula climbs a tree and sees a pond in the distance. Yudhiṣṭhira sends him there to fetch water in the quivers. He comes to a nice pond of beautiful clear water surrounded by cranes. But as he is just about to drink the water an invisible spirit (Yakṣa) speaks out from the air: "Do not commit any outrage, friend, this is my property; first answer my questions, then drink and take the water!" But on hearing these words Nakula does not turn back; he drinks and sinks lifeless to the ground. His brothers wait for a long time, and as he does not come back, Sahadeva goes to search for him, he too meets with the same fate. Now Yudhiṣṭhira sends Arjuna who meets with the same fate and then Bhīma who makes a vain bid to fight with the invisible Yakṣa. He too drinks of the pond and falls down lifeless. Suspecting some evil, Yudhiṣṭhira goes at last to search for his brothers. With horror he finds his brothers there, lying dead, and laments bitterly. As he approaches the pond he too hears the voice of the spirit which warns him from drinking before answering his questions. Yudhiṣṭhira says, he is ready to answer the questions and there follows now an extremely interesting game of questions — and answers in which – if we exclude some riddles in the ancient Vedic Brahmodayas[1] — almost the entire moral teaching of India is given. Only a few specimens may be given here:

The Yakṣa: What is heavier than the earth? What is higher than the sky? What is faster than the wind? What is more numerous than grass?

Yudhiṣṭhira: The mother is heavier than the earth. The father is higher than the sky. The mind is faster than the wind. Thoughts are more numerous than the grass.

The Yakṣa: Who is the friend of the traveller? Who is the friend of the one staying at home? Who is the friend of the sick man? Who is the friend of the dying man?

1. Cf. p. 170 f. above. The riddle quoted there from Vājasaneyi-Saṃhitā XXIII, 45 f. reappears here. (Mahābh. III, 313, 65 f.).

Yudhiṣṭhira: A caravan is the friend of the traveller. The wife is the friend of the one who stays at home. The doctor is the friend of the sick man. Generosity is the friend of the dying man.

The Yakṣa: Who is the enemy hard to defeat, and which the endless disease ? Which man is considered as good and which one as bad ?

Yudhiṣṭhira: Anger is the enemy hard to defeat, avarice the endless disease. He is considered as good who is kind to all beings; as bad is considered he who knows no pity.

The Yakṣa: What is called delusion, O King, and what is pride ? What is meant by indolence and what suffering ?

Yudhiṣṭhira: Being deluded in matters of moral[1] is delusion, being proud of one's own self is pride; inaction in matters of moral is indolence, and ignorance is real suffering.

The Yakṣa: What is called firmness by the ṛṣis and what bravery ? What is called the best bath ? What is generosity ?

Yudhiṣṭhira: Being firm in fulfilling one's duty is firmness; bravery is taming the senses. The best bath is what frees from mental impurity, generosity lies in affording protection to all beings.

The Yakṣa: Tell me, O King, when one considers properly, does Brahminship lie, in birth, in the way of life, in Veda-study or in scholarship ?

Yudhiṣṭhira: Listen my dear Yakṣa ! Neither birth nor Veda-study, nor scholarship is the basis of Brahminship, but only a good way of life — there can be no doubt about that. More than to anything else should

1. There is in our language no word which would exactly mean what the Sanskrit word "Dharma" means. "Dharma" means "the norm of doing" and includes the concepts of "law, justice, custom, moral and religion, duty and virtue". It is therefore impossible, to translate the word in the same way everywhere. Cf. p. 304 above.

> a Brahmin pay attention to his way of life; as long as his good way of life is not weakened, is he himself not weakened; if his good way of life has come to an end, then that is also his end as well. Those who learn and those who teach and those who reflect on the sciences — fools are they all, if they are slaves to passions. He who does his duty is a wise man. A villain, even if he knows all the four Vedas, is not superior to a Śūdra. He who performs nothing more than the fire-sacrifice, but tames his senses, such a one is considered to be a Brahmin.[1]

The Yakṣa is so much pleased with the answers of Yudhiṣṭhira that he wants to bring back to life one of his brothers. Yudhiṣṭhira may choose which of the brothers is to be revived. He chooses Nakula and substantiates his choice as follows: His father had two wives and it was just and proper that also one son of Mādrī; the second wife, lives. The answer pleases the Yakṣa so much that he makes all his brothers come back to life. The Yakṣa however is in reality none other than God Dharma himself, the "father"[2] of Yudhiṣṭhira, the god of justice and morals. Before disappearing he grants the Pāṇḍavas one more favour — that they may remain unrecognised in the thirteenth year. For, the twelve years of forest-life are over now and as per the agreement they must spend the 13th year unrecognised among men.

The Pāṇḍavas at King Virāṭa's Court[3]

The Pāṇḍavas decide to go to the court of Virāṭa, the king of the Matsyas and to introduce themselves there under false names, properly disguised. They hide their weapons on a tree

---

1. III, 313. Similar definitions of "Brahmins" are frequent in Buddhist texts. Cf. for example Vinayapiṭaka, Mahāvagga I, 2, 2f. Suttanipāta, Vasettasutta and Milindapañha IV, 5, 26. A version of this story of Yudhiṣṭhira and the Yakṣa is found in the Jaina Hemavijaya's "Kathāratnākara," No. 21 (German translation by J. Hertel, Vol. I, pp. 58 ff.).

2. See p. 309 above.

3. The experiences at Virāṭa's court form the contents of the fourth book called Virāṭaparvan.

near the cremation grounds on the outskirts of the town. Hanging from the tree they look like dead bodies so that no one dares approach them; to the herdsmen who are watching them, they say that in the manner of their forefathers they are thus disposing of the dead body of their 180-year old mother. Yudhiṣṭhira now goes at first to Virāṭa, pretends to be an excellent gambler and is appointed as his comrade and confidence-man. Then the others come one after another. Bhīma joins the service of the king as a cook. Arjuna under the feminine name of Bṛhannalā pretends to be a eunuch and is appointed as dance-master to Uttarā, the king's daughter. Nakula is taken as a horse-breaker, Sahadeva as a cattle-inspector, while the queen makes Draupadī her chamber-maid.

The Pāṇḍavas endear themselves to Virāṭa, especially by virtue of Bhīma who once distinguished himself by killing the famous athlete Jīmūta in a wrestling match organised in honour of god Brahmā.

But Draupadī experienced an unpleasant adventure. Kīcaka, the commander-in-chief and brother-in-law of the king falls in love with the pretty chamber-maid and waylays her. But even at the time when she was appointed by the queen, Draupadī had given out that she was the wife of five Gandharvas who would protect her in difficulties. By fixing an appointment with him Draupadī induces Kīcaka to come at night to the dancing hall where Bhīma lies in wait for him and after a violent wrestling with him strangles him to death. Thereupon Draupadī calls the watchman and tells him that one of her Gandharvas has killed Kīcaka because he followed her making love. The powerful relatives of Kīcaka want to burn the chambermaid along with the dead body of Kīcaka; but Bhīma again comes to her rescue and passing for a Gandharva he kills 105 Sūtas (Kīcaka is a Sūta) and sets Draupadī free. Then the people of the town demand that the chambermaid be dismissed, who is dangerous because of her Gandharvas. The king also issues necessary orders. But Draupadī requests the queen for permission to stay for thirteen days more, for then the Gandharvas would take her. (In 13 days the 13th year will have passed).

In vain did Duryodhana send out spies to discover the whereabouts of the Pāṇḍavas. The spies bring only the news that Kīcaka has been killed by Gandharvas which however is a pleasant news to Duryodhana because the Matsyas are his enemies. Kīcaka had also often oppressed Suśarman, the king of the Trigartas. Now the Trigartas join the Kauravas in a common attack on the Matsyas. Just when the 13th year of banishment is over, news comes that the Trigartas have attacked and seized the cattle of King Virāṭa. Virāṭa mobilises for war, equips Yudhiṣṭhira, Bhīma, Nakula and Sahadeva with arms and marches against the Trigartas. A mighty battle follows. Virāṭa is taken prisoner but is soon freed by Bhīma, and finally the Trigartas are defeated, thanks to the aid of the Pāṇḍavas, who still remain unknown.

While Virāṭa is fighting with the Trigartas, the Kauravas attack his country from another side and rob many cows. The cowherds come to Uttara, the young prince, who has stayed back in the town, and exhort him to march against the Kauravas. But he has no charioteer. Draupadī then mediates through the princess to make Uttara take Arjuna as charioteer. He gets ready and they go to the battlefield. When Uttara sees the mighty army of the Kauravas he is frightened, jumps down from the chariot and wants to run away. But Arjuna catches him again, drags him by the hair to the chariot and encourages him with his words. Then they drive to the tree where the Pāṇḍavas' weapons are hidden and Arjuna takes his weapons. As he discloses himself to Uttara as the great hero Arjuna, Uttara takes courage. He becomes now the charioteer to Arjuna. A terrific battle ensues now in which Arjuna fights with Duryodhana, Karṇa, Bhīṣma and the other heroes of the Kauravas and naturally wins a glorious victory. Although the Kauravas suspect that it may be Arjuna, still they have not recognised him.

After winning the battle Arjuna puts the weapons again on the tree and returns to the town as dance-master Bṛhannalā and Uttara's charioteer, after dinning into Uttara's ears that he should not reveal him. In the meanwhile Virāṭa and the Pāṇḍavas have returned after defeating the Trigartas. The king is much worried when he hears that his son has marched against the Kauravas. But soon news comes of the victory. Uttara is received in triumph. He says, it was not he who defeated the

Kauravas but a god in the form of a beautiful youth has helped him. Three days later the thirteenth year has ended. To the great surprise of the king the five Pāṇḍavas appear in their rue form in the hall and reveal their identity. Virāṭa is very pleased and offers his daughter to Arjuna in marriage. Arjuna however does not take her for himself, but for his son Abhimanyu, because by making her his daughter-in-law, he says, he proves that in spite of his having been in close contact with her for one year, she has remained pure. With great pomp they celebrate now the marriage of Abhimanyu with Uttarā to which numerous kings, of course Drupada and Kṛṣṇa also, come with rich presents.

Peace-Negotiations and War-Preparations[1]

During the celebrations of this marriage the Pāṇḍavas and their friends hold discussions as to how they should behave towards the Kauravas. Kṛṣṇa proposes that they may send an emissary to Duryodhana to ask him to give back to the Pāṇḍavas their kingdom. During long deliberations it is resolved to send the old family-priest of King Drupada as emissary to the Kauravas.

But before the negotiations begin the Pāṇḍavas as well as the Kauravas endeavour to get as many allies as possible to their side. And both parties make simultaneous efforts to enlist the support of some powerful kings. Thus Duryodhana tries to win over to his side Kṛṣṇa himself whom we know till now as an intimate friend of the Pāṇḍavas. It is a chance coincidence that Duryodhana comes to Kṛṣṇa while he is just sleeping and immediately after comes Arjuna. Because Duryodhana has come first but Arjuna has been seen first, Kṛṣṇa thinks he must not disappoint either of them and so he tells that he will help one of them with his advice and the other by placing an army of herdsmen at his disposal. Duryodhana chooses the latter, Arjuna the former. Therefore Kṛṣṇa promises not to actually take part in the battle, but only to help as charioteer to Arjuna and

1. These are the contents of the fifth book (Udyogaparvan).

advisor to the Pāṇḍavas. Also Śalya, who, accompanied by an army is on his way to Yudhiṣṭhira to join him, is exhorted by Duryodhana to go over to the side of the Kauravas, Śalya accepts, but yet he goes to Yudhiṣṭhira. And the latter, who is otherwise always described as an embodiment of Virtue, makes a disgraceful agreement with Śalya. According to this, Śalya has to fight on the side of the Kauravas, but as charioteer to Karṇa when there is a duel between him and Arjuna, he is to drive the chariot improperly and thus bring about the downfall of Karṇa.

While in this manner both parties are already thinking in terms of war, Drupada's aged priest comes as emissary to King Dhṛtarāṣṭra, to whom he brings the conditions of peace from the Pāṇḍavas. The king receives him respectfully but gives no conclusive reply; he says he will himself send his own charioteer Sañjaya as ambassador to Yudhiṣṭhira. That happens in a few days; but Sañjaya brings only the message that Dhṛtarāṣṭra wants peace without offering anything to the Pāṇḍavas. Thereupon Yudhiṣṭhira sends back the reply: Either I must get Indraprastha and half the kingdom, or the war shall start. Indeed, he says, in order to prevent bloodshed among relatives, he is prepared to accept peace even if Duryodhana puts at his disposal at least five villages. On this reply brought by Sañjaya there is a discussion among the Kauravas. Bhīṣma, Droṇa and Vidura try in vain to persuade Duryodhana to yield and make peace. As it is seen that Dhṛtarāṣṭra is very weak and powerless this discussion comes to an abrupt end without any result.

The Pāṇḍavas too hold consultations once again on peace. And Kṛṣṇa offers to make one more attempt and is himself ready to go to the Kauravas as an emissary of peace. The Pāṇḍavas accept this offer gratefully. Even the stubborn Bhīma speaks in words whose softness is so surprising, "as if the mountains have become light and fire cold," in support of peace, so that even Kṛṣṇa is astonished. On the other hand some of the heroes, especially the heroic wife Draupadi, dismiss the idea of peace-negotiations, but would like to declare war immediately.

However, Yudhiṣṭhira insists on sending a peace-maker. Turning his gentle thoughts to Kuntī, his mother, he requests

Kṛṣṇa to visit her who is living with Vidura at the court of the Kauravas and make enquiries about her welfare.

Accompanied by wishes and blessings Kṛṣṇa goes to the Kauravas. He is splendidly received by Dhṛtarāṣṭra but he accepts only the hospitality of Vidura. He visits also Kuntī at once and conveys to her the best regards of Yudhiṣṭhira. The hero-mother laments bitterly the separation from her sons. But she feels still more painfully the humiliation to which Draupadī was put, and she reproaches Yudhiṣṭhira of being too weak. She asks Kṛṣṇa to tell her sons not to forget their duty as warriors and not to hesitate to risk their life, further that the time was now come, "for the sake of which a warrior's wife bears children". On the next morning Kṛṣṇa goes in ceremonious pomp to the assembly of the Kaurava princes and gives there a speech exhorting them to peace. Dhṛtarāṣṭra explains that although he himself wants only peace, still he cannot do anything against the wishes of his son Duryodhana. Then Kṛṣṇa addresses his entreaties to Duryodhana and also Bhīṣma, Droṇa and Vidura do their best to make Duryodhana accept the conditions for peace. The latter however declares that he does not want to cede to the Pāṇḍavas even as much land as would cover the tip of a needle. After he has angrily left the assembly, Kṛṣṇa suggests that the well-meaning people among the Kauravas should deliver Duryodhana and his comrades as prisoners to the Pāṇḍavas. Dhṛtarāṣṭra does not give any consideration to this suggestion, but he sends for his wife Gāndhārī in order that she might try to persuade their obstinate son make peace. Gāndhārī comes and reproaches the old king strongly for handing over the kingdom to his son. The admonitions which she gives to Duryodhana are futile like those of the others. On the other hand Duryodhana and his comrades hatch a plan to take Kṛṣṇa prisoner and thus get rid of a powerful enemy. The plan does not remain secret and Duryodhana is strongly rebuked by Dhṛtarāṣṭra and Vidura for this plan to violate the rights of an ambassador. After Bhīṣma and Droṇa have in vain exhorted to peace, even this peace-mission of Kṛṣṇa must be considered as having failed.

Before Kṛṣṇa departs he has one more secret meeting with Karṇa. This brave hero is generally considered to be the son of a charioteer (Sūta). But it is said that in reality he is born of Sūrya, the sun-god to Kuntī as she was still a virgin, in a peculiar way, without her virginity being in any way violated. But after she has borne him, she felt ashamed and put the boy in a water-tight basket which she then hoisted out in a river. There a charioteer found him, rescued him and brought him up. So Karṇa is actually only an elder brother of the Pāṇḍavas. Kṛṣṇa points to this and tries to persuade him to take the throne and instal Yudhiṣṭhira, his younger brother, as his successor to the throne, which would be acceptable to the Pāṇḍavas. Karṇa dismisses the suggestion of such a treason against his friend Duryodhana. Even as Kuntī, supported by Sūrya himself, persuades him similarly to go over to the side of the Pāṇḍavas, Karṇa replies to her only with harsh words saying that she has never been a good mother to him, so he will not also be a good son to her now.

Thus Kṛṣṇa returns unsuccessfully to the Pāṇḍavas and reports on his unsuccessful attempts to establish peace. A wild war-cry is heard when Kṛṣṇa says that they even wanted to take him prisoner. Both parties make zealously their preparations for war. The Pāṇḍavas choose Dhṛṣṭadyumna, son of Drupada as commander-in-chief and the Kauravas choose Bhīṣma. Forces are arrayed and arranged. Bhīṣma enumerates to Duryodhana the heroes according to their rank as chariot-fighters and while doing so he puts Karṇa lower than all other heroes and this insults him fatefully. Karṇa swears that he will not take part in the battle until Bhīṣma is killed. Then Bhīṣma enumerates the chief heroes of the Pāṇḍavas and explains that he will fight with all, with the exception of Śikhaṇḍin. This Śikhaṇḍin was born as a girl, as daughter of Drupada and later transformed into a male only when a Yakṣa exchanged his sex with hers.[1] But Bhīṣma sees in this warrior still only the woman, and with a woman he does not fight.

After completing the preparations for war, the Kauravas send Ulūka, the son of an actor, to the camp of the Pāṇḍavas with a declaration of war in the form of objurgations and the Pāṇḍavas in their turn send him back with words which are no less

1. About this and similar sex-changes in the literature of fairy tales compare Th. Benfey, *Das Pantschatantra* I, p. 41 ff.

humiliating and defiant. Thereupon the two armies march towards Kurukṣetra.

The Great Eighteen-Day Battle[1]

Drawn up in endless rows both armies stand with their auxiliaries on both sides of the great Kurufield (the Kurukṣetra). Watchwords and insignia are fixed, by which friends and foes can be distinguished from one another. After this agreements are reached between the fighting armies as on the basis of international law: Fighting must be only between opponents of equal birth and between those armed with the same kinds of weapons; chariot-fighters must fight only with chariot-fighters, elephant-fighters with elephant-fighters, horsemen with horsemen, infantry with infantry, no one should fight without challenging the opponent in advance; those who have surrendered or have been incapacitated as well as who are refugees shall not be killed; coachmen, beasts of burden, carriers of arms and musicians shall also be spared.

Before the battle commences the holy Vyāsa appears once and bestows on Sañjaya, Dhṛtarāṣṭra's charioteer the gift of seeing all the happenings on the battlefield. He makes him also invulnerable so that he can give daily report to the old blind king. And as the following descriptions of war are given out as narrated by Sañjaya who reports them as an eyewitness, they receive an unusually realistic character.[2]

The venerable Bhīṣma, the great uncle of the Kauravas as well as of the Pāṇḍavas commands the armies of the Kauravas in the first ten days of the battle. In a fiery speech he exhorts the warriors to a bold fight: "The great gate of heaven stands

1. The sixth book (Bhīṣmaparvan) begins here and ends with the fall of General Bhīṣma.

2. Similarly the Langobardian poets frequently resort to the artifice "of observing the progress of the battle through the eyes of a scout who is set on an eminence, and then reports what he has seen; by this means the artist avoids a tedious description, and has the twofold advantage of being in a position to limit himself to the main incidents, and of thrilling his hearers to a greater degree." (R. Koegel, *Geschichte der deutschen Literature*, I, 1, Strassbourg 1894, p. 120).

wide open today oh warriors! March through this gate to the world of Indra and of Brahman! ... It is improper for a warrior to die of disease at home, to find death in the battlefield, that is a warrior's eternal duty".[1] So they march bravely to the battlefield, and in burnished adornment of their weapons and their armours the two armies stand facing each other.

Thundering war-cry and booming war-music give the signal for the war to begin. And in a terrific fight the Kauravas and the Pāṇḍavas encounter each other — without any consideration for relationship: The father knows not the son any more, nor brothers one another, the uncle does not know the nephew anymore and friends one another. Elephants cause great havoc and a bloody massacre follows. Sometimes heroes of this side, sometimes those of the other side distinguish themselves in duels; victory is now on the side of the Pāṇḍavas, now on the side of the Kauravas. But when night falls, the fighters withdraw, and only on the following day the armies are arrayed anew and the fighting begins once again. Again and again Bhīṣma and Arjuna encounter each other and both fight so bravely that gods and demons witness the fighting with astonishment. But whenever the Kauravas suffer losses, Duryodhana reproaches Bhīṣma of being too considerate towards the Pāṇḍavas; and when the Pāṇḍavas suffer losses Kṛṣṇa reproaches Arjuna that he is not aiming his arrows against Bhīṣma. Many brothers of Duryodhana have already fallen in the battle. Then Duryodhana again reproaches Bhīṣma of showing too much pity towards the Pāṇḍavas. He asks him to win the battle or hand over the supreme command to Karṇa. Overpowered by pain and anger Bhīṣma promises to fight unsparingly against all — excepting Śikhaṇḍin who has been a woman. "Have a quiet sleep, O son of Gāndhārī", he says,[2] "tomorrow I will fight a great battle of which people will talk as long as the world will exist". And indeed on the ninth day of the battle the Pāṇḍavas suffer heavy losses. Bhīṣma rages in the enemy's army like the God of Death while Arjuna who still reveres Bhīṣma as "grandfather"[3] fights with too great regard for him. As Kṛṣṇa notices this he

1. VI, 17, 8 ff.
2. VI, 99, 23.
3. This is how Pāṇḍu's sons address Bhīṣma mostly.

himself springs on to Bhīṣma in order to kill him, but Arjuna pulls him forcibly back reminding him of his promise not to fight. Suffering heavy losses in the hands of Bhīṣma, the Pāṇḍavas take to a wild flight, and as night approaches they withdraw into their camp.

The Pāṇḍavas use the night for consultations. As they know that Bhīṣma will not fight with Śikhaṇḍin, they decide[1] to put the latter against Bhīṣma; but standing hidden behind Śikhaṇḍin Arjuna shall shoot at Bhīṣma. Only unwillingly Arjuna makes up his mind in favour of this treachery and with pain and shame he remembers that as a child he had played in Bhīṣma's lap and called him"daddy". But Kṛṣṇa can persuade him to believing that only he can defeat Bhīṣma and that he is simply discharging his duty as a warrior when he kills his powerful opponent.

Thus breaks the morning of the tenth day of the battle and Śikhaṇḍin is placed in the forefront by the Pāṇḍavas while the Kauravas advance with Bhīṣma at their head. Bhīṣma is the focus of the battle between the Pāṇḍavas and the Kauravas, the whole day. Thousands and thousands on both sides sink into the dust. At last Śikhaṇḍin behind whom Arjuna hides himself succeeds in getting at Bhīṣma, who smilingly receives his arrows without defending himself. However rapidly Śikhaṇḍin shoots his arrows at Bhīṣma, they cannot do him any harm. Soon however, Arjuna hiding behind Śikhaṇḍin begins to shoot arrow after arrow at the venerable Bhīṣma. And turning to Duśśāsana fighting by his side, Bhīṣma says, "These arrows, which like Yama's messengers destroy my life-spirits fully, are not

1. In the old poem it was probably Kṛṣṇa who gave this advice. The presentation in our present Mahābhārata is quite absurd. Here it is said that the Pāṇḍu-sons go at the time of nightsleep to Bhīṣma in the enemy camp and ask him very naively, how best they could kill him. Bhīṣma himself gives them the advice, to place Śikhaṇḍin opposite to him and make Arjuna stand behind Śikhaṇḍin and fight. This we read in the beginning of Chapter VI, 107; in the middle of the same chapter we read the beautiful texts in which Arjuna so full of delicate feelings thinks of his "grandfather" Bhīṣma who has rocked him on his knees as a child; and at the end of the same chapter it is the same Arjuna who comes forward to kill Bhīṣma in such a disgraceful manner. Cf. Ad. Holtzmann, *Das Mahābhārata* II, 172 f.

Śikhaṇḍin's arrows, these arrows, which like enraged poison-spitting snakes penetrate with their tongues into my limbs are not Śikhaṇḍin's arrows, they are Arjuna's missiles".[1] He pulls himself together for the last time and shoots an arrow at Arjuna which however the latter meets half-way with his own and smashes into three pieces. Then he takes sword and shield to defend himself. But Arjuna breaks his shield into a hundred pieces. Then Yudhiṣṭhira orders his people to attack Bhīṣma and the Pāṇḍavas rush to him attacking him from all sides who is now standing alone until at last bleeding from innumerable wounds, he falls down from his chariot[2] shortly before sunset. But so many arrows are sticking to his body on all sides that while falling his body does not touch the ground but rests on a bed of arrows.

Loud is the jubilation among the Pāṇḍavas and boundless the lamentation in the camp of the Kauravas. In honour of the fallen hero, who was closely related to both parties however, a truce is agreed upon. And both Pāṇḍavas and Kauravas, filled with admiration and grief stand round the dying hero. He greets the warriors and wants to speak to them. Exhausted, his head hangs down. He asks for a cushion. They go to fetch fine cushions. Smilingly he turns them down. Then Arjuna takes three arrows from his quiver and supports with them, the head of Bhīṣma who tells satisfied, that is what he wanted, that is the proper bed for a hero. The dying man addresses in powerful words an advice to Duryodhana, to conclude peace. "Let this battle end with my death," my son, he exhorts him, "make

1. VI, 119, 63 f.

2. In contradiction to this description (VI, 120, 58 ff) is the foolish story (VI, 116) where Bhīṣma tells Yudhiṣṭhira in the midst of the battle, that he is tired of his life whereupon the latter, with cheap courage, exhorts his men to fight against the hero, as also the childish tale (VI, 120, 32 ff.) which tells how the Vasus (divine beings) and Ṛṣis appear in the sky and welcome Bhīṣma's determination to die. They are later interpolations which pursue the double purpose of clearing the Pāṇḍavas and making Bhīṣma himself into a demigod. In the old poem Bhīṣma was certainly only a mighty hero whom the Pāṇḍavas ruined in a manner unworthy of noblemen. But the story of VI, 116 is known in the "Dūtaghaṭotkaca" (v. 19), ascribed to Bhāsa.

peace with the Pāṇḍavas". But Duryodhana like a man in death-bed who refuses medicine, rejects the advice of the wise Bhīṣma.

The defiant but noble Karṇa also comes to pay his respects to the dying hero. With failing eyes the old man embraces him and exhorts him to make peace with the Pāṇḍavas all the more because as Kuntī's son he is their brother. But Karṇa declares that he must be loyal to Duryodhana and discharge his duty as warrior in the battle with the Pāṇḍavas. He pleads helplessness. And Bhīṣma reconciling himself gives the brave fighter permission to fight, although it is painful to him to see all his efforts at peace have gone in vain.[1]

Now that Bhīṣma has fallen, Karṇa again takes part in the battle and on his suggestion the old teacher Droṇa is installed as the supreme commander.[2] Under his generalship they fight from the 11th to the 15th day.

The 13th day of the battle brings a sad event for the Pāṇḍavas. Abhimanyu, the youthful but courageous son of Arjuna, ventures too deep into the ranks of the enemies, is isolated from his protectors by Jayadratha, the Sindhu-king, and killed by Duśśāsana's son. Arjuna swears to take terrible revenge on the "murderer" of his son as he calls Jayadratha. The main event of the 14th day is therefore the fight between Arjuna and Jayadratha which lasts the whole day and ends

1. In the old poem Bhīṣma after his fall has lived certainly no longer than was necessary to say some more words to Duryodhana and Karṇa. Our Mahābhārata tells the funny story that Bhīṣma fell when the sun was in his south course. i.e. in the half year before winter-solistice (but that he postponed his death till the northern course (Uttarāyaṇa) i.e. to the half year before the summer-solistice. The Upaniṣads teach that the soul that goes to the Brahman-world on the divine path must pass through Uttarāyaṇa (Chānd. Up. V, 10, 1, Bṛh. Up. VI, 2, 15). From this the theologians have ingeniously deduced that a holy man or Yogi who wants to be united with Brahman must die in Uttarāyaṇa. (Thus Bhagavadgītā VIII, 24). Even philosopher Śaṅkara (on Vedānta-Sūtra, IV, 2. 20 f) says that Bhīṣma must have chosen the Uttarāyaṇa for his death. In those days (8th century A.D.) the story of Bhīṣma's death must have been already told as in our Mahābhārata.

2. The battle under the command of Droṇa forms the contents of the seventh book (Droṇaparvan).

with the latter's death. He falls, as Arjuna has sworn, before the sun has set. At the same time Bhīma has raged over the army of the Kauravas and killed numerous sons of Dhṛtarāṣṭra.

But today the fighting is not interrupted at sunset as on the other days. The fighters are so bitter that they do not pause even as darkness sets in. In the light of faggots and lamps the fighting goes on. Astonishing fights are fought out by individual heroes. Karṇa inflicts very heavy losses on the Pāṇḍavas, and on Kṛṣṇa's advice the Rākṣasa Ghaṭotkaca is sent out against Karṇa. The hero has a tough fight with the gigantic monster, and the Rākṣasa causes the army of the Kauravas heavy losses, until he is at last killed by Karṇa. Even while falling, the Rākṣasa Ghaṭotkaca pulls down a whole troop of the Kauravas and kills them. The Pāṇḍavas are depressed over the death of Bhīma's son Ghaṭotkaca — only Kṛṣṇa is jubilant. Karṇa has used against the Rākṣasa the spear that Indra had presented him and which he had reserved to be used against Arjuna.[1] This is exactly what Kṛṣṇa has wanted.

The battle rages forth until the warriors of both armies are overcome with sleep. Only with great effort the most dutiful warriors remain firm. Many people even tired and sleepy fall down from their elephants, chariots and horses while others even grope blindly due to sleep and kill their own friends. Then Arjuna the warrior gives in a voice loudly heard in the distance, permission to sleep for a while. Friends and foes welcome his suggestion joyously and bless Arjuna for this. And in the midst of the battlefield horses, elephants and warriors lie down to slumber.

Of the poetic beauty of the night-scene described here — the style reminds us sometimes of the lyric of Kālidāsa[2] — the following literal prose-translation can give only a poor idea:

"Then overcome with sleep all the great chariot-fighters became still. Then they lay down, some on the back of their horses, others in their chariots, and yet others on the backs of their elephants and many even stretched themselves on the

1. He was allowed to use it only once. See p. 332 above.

2. Also some verses of interpolation excepted, which were inserted by a later art-poet.

floor. With their weapons, with maces, swords, hatchets and lances, in full armour, they lay down to sleep, some here, some there. The elephants which heavily breathing lay on the earth looked like mountains on which gigantic snakes were hissing along. And this slumbering army, as it lay there unconscious, absorbed in sleep resembled a wonderful picture, painted on canvas by a skilful artist. Then suddenly the moon rising in the east radiated her reddish light ... In the trice of a second the earth was filled with light and the deep bottomless darkness flew rapidly away ... From the rays of the moon this army of warriors woke up like a garden of lotus flowers from the rays of the sun. And as the sea-breeze rises when the moon shines, so this sea of troops rose with the rising of the planet of night. But then O king, began once again the battle for destroying the world of these men who longed for the highest celestial world".[1]

And the bloody fighting continues uninterruptedly lasting till day break. The 15th day of the battle breaks. The sun rises in the east and the warriors of both sides get down from their horses, elephants and chariots; raising their eyes to the sun-god, they perform, with folded hands, their morning worship. But only one moment lasts this interruption and the battle continues to rage. Two of the best heroes, the kings Drupada and Virāṭa fall at Droṇa's hands. The Pāṇḍava heroes make an unsuccessful bid to kill this valiant warrior. An astonishing duel between Droṇa and Arjuna – teacher and pupil – which even the gods themselves witness with admiration, has no decisive outcome, as the pupil is in no way inferior to the teacher in the art of warfare. It is then again Kṛṣṇa who hits upon a treacherous deceit, spurned by him, Bhīma kills an elephant which by chance, is called Aśvatthāman and cries then loudly, going towards Droṇa, that Aśvatthāman – this is also the name of Droṇa's son – has been killed. Droṇa trembles, but does not believe the news yet. Only when Yudhiṣṭhira famous for his love of truth, now persuaded by Kṛṣṇa, repeats the lie, Droṇa is forced to believe it. Overcome by pain, he puts the weapons aside and stands engrossed in deep contemplation, seizing this

1. VII, 185, 37 ff.

moment Dhṛṣṭadyumna, Drupada's son, cuts off the head of the 85 year old Droṇa. In vain does Arjuna shout, the venerable teacher must not be killed. Dhṛṣṭadyumna has performed the deed and thrown the head of the commander in the midst of the Kauravas, who terrified, now take to flight. Only now does Aśvatthāman learn the news of his father's death and he swears bloody revenge on the Pāñcālas and the Pāṇḍavas.

After Droṇa's fall Karṇa is chosen as the supreme commander of the Kauravas. Under him they fight only for two days.[1] On the 16th day of the battle Bhīma and Aśvatthāman, Arjuna and Karṇa perform miraculous acts of bravery but there is no decisive outcome. On the morning of the 17th day Karṇa asks Śalya, the king of the Madras to be given to him as chariot driver for only then he would be equal to Arjuna who has an excellent chariot-driver in Kṛṣṇa. Śalya protests at first against being asked to perform a subordinate service, agrees however at last, under the condition that he may be permitted to talk before Karṇa in any manner he likes. Of this permission he makes unlimited use. While he is driving Karṇa's chariot, he heaps scorn and mockery on him. Karṇa remains no defaulter, but attacks with his sharp tongue the Madras, the subjects of Śalya, whom he terms false, hypocritical, given to drinking, victims of immorality and incest. Śalya on the other hand makes reproaches on Karṇa that the Aṅgas over whom he is ruling, sell their wives and children.[2] At last Duryodhana establishes again peace between the two and both go to the battlefield.

While Arjuna tries to approach Karṇa, Bhīma causes a terrible blood-bath among the sons of Dhṛtarāṣṭra, of whom he kills many. With his massive mace he hurls down Duśśāsana from his chariot, springs on him, breaks his breast open and drinks the warm blood of his heart—as he had sworn once upon a time.[3] Shuddering with fear on seeing this, the enemies

1. This fighting forms the contents of the 8th book (Karṇaparvan).

2. The whole peculiar chapter (VIII, 33-45) is extremely interesting from the point of view of cultural history and ethnography.

3. See p. 325 above.

withdraw. In the meanwhile Arjuna and Karṇa are entangled in a terrible duel in which even gods take sides. Indra for Arjuna Sūrya for Karṇa. Like two wild elephants fighting each other with their tusks the two heroes shower arrows on each other. Arjuna tries unsuccessfully to throw Karṇa down. Then the chariot of Karṇa begins to sink with one wheel into the earth.[1] Karṇa tries hard to pull out the chariot and exhorts Arjuna in view of the rules of war to stop fighting for a little while. But Kṛṣṇa persuades Arjuna not to show any consideration. And Arjuna who is otherwise ideally chivalrous kills Karṇa treacherously while he is still occupied with setting right his chariot. From the body of the fallen hero radiates a light and even when dead he retains his beauty.

Great jubilation prevails in the camp of the Pāṇḍavas, the Kauravas however flee for fear.

Only with great difficulty does Duryodhana succeed in collecting his troops to renewed fighting and encouraging them. Śalya is the supreme commander on the 18th day of the battle.[2] Yudhiṣṭhira is selected to take up the duel with Śalya. After a long and violent fighting Śalya is killed by Yudhiṣṭhira about noon. The Kauravas flee. Only Duryodhana and Śakuni with a small group still put up desperate resistance. Sahadeva kills Śakuni. Arjuna and Bhīma cause a terrifying massacre. The army of the Kauravas is completely destroyed.

Duryodhana flees alone to a pond, where he hides himself. Besides him there are only three heroes still alive: Kṛtavarman, Kṛpa and Aśvatthāman. The sun has already set. Devastated and empty lies the camp of the Kauravas. The Pāṇḍavas search for the fugitive Duryodhana and find him in the end. Yudhiṣṭhira

1. Although we know already (See p. 339) that this happens as a consequence of a treachery by Śalya, it is presented here in such a way as to make it appear that this accident has occurred to Karṇa as a consequence of the curse of a Brahmin who had been insulted by him (VIII, 42, 41 and 90, 81). The entire narrative of the fight between Arjuna and Karṇa (VIII, 86-94) has been touched up to a great extent. Cf. Oldenberg, *Das Mahābhārata*, pp. 50 ff., where he says that in this instance nothing is left of the old poem, but that "a new poem was created on the old theme."

2. This day of the battle forms the contents of the 9th book (Śalyaparvan).

challenges him to a duel. Duryodhana says, he will fight only on the next morning: Out of exhaustion, not out of fear, says he has run to the pond. But Yudhiṣṭhira says that the duel must take place at once and promises to him that he shall remain king if he kills even one of them. It is Bhīma, with whom Duryodhana shall fight. The mace-fight is started with the usual wordy-duel. From a long distance comes Baladeva, Kṛṣṇa's brother, (who had not taken part in the battle) to be a spectator to the mace-fighting. The gods too watch the scene with astonishment and admiration. As two bulls attack each other with their horns the two heroes strike with maces at each other. Their bodies overrun with blood they continue their fight. With their maces they cut into each other's flesh like two cats fighting for a piece of meat. Both of them demonstrate extraordinary courage and neither is inferior to the other. Then says Kṛṣṇa to Arjuna, never shall Bhīma be in a position to defeat Duryodhana in an honest fight, because although Bhīma is stronger, Duryodhana is a more skilled fighter. He reminds him of Bhīma's words, as he once, when Draupadi was insulted[1] swore to smash Duryodhana's thigh. Then Arjuna beats with his hands on his thigh in such a way that Bhīma sees it. Bhīma understands this gesture — and while his opponent springs to strike the next blow, Bhīma shatters his thighs with one blow that he collapses like a tree uprooted by the storm. Baladeva however, who has been watching the duel hurls wrathful words at Bhīma who has fought disgracefully, for in a proper mace-fighting it is forbidden to strike the enemy below the navel. Only with great difficulty his brother Kṛṣṇa holds him back from chastising Bhīma. In vain does Kṛṣṇa try to convince his brother with his sophistications that Bhīma has acted rightly. The righteous Baladeva mounts his chariot in anger and rides away, assuring that Bhīma will be known in the world as an unjust fighter and Duryodhana as an honourable one for ever.

After this Yudhiṣṭhira sends Kṛṣṇa to Hastināpura to console and pacify Dhṛtarāṣṭra and Gāndhārī and Kṛṣṇa does this to

1. See p. 325 above.

the best of his ability. The Pāṇḍavas decide to spend the night outside their camp on the bank of the river.

As soon as Aśavatthāman and his two companions have heard about the death of Duryodhana, they hurry to the scene of action and lament the hero lying there with his thighs smashed. And Aśvatthāman swears to kill all Pāṇḍavas, whereupon Duryodhana formally makes him the supreme commander (we do not know of what)!

The Nocturnal Bloodbath in the Pāṇḍava Camp[1]

The three surviving heroes of the Kaurvas, after taking leave of Duryodhana, went to a tree at a short distance from the battlefield in order to spend the night there. Kṛpa and Kṛtavarman have fallen asleep, but Aśvatthāman is kept awake by wrath and thirst for revenge. Then he sees how in the branches of the tree under which they are resting, a flock of crows are sleeping in their nests and how suddenly in the midst of the night a horrifying owl comes flying and kills all the sleeping birds.[2] This sight suggests him to attack the enemies while they were sleeping and murder them all. He wakes the other two heroes and explains them his plan. Kṛpa tries to hold him back, saying it is unjust to kill sleeping and unarmed men. Aśvatthāman nevertheless replies, that the Pāṇḍavas "have broken the bridge of justice into hundred pieces" long ago: now he must take revenge and no man shall prevent him from putting his idea into action. "The Pāñcālas will I kill, the murderers of my father, while they are sleeping in the night – may I be then born in my next birth even as a worm or an insect!"[3] So determined, he mounts his chariot and drives to the enemy's camp. Like a thief he creeps in while the other two heroes are keeping guard at the gate in order to kill anyone that tries to flee. He rushes into the tent of Dhṛṣṭadyumna, who killed his father, awakens him with a kick and stramples him to death like an

1. This forms the contents of the 10th book (Sauptikaparvan).
2. Cf. with this scene: Th. Benfey, *Das Pantschatantra*, (I, p. 336 ff).
3. X, 5, 18-27.

animal. Then he goes like the god of death from tent to tent, from camp to camp and pitilessly murders one after another the sleeping and drowsy heroes, among them also the five sons of Draupadī and also Śikhaṇḍin. Even before midnight all the warriors of the enemy-camp are killed. Thousands of them are immersed in their blood. Rākṣasas and Piśācas, the demons revelling in the night and eating flesh, come in large numbers to enjoy the flesh and blood of the murdered ones. As the day breaks there is again deadly quiet prevailing everywhere in the camp.

But the three heroes rush to the place where the dying Duryodhana is still lying, in order to convey to him the news of the massacre of the warriors of the enemy camp. And after Duryodhana has heard this, which is a joyful news for him he gives up his life gratefully and gladly.

In the meanwhile Dhṛṣṭadyumna's chariot driver, the only survivor has brought to the Pāṇḍavas the terrible news that their and Drupada's sons have been murdered and the whole army destroyed. Yudhiṣṭhira falls unconscious and is kept up by his brothers only with very great difficulty. Then he sends for Draupadī and other relatives. He goes to the camp and on seeing what is visible then he almost collapses. Then Draupadī also reaches there and in her immense grief for her murdered sons and brothers she congratulates her husband Yudhiṣṭhira in most bitter irony on his splendid victory. As boundless as his misery is also her wrath on the murderer Aśvatthāman and she refuses to take food until this terrible deed is avenged.

Whether and how in the original epic this deed of Aśvatthāman was avenged is not clear to us from our Mahābhārata because there are so many interpolations and mutilations in this. In a very unclear and confused way the following is narrated:

Bhīma chases Aśvatthāman, fights with him, but actually loses; in any case he does not kill him, but Aśvatthāman gives him voluntarily a jewel desired by Draupadī which he had on his head even from the time of his birth (There was no mention of this strange crest-jewel earlier). Moreover he is in possession of a miraculous weapon with which he kills the last progeny of the Kuru-race who is still lying as an embryo in the womb of Uttarā, the daughter-in-law of Arjuna; as a result of this Uttarā delivers later a dead child which however is brought to life by Kṛṣṇa. This is Parīkṣit, the father of Janamejaya during whose serpent-sacrifice the Mahābhārata is said to have been recited for the first time. But Kṛṣṇa curses Aśvatthāman, that he shall wander on the earth for three thousand years — as a sort of Ahasver — alone, avoided by all men, spreading the foul smell of blood and pus and laden with all kinds of diseases.

Whether anything of all this belongs to the old poem, is difficult to say. But the lamentation certainly belonged to it.

The Lamentation of the Women[1]

Sañjaya and Vidura try to console the old king Dhṛtarāṣṭra in his boundless grief, but in vain. Again and again he breaks down and finally even Vyāsa comes to console him. Now obsequies must be performed to the dead. For this purpose the king sends for his wife Gāndhārī and the other women, and wailing loudly they go out of the town to the battlefield. On the way they meet the three surviving Kaurava heroes, who tell them of the horrible blood-bath that they gave the enemy camp in the night. They do not stay, but of fear of vengeance by the Pāṇḍavas they run away. Actually the five Pāṇḍavas also come that way immediately thereafter and meet the grief-stricken funeral procession. With great difficulty Kṛṣṇa succeeds in reconciling the Pāṇḍavas with the old royal couple however much difficult it is for Gāndhārī to forgive Bhīma, who of all her hundred sons did not leave even one alive. Of course Draupadī too has lost all her sons, and the commonness of grief contributes to reconciliation.

There follows now the lamentation of Gāndhārī, which, both as a piece of elegic poetry and by means of the clarity of portrayal which reminds us of the descriptions of the battlefield by Wereschagin belongs to the most beautiful portions of the whole epic. The fact that the poet does not narrate it himself,

1. This forms the contents of the 11th book (Strīparvan).

but makes the aged mother of the heroes narrate what she witnesses with her own eyes, makes the whole text appear all the more effective.[1]

The procession of the mourners reaches the battlefield. Horrifying is the sight of the dead bodies torn to pieces round which birds of prey, jackals and carnivorous demons are swarming while mothers and wives of the fallen heroes wander about the corpses wailing. Gāndhārī sees all this when she, addressing Kṛṣṇa, begins to lament. She sees also Duryodhana and remembers with melancholy how he took leave of her on the evening before the fight. "Him, whom once beautiful women were serving with cool breeze from their fans, only birds of prey are now fanning with their wings". But more than the sight of their brave son, more than the sight of all her hundred sons who are lying in the dust, who are however assured of heaven, they lament their daughters-in-law, who, in wild despair, are running with their hair helter-skelter hither and thither between the corpses of their husbands and sons. They see their clever son Vikarṇa lying in the midst of dead elephants, with his limbs chopped — "as if in the autumn-sky the moon is surrounded by dark clouds". Then she sees the youthful Abhimanyu, Arjuna's son whose beauty not even death could destroy completely. His unfortunate young wife comes up to him, strokes him gently, removes his armour, takes the bloody locks in her hand, lays his head in her lap and speaks to the dead man in the most delicate words, she asks him to remember her sometimes even when he is happily enjoying himself in heaven in the company of celestial damsels. Then her eye falls on Karṇa, the hero, whom all had feared once and who is now lying down as a tree broken by a storm. Then she sees her son-in-law Jayadratha, the Sindhu-king, whose wives try in vain to frighten away the greedy birds of prey from the corpse whereas

1. Although it is clearly mentioned (XI, 16, 10 f) that Dhṛtarāṣṭra and the women have arrived in Kurukṣetra and see the bloody battlefield before them, it is said at the beginning of the chapter that because of their piously practising penance Gāndhārī obtained, through the grace of Vyāsa, a divine eye, the eye of a seer with which she could see the battlefield from a distance. It is centainly a feature foreign to ancient poetry — an inept brain-wave of a later day pedant.

her own daughter searches wailing for her husband's head. Then she again sees Śalya, the Madra-king, lying, whose tongue is just being eaten by vultures, whereas surrounding him his lamenting wives are sitting, "like ardent wives of an elephant who has sunk into the mud". She also sees Bhīṣma lying on his bed of arrows — "this sun among men goes to rest, as the sun in the sky sets". And after she has mourned Droṇa and Drupada and all great heroes who have fallen, she turns with angry words to Kṛṣṇa and reproaches him for not having prevented the destruction of the Pāṇḍavas and the Kauravas. And then she pronounces the curse on him that 36 years later he will cause the destruction of his own clan and will come to a miserable end in the forest.

Thereupon Yudhiṣṭhira gives the order for performing the funeral rites for all the dead. Pyres are erected, butter and oil are poured over them. Sweet-smelling wood and valuable silk-clothes, broken chariots and weapons are burnt with the dead bodies. After performing the rites and the wakes at which even strangers and friendless persons are not forgotten, they all go to the bank of the Ganges to offer the usual oblations to the dead.

The old poem has perhaps ended here. Our Mahābhārata pursues the story of the heroes still further.

THE HORSE-SACRIFICE[1]

Only at the time of performing the oblations to the dead did Kunti inform her son Yudhiṣṭhira that Karṇa too was a son of hers and so she asks him to offer oblations to him as to the eldest brother. Now Yudhiṣṭhira is very sad that he has been not only guilty of the ruin of so many relatives and friends but also committed fratricide by causing the death of Karṇa. Quite disconsolate that he is, he announces his intention to go to the forest and become an ascetic. His brothers and Kṛṣṇa try to persuade him to take over the rule, but with no success—he remains firm in his decision, until at last Vyâsa comes and advises him to perform the horse-sacrifice and thus purify

1. This forms the contents of the 14th book (Aśvamedhaparvan) Regarding the 12th and 13th books see further down (p. 405.)

himself from his sins. Yudhiṣṭhira follows this advice. Preparations are made for the horse-sacrifice. As required by the ritual the sacrificial horse is set free so that it might roam about freely for one year. Arjuna is chosen to accompany the horse and protect it. From country to country he follows the horse over the whole earth. While wandering thus he has to win many battles, for everywhere he encounters clans, whose warriors have been defeated in the Kuru-battle and who are therefore antagonistic to him. He performs great heroic deeds, but avoids as far as possible, unnecessary bloodshed and invites all subjugated kings for the horse-sacrifice. After one year he returns with the sacrificial horse to Hastināpura where he is received with great jubilation. Now begins the sacrificial festival to which the royal invitees flock from all sides. With strict adherence to all ritual regulations the horse is slaughtered and sacrificed in fire. The Pāṇḍavas inhale the smoke of the burnt marrow by which all their sins are destroyed. After completing the sacrifice Yudhiṣṭhira "gifts the whole earth" to Vyāsa who, in his generosity, gives it back to Yudhiṣṭhira and exhorts him to present plenty of gold to the priests. After Yudhiṣṭhira has accordingly gifted away lots of gold to the priests, he is purified from the sins and rules from then onwards as a good and pious king over his country.

Dhṛtarāṣṭra's End

The old king Dhṛtarāṣṭra[1] as the head of the family is even now requested to give advice in all matters. And he and his queen are always held in high respect. Thus the old king lives at Yudhiṣṭhira's court for 15 years on the best terms with the Pāṇḍavas which is somewhat disturbed only by his relationship with Bhīma. The old king could never completely forgive Bhīma who had deprived him of all his sons, and even the defiant Bhīma only too often vexed his aged uncle by his improper speech. So after 15 years the old king decided to retire into the forest as a hermit. Only reluctantly Yudhiṣṭhira consents to this. Kṛṣṇa however says that it has been the custom of pious kings to die either as kings on the battlefield or as hermits in the forest. So

1. Here begins the 15th book (Āśramavāsikaparvan).

Dhṛtarāṣṭra and Gāndhārī leave for the forest and also Kuntī, Sañjaya and Vidura join them. After sometime when the Pāṇḍavas visit their relatives in the hermitage, the wise Vidura is just breathing his last. Two years later news reaches the Pāṇḍavas that Dhṛtarāṣṭra, Gāndhārī, and Kuntī had died in the course of a forest-fire while Sañjaya had left for the Himālayas.

The Destruction of Kṛṣṇa and His Race[1]

Thirty six years after the great battle in the Kurukṣetra the Pāṇḍavas receive the sad news that the curse of Gāndhārī[2] has been fulfilled and Kṛṣṇa has been destroyed along with his race. In a drinking bout two clan-chiefs begin to quarrel with each other and others join them. A general mace-fighting ensues — stalks of reed are transformed by Kṛṣṇa into maces — and the men of the Yādava-race kill one another. Kṛṣṇa searches for his brother Baladeva, but finds that he is just breathing his last. A white serpent comes running out of Baladeva's mouth and goes swiftly into the ocean[3] where it is received by most famous serpent-demons. Then Kṛṣṇa lies in the desolate forest and is engrossed in deep contemplation. Here he is mistaken for an antilope by a hunter named Jarā (i.e. old age) is shot at by him in his heel— the only spot where he is vulnerable— and killed.

The Last Journey of the Pāṇḍavas

Disconsolate over the death of their faithful friend, the Pāṇḍavas decide to go on their last journey.[4] Yudhiṣṭhira installs Parīkṣit on the throne and takes leave of his subjects. Then the five brothers with their wife Draupadī, all clad in bark-clothes, followed only by a dog, wander into the Himālayas, climb them and reach the divine mountain Meru. On their way to heaven first Draupadī falls down dead, then

1. Told in the 16th book (Mausalaparvan).
2. See page 356 above.
3. A beautiful example of the soul in the guise of a serpent, a notion prevailing among so many folks. In the German legend of King Guntram too the soul comes out of the mouth of the sleeping king and hurries into a mountain.
4. With this begins the 17th book (Mahāprasthānikāparvan).

Sahadeva, then Nakula, soon after that Arjuna and at last Bhīma. Then Indra comes in his divine chariot in order to take Yudhiṣṭhira to heaven.[1] The latter does not want to go with him because he does not want to be in heaven without his brothers. Then Indra promises him that he will see his brothers as well as Draupadī in heaven. Yudhiṣṭhira insists that his dog also must go with him, which Indra of course does not at all allow. At last the dog reveals itself as God Dharma, who is greatly pleased with Yudhiṣṭhira for his loyalty. So then they come to heaven where however Yudhiṣṭhira does not want to stay at all, because he finds neither his brothers nor Draupadī there. As he sees even Duryodhana sitting on a heavenly throne[2] and respected by all, he does not wish to have anything to do with heaven and asks to be taken to those worlds where his brothers and heroes like Karṇa are staying. Then the gods send a messenger with him who then takes him to the hell where he sees the horrible tortures of those condemned to hell. When he is about to turn his eye away from the terrifying sight, he hears voices which beg him to stay on because a pleasant breeze is blowing from him. Moved with pity he asks those undergoing the tortures who they are, and learns that they are his brothers and friends. Then he is overcome with grief and anger at the injustice of providence and he sends the messenger back to the gods saying that he does not want to go to heaven but likes to remain in hell. Soon however the gods come down to him and Indra explains to him that those who have sinned most come to heaven first and then they will be sent to hell whereas those who have committed only few sins pay for these few sins first in the hell, go to heaven after

1. In his essay "Points de contact entre Mahābhārata et le Shahnamah" (*Journal Asiatique*, Serie 8 ème, t. X, 1887, p. 38 ff.) J. Darmesteter has compared the ascent to heaven of Yudhiṣṭhira with the vanishing of Kai Khosru in the Persian hero-epic. Also Kai Khosru climbs on a high mountain to go to heaven with his physical body in tact. Just like Yudhiṣṭhira's brothers, so also the Pehlewans accompanying Kai Khosru die on the way. Still the two epics are so fundamentally different from each other that it cannot be believed that they are connected with each other. (Cf. also Barth in *Revue de l' histoire des Religions* (19, 1889, p. 162 ff.).

2. Here begins the 18th (and the last) book (Svargārohaṇaparvan).

that to enjoy eternal bliss. He himself had to visit the hell because of his cheating Droṇa and similarly his brothers and friends had to atone for their sins in the hell. Very soon however the entire horror of the hell disappears; they find themselves all in heaven and assume divine forms.[1]

The main story briefly sketched here makes roughly one half of the 18 books of the Mahābhārata.[2] The other half is made up of those partly narrative and partly didactic constituents of the work which have, if at all, only a very loose connection with the battle of the Kauravas and the Pāṇḍavas. We shall speak about them in the following chapters.

Ancient Hero-Poetry in the Mahābhārata

It was also one of the duties of the bards of ancient India to follow up the genealogies of the kings, or, if necessary, even to create them. Genealogical verses (anuvaṃśaśloka) form therefore an essential constituent of ancient heroic poetry. And the first book of the Mahābhārata contains a whole chapter called "Sambhavaparvan", i.e., the chapter of the origins in which many interesting legends of the heroes are traced back right upto their initial forefathers descending from the gods and many interesting legends of these ancient kings of prehistoric times are narrated in them. It is natural that among the names of these forefathers of the Kauravas and the Pāṇḍavas belonging to the Bhārata-House the name of that Bharata also must find a place from whom the Mahābhārata itself gets its name. But Bharata is the son of king Duṣyanta and Śākuntala who has become so famous through Kālidāsa's drama and whose story is also narrated in the Sambhavaparvan.

But it is regrettable that just the Śākuntala-episode of the Mahābhārata[3] has been handed down to us by tradition in

1. Cf. on this episode also Lucian Scherman, *Materialien zur Geschichte der ndischen Visionsliteratur*, Leipzig 1892, p. 48 ff.; also the legend of Vipascit in the Mārkaṇḍeya Purāṇa.

2. The 18 parvans or books of the Mahābhārata contain altogether 2109 Adhyāyas or chapters; of these, 1070 make up the main story.

3. I-68-75. A complete translation was given by B. Hirzel in the appendix to his translation of Kālidāsa's "Śākuntala" (Zurich 1833, 2nd edition 1849). A condensed poetic treatment offering a profitable study was given by Ad. Friedr. Graf von Schack in *Stimmen von Ganges*

such a bowdlerized and perhaps even multilated priestly form which retains only few characteristic features of the ancient heroic poetry and might have been hardly the basis for Kālidāsa's poetry. The descriptions of the forest, of hunting, and of the hermitages are all woven not with "epic" but with pedantic range and partly even according to the pattern prescribed by later day ornate poetry of royal courts. The narrative is in itself based on an unattractive, inartistic foundation. That Śakuntala is not recognised by the king is not motivated through a curse and the story of the lost ring, as in the case of Kālidāsa, but through the desire of the king to remove every doubt of the royal parentage of his son in the eyes of the courtiers. Therefore he causes a divine judgement. He pretends not to know Śakuntala and not to have anything to do with the son until a heavenly voice proclaims in the presence of the whole court that Śakuntala has spoken the truth and that her child is really the son of King Duṣyanta. Here we come across two verses of which we know certainly that they belong to the oldest portion of the Śākuntala-poem and are taken from the ancient bard-poetry.[1]

"The mother is only the leather bag (for bearing the seed), to the father belongs the child; the son whom he produced, is he himself.[2] Receive[3] your son, Duṣyanta, do not insult Śakuntala !

The son O king, saves the manes from the hold of Yama (the God of death). But you are the creator of this child, Śakuntala spoke the truth".

(Stuttgart 1877) p. 32 ff., J. J. Meyer, *Das Weib im altindischen Epos*, pp. 68ff., and W. Perzig (*Indische Erzähler*. Vol. 12, Leipzig 1923, pp. 50 ff.). The Kumbakonam edition has enlarged and spoiled the traditional text still more; see M. Winternitz, *Ind. Ant.* 1898, p. 136; J. J. Meyer, ibid., p. 76, and Perzig, ibid., pp. 123 ff.

1. We find the same verses (I, 74. 109 f.) in the Mahābhārata (I. 95, 29 f.) quoted once again as "genealogical verses" (Anuvaṁśaślokau), and they reappear in the Harivaṁśa (32, 10 ff.), in the Viṣṇupurāṇa (IV, 19) and in the Bhāgavata-Purāṇa (IX, 20, 21 f.)

2. Cf. The verses translated on p. 196 above.

3. On account of this word "bear" (bhara) the boy got the name Bharata.

Also in the dialogue between Śakuntala representing her son's and her own claims and the king not willing to recognise them, we find many old and original verses preserved. In any case such a dialogue must have been the main constituent of the old story, and in Śakuntala's speech moralising sentences may have occurred like the following beautiful verses :

"If you think 'I am alone', then you know not the old wise man, who lives in your heart and who knows each evil deed. In his presence you commit your sin. Many a man thinks, who has committed evil, that no one has seen him; but the gods have seen him and also the spirit that lives in his heart."[1]

Śakuntala will have also spoken of the happiness and blessing that a son causes to his father, as in the verses:

"He himself has produced himself as son again through himself,[2] the wise men say usually. Therefore man shall look upon his wife, the mother of his sons, as his own mother".

"Is there a greater happiness, than that given by the son when he, covered with dust, comes home after playing and embraces his father's body ?"

"From out of your body is this one born, from out of one soul a second soul. See here your son, as your second self in the crystal-clear pond."[3]

Yet it is not probable that all the beautiful texts which Śakuntala is made to say — texts which deal with happiness and marriage and the duties of the husband, with the duties of the father and truthfulness — belong to the ancient heroic poem. Some verses referring to the law of marriage and succession which are taken from the law books indicate rather that Brahminical scholars have used the speeches of Śakuntala to include as many texts on morals and law as was possible. This does not prevent us from finding in these speeches some of the most splendid specimens of Indian epigrammatic poetry, as the following:

1. I, 74, 17.
2. Similarly Aitareya-Brāhmaṇa VII, 13; Cf. p. 196 above.
3. I, 74, 47; 52; 64.

"The wife is the husband's half, the wife is the best friend, The wife is the root of the three ideals of life, the wife is the root of the highest prosperity".

"They, the gently-speaking women are friends in loneliness, fathers while performing sacred acts, mothers for the unhappy ones".

"Tortured by pains of sorrow and pestered by diseases, men are revived by their wives as those who are tortured revived by fresh water".[1]

Among the forefathers of the heroes of the Mahābhārata is also a certain King Yayāti mentioned, whose story is similarly mentioned in the Sambhavaparvan, the chapter of the genealogical bard-poetry.[2] But just as the old Śakuntala poem was used for giving expression to Brahminical teachings on law and morals, so also the ancient Yayāti-legend, which must have been originally a sort of Titanic legend, was transformed into a moral story by which it became a popular theme for ascetic poetry. Of course the traces of the ancient heroic-poetry have not been completely wiped away, they are seen particularly in a certain blunt humour with which the story of the two wives of the king is told. From the contents of the Yayāti-episode only the following may be mentioned in particular.

Devayānī, the daughter of the Asura-priest Śukra, has been insulted by the daughter of the Asura-king. Therefore the priest wants to leave the king. The latter however, in order to pacify the priest, gives his daughter to Devayānī as her servant. Soon after this Devayānī becomes the wife of King Yayāti who must promise not to have any relation with her "servant" the princess Śarmiṣṭha. But the king breaks his word and produces three sons after a secret marriage with Śarmiṣṭha. The jealous Devayānī finds this out and complains to her father Śukra,

1. I, 74, 40; 42; 49.

2. The story is told at first briefly I, 75, and then repeated with many details I, 76-93. The last part of the legend is told once again with some additions V, 120-123. A free poetical treatment of the Yayāti-episode is found in Ad. Holtzmann, Indische Sagen I (Karlsruhe 1845), p. 139-88. A mythological interpretation of the legend has been attempted by A. Ludwig in "Die Geschichte von Yayati Nahuṣya, Analyse und Rolle derselben im Mahabharata", Prag 1878. (Sitzungsberichte der k. böhm. Ges. d. Wiss.)

who curses Yayāti that he shall immediately lose his youth and become old and infirm. However, on Yayāti's begging him, he lightens the curse to this extent that he may transfer his old age to anyone else.

Now Yayāti, on becoming suddenly old and wrinkled and grey-haired, asked his sons one after another, to take his old age and give him their youth because he had not yet enjoyed enough pleasures in life. Neither of the elder sons was prepared to consider his suggestion and they are therefore cursed by their father. Only the youngest, Puru, is prepared to do as his father wishes. He takes over the old age of his father and gives him in return his own youth. Thereupon Yayāti enjoyed the finest bloom of youth for a thousand years and enjoyed life in all its perfection. He shared the pleasures of life not only with his two wives but also with a celestial nymph, the pretty Apsaras Viśvāci ("inclined to all"). But however much he enjoyed, he never had enough. And as the 1,000 years were over, he realised the knowledge that he pronounced in the following verses:

> "Truly not through fulfilling the desires is desire pacified;
> No, it simply grows and becomes stronger, like the fire through the sacrificial butter.
>
> Only he who never did harm to any being whatsoever, whether with deeds, with thoughts or words, he will be united with Brahman,
>
> He who fears nothing and whom no being fears,
>
> He who nothing desires and knows no hatred, he will be united with Brahman".[1]

1. I, 75, 49-52. Only the first verse literally reappears at all other places where the Yayāti-legend is told. (It occurs also in Manu II, 94). The remaining verses are also found in I, 85, 12-16, Harivaṁśa 30, 1639-1645, Viṣṇu-Purāṇa IV, 10, Bhāgavata-Purāṇa IX, 19, 13-15 with variants. But only I, 75, 51-52 and Harivaṁśa 30, 1642 speak of the union with Brahman in the sense of the Vedānta-Philosophy. At all other places in the corresponding verses there is always only the talk of controlling the desires as the goal worthy of aiming in the practice of the ascetic moral. And this moral is the same for Buddhists and Jains as well as Brahminic and Vaiṣṇavite ascetics. Hence we find quite similar texts in all the Indian sects which know an asceticism.

Then he gave back to his son Puru his youth, took his own age upon himself, and after giving the kingdom to Puru, he went to the forest, lived there as a hermit and practised for a thousand years most severe penitent exercises. As a result of it he reached heaven where he lived long, honoured by all gods and saints. But one day he behaved arrogantly during a conversation with Indra and was therefore expelled from heaven. Later however he goes again to heaven along with his four pious grandsons.

A kind of Titanic legend that ends with a fall from the heaven is also that of Nahuṣa, the father of Yayāti that is often narrated in the Mahābhārata:[1]

Nahuṣa, a grandson of Purūravas[2] was a powerful king, who destroyed the robber-bands (dasyusaṅghātān). But he imposed taxes on the Ṛṣis also and made them carry him on their backs like beasts of burden. He overpowered even the gods and, instead of Indra, he ruled the heaven. He coveted Śaci, Indra's wife, for wife and became so haughty that he harnessed the celestial ṛṣis to draw his chariot and kicked Agastya on his head. This was of course too much for the great holy man and he cursed Nahuṣa so that he fell down from heaven and had to live as a serpent for 10,000 years.[3]

Some of the poems included in the Mahābhārata are so extensive and form a compact whole that they can be even called epics in the epic. To this type belongs the poem of Nala and Damayantī,[4] a poem whose claim to fame is well established. While the Pāṇḍavas are living in exile in the forest they are once visited by the Ṛṣi Bṛhadaśva. Yudhiṣṭhira complains to him of his misfortune and that of his people and puts him the question, whether there has ever been a more unfortunate king than he himself. Thereupon Bṛhadaśva narrates the story

1. At first I, 75 as introduction to the Yayāti-episode, then more elaborately V, 11-17, in a shorter extract also XII, 342 and XIII, 100. A free poetic treatment in Ad. Holtzmann's *Indische Sagen*, I, p. 9-30.

2. Also Purūravas (Cf. p. 94 f., 193 f. above) was, like Nahuṣa, according to the Mahābhārata, an enemy of the priests, who oppressed the Ṛṣis and was destroyed through their curse.

3. Then he was freed by Yudhiṣṭhira (III, 179 f) See p. 330-31 above.

4. III, 52-79: Nalopākhyāna.

of the unfortunate king Nala, who in the game of dice with his brother Puṣkara loses all his property and his kingdom and is then banished to the forest together with his faithful wife Damayantī; persecuted and blindened still by the wicked demon of gambling, he leaves his faithful wife in the midst of the forest while, tired of the long walk, she lies in deep slumber. The adventure of King Nala and of Damayantī forsaken by her husband, how they roam about the forest separated from each other, how Damayantī, after much suffering and hardship is kindly received by the Queen-mother of Cedi, how Nala, after being made unrecognisable by the serpent-king Karkoṭaka, serves King Ṛtuparṇa as horse-breaker and cook until at last husband and wife after long and painful separation are united again in love — all this is narrated in the fairy tale-style which is affectionately simple, really appealing to the masses and not without occasional glimpses of humour.

Ever since 1819 when Franz Bopp published for the first time this poem with a Latin-translation, it has been one of the most distinguished pearls of Indian literature, nay, even of the literature of the whole world. And it has been translated into German several times and adapted. Bopp's translating and editing of the poem was greeted by A. W. von Schlegel with the following words:[1]

"Here I will say only this much, that to my feeling this poem can be hardly surpassed in its pathos and ethos, in its enchanting force and delicacy of sentiments. By its very nature it appeals to young and old, high and low, connoisseurs of art and dilettantes, ... heroic faithfulness and loyalty of Draupadī is well-known as is that of Penelope in our own country; and in Europe the meeting place of the products of all continents and ages it deserves to be equally well-known". And it has become so. Friedrich Rückert, the genius of a translator has translated this poem into German in the year 1828[2] making it as popular

1. *Indische Bibliothek.*

2. New impressions appeared in 1838, 1845, 1862 and 1873. A very free rendering was given by Ad. Holtzmann in his "*Indische Sagen*".

in Germany as Dean H. H. Milman[1] did in England. Of course Rückert's translation certainly shows a daring use of the German language especially in the matter of compound words modelled according to Sanskrit. This intrepid use of the language, although often admissible, is still as ill-suited to the marvellous simplicity and epic dignity of the original[2] as the "knittel-verses" with their gushing, effervescent rhymes reflect the spirit of the calm river of the Indian Śloka. A better picture of the Indian poetry can be had perhaps from the poetical translation by Ernst Meier[3] who with great skill made a very successful use of the Niebelungen-stanzas, and even a much better idea can be had perhaps from the prose-translation of Hermann Camillo Kellner[4] which is very precise, careful and true to the original.

One can judge for oneself by comparing the translations of the first two verses:

Rückert

"There was a prince known with fame
Nala the son of Vīrasena called
Endowed with every virtue
Bravery, beauty and youth;
Excelling amidst princes of men
Like the king of gods in propriety
Radiating over the whole
Country like the sun in splendour".

Meier

"There was a king Nala
Son of Vīrasena,
Beautiful, clever and powerful
Versatile in horse and chariot
Surpassing the kings
Like Indra the world of gods
And excelling all in lustre
Like the sun in heaven's canopy".

---

1. *Nala and Damayantī and other poems translated from the Sanskrit into English verse*, Oxford, 1835.

2. Sometimes Rückert has added metaphors and ideas that do not at all occur in the original. In contrast to this is the free treatment of Ad. Holtzmann (*Indische Sagen* III) very much condensed. However this author feels that he "has not shortened the poem as such, but has only purified it from artificial accessories which only spoil the beauty of the original work". In doing so he has however acted also as arbitrarily as in the Kuruingen". See p. 306 above.

3. "*Die klassischen Dichtungen der Inder*" (Stuttgart 1847), I. Teil. Also E. Lobedanz has published a metrical treatment in 1863 in Leipzig.

4. *In Reclams Universalbibliothek.*

Kellner: "Once there was a king, Nala was his name, mighty son of King Vīrasena (Army-hero). He was endowed with covetable virtues, beauty of form and an expert horse-breaker. Far, far did he exceed all princes of men as the king of gods exceeds the gods; in lustre he was comparable to the sun".

Nala Naiṣadha, the hero of the story is certainly none other than Nada Naiṣadha, mentioned in the Śatapatha-Brāhmaṇa[1] of whom it is said that he "carries day after day (the death-god) Yama to the south". Therefore he must have lived in those days and led campaigns to the south. The name of the hero indicates therefore that he must have lived in very ancient times. The poem too might belong to the older though not to the oldest constituents of the Mahābhārata. It is in any case free from all Purāṇa-like accessories and only the Vedic gods like Varuṇa and Indra are mentioned, but not Viṣṇu or Śiva. Also the cultural conditions described in the poem are in general, simple and antiquarian. On the other hand we find scarcely anywhere in the most ancient poetry such a gentleness and so much romanticism in the description of courtships and love in general as for instance in the initial chapters of the Nala-poem. Only the very ancient poem of the love of Purūravas and Urvaśī makes us surmise that the romance of love was not unknown to India even in the earliest times. How much the romantic element appeals to the Indian mind in general is shown by the immense popularity of this poem which has been again and again followed as model by later poets — in Sanskrit as well as other modern Indian languages and dialects.[2] Moreover few Indian poems suit the European taste so much as the Nala-song. It has been translated into almost all the languages of Europe,[3] and a theatrical adaptation by

1. II, 3, 2, 1 f.
2. Cf. the enumeration in A. Holtzmann, *Das Mahābhārata*, II, 69 ff.
3. A. Holtzmann, ibid., II, 73 ff. mentions translations into German, English, French, Italian, Swedish, Czech, Polish, Russian, Modern Greek and Hungarian. There are also translations into English by Monier Williams (1860), Charles Bruce (1864), Edwin Arnold (Indian Idylls, 1883,

A. de Gubernatis was even staged in Florence in 1869. And at all universities of the west it has been the custom since a long time, to begin the study of Sanskrit by reading this poem, for which purpose it is admirably suited both from the point of view of its language as well as of its contents.[1]

A kind of epic in epic is also the Rāma-episode.[2] But whereas the Nala-song is (in spite of many deforming additions and interpolations from which of course no part of the Mahābhārata is completely free) a piece of art and a precious remnant of the ancient bard-poetry, the story of Rāma has, for us any significance for the history of the second great epic of the Indians, the Rāmāyaṇa, only from the standpoint of the History of Literature. For, the Rāma-episode is scarcely anything other than a rather inartistically condensed reproduction of either the Rāmāyaṇa itself[3] or of those hero-songs from which Vālmīki took the material for his poetry. The narrator of the Rāma episode is the Ṛṣi Mārkaṇḍeya who tells it in order to comfort Yudhiṣṭhira who is very melancholy on account of the kidnapping of Draupadī[4] because, also Rāma's wife Sītā was kidnapped and was in the prison of Rāvaṇa, the demon. Suggestive references to the Rāma-legend are also found frequently in the Mahābhārata. We may recall to our minds the meeting between Bhīma and the monkey Hanumat.[5]

Poetical Works. 1885); into German by E. Lobedanz (1863), H. C. Kellner (in Reclams Universalbibliothek), L. Fritze (1914); into French by S. Lèvi, (Paris, 1920 in *Les classiques de l' orient*, Paris 1920).

1. The text of the Nala story has often been published, with glossary and notes, for beginners in Sanskrit, e.g. by G. Bühler (*Third Book of Sanskrit*, Bombay, 2nd Ed. 1877), Monier Williams (London, 1879), J. Eggeling (London, 1913), H. C. Kellner (Leipzig, 1885), W. Caland (Utrecht, 1917).

2. III, 273-90; Rāmopākhyāna.

3. For this opinion H. Jacobi has brought in his *Das Rāmāyaṇa* (Bonn 1893), p. 71 ff. such strong proofs that in spite of the objections raised by A. Ludwig in his *Über das Rāmāyaṇa und die Beziehungen desselben zu Mahābhārata*, p. 30 ff and by Hopkins in his *The Great epic of India*, p. 63 f, they still appear as most probable. Cf. also A. Weber in "*Über das Rāmāyaṇa*", p. 34 ff.

4. See p. 332 above. Perhaps this story of the kidnapping of Draupadī is itself only a plump imitation of the kidnapping of Sītā in the Rāmāyaṇa.

5. See p. 329 above.

A much more valuable remnant of the bard-poetry of ancient times, that is unfortunately available only in parts, is from the fifth book of the Mahābhārata. It is the story of the heroic mother Vidula.[1] Kuntī sends a message to her sons through Kṛṣṇa that they should not forget their duty as warriors.[2] Then she tells also how once upon a time the warrior's wife Vidula incited her son Sañjaya to fight. This Sañjaya was leading a miserable life despondently with his wife and his mother after a disgraceful defeat that the king of the Sindhus had inflicted on him. Then Vidula in very strong words reproaches him for his cowardice and inaction and incites him in a fiery speech to new heroic deeds. In order to give an idea of the blunt force of the language of this fragment of ancient hero-poetry, at least a few verses from this speech may be translated.

"Up, coward, do not lie there so lazily, after you have been defeated thus, to the joy of your enemies, to the sorrow of your friends!"

"Soon is a shallow stream full, easy it is to fill the hand of a mouse. Soon is the coward pleased, with the least is he satisfied."

"Die not like a dog, but at least only after you have broken the fangs of the snake! Show courage, even if your life be threatened!"

"Why are you lying like a dead man, like one struck by thunder? Up coward! Sleep not, after you have been defeated by the enemy!"

"Burn in flames like a faggot of the Tinduka-wood[3] even if

---

1. V, 133-36: Vidulaputrānuśāsana. Cf. H. Jacobi, Über ein verlorenes Heldengedicht der Sindhu-Sauvīra (in *Melanges Kern*, Leyden, 1903, pp. 53ff.). A free poetical rendering of the poem is given by J. Muir, Metrical Translations from Sanskrit Writers, pp. 120-33. He justly refers to the women of Rajputana who "maintain in more recent times the character of heroism ascribed to Vidula in this passage of the Mahābhārata. (ibid., p. 132).

2. See p. 340 above.

3. Tinduka, the tree *Diospyros embryopteris*.

it should be for one moment, but do not be lying in smoke like a flameless straw-fire, only in order to be alive!"

"Better flame up for a moment than lie simply fuming for a long time! O let it not be that in a king's house a meak donkey was born!"

"Whose deeds men do not admire as miracles, who serves only for increasing the great multitude, he is no woman, he is no man".[1]

For all the admonitions and reproaches of the mother the son, who is characterised by his short speeches, can only reply that he is lacking in the means to a victorious battle and that there is no purpose served to her by his dying.

"Made of steel is your heart, O my heroic mother, you, who know, no sympathy, no pity.

"Woe to the life of the warrior, that you urge me to fight, as though you were another man's mother and I a stranger to you;— that you say such words to your only son ! Of what use would the whole earth be to you, if you would not see me any more ?"[2]

But his mother replies to him only with new admonitions, that the warrior must not know any fear and in any case must discharge his duty as a warrior. And at last she succeeds in shaking up her son although he has only very little understanding.

"Like a noble horse, when he is blamed, so did the son do, through the mother's play of words, all that she asked of him."[3]

This torso of a hero poem is one of the few pieces in the Mahābhārata which have remained totally unaffected by the Brahminical influence. Only too often the ancient bard-poetry whose very soul is the warrior-spirit has been diluted in form and content under the influence of Brahminical scholars. Thus we find — this is only one of many examples — in the 12th book of the Mahābhārata "an old Itihāsa" quoted, which Nārada narrates to Sañjaya, in order to console him in his grief over the loss of his son. Many kings of prehistoric times are named all of whom had to die although they were famous heroes. What do the "heroic deeds" of these kings consist in? — In this,

1. V, 132, 8-10, 12, 15, 22.
2. V, 134, 1-3.
3. V, 135, 12; 16.

that they performed numberless sacrifices and, what is more important, that they gave huge presents to the priests. One king, for example, gives to the priests as sacrificial reward, "thousand times thousand" virgins wearing gold ornaments, of whom each one sits on a chariot drawn by four horses; each chariot is accompanied by a hundred elephants with gold garlands; behind every elephant follows a thousand horses, behind every horse a thousand cows, behind every cow a thousand goats and sheep.[1] Often it is hard to say whether we are reading remnants of ancient hero-poetry in priestly bowdlerizations or independent Brahminical poetry.

Brāhminical Myth and Legend Poetry in the Mahābhārata

That the ancient Indian bard-poetry has not been preserved to us in its original purity is to be attributed to the fact that the Brahmins have taken control of the Mahābhārata. But we also owe it to the same fact that we find to day preserved in the Mahābhārata, not only numerous sagas of gods and legends but also important creations of Brahminic art of poetry and valuable testimonies of Brahminical wisdom.

Of mythological and legendary interest is the frame narrative of the serpent sacrifice of Janamejaya[2] in which again a veritable criss-cross texture of stories — serpent sagas myths or the garuḍa-bird etc.—are all woven into one another. But what is called here the serpent-sacrifice is in reality a serpent-spell, i.e. a charm to destroy the snakes. Janamejaya's father Parīkṣit had been bitten to death by the serpent king Takṣaka. In order to avenge his father's death, king Janamejaya performs a great sacrifice[3] during which, forced by the exorcisms of the priests

1. XII, 29. A similar list of ancient kings who were famous for their generosity is also found in VII, 56-71.

2. I, 3, A3-58; XV, 35. A free poetic treatment under the title "Das Schlangenopfer" is found in A. Holtzmann's *Indische Sagen*, Band III. Similar sagas are found in Europe also, especially in Tirol, cf. The treatise, 'Das Schlangenopfer des Mahabharata' (in *Kulturgeschichtliches aus der Tierwelt* of the Verien für Volkskunde und Linguistik in Prag 1904)—Winternitz.

3. In the pauses of this sacrifice the Mahābhārata is supposed to have been recited. See page 303 above. Porzig (ibid.) suggests that the

all the serpents of the earth come from far and wide and jump into the fire. This is described with great clarity in our epic.

"Now there began the sacrificial act in the manner prescribed for the serpent-sacrifice. The priests hurried here and there each zealous in his work. Covered in black clothes, eyes reddened with smoke, they poured sacrificial butter in the flames of the fire. They made the hearts of all the serpents tremble and summoned them all into the jaws of fire. Then the snakes fell into the flames of the fire, bending and calling one another pitiably. Gasping and hissing with their tails and heads winding round one another, they jumped in lots into the brightly glowing fire, big and small, many, of many colours, overflowing with poison, horribly stinging like pestles of mighty power-driven by the curse of their mother, the snakes fell into the fire".[1]

The old myth, which already occurred in the Vedic texts[2] of Kadru and Vinata, is also combined with this serpent-sacrifice. Kadru, the "red-brown one", is the earth and the mother of the snakes, Vinata the "bent one" is the canopy of the sky and the mother of the mythical bird Garuḍa. And further here the myth of the churning of the ocean [3] is interwoven which also occurs in the Rāmāyaṇa and the Purāṇas and is narrated again and again by later poets or is used as a source for metaphors and

Āstīkaparvan was originally much more closely connected with the Mahābhārata as a frame-story, and that it was not Vaiśampāyana, but Āstīka himself who related the whole of the Mahābhārata, and thereby saved the snake-king Takṣaka. There are but very weak grounds for this hypothesis. It is more probable that the whole of the Āstīkaparvan was originally an independent poem, which was only later connected with the recitation of the Mahābhārata. Cf. V. Venkatachellam Iyer, Notes of a Study of the Preliminary Chapters of the Mahābhārata, Madras, 1922, pp. 352 ff.

1. I, 52.

2. Śatapatha-Brāhmaṇa III, 6, 2. Taittirīya-Saṃhitā VI 1, 6, 1. Kāṭhaka 23, 10. *Der Suparṇādhyāya* (published by E. Grube, Berlin 1875 and reprinted in *Indische Studien,* Bd. 14) a late-vedic text in which Oldenberg has recognised (*ZDMG* Bd. 37, 1883, p. 54 ff) one of the oldest earlier phases of the Indian epic, is connected to some extent, with the story in the Mahābhārata.

3. I, 17-19.

similes. How gods and demons unite and, working hard, churn the ocean to obtain the drink of immortality, while the Mandara mountain serves as churning-stick and the serpent-king Vāsukī as the churning-rope, how then out of the foaming mass the moon, and then Lakṣmī, the goddess of luck and beauty, the intoxicating drink Surā and other precious things are born until at last the beautiful god Dhanvantari, holding in his hand the drink of immortality in a shining white vessel, springs up from the ocean — is described, if we may say so, with lively "lucidity".

One more serpent saga interwoven with the frame narrative deserves special mention — the story of Ruru, partly only a doublet of the saga of the serpent-sacrifice itself, for just like Janamejaya so also Ruru vows to kill all snakes. This happened, however, in the following way:

Ruru the son of a Brahmin saw once the beautiful damsel Pramadvarā, daughter of an Apsarasa and was seized with love for her. She is engaged to him, but a few days before the wedding she is bitten by a poisonous snake while playing. Lifeless she is lying there, as in sleep, more beautiful than ever. All the hermits of the forest come along and, seized with pity, burst into tears. But Ruru, in his sorrow, goes out into the thickest of the forest. Wailing loudly he addresses the gods on the strength of his penance and his pious life, to give back his beloved to him. Then a messenger of the gods appears to him and proclaims that Pramadvarā can be brought back to life again only when he gives half of his own life for her. Immediately Ruru is ready to do so and the god of Justice, i.e. the god of death agrees, that Pramadvarā be made alive again. On an auspicious day afterwards the two are married. Ruru, however vowed to kill all the snakes of the earth and thereafter whenever he saw a snake, he killed it. One day however he came across a harmless snake, which begged him to spare him. It was in reality a ṛṣi, who, as a result of a curse, had to live as a snake and was freed from the spell by his meeting with Ruru. In his human form he exhorts him to give up killing living beings.[1]

1. Extract from I, 8-12.

Ruru the hero of this legend, is a grandson of that Cyavana, of whom even the Ṛgveda[1] says that the Aśvins have made him alive again. The story of this rejuvenation is told exhaustively in the Brāhmaṇas[2] and a version of the legend is also found in the Mahābhārata.[3] It is instructive to compare the Vedic form of the legend with that in the epic. Hence the contents are given hereunder according to the Mahābhārata and in the notes the most important deviations of the Brāhmaṇa Stories are pointed out.

Cyavana, a son of Bhṛgu devoted himself to intense exercises of penances on the bank of a pond. He stood motionless like a pillar so long that a whole hillock of earth grew on him, and ants were crawling all over it and he himself was looking like an ant hill.[4] Once king Śaryāti came near this pond with his retinue. His youthful daughter Sukanyā sporting around with her companions, stumbled on the ant hill in which only the two eyes of the ascetic were visible like two glow-worms. Out of arrogance and curiosity the young girl poked around the two glowing objects with a thorn and pierced the two eyes of the ascetic.[5] Filled with anger the holyman caused obstruction to the urination and passing of stools of Śaryāti's army.[6] The king investigated the cause of the misfortune for a long time, and as it was found out that the great penitent was

1. Ṛgveda I, 116, 10, where he is called Cyavāna.

2. Śatapatha-Brāhmaṇa IV 1, 5 translated into German by A. Weber, *Indische Streifen* I (Berlin 1868), p. 13 ff Jaiminiya-Brāhmaṇa III, 120 f. cf. the interesting study of E. W. Hopkins in "The fountain of youth" (in the *Journal of the American Oriental Society*, vol XXVI, 1905 pp. 1-67 and 411 ff.) which pursues the legend of the Fountain of youth not only among the Indians but also among other peoples.

3. III, 122-25 Allusions to the last part of the story also in XII, 342, XIII, 156 and XIV, 9.

4. Of these exercises of penances there is no mention in the Brāhmaṇas. There Cyavana is only an "old saint with a ghostly appearance".

5. In the Brāhmaṇas it is the young lads in the retinue of the king who abuse the old ṛṣi and throw lumps of mud at him.

6. According to the Brāhmaṇas the punishment consisted in causing disunity in the king's retinue: "Father fought with son, brother with brother" (Śat. Br.). "The mother did not know the son, nor the son knew the mother" (Jaim. Br.).

insulted, he went to him to beg to be forgiven. The latter could be pacified only when the king agreed to give him his daughter in marriage. Thus the young girl becomes the wife of the old and infirm man. One day the two Aśvins see the young woman when she is just coming out from her bath and desire to make her choose one of them as husband in the place of the ugly old man. But she says she would be faithful to her husband. Then the two divine doctors propose to her that they would make her husband young and she should then choose between them and the rejuvenated Cyavana. Because Cyavana agrees to this, she too consents. The Aśvins thereupon make the old ascetic get into the pond and they themselves dive into the water then. After this all the three of them come out, identical with one another and in the splendid beauty of their youth. Now Sukanyā should choose and she decides, after proper comtemplation, in favour of her own husband Cyavana.[1] The latter however grateful to the Aśvins for having made him young, promises them to enable them drink Soma. During a big sacrifice which he performs for Śaryāti he offers Soma to the Aśvins. But Indra, the king of the gods, does not want to concede that the Aśvins, who wander about human beings as doctors should be worthy of the Soma. Cyavana however does not care for Indra's objections and continues to make offerings to the Aśvins. Then the angry Indra is about to hurl the thunderbolt at him. But at this moment the holy man paralyses the arm of the god; and in order to humiliate him thoroughly[2] he creates, by virtue of his asceticism, a horrible, gigantic monster — Mada, the

1. There is no mention in the Śat. Br. about the Aśvins also getting into the water of the pond. But the Jaim. Br. tells that Cyavana made Sukanyā familiar with a sign by which she would recognise him.

2. In the Śat. Br. there is absolutely no mention of a humiliation of the god (Indra), but it is told that Cyavana gives to the Aśvins only a means by which they are made by Indra and the other gods voluntarily participants in the Soma-drinking. In the Jaim. Br. however it results already in a test of strength between the Ṛṣis and the gods, and the Ṛṣis create the Mada to help them. But as Indra and the gods flee from the monster, the sacrifice threatens to become an Indra-less and a god-less one and the Ṛṣi requests Indra with prayers and invocations very politely to come back. Only in the description of the Mahābhārata is the god Indra totally humiliated by the holy man.

intoxication. With his gigantic mouth (one of the jaws is on the earth while the other reaches upto the heaven) he rushes to Indra and threatens to devour him. Trembling with fear the king of the gods asks the holyman to show mercy and the latter, pacified, lets the intoxication vanish again, by distributing it over the intoxicating drink Surā, women, dice and the hunt.[1]

It is seen here, as in many other cases, clearly that the Brahminical poetry contained in the epic portrays a much younger phase of development than that of the Vedic literature. The characteristic of this younger Brahminic poetry is however, exaggeration, vehemence in general, and in particular the intemperate superiority of the holy men — Brāhmins and penitents — over the gods. Even in the actual Indra-myths, which follow the old vedic sagas of the gods, Indra is not any more the mighty champion and the demon-vanquisher, as we know him from the hymns of the Ṛgveda.[2] Although the old saga of Indra's battle with Vṛtra still lives on, (it is narrated rather exclusively even twice in the Mahābhārata,[3] yet the main stress is laid on this that by killing Vṛtra, Indra has made himself guilty of Brahmin-murder. How he had to free himself from this terrible guilt and had to subject himself to many humiliations in doing so, is related at great length. As we have seen, he was even deprived of his celestical throne for some time and Nahuṣa occupied his place.[4] That by exercises of penance made by pious Brāhmins Indra's power is shaken, follows from numerous sagas. It is said in particular[5] that penance can force Indra himself to go to the seat of Yama (the god of death). And even quite often Indra takes to the proven means of sending a beautiful Apsaras to lead astray[6] any

1. In the Jaim. Br. the demon "intoxication" is transferred only to Surā (brandy).

2. Cf. p. 75 ff above.

3. III, 100 f V, 9-18. Many are the allusions to this battle. A doublet of this legend of the Vṛtra-battle is the one describing the battle of Indra with Namuci IX, 43.

4. See p. 365 above.

5. III, 126, 21.

6. Cf. A. Holtzmann, Indra nach den Vorstellungen des Mahābhārata in *ZDMG*, Vol 32, p. 290 ff.

holy man who by means of his exercises of penance, threatens to become dangerous to the gods.

Also Agni the friend of Indra has lost much of his earlier divine splendour in the myths of the Mahābhārata. Of course the myths told about him are on the background of the Vedic notions on fire and fire-god. Even in the Ṛgveda fire is called "the lover of damsels, the husband of women".[1] But the Mahābhārata can tell us real love-stories of Agni. Thus we read that he fell in love with the beautiful daughter of king Nīla and that the holy fire in the palace of the king would burn only when it was fanned by the beautiful lips and the sweet breath of the king's daughter. The king had no choice, but to give his daughter to Agni in marriage. In gratitude for this the god granted that he would be indefatigable and that the women of his town would enjoy absolute freedom in matters of sexual intercourse.[2] There is also mention of Agni's gluttony already in the vedas. But the legends of the Mahābhārata tell us that he has become "all-eater" as a result of a curse by the Ṛṣi Bhṛgu. That Agni has many brothers and that he hid himself in water or in the pieces of friction-wood are also Vedic ideas which already led to the origin of myths already in the Brāhmaṇas;[3] but only in the Mahābhārata exhaustive stories are told as to why Agni hid himself[4] and how the gods found him again.

To the legends which are already known in the Veda, and recur in the Mahābhārata, belongs also the deluge legend of Manu and the fish, which we have already heard as narrated in the Śatapatha-Brāhmaṇa.[5] The story in the Mahābhārata, the first episode[6] as it is called, is distinguished from the

---

1. See p. 80 above.
2. II, 31. A similar love-story on Agni XIII 2.
3. For example Śatapatha-Br., I, 2, 3, 1; Taittirīya-Saṃhitā II, 6,6.
4. Cf. A. Holtzmann, Indra nach den Vorstellungen des Mahābhārata in *ZDMG*, vol. 32, p. 290 ff.
5. See p. 194 f.
6. Matsyopākhyāna, III, 187 translated often — at first by Franz Bopp, *Die Sündflut nebst drei anderen der wichtigsten Episodan des Mahābhārata*, Berlin 1829. A later translation (by H. Jacobi) with H. Usener, *Die Sintflutsagen*, Bonn 1899, p. 28 ff.

legend, as told in the Brāhmaṇa, by its greater elaborateness and poetic presentation which is also combined with imagination. For example in a description as to how the sky is tossed up and down "like a drunken harlot" on the excited ocean. In the matter of contents it is of importance that in the Mahābhārata exactly like in the Semitic deluge-legends, it is mentioned that seeds are taken aboard the ship.[1] In this we find one of the strongest proofs to show that the Indian deluge-legend has been taken from the semitic legend.[2] The end of the story in the Mahābhārata is different from that in the Brāhmaṇa. Here the fish says that he is the god Brahman and asks Manu to create the world anew, and the latter does it by subjecting himself to hard exercises of penance.[3]

Less famous is the profound, beautiful myth of the goddess death which is told twice in the Mahābhārata[4] "whose child is the death? Where from does death come ? Why does the death snatch away the creatures of this world ? These are the questions put by Yudhiṣṭhira depressed over the death, of so many heroes who have fallen in the battle. Then Bhīṣma tells him (or Vyāsa[4]) the story. Nārada once told king Anukampaka

1. Similarly in the Matsya-Purāṇa and in the Bhāgavata-Purāṇa where the legend is told once again.

2. Cf. The treatise "Die Flutsagen des Altertums und der Naturvölker" in the XXXI volume of *Mitteilungen der Anthropologischen Gesellschaft in Wien*, 1901 especially on p. 321 f and 327 ff. We do not know, how those people who like R. Pischel (Der Ursprung des christlichen Fischsymbols *Sitzungsberichte der Berliner Akademie der Wissenschaften*, XXV, 1905) deny the connection between the Indian and the Semitic deluge-legends, can explain this certainly conspicuous concurrence between the two.

3. Of the "seeds" which he has taken with him, there is no further mention during the creation of the world again.

4. VII, 52-54, where Vyāsa consoles Yudhiṣṭhira who is overcome with grief over the death of Abhimanyu (see p. 346 above) by narrating the story and XII, 256-58 where Bhīṣma once again tells this same comforting story to Yudhiṣṭhira when he bemoans the loss of many heroes who have fallen in the great battle. But probably the story was found originally only in the XII book, for the verses XII, 256, 1-6 in which there is a talk of the many peoples killed in plural, VII, 52, 12-18 are found verbatim again repeated although here actually only the lamenting for Abhimanyu is the occasion for the story. This piece is translated by Friedrich Rückert (in R. A. Boxberger's *Rückert Studien*, Gotha 1878, p. 114 ff.) and by Deussen in *Vier philosophische Texte des Mahābhāratam*, p. 404-13.

when the latter was disconsolate on the death of his son. Following is the summary of the story:

As the first forefather Brahman had created the world they multiplied themselves incessantly and did not die. The world became more and more overcrowded and the earth complained to Brahman, that she cannot bear her burden any longer. Then the father contemplated as to how he could reduce the beings, but he could think of no means, so he grew angry and the fire of his wrath came out rustling through the pores of his body, flames spread all over the world and threatened to destroy everything. But god Śiva felt pity for the world and upon his intervention Brahman withdrew the fire born out of his wrath into himself again and ordered the birth and death of the beings, but then came out of the pores of his body a dark-eyed, beautifully, decorated woman covered in a bright red costume. She wanted to go her way towards south, but Brahman called her and said: "Death, kill the beings of this world! You are born out of my thought of world-destruction and of my wrath, so kill the creatures, fools and wisemen, all together!" The lotus-garlanded goddess of death wept loudly, but the lord of the creation caught her tears in his hands. But she begged him to excuse her from this cruel duty.

"May you be venerated, O Lord of the beings, be merciful to me, that I need not kill innocent creatures — children, old people and people in the prime of their youth, beloved children, best friends, brothers, mothers and fathers! I shall be cursed when they die away. I am afraid of that. And I am afraid of the tears of the unfortunate ones, the dampness of which will burn me in all eternity".

But a decision of Brahman is unalterable. She must adapt herself; of course the father grants her the favour that greed, anger, jealousy, envy, hatred, delusion and shamelessness ruin the men and that the tears which the goddess has shed and which he is holding in his hand, develop into diseases which kill the creatures. So she is not affected by any guilt of the death of the beings. The contrary is the case. The sinners are ruined by their own sins. But she, the goddess of Death, is justice himself and the goddess of justice[1] by snatching the living beings away unaffected by love or hatred.

A proof for the rather old age that must be attributed to this myth as well as to that of Manu and the deluge, is the high rank accorded to God Brahman in them. God Śiva is subordinate to Brahman in the myth of the goddess Death who addresses him as "son". Myths in which God Śiva takes a position superior to all other gods, mark a much later phase of Brahminical poetry in the Mahābhārata. The same is true also of the myths in which God Viṣṇu plays the main role. Often older myths and legends of Brahman have been rewritten to suit Viṣṇu or Śiva worship which can be mostly recognised without any difficulty. Such Vaiṣṇavite and particularly Śaivite ornamentations distinguish themselves often like blots on a painted picture. They can be easily separated and their removal only goes to enhance the value of the poetry. As poetical products the stories which are devoted to the glorification of the gods Viṣṇu and Śiva are of absolutely poor quality.[2]

But for this, a goddess Death does not play any role in Indian mythology.[3] Just as in the above mentioned myth the goddess of death becomes the goddess of Justice, so also in the whole of Mahābhārata the notion is current that Yama, the god of Death is identical with Dharma, the personified justice.[4] But nowhere does this identification of the king of the world of this dead with the lord of justice and righteousness find such beautiful expression as in the most splendid of all Brahmanical poetries which the epic has preserved for us, namely in the

1. VII, 54, 4-1.

2. Devoted exclusively to the sectarian cult are the pieces like the Viṣṇusahasranāma-Kathana (XIII, 149), the enumeration of thousand names of Viṣṇu, the Śatarudrīya (VII, 202). "the hundred names of Śiva", and the Śivasahasranāma-stotra (XII, 284, 16 ff.), "Praise of Śiva in thousand names" cf. above p. 172 f.

3. She is mentioned only once more in addition to Yama in the Brahmavaivarta-Purāṇa (Th. Aufrecht, *Catalogus codium MSS. Sanscriticorum in Bibl. Bodleiana,* p. 229).

4. On god Dharma see also above on p. 308 and 359.

wonderful poem of Sāvitrī, who is faithful to her husband.[1] The partly religious character of the poetry, the intermixing of mythology — of course old Brahmanic mythology in which Brahman the first forefather determines the destiny of men and neither Śiva nor Viṣṇu play any role — and the scenery of the penance-garden in which the action takes place for the most part, make us classify the Sāvitrī episode together with the Brahminical legend-poetry. Yet we cannot stop doubting and asking whether this is perhaps a pious piece of the ancient bard-poetry. For, the independent deportment of the princess Sāvitrī, who goes out in search of a husband for herself and insists upon her own choice although the holyman and her father raise an admonishing objection; the independence with which she practises penance, performs sacrifice and takes vows;[2] and above all her bold pleading for the life of her husband as well as her knowledge of wise sayings, by which she impresses even the god of death – all this reminds one rather of the women of the heroic-poetry like Draupadī, Kuntī and Vidula than of the Brahmanic ideal of a woman.[3] Whosoever it was, who has sung the song of Sāvitrī, whether a Sūta or a Brahmin, in any case, he was one of the greatest poets of all times. Only a great poet was in a position to present this marvellous character of a woman so lively to us that we think, we are seeing her in front of our eyes. Only a true poet could describe the victory of love and loyalty, of kindness and wisdom over destiny and death in such a moving and solemn manner without

---

1. III, 293-99: Sāvitryupākhyāna, "Episode of Sāvitrī" or Pativratā-māhātmya, "the song in praise of the woman who is faithful to her husband". The story is told by the seer Mārkaṇḍeya who is many thousands of years old but eternally youthful to Yudhiṣṭhira in order to console him over the fate of Draupadi

2. According to Brahmanic rules a woman as such (separated from her husband) is not entitled to perform sacrifices or to undertake fasting and other vows (Manu V, 155).

3. This ideal is, in short, the "Griselda-ideal" — the unconditionally obeying, subordinate woman of whom Manu V, 154 speaks: "Even when a husband is devoid of all virtues, is only a slave to pleasures, and possesses no good properties whatsoever, he must be ever respected by a virtuous woman like a god".

degenerating even for a moment into a dull preacher of morals.[1] And only an artist blessed with divine grace could conjure up such wonderful images before us. There we see the horrified woman boldly march by the side of her husband who has fallen down dead; the fatally ill husband who lays his head, tired in the lap of his wife; the terrible figure of the god of death who puts the soul of the man in fetters and draws it along; the wife fighting for her husband's life with the god of death; and finally, the happy re-united couple who, clasping their arms with each other, tread their way homeward in the moon-light. And we see all these images in the glorious frame-work of an Indian jungle the feeling of whose profound calm and the breathing of whose sweet fragrance are experienced by us so to say when we devote ourselves to the magic of this incomparable poetry.

What a great value is recognised by the Indians themselves in the treasure that they possess in the form of this immortal poetry is shown to us by the concluding words which are appended to the poem in our Mahābhārata:

"Whosoever hears the splendid story of Sāvitrī with his heart full of faith, he is happy, he is assured of salvation, and never will he have any grief".

Even today, Indian women celebrate every year a festival (Sāvitrī-vrata) in memory of the faithful Sāvitrī in order to be assured of conjugal happiness, and the recitation of the

---

1. The dialogue between Sāvitri and the God of death, Yama, who is at the same time Dharma, forms the nucleus of the poem. Some of the verses may not have come down to us in their original pure form. But the basic idea of all the epigrams with which Sāvitrī so much pleases and compels, is recognisable sufficiently clearly, it is the doctrine of wisdom which is identical with love and kindness. It is no specially Brahminical wisdom, as little as Sāvitrī is "a pious ideal woman endowed with all Brahminical knowledge who is imagined according to the heart's desire of the priest" as Paul Horn says in "Der dumme Tod im Savitri-liede", Beilage Zur Allg. Zeitung 1902, No. 55 p. 478). We cannot at all say that this dialogue is "an interpolation" or "a special text by the priests". Just as little can one agree with Paul Horn when he sees in the Sāvitrī-legend a parallel to the German legends of the Dummen Tod".

poem from Mahābhārata forms an essential constituent of the celebrations.[1]

The poem has been often translated into European languages and also into German. A single prose translation was already given by Franz BOPP,[2] the first poetical treatment was by Friedrick Rückert.[3] Yet all translations, modifications and adaptations can give us only a poor idea of the incomparable charm of the Indian poem.

Not all Brahmanical legends are so pious and moral as that of Sāvitrī. Indeed we can easily compile from the Mahābhārata a volume of dirty and beastly stories in which the Brahmins find pleasure — stories which in faithful translation into German must be published with the label "only for scholars". But one of these stories has attained a certain fame and is also of no little importance to the criticism of the Mahābhārata itself. This is the legend of Ṛṣya Sṛṅga[4] of the Ṛṣi who had never seen a woman. The content of this funny tale is, in short, as follows :

---

1. Cf. Shib Chunder Bose, *the Hindoos as they are*, 2nd Ed. Calcutta 1833, p. 293 ff.

2. *Die Sindflut nebst drei anderen der wichtigsten Episoden des Mahābhārata* Berlin, 1829, p. 11-70.

3. In the *Brahmanische Legenden* 1836, Werke published by C. Beyer, vol. vi, p. 412 ff. All too free treatments with arbitrary and unnecessary changes are given by A. Holtzmann in the *Indische Sagenn* I (Karlsruhe 1845, 2. Aufl. 1854) and Luise Hitz in the *Ganga-Wellen* (Munich 1893). Entirely out of taste is the translation of Albert Hofer, *Indische Dichtungen* (Leipzig 1844). The translations of J. Merkel (Aschaffenburg 1839) and of Ernst Meier (in the *Morgenblatt fur gebildete Leute*" 1854) are not known to me. The exact translation (in prose; only the epigrams are in verse) by Hermann Camillo Kellner (in *Reclams Universalbibliothek*, No. 3504, Leipzig 1895) gives us a good idea of the original. For other translations, see Holtzmann, "*Das Mahābhārata* II, pp. 92 f. The Sāvitri-poem has also been adapted for the stage by Ferdinand Graf Sporck, with music by Hermann Zumpe, and produced in German theatres.

4. III, 110-13. Freely rendered into German by Holtzmann in *Indische Sagen*, and by J. V. Widmann (*Buddha*, Bern 1869, pp. 101 ff.). Very freely dramatised by A. Christian Albers in *Calcutta Review*, Nov. 1923, pp. 231 ff. (*The Great Drought*). J. Hertel (*WZKM*. 18, 1904, pp. 158 f.) and L. V. Schroeder, *Mysterium und Mimus im Rigveda*, pp. 292 ff., have tried to

Ṛṣyaśṛṅga[1] is the son of a holyman born in a strange manner of a gazel. He grows up in a hermitage in the forest without having ever seen any person other than his own father. In particular he has never seen a woman. Now there broke out a great famine in the kingdom of King Lomapāda and wise men explained: the gods are angry, and there will be rain only if the king would succeed in bringing Ṛṣyaśṛṅga to his country.

The king's daughter Śānta[2] takes upon herself the task of enticing the young saint into the country. A floating hermitage is erected with artificial trees and shrubs, and in this hermitage Śānta sails to the abode of Ṛṣyaśṛṅga. Arriving near the forest hermitage the king's daughter gets on the land and uses the absence of Ṛṣyaśṛṅga's father to approach the youthful penitent. She gives him magnificent fruits and wonderful wine, plays coquettish games with a ball and presses herself in gentle embraces against the youth who thinks he has before himself another boy of the hermitage. Then the damsel goes back to her ship again because Ṛṣyaśṛṅga's father approaches the hermitage. The old man notices the excitement of his son and asks him what has happened. The latter describes his experience in the following words:

"A Pupil with plaited hair
was here, quite white in face

---

explain the Ṛṣyaśṛṅga poem as an ancient drama, a kind of "mystery-play". It is really a *ballad* of the type of the Vedic Ākhyānas. H. Lüders (*NGGW.*, 1897, pp. 1 ff.; 1901, pp. 1 ff) has traced the older forms of this ballad; by comparing its different versions in Indian literature.

1. The name means "gazel's horn". Because he has a horn on his head, he is called in Buddhistic versions also "Ekaśṛṅga" (i.e. "one-horn").

2. In our Mahābhārata it is not Śānta, but a courtesan who seduces the holyman. Lüders (ibid) has however proved very clearly that Śānta, the princess has been the seducer not only in the original form of the legend as it is preserved to us even today in the Jātaka book belonging to the Buddhistic Tripiṭaka but also in a more original form of the Mahābhārata itself. Only some later rhapsode or copyist found it objectionable that a king's daughter should have seduced Ṛṣyaśṛṅga and so substituted her with a courtesan so that one does not know why the king at last gives his daughter in marriage to the holyman. Besides, Holtzmann has in his free adaptation (ibid) already made the princess Śānta the seducer of Ṛṣyaśṛṅga.

with black eyes and smiling mouth
with thin body and high breast
As if in May the cuckoo sings
So sweet did it sound, when he spoke
And around him fluttered sweet fragrance
As when the wind blows in spring
Of our fruits he did not want any
And did not drink of our well.
He gave me other fruits which tasted
So magnificent, and of his drink
As I tasted it, I felt so well;
The earth began to shake
Then the boy caught me by my hair
And drew down my head towards himself
And placed his lovely mouth
On my mouth and then made
A small noise; that made
A shudder go through my limbs.
To see this pupil I am yearning;
Where he is, I too should always like to be;
I feel so bad, in my heart is pain,
Since I am missing him.
The penance that the boy learnt
That I should like to learn, that I find
Better, than the penance that you
My father, have taught to me."

Thereupon the father:

"My son, in such beautiful form
Go the devils in the forests round and round
To disturb the penance and salvation
Of pious people; trust them not. [1]

1. The verses according to A. Holtzmann. Ibid.

But hardly has the father gone away again, when Ṛṣyaśṛṅga goes in search of his young "friend". Soon he has found the beautiful Śānta, is enticed by her to the swimming hermitage and led away into Lomapāda's kingdom. At the moment when the holyman enters the country, it begins to rain in cats and dogs. The king however, makes him his son-in-law after pacifying his old father with rich presents.

Various versions of this legend are also found in other Indian literary works, especially in the Rāmāyaṇa, in the Padma-Purāṇa and the Buddhistic collections of fairy tales. It can be easily recognised that the story was originally as much a merry as a vulgar farce, whose vulgarities, the various adapters sought to mitigate. The scene in which the penitent son, who has never seen a woman, sees the beautiful damsel whom he takes for an ascetic, while the charms of the pretty one do not leave him cold, was found in the original version in any case to be the centre of the whole story and was described with a vulgar humour of whose vehemence some specimens are preserved to our present day in the Buddhist Jātaka-book.[1] But how popular this farce was is shown by the fact that it is also known in various versions in Tibet, China and Japan and has left behind its traces even in the unicorn-legend of the occident.[2]

The Ṛṣyaśṛṅga legend is found in the so-called Tīrtha-yātra-chapter.[3] The Ṛṣi Lomaśa who has come to console the brothers of Arjuna[4] makes a pilgrimage with them. In every holy place (Tīrtha) which they visit the Ṛṣi narrates a story relating to that place. Thus in this portion (certainly not belonging to the oldest constituent of the Mahābhārata)

1. In the Gāthās of the Jātakas Nos. 523 and 526. These Gāthās are according to Lüders(ibid., 1897) "the oldest literary version of the Ṛṣyaśṛṅga legend," and these stanzas were atleast in parts known to the author of the Mahābhārata version and must have been included in his book translated into Sanskrit and more or less modified.

2. Cf. F. W. K. Müller, Ikkaku seunin, a Japanese Opera of the middle-ages transcribed and translated. Together with a digression on the Unicorn-legend (in the *Festschrift fur Adolf Bastian zu seinem* 70. *Geburtstage*, Berlin 1896, pp. 513-38).

3. i.e., "Chapter of pilgrimages III, 80-156. Holy places to which pilgrimages ("yātrās") are undertaken, are called "Tīrthas".

4. See above p. 329.

numerous Brahminical legends are combined. Here is for example also the legend of Cyavana[1] already mentioned above, like the legends of the famous Ṛṣi Agastya. This great holyman is, moreover, requested by the gods, to dry up the ocean in order that they could fight some demons who are living on its bed. The holy man does so by simply drinking out the whole ocean. He is also the hero of many other Brahminical legends.[2]

While these Agastya-legends are supposed to describe the mighty superiority of Brahminic saints over men and gods, we find in the Mahābhārata also a whole cycle of legends whose heroes are the famous Ṛṣis Vasiṣṭha and Viśvāmitra,[3] which although serving to glorify the Brahmins still show clearly traces of a fight for hegemony between priests and warriors. These legends whose roots reach deep into the Vedic times appear again and again in various versions also in the Rāmāyaṇa-epic and in the Purāṇas. The most famous of these legends is that of Vasiṣṭha's cow, which has inspired Heine to the verses.

"O king Visvāmitra
O what a fool you are
That you so much fight and do penance
And all for the sake of one cow"

The content of the legend is according to the Mahābhārata briefly as follows:

Viśvāmitra was a warrior, the son of king Gādhin of Kānyakubja (Kanouj). Once on a hunt he came to the hermitage of Ṛṣi Vasiṣṭha. The latter had a wonderful cow, which fulfilled all his desires. If he wanted anything, be they foods or drinks, precious stones or clothes or whatever it may be he needed only to say: "Give" and the cow Nandinī gave it to him. When Viśvāmitra saw this excellent cow, he wanted to have it for himself and offered to Vasiṣṭha 10,000 ordinary cows in exchange for it. But Vasiṣṭha did not want to give

---

1. See 375 f.
2. III. 96-109.
3. I, 177-82; V, 106-19; ix 39 f; 42 f; xii 141; xiii 3f. cf. J. Muir: *Original Sanskrit Texts*, vol. I, 3rd. ed., London 1890, p. 388 ff., 411 ff. and F. E. Pargiter, in *JRAS*, 1913, pp. 885 ff.

away the cow, which offered him everything needed for sacrificial purposes. Nevertheless Viśvāmitra wanted to take the cow by force following the custom of the warriors. Vasiṣṭha as a gentle Brahmin did not of course hinder him from doing so, but the strange cow herself produced from her body mighty armies of warriors, who defeated the troops of Viśvāmitra and put them to flight. Then the proud king sees that Brahmin-power is certainly superior to warrior-power; he gives up his kingdom and does mighty penance in order to become a Brahmin which of course he achieves after indescribable exertions.

Another peculiar legend from this cycle of legends should be mentioned in particular because it reminds us of some traits of the Ahasver-legend.

Even after Viśvāmitra has become a Brahmin, his enmity with Vasiṣṭha continues. Induced by Viśvāmitra, Kalmāṣapāda who is possessed by a Rākṣasa kills the sons of Vasiṣṭha. This Vasiṣṭha is however so full of gentleness that he would rather die than let his wrath run riot. He wanted to put an end to his life and springs down from the Meru mountain but falls as on a heap of wool. He enters the fire but it does not burn him. With a stone round his neck he throws himself into the sea, but he is thrown back alive. So he returns depressed to his hermitage. But as he sees his house devoid of children, grief brings to his mind thoughts of suicide once again. Tying his hands and feet tightly, he throws himself into a mountain-stream in floods but the current cuts the ropes and sets him free and throws him back to the bank. Wandering further, he comes to a river which is full of crocodiles and horrifying monsters; he jumps into it but the wild animals timidly recede from him. As he sees that he cannot commit suicide, he goes back to his hermitage after wandering through many mountains and countries. On the way he meets his daughter-in-law Adṛśyantī and he hears a voice like that of his sons singing Veda-hymns. It is the voice of his grand-son, not yet born, who even in his mother's womb — Adṛśyantī is pregnant with him for twelve years now — has learnt all the Vedas. As soon as he comes to know that his family line will be continued he gives up his thoughts of suicide.

Whereas this kind of Brahmnical legend is not devoid of a certain literary value, there are also numerous stories in the Mahābhārata which have been invented purely for the purpose of glorifying the Brahmins or for impressing some Brahminic teachings. We have for example, stories of pupils in the matter of obedience to their teachers go to extremes, like that of Uddālaka Āruṇi who is commissioned by his teacher to stop the leakage in a dam and does so with his own body as he has no other means at his disposal. Or there is the story told of a king who as a penalty for giving a cow that belonged to one Brahmin to another as a present, was transformed into a lizard.[1] There are other stories to show that there is no higher meritorious deed than rewarding the Brahmins with cows. In a famous Upaniṣad the lad Naciketas thirsting for knowledge uses his stay in the nether world for storming the god of Death with questions on the life beyond death. In the Mahābhārata the lad — here he is called Naciketa — lets himself be shown the paradise of those who have given away cows as gifts, and Yama gives him a long lecture on the merit one acquires by making gifts of cows.[2] In order to prove that it is a meritorious act to present umbrellas and shoes, it is said that the Ṛṣi Jamadagni was once angry with the Sun and was about to shoot him down from the sky when he (the Sun) pacified the Ṛṣi before it was too late by presenting an umbrella and a pair of shoes to him.[3] Such stories are not at all rare especially in the didactic portions and books (xii and xiii). Finally in these instructive portions of the Mahābhārata we also find numerous frame work narratives termed as "Itihāsas", which serve only the purpose of introducing and clothing dialogues on topics of law, morals or Philosophy. It is noteworthy that we find in these Itihāsas as speakers, incidentally the same personalities whom we find in the Upaniṣads — for example Yājñavalkya and Janaka.[4] And as in the Upaniṣads and the Buddhistic dialogues we find in the didactic Itihāsas of the Mahābhārata also

1. I. 3; xiii 70 f.
2. xiii, 71, cf. p. 242 f. above.
3. xiii, 95 f.
4. xii, 18; 290; 310-20.

learned women[1] discussing on an equal footing with kings and wise men.[2]

Fables, Parables, and Moral Stories in the Mahābhārata[3]

These Itihāsa-Saṃvādas, as we can call these dialogues (saṃvāda) clothed in stories mostly do not belong to the Brahminic legend-poetry, any more, but to what we have termed, for want of a better expression, as "ascetic poetry".[4] This is clearly distinguished from the Brahminical poetry which is connected with the ancient legends of gods which are already almost forgotten by the masses; it is more closely connected with the popular literature of fables and fairy tales, partly because it draws its material from these sources, partly because it is closely adapted to them. And while the Brahminic legends as well as the Brahminic Itihāsa-Saṁvādas serve the special interests of the priests and teach a restricted priestly moral, which culminates in sacrificial service and worship of Brahmins (more than the gods,) the ascetic poetry rises to the level of a general moral which teaches, above all, love of all beings and renunciation of the world. This literature has left its mark firstly on the Upaniṣads and then also to an equal degree in the Mahābhārata and in some purāṇas as well as in the holy scriptures of the Buddhists and the Jains. It is therefore no wonder that we often come across the same legends of saints and epigrams of wisdom and morals repeated verbatim in these various literatures.

But the oldest Indian fables are found already in the actual epic and they serve to stress the importance of both the nīti i.e., practical wisdom as well as the Dharma or moral.

---

1. Incidentally also gods, for example Indra and Bṛhaspati xii, 11, 210, 68; 84; 103, xiii, 111-13.

2. King Janaka debates with nun Sulabhā, xii, 320, King Senajit is consoled by the courtesan Piṅgalā with her verses, xii, 174.

3. A selection of moral stories, especially from the xii book of the Mahābhārata is given in French translation by A. Roussel, *Legends Morales de l' Inde au Bhāgavata Purāṇa et au Mahābhārata*, traduit du Sanskrit (Les littératures populaires t. 38 et. 39, Paris 1900). On Fables and parables see Oldenberg, *Das Mahābhārata*, p. 66 ff.

4. See M. Winternitz in *Calcutta Review*, Oct. 1923, pp. 1 ff.

Thus a minister advises Dhṛtarāṣṭra to treat the Pāṇḍavas in the same way as a certain jackal who knew how to exploit his four friends — a tiger, a mouse, a wolf and an ichneumon for getting a prey, and then got rid of them all very cleverly so that he could enjoy the prey all for himself.[1] At another place Śiśupāla compares Bhīṣma to the hypocritical old flamingo who always spoke only of morals and enjoyed the confidence of all the birds living in the neighbourhood so that they deposited their eggs with him until they discovered only when it was too late that the flamingo eats their eggs away. Also very nice is the fable of the deceitful cat which on behalf of Duryodhana Ulūka is supposed to tell Yudhiṣṭhira for whom it is meant. With its arms raised high the cat performs severe penance on the banks of the river Ganges; and he can pretend to be so pious and good that not only the birds honour him but also even the mice place themselves under his protection. He is ready to protect them, but he says he is, due to his ascetic practices so weak that he cannot move about. Hence the mice have to carry him to the river—where he eats them up and becomes stout and fat.[2] The clever Vidura to whom many wise sayings are attributed, knows also many fables. So he advises Dhṛtarāṣṭra, not to persecute the Pāṇḍavas out of selfishness, lest he should be like the king who killed the gold-spitting birds due to greed so that he had afterwards neither gold nor birds any more.[3] In order to exhort him to peace he tells him also the fable of the birds which flew up with the net cast by the hunter, but finally by quarrelling with one another, fell into the hands of the hunter.[4]

1. I, 140 translated by Albert Hoefer. *Indische Gedichte* II, 187-92. On similar fables cf. Th. Benfey Pantschatantra I p. 472 f.

2. —ii, 41, v, 160. Such fables in which animals appear as hypocritical asceties are not at all rare in the Indian fable-literature. Cf. Th. Benfey ibid I, 177 f, 352. and M. Bloomfield, *JAOS*, 44, 1924, pp. 202 ff.

3. II. 62. Related to the fairy-tale of Suvarṇaṣṭhīvin (gold-spitter), the son of king Sṛñjaya. This king had desired a son whose entire evacuation of bowels should be gold. The desire is fulfilled and the gold heaps up in his palace. But at last the son is kidnapped and murdered by robbers (Dasyus) and all the gold vanishes. vii, 55. Cf. Benfey, ibid I, 379.

4. v, 64. cf. also the fable of the crow which wants to enter a flying race with the flamingoes; viii, 41, translated by Benfey ibid. I p. 312 ff. where connected fables are indicated.

But most of the fables and perhaps all the parables and moral stories are found in the didactic portions and in the books xii and xiii. Many of these occur again in the Buddhistic and later collections of fables and fairy tales and some have entered even European narrative literature. Thus Benfey has followed through world-literature a series of fables which have for their theme the impossibility of the friendship between cat and mouse.[1]

Some beautiful parables are found in the didactic portions of the Mahābhārata. Thus "the old Itihāsa, the dialogue between the river and the ocean"[2] narrated in order to impress the wise lesson of endurance that it is good to bend down and be humble.

The ocean asks the rivers, how it happens that they uproot strong powerful trees and bring them to him, whereas they never bring the thin weak reeds. The Ganga replies to him: "The trees stand, each in its place firmly rooted at one spot. Because they offer resistance to the current they must be removed from their place. Not so the reeds. The reed bends as soon as it sees the current advance — not so the trees — and when the force of the river is over, it again stands erect".

The parable of the man in the well which the wise Vidura tells to king Dhṛtarāṣṭra[3] has attained great fame and has spread even in the whole world. Both for its own sake and also on account of its significance for world-literature an extract of it deserves to be reproduced here:

A Brahmin loses his way in a dense forest infested with robbers. Seized by great fear he runs here and there, looking in vain for a way out. Then he sees, that the terrible forest is surrounded on all sides with snares and is encompassed by both arms of a horribly "looking woman". Huge and terrible five-headed dragons

1. xii 111; 138; 139 (also Harivaṁśa 20, 117 ff.) translated and proved by Benfey ibid. I, 575 ff, 545 ff, 560 ff. Other fables of the Mahābhārata which belong to the world-literature are that of the three fishes xii, 137 (Benfey ibid I, 243 f) and the dog of the saint which is transformed one after another into a leopard, a tiger, an elephant, a lion, a śarabha and finally again into a dog, xii, 116 f. Benfey ibid I, 374 f.

2. xii, 113.

3. xi 5.

which rise to the sky like gigantic rocks surround this big forest. And in the midst of this forest is a well. Over-grown with bushes and creepers. The Brahmin falls into it and remains hanging in the entangled branches of a liana. "As the big fruits of a bread-fruit tree hang down from the stem, so he was hanging there, feet upward head down-ward. And one more still greater danger threatened him there. In the midst of the river he saw a big, strong dragon and at the edge of the well-top he saw a black gigantic elephant with six mouths and twelve feet slowly come towards him". But in the branches of the tree that covered the well all sorts of terribly-looking bees were swarming and making honey. The honey trickles down and is assiduously drunk by the man — hanging in the well. For he was not vexed of life and did not give up hope of life although white and black mice were nagging at the tree from which he was hanging. The forest — thus Vidura explains the allegory to the king who is afflicted with pity — is the saṁsāra, the life in the world: the animals of prey are the diseases, the ugly gigantic woman is the old age, the well is the body of the beings, the dragon at the bottom of the well is time, the entangled creepers in which the man remained hanging is the hope of life, the elephant with six mouths and twelve feet the year and the six seasons and twelve months, the mice are the days and nights and the honey-drops the sensual pleasures.

That this parable is a truly Indian product belonging to the ancient poetry cannot be doubted. It has been described as "Buddhistic"[1] but it corresponds no more to the life-view of the Buddhists than to that of the Jains and other Indian ascetic sects. Nevertheless it is likely that it was the Buddhistic versions that have prepared the way for it to the west. For it has penetrated into the literatures of the west with that literary current which has flown to the occident through the chapbooks "Barlaam and Joasaph" and "Kalilah and Dimnah" which although originating in India, became entirely international. In Germany it is best known through Rückert's beautiful poem, *Es war ein*

1. Thus Benfey, ibid I, p. 80 ff and M. Haberlandt, *Der altindische Geist* (Leipzig 1887) p. 209 ff.

Mann im Syrerland, which was directly drawn from a Persian source, a poem by Jelal-ed-din-Rumī[1] Ernst Kühn has finally traced[2] the whole "circuit of this really non-confessional allegory, which has sewn Brahmins, Jains, Buddhists, Mohammadens, Christians, Jews in the same way for finding edification.

Just as in this case of the parable, so also in the case of many moral stories of the Mahābhārata one could be at first inclined to trace them back to Buddhistic sources. On a closer observation it will become clear that they could have been drawn from that fountain of popular stories which was equally at the disposal of Brahmins, Buddhists and other sects. Thus for instance the stories of king Śibi appear not only very much Buddhistic, but actually in one of the texts belonging to the Tripiṭaka[3] the legend is already told as to how this self-sacrificing king pulls out both his eyes in order to make a present of them to a beggar. In the Mahābhārata there are three different versions[4] of the story of this king who cuts the flesh of his own body piece after piece and gives up his life in order to save the life of a dove chased by a hawk. The very same king Śibi also plays a role in the ancient heroic legends of Yayāti. He is one of the four pious grandsons of this king who offer their places in heaven to him and finally go to heaven with him.[5] And the description of the immeasurable wealth and immense generosity of Śibi at another place bears decidedly a Brahminic colouring. Here Śibi is glorified as a pious sacrificer who presents the Brahmins with as many cows as rain drops

1. *Friedrich Rückerts Werke*, published by C. Beyer, Vol. I, p. 104 ff. The Persian poem translated from the Diwane-Jelal-ed-din-Rumis translated by Joseph v. Hammer, *Geschichte der schönen Redekünste Persiens*, Wien 1818, p. 83. cf. also R. Boxberger, Rückert-Studien, p. 85 f., 94 ff.

2. In the *Festgruss an O. v. Böhtlingk*, Stuttgart 1888, p. 68-76.

3. Cariyāpiṭaka I, 8. cf. also the Śivi-Jātaka (Jatakas ed: v. Fausböll, iv, 401 ff No. 499) and Benfey ibid I, 388 ff.

4. III, 130 f., 197, XIII, 32. See Griffith, *Idylls from the Sanskrit*, pp. 123 ff. (*The Suppliant Dove*).

5. I, 86 and 93. Cf. p. 364 above.

which fall on the earth, as there are stars in the sky and grains of sand, in the bed of the river Ganges.[1]

Among the popular stories of self-sacrifice found in the ascetic poetry is also the touching story of the hunter and the doves[2] which is also included in the collection of fables "Pancatantra".[3] Love even towards enemies and self-denial can hardly be practised more fervently than in this "holy Itihāsa which destroys all sins", that narrates how the cock-pigeon burns itself up in fire for the wicked hunter who has caught his beloved wife because he cannot offer any other food to the "guest"; how the dove follows her husband to death and how the wicked hunter, amazed at the love and self-sacrifice of the dove-couple, gives up his wild life, becomes an ascetic and finally also seeks death in fire.[4]

Yet another side of ascetic moral is brought into the limelight by the story of the pious ascetic Mudgala who does not want to go to heaven:

As Mudgala is so wise and pious a messenger of the gods appears in order to take him to heaven. But Mudgala is so cautious as to enquire, what sort of a condition is there regarding this heavenly existence. The messenger of the gods describes then all the splendours of heaven and all the bliss which is waiting for the pious there. Of course he has to say that this bliss is not eternal. Everyone should reap the fruits of his deeds. If the Karman is exhausted once, then it means that he must come

1. VII, 58. Completely Brahmanic is also the legend of Śibi told in III, 198. In this legend he kills unhesitatingly his own son as desired by a Brahmin and even eats himself because the Brahmin orders it. In contrast to this, the story of King Sihotra and Śibi (III, 194) looks more Buddhistic and appears again indeed in the Buddhistic literature (Jātaka No. 151) although not relating to Śibi any more. Cf. T. W. Rhys Davids, *Buddhist Birth Stories*. London, 1880, p. XXII-XXVIII; R. O. Franke, *WZKM*, XX, 1906, p. 320 ff.

2. XII, 143-49.

3. At least in one recension of it. See Benfey ibid. I, p. 365 f., 152, translation II, 247 ff. A poetical treatment was given by M. Haberlandt, *Indische Legenden*, Leipzig 1885, p. 1 ff.

4. The story can be hardly Buddhistic, because Buddhism does not recommend religious suicide. Other sects, e.g. the Jains recommend it.

down from the heaven and begin a new life. Then Mudgala says he does not want anything to do with such a heaven, he devotes himself again to severe ascetic exercises and attains at last through deep meditation (dhyānayoga) and complete disinterestedness towards the sensual world that highest resort of Viṣṇu in which alone the eternal bliss of Nirvāṇa is to be found.[1]

The theory of Karman, the act, which is the destiny of men, whose first appearance we could observe in the Upaniṣads[2] constitutes the object of many profound stories of the Mahābhārata. One of the most beautiful of them is that of the snake, death, destiny and the act. The story is, in short, as follows:

Gautamī, an old and pious Brahmin woman one day finds her son dead. A snake has bitten him. Arjunaka, the furious hunter brings the snake dragging with a rope and asks Gautamī how he should kill the wicked murderess of his son. Gautamī replies that by killing the snake her child will not become alive any more and even otherwise no good would come out of it. The hunter contradicts saying that it is good to kill enemies as Indra has killed Vṛtra, as we all know. But Gautamī cannot find anything good in torturing and killing enemies. Then the snake also joins the conversation. It says that it is not at all to blame for the death of the boy. It was Mṛtyu, that is, death, who used it only as a tool. Now while the snake and the hunter are vehemently quarrelling as to whether the snake was guilty of the child's death or not, the god of death, Mṛtyu, himself appears and explains that neither the snake nor he himself, but destiny (Kāla, "the time") was guilty of the boy's death: because, everything that happens, happens through Kāla; everything that exists, exists through Kāla. "As the clouds are driven hither and thither by the wind, so also death is subordinate to destiny". While the hunter persists in his opinion that the snake as well as the death are guilty of the child's death, there

1. III, 260 f. E. Windisch (*Festschrift Kuhn,* pp. 4 f.) sees in this Mudgala the prototype of the Buddhist Maudgalyāyana who visits the heaven and hells.

2. See above, p. 240.

appears Kāla, the destiny himself and explains; "Neither I nor the death (Mṛtyu) nor the snake here is guilty of the death of any being, O hunter, we are not those who cause anything. The act (Karman) it is, which drives us to do; there is no other agency causing his death, by his own act (Karman) was he killed. ... As the potter shapes from out of a lump of mud whatever he wants, so also man shapes his destiny himself through his acts. As light and shade are most intimately and eternally connected with each other so also the deed and the doer intimately connected through everything that the doer himself has done". Then Gautamī also finds consolation in the thought that the death of her son is necessarily the result of his own Karman.[1]

How men should behave towards death is a question that Indian thinkers and poets have very often treated in innumerable wise sayings and also in many comforting tales.[2] One of the most beautiful of these stories is that of the vulture and the jackal and the dead child of which only a short summary is given here:

The only son of a Brahmin had died. Wailing and weeping his relatives carry the dead body of the small child to the graveyard. In their grief they cannot at all go away from their dear dead child. Then attracted by their wails there comes a vulture flying and explains to them how futile all wailing for the dead child is. No dead man comes back again to life, when once he has fallen a victim to Kāla;[3] therefore they must go home immediately. Somewhat consoled, the mourners turn homeward. Then a jackal accosts them and reproaches them of lack of love, because they have abandoned their child so soon. They turn back sadly. Here the vulture is waiting and scolds them for their weakness. One should not weep for the dead, he says, but for ones ownself. This self, one should purify above all and not mourn for the dead. All good and bad of men depends only on Karma. "The wise man as well as the fool, the rich man as well as the poor, they all come under Kāla's power,

1. XIII, 1.
2. See pages 291 above and Lüders in *ZDMG*, Vol. 58, p. 707 ff.
3. Kāla is not only "time" and "destiny", but also "fate".

with their good and bad deeds. What do you want to achieve with your mourning? Why are you complaining of death? etc. Again the mourners turn, homeward. And again the jackal admonishes them not to give up their love for the child; they must fight against destiny, it says, for, it may perhaps be still possible to bring the child back to life. As against this the vulture remarks: I am well over a thousand years old, but I have never seen that a dead man was ever brought back to life. "Those who do not care for their mother, father, relatives and friends as long as they live, violate the moral. What should your wailing help him who does not see with his eyes, who is motionless and is absolutely dead?" And again and again the vulture incites the mourners to go home whereas the jackal asks them to go back to the graveyard. This is repeated many times. Vulture and jackal pursue their own object thereby, for they are, both of them, hungry and greedy after the dead body. At last God Śiva, induced by his consort Umā, takes pity on the relatives and brings the child back to life. [1]

But it is not only the ascetic moral that finds expression in the moral stories of the Mahābhārata. Many of them appeal to us just because they teach us rather the moral of everyday life having its roots in the love between husband and wife, and parents and children. One of the most beautiful of these stories is that of Cirakārin or of the contemplating youth[2] who is ordered by his father to kill his mother who has gone astray. As he is slow by nature and contemplates for a long time, he hesitates to execute the order and ponders over the pros and cons at length, whether he should execute his father's order and commit a matricide or he should fail in his duty towards his father. While he is contemplating thus his father comes back and as his anger has subsided in the meanwhile he is really happy that true to his name, his son Cirakārin has been contemplating on it so long, without acting. The focus of the story narrated in simple popular tone with a certain humour is the monologue of the lad. He speaks in a beautiful language, of

1. XII, 153.

2. XII, 265, translated into German by Deussen, "*Vier Philosophische Texte des Mahābhāratam*", p. 437-444.

father's love, filial duties and still more beautifully of mother's love:

As long as one has a mother, one is well-protected; if one has lost her one has no protection. Even if one has lost all wealth, still no worry oppresses him, no age wearies him, if he can call out "mummy" while entering his house. If one has also sons and grandsons and he comes to his mother, even if he is a hundred years old, he behaves like a two year old child. ... A man is then old, becomes then unhappy, finds the world then empty when he has lost his mother. There is no cooling shade like the mother, there is no refuge like the mother and no beloved like the mother". . . .

The emphasis in all these stories lies in the speeches of the persons appearing. But we have already mentioned that many so-called Itihāsas are actually only short introductions and clothing for didactic dialogues so that we may call them Itihāsa-Saṃvādas. Some of these dialogues are on a par with the best products of a similar character in the Upaniṣad and the Buddhistic literature. The exclamation of King Janaka of Videha after he has attained the soul-peace reads like a text of an upaniṣad, "Oh immeasurable is my wealth, as I possess nothing. If the whole of Mithilā burns, nothing of mine is burnt.[1] And we are reminded of the Buddhistic nun-songs (Therī-gāthā) when we read the verses of the courtesan Piṅgalā who at the time of rendezous is robbed of her lover and after overcoming her grief, attains that profound tranquillity which has ever been the highest goal of all Indian ascetic wisdom-verses which end thus: Calmly is Piṅgalā resting, after replacing desires and hopes with a state of perfect contentment".[2] As sometimes

1. XII, 178 Mithilā is the residential town of Janaka. Cf. Jātaka (ed. Fausböll), vol V, p. 252 (Verse 16 of the Sonakajātaka, no 529) and vol VI, p. 54 (no. 539). R. O. Franke, *WZKM*, XX, 1906, p. 352 f. J. Muir (*Metrical translations*, p. 50) translates as follows:

"How vast my wealth, what joy I taste,
Who nothing own and nought desire!
Where this fair city wrapped in fire,
The flame no goods of mine would waste."

2. XII, 174; 178,7 f. Buddhistic parallels are produced by R. O. Franke. *WZKM*, XX, 1906, p. 346 f.

in the Upaniṣads[1] so also in the dialogues of the Mahābhārata it is often people from the contemptible castes and low social positions who are in possession of the highest wisdom. Thus the Brahmin Kauśika is taught a lesson in philosophy by Dharmavyādha, the pious hunter and meat-dealer who makes it particularly clear that not birth but virtuous conduct makes one a Brahmin.[2] Thus the merchant Tulādhāra also appears teacher of the Brahmin ascetic Jājali.[3] This Itihāsa-dialogue is so important for Indian ethics that an extract of it deserves to be reproduced.

Jājali, the Brahmin lived as a hermit in the forest and devoted himself to most terrible practices of penance. Clothed in rags and hides of animals, his body caked with mud, he roamed about the forest in rain and storm, observed strict fasting and defied every inclemency of the weather. Once he was standing, absorbed in yoga, in the forest, motionless like a wooden post. There came a bird-couple flying towards him and built their nest in the hair of his head dishevelled by the storm and made knotty by dirt and dampness. As the yogi noticed this, he did not move, but remained standing motionless like a pillar, until the female bird had laid eggs in the nest on his head, until the eggs were hatched, until the young birds were fledged and flew away. After this powerful asceticism Jājali cried out in the forest jubilant and filled with pride, "I have attained the very personification of all piousness". Then a heavenly voice answered him from the air, "In piousness you are not at all equal to Tulādhāra, O Jājali and not even this wise Tulādhāra who lives in Benares, may say of himself, what you are saying of yourself". Then Jājali was very much depressed and went to Tulādhāra in Benares, in order to see how this Tulādhāra had attained such a standard in piousness. But Tulādhāra is only a merchant in Benares, where he runs on open shop and sells all sorts of spices, medicinal herbs and similar things. On being questioned by the Brahmin Jājali in what does the piousness

---

1. See page 211 f above.
2. III, 207-216.
3. XII. 261-264. Now completely translated into German by Deussen, *Vier philosophische Texte des Mahābhāratam*, p. 418-435.

consist which people admire so much, he replies with a long speech on moral beginning with the words:

"I know the eternal law, O Jājali with all its mysteries: it is known to me as the ancient doctrine of love doing good to all beings.[1] A way of life which is associated with absolute harmlessness or in any case with little harm for all beings — that is the highest piousness; according to this I live O Jājali. With wood and grass which others have cut I have built this hut. I buy and sell honestly red lac, lotus-roots, lotus fibres, all kinds of scents, many kinds of juices and drinks — with the exception of intoxicating drinks. O Jājali, he who is a friend of all beings and who finds happiness in thought word and deed in the well-being of all, he knows the moral law. I know neither favour nor anger, neither love nor hatred. I treat all beings equally: see Jājali, that is my vow. I have the same balance[2] for all beings, O Jājali, when one is afraid of none and none is afraid of him, when one has preference for none and hatred for none then he is united with the Brahman ..."

Then follows a long discussion on Ahiṁsā, the precept of non-injury. There is no higher law than having consideration for all beings. Therefore even cattle-breeding is cruel because it leads to torturing and killing of animals. Cruel is also maintaining slaves and trading in living creatures. Even agriculture is full of sins because the plough wounds the earth and kills many innocent animals. Jājali disagrees saying that without agriculture and cattle-breeding men could not exist and could not find food and that even sacrifices would be impossible, if animals might not be killed and plants might not be destroyed. To this Tulādhāra replies with a long discussion on the true sacrifice which must be performed without asking for reward and without the killing of living beings. Finally Tulādhāra calls upon the birds also which had built their nest in Jājali's hair

1. Maitra (in the Pāli of the Buddhists "metta") means "friendship" and is the technical word for the love towards all beings, which distinguishes itself from the brotherly love of christianity in this that it extends beyond human beings to animals as well.

2. The name of the merchant, Tulādhāra means "He who holds the balance".

to testify to his doctrine and they too vouchsafe that true religion consists in having consideration for all living beings.

We can observe the sharp contrast between the Brahmanic moral and that of the Indian asceticism nowhere so beautifully as in the dialogue between father and son[1] in which the father represents the viewpoint of the Brahmin and the son that of the ascetic who has broken away from the priestly religion. The view of life represented by the son is that of the Buddhists and the Jains,[2] without however being restricted to these. It would be hasty if one would declare the dialogue of which a partial translation follows here or even only individual verses of the same as "Buddhistic or as "borrowed from the Buddhists":

A Brahmin who found pleasure in learning the Veda had an enlightened son, by name "Intelligent" (Medhâvin). This son who was well-versed in everything connected with salvation, moral and practical life and understood the true essence of the world, spoke to his father who found pleasure in learning the Veda.

The son spoke, "What should, O father, the wise and enlightened one do ? Quickly vanishes the life of men. Do tell me, O father, one after another in a purposeful order in order that I may do what is good and proper".

The father spoke, "My son ! As a Brahmin pupil he should first study the Veda. Then he should wish for sons in order that he might purify the manes of the forefathers from guilt. And after he has set up fire and performed offerings, he should go to the forest and try to live as an ascetic."[3]

The son said, "How can you, being a wise man, speak like this ? While the world is infested and threatened on all sides, whereas the inescapable ones are incessantly flowing past".

1. XII, 175, in a slightly deviating version repeated in XII, 277. Now translated into German by Deussen, *Vier Philosophiesche Texte des Mahābhāratam*, p. 118-22.

2. Almost every verse which is spoken by the son in the Mahābhārata could be found as well in a Buddhistic or Jaina text. Actually XII, 174. 7-9 is found again in the Uttarādhyāyana-Sūtra (14, 21-23) of the Jains, and XII, 174, 13 corresponds almost verbatim to the verses of the Buddhistic Dhammapada, 47 f. A similar dialogue occurs also in the Jātaka No. 509, cf. J. Charpentier, *ZDMG*. 62, 1908, 725 ff.

3. This is the Brahmanic doctrine of the Āśramas, See p. 215 above.

The father said, "How is the world infested ? By whom is it threatened on all sides ? Who are the inescapable ones who are incessantly flowing past ? Why do you frighten me thus ?

The son said, "With death is the world infested, by old age is it threatened on all sides. And the inescapable nights[1] come and go always. If I know that death does not stop how can I still wait patiently ? How can I live along filled that I am with such knowledge ? When life becomes shorter and shorter, as night by night passes the wise one must realise that our days are useless. Like a fish in shallow waters, who could feel happy any more ? Even before man's desires are fulfilled death approaches man. Even if he is, so to say, plucking flowers death attacks him as the she-wolf does a lambkin and runs away with him ... What can be done tomorrow, do today; do in the morning, what is to be done in the evening. For death does not wait whether you have completed your work or not. And who knows, whose hour of death comes today ? Even as a youth, do what is just and good; fleeting is the life. ... Immediately after a mortal's birth old age and death begin to follow him till the end; all beings movable or immovable are subjected to them.[2] Indeed, only the beginning of death is this pleasure of the senses (of the householder living) in the village; but the forest (where the hermit lives) is, as the Veda teaches, a place where gods are gathered. This pleasure of the senses of the villagers — it is a chain that binds us. Good people immediately break it off, wicked ones break it never. He who wounds no living being through thoughts, words or deeds, he will not be bound by actions which make him miss the goal of life ... How should a man like me perform murderous animal-sacrifices ? How should a wise man perform murderous warrior-sacrifices as if he were a Piśāca ?... There is no eye equal to the eye of knowledge; there is no asceticism equal to that of truth; there is no happiness equal to that of renunciation. In the self (Ātman), produced by the self, firmly rooted in the self will I also live without progeny, alone in the self; no progeny need save me. There is no greater

1. Indians reckon time usually in terms of nights and not days.

2. The immovable "beings" are the plants and trees.

pleasure for Brahmins than loneliness, equanimity, truth, virtue, firmness, gentleness, straightforwardness and renunciation of all actions. Why do you need treasures, why relatives, why a wife, O Brahmin, as you are certain to die? Seek the self hidden in yourself (the Ātman)! Whither have your forefathers gone? Whither your father?"

Thus this dialogue which apparently operates within the range of Buddhistic thought regions ends up with the Ātman-theory of the Vedānta that we have met with in the Upaniṣads.[1] And it is not at all conspicuous. There were no greater differences among the various ascetic sects of ancient India than there are among the various protestant sects of present day Great Britain. It is therefore no wonder that in the stories of holymen, in the dialogues and sayings of wisdom of the ascetic poetry which have been included in the Mahābhārata there are so many similarities to the Upaniṣads as well as to the holy scriptures of the Buddhists and the Jains.

The Didactic Portions of the Mahābhārata[2]

Most of the Itihāsas and Itihāsa-Saṁvādas discussed in the previous chapter are found in the numerous and extensive didactic portions of the Mahābhārata. Such portions of varying length are found scattered over all the books and they treat three things which Indians term as the final aim of all philosophy — Nīti, i.e. worldly wisdom, especially for kings and hence also "policy", Dharma, i.e. both systematic justice as well as general moral and Mokṣa, i.e. "salvation". Nevertheless it is not always that we find these things told in the form of attractive stories and beautiful sayings, but we find also lengthy chapters which contain the dullest discussions — especially on philosophy in the XII and on justice in the XIII book.

Even from our synopsis[3] it can be seen that books XII and XIII do not at all have anything to do with the actual epic, but

---

1. See p. 225 ff. above.

2. On the style and contents of these didactic portions cf. O. Strauss, *ZDMG.* 62, 1908, pp. 661 ff., and *Ethische Probleme aus dem Mahābhārata*, Firenze 1912 (from *GSAI.* 24, 1911).

3. Cf. p. 356 above.

that the events narrated in the XIV book directly come after the close of the XI book. But the interpolation of these two extensive books has been rendered possible through the legend to which we have already referred. Pierced through innumerable arrows, Bhīṣma is lying in the battlefield, but because he can himself choose the hour of his death, he decides to die only half a year later.[1] This interval time is used by the fatally wounded hero who is at the same time a learned jurist, theologian and yogin, to give discourses to Yudhiṣṭhira on philosophy, moral, and justice. And the XII book begins with Yudhiṣṭhira's profound despair over the death of so many valiant warriors and close relatives of his. He indulges in self-reproaches and resolves, in his despair, to withdraw from the world and to end his life as a hermit. His brothers try to prevent him from doing so, and this gives rise to lengthy discussions as to whether renunciation and seclusion are proper or the fulfilment of one's duties as householder and king. The wise Vyāsa is also present and explains that a king should first fulfil all his duties and that only in the evening of his life he should retire into the forest. But he directs Yudhiṣṭhira to Bhīṣma who shall instruct him what the duties of a king are. So after he got himself crowned Yudhiṣṭhira accompanied by a large number of courtiers actually goes to Bhīṣma who is still lying in the battlefield to put him questions on the duties of a king and also about other things. The speeches of Bhīṣma on justice, moral, and philosophy fill the books XII and XIII.

The first half of the XII book (Śānti-parvan) consisting of the two portions "Instruction on the duty of a king" and "Instruction on the Law in cases of emergency (crisis)"[2] deals specially with the dignity and the duties of a king, in the course of which also instructions on politics (nīti), are brought in and further also on the duties of the four castes and of the four

1. See the Note on p. 346 above. V. V. Iyer, *Notes of a Study of the Preliminary Chapters of the Mahābhārata*, pp. 271 ff.; and Oldenberg, *Das Mahābhārata*, pp. 76 ff., Hopkins, *Great Epic of India*, pp. 381 ff., applies to these books (XII, XIII) the term "pseudo-epic."

2. Rājadharmānuśāsana-parvan (I-130) and āpaddharmānuśāsana-parvan (131-173).

life-stages (Āśramas) in general, on the duties of parents and children to one another, on the proper conduct when in peril and danger, on self-discipline, asceticism and love of truth, on the relationship of the three ideals of life[1] and many more similar things. The second half of the book, containing the chapter on "Advice on the duties which lead to salvation"[2] is mainly of philosophical content. But even here we find beside long, dull and often confused discussions on cosmogony, psychology, fundamentals of ethics or the theory of salvation also many of the most beautiful legends, parables, dialogues and moral sentences of which some have been already discussed in the foregoing chapter. And while as a whole this XII book represents only an inartistic, mostly hotch-potch, compilation, still it contains many precious pearls of poetry and wisdom. Even as a source for the story of Indian philosophy this book is of inestimable value.

While the XII book can be described in a certain way as a "texbtook of philosophy" the XIII book (Anuśāsana-parvan) is in essence nothing but a textbook of law. Indeed in this book there are quite large passages which contain either quotations from or exactly parallel texts to well-known law books — for example that of Manu. We shall see in a subsequent chapter that even the Indian Law literature consists to a large extent of metrical textbooks and belongs to didactic poetry. The XIII book of the Mahābhārata distinguishes itself from the other lawbooks (Dharmaśāstras) only in this that the dull description is often interrupted by the narration of legends[3] which are mostly lacking in depth and taste. Whereas the XII book although not a part of the original epic still might have been interpolated at a comparatively earlier time, with respect to the XIII book there can be hardly any doubt that it has become a part of the Mahābhārata at a much later date. It bears all the features of a quite modern work of an inferior quality. To mention only one, we may say that nowhere in the Mahābhārata

---

1. Dharma, Artha, and Kāma, Cf. note on p. 304 above.
2. Mokṣadharmānuśāsana (174 ff.), completely translated into German by Deussen in *Vier philosophische Texte des Mahābhāratam.*
3. Of the sort mentioned on p. 390 above.

are the claims of the Brahmins to superiority to all other strata of society asserted in such a presumptuous and exaggerated manner as in the XIII book. A great part of the book concerns itself with the Dānadharma, i.e. with the rules and regulations on generosity. What is meant by "generosity" is however always giving gifts only to Brahmins.

In addition to what is in these two books we also find apart from small texts not exceeding one or two cantos, also larger didactic chapters in the III, V, VI, XI and XIV book. In the III book (28-33) we find a long conversation between Draupadī, Yudhiṣṭhira and Bhīma on ethical questions in the course of which Draupadī quotes a conversation between Bali and Prahlāda and a "Nīti of Bṛhaspati".[1] In the same book we find (205-216) the discussions of Mārkaṇḍeya on the virtues of women (205 f), on the kindness to all living beings (Ahiṃsā), (206-208) on the power of destiny, renunciation of the world and salvation, on the teachings of the Sāṅkhya-philosophy(210) and of the Vedānta (211) on the duties towards parents (214 ff) and similar things. The V book contains long speeches of Vidura on morals and practical wisdom (33-40) and the philosophic teachings of the eternally young Sanatsujāta (41-46). In the VI book we come across the famous Bhagavadgītā (25-42) to which the Anugītā contained in the XIV book (16-51) constitutes a sort of continuation or supplement.[2] Moreover Vidura's words of consolation in the XI book (2-7) belong to the field of ethics.

Of all these didactic pieces of the Mahābhārata none has attained such popularity and fame as the Bhagavadgītā[3] or

---

1. III, 32, 61.

2. The three philosophical poems Bhagavadgitā, Sanatsujātiya and Anugitā have been translated into English by Kāśināth Trimbak Telang in the 8th volume of the *Sacred Books of the East*; now also into German by Deussen in *Vier Philosophische Texte des Mahābhāratam.*

3. The complete title is Bhagavadgītā-upaniṣadaḥ, "the secret teachings given by the Exalted One". "Bhagavat, the Exalted One, the venerable one" is the attributive of God Viṣṇu who is personified in Kṛṣṇa who gives to Arjuna the teachings contained in the poem. Besides "Bhagavadgītā" in India the short title "Gitā" (i.e. the song par excellence) is also quite well known.

the "Song of God". In India itself there is hardly a book, that is read so much and respected so highly as the Bhagavadgītā. It is the holy book of the Bhāgavatas, a Vaiṣṇavite sect, but it is also a book of worship and edification for every Indian, to whichever sect he may belong. Of Avantivarman, a king of Kashmir, born in 883 A.D. the historian Kalhaṇa[1] says that at the time of his death he let the Bhagavadgītā be read from the beginning to the end and then, thinking of Viṣṇu's heavenly abode he died cheerfully. And he was not the only Indian who found consolation in this book in the hour of his death. There are, even today, many educated Hindus, who know the whole poem by heart. Innumerable are the manuscripts which are preserved of this book. And since 1809, when it was printed for the first time in Calcutta, not a single year passes when some new print of this work does not appear. Numerous are also the translations in modern Indian languages.

Outside India, too, the Bhagavadgītā has won many admirers. The Arabian traveller Alberuni knew the poem perfectly and appreciated it very highly.[2]

In Europe the poem was made known for the first time through the English translation of Cha. Wilkins (London 1785). Of great importance was the critical textual edition by August Wilhelm von Schlegel[3] to which a Latin translation was appended. Through this work Wilhelm von Humboldt was introduced to the poem and it was already mentioned[4] how greatly he was enraptured by the same. He placed the Bhagavadgītā at a higher level than Lukrez and even Parmenides and Empedocles and declared that "this episode of the Mahābhārata is the most beautiful, indeed perhaps the only truly philosophical poem that all the literatures known to us have". In a big treatise of the Berliner Akademie (1825-1826) "On the

1. Rājataraṅgiṇī V, 125.

2. See E. C. Sachau, *Alberuni's India*, I, p. xxxviii; II, Index. s.v. Gitā.

3. Cf. p. 9 and 13 above. The English translation of Wilkins has been translated into German by Fr. Majer in Jul. *Klaprothy's Asiat Magazin*", vol. I and II, (Weimar 1802). Also Herder has translated some verses of the Bhagavadgītā into German in *Gedanken einiger Brahmanen*.

4. See p. 15 f. above. Cf. *Collected Works of Wilhelm von Humboldt*, I, p. 96 and 111.

episode of the Mahābhārata known as Bhagavadgītā"[1] and in an elaborate review of the Schlegelian edition and translation[2] Wilhelm von Humboldt deals with the poem in great detail. It was translated into German many times, by C.R.S. Peiper in 1834, by Fr. Lorinser in 1869, and by R. Boxberger in 1870.[3] But the most exact and reliable translations are now those by R. Garbe[4] and by P. Deussen.[5] The Bhagavadgītā was translated into other European languages too, notably into English.[6]

The poem is found however at a place where one would least expect it — at the beginning of the VI book where the descriptions of the Great war begin. All preparations for war have been made. Both armies stand facing each other, ready for war. Then Arjuna lets his chariot be stopped between the two armies and surveys the armies of Kauravas and Pāṇḍavas mobilised for war. And as he sees on both sides "fathers and grandfathers, teachers, uncles and brothers, sons and grandsons, fathers-in-law and comrades", he is overcome with a feeling of the deepest pity; he is horrified at the thought that he had to

1. Also *Coll. works* I, 26-109.

2. In Schlegel's *Indische Bibliothek*, vol. II, 1824, p. 218 ff, 328 ff. Also *Coll. works* I, 110-84.

3. Very valuable is the English translation by Telang mentioned above in note 2 on p. 408. On the contrary the German translation by Franz Hartmann (Braunschweig 1892) has been made for modern theosophists who are in a position to read it in the sunlight of the divine spirit". (Foreword to the translation), and hence it cannot be recommended for ordinary mortals.

4. *The Bhagavadgītā* translated from Sanskrit with an introduction of its original form, its teachings and its age. Leipzig 1905. This translation is philologically exact and reproduces the philosophical content of the poem reliably. Of its poetic import however it does not give us any idea, nor is that its intention. Among the poetic translations I prefer that of Peiper's without rhyme to the verses of Boxberger with rhymes. Lorinser's translation is as unpoetic as ungerman.

5. See Note 3 on p. 305 above.

6. English translations by J. C. Thomson, Hertford, 1855; K. T. Telang (in verse, Bombay, 1875; prose in *SBE*. Vol. 8); John Davies (1882); Edwin Arnold (1885); C. C. Caleb (1911); L. D. Barnett (in Temple classics). Sanskrit text with English Translation by Annie Besant and Bhagavan Das, Benares, 1905.

fight against relatives and friends. It appears to be a sin and madness to him, to be wanting to murder those people, for whose sake one normally goes to war. But as Kṛṣṇa reproaches him of weakness and softness, Arjuna explains that he is absolutely perplexed, that he does not know whether it is better to defeat or be defeated by the enemy, and he at last requests Kṛṣṇa to enlighten him as to what he should actually do in this embarrassing situation of conflicting duties. Then Kṛṣṇa answers with a detailed philosophical discussion,[1] whose direct object it is to convince Arjuna that it is his duty as a warrior to fight whatever the consequences may be. Thus he says:

"You are mourning for those for whom you need not mourn, although you are talking sensibly. The wise man does not feel sorry for either the living or the dead. Never was there a time when I did not exist, never a time when you did not exist, never a time when the kings were not; and none of us will ever cease to exist. As man attains in this body of his childhood, youth and age, so does he also attain another body (after death): the wise man is not bewildered at this. ... Perishable are only these physical bodies of the eternal, imperishable indestructible men; therefore simply fight, O Bharata-child! He who declares the one as the killer and the other as the killed one — they both know nothing. For man does not kill and is not killed. He is not born and dies never and never will be, when he has come into existence once, cease to exist. Unborn, everlasting, permanent and eternal he is not killed when the body is destroyed. As a man throws away old clothes and puts on other new clothes, so man throws away the old bodies and takes up new ones. No sword wounds him, no fire burns him, no water makes him wet, no wind dries him up. ... If you have known all this you should not mourn for him ..."[2]

Kṛṣṇa says therefore: There is no cause for mourning for the impending killing, for man himself, i.e. the spirit is

1. On the teaching of the Bhagavadgītā see R. G. Bhandarkar, Vaiṣṇavism, Śaivism, etc. (*Grundriss* III, 6), pp. 14 ff.; and J. E. Charpentier, Theism in Mediaeval India, London, 1921, pp. 250 ff. Some less known monographs on the Gītā are discussed by P. E. Pavolini, *GSAI.*, 24, 1911, pp. 395 ff.

2. II, 11-13. 18-20. 22. 23. 25.

eternal and indestructible, it is only the bodies which are destroyed.[1] And he adds the admonition to Arjuna, that he may think of his duty as warrior and begin the justified battle. Happy is the warrior to whose lot falls such a battle, which opens the gate of the heaven to him! If he does not fight, then he brings only shame upon himself which is worse than death. If he falls in the battle, he is assured of heaven, if he wins, then he rules over the earth. Therefore he must fight in any case. With this speech of Kṛṣṇa, the hero, are all subsequent discussions of Kṛṣṇa, the sage and later of Kṛṣṇa the God — for in the course of the poem it is more and more the God Kṛṣṇa who speaks to Arjuna — in conflict. For all further discussions of the Bhagavadgītā on the ethics of action culminate in the theory that man should do his duty, but without any consideration for success or failure, without caring for the reward to be expected. For only such a desireless action which — consists in giving up all action, in non-action, in the absolute world-renunciation is somewhat compatible with the actual ideal of morality. And yet actually we can trace through the whole poem an irreconcilable contradiction between the quietistic moral of asceticism to which meditation practised in seclusion from the world and endeavouring for the highest knowledge appears as the way to salvation and the moral of action which has been never at least properly recognized. Of course Kṛṣṇa teaches that there are two paths of salvation, the path of knowledge and the path of action. But as long as the spirit is bound to the body it is only hypocrisy to say that man can live without acting. For eternally connected with matter are the three "qualities"[2] (Guṇas) — gentleness, passion and darkness through which actions are necessarily born. What man can do is therefore only this — that he does his duty without desires, without wishes. For as fire is covered with smoke and as a mirror with dirt, as the embryo in the womb by the amnion so also is knowledge

1. There is no murder or act of violence which could not be justified by this miserable sophistry. It is surprising that the pious readers of the Gītā do not see this. On the unsolved and insoluble contradiction between the principles of the Gītā and the morality of war forming the starting-point of Kṛṣṇa's speeches, see W. L. Hare, *Mysticism of East and West*, London, 1923, pp. 159 ff.

2. The theory of the three guṇas belong to the Sāṅkhya philosophy.

concealed by desire, the eternal enemy of the "knower."[1] Therefore whoever acts without desire approaches best the actual ideal which is on the path to knowledge. How highly the Bhagavadgītā esteems knowledge as the way to salvation is shown by the verses (IV, 36 f):

"And should you be even the worst sinner amongst all the sinners, with the boat of knowledge you will cross all sins. As the fire which, as soon as it is inflamed transforms the fire wood into ash, O Arjuna, so does the fire of knowledge transform all actions into ash".

And also according to the Bhagavadgītā he is a Yogin — the ideal of the holy and the wise man — who, turning away from all that is earthly, only contemplating, aspires for knowledge. The Yogin maintains his peace of mind "in cold and heat, in joy and sorrow, in honour and dishonour". A lump of mud, a stone and a lump of gold are all equal in his eyes. He treats alike friends and foes, strangers and relatives, good people and bad ones. Sitting in meditation at a lonely place "he motionless fixes his eye on the tip of his nose." "As a light in an air-tight place does not flicker" — this is the classical simile for the Yogin who holds his thinking in check and devotes himself completely to meditation (Yoga).[2] While evidently in the Upaniṣads[3] contemplation and thinking is considered as the only way to knowledge and salvation, the Bhagavadgītā knows yet another way, that of Bhakti, i.e., of love of God.[4] To

1. Bhāg. III, 38 f.

2. VI, 7-19. In a letter to Gentz, Wilhelm von Humboldt writes, he (Gentz) will understand, how much the Indian poem must influence him. "For, I am not at all unlike the 'deeply engrossed ones' (i. e. the Yogins) of whom there is mention in it." (*Works of Friedrich von Gentz*, published by G. Schlesier, Mannheim, 1840, V, p. 300).

3. Cf. p. 242 above.

4. It is this idea of Bhakti or love for God which more than anything else in the Bhagavadgītā reminds us of Christian thought currents. Even otherwise the echoes of Christian currents are so strong that the attempt of F. Lorinser in the appendix to his translation (Breslau 1869), to prove Christian influences in the Bhagavadgītā cannot be condemned outright. But it is precisely the thorough investigation of Lorinser which also proves

Arjuna's question, whether in that case whoever is not in a position to direct his mind completely to meditation is lost, Kṛṣṇa gives the following reply: "Nobody who has done good is completely lost." He who has done his duty in this world will be reborn after his death depending on the merit of his deeds, in a good family and will attain gradually, after many re-births, the ability to become a Yogin. "Among all the Yogins" says Kṛṣṇa,[1] "that one is deemed by me to be most

that here it is a case of a parallelism which is highly interesting from the point of view of the history of religion and that it is not a case of one religion borrowing from another. Lorinser is convinced that "the author of the Bhagavadgītā not only knew the books of the New Testament and used often, but also wove into his system Christian ideas and views in general," and he wants to prove that this greatly admired monument of ancient Indian mind, this most beautiful and exalted didactic poem which can be considered as the noblest of the flowers of heathen wisdom owes its purest and most admirable teachings largely to Christian sources. Guided by such tendencies Lorinser compared all that can be compared even to a small extent. But among the over 100 texts of the Evangelia which Lorinser quotes as parallel to texts of the Bhagavadgītā, there are utmost 25 of such a nature as would make a borrowing even thinkable. In not a single case however is the similarity of such a nature as would make the presumption of a borrowing more probable than that of a chance coincidence. Even the love of God is not restricted to Christianity. We need think only of Sufism in which it plays no smaller role than with the Christian mystics. The explanations of Lorinser have also not convinced any Indologist till now. Even A. Weber, who traces back Bhakti to Christian influences (*Griechen in Indien, SBA.*, 1890, p. 930), thinks, Lorinser goes too far. Cf. also A. Barth, The Religions of India, transl. by J. Wood, London 1889, p. 220 f. and Garbe ibid., p. 32 f. and 55 ff. E. W. Hopkins, *India, Old and New*, New York, 1902, 146 ff.) is the only scholar who has expressed a decided opinion in favour of the theory that the Bhagavadgītā was influenced by Christianity. G. Howells (*The Soul of India*, London, 1913, 425 ff.) compares the doctrines of the Gītā with those of the New Testament, and seeks to trace points of agreement, without asserting that the Gītā was dependent on Christianity. Most scholars agree that the doctrine of Bhakti can be explained by earlier Indian teachings, and that the hypothesis of Christian influence on the Bhagavadgītā is unlikely, on historical grounds. Cf. J. Muir, *Ind. Ant.*, 4, 1875, pp. 77 ff.; A. Barth, *RHR*, 11, 1885, pp. 57 f. (*Oeuvres* I, 370 f.) and the Religions of India, transl., London, 1889, 220 f.; J. van den Gheyn, *Le Muséon* 17, 1898, pp. 57ff.; L. J. Sedgwick, *JBRAS.*, 23, 1910, 111 ff.; A. B. Keith, *JRAS*, 1907, 490 ff.; Grierson, *ERE*. II (1909), pp. 547 ff.; and esp. R. Garbe, *Die Bhagavadgītā* (2nd Ed.), pp. 66 ff., and *Indien und das Christentum*, 1914, pp. 227 ff.

1. VI, 47.

sincere who loves me with his inner self faithfully directed towards me." Only out of love of God arises knowledge of God and true salvation. This is taught by Kṛṣṇa again and again: "Even if a very ill-conducted man worships me, not worshipping any one else, he must certainly be deemed to be good, for he has well resolved. He soon becomes devout of heart, and obtains lasting tranquillity. (You may) affirm, O son of Kuntī ! that my devotee is never ruined. For, O son of Pṛthā, even those who are of sinful birth, women, vaiśyas and śūdras like wise, resorting to me, attain the supreme goal. What then (need be said of) holy Brahmins and royal saints who are my devotees ? ..."[1]

Also moral action and all virtues of the Yogin receive their essential value only through this love of God:

"Hateless toward all born beings, friendly and pitiful, void of the thought of a Mine and an I, bearing indifferently pain and pleasure, patient,

ever content, the Man of the Rule subdued of spirit and steadfast of purpose, who has set mind and understanding on Me and worships Me, is dear to Me.

He before whom the world is not dismayed and who is not dismayed before the world, who is void of joy, impatience, fear and dismay,

desireless, pure, skilful, impartial, free from terrors, who renounces all undertakings and worships Me, is dear to Me."[2]

The substance of all ethical teachings of the Bhagavadgītā is however contained in the verse that the commentators rightly term as the "Quintessence-verse".[3]

"He who performs all his actions for my sake, he who is faithful to me, he who loves me, is free from attachment to the earth and without hatred towards any being, he comes to me, O son of Pāṇḍu !"

Here it is also said in what according to the Bhagavadgītā the salvation of the highest welfare consist — in the union with God.

1. IX, 30-33. translated by K. T. Telang, *SBE.*, Vol. 8, p. 85.
2. XII, 13-16, translated by L. D. Barnett.
3. XI, 55.

This is however to be understood "as exaltation of the soul to God-like existence, as continued individual existence in the presence of God."[1]

There are thus three paths, which lead to this goal; the path of the dutiful action, the path of knowledge and the path of love of God. And it is at least attempted —although the attempt does not meet with success always—, to reconcile the three paths with one another. The first path can be reconciled with the third and the love of God leads to the knowledge of God, it therefore coincides with the second path. Thus one can overcome to a certain extent the contradictions in the ethical teachings[2] of the Bhagavadgītā.

There are, however, other contradictions in the poem staring us in the face at every turn. Kṛṣṇa invariably speaks of himself as a personal god, as the creator, who is eternal and imperishable, but is nevertheless born into the world or creates himself at such times when a decrease in religion is imminent; this is especially the case in the passages dealing with bhakti (IV,5 ff.). In other places, again, he teaches that *he* is in all beings, and all beings are in *him* (VI,30 f.). "This All is strung on me, like pearls on a string. I am the taste in the water, O son of Kuntī, I am the light in the sun and moon, the syllable Om in all the Vedas, the sound in the atmosphere and the bravery in men," etc. (VII, 7 ff.). This doctrine, according to which God is separate from the world, though at the same time immanent in it, is taught as a great secret (IX, 1 ff.). There is, however, a third category of passages where Kṛṣṇa is not mentioned at all, but which speak quite abruptly of the brahman (neuter) as the sole and highest world principle in the sense of the monism of the Upaniṣads. Moreover, side by side with verses mentioning the Veda in an almost scornful tone (II,42 ff.), we find other passages recommending the sacrifices prescribed in the Veda, and even describing the sacrifice as "a magic cow

1. Garbe, *Die Bhagavadgītā* (2nd Ed.), p. 65.

2. Otto Strauss, *Ethische Probleme aus dem "Mahābhārata,"* Firenze 1912 (*GSAI.* 24,1911), pp. 309 ff., gives a good summary of the ethics of the *Gītā*, which he presents as a compromise between the contradictory doctrines.

which fulfils all wishes." (III,10), which is difficult to reconcile with that "desireless action" that is so often praised.

This doctrine of desireless action is sometimes described by the term *Yoga.* The same term is, however, used to denote various things. The usual meaning is what is generally understood by Yoga in Indian literature, i.e., the doctrine of absorption, and of the methods by which man can withdraw from the sense-world and become entirely absorbed in the deity. It is in this sense that the Bhagavadgītā is sometimes called a *Yogaśāstra,* or manual of Yoga. This "practical philosophy" of the yoga has its psychological and metaphysical foundation in the Sāṁkhya.[1] The Sāṁkhya, however, teaches differentiation between spirit (puruṣa) and matter (prakṛti), plurality of souls, and independence and eternity of matter, and explains the creation as an unfolding of the world from original matter. Now all these are doctrines diametrically opposed to the doctrine of unity taught by the Upaniṣads and the Vedānta. In spite of this, the passages dealing with the brahman, teach the doctrine of universal unity as well.

How can all these contradictions be explained ? Scholars are by no means unanimous on this point. Some are content to say that all these contradictions simply result from the fact that the Bhagavadgītā is not a systematic philosophical work, but a mystical poem, and that, in the words of Franklin Edgerton, the most decided and consistent exponent of this opinion, it is "poetic, mystical, and devotional, rather than logical and philosophical." W. von Humboldt had already said: "It is a sage, speaking out of the fulness and inspiration of his knowledge and of his feeling, not a philosopher trained in a school, classifying his material in accordance with a definite method, and arriving at the last principles of his doctrine by a skillful chain-work of ideas."[2] On the other hand, other scholars maintain that there

1. In V. 4 f., it is explained with great emphasis that Sāṁkhya and Yoga are one. In XVIII, 13, *sāṁkhye kṛtānte* cannot mean anything but "in the *Sāṁkhya*-system. "In XVIII, 19, *guṇasaṃkhyāna* is explained by *Śaṅkara* as Kapila Śāstra. Kapila, the founder of the Sāṁkhya system, is called the first of the perfect sages, in X, 26.

2. "Über die ünter dem Namen Bhagavadgītā bekannte Episode des Mahābhārata," 1825 (*Gesammelte Schriften* V, p. 325). The following take up more or less the same point of view : K. T. Telang, *SBE.*, Vol. 8, pp. 11 ff.;

are limits even for mystical poetry, and that the contradictions in the Gītā can better be explained by the assumption that the poem has not come down to us in its original form, but like most parts of the Mahābhārata has only received its present form as a result of interpolations and revisions. Some scholars had assumed that the Bhagavadgītā had originally been a pantheistic poem, which was remodelled later by the devotees of Viṣṇu into a theistic peom. This is very improbable, for in spite of all the contradictions the whole character of the work is predominantly theistic. God appears as an essentially personal god, who, as a teacher, and in human incarnation, requires devotion (bhakti) of his worshippers.

Taking this for granted, R. Garbe[1] made a direct attempt to reconstruct the original poem, by printing in small type in his translation all verses which he considers unauthentic i.e. interpolated from the view-point of the Vedānta philosophy and the orthodox brahmanical religion. We are at first likely to be in entire agreement with Garbe.[2] However, after repeated readings of the Gītā and the most thorough investigation of the passages cut out by Garbe, we come to the conclusion that even the original poem did not teach pure theism, but theism tinged with pantheism. we do not now believe that we are justified in pronouncing as interpolated all those passages where Kṛṣṇa

---

E. W. Hopkins, *JRAS.* 1905, pp. 384 ff.; and *Cambridge History* I, 273; L.v. Schroeder in the introduction to his German translation; B. Faddegon, *Camkara's Gītābhāṣya, toegelicht en beoordeeld*, Diss., Amsterdam 1906, pp. 12 ff.; D. van Hinloopen Labberton, *ZDMG.* 66,1912, 603 f.; R. G. Bhandarkar, Vaiṣṇavism, Śaivism, etc., pp. 157 ff.; O. Strauss, Ethische Probleme aus dem *Mahābhārata.* (GSAI. 24,1911), p. 310; ZDMG. 67, 1913.714 ff.; A. B. Keith, *JRAS.* 1913, p. 197; 1915, p. 548; H. Oldenberg, *NGGW.* 1919, 321 ff., and Das Mahābhārata, pp. 39,43, 70 ff.; J. N. Farquhar, *Outline of the Religious Literature of India.* London 1920, pp. 90. f.: H. Jacobi, *DLZ*, 1921, 715 ff.; 1922, 266 ff.; F. Edgerton, *The Bhagavadgītā* interpreted, Chicago 1925.

1. In his translation of the *Bhagavadgītā*, see also *ERE.* II, 535 ff. and *DLZ*, 1922, 98 ff., 605 f.

2. Also F. O. Schrader, *ZDMG.* 64, 340, and A. Hillebrandt, *GGA.* 1915, p. 628, agree with Garbe. Grierson, too (*ERE.* II, 540 f.; *Ind Ant.* 37, 1908, 257) agrees with Garbe in counting the passage where "Brahminism" is taught, among the "later" portions of the *Gītā*. The scholars mentioned in Note 2 are the opponents of the view adopted by Garbe.

speaks of himself as immanent in the world, as for instance the beautiful verses VII, 7 ff. On the other hand, we still agree with Garbe that those passages where mention is suddenly made of the *brahman* (neut.) without any reference to Kṛṣṇa whatsoever, are interpolated (e.g. II, 72; V 6,7,10; VII, 29-VIII, 4 etc.), as well as the passages where ritual and sacrifices are recommended or glorified (e.g. III, 9-18; IX, 16-19 etc.). It is also likely, that the original Bhagavadgītā was much shorter, and that the work in its present form contains many more interpolations and additions than are assumed by Garbe. The very fact that the Bhagavadgītā contains exactly 18 Adhyāyas, just as the Mahābhārata is divided into 18 Parvans and as there are 18 Purāṇas, is suspicious.[1] Canto XI, where Kṛṣṇa reveals himself to Arjuna in his godlike form, is of the nature of a Purāṇa rather than like the work of the poet of the first sections. It is this very conviction that the author of the original Gītā was a great poet, that makes us hesitate to attribute to him such verses as XI, 26 ff., where the heroes of the epic are visioned as hanging between the teeth of the god,—a vision by which a further excuse for the killing of the enemy is added to those already given in Canto II: namely Arjuna need not hesitate to kill the enemies, because in reality they have "already been killed (by God)."[2]

There can hardly be any doubt that the Bhagavadgītā did not belong to the original heroic poem. It is scarcely imaginable that an epic poet would make his heroes hold a philosophical conversation of 650 verses in the midst of the description of a battle. In all probability the original epic included only a very short dialogue between Arjuna and the hero and charioteer (not the god) Kṛṣṇa. This dialogue was, as it were, the germ from which the present didactic poem grew.[3] This didactic poem was

1. Cf. Hopkins, *Great Epic*, p. 371.

2. Those scholars, too, who reject Garbe's views, do not all believe in the unity of the Gītā. Hopkins (*Great Epic*, pp. 215-34 f.) speaks of the Gītā as "clearly ... rewritten by a modernising hand." Oldenberg, too, thinks it likely that the earliest Gītā concluded with II, 38, and that Adhyāyas XIII-XVIII are an appendix or appendices (*NGGW*. 1919, 333 f., 336 f.). See also Strauss, *Ethische Probleme*, pp. 312 f.

3. H. Jacobi (*ZDMG*. 72, 1918, 323 ff.) has endeavoured to trace in the poem those verses (of *Adhyāyas* I and II) which belonged to the old epic. But

originally, by its very nature, a text of the Bhāgavatas, wherein the doctrine of bhakti in conjunction with the yoga doctrine of desireless action was taught on the foundation of the Sāṃkhya. There is evidence from inscriptions that, as early as the beginning of the 2nd century B.C. the religion of the Bhāgavatas had found adherents even among the Greeks in Gāndhāra.[1] It is perhaps not too bold to assume that the old Bhagavadgītā was written at about this time as an Upaniṣad of the Bhāgavatas.[2] Its language, style and metre, too, prove the work to be one of the earlier parts of the Mahābhārata. There are references to the Gītā in later sections of the epic,[3] and the *Anugītā* (XIV, 16-51) is surely nothing but a late imitation and continuation of the Bhagavadgītā, than which it contains a still greater variety of doctrines.

The Bhagavadgītā was already known to the poet Bāṇa (in the 7th century A.D.) as a portion of the Mahābhārata,[4] and side by side with the Upaniṣads and Vedānta-sūtras it formed one of the foundations of the philosophy of Śaṅkara. Most likely it was already in the early centuries A.D. that it received its present form at the hands of orthodox Brahmins; in this form it became and has remained until today the most popular religious book for all Hindus. The work owes this great popularity to the very circumstance that the most conflicting philosophical doctrines and religious views are united in it, so that adherents of all schools and sects could make use of it, and even today the

it is not impossible that there was no dialogue whatsoever between *Kṛṣṇa* and *Arjuna* in the old heroic poem, and that the whole poem was originally a text independent of the epic, an *Upaniṣad*, which was inserted bodily into the epic.

1. See J. H. Marshall, *JRAS.* 1909, pp. 1053 ff.; J. F. Fleet. ibid. 1087 ff.; D. R. Bhandarkar, *JBRAS.* 23,1910, 104 ff.; R. G. Bhandarkar, *Ind. Ant.* 41, 1912, pp. 13 ff.; *Vaiṣṇavism, Śaivism,* etc., pp. 3 f.; H; Raychaudhuri, *Early History of the Vaiṣṇava Sect*, Calcutta, 1920, pp. 13, 52 f., 58 ff.

2. According to K. T. Telang (*SBE.*, Vol. 8, p. 34) the Gītā is "earlier than the third century B. C.," according to R. G. Bhandarkar (*Vaiṣṇavism, Śaivism,* etc., p. 13) it is "not later than the beginning of the fourth century B.C." Edgerton is right when he says (ibid. p. 3): "All that we can say is that it was probably composed before the beginning of our era, but not more than a few centuries before it."

3. XII, 346, 11 with "Harigītāḥ" and XII, 348, 8.

4. K. T. Telang, *SBE.*, Vol. 8, p. 28.

strictest Brahmin is just as much edified by it as the adherent of the Brahmo-Samaj and the believing theosophist under the leadership of Annie Besant.

It is scarcely possible, however, that the Bhagavadgītā can have arisen from the start on the basis of syncretism, as the latter only made its appearance more and more in later times. It is certain that the old and authentic Gītā was the work of a true and great poet. It is on the strength of its poetic value, the forcefulness of its language, the splendour of the images and metaphors, the breath of inspiration which pervades the poem, that it has made such a deep impression on impressionable minds of all ages; and we are convinced that the poetical beauties as well as the moral value of the poem would find still greater appreciation, had the poem not been mutilated by additions and interpolations.[1]

Another text-book of the Bhāgavatas is the Nārāyaṇīya (XII, 334-51); this is certainly a later work than the Bhagavadgītā, but even this has been augmented by additions.[2] It is a work in true purāṇa style, which teaches that perfection can only be attained by bhakti and the grace of God, who appears here under the name of Nārāyaṇa. Here, too, we find the Bhāgavata religion and the philosophy of Sāṃkhya and Yoga mingled with Vedānta ideas. The paradise of the pious devotees of Nārāyaṇa, Śvetadvīpa or "the white island," is described in very fantastical fashion:

The sage Nārada desires to look upon the only god Nārāyaṇa, whose faithful worshipper he is, in his original nature. He therefore raises himself aloft by the strength of yoga, and reaches the divine mountain Meru. Gazing thence to the north-west, he espies north of the ocean of milk the famous "white island"

1. Attention has often been called to the fact that, notwithstanding the many beauties and lofty thoughts, the poem has many weak points. Cf. O. Böhtlingk, Bemerkungen zur Bhagavadgītā (*BSGW.*, 1897); E. W. Hopkins, *Religions of India*, pp. 390, 399 f., quoted in assent by R. Garbe, *Die Bhagavadgītā*, p. 16; and V.K. Rajwade, *Bhandarkar Com. Vol.*, pp. 325 ff.

2. See R. G. Bhandarkar, *Vaiṣṇavism, Śaivism*, etc. pp. 4 ff., Grierson, *Ind. Ant.* 37, 1908, 251 ff., 373 ff. Translated into German by Deussen, *Philosophische Texte des Mahābhāratam*, pp. 748 ff., into Dutch by C. Lecoutere in *Mélanges Charles de Harlez*, Leyden 1896, pp.162 ff.

lying 32,000 yojanas from Meru. On this island he sees "white men without sense organs, who take no nourishment, whose eyes do not blink, from whom a most pleasant scent emanates, who are free from all sin, at the sight of whom evil men are dazzled. whose bodies are of bone, hard as diamond, who are indifferent both to honour and scorn, like unto the children of heaven in form, endowed with shining strength, with heads in the shape of sunshades. Their voice resembles the rushing of torrents of rain, they have four equal testicles, feet like lotus-leaves, sixty white teeth and eight fangs; they lick their sun-like faces with their tongues, and all full of love for God."[1]

It seems evident that the "white island" as well as the divine mountain Meru and the ocean of milk, belong to the province of mythology, and not to that of historical geography. A few scholars have, however, tried to identify the ocean of milk with Lake Issyk-Kul or Lake Balkash, and the "white island" with a land of "white men" in the north, inhabited by Nestorian Christians,[2] so that we should have to assume that there was Christian influence in the Nārāyaṇīya. But the description of Śvetadvīpa does not remind us of the Christian Eucharist, but of heavenly regions such as Vaikuṇṭha, Goloka, Kailāsa and the Sukhavatī paradise of the Buddha Amitābha.

Though Sāṁkhya and Yoga stand in the foreground of most of the philosophical sections of the Mahābhārata, we nevertheless find everywhere interpolated passages where the Vedānta is taught, and a few longer passages like the *Sanatsujātiya* (V, 41-46) have been inserted with an entirely Vedantist teaching.[3]

---

1. XII, 335, 6-12. A tongue of this kind also belongs to the 32 characteristics of a Buddha, who, however, has only forty white teeth, e. g. *Suttanipāta, Selasutta* (*SBE.*, Vol. 10, II, p. 101).

2. Cf. J. Kennedy, *JRAS*. 1907, 481 f., R. Garbe, *AR*. 16, 1913, 516 ff., and *Indien und das Christentum*, Tübingen 1914, pp. 192 ff., Grierson, *ERE*. II, p. 549. On the other hand, see Winternitz, *Oesterreich. Monatsschrift füdenr Orient*, 41, 1915, pp. 185 f., and H. Raychaudhuri, *Early History of the Vaishnava Sect*, pp. 79 ff.

3. For the philosophical doctrines contained in the Mahābhārata, see E. W. Hopkins, *The Great Epic of India*, pp. 85-190, J. Dahlmann, *Die Sāṃkhya-Philosophie als Naturlehre und Erlösungslehre nach dem Mahābhārata*, Berlin 1902, P. Deussen, *AGPh* I, 3, pp. 8-144. Contrary to Deussen and Dahlmann,

However, as regards poetical value, there is none of the philosophical sections of the Mahābhārata which could bear the least comparison with the Bhagavadgītā.

As against this we find many beautiful flowers of Indian poetics in those didactic pieces which are concerned with ethical questions, for example with the frequently debated question of the relationship between destiny and human action (*karman*) or which contains general moral teachings without the least regard for any philosophical or religious views of the richness of beauty and wisdom which is concealed in these sayings of the Mahābhārata, the following translations may give at least a small specimen;

"A wound caused by arrows is healed leaving behind only a scar, a forest felled by the axe grows again, but a wound cut by speech — a detestable, wicked speech — does not heal again".

"Of the man whom the gods want to ruin, they rob the brains, then he sees everything upside down".

"The gods protect not like the shepherd with the stick in his hand, but whom they want to protect, to him they give intelligence".

"He who speaks no wounding words, nor lets them be spoken; he who although beaten does not beat back, nor cause to be beaten back, he who does not seek to beat even the wicked man, him do the gods yearn to see".

"Another man enjoys the wealth of the deceased (one), birds and fire consume the constituents of his body; only with these two does he go to the other world — with his good and evil deeds, which always accompany him".

"Friends, relatives and sons leave the dead man and go home, as birds turn away from trees devoid of flowers and fruits. But the act that he himself has committed, follows him when he is thrown into the fire. Therefore man should, to the best of his energy, collect by and by good deeds."

---

it is wrong to speak of an "epic philosophy" as a "transition philosophy" between the philosophy of the *Upaniṣads* and that of the later systems. The epic proper has no connection with philosophy at all, and the "pseudo-epics" contains a mixture of philosophical doctrines belonging to widely different times.

"Good it is, to speak the truth: there is nothing higher than the truth. Through the truth everything is maintained in order; on the truth is everything founded.

Even criminal robbers are bound to truth among themselves and avoid, based on it, betrayal and quarrel; if they did not practise truth among themselves, they would be certainly ruined".

"From all sides the thief fears danger as a wild animal that has come into a village; as he himself does so much evil, he expects it also from others.

Always and every where the pure one goes merrily and fearlessly, for as he himself does nothing bad, so he expects also nothing evil from others".

"What a man does not wish that others may—do (it) to him that let him not do also to others, as he knows how unpleasant it is to him."[1]

The Harivaṁśa, an Appendix to the Mahābhārata[2]

The explanations of the preceding chapters must be sufficient, to give an idea of the variegated contents of the 18 books (Parvans) of the Mahābhārata. But the Indians consider the Harivaṁśa, a work which is in reality a purāṇa and also occasionally called "Harivaṁśa Purāṇa", also as a constituent of the Mahābhārata. Yet the book is considered even by the Indians not as a 19th Parvan but as a Khila, i.e., as a supplement or Appendix to the Mahābhārata. Now this "appendix is certainly a work of 16374 couplets (ślokas), and therefore longer than the Ilias and the Odyssee put together. Still its literary importance is not at all proportional to its volume. It is above all no "poetry", in no sense the work of any poet but a heaping up or very loosely arranging side by side of texts—legends, myths, hymns—which serve to glorify God Viṣṇu. The Harivaṁśa is

---

V. 33,77; 80; 34, 41; 35,11; 39, 16-18; xii 258, 10 f; 15 f; 19. See also above p. 296 f, 320 f, 323, 357, 359-362.

2. Cf. A. Holtzman, *Das Mahābhārata* II, p. 272-298, and E. W. Hopkins, Gleanings from the Harivaṁśa in *Festschrift Windisch*, p. 68. There is a French translation of this appendix by S. A. Langlois: *Harivamsa ou histoire de la famille de Hari*, Paris 1834-1835.

also not the work of one compiler. The last third of it is certainly a later appendix to the appendix and in the remaining parts of the work also many pieces have been probably inserted later at quite different times.

The connection of the Harivaṁśa to the Mahābhārata itself is largely an external one and is limited in essence to this, that the same Vaiśaṁpāyana who is supposed to have recited to Janamejaya the whole Mahābhārata[1] is also considered to be the reciter of the Harivaṁśa. Connected with the frame-narrative of the Mahābhārata Śaunaka requests Ugraśravas at the beginning of the appendix that he may tell him now after he has told him all the nice stories about the Bharatas, also something about the Vṛṣṇis and Andhakas — about the families to which Kṛṣṇa belongs. Thereupon Ugraśravas remarks, exactly the same request was made by Janamejaya to Vaiśaṁpāyana after the recital of the Mahābhārata and the latter told at once all that he will tell now. Thus all that follows now is attributed to Vaiśaṁpāyana. Moreover, in some verses in the beginning and in the whole of one long canto at the close of the appendix[2] the praise of the Mahābhārata including the Harivaṁśa is sung in extravagant verses and the religious merit is stressed which one acquires by reciting and hearing the whole poem. This exhausts actually everything which characterises Harivaṁśa as belonging to the Mahābhārata. In the matter of contents the Harivaṁśa has nothing more common than the Purāṇas have with the Mahābhārata. There are of course many legends, especially Brahminic legends and myths which occur in the Mahābhārata which are also found in various versions in the Harivaṁśa as well as in the Purāṇas.

The Harivaṁśa consists of three big parts, of which the first is entitled "Harivaṁśaparvan". The title "Harivaṁśa", i.e. "lineage of Hari"[3] which is given to the whole appendix is suitable only to this first book. It begins in the manner of the Purāṇas with a rather confused version of the story of creation

1. See p. 303 above.
2. Adhyāya 323.
3. Of the innumerable names of God Viṣṇu, Hari is one of the most frequent.

and all kinds of mythological stories, for example of Dhruva who became the Pole Star (62 ff), of Dakṣa and his daughters, of the ancestresses of gods and demons (101 ff) etc. Exhaustive stories are told of the Titan Vena, an enemy of the Veda and the sacrifice and of his son Pṛthu the first king of men.[1] In the genealogy of the solar dynasty (545 ff) i.e., of the king Ikṣvāku and his descendants, who trace their origin back to the Sun-god numerous legends are included, for example, that of Viśvāmitra and Vasiṣṭha (706 ff). Out of all context of this genealogy we find here a ritual piece on the manes and the sacrificial services due to them.[2] Then follows (1312 ff) the genealogy of the lunar dynasty which was founded by Atri the son of the moon god (Soma). A grandson of Soma was the famous Purūravas whose amorous adventures with Urvaśī are narrated in an antiquarian form rather closely connected with the Śatapatha-Brāhmaṇa.[3] To the descendents of Purūravas belong Nahuṣa and Yayāti. The latter's son Yadu is the ancestor of the Yādavas of whom Vasudeva is one, and as his son Kṛṣṇa the god Viṣṇu has been born on the earth. After the genealogy of the earthly Kṛṣṇa has been given, there follow a series of songs (2131 ff) which are wholly concerned with God Viṣṇu and so contain in a certain way the divine history of Kṛṣṇa previous to this stage.

The second great part of the Harivaṁśa entitled Viṣṇupurāṇa[4] is concerned almost exclusively with Kṛṣṇa, the incarnation of god Viṣṇu. At great length all the stories are told of the birth and childhood, of the heroic deeds and love adventures of the human, sometimes all too human cowherd-god: All these stories are told with more or less exhaustiveness also in some of the Purāṇas and they have made the name of Kṛṣṇa one of the names most familiar to every Hindu. Whereas the best and

1. Pṛthūpākhyāna, Adhy. 4-6 verses 257-405.

2. "Pitṛkalpa" (Manes-rituals) Adhy. 16-24. vss. 835-1311. Interpolated is the story of Brahmadatta who understands the languages of animals. Adhy. 21. vss. 1185 ff translated and discussed by Th. Benfey in *Orient and Occident* vol. II, 1862 p. 133-71, and by Leumann, *WZKM.*, 6, 1892, pp. 1 ff.

3. Adhy. 26 verses 1363-1414—translated by K. Geldner in the "*Vedische Studien*". I, p. 249 ff. of above p. 193 f.

4. Adhya. 57 ff—vss. 3180 ff.

wisest among the Viṣṇu-worshippers adore Kṛṣṇa above all as the proclaimer of the pious teachings of the Bhagavadgītā, it is the Kṛṣṇa of the legends as they are narrated in the Harivaṁśa and in the Purāṇas, who is worshipped and prayed to by the millions of the actual folk in the whole of India upto the present day sometimes as a supreme God, and sometimes esteemed as an ideal of the perfect humanness. And it is also just this God of the legends but not the Kṛṣṇa of the Mahābhārata, the treacherous, hypocritical friend of the Pāṇḍavas. of whom already the Greek Megasthenes speaks as of the "Indian Hercules". In order to give an idea of these Kṛṣṇa-legends which are equally important from the point of view of the history of literature as that of the history of religion, we may sketch here very briefly the contents of this second part of the Harivaṁśa:[1]

In the town of Mathura[2] a wicked King named Kaṃsa was reigning. He was informed by Nārada that he would be killed by the eighth son of Devakī, his father's sister and wife of Vasudeva. So Kaṃsa decides to kill all the children of Devakī. He places Devakī under strict supervision of his servants and six of her children are killed immediately after birth. The 7th child — it is Kṛṣṇa's brother who is better known as "Rāma with the ploughshare", "Balarāma" or "Baladeva"—is saved by Nidrā[3] the goddess of sleep who transplants the boy even before his birth from the womb of Devakī into that of Rohiṇī, another wife of Vasudeva. However, in order to save his eighth child (and this was Kṛṣna) from Kaṃsa Vasudeva himself replaced him by the daughter of the cowherd Nanda and Yaśodā who was born at the same time. Thus this child is

1. Cf. E. Windisch, "on the Drama of Mṛchakaṭika and the Kṛṣṇa-legend in *Berichte über die Verhand. der Kgl. Sachsischen Gesellschaft der Wiss. Zu. Leipzig, phil.-histor. el.*" 37 Vol. 1885, P. 439 ff 456 ff.

2. Even to-day the temples of Mathura are full of statues which relate to the Kṛṣṇa-legend. Cf. P. Deussen, *Erinnerungen an Indian* (Kiel and Leipzig 1904), p. 112.

3. Perhaps the fact that Nidrā is also considered as a name of Durgā caused the interpolation of a hymn to this goddess. Āryāstava (Adhy. 59—vss 3268-3303). Of course the interpolations of such hymns (stories) is characteristic of all Purāṇas.

smashed to death on a rock by Kaṃsa while Kṛṣṇa grows up among the cowherds as the son of a cowherd.

Rāma is also entrusted to the care of the same family and both boys grow up together in the village of cowherds. Even as child Kṛṣṇa performs miraculous deeds. Once when his foster-mother Yaśodā makes him wait too long for food while he was lying under a cart, he begins to kick impatiently with his hands and feet and with one foot finally throws the big cart upside down. On some other day after this the two boys Kṛṣṇa and Rāma in the high spirits of their wantonness wander through the fields and forests and cause no small worry to the simple cowherd's wife that Yaśodā is. Once she does not know in her despair what to do and ties the little Kṛṣṇa with a string round the belly tightly to a heavy mortar saying in her anger, "Now run, if you can!" The boy however, drags away not only the mortar with himself, but as it is obstructed by two huge trees between which it is dragged, he uproots them too and drags them along. With great amazement the cowherds and the foster mother see that the boy is sitting laughing in the midst of the branches of the trees. He is not in the least hurt.

After seven years had passed, life in the village of cowherds seemed too uninteresting for the boys. So Kṛṣṇa made wolves issue out from his body which frightened the cowherds so much that they decided to wander further. They moved with their cattle to the Vṛndā-forest. Here the boys are moving about gaily through the forest. One day he strolls about alone-singing and playing, whistling on a leaf, playing on the flute on the bank of the river Jumnā and reaches a deep lake in which Kāliṅga, the serpant king lives who with all his courtiers makes the water of Jumnā poisonous and menaces the whole region. Quickly resolving Kṛṣṇa jumps into the lake to vanquish the terrible dragon. Immediately the five-headed fire-splitting monster appears and an army of snakes rushes towards the young hero, surrounding and biting him. He however frees himself from them, presses the head of the monster to the ground and springs energetically on to the central head of the monster so that the dragon surrenders and withdraws with the entire serpent-race into the ocean.

Soon after he kills also the demon Dhenuka, who in the form of a donkey is guarding the mountain Govardhana. Another demon, the giant Pralamba avoids Kṛṣṇa at the beginning, but is killed in the end by his brother Rāma.

In the autumn season the cowherds want to arrange as usual a great festival in honour of Indra the rain-god. Kṛṣṇa is against this honour to Indra. We are herdsmen wandering through the forest and live by our cattle wealth; cows are our gods, the mountains and the forests" (3808). With such speeches he exhorts the herdsmen, to perform a sacrifice to the mountain instead of a festival to Indra. This makes Indra so angry that he sends down a terrible storm. But Kṛṣṇa lifts up the Govardhana mountain and holds him as an Umbrella over the heads of the herds and herdsmen so that they are all fully protected. After seven days the storm stops. Kṛṣṇa puts the mountain back in its place and Indra humbly recognises in Kṛṣṇa the exalted God Viṣṇu.

Then the herdsmen praise and worship him as a God, but he says smilingly that he wants to be only their kinsman and the time will come when they would recognize his true nature. And as a herdsman amongst herdsmen he spends his time in youthful gaiety. He organises bull fighting and competitions among the strongest of the herdsmen. But in the beautiful autumn nights his heart enjoys the round-dances[1] performed in the moonlight by the herdsmen's pretty daughters, who are all in love with the youth, singing the glory of his deeds and imitate merrily his acts and his sports — his joyous looks, his singing, his dancing and his songs.

Once as Kṛṣṇa was enjoying himself with the damsels of his village, Ariṣṭa, a demon appeared in the form of a bullock. Kṛṣṇa breaks one of his horns and kills him with it.

The fame of all these heroic deeds of Kṛṣṇa reaches Kaṃsa's ears and causes him worry. In order to render him harmless he makes the two young heroes come to Mathura where they

1. There are dances called Rāsa or Halliśa accompanied by mini-performances which are performed even to-day in some parts of India and are still known in Kathiawad by a name corresponding to the Sanskrit name of "Halliśa (cf. the Indian monthly *East and West*, Vol. I, 748 f, May 1902).

should contest with his best wrestlers during a festival. But no sooner did they arrive in the town than Kṛṣṇa performed miraculous deeds and acts of strength. Thus he bent the great royal bow which even the gods could not bend, with such great power that it broke into pieces with a loud noise. When an elephant was let loose by Kaṃsa on the youths, Kṛṣṇa broke its tusk and killed it with it. Also the two wrestlers who were sent by Kaṃsa to oppose the lads were killed by them.

Fiery with rage the king now orders that all the cowherds and their lads be expelled from his kingdom. Then Kṛṣṇa springs like a lion on Kaṃsa, drags him by the hair into the midst of the arena and kills him.

After a time the two brothers go to Ujjain to learn the art of archery from a famous teacher there. A son of this teacher had died in the sea and the teacher asks Kṛṣṇa to bring this son back to him as his tuition fee. So Kṛṣṇa descends to the nether-world, vanquishes the god of death Yama and brings the boy back to his father.

To take vengeance for the death of Kaṃsa his father-in-law Jarāsandha with many allies goes to war with the Yādavas, besieges Mathura but he is beaten back by Kṛṣṇa again and again. However he repeats his attacks again and again until he is at last forced to withdraw. These battles with Jarāsandha are described in a long series of songs.

Similarly the following story of the abduction of Rukmiṇī is also woven very elaborately.[1] King Bhīṣmaka of Vidarbha promised to give his daughter Rukmiṇī in marriage to king Śiśupāla and the wedding was to be performed. Then Kṛṣṇa comes with his brother Rāma to the wedding ceremony and kidnaps the bride. The princes, seriously insulted by this, chase him but are thrown back by Rāma. Rukmin, the brother of the kidnapped swears that he will not go back to his home town without killing Kṛṣṇa and getting his sister back. A violent fight ensues in which Rukmin is defeated; on being requested by Rukmiṇī however Kṛṣṇa spares his life. In order to be faithful to his vow Rukmin founds a new town. In

1. In the old legend in which Kṛṣṇa appears as hero, later pieces are interpolated in which he appears as god Viṣṇu in his entire godliness.

Dvārakā Kṛṣṇa's marriage with Rukmiṇī takes place. He has ten sons by her but then he marries seven more queens and 16,000 other women with whom he begets thousands of sons. Pradyumna,[1] a son of Kṛṣṇa and Rukmiṇī later marries a daughter of Rukmin and their son Aniruddha marries a grand daughter of Rukmin. During the marriage of Aniruddha a quarrel breaks out between Rāma and Rukmin while they are at a play of dice and the latter is killed by Rāma. On this follows a glorification of Rāma's deeds.[2]

Then follows the story of the killing of Naraka.[3] This Naraka is a demon who has robbed Aditi of her ear-rings and who has also caused great trouble to the gods. On being requested by Indra, Kṛṣṇa fights against him and kills him.

The next story[4] shows us Kṛṣṇa in war against Indra. The sage Nārada once brought to Kṛṣṇa a flower of the celestial tree Pārijāta, which Kṛṣṇa then presented to his beloved wife Rukmiṇī. Then one of his other wives Satyabhāmā becomes jealous and is sulky until Kṛṣṇa promises her to bring the entire Pārijāta-tree from Heaven. But as Indra does not part with the tree willingly, Kṛṣṇa challenges him to a battle. This leads to a long violent fighting between the two gods—which is settled amicably by the divine mother Aditi.

Only loosely connected with this long chapter there follows a rather long and extensive piece[5] which really belongs to scientific erotics, to the Kāmaśāstra. It is an instruction (in the form of a conversation between the wives of Kṛṣṇa and the sage Nārada who quotes the authority of Umā, the consort of Śiva) in the observance of Puṇyakas and Vratakas, i.e., of ceremonies, celebrations and vows by means of which a wife can make her body pleasant to her husband and ensure his favour to herself. But as these ceremonies can be used successfully only by virtuous women they are preceded by some teachings on the duties of wives (7754 ff).

1. He is an incarnation of the God of Love.
2. Baladevamāhātmyakathana, Adhy. 120, 6766-6786.
3. Narakavadha, Adhyāyas 121-123—6787-6988.
4. Pārijātaharaṇa, Adhy. 124-140—6989-7956 A hymn to Śiva (Mahādevastavana), Adhy. 131—7415 to 7455 is interpolated.
5. Puṇyakavidhi, Adhy. 136-140—vers. 7722-7956.

Again the next chapter[1] tells about the battles of Kṛṣṇa with the demons. The Asuras of the six towns (Ṣaṭpura) rob the pious Brahmadatta of his daughter. Kṛṣṇa comes to his rescue, defeats and kills Nikumbha the king of Asuras and gives his daughter back to the Brahmin.

Then follows a completely sivite piece[2] which has nothing at all to do with Kṛṣṇa and tells how the thousand-headed demon Andhaka is killed by Śiva.

The following chapter[3] comes back to Kṛṣṇa again and tells another story of the killing of Asura Nikumbha. The Yādavas with Kṛṣṇa and Rāma at their head undertake a pilgrimage to a sacred place of bathing on the sea-shore in order to celebrate a festival of gaiety there. Kṛṣṇa with his 16000 wives, Rāma with his only wife Revatī and the Yādava youths with thousands of mistresses indulge in all sorts of pleasures in water and on the sea shore to the accompaniment of playing, singing, eating and drinking.[4] In the course of these festivities the demon Nikumbha abducts Bhānumatī, a daughter of the Yādavas Bhanu Krishna's son, Pradyumna chases the Asura and brings back the abducted while Kṛṣṇa himself kills Nikumbha.

The Cantos following this[5] are concerned almost exclusively with Pradyumna, the son of Kṛṣṇa. At first the story of Pradyumna's marriage with Prabhāvatī, the daughter of the Asura Vajranābha is told, in which the celestial flamingoes bring about the marriage just as in the Nala-song flamingoes are the love messengers between Nala and Damayantī. In order to win Prabhāvatī, Pradyumna comes disguised as an actor along with a dramatic troupe to the court of Vajranābha. Then all sorts of dramas are enacted[6] by which the Asuras

1. Ṣaṭpuravadha, Adhy. 141-144—vers. 7957-8198.

2. Andhakavadha, Adhy. 145 f —vers. 8199-8300.

3. Bhānumatīharaṇa, Adhy. 147-149—vers. 8301-8549.

4. The splendid description of this voluptuous scenes fills two cantos (147 f=8301-8470).

5. Adhy. 150 ff=vers 8550 ff. Freely translated into German in the beautiful poem "Pradyumna" by Schack. *Stimmen von Ganges*, p. 67 ff.

6. This 8672 ff. is perhaps one of the oldest, and in any case the most interesting mention of dramas and dramatical performances in the Indian

are completely charmed. Pradyumna however uses the cosy nights for indulging in the enjoyment of love with Prabhāvatī. At last Vajranābha hears about the love-affair; enraged he wants to have Pradyumna bound in fetters. But the latter kills the approaching warriors and the Asura king himself. Then he comes to Dvārakā with his beloved.

The second story[1] deals with the early love of Pradyumna; how he is kidnapped, just seven days after birth, by the Asuras and grows up in the house of the demon Śambara; how the latter's wife Māyāvatī is consumed with love for this beautiful youth and discloses to him that he is not her son but of Kṛṣṇa and Rukmiṇī; then Pradyumna kills Śambara in a desperate fight[2] and united at last with Māyāvatī he comes back to his home-town where he is happily received by his parents.

Here without any obvious relationship, there is an interpolation of the daily prayer of Rāma[3] a litany consisting of an enumeration of divine beings.

After a few smaller pieces — legends and speeches — which serve to glorify Kṛṣṇa, the book comes to a close with the story of the "Battle with Bāṇa"[4] and of the love-affair of Aniruddha; the son of Pradyumna with Uṣā the daughter of the Asura-king Bāṇa. The latter is a favourite of God Śiva. When Aniruddha is oppressed by Bāṇa, Kṛṣṇa, comes to his rescue; and the fighting against Bāṇa leads to a violent fighting between Śiva and Viṣṇu, by which the whole world is threatened terribly. But Brahman comes to the rescue of the world and establishes peace between the two gods by explaining that Śiva and Viṣṇu are one and the same. There follows a hymn (stotra)

literature. Here not only scenes from the life of Kṛṣṇa are enacted, but there is also a clear mention of dramatising the great epic *Rāmāyaṇa* and of the story of *Ṛṣyaśṛṅga* (cf. p. 384 ff. above). Unfortunately the age of this piece called *Pradyumnottara* is very uncertain. Cf. Sylvian Levi, *Le Théatre Indien*, Paris 1890, p. 327 ff., and also A. B. Keith, *The Sanskrit Drama*, Oxford 1924, pp. 28, 47 f.

1. Śambaravadha, Adhy. 163-167=verses 9208-9487.

2. In this, Durgā whom he invokes with a hymn Pradyumnakṛta-Durgāstava, (Adhy. 166=verses 9422-9430) helps him.

3. Baladevāhnika, Adhy. 168=verses 9488-9591.

4. Bāṇayuddha, Adhy. 175-190=verses 9806-11062.

for glorifying these two as identical deities.[1] The book ends with the wedding of Aniruddha with Uṣā which is celebrated in a splendid manner in Dvāravatī.

The interweaving of stotras (hymns) as the one here on Viṣṇu-Śiva, shows in particular how largely the Harivaṁśa is a collection of texts for religious purposes and not an epic poetry.[2]

But whereas in the second book there are certainly some remnants of a Kṛṣṇa-epic which might have likewise existed once, the third book called the "Bhaviṣya-Parvan" (11063 ff) is only a loose collection of Purāṇa-texts. The title "Bhaviṣya-parvan" that is "Chapter of the future" relates only to the earlier cantos of this book which contains predictions on the coming world-epoques. Here we are told of a horse-sacrifice that Janamejaya wanted to perform; but Vyāsa forecasts that this sacrifice will not come to a successful end because a godless epoque will begin only long after which the Kṛta-epoque of virtue and piety will follow. This chapter[3] forms a compact whole and is also described as an independent poem. This is followed by two different creation-stories without any context.[4] A third chapter treats very exhaustively the incarnations of Viṣṇu as wild-boar, man lion and dwarf.[5] Then follows a chapter which like the last of the II book follows the tendency

1. Hariharātmakastava, Adhy. 184=verses 10660-10697. This is one of the few places in the Indian literature where there is mention of the Trimūrti. For Hari (Viṣṇu) and Hara (Śiva) are not only with each other identical but also with Brahman.

2. How great is the honour given to the Harivaṁśa as a religious book is shown by the fact that it is a custom in the lawcourts of Nepal to place a copy of Harivaṁśa on the head of the witness if he is a Hindu as a copy of the Koran is placed on the head of a Mohammadon (A. Berth, *Religions of India*, p. 156 note).

3. Adhy. 191-196=verses 11063-11278. This piece (11270 ff) is praised as a great kāvyam (Mahākāvyam). But even the verses 11082 ff say clearly that the Harivaṁśa has ended and that the story of Janamejaya's horse-sacrifice forms only an appendix to the Harivaṁśa. The chapters following this are certainly only later additions.

4. Pauṣkaraprādurbhāva, Adhy. 197-222=verses 11279 to 12277.

5. Adhy. 223-263=verses 12278-14390. A hymn to Viṣṇu (Viṣṇustotra) 12880 ff (Adhy. 238) is begun by Brahman. A hymn in prose to the "great spirit" (Mahāpuruṣastava) is sung by Kaśyapa 1414 ff (Adhy. 259).

of reconciling the worship of Viṣṇu and of Śiva with each other. In turns Viṣṇu and Śiva sing a hymn on each other.[1] Again the next piece deals with a heroic deed of Kṛṣṇa namely the killing of King Pauṇḍra who rebels against Kṛṣṇa.[2] The last big chapter of Harivaṁśa is the legend (Upākhyāna) of the two Śiva-Worshippers Haṃsa and Ḍimbhaka, who are humiliated by Kṛṣṇa-Viṣṇu.[3]

Further one more long canto is added which speaks in the most extravagant language of the religious merit of reading the Mahābhārata and of the reward that is waiting in heaven for the reader. This canto also prescribes the presents that should be given to those who read out (vācaka) each parvan on completing the reading. Finally the canto ends in a song which brings the glory of the Mahābhārata as the most sacred and exalted of all textbooks (śāstra).[4] Above all it is said in praise of this work that it served the glorification of Viṣṇu for: "In the Veda, in the Rāmāyaṇa, in the holy Bhārata, O bravest child of Bhārata, everywhere in the beginning, in the end and in the middle, Hari's glory is sung."[5]

Strangely enough there follows after all the glorifications of Viṣṇu and after the book has actually already come to an end, one more Canto[6] in which God Śiva is praised and it is told how he has destroyed the three fortresses (Tripura) of the demons. Of course even here a concluding verse is added in praise of the "great Yogin" Viṣṇu.

The book finally closes with a short summary of the contents of the Harivaṁśa and an enumeration of the religious merits that one acquires by hearing this "Purāṇa".

---

1. Kailāsayātrā, Adhy. 264-281=verses 14391-15031. Adhy. 278. Īśvarastuti, Adhy. 279 and 281; Viṣṇustotra.
2. Pauṇḍrakavadha, Adhy. 282-293=verses 15032-15375.
3. Haṃsaḍimbhakopākhyāna, Adhy, 294-322=verses 15376 to 16139.
4. Adhy. 323=verses 16140-16238: Sarvaparvānukīrttana. The enumeration of the Parvans contains partly other names than as given out by our editions. The contents of this Adhyāya is connected to similar songs of praise in the I book of the Mahābhārata. cf. above p. 304 f.
5. Verse 16232.
6. Tripuravadha, Adhy. 324=verses 16239-16324.

That the Harivaṁśa is wholly and entirely a Purāṇa is also shown by its numerous and often verbatim agreements with many of the most important Purāṇas.[1] It was nevertheless necessary to speak about the Harivaṁśa here and not wait till the chapter on the Purāṇas, not only because this work is considered by the Indians as a part of the Mahābhārata but also because just this supplement and its addition is specially suited for throwing light on the history of the Mahābhārata itself. We will now turn out attention to this history.

The Age and the History of the Mahābhārata

We have now given a survey of all that has been handed down to us in manuscripts and publications on "Mahābhārata" and are now faced with the question: How and when did this huge work originate ?

The reader must have already noticed even in the short summary of the actual hero-poetry (p. 307-60) a contradiction that becomes still more prominent while reading the Mahābhārata itself, whereas the poem in its present form throughout supports the stand of the Pāṇḍavas and describes the Pāṇḍava-heroes not only as extremely courageous but also noble and good, and on the other hand paints the Kauravas as deceptive and wicked, — the poem tells us, strangely contradicting itself, that all the Kaurava-heroes have been killed in the war by treacherous and dishonest means.[2] It is still more conspicuous that all treachery comes from Kṛṣṇa that he is the originator of all deception and defends the conduct of the Pāṇḍavas. And it is the same Kṛṣṇa who is praised and glorified as in the Harivaṁśa as an incarnation of the highest God Viṣṇu and as a true ideal and model of all virtues.

How are these strange contradictions to be explained ? We can only make some presumptions regarding this. Firstly, perhaps the presumption is justified, although it is supported only by the Mahābhārata itself, that once in northwestern India a change

1. Brahma-, Padma-, Viṣṇu-, Bhāgavata and especially Vāyu-Purāṇa. The Garuḍa-Purāṇa gives the contents of the Mahābhārata and of the Harivaṁśa in extracts. See A. Holtzmann, "*Das Mahābhārata,*" IV p. 32, 35, 37 ff, 40, 42 ff, 47 ff, 56.

2. See p. 344 f, 348, 350, 351 above.

of dynasty has taken place as a result of a terrific battle and that these quasi-historical events form the basis for the actual epic.[1] Proceeding from this we can very well imagine that the original hero-songs which treated the battle of the hostile cousins, were sung in the circles of bards who were close sympathisers of Duryodhana himself or of the house of the Kauravas; but that in course of time, as the power of the victorious Pāṇḍavas grew stronger and stronger these songs went over into the possession of bards who were in the service of the new rulers. In the mouths of these bards those changes were made which made the Pāṇḍavas appear in a favourable and the Kauravas in an unfavourable light, without changing very much the original tendency of the songs. In our Mahābhārata the nucleus of the epic, the description of the great battle, is attributed to Sañjaya, the chariot-driver of Dhṛtarāṣṭra i.e. to a bard of the Kauravas. But precisely in these battle-scenes the Kauravas appear in a favourable light. On the other hand the whole Mahābhārata itself is recited according to the framework — narrative of Vaiśampāyana, the disciple of Vyāsa during the serpent-sacrifice. But Janamejaya is considered as a great grand son of Arjuna, the Pāṇḍava, which agrees with this that in the Mahābhārata as a whole the Pāṇḍav as are given preference over the Kauravas.[2]

---

1. Even those who believe to find a mythological kernel in the saga (legend) which is the basis for the epic, admit that historical elements are also in it. Thus A. Ludwig, on the relation of the mythical elements to the historical basis of the Mahābhārata (*Abhandlungen der K. böhmischen Ges. d. Wissensch* VI. 12 : Über das Verhältnis des mythischen Elementes zu der historischen Grundlage des Mahābhārata.) Prague, 1884. Pargiter and Grierson (*JRAS.*, 1908, pp. 309 ff., 602 ff.) have expressed the opinion that, underlying the war between the Kauravas and the Pāṇḍavas there may be the historical fact of a battle of nations (a fight between the nations of Madhyadeśa and the other nations of India) and at the same time a fight between a warrior party on the one side and a priestly party on the other. There is no justification of this historical construction. Cf. Hopkins, *Cambridge History*, I, p. 275.

2. There was no systematic remodelling (as is the view of Holtzmann), but that gradual changes were made. J. v. Negelein (*OLZ.* 1908, 336 f.) refutes this theory by observing that the ancient epic took no stock whatsoever of the moral point of view, that it portrayed both parties in almost equal light and shade, and that it merely rejoiced in the

As far as Kṛṣṇa is concerned, the clan of Yādavas, to whom he belongs, is described in many places of the Mahābhārata a clan of herdsmen of rude manners and he himself is treated with scorn again and again as "herdsman" and "slave". In the ancient hero-poetry he was only an excellent leader of that clan of herdsmen and had nothing godly in him. Even the Kṛṣṇa legends of the Harivaṁśa seem to have as their basis older sagas in which Kṛṣṇa was not a God but the hero of a rude folk of herdsmen. It is possible that the legend knew more than one Kṛṣṇa who later on got all fused into one; or that (as it has been presumed by some the Kṛṣṇa of the hero-poem and of the legend was also a founder of a religion or of a sect whose main teachings are found in the oldest portions of the Bhagavadgītā and that this Kṛṣṇa was then made into an incarnation of God Viṣṇu by his followers who worshipped him. It is far more likely that there were two or several traditional Kṛṣṇas, who were merged into *one* deity at a later time. Kṛṣṇa, the son of Devakī, is mentioned in the Chāndogya-Upaniṣad (III, 17) as a pupil of Ghora Aṅgīrasa, who expounds doctrines which at least in a few points coincide with those of the Bhagavadgītā. For this reason we can scarcely separate this old saga of the time of the Upaniṣads from the Kṛṣṇa of the Bhagavadgītā.[1] It is possible that this Kṛṣṇa was the founder of the Bhāgavata religion, and that like so many other founders of religions in India, he was made into an incarnation of the

---

actual display of strength. A similar view is taken by Oldenberg (*Das Mahābhārata*, pp. 35 ff.) who, like Hopkins (*Cambridge History*, I, 265) believes that the moral reflections cast on the conduct of the Pāṇḍavas belong to a more modern age, "when a finer morality had begun to temper the crude royal and military spirit." Hertel (*WZKM*. 24, 1910, 421) seeks to explain the contradiction of the treacherous behaviour of the Pāṇḍavas and the poet's siding with them, by saying that the Mahābhārata has the character of a nītiśāstra and that, according to the rules of politics, the king is justified in or even is duty bound to the utilisation of cunning. These scholars, however, forget that the speeches in which the Pāṇḍavas' manner of fighting is condemned as dishonourable, do not belong to the didactic additions to the epic, but are interwoven with the description of the fight itself, and do not in the least bear the stamp of later additions.

1. Cf. H. Raychaudhuri, *Early History of the Vaishnava Sect*, pp. 23, 30 f., 48 ff.

god worshipped by his adherents.[1] It is possible, moreover, that Kṛṣṇa did not figure at all in the original epic, and was introduced only later, perhaps with the express intention of justifying the actions of the Pāṇḍavas, which were shady from the moral point of view, by representing them as inspired by the "god" Kṛṣṇa.[2] Much as has been written on the problem of Kṛṣṇa, we must admit, nevertheless, that no satisfactory solution has been found.[3] In any case, it is a far cry from Kṛṣṇa, the friend of the Pāṇḍavas, to Kṛṣṇa of the Harivaṁśa and the exalted god Viṣṇu.

Thus an account of the political and religious development which is reflected in the cantos of the Mahābhārata relating to the great war makes us presuppose — namely the transfer of power from the Kauravas to the Pāṇḍavas and the deification of Kṛṣṇa — the passage of a very long period of time; and it is not likely that even these cantos which constitute the kernel of this work originate from one and the same poet. Such a presumption becomes even more unlikely when we consider the innumerable contradictions which occur in the details of the main story. We may remind here only of the stories of the marriage of the Pāṇḍavas (see on page 316 above) and the adventures of Arjuna (p. 319). In the fourth book we find a doublet of the whole battle in the Kuru-field; Bhīṣma and all the heroes of the Kauravas are put to flight by Arjuna in a split second; which

1. This view is advocated especially by Garbe, *Die Bhagavadgītā*, 2nd Ed., pp. 27 ff.

2. Thus Oldenberg, *Das Mahābhārata*, pp. 37, 43. Cf. also Jacobi, *ERE*. VII, 195 f. and Sir Charles Eliot, *Hinduism and Buddhism* (London, 1921), II, 154, who emphasizes the point that Kṛṣṇa is not so essentially important in the story of the Mahābhārata as is Rāma in that of the Rāmāyaṇa. It seems however, that the *warrior* Kṛṣṇa, *not the god* Kṛṣṇa is too closely bound up with the main narrative for the epic to be imaginable entirely without him.

3. Cf. Holtzmann, *Das Mahābhārata* I, 132, ff.; A. Weber, *Zur indischen Religionsgeschichte* (*Sonderabdruck aus "Deutsche Revue"* 1899), pp. 28 f., L. J. Sedgwick, *JBRAS*, 23, 1910, pp. 115 ff.; Grierson, *ERE*, II, 539 ff; Jacobi, *ERE*, VII, 193 ff. and *Streitberg-Festgabe*, p. 168; A. B. Keith, *JRAS*. 1915, 548 ff; R. G. Bhandarkar, *Vaiṣṇavism*, etc., pp. 3 f., 8 ff., 33 ff.; Raychaudhuri, ibid., pp. 18 ff. and passim; Garbe, ibid.; Eliot, *Hinduism and Buddhism* II, 152 ff.; Hopkins in *Cambridge History* I, 258; Oldenberg, *Das Mahābhārata*, pp. 37 ff.

cannot be reconciled with the later description that makes it possible for the Pāṇḍavas to defeat the Kauravas only after 18 days and that too by employing cunning and deceit. There can be no doubt that the whole fourth book (Virāṭaparvan) is a product of later times[1] than the splendid descriptions of war in the following books. But also in those books, which contain those portions of the epic which are certainly the oldest, we find again and again contradictions which cannot be explained by the "ingenious carelessness" of any poet.[2] Further, we find by the side of the most splendid descriptions full of blunt power also very long cantos in which with dull monotony and continued repetitions the description of the eighteen day battle is only spun out as much as possible.

Thus even that what we can call the "actual epic", as it has come down to us, is certainly not the work of one poet. Even this "kernel" of the Mahābhārata is not the old hero-poetry any more, but this old poetry is contained in it in a very adulterated form.

But now we have seen that around this kernel a huge mass of the most diverse poetries got collected; hero-songs from various sources of legends, Brahmanical, mythical and legendary poetry, ascetic poetry and didactic poetry of all sorts from simplest moral sayings upto extensive philosophical poems, regular law books and whole Purāṇas. Though J. Dahlmann has applied an enormous amount of erudition[3] in an attempt to

---

1. According to Holtzmann, *Mahābhārata* II, p. 98 and Hopkins,—*The Great Epic of India*, p. 382 f. Cf. also N. B. Utgikar, *The Virāṭaparvan of the Mahābhārata* (Poona, 1923), pp. xx f.

2. Cf. note on p. 344, 345 f, 350, 355 above.

3. Although Joseph Dahlmann in his book *Das Mahābhārata als Epos und Rechtsbuch* (Berlin, 1895) speaks only of a "unitary diaskensy", still he ascribes to the "diaskenast" an activity that would brand him as a poet; and finally (see p. 302) he speaks of the Mahābhārata as the work of a "single poetically active power". In his book *Genesis of the Mahābhārata*" (Berlin, 1899), he says in particular: "The poet was a diaskenast, the diaskenast a poet." Moreover it is noteworthy that even such a naive and rather strictly religious Indian like C. V. Vaidya (*The Mahābhārata, A Criticism*, Bombay, 1905) who speaks with reverence of Vyāsa, the contemporary of Kṛṣṇa as of the "poet" of the Mahābhārata (he ranks him higher than Homer, Milton

prove that the Mahābhārata is one unified work which was composed by *one* poet in pre-Buddhist times both as an epic and a law-book, only few scholars agree with him. Sylvain Lévi'[1] too, has recently attempted to explain the Mahābhārata as a "deliberate composition organically and artistically spread around a central fact and inspired by a dominant sentiment which penetrates and permeates it." He compares the Mahābhārata with the Vinaya, the code of discipline of the Mūla-Sarvāstivādin Buddhists, and is of opinion that the whole great epic "with all its exaggerations and episodes, with all its varied and luxuriant mass of detail" is based on nothing but "a code of Kṣatriya discipline as practised by the Bhāgavatas." Of course, if we take it that the nucleus of the epic is to be found in the Bhāgavata, Nārāyaṇīya and Harivaṁśa, such a point of view is justifiable. If, however, the real nucleus of the Mahābhārata is a hero-poem of the conflict between the Kauravas and the Pāṇḍavas, Lévi's interpretation is just as impossible as that of Dahlmann. Those scholars who see in the Mahābhārata a "scripture of the warrior caste,"[2] forget that the Mahābhārata as we have it in our present-day text contains much which would be quite out of place in a work intended for warriors. The ascetic morality of ahiṁsā which is preached in so many passages in the didactic sections, of the love towards all creatures and complete resignation, is just as incompatible with the very sensual pleasures promised to the warrior in Indra's heaven, as with the eating of meat and the drinking of strong drinks in which the heroes and even their wives indulge, in many a vivid description of the warriors' life in the actual epic.[3] Anyone who has really read the whole of the Mahābhārata and not only the most magnificent portions of it, is bound to admit that our present-day text of the epic contains not only much that is diverse in content, but

---

and Shakespeare) and calculates in all seriousness that Vyāsa and Kṛṣṇa lived at the time of Mahābhārata battle about 3101 B.C., straightaway admits that the Mahābhārata in its present form is the enlarged form of an originally much smaller work and contains numerous additions and interpolations.

1. *Bhandarkar Com. Vol.*, pp. 99 ff. (English in *Ann. Bh. Inst.* I, 1, 13 ff.)
2. Eliot, *Hinduism and Buddhism* I, pp. xc f. Cf. also Hopkins in *Cambridge History* I, p. 256.
3. See Hopkins, *Great Epic*, pp. 373, 376 ff.

also much that is diverse in value. In truth, he who would believe with the orthodox Hindus and the above-mentioned western scholars, that our Mahābhārata, in its present form, is the work of one single man, would be forced to the conclusion that this man, was, at one and the same time, a great sage and an idiot, a talented artist and a ridiculous pedant — apart from the fact that this marvellous person must have known and confessed the most antagonistic religious views, and the most contradictory philosophical doctrines.[1]

Even with respect to language, style and metre the constituents of the Mahābhārata show absolutely no uniformity. Only in a very general way can we speak of the "epic Sanskrit as the language of the popular epics.[2] In reality the language of the epic is in some portions more antiquarian, i.e., more closely related to the ancient Indian language of the Vedic prose works than in the other portions. And by the side of linguistic phenomena which sound like Pāli and which can be described as popular, there are also others, which must be explained simply as linguistic irregularities like the ones which uneducated and inferior writers of the calibre of Purāṇa-writers are often guilty of. Also in the matter of style it can be said only in a general way that it is still far from the so-called Kāvyastyle of the later ornate poetry, i.e., a style marked by an excessive use of artistic means (Alaṃkāras). But there is no want of passages in the Mahābhārata which remind us already of this Kāvyastyle.[3] Beside them we find also passages which are in the naive style of the ancient Itihāsas, as they are told in the Brāhmaṇas and Upaniṣads, while in numerous other places the

1. Oldenberg (*Das Mahābhārata*, p. 32) calls it a "scientific monstrosity" to suppose that the Mahābhārata was a unified composition.

2. On the epic language H. Jacobi writes in his *Das Rāmāyaṇa* p. 112 ff. cf. also above p. 37 and Hopkins, *The Great Epic of India*, p. 262. A. Ludwig, *Mahābhārata als Epos und Rechtsbuch*, pp. 5 ff.; J. Wackernagel, *Altindische Grammatik* I, pp. xliv ff.; W. Kirfel, *Beiträge zur Geschichte der Nominalkomposition in den Upaniṣads und im Epos*, Bonn 1908; Keith, *JRAS*, 1906, pp. 2 f; Oldenberg, ibid., pp. 129 ff., 145 ff.

3. Cf. above p. 347. But these passages are not numerous, in any case not at all so numerous as those in the Rāmāyaṇa.

most sloppy Purāṇa-style dominates. As regards the metre,[1] the śloka, which is born out of the ancient anuṣṭubh is perhaps the epical metre par excellence. But of this śloka there are more archaic and younger forms which are all represented in the Mahābhārata. Further there is in our epic also old prose passages whose prose is sometimes rhythmical and is sometimes intermingled with stanzas.[2] Also of the Triṣṭubh-metre, which is more used in the Mahābhārata — though the śloka is about twenty times as common as the triṣṭubh — we find not only the archaic form that resembles the Vedic but also later forms; and we come across even the artistic metres of classical Sanskrit poetry scattered in the Mahābhārata already.

Lastly, we must not forget that the opening sections of the Mahābhārata themselves give clear indications that the epic had not always its present form and extent. Even the tables of contents which we find in the first two adhyāyas, are not always in agreement with our text.[3]

All this therefore indicates that the Mahābhārata has more than one origin and that it consists of earlier and later pieces which belong to various centuries. Form and content equally testify that some parts of the Mahābhārata go back to Vedic times, whereas others must be contemporaneous with the later products of the Purāṇa literature.

Now it has been presumed — especially by A. Holtzmann— that there was an old hero-poem of the Kauravas which was the "original Mahābhārata", that this has undergone a "tendencious modification" in favour of the Pāṇḍavas; and that it has been "modified tendenciously" more than once—at first by the

1. See Hopkins, *Great Epic*, pp. 191 ff.; J. Zubaty, *ZDMG*, 43, 1889, pp. 619 ff.; Ludwig ibid., p. 37; Jacobi in *Gurupūjākaumudī*, pp. 50 ff.; Oldenberg, ibid., pp. 137 ff; see also above, p. 55.

2. Cf. Hopkins, ibid., p. 266 ff. and above, p. 92.

3. Cf. V. V. Iyer, Notes of a Study of the Preliminary Chapters of the Mahābhārata, pp. 17 ff. and passim; Oldenberg, ibid., pp. 33 ff., 43 ff. Though the division into 18 Parvans is traditional, it is not certain that the division was originally the same as we find it in our text at the present day. Alberuni mentions other titles of the 18 Parvans, see E. Sachau, *Alberuni's India*, I, pp. 132 f. The Southern Indian MSS and the Javanese translation also have other titles. Cf. also Brockhaus, *ZDMG*. 6, 1862, pp. 528 ff.

Buddhists and then by the Brahmins. The second "Purāṇa-like modification" took place according to Holtzmann by about 900-1100 A.D., which was then followed by the final fixing and settling of the text."[1]

It is important to state that this last presumption according to which the Mahābhārata received its present form in the 15th or 16th century is absolutely wrong. For it has been proved through literary and epigraphical evidences[2] that the Mahābhārata was, even as early as about 500 A.D., not merely an epic any more but a holy text book and an edifying work and it was to a large extent essentially not different in content and volume from the work as it is available to us now. The philosopher Kumārila (about 700 A.D.) quotes numerous passages from almost all the books of the Mahābhārata, which to him was a great smṛti expounded by Vyāsa.[3] The poets Subandhu and Bāṇa (about 600-650 A.D.) knew the Mahābhārata chiefly as a poem, indeed Bāṇa considered it as the culmination of all poetry.[4] In his novel "Kādambarī" the latter tells that Queen Vilāsavatī of Ujjain attended a public recitation of the Mahābhārata at a festival in a temple. Such public readings of the Mahābhārata take place even today in India on the occasion of festivals in temples — and of course more for edifying and instructing in religion rather than for entertaining.[5] By about 600 A.D., however, an inscription of Cambodia testifies to the prevalence of such public readings and that especially using the

1. Holtzmann, *Das Mahābhārata*, I, 194.

2. See R. G. Bhandarkar *JBRAS*. 10, 1871-72, pp. 81 ff.; K.T. Telang, *SBE*., Vol. 8, pp. 28 ff.; and especially G. Bühler and J. Kirste, *Indian Studies* II, *SWA*. 1892.

3. See Bühler, ibid., pp. 5 ff.

4. Harṣacarita, introductory verses 4-10. But from this passage it does not follow, as Peterson (Kādambarī, Introd., p. 68) thinks, that in Bāṇa's time the Mahābhārata "was as yet comparatively a fresh wonder in the world," but rather that its fame had already "penetrated the three worlds," as Bāṇa himself says. On the Mahābhārata in the works of Subandhu and Bāṇa, see W. Cartellieri, *WZKM*. 13, 1899, 57 ff.

5. In another place in the "Kādambarī" (ed. Peterson, p. 209) we read that Kādambarī listens to a recitation of the Mahābhārata, Nārada's daughter reciting it "in a gentle singing voice," whilst a pair of Kinnaras seated behind her accompany the recitation on the flute.

manuscripts which were presented for this purpose in that distant Indian colony to the east of India.

Finally, we possess also documents of land-gifts from the 5th and 6th centuries in which the chapters of the XIII book (above p. 408) dealing with the moral of gifting are quoted as sacred texts and in one of such inscription the Mahābhārata is already described as the "collection of a hundred thousand verses". The number of 100000 verses cannot be reached even approximately if the books XII and XIII and even a portion of the Harivaṁśa are not added.[1] But if even in the 5th century the Mahābhārata contained the undoubtedly latest portions like Book XIII and the Harivaṁśa,[2] if it was already then a text book and devotional book and if a hundred years later manuscripts of the

---

1. In the Mahābhārata itself there is a mention of the "hundred thousand" verses of the Mahābhārata (I, 1, 107; xii, 343, ii; cf. above p. 304 and Hopkins ibid., p. 9).

The 18 books of the Mahābhārata have 90092 verses in the Calcutta edition, of which 13935 are in Book XII and 7759 in book XIII. With the whole of the Harivaṁśa the number of the verses amounts to 106,466. If we omit the Bhaviṣyaparvan (see p. 434 above), then we have the number of verses as 101,154, which comes nearer to the round number of "hundred thousand". Even the existence of various recensions of the Mahābhārata which often deviate from one another in this way that one recension omits a number of verses which are found in another, but on the other hand adds somewhere else just an equal number of verses which are missing in the other, prove that the contents of the Mahābhārata could also be different without there being any change in its volume.

2. We cannot form any definite conclusion as to the date of the Harivaṁśa ("about the third century of the Christian era," R. G. Bhandarkar, *Vaiṣṇavism*, etc., p. 36) on the basis of the occurrence of the word "dinar"= denarius. We may assume, however, that this appendix to the Mahābhārata did not come into existence very long before the 4th century A.D.; for though Roman gold coins were known in India as early as in the 1st century A.D. (see E. J. Rapson, Indian Coins, *Grundriss* II, 3 B., pp. 4, 17 ff., 25, 35; R. Sewell, *JRAS.* 1904, 591 ff.), the Indian word dinar is only traceable from 400 A.D. onwards in Gupta inscriptions (Sewell, ibid., p. 616). Cf. B. C. Mazumdar, *JRAS.* 1907, pp. 408 f.; A. B. Keith, *JRAS.* 1907, pp. 681 ff.; 1915, pp. 504 f. If the Buddhist poet Aśvaghoṣa should really be the author of the Vajrasūci which is ascribed to him, the Harivaṁśa would already have been a part of the Mahābhārata in the 2nd century A.D., for two verses from the Harivaṁśa (1292 f.) are quoted in the Vajrasūci 3 (see Weber, *Indische Streifen* I, p. 189) with the words "for it is written in the Bhārata."

Mahābhārata had already reached upto the east of India and were read out there in temples, then we are right in concluding that it must have received the form which it has even today at least one or two centuries earlier i.e., in the 3rd or 4th century A.D. Alternatively[1] however it is possible that it has received this form only after the origin and the spread of Buddhism to which there are many allusions in it and that too only after Alexander's invasion of India, because the Yavanas, i.e., the Greeks (Ionians) are often mentioned in it and there is also mention in it of stone constructions whereas earlier to the Greeks only wooden constructions were known in India. Accordingly the Mahābhārata can have received its present form not earlier than in the 4th century B.C. and not later than in the 4th century A.D.[2]

A greater modification of the Mahābhārata or even the addition of one of the bigger books cannot have therefore taken place any more after the 4th century A.D. But we cannot at all hold the hypothesis of one or even more modifications either to be necessary or probable.[3] Just as in later times the copyists dealt with their text rather arbitrarily so also in earlier times

1. See Hopkins, *Great Epic*, pp. 391 ff. If Dio Chrysostomos' statement that even the Indians sang Homer's poems and that they were well acquainted with the sufferings of Priam, etc., alluded to the Mahābhārata (as is the view of A. Weber, *Ind. Stud.* II, 161 ff.; Holtzmann, *Das Mahābhārata* IV, 163; Pischel, *KG*, 195; H. G. Rawlinson, *Intercourse between India and the Western World*, Cambridge, 1916, pp. 140 f., 171), then this statement would constitute our earliest external evidence of the existence of the Mahābhārata in the 1st century A.D. It is possible, however (in fact, according to Jacobi in *Festschrift Wackernagel*, pp. 129 f., probable), that Dio's statement, which was repeated by Aelian, refers to an actual Indian translation of Homer. On various Greek words in the Mahābhārata, see Hopkins, ibid., p. 372; Rawlinson, ibid., p. 172 note.

2. Hopkins, *Epic Mythology* (Grundriss III, 1 B 1915, p. 1) considered 300-100 B.C. to be the probable date of the Mahābhārata, but in *Cambridge History* I, p. 258, he also gives the limits 4th century B.C. to 4th century A.D. S. Lévi (*JA*. s. 11, t. V, 1915, p. 122) concludes from the agreement between the geography of the Buddhist Mahāmāyūrī with that of the Mahābhārata, that the latter received its final redaction in the first three or four centuries. A.D.

3. This shall not mean that individual portions like for example the Virāṭa-Parvan have not been modified. (cf. Hopkins in the *J. Am. O.S.* Vol. XXIV, 1903, p. 54).

the rhapsodes among whom the hero-songs must have been propagated only orally for a number of centuries took all the liberties with the recitation of their songs; they elaborated the scenes which were liked by their audiences and shortened the scenes which did not impress them. But the greatest modifications through which the old hero-poetry gradually became a collected-work, that brought "much" and therefore "something to everybody", are perhaps to be explained only as follows — that the preserving of this hero-song and handing it down to the successive generations changed hands from the original singers to other circles and the result was that the songs were transplanted to other religions and were adapted to suit other times and a changing audience. As we have seen the songs of the bards must have gone from the bards who were loyal to the Kuru family to those who were connected with the Pāṇḍava family. From the regions where the Viṣṇu-cult was predominant they spread to the regions where Śiva was worshipped as the supreme deity. Even the phases which the Kṛṣṇa cult had undergone left their trace in the epic-poetry. As in the case of other folks so also in the case of the Indians a time must have come when the creative power of the poet was not active in the field of hero-poetry and so the hero-poetry did not exist any more as a living poetry and so only the old songs were sung by the bards.[1] Moreover those days had gone when the bards went to the battlefield as chariot-drivers with the warriors in order to sing the glory of their deeds, for instance at a great sacrifice after the war was won. The descendents of these bards were an inferior class of literates — the same people who occupied themselves with preserving and handing down the Purāṇas. These people were perhaps neither proper warriors nor proper Brahmins — in the law books the Sūtas are rightly termed bastards who are supposed to have been born to Kṣatriyas in Brahmin-women or to Brahmins in Kṣatriya-women. And it is exactly also the peculiarity of the Mahābhārata in its present form that it is neither proper warrior-poetry nor priestly-poetry, it is no more an epic, but also no more a Purāṇa actually.

1. Cf. H. Jacobi in *GGA*, 1892. p. 632.

The Mahābhārata might have attained any kind of a final form only when it was written down after oral transmission of many centuries. In editing and copying it perhaps only Brahmins and Pandits took part. But if we must say that the Mahābhārata was even in the 4th century A.D. or even earlier on the whole with respect to extent and content not essentially different from the work that we have today, then we must particularly stress the words "on the whole" and "not essentially". For additions and changes, and not only additions of individual verses but also of whole cantos (like the hymns to Durgā etc.) have been made till the most recent times[1] and a critically established text of the Mahābhārata does not at all exist.

When one speaks of the Mahābhārata, one means by that in general one of the two editions made by the native scholars in India, the "Calcutta edition" (1834-1839)[2] in four quarto-volumes the last of which contains the Harivaṁśa or the "Bombay edition" with the commentary of Nīlakaṇṭha. This latter edition has appeared in many reprints since 1862.[3] It does not contain the Harivaṁśa. These two recensions differ from each other in such a manner that one of them contains verses and even entire cantos which are missing in the other or that verses appear in a different order etc.

From all this the important lesson follows that in reality the age of each section of the Mahābhārata, indeed that of every single verse must be determined in itself and that remarks like "That is already said in the Mahābhārata" have no justification whatsoever and make no sense whatever with respect to

1. R. G. Bhandarkar (*JBRAS.* 20, 1900, p. 402) points out that interpolations were made in the Anuśāsanaparvan as late at the Gupta period.

2. This edition was begun by the Committee of Public Education and completed under the auspices of the Asiatic Society of Bengal, and contains also the text of the Harivaṁśa.

3. It has appeared in several editions since 1862. See Holtzmann, *Das Mahābhārata*, III, pp. 2 ff., 9ff., on this and other Indian editions. The edition by Pratapa Chandra Roy (Calcutta, 1882 ff.) is very handy, but is unfortunately spoiled by misprints. This edition is a work of true Indian piety and charity: it was printed by the aid of collections organised by the editor, for the purpose of free distribution, and, 10,000 copies were given away gratis.

chronology. There is still less justification for associating certain dates with the Mahābhārata as a whole because not only in distinctly "old" portions more recent interpolations have taken place but even in the "younger" portions very old pieces are found. Thus the whole first book of the Mahābhārata is certainly not "old", this does not however disprove that many sagas, legends and genealogical verses occurring in it are old. Even in the Harivaṁśa which was certainly added only late there are very old verses and legends. But of course the expressions "old" and "young" are to be applied to entire books and larger pieces of the Mahābhārata always with caution and reserve.

And this takes us to the most difficult question: What do we mean when we say "old" and "oldest" portions of the Mahābhārata? In other words: Upto what time do the beginnings of the Mahābhārata go back ?

Let us adhere to facts. In the entire Vedic literature there is no mention of a Mahābhārata although very often in the Brāhmaṇas and the Upaniṣads there is a talk of Ākhyāna, Itihāsa, Purāṇa and Gāthā-Nārāśaṃsī (p. 293 f). Even of the great and historical event around which the whole epic revolves —the bloody battle in the Kuru-field—the Veda knows nothing although in the Brāhmaṇas precisely this Kuru field is so often mentioned as a place where gods and men performed great sacrifices, that this event would have been certainly mentioned, if it had already taken place.[1] Of course Janamejaya, the son of Parīkṣit and Bharata, the son of Duṣyanta and Śakuntalā are mentioned in the Brāhmaṇas, and even in a Kuntapa-song of the Atharvaveda, Parīkṣit is praised as a peace loving king under whose reign the Kuru country flourished. In the works belonging to the Yajurveda Kurus and Pāñcālas or Kurupāñcālas are often mentioned, and in the Kaṭhaka (8,6) an anecdote on Dhṛtarāṣṭra the son of Vicitravīrya is told in connection with a sacrificial festival of the Kurupāñcālas. As against this nowhere in the entire Veda do we find the name of Pāṇḍu or his sons, the Pāṇḍavas, nowhere names like Duryodhana,

1. See A. Ludwig, *Über das Verhältnis des mythischen Elements zu der historischen Grundlage des Mahābhārata*, page 6.

Duśśāsana, Karṇa etc. Although the name Arjuna occurs in a Brāhmaṇa, still it occurs only as a pseudonym of the god Indra. The Sāṅkhāyana-Śrautasūtra (XV, 16) is the first place where we find mention of a war in Kurukṣetra which was disastrous for the Kauravas.[1] In the Āśvalāyana-Gṛhyasūtra,[2] "Bhārata and Mahābhārata" are mentioned in a list of teachers and sacred books which are honoured by libations at the end of the study of the Veda. Pāṇini[3] teaches the formation of the names of "Yudhiṣṭhira," Bhīma" and "Vidura", and the accent of the compound word "Mahābhārata." Patañjali, however, is the first to make definite allusions to the story of the battle between the Kauravas and the Pāṇḍavas.

How is it with the Buddhist literature ? In the Tipiṭaka, the Pali-canon of the Buddhists, there is no mention of the Mahābhārata. As against this, in the oldest texts of the Tipiṭaka we find poetries of the kind of the Ākhyāyanas, which we have already come across in the Brāhmaṇas as an earlier stage of the epic.[4] The Jātakas, whose metrical constituents (the Gāthās)

1. Cf. Leumann, *ZDMG*, 48, 1894, 80ff, Ludwig, *Das Mahābhārata als Epos und Rechtsbuch*, pp. 77 ff, Hopkins in *Cambridge History* I, 252 f. B.C. Mazumdar (*JRAS*. 1906, 225f.) suggest that the author of the Mahābhārata grafted the Kuru-Pāṇḍava story upon an older story of a war between Kurus and Pāñcālas.

2. III, 4,4. This passage has been much discussed. Cf. Hopkins, *Great Epic*, pp. 389 f. Dahlmann, *Das Mahābhārata als Epos und Rechtsbuch*, pp. 152 ff. Winternitz, *WZKM*, 14, 1900, pp. 55f. Utgikar in *Proc. IOC*, Vol. II, pp. 46 ff. Oldenberg, *Das Mahābhārata* pp. 18, 33. Utgikar is right in explaining the mention of the Mahābhārata in the Āśvalāyana-Gṛhyasūtra (and not in other Gṛhyasūtras) by the fact that Āśvalāyana counts as the pupil of Śaunaka, and according to the frame story of the Mahābhārata. Ugraśravas relates the Mahābhārata to Śaunaka. The date of the Āśv.-Gṛhyas. is however, entirely unknown, and lists of this nature could easily have been enlarged at any time in Āśvalāyana's school. For this reason we are not justified in drawing a chronological conclusion from this passage.

3. VIII, 3, 95; III, 2, 162; 4, 74; VI, 2, 38. But these scanty references do not admit of our drawing any conclusion as to the contents and extents of the epic known to Pāṇini.

4. See above, p. 291, E. Windisch, Māra und Buddha (*ASGW*., Vol. XV, Leipzig, 1895), pp. 222 ff. and T. W. Rhys Davids, *Buddhist India*, London, 1903, p. 180 ff. In the Brahmajālasutta (*Dialogues of the Buddha*, translated from Pāli by T. W. Rhys Davids, London, 1899, p. 8) recitations of Ākhyānas are mentioned by the side of entertainments and theatrical performances which the monk shall avoid. If, as the commentator says, recitations of the Mahābhārata and the Rāmāyaṇa were meant, then the author would have certainly mentioned their names.

belong to the Tipiṭaka, show an acquaintance with the Kṛṣṇa-legend but not with the Harivaṁśa and the Mausalaparvan of the Mahābhārata.[1] The names found in the Jātaka-books, viz. Pāṇḍava, Dhanañjaya (a common attribute of Arjuna in the Mahābhārata), Yudhiṭṭila (Pāli form for Yudhiṣṭhira), Dhataraṭṭha (Pāli form for Dhṛtarāṣṭra), Vidhura or Vidhūra (the Vidura of the Mahābhārata)—indeed even the story of the self-selection of the husband and Draupadī's marriage with five husbands occurring there prove not only that the Mahābhārata was not known at this time, but also rather that the contrary was the case. For Pāṇḍava appears in the Jātaka as the name of a horse,[2] Dhṛtarāṣṭra as the name of a flamingo,[3] Dhanañjaya and Yudhiṣṭhira are named only as Kuru-kings who live in Indraprastha and Vidura is a wise man who makes his appearance sometimes as a family priest, sometimes as a minister in the court of Dhanañjaya or of Yudhiṣṭhira.[4] But

1. This has been proved by H. Lüders in *ZDMG.*, Vol. 58, p. 687 ff. Cf. also, E. Hardy in *ZDMG*, Vol. 53, p. 25 ff. The Kṛṣṇa-saga is told in the Ghaṭajātaka (No. 454); allusions to it are found also in the Jātaka No. 512 and No. 530 (Gāthā 20). The Jains have — according to Jacobi (*OC*, VII, Vienna, 1886, p. 75 ff., and *ZDMG.* Vol. 42, 1888, p. 493 ff.) — not only known the Kṛṣṇa-saga but they also have included already in the 3rd or 2nd century B.C. the Kṛṣṇa-cult in their religion, by including Kṛṣṇa to the number of their holy men. This does not prove anything in the matter of the Age of the Mahābhārata.

2. Jātaka No. 185.

3. Dhataraṭṭha is a king of the gods in Jāt. No. 382, a king of the Nāgas in Jāt. No. 543, a king of the flamingoes in Jāt. Nos. 502, 533, 534. In Jāt No. 544 he heads a list of righteous kings. In the Mahāvastu Dhṛtarāṣṭra is the name of a Buddha, and once the name of a palace, see E. Windisch, Buddhas Geburt (*ASGW.*, 1908), pp. 101, 168.

4. In the Jātaka No. 413 Dhanañjaya is a Kuru king residing in the city of Indapatta (Indraprastha) of the family of Yudhiṭṭhila (Yudhiṭṭhila-gotta), and Vidhura is his purohita. In Jāt. No. 515, Dhanañjaya Korabya is a pious Kuru king, called Yudhiṭṭhila in the Gāthās, while the sage Vidhura is living at Benares. In the Vidhurapandita-Jātaka (No. 545, already mentioned in the second century B.C. with the title "Vitura-Punyakīya-jātakam" in a Bharhut inscription, see E. Hultzsch, *Ind. Ant.*, 1892, p. 234) Vidhura a minister of the Kuru King Dhanañjaya who (like Yudhiṣṭhira in the Mahābhārata) is fond of playing at dice. But there is no allusion at all to the story of the Mahābhārata. In Jāt. No. 329 Dhanañjaya is a king of Benares. Vidhura also occurs as the name of a wise monk in the Therīgāthā 1188 and in the Majjhimanikāya 50.

Draupadī, one of the most splendid female characters of the epic appears in the Jātaka as a model of womanly infamy as she is not contended with her five husbands but also indulges in adultery with a hunchbacked servant.[1]

From these facts one must perhaps infer that an epic Mahābhārata, i.e., an epic poem that treated the battle of the Kauravas and the Pāṇḍavas and the battle in the Kuru-field and bore the title "Bhārata or Mahābhārata" cannot have existed before the conclusion of the Veda; that on the contrary such a poem must have already existed in the 4th century B.C. because the sūtra-works of Sāṅkhāyana, Āśvalāyana and Pāṇini must be placed before this time. But as the Pāli canon of the Buddhists which originated in the 3rd and 4th century B.C. show only a very superficial if at all any knowledge of the Mahābhārata, it might have been known still less in eastern India where Buddhist literature originated.

But we have seen that some elements of our present Mahābhārata can be traced back to the Vedic time and that much, especially in the didactic chapters, is drawn from the common literary possession from which also Buddhists and Jains (perhaps even as early as in the 5th century B.C.) have drawn.[2]

Finally it should also be mentioned that not only the events described in the epic but also the innumerable names of kings and royal dynasties—however much some of the events and many of the names may produce the semblance of the historical—do not at all belong to Indian history in the real sense of the word. It is true that the Indians set the reign of Yudhiṣṭhira and the

1. Jātaka No. 536 (gāthā 288). Cf. Winternitz, *JRAS.*, 1897, pp. 752 ff.

2. Verses Mahābh. XI, 7,23 ff., which H. Raychaudhuri (*JASB.*, *N.S.*, 18, 1922, pp. 269 ff.) believes to be quoted in the Besnagar inscription, also belong to this literary common property. See above, pp. 294, 393, f., 401, 403. On the Ṛṣyaśṛṅga-legend in the Jātaka, cf. above, pp. 399 ff. and H. Lüders in the treatise there cited. Another legend which the Mahābhārata (I, 107 f.) has in common with the Jātaka (No. 444) is that of Māṇḍavya, who, as a punishment for having in his childhood impaled a fly on a thorn, was taken for a robber and impaled. (Cf. L. Sherman, *Materialien zur Geschichte der indischen Visionsliteratur*, Leipzig, 1892, pp. 53 f., and N. B. Utgikar in *Proc. II OC.* 1922, pp. 221 ff. In the Jātaka this Māṇḍavya is a friend of Kanhadīpāyana, i.e. of Kṛṣṇa Dvaipāyana Vyāsa.)

great war of the Mahābhārata at the beginning of the Kaliyuga, or Iron Age, i.e. 3102 B.C.; but this date for the beginning of the Kaliyuga is based upon the artificial calculation of Indian astronomers, and the association of this date with the conflict of the Kauravas and Pāṇḍavas is, of course, quite arbitrary.[1] The political history of India begins with the kings Bimbisāra and Ajātaśatru, who are testified as contemporaries of Buddha. In any case we can attribute historical character to the kings of Śaiśunāga and Nanda-dynasties mentioned in the Purāṇas.[2] With the great Candragupta (321 B.C.) the founder of the Maurya-dynasty, we set foot on the firm soil of history in India.

Of all these historic personalities no trace is found in the Mahābhārata.[3] This "pre-historic" character of the narrative and of the heroes points doubtless to a great antiquity of the epic.

Summing up, we can therefore say the following about the age of the Mahābhārata:

(1) Individual sagas, legends and poems which were included in the Mahābhārata reach back to the Vedic period.

(2) An epic "Bhārata or Mahābhārata" did not however exist in the vedic period.

(3) Many moral stories and sayings which are contained in the Mahābhārata belong to the ascetic poetry, from which source, Buddhists and Jains have drawn from the 6th century B.C. onwards.

(4) If between the 6th and the 4th centuries B.C. an epic Mahābhārata has already existed, then it was not yet known in the motherland of Buddhism.

(5) The existence of the epic called the Mahābhārata before the 4th century B.C. has not been proved beyond doubt.

---

1. See R. Rāmakrishna Bhagwat, *JBRAS.*, 20, 1899, pp. 150 ff. and J. F. Fleet, *JRAS*, 1911, pp. 479 ff., 675 ff. In a similar way the Arabian astronomers have connected the same era with the Deluge.

2. According to V. A. Smith, *The Early History of India* (Oxford, 1904), p. 41, the founding of the Śaiśunāga-dynasty would have to be fixed about 600 B.C., Bimbisāra's ascent to the throne about 519 B.C. and the founding of the Nanda-dynasty about 361 B.C. Cf. E. J. Rapson, *Cambridge History,* I, pp. 312 ff., 697.

3. E. W. Hopkins (in the *Album Kern*, p. 249 ff.) believes however that allusions to the Mauryas, Aśoka and Candragupta are found in the Mahābhārata. But why should this be so concealed ?

(6) Between the 4th century B.C. and the 4th century A.D. the transformation of the epic Mahābhārata into our present collected work has taken place—probably gradually.

(7) In the 4th century A.D. the work had on the whole already its present volume, content and character.

(8) But small changes and additions have been still made even in later centuries.

(9) There is no "epoque" of the "Mahābhārata", but the age of each one of the sections or parts must be determined in itself.

The Rāmāyaṇa[1]

Popular Epic and Ornate Poetry in One

In more than one respect the Rāmāyaṇa is essentially different from the Mahābhārata. First of all, it is much less in volume and has much more uniformity. Whereas the Mahābhārata in its present form can be hardly called an actual epic, the Rāmāyaṇa is still a considerably uniform hero-poem even in the form in which we find it to-day. Further, whereas the native tradition makes Vyāsa, a quite mythical seer of prehistoric times who is at the same time also, the compiler of the Vedas and of the Purāṇas the author or publisher of the Mahābhārata, it calls a poet named Vālmīki the author of the Rāmāyaṇa; and we have no reason to doubt, that there has once nearly lived a poet of this name and composed in the form of a unitary poem all those songs living scattered in the mouths of the bards. The Indians call this Vālmīki the "first ornate poet" (ādikavi) as well as the Rāmāyaṇa "the first ornate poem" (ādikāvya). Indeed the beginnings of epic ornate poetry can be traced back to the Rāmāyaṇa and Vālmīki has always been the model which all subsequent Indian authors of ornate poetry emulated with admiration. The essential character of the so-called Kāvya lies in this that it lays

1. The problems of the Rāmāyaṇa have been thoroughly treated at first by Albrecht Weber in, Über das Rāmāyaṇa" *Abhandlungen der Berliner Akademie aus dem Jahre* 1870, p. 1-88). Forming the basis and partly also serving as the basis for the following chapters is Hermann Jacobi's "*Das Rāmāyaṇa, Geschichte und Inhalt.*" Bonn 1893. A good survey of the whole Rāmā literature is given by Al. Baumgartner S. J. *Das Rāmāyaṇa und die Rāmalitterature der Inder*, Freiburg i. B. 1894. Also C. V. Vaidya's *The Riddle of the Rāmāyaṇa*, Bombay and London 1906 contains also some good remarks.

greater stress on form than on matter and content of the poetry and that so-called Alaṁkāras, that is, "ornaments" like similes, poetic-figures, alliterations etc. are used in plenty, and even in excess. Similes are heaped upon similes, and descriptions, especially nature-descriptions are woven endlessly with more and more new metaphors and epithets. Of these and other peculiarities of classical ornate poetry we find the earliest beginnings already in the Rāmāyaṇa. Thus whereas we could find in the Mahābhārata mixture of a popular epic and theological didactic poetry (Purāṇa) we see the Rāmāyaṇa as something between a popular epic and ornate poem.

It is a truly popular epic just like the Mahābhārata because like this it has become the property of the entire Indian folk and—as perhaps no other poem in the entire world literature—has influenced the whole thinking and writing of the folk through all the centuries. In the introduction (composed later) to the epic it is said that God Brahman himself had asked the poet Vālmīki to sing the glory of Rāma's deeds in verses; and that the God has promised him:

"As long as the mountains stand,
As long as the rivers are on the earth,
So long will in this world,
The song of Rāma continue to live."[1]

This statement has proved itself to be prophetically true to this day. Since more than 2,000 years the poem of Rāma has remained alive in India and it continues to live in all strata and classes of the folk. High and low, princes and peasants, landlords and artisans, princesses and shepherdesses are well versed with the characters and stories of the great epic. Men find the celebrated deeds of Rāma elevating and his wise speeches exalting; women love and praise Sītā as the ideal woman faithful to her husband, as the highest feminine virtue. But young and old take delight in the miraculous deeds of the loyal monkey Hanumat and no less in the horrifying tales of the man-eating giants and demons endowed with powers of magic. Popular sayings and proverbs testify to the familiarity of the folk with the stories of the Rāmāyaṇa. Moreover, teachers and

1. 1,2,36 f.

masters of the various religious sects take the support of the authority of the Rāmāyaṇa and draw from it when they want to spread religious and moral teachings in the folk. And the poets of all later ages, from Kālidāsa to Bhavabhūti had always drawn their material from the Rāmāyaṇa and processed it anew.[1] If we take the modern Indian literature of the languages of the masses, then we find already by the beginning of the 12th century a Tamil translation of the Sanskrit epic and soon follow adaptations and translations into the popular languages from north to south. The religious-philosophical Hindi poem Rām-Caritmānas based on the ancient epic, composed by the famous Tulsi Das has become an evangelium for millions of Indians. Generations of Hindus in all parts of India have known the old legend of Rāma in such modern translations. Even in our days they arrange recitations of this poem in the houses of the rich. Also dramatic adaptations of the story of Rāma, as the ones already mentioned in the Harivaṁśa (note on p. 432, above) can be seen enacted in the villages and towns of India on religious and festival occasions. Thus in northern India for example in Lahore, every year the Daśahrā festival is celebrated by the "Rāma-play" (Rām Līlā), in which the most popular scenes from the Rāmāyaṇa are enacted[2] in the presence of a very large audience. We can answer the question whether the widespread worship of the monkey-king as a local deity in India and the monkey worship in general is to be traced back to the popularity of the Rāmāyaṇa or whether on the other hand the significant role which the monkeys play in the Rāma-legend must be explained as originating in an earlier monkey-cult. But it is certain that an image of the monkey-king Hanumat must not be missing in any big village and that there are lots of monkeys in many temples which are treated

---

1. A. Baumgartner, *Das Rāmāyaṇa und die Rāmaliteratur der Inder*. Freiburg B., 1894, has given a survey of the whole Rāma-literature.

2. J. C. Oman who was an eye-witness gives a vivid description of this festival in *The Great Indian Epics, the stories of the Rāmāyaṇa and the Mahābhārata*, London 1899, p. 75 ff. Cf. M. M. Underhill, *The Hindu Religious Year*. Heritage of India Series, 1921, pp. 79 f.

with great consideration and love. This is so in particular in Oudh, the ancient residence-town of Rāma.[1]

Rāma himself, the hero of the Rāmāyaṇa, was made into an incarnation of God Viṣṇu only later and then worshipped as a demi-god. It cannot be a surprise to us that the epic dealing with a demi-god Rāma assumed then the character of a holy book. Thus even in the first canto (of course not originating from Vālmīki) it is said:

"Whoe'er this noble poem reads
That tells the tales of Rāma's deeds,
Good as the scriptures, he shall be
From every sin and blemish free.

Whoever reads the saving strain
With all his kin the heavens shall gain
Brahmins who read shall gather hence
The higher praise for eloquence.

The warrior o'er the land shall reign
The merchant luck in trade obtain;
And śūdras listening ne'er shall fail
To reap advantage from the tale".

(Translated by R.T.H. Griffith)

There is also a typical story of Dāmodara II, a king of Kashmir, who was transformed into a serpent by a curse and cannot be redeemed from the curse until he gets the whole Rāmāyaṇa read out to him in one single day.[2]

But it is just this popularity of the Rāmāyaṇa, as also in the case of Mahābhārata, which is also a reason for this that the poem has been handed down to us not in its original form but enlarged through additions and changes and mutilated in many ways. The work, as we have it today consists of seven books and contains 24,000 couplets (ślokas); but of these what is old or new or real or spurious, can be determined only when we have given a short summary of the contents of the poem.

---

1. Cf. W. Crooke, *Popular Religion and Folklore of Northern India*, 2nd. ed., 1896, p. 85 ff., W. J. Wilkins, *Hindu Mythology*, 2nd ed., Calcutta 1882. p. 405, Underhill, ibid., pp. 119 f.

2. Kalhaṇa's Rājataraṅgiṇī I, 166.

CONTENTS OF THE RĀMĀYAṆA[1]

The first book, called Bālakāṇḍa (Book of the childhood) begins with an introduction on the origin of the poem and tells the story of Rāma in his boyhood days.[2] But just like in the Mahābhārata in this book also the course of the narrative is interrupted by the interpolation of numerous Brahmanical myths and legends; and some of these are all the same as occur in various versions also in the Mahābhārata. Thus even the mention of Ṛṣyaśṛṅga is enough to tell us the legend already known to us.[3] The appearance of Vasiṣṭha and Viśvāmitra is the occasion for narrating numerous stories referring to these two well-known ṛṣis of antiquity. Thus in particular we are told the story of Viśvāmitra's expiatory exercises which he performed to become a Brahmin. Likewise it is also told exhaustively how this ṛṣi was tempted by the apsaras Menakā and Rambhā.[4]

1. There is no complete German translation. There is an Italian translation by Gaspare Gorresio, Parigi 1847-1858, (5 volumes), a French one by H. Fauche 1854-1858 (9 volumes), and one by A. Roussel, Paris 1903-1909, an English version by Ralph T. H. Griffith. Benares and London 1870-1874 (5 volumes, reprinted in 1 volume, Benares 1895, new edition with a memoire by M. N. Venkataswami, Benares 1915) and an English prose translation by Manmatha Nath Dutt, Calcutta 1892-1894 (7 volumes). A condensed reproduction of the whole poem in beautiful English verses is Romesh Dutt's splendid book *Ramayana, The Epic of Rama, Prince of India, condensed into English Verse*, 1900. Summaries in the above mentioned (p. 454 — Note) works of Jacobi and Baumgartner. F. Rückert has given the summary in a highly condensed form in his poem *Rama's Ruhm und Sitas Liebesleid* (Ges. poetische Werke in 12 Bänden, Frankfurt a. M., 1868, III, 268 ff.) Only Book I has been translated into German by J. Menrad, München, 1897. Also, see R. T. H. Griffith, *Scenes from the Rāmāyaṇa*, reprinted and published by the Pāṇini-Office. Allahabad, 1912.

2. Only this first book has been fully translated into German prose by J. Menrad, *Rāmāyaṇa, das Lied vom König Rama ein altindisches Heldengedicht des Vālmīki* etc., Munich 1897.

3. I, 9-11. Translated by Otto Wilmans in, *Polyglotte der Orientalischen Poesie of H. Jolowicz*. 2nd Ed., Leipzig 1856, p. 83 ff. cf. H. Lüders in the *Nachrichten der K. Ges. der Wiss. zu Göttingen, phil.-hist. Kl.* 1897, Nr. 1. p. 18 ff. and above p. 384 ff.

4. I, 51-65 Translated by Franz Bopp, *Über das conjugations-system der Sanskritsprache usw.* Frankfurt a. M. 1816, p. 159 ff. From this translation Heine got acquainted with the legend above on pp. 388-89.

The ancient legend of Śunaḥśepa belongs also to the ancient cycle of Viśvāmitra-legends.[1] Of the other myths and legends we may mention also that of the dwarf-incarnation of God Viṣṇu (I.29), of the birth of the war-god Kumāra or Kārthikeya (I.35-37), of the 60,000 sons of Sagara (of the ocean) and of the descent of the Gaṅgā from the heaven[2] and of the churning of the ocean by gods and demons.[3]

From the introduction we may mention in particular only the beautiful story of the invention of the śloka.[4]

Vālmīki is wandering on the bank of a river through the forest. Then he notices a plover-couple which is hopping about in the grass singing charmingly. Suddenly a wicked hunter comes that way and kills the male with an arrow. As the bird now rolls in its blood and the female wails in its miserable voice, Vālmīki is afflicted with profound sympathy and out of his breast springs a curse against the hunter. The words of the curse however take themselves the form of śloka and God Brahman commissions the poet to sing the deeds of Rāma precisely in this manner.

On the boyhood of Rāma the following is told in the first book. In the town of Ayodhyā (the Oudh of the present day) in the country of Kosala (north of the Ganges) a powerful and wise king by name Daśaratha was ruling. He was childless for a long time. So he decided to perform the horse-sacrifice. The sage Ṛṣyaśṛṅga was won over to direct the details of the great performance and he performs a specially effective offering which with its powers of magic could effect the birth of sons. Precisely at this time the gods in heaven had to suffer much from the demon Rāvaṇa. They therefore approach Viṣṇu requesting him

1. I. 62, cf. above p. 195 ff.

2. I. 38-44. This piece has already been translated into German by A. W. Von Schlegel in his *Indischen Bibliothek* I (Bonn 1823), p. 50 ff. and also A. Hoefer, *Indische Gedichte*, II. 33 ff. An outline of the story is given by J. C. Oman, in *The Great Indian Epics*, pp. 87 ff.

3. I, 45, cf. above p. 374.

4. I, 2. Translated by F. von Schlegel, *Über die Sprache und Weishiet der Indier*, p. 266. H. Jabobi *Das Rāmāyaṇa*, p. 80 f. presumes that this legend is based on the fact that the epic śloka in its final form is traced back to Vālmilki.

to become a human being in order to kill Rāvaṇa as such Viṣṇu agrees and decides to be born on the earth as the son of Daśaratha. After the horse sacrifice was completed, the three wives of king Daśaratha bore him four sons; Kauśalyā gave birth to Rāma (in whom Viṣṇu had personified himself), Kaikeyī to Bharata, Sumitrā to Lakṣmaṇa and Śatrughna. Of these four princes, Rāma the eldest was the declared favourite of the king. From his youth onwards Lakṣmaṇa was however most intimately affectionate towards his elder brother Rāma. He was like his second life and did all that he desired, reading his desires even from his eyes.

As the sons had grown up, the great Ṛṣi Viśvāmitra came to the court of Daśaratha. With him went Rāma and Lakṣmaṇa in order to kill demons for which the Ṛṣi rewarded them with magic weapons. Viśvāmitra also accompanies the princes to the court of Janaka of Videha. This Janaka had a daughter named Sītā. She was no ordinary human child, but as the king was once ploughing the field she had come out of the earth — hence her name Sīta, "the furrow"— and Janaka had brought her up as his own daughter. But the king possessed a wonderful bow and had proclaimed that he would give his daughter in marriage only to him who would bend this bow. Many princes had already tried but in vain. Then came Rāma and bent the bow so that it broke into pieces with a thundering noise. Greatly pleased the king gives him his daughter in marriage. Daśaratha is informed and is brought and then the wedding of Rāma and Sītā is performed with great joy. And they both lived in happiness and bliss for many years.

The actual plot begins with the second book which describes the events of the royal court of Ayodhyā and is therefore called Ayodhyā-Kāṇḍa.[1]

As Daśaratha felt old age approaching him, he decided to crown his favourite son Rāma as his successor and asked his family-priest Vasiṣṭha to make all the preparations necessary for the coronation. The hunchbacked maid of Queen Kaikeyī notices this and incites her mistress that she should prevail

1. A free and brief poetic treatment of this book in German is *Rāma, ein indisches Gedicht nach Walmiki*, deutsch von Adolf Holtzmann, 2nd ed. Karlsruhe 1843.

upon the king to make her son Bharata the successor to the throne. The king had granted her once upon a time two boons which she had not taken till now. Now she asks of the king that he should send Rāma into exile for 14 years and make her son Bharata his successor to the throne. The king is crushed down, but Rāma himself as soon as he has heard about the matter, does not hesitate even a moment to go into exile, in order that his father may not break his word. In vain do his mother Kauśalyā and his brother Lakṣmaṇa try to hold him back. He insists that it is his highest duty to be helpful to his father in fulfilling his promise. He at once informs his wife too, that he is determined to go into exile. He exhorts her to be kind to Bharata, to lead pious and temperate life at the court of Daśaratha and to serve his father and mother[1] obediently. But Sītā replies to him in a magnificent speech on the duties of a wife, that nothing would stop her from following him to the forest:

"My lord, the mother, sire and son
Receive their lots by merit won;
The brother and the daughter find
The portions to their deeds assigned.
The wife alone, whate'er await,
Must share on earth her husband's fate.
So now the king's command which sends
Thee to the wild, to me extends.
The wife can find no refuge, none,
In father, mother, self, or son:
Both here, and when they vanish hence,
Her husband is her sole defence.
If, Raghu's son, thy steps are led
Where Daṇḍak's pathless wilds are spread,
My feet before thine own shall pass
Through tangled thorn and matted grass.
And as with thee I wander there
I will not bring thee grief or care.

1. It is interesting that Rāma always speaks of all the wives of his father as his "mothers".

I long, when thou, wise lord, art nigh,
All fearless, with delighted eye,
To gaze upon the rocky hill,
The lake, the fountain and, the rill;
To sport with thee, my limbs to cool,
In some pure lily-covered pool,
While the white swan's and mallard's wings
Are playing in the water springs.
So would a thousand seasons flee
Like one sweet day, if spent with thee.
Without my lord I would not prize,
A home with gods above the skies;
Without my lord, my life to bless,
Where could be heaven or happiness ?"[1]

Rāma describes to her all the terrors and dangers of the forest, in order to dissuade her from her decision. But she remains firm and does not like to entertain the idea of a separation; like Sāvitrī once upon a time in the past followed Satyavat, she would go away from him.

Then at last Rāma consents that Sītā goes with him to the forest. Lakṣmaṇa, the faithful brother cannot naturally be prevented from following his brother into exile. Clothed only in tree-barks they go into exile much to the distress of all the people.

But king Daśaratha cannot suppress his grief at the banishment of his son. A few days after Rāma had gone into exile, the king gets up from sleep at midnight. Then he is reminded of a misdeed he had committed in his youth; he tells Kauśalyā how once upon a time he had killed a young ascetic by mistake while hunting and how his blind father had cursed him, that he shall die out of grief or separation from his son. Now this curse was being fulfilled:

"I see thee not: these eyes grow blind,
And memory quits my troubled mind.
Angels of Death are round me: they
Summon my soul with speed away.

1. II, 27 translated by R. T. H. Griffith.

What woe more grievous can there be,
That, when from light and life I flee,
I may not, ere I part, behold
My virtuous Rāma, true and bold?
Grief for my son, the brave and the true,
Whose joy it was my will to do,
Dries up my breath, as summer dries
The last drop in the pool that lies. . . .
Ah Raghu's son, ah mighty-armed,
By whom my cares were soothed and charmed,
My son in whom I took delight,
Now vanished from thy father's sight!
Kauśalyā, ah, I cannot see;
Sumitrā, gentle devotee!
Alas Kaikeyī, cruel dame,
My bitter foe, thy father's shame!
Kauśalyā and Sumitrā kept
Their watch beside him as he wept.
And Daśaratha moaned and sighed,
And grieving for his darling died."[1]

After the death of the king, Bharata who stays in Rājagṛha is brought and is exhorted by his mother Kaikeyī and by the ministers to ascend the throne. But Bharata flatly refuses and declares with resolve that the kingdom was Rāma's and he would bring him back. With a great retinue he starts off to fetch his brother. In the meanwhile Rāma stays in the Citrakūṭa mountains and is just describing to Sītā the beauties of the landscape.[2] When they see clouds of dust being raised and hear the noise of an approaching army, Lakṣmaṇa climbs up a mountain and sees the army of Bharata approach. He thinks it is an enemy attack and is enraged. But soon he sees that Bharata leaves his army back and approaches alone. He comes near Rāma, falls on his feet and the brothers embrace each other. Now Bharata, shedding tears reproaching himself and

1. Translated into German by Ad. Friedr. Grafen von Schack, *Stimmen vom Ganges* (Stuttgart, 1877), p. 106-19; *Der Tod des Dasaratha*. The English translation is by Griffith (II, 64).

2. II, 94. A splendid description of nature such as this are not seldom in *Rāmāyaṇa*.

his mother Kaikeyī, reports to Rāma the death of their father and exhorts him to come back and rule the country. Rāma says he cannot reproach him or his mother; but what the father had ordered was dear to him even now and his resolve, to spend 14 years in the forest, he would never give up. In vain are all the entreaties of Bharata, who reminds him of the death of their father. Mourning deeply Rāma performs the oblations to the departed father, but he remains firm in his decision. Rāma consoles the mourning brother with a splendid speech on the natural necessity of the transitoriness of life and the inevitability of death which makes any mourning foolish.

In scatterings end collections all;
High towering piles at length must fall;
In parting every meeting ends;
To Death all life of creatures tends.

The early fall to earth is sure,
Of fruits on trees that hang mature,
Of mortals here behold a type;
They, too, succumb, for death when ripe.

As houses fall when long decay
Has worn the posts which formed their stay,
So sink men's frames, when age's course
Has undermined their vital force . …

As logs that on the ocean float,
By chance are into contact brought,
But tossed about by wind and tide,
Together cannot along abide,
So wives, sons, kinsmen, riches, all
Whate'er our own we fondly call,—
Obtained, possessed, enjoyed, today,
Tomorrow all are snatched away.

As, standing on the road a man
Who sees a passing caravan,
Which slowly winds across the plain,
Cries, "I will follow in your train",

So men the beaten path must tread
On which their sires of yore have led.
Since none can nature's course elude,
Why o'er thy doom in sorrow brood ?[1]
(II, 105, 16 ff. translated by J. Muir).

The Councillors too come in order to ask Rāma to take over the reign. One of them, Jābāli, a thorough heretic tries to counteract his moral hesitation by saying that—everyone should live only for himself and need not care for father or mother, that death was an end of everything, that the senseless talk of a world beyond is spread only by cunning priests in order to obtain gifts, therefore he should consult only his power of understanding and ascend the throne. But Rāma rejects outright these teachings of the nihilist.[2] Even the ideas of the pious priest Vasiṣṭha cannot change his mind. And in the end Bharata must yield and agree to govern the kingdom in the name of Rāma. Rāma gives him his sandals as the symbol of government[3] and Bharata goes back to Ayodhyā where Rāma's sandals are ceremoniously installed on the throne to represent the king while he himself goes over to Nandīgrāma in order to mind the affairs of the kingdom from there in the name of Rāma.

1. II, 105, 16 ff. according to Holtzmann, *Rāma*. 1930 ff. "sayings of this sort belong to the oft-quoted common possession of Indian poets. We find them almost verbatim also in the Mahābhārata, in the Purāṇas, in the legal literature (for example Viṣṇusmṛti xx, 32) in the Buddhistic aphoristic wisdom, in the sayings of Bhartṛhari etc., Rāma's speech of consolation forms the nucleus of the Daśaratha-Jātaka; cf below p. 487.

2. This expression corresponds exactly to the Sanskrit "nāstika i.e., one who teaches that there is nothing, "nāsti". Here Rāma is made to say, "Like a thief is the Buddha, and the Tathāgata, you must know, is a nāstika". This verse which does not occur in all recensions has been distinctly proved long ago as spurious (Jacobi, ibid., p. 88 f.). Jacobi considers the entire Jābāli episode to be an interpolation. A. Hillebrandt, however, observes (Festschrift Kuhn, p. 23): "The situation is described very well, and such an effective contrast has been made between the materialist and the pious Rāma that I cannot consider this passage as spurious."

3. On the shoe as a legal symbol in Old Norsic and Old Germanic law, compare Jacob Grimm, *Deutsche Rechtsaltertümer*, 4th edition, 1899, I, 213 ff. Even A. Holtzmann makes a comparison with strikingly similar Hebrew custom, Ruth 4, 7.

The third book which describes the forest life of the banished ones and is therefore called "Āraṇya-Kāṇḍa", "Forest-Chapter" takes us so to say from the world of reality into a colourful world of fairy tales which we do not leave any more till the end of the book. Whereas the second book shows us the life and activity at a royal court in India and is the result of a court-intrigue as similar intrigues have actually occurred in the past in India — thereby is only the exaggerated nobility of the two brothers Rāma and Bharata rather imaginary with the third book the battles and adventures of Rāma commence which he encounters with the fantastic figures and demonic beings.

When the banished ones had lived for a long time in the Daṇḍaka-forest, the hermits living in the forest requested Rāma for protection from the Rākṣasas. Rāma promises this and is engaged from then on incessantly in battles with those diabolical monsters. The man-eating giant Virādha is the first one who is killed.[1] It is a fatal meeting that the exiled ones have with Sūrpaṇakhā (having claws as big as winnows), the sister of Rāvaṇa. This female devil falls in love with Rāma and makes advances to him. But he directs her to his brother Lakṣmaṇa who is not yet married.[2] Lakṣmaṇa turns down her advances scornfully. Boiling with rage she wants to devour Sītā. Upon this Lakṣmaṇa cuts off her ears and nose. She runs shreiking to her brother Khara who then attacks Rāma first with 14 and then with 14,000 Rākṣasas who are all killed by Rāma. After Khara also has fallen. Sūrpaṇakhā runs to Laṅkā, a fabulous country beyond the ocean,[3] and instigates her brother Rāvaṇa, a ten-headed monster and ruler of Laṅkā, to take vengeance on Rāma. At the same time she describes to him the wonderful beauty of Sītā in the most attractive colours

1. Here follow again in cantos 8-14 all sorts of legends, for example of the Ṛṣi Agastya among others, just like in Book I and in the Mahābhārata.

2. This text is one of the many proofs for the spuriousness of the first book in which it is told that Rāma's brothers have married at the same time as he himself.

3. Not Ceylon, as one is used to presume in general. Only at a much later time Laṅkā was equated with Ceylon. See Jacobi, *Rāmāyaṇa* p. 90 ff. M. V. Kibe, *Rāvana's Laṅkā Discovered*, 2nd Ed., 1920, attempts to determine the geographical position of Laṅkā.

and provokes him to win her and make her his wife. So Rāvaṇa starts off, drives in his golden chariot through the air over the ocean and meets on the other side Mārīca who is living there doing penance. With the help of this friend Rāvaṇa succeeds in isolating Sītā from her protectors and to abduct her. He kidnaps her in his chariot through the air. Jaṭāyus the vulture, an old friend of Daśaratha comes flying and succeeds in smashing Rāvaṇa's chariot, but he is at last beaten by Rāvaṇa who now takes Sītā in his clutches and flies away with her. As she is carried through the sky, the flowers in her hair fall down to the earth and the anklets studded with precious stones slip down from her feet and fall to the earth. The trees in whose twigs the wind is rustling seem to call out to her "Do not fear"; the lotuses let their flower heads hang down as though they were lamenting their dear friend; lions, tigers and other wild animals go running as if in anger behind Sītā's shadow; the mountains seem to mourn for Sītā with their faces overflowing with tears (the waterfalls) and their hands stretched out (the peaks shooting up into the sky). Even the exalted sun himself, his rays becoming dark and his face pale on seeing Sītā being kidnapped, seems to bewail; "There is no law any more, no truth, no righteousness and no innocence when Rāvaṇa kidnaps Sītā, the wife of Rāma" (iii, 52, 34-39). But Rāvaṇa flies with his booty over the ocean to Laṅkā where he accommodates her in his harem. He takes her round his palace, shows her all his splendours and describes to her the immeasurable riches and wonderful things at his command. With flattering words he tries to persuade her to become his wife. But Sītā replies to him in anger that she would never be faithless to Rāma and let her be touched by Rāvaṇa. Then Rāvaṇa threatens that if she would not yield to him within 12 months, he would let her have cut into pieces by the cooks and eat her for breakfast. Then he sends her to a grotto and hands her over to Rākṣasa-women for being guarded strictly.

In the meanwhile Rāma and Lakṣmaṇa have returned and to their amazement they find the hut empty. They look in vain in the forest for Sītā. Rāma laments bitterly and questions the trees, the rivers, the mountains and the animals — but none can give him news of Sītā. At last they find the flowers and ornaments which Sītā has dropped on the way while on flight, and soon also the wreckage of Rāvaṇa's chariot, the weapons lying about and other traces of a fight. Rāma has no other thought but that Sītā has been killed by the Rākṣasas and in mad rage he declares that he would destroy the whole world: He would fill the whole atmosphere with his arrows, he would arrest the blowing of the wind, destroy the rays of the sun and cover the earth in darkness, send the peaks of mountains rolling down, dry up the ponds, smash the ocean to pieces, uproot the trees; indeed he would even annihilate the gods themselves if they did not give him his Sītā back. Only with very great difficulty does Lakṣmaṇa succeed to pacify the infuriated Rāma and make him continue his search. Then they find the vulture Jaṭāyus who is rolling in blood. While dying he tells them what has happened, but he dies even before completing his narration. Wandering southward they come across a crying headless monster, Kabandha, whom they free from a curse. As an expression of his gratefulness he gives Rāma the advice that he should ally himself with the monkey-king Sugrīva who will help him for winning back Sītā.

The fourth book — the Kiṣkindhā-kāṇḍa — tells of the alliance that Rāma makes with the monkeys in order to win back Sītā.

The brothers arrive at the Pampā-lake, the sight of which strikes a melancholy note in Rāma's heart. For it is spring and the sight of nature waking up rouses in him a yearning to see his beloved from whom he is now separated.[1] Here they soon meet the monkey-king Sugrīva. He tells them he has been robbed of his wife and kingdom by his brother. Rāma and Sugrīva now make an alliance of close friendship. Rāma promises to help Sugrīva against Vālin while Sugrīva promises to help Rāma in winning back Sītā. In front of Kiṣkindhā[2] the residence of Vālin, the two antagonistic brothers fought with each other. Rāma comes to Sugrīva's rescue and kills Vālin. Sugrīva the monkey becomes the king and Aṅgada, the son of Vālin is installed as successor to the throne.

1. The entire first canto is an elegy, which one could call "Yearning for the Beloved in Spring" quite in the style of later ornate poetry.

2. Hence the title of the IV Book.

Among the Councillors of Sugrīva is however Hanumat,[1] the son of the Wind-god, the wisest. Sugrīva has the greatest confidence in him and he commissions him with the discovery of Sītā. Accompanied by an army of monkeys under Aṅgada's command the clever Hanumat sets out on the way to the south. After many kinds of adventures they meet Sampāti, a brother of Jaṭāyus the vulture. This Jaṭāyus tells them, how, as he wanted to compete with his brother in flying[2] his wings were burnt down so that he had to remain wingless on the Vindhya mountain. But he had seen how Rāvaṇa had kidnapped Sītā to Laṅkā. He describes to them the location of Laṅkā and the monkeys get down to ocean. When they see the immeasurably surging sea before them they are seized with sheer despair as to how they could cross it over. But Aṅgada implores them not to despair, "because despair kills men like the angry serpent kills a boy." (IV, 64,9). Then they hold a council as to who can jump farthest and it is seen that no one can jump so far as Hanumat. So he climbs the Mahendra mountain and gets ready to jump over the ocean.

The fifth book describes the wonderful island Laṅkā, the residential town, the magnificent palace and the harem of Rāvaṇa and tells how Hanumat gives Sītā the news of her beloved Rāma and finds out also the strength of the enemy. The title "Sundara-Kāṇḍa" that is, "the pretty chapter" might have been given to the book because of the many poetical descriptions[3] which it has, or because it contains fabulous things more than all other books. If the entire second half of the Rāmāyaṇa is a "romantic epic", this fifth book is especially romantic — and for the Indian taste what is romantic is always the most beautiful.

With a mighty spring which makes the Mahendra mountain tremble in its depths and transports all the beings living on the mountain into fear and fright, Hanumat the monkey leaps

1. Also Hanumat the name means, "The one with the jaws". According to IV, 66, 24 he is called so because Indra smashed his jaws with the thunderbolt.

2. Like the Ikarus. This myth is treated only brieflv in (IV, 58), and then in IV, 59-63 in a Purāṇa-like enlargement.

3. According to Jacobi, *Rāmāyaṇa*, p. 124.

into the air and flies off over the ocean. After a four day flight in the course of which he experiences various adventures and performs miracles, he at last reaches Laṅkā. From a mountain he observes the town which appears invincible to him. He makes himself as small as a cat[1] and enters the town after sun-set. He looks round the enitre demon city, the palace of Rāvaṇa and the wonderful chariot called Puṣpaka, on which the Rākṣasa usually drives through the air. He also gains entry into Rāvaṇa's harem where he espies the powerful demon-prince resting in the midst of his beautiful women.[2] After searching in vain for a long time he at last finds Sītā, consumed with grief, in the Aśoka-grove. He reveals himself as a friend and messenger of Rāma. She tells him that Rāvaṇa has threatened to eat her up and that she must die after two months if Rāma does not set her free before that. But Hanumat assures her that Rāma will come to set her free.[3]

---

1. According to another explanation: "like a horsefly". Hanumat can change his form as he likes.

2. This nocturnal harem-scene (V, 9-11) is described in a lively manner in the style of ornate-poetry and reminds us very much of the description in the Buddha-legend, where Prince Siddhārtha, surrounded by his wives, wakes up at the hour of midnight and is afflicted with contempt for the pleasures of the world. The similarity of the situation and the description is striking enough to justify the presumption that it is an imitation of the description of Aśvaghoṣa in the Buddhacarita (V, 47 ff.). For as E. B. Cowell aptly remarks (in the foreword to his edition of the *Buddhacarita*), this scene forms an essential constituent of the Buddha-legend, whereas in the Rāmāyaṇa it is only a quite superfluous decoration. Of course this piece cannot be ascribed to Vālmīki himself, but some Vālmīkites (as following Jacobi we may call the successors of Vālmīki who have enlarged his work) may be guilty of this imitation.

3. With this Hanumat's mission is fulfilled and the following story (41-55) is doubtless a later interpolation. In order to test the strength of the enemy Hanumat starts a quarrel by destroying the Aśoka-grove. From violent fights with thousands of Rākṣasas he emerges as the lonely victor. But finally he is handcuffed, and brought before the demon-king. Hanumat reveals himself as Rāma's messenger and demands the return of Sītā. Rāvaṇa wants to kill him but is persuaded to spare him as he is a messenger. But in order to punish him he lets clothes soaked in oil be tied round the tail of the monkey and set fire to it. Sītā hears of this and prays to Agni, the god of fire, that he may not burn Hanumat. The monkey now springs with his

Then Hanumat returns to the mountains, flies over the ocean back and tells his experiences in Laṅkā to the monkeys waiting there for him. Then he goes to Rāma, reports to him that he has met Sītā and brings him her message.

The sixth book, that describes the great battle between Rāma and Rāvaṇa — hence called Yuddha-Kāṇḍa, "Battle-Chapter" — is the most voluminous of all.

Rāma praises Hanumat for the successful fulfilment of his mission and embraces him heartily. Nevertheless he is in despair when he thinks of the difficulty of crossing the ocean. Sugrīva advises him to build a bridge over the ocean to Laṅkā. Hanumat gives an exact description of the town of Rāvaṇa and its fortress and explains that the chiefs of the monkey-army would be in a position to take it. Rāma therefore gives orders to array the army ready to march and soon the huge monkey-army marches southwards towards the sea.

When the news of the approaching army of monkeys had reached Laṅkā, Rāvaṇa summoned his councillors — all great and powerful Rākṣasas — for a consultation. While all relatives and councillors incite Rāvaṇa with pompous speeches to fight, Vibhīṣaṇa, Rāvaṇa's brother points to unfavourable omens and advises to give back Sītā. At this Rāvaṇa is very angry and accuses him of jealousy and dislike. Relatives, says he, are the worst enemies of a king and hero. Greatly vexed with his brother, Vibhīṣaṇa parts company with him, comes flying with four other Rākṣasas over to Rāma's side and becomes his ally. On Vibhīṣaṇa's advice Rāma turns to the sea-god himself with a request to help him across the ocean. This ocean calls out Nala, the son of the divine architect Viśvakarman and commissions him to construct a bridge over the ocean. On Rāma's order the monkeys fetch rocks and trees. In a few days a bridge is constructed over the ocean and the whole great army crosses over to Laṅkā.

Now the residential town of Rāvaṇa is surrounded by the monkey-army. Rāvaṇa orders a general attack. There ensues a battle and a number of individual duels take place between

burning tail from house to house and sets fire to the whole town while he himself escaped unscathed. The spuriousness of this piece has been irrefutably proved by Jacobi, ibid., 31 ff.

the chief heroes of the two fighting armies. Lakṣmaṇa, Hanumat, Aṅgada and the bear-king Jāmbavat are the best allies of Rāma, whereas on the side of Rāvaṇa his son Indrajīt distinguishes himself in particular. He is adept in all arts of magic and can make himself invisible at any moment.

So he once inflicts dangerous wounds on Rāma and Lakṣmaṇa. But in the night Hanumat, on the advice of the bear-king Jāmbavat flies to the Kailāsa-mountain in order to fetch from there four specially powerful medicinal herbs. As these herbs lie concealed, he simply takes the whole peak of the mountain and carries it to the battle-field where through the fragrance of the medicinal herbs Rāma, Lakṣmaṇa and all the wounded recover immediately. Now Hanumat transports the mountain back to its place.

At another time Indrajīt, the magician, comes out of the town bringing with him in the war chariot an image of Sītā—conjured up by him to abuse and behead it in the presence of Hanumat, Lakṣmaṇa and the monkeys and Hanumat is enraged and brings to Rāma the news that Sītā has been killed, Rāma falls down unconscious. Lakṣmaṇa breaks out in mourning and speaks bitterly disparaging gods, complaining against fate which is unmindful of virtue (vi, 83, 14 ff)—but he is soon enlightened by Vibhīṣaṇa that all that was only a deception of Indrajīt. At last Indrajīt too is killed by Lakṣmaṇa in a violent duel.

Furious at the death of his son, Rāvaṇa himself appears now on the battle-field. A terrific duel takes place between Rāma and Rāvaṇa which lasts for days and nights. The gods themselves come to the rescue of Rāma, especially Indra with his chariot and missiles. However often Rāma cuts off Rāvaṇa's heads, they grow again afresh. At last he succeeds in piercing through Rāvaṇa's heart with a weapon made by god Brahman himself. The army of the monkeys rejoices greatly, the Rākṣasas take to flight. After a ceremonious funeral to Rāvaṇa, Vibhīṣaṇa is installed as the king of Laṅkā by Rāma.

Only now Rāma lets Sītā be fetched, proclaims to her the glad news of the victory achieved — but he rejects her in the presence of all monkeys and Rākṣasas. He declares that he took vengeance for the dishonour committed on him, but he would not have anything to do with her any more; for a.woman who has sat on another man's lap and who has been viewed with lustful eyes by another man cannot be accepted as wife by Rāma any more. Then Sītā laments bitterly the unjustified suspicion of Rāma and asks Lakṣmaṇa to set up a pyre; for now there is no other go for her than to throw herself into fire. Rāma gives his consent, the pyre is set up and is set fire to, and calling the fire to be her witness, Sītā jumps into the flames. Thereupon the god Agni rises from the burning pyre with the unscathed Sītā on his arm and hands her over to Rāma, assuring in a solemn speech that she has always remained faithful to him and has remained pure and prestine even in the palace of Rākṣasa. Hereupon Rāma declares that he never doubted the purity of Sītā but it was necessary to prove her purity in the presence of the folk.

Now Rāma and his people, accompanied by Hanumat and the monkeys, return to Ayodhyā, where they are received with open arms by Bharata, Śatrughna and the mothers. To the jubilation of the people they enter Ayodhyā, Rāma is crowned king and rules now happily over his people to the great prosperity of all his subjects.

With this the story of Rāma actually comes to an end, and there cannot be any doubt that with the sixth book the original poem has come to a close and that the 7th book coming after this still further, is an addition. This seventh book — it is called Uttara-Kāṇḍa, "last chapter"— contains again numerous sagas and legends as they occur in a similar way also in the Mahābhārata and in the Purāṇas, which do not at all have anything to do with the saga of Rāma. The earlier cantos deal with the birth of the Rākṣasas and the battles between Indra and Rāvaṇa[1] after which the story of Hanumat's boyhood is told (vii, 35 f). Only about a third of the book is concerned with Rāma and Sītā, and in particular, the following is told:

One day Rāma is told that the people are expressing their disapproval of the fact that he has accepted Sītā even though she has sat (at the time of kindnapping) on Rāvaṇa's lap, they feared that this will have a bad influence on the morals of women in the country. Rāma, the ideal king is very much

1. vii, 1-34, Jacobi calls the piece "Ravaneis".

depressed at this; he cannot bear the reproach that he sets a bad example to his subjects, and orders his brother Lakṣmaṇa to take her away and leave her outside the country. With a heavy heart—Lakṣmaṇa takes her in his chariot to the Ganges and brings her to the other bank of the river where he discloses to her that Rāma has rejected her owing to the aspersions cast by the people. In profound grief, but yet fully resigned to her fate, Sītā sends Rāma only best regards. Soon after this children of the hermitage of Vālmīki find the weeping Sītā in the forest and take her to the hermitage, where Vālmīki entrusts her to the care of the women folk of the hermitage. There she gives birth to the twins Kuśa and Lava after some time.

Many years pass. The children have grown up and have become pupils of the ascetic and singer Vālmīki. Then Rāma organises a horse-sacrifice. For this Vālmīki too comes with his pupils. He asks two of them to recite the Rāmāyaṇa composed by him in the sacrificial assembly. All hear the wonderful recitation with rapt attention. Soon however, Rāma learns that the two youthful singers Kuśa and Lava[1] who have recited the poem to the accompaniment of the lute, are sons of Sītā. So he sends messengers to Vālmīki requesting him to make Sītā purify herself by means of an oath in the presence of the sacrificial assembly. The next morning Vālmīki fetches Sītā and in a ceremonious speech the great ascetic himslf declares that she is blemishless and her children the twin brothers Kuśa and Lava are the actual sons of Rāma. Thereupon Rāma explains that although he himself is satisfied with the words of Vālmīki, still he would like Sītā to purify herself by means of an oath. Then all the Gods descended from the heaven. Sītā, however, spoke turning her look downward and folding her hands, "As truly as I have never even thought of another man than Rāma — may Goddess Earth open her womb to me ! As truly as I have worshipped only Rāma in thought, word and deed,— may Goddess Earth open her womb to me ! As truly as I have spoken the truth here, and never known a man other

1. Professional "travelling singers" who sang epic songs to the accompaniment of the lute were called "Kuśīlava"; the names of Kuśa and Lava have been invented to signify etymologically in a way the word "Kuśīlava" Jacobi, p. 62 f., 67 f.

than Rāma — may Goddess Earth open her womb to me!" Scarcely was this oath taken, than a heavenly throne rose out of the earth, borne by the serpent-demons on their heads, and Mother Earth, sitting on the throne, embraced Sītā and disappeared with her into the depths. Rāma now implores Goddess Earth to give him back his Sītā, but in vain. Only god Brahman appears and consoles him with the hope of reunion in the heaven. Soon after this Rāma hands the government over to his two sons Kuśa and Lava and he himself disappears into the heaven where he becomes Viṣṇu once again.

The thread of the narration of this story is interrupted through the interpolation of numerous myths and legends again and again. We find there again the well-known legends of Yayâti and Nahuṣa (vii, 58 f) of the killing of Vṛtra and Indra, who thus makes himself guilty of Brahmin-murder (VII, 84-87), of Urvaśī, the beloved of the gods Mitra and Varuṇa who produce in a miraculous way the Ṛṣis Vasiṣṭha and Agastya (VII, 56 f.) of king Ila who as the woman Ila gives birth to Purūravas (VII, 87-907) and similar ones. Many legends with a really strong Brahmanic tendency resemble stories of the 13th book of the Mahābhārata in their dignity. Thus we find for example the story of the ascetic Śambūka belonging to the Śūdra-caste whose head is cut off by Rāma for which act he is praised by the gods, because a Śūdra should not dare practise asceticism, and that of the god who must consume his own flesh because in an earlier life he had practised asceticism but failed to make gifts to Brahmins (VII, 73-81) and similar legends of edification. The whole book bears throughout the character of the latest portions of the Mahābhārata.

The Genuine and the Spurious in the Rāmāyaṇa[1]

It cannot be doubted that the entire seventh book of the Rāmāyaṇa has been added only later on. But it has been

1. The problems of the Rāmāyaṇa have been fully dealt with first by A. Weber, "Über das Rāmāyaṇa" (*ABA.*, 1870). The fundamental work on these problems is that of H. Jacobi, *Das Rāmāyaṇa, Geschichte und Inhalt*, Bonn, 1893. See also C. V. Vaidya, *The Riddle of the Rāmāyaṇa*, Bombay and London, 1906; and Dinesh Chandra Sen, The Bengali Rāmāyaṇas, Calcutta, 1920.

known since a very long time that the entire first book cannot have belonged to the original work of Vālmīki. Not only are there numerous internal self-contradictions in this book but also the language and style show themselves as inferior in quality to those of Books II to VI. Further, nowhere in the genuine parts of the poem is any reference made to the events of the first book. In fact, in this book we find statements which exactly contradict statements of the later books.[1]

Only in the first and seventh book is Rāma understood as a divine being, an incarnation of god Viṣṇu. But for a few certainly interpolated texts[2] he is, in the books II to VI, throughout always only a human hero and in all the parts of the epic which are doubtlessly genuine, there is not a single trace to show that he would have been thought as an incarnation of Viṣṇu. Wherever in the genuine parts of the poem mythology is in play, it is not Viṣṇu, but god Indra who is considered as the highest god in the Veda.

For the two books I and VII it is also typical that in them, as we have seen, the thread of the narration often snaps and numerous Brahmanic myths and legends were interpolated as in the case of the Mahābhārata and the Purāṇas. Such things occur only at very few places in the Books II and VI. The additions and enlargements in these books — they are numerous enough — are of a quite different type. They consist mainly in this that just the most beautiful and popular texts have been, as far as possible, elaborated by the reciters, and increased by their own inventions. In fact we must imagine the transmission of the Rāmāyaṇa through centuries in the following manner: It was transmitted orally — as in the manner of Kuśa and Lava in the Uttara-Kāṇḍa for a long time (perhaps for centuries). These reciters and travelling musicians considered the epic songs as their property with which they took all sorts of liberties. Now, if they noticed that the listeners were moved with the touching lamentation of Sītā, of Daśaratha or of Kauśalyā they composed some more verses in addition in order to spend some more time in that context, if the battle-scenes found special

1. For example, the wedding of Lakṣmaṇa above, p. 466, note 2.
2. Thus for example at the end of the VI book where at the moment Sītā mounts the pyre, all gods come down and praise Rāma as god Viṣṇu.

favour with a war like public then it was always easy for the reciters to bring new heroes to fight duels; they could always get a few thousands or tens of thousands of monkeys or Rākṣasas slaughtered or narrate a heroic deed already once narrated in a slightly altered form, if listeners found pleasure in comic scenes particularly where the monkeys appear, then it was a temptation for the reciter, not only to spin out such scenes but also to compose more such new ones; if he had a learned audience consisting of Brahmins then he sought to win their favour by spinning out the didactic pieces, by adding new moral verses or by interpolating moral sayings that they had taken from somewhere; lastly many ambitious rhapsodes have elaborated the descriptions of nature found popular certainly in the ancient and genuine poetry by means of additions in the style of the ornate poetry of royal courts.[1] But the Rāmāyaṇa got a somewhat fixed form — just like the Mahābhārata — perhaps only when it was reduced to writing.[2] This must have happened at a time when the poem was already so famous and beloved, that it was already considered as an act of religious merit, to read and hear it and that the heaven was promised to those who copied it down.[3] But the more one copied of such a splendid and salutary poem "that bestows long life, health, fame, good brothers and understanding",[4] the more certainly did one go to heaven. Therefore the early collectors and compilers who reduced the poem to writing did not consider it as their duty to sift critically what they received, to separate the genuine from the spurious but to them everything was rather welcome which offered itself under the title "Rāmāyaṇa".

---

1. It was favourable for the elaborations and unfavourable for the retention of the genuine, that the śloka is a verse-metre that is easy to use. It is very easy for even a half-educated man who knows Sanskrit, to just heap śloka after śloka in a spur of a moment.

2. The activity of the commentators through whom the text was made more secure began in any case much later.

3. VI, 128, 120: Those men who full of love for Rāma write down this collection (Saṃhitā) composed by the Ṛṣi, acquire an abode in Indra's heaven.

4. VI, 128, 122, see also above p. 457.

But we can speak only of a "somewhat" fixed form of the Rāmāyaṇa, because the manuscripts in which the epic has come down to us vary from one another very much, and there are at least three different recensions of the text which represent the transmission in the various regions of India. These recensions differ from one another not only with respect to individual readings but also in this that in each of them verses, longer texts and even whole cantos occur which are missing in the others; also the order of the verses is not the same in the different versions. The most widely spread (both in the north and the south of India) and probably also the oldest recension is the one which Jacobi designated as "C" and which has been printed many times in Bombay.[1] The only complete edition that appeared in Europe, that of G. Gorresio[2] contains the Bengal recension. The text of the North-Western Indian (Western Indian, Kashmiri) recension is now being printed at Lahore.[3]

That there are great differences between the recensions proves only the presumption of oral transmission of the text. It is understandable that the order of the verses in the memory of rhapsodes gets shifted, that the text had to undergo often significant changes and that the reciters of the various regions made their own additions and elaborations.

---

1. Our quotations are from this recension in the edition of the NSP, by K. P. Parab, 2nd Ed., Bombay, 1902. It was a mistake to call this recension "Northern Indian," for the Southern Indian MSS give the same text; See Winternitz, *Catalogue of South Indian Sanskrit Manuscripts*, London, 1902, p. 67; M. Winternitz and A. B. Keith, *Catalogue of Sanskrit MSS.*, in the Bodleian Library, II, pp. 145 f.

2. Turin, 1843-1867. See on this edition E. Windisch, *Geschichte der Sanskrit-Philologie* (Grundriss I, 1B) pp. 145 f. Only the two first Books have been edited (with a Latin translation) by A. W. von Schlegel, Bonnae, 1829, 1838, on eclectic principles. An edition from a Bengali MS with comparative footnotes was published by Pandit Rasiklal Bhattacharya in the *Pandit*, N. S., Vols. 28-34. A comparative study of the recensions C and B (Bengali) has been made by M. Vallauri, *GSAI*, 25, 1912. pp. 45 ff.

3. Critically edited by Pandit Ram Labhya, published by the Research Department, D. A. V. College, Lahore, 1923 ff. Cf. Hans Wirtz, *Die Westliche Recension des Rāmāyaṇa*, Diss. Bonn, 1894; S. Lévi, JA. 1918, s. 11, t. xi, pp. 5 ff. Only when we shall have critical editions of all the three recensions will it be possible to decide which of them contains the more authentic text.

What is common to all the three recensions is that all of them contain seven books, and that in each of them spurious texts occur by the side of the genuine ones. An "original text" of the Rāmāyaṇa is therefore not to be had in any of the recensions; but the absence of a text in one of the recensions is always a justified ground for suspicion against its genuineness. And in general it is in any case more easy in the case of the Rāmāyaṇa than in that of the Mahābhārata to isolate the spurious and the more recent portions. "As in the case of some of our old venerable cathedrals", says Jacobi[1] "every coming generation has added something new and repaired the old without the original layout being in any way obliterated in spite of all built up chapels and steeples; thus many generations of singers have been working at the Rāmāyaṇa; but the old nucleus, round which so much has grown about is easily recognisable in its main features even if not in minute details". Jacobi himself has proved irrefutably in his work, "Das Rāmāyaṇa" a large number of additions and elaborations as such. That when an attempt is made to prepare a critical edition of the text perhaps only one fourth of the 24,000 verses of the Rāmāyaṇa handed down to us would turn out to be "genuine", does not speak anything against the justification of the criticism.[2] It is only on account of the large number of the "spurious" in the Indian epics that we are more often disappointed while reading those which rouse great admiration in us. And when we compare the Indian with the Greek epics with respect to their artistic value if the result should necessarily turn out against the former ones, then the people responsible for this are not the poets of ancient India but rather those poetasters who have elaborated and mutilated the old cantos by means of their own additions and changes. The "shapelessly fermenting verbosity" of which Friedrich Rückert reproaches the Rāmāyaṇa, is certainly more often on account of the Vālmīkites than of Vālmīki himself. On the whole however the German poet is certainly right when he

1. *Das Rāmāyaṇa*, p. 60.

2. In the 51st volume of the *ZDMG* (1897) p. 605 ff., Jacobi has made an attempt to deal critically with considerable connected portion of the Rāmāyaṇa, and in that attempt, of 600 verses not even a quarter has been left behind.

seeks the beauty of the Indian poetry somewhere else than that of the Greek, saying:

> "Such fantastic grievances, such shapelessly
> fermenting verbosity,
> As the Rāmāyaṇa offers you, that Homer has
> Certainly taught you to despise, but yet
> such high thinking
> And such profound heart even the Ilias
> does not show you".[1]

The Age of the Rāmāyaṇa[2]

Closely connected with the question of the genuine and spurious in the Rāmāyaṇa is that of the age of the poem -- unfortunately there again we have to depend only on presumptions. Of course for answering this question it is certainly not immaterial if we can at least imagine to ourselves what time could have possibly passed between the original poem whose genuine constituents are to be sought in Books II-VI and the two appended Books I and VII. In this connection the following considerations of Jacobi deserve our special attention. Rāma, originally doubtless a clan-hero, became a national hero only through the Rāmāyaṇa. As a demi-God vanquishing the demons, this national hero became in Books I and VII (and in a few interpolations) also an incarnation of god Viṣṇu. This transformation of Rāma from man to demi-God and finally to an incarnation of Viṣṇu, the supreme God can have been accomplished only in a long period of time. Secondly in the first and the last books of the Rāmāyaṇa poet Vālmīki appears as a pious hermit in a forest and a Ṛṣi and as a contemporary of Rāma, the hero. Both of them were possible only when Vālmīki had receded chronologically into such a long distance from later poets that the formation of foggy legends could make his person unclear to their eyes. The time that was necessary for this cannot be estimated even approximately by

1. F. Rückert, *Poetisches Tagebuch*, Frankfurt a. M. 1888, p. 99.
2. Cf. Jacobi, ibid., p. 100 ff.; A. B. Keith, *JRAS*, 1915, p. 318 ff.

us; only this much is certain: that it will have to be reckoned in terms of centuries rather than in decades.[1]

But we must hasten to add that in our Mahābhārata too which knows not only the Rāma-legend but also the Rāmāyaṇa of Vālmīki, Rāma is considered as a personification of Viṣṇu and Vālmīki is mentioned as an ancient Ṛṣi. It has been already mentioned above (p. 369) that in all probability the Rāmopākhyāna of the Mahābhārata is only a free condensed rendering of the Rāmāyaṇa -- here, we can add: of the Rāmāyaṇa in a very recent form, rather closely approaching the present one. For, Rāma is, for the author of the Rāmopākhyāna, already an incarnation of Viṣṇu,[2] he knows that Hanumat has burnt Laṅkā — a text that has been proved to be an interpolation[3] and he knows already the portion of the seventh book relating to Rāvaṇa.[4] The story of Rāma is told in the Mahābhārata in order to console Yudhiṣṭhira in his grief over the abduction of Draupadī. The whole episode of Draupadī's abduction is certainly only a duplicate of Sītā's abduction in the Rāmāyaṇa. In the latter this abduction is the nucleus of the whole legend and the poem whereas in the Mahābhārata Draupadī's abduction has almost no significance for the course of the story. Other conspicuous concurrences between the individual features of the two epics especially the similarity of the two heroes — Arjuna and Rāma — has been pointed out, the banishment into the forest for a period of 12 to 14 years, the bending of the bow, the awarding of the divine weapons to the heroes, who get them from the gods[5] these are points where the influencing of the one by the other is possible but can hardly be proved. Yet it is highly probable that the Mahābhārata has borrowed its features from the Rāmāyaṇa, rather than the other way about.

1. Jacobi, p. 65.
2. Mahābh. III, 147, 31; 275, 5 ff.
3. Mahābh. III, 148, 9, cf. above. p. 470. Note 1.
4. Jacobi, p. 73 f. Also Mahābh. VII, 59 and xii, 29, 51 ff. shortly touches upon the Rāma-legend and makes references in some verses which coincide partly with Rāma. vi, 128, 95 ff. to the heavenly condition in which the subjects of Rāma lived i.e., "which lasted ten thousand and ten hundred years of reign".
5. Cf. A. Holtzmann, *Das Mahābhārata* iv, 68 f. *E. Windisch in the Literar-Central.* bl 1879. No. 52. Sp. 1709.

For whereas the Rāmāyaṇa does not show any sort of acquaintance with the Pāṇḍava-legend or of the heroes of the Mahābhārata,[1] the Mahābhārata knows, as we have seen, not only the Rāma legend but also the Rāmāyaṇa itself. In the Harivaṁśa there is mention of even a dramatic performance of the Rāmāyaṇa (see above note on p. 433). It is still more important that in the Mahābhārata (VII, 143, 66) a śloka is quoted — that was sung even before Vālmīki's time which is actually in our Rāmāyaṇa (vi, 81, 28). In many places of the Mahābhārata Vālmīki is called a "great penitent and great Ṛṣi along with Vasiṣṭha and other Ṛṣis of pre-historic times.[2] Once he tells Yudhiṣṭhira that in the course of a debate he was once cursed by holy Munis as "Brahmin-murderer" and that by this the sin of Brahmin-murder came upon him from which he could purify himself only by worshipping Śiva.[3] All these facts entitle us to support Jacobi's statement (ibid., p. 71) that the Rāmāyaṇa must have been generally known as an old work, "before the Mahābhārata had been completed". This is in perfect agreement with the fact that the "degeneration process", if one may say so, i.e. the usurping of the genuine by the spurious and the permeation of the old with the later portions has reached such an advanced state in the Mahābhārata that it has penetrated into the whole work whereas in the case of the Rāmāyaṇa it is found only in the initial stage and extends only to the first and seventh book and few portions of the remaining books.

---

1. If Sītā declares that she wants to be faithful to Rāma as Sāvitri to Satyavat (ii, 306) or Damayanti to Nala (v. 24,12) this does not prove that the poet must have known the Sāvitrī-poem or the Nala-song as parts of the Mahābhārata as presumed by Hopkins in *The Great Epic*, p. 78.

2. Mahābhārata I, 2, 18; II, 7, 16; V, 83, 27; XII, 207, 4; Hariv. 268, 14-539.

3. Mahābh. XIII, 18, 8. According to the Adhyātma-Rāmāyaṇa, Vālmiki lived among robbers when he was a young man, though he was a Brahmin by birth. The same tradition is to be found in the Bengali Rāmāyaṇa. Cf. Jacobi. ibid., p. 66 note; D. Ibbetson and A. K. Mojumdar in *Ind. Ant.*, 24, 1895, p. 220; 31, 1902, p. 351; D. Ch. Sen, *Bengali Rāmāyanas*, p. 125 (a similar Mohammedan legend, pp. 127 ff.). Balmik, i.e. Vālmiki, is worshipped as a kind of saint by the caste of the scavengers in Eastern Punjab, see R. C. Temple, *The Legends of the Punjab*, I (1884), pp. 529 f.

But if the Mahābhārata had on the whole its present form even as early as in the 4th century A.D. (above p. 446) then the Rāmāyaṇa must have been "completed" (the word is to be taken cum grano salis) already at least one or two centuries before this.[1]

This by no way answers the question which of the two great epics is the older one. After all this has been said about the history of the Mahābhārata as well as that of the Rāmāyaṇa, it is clear that this question has no sense, but that it gets resolved into three different questions as follows: (1) Which of the two works, in the form in which we find them today, is the older one? (2) What are the relations between the epoque in which an original epic Mahābhārata gradually became the great collected work combining in itself the hero-song and the didactic poem and the age in which the ancient poem of Vālmīki was elaborated into the Rāmāyaṇa of our day first by means of big and small additions in the earlier books and finally by the addition of Books I and VII? (3) Was there in ancient times an epic Mahābhārata or an epic Rāmāyaṇa at all?

We could answer only the first question by saying that our present day Rāmāyaṇa is older than the Mahābhārata in its present form. As regards the second question, we may perhaps presume that the Rāmāyaṇa which is so much smaller required a shorter time than the Mahābhārata. Now we have already pointed out that the character of the two spurious books of the Rāmāyana bears a striking resemblance to that of the Mahābhārata and often the same Brahmanic legends reappear in both the works. However these stories which are common to both works are told so differently that we do not have to think of a borrowing but we must presume that they come from the same source — from the Itihāsa literature transmitted orally in Brahmin circles. Moreover all the books of the Rāmāyaṇa and of the Mahābhārata have many usages, hemistiches, epigrams and complete texts in common[2] and there is agreement to a

1. Besides this we know from Chinese sources that already in the 4th and 5th centuries A.D. the Rāmāyaṇa was a well known and popular poem in India. (K. Watanabe in the *JRAS*, 1907, p. 99 f.)

2. This has been proved especially by E. W. Hopkins in the *American Journal of Philology*. Vols. XIX, pp. 138 ff. and XX, pp. 22 ff., and in his book *The Great Epic of India*, pp. 58 ff., 403 ff.

large extent between the two works in the matter of language, style and prosody.[1] From these facts we infer that the period of growth of the Rāmāyaṇa falls within the longer period of growth of the Mahābhārata.

The third question as to which of the two *original* epics is the older one cannot be answered easily. The Hindus declare the Rāmāyaṇa to be earlier than the Mahābhārata, because, according to the traditional list of Viṣṇu's incarnations, the incarnation as Rāma preceded that as Kṛṣṇa.[2] This argument has no force, because in the old, genuine Rāmāyaṇa, as we have seen, Rāma does not as yet appear as an incarnation at all. It is a fact, however, that allusions to Vāsudeva (Kṛṣṇa), Arjuna and Yudhiṣṭhira already occur in Pāṇini's grammar, whereas Rāma is not mentioned either by Pāṇini or Patañjali, nor in inscriptions of the pre-Christian era.[3] It is likely, too, that the theory of incarnation arose out of the Kṛṣṇa cult, and that the transformation of the hero Rāma into an incarnation of Viṣṇu resulted only later, by analogy to the Kṛṣṇa incarnation.[4] A few scholars[5] have declared the Rāmāyaṇa to be the earlier of the two epics, because the burning of windows does not occur in it, whilst it is mentioned in the Mahābhārata. The fact of the matter, however, is that in the old, genuine Mahābhārata the burning of widows is just as much absent as in the genuine Rāmāyaṇa, whilst there are allusions to it in the later portions of the Rāmāyaṇa, though less frequent than in the Mahābhārata.[6] Jacobi holds the Rāmāyaṇa so certainly to be the older poem, that he even presumes that the Mahābhārata has become an epic only under the influence of Vālmīki's poetic art.[7]

1. On the Śloka in the two epics see Jacobi, ibid., pp. 24 ff., and *Gurupūjākaumudī*, pp. 50 ff.

2. According to the Purāṇas, Rāma appears in the Kṛtayuga, but Kṛṣṇa not until the Dvāparayuga. Cf. A. Govidacarya Svamin in *JBRAS.*, 23, 1911-1912, pp. 244 ff.

3. Cf. R. G. Bhandarkar, *Early History of the Deccan*, 2nd ed., Bombay, 1895, p. 10: Vaiṣṇavism, etc., pp. 46 f.

4. Jacobi in *ERE.*, VII, 194 f. R. Chanda, *The Indo-Aryan Races*, 1, 1916, pp. 88 f., 111 ff.

5. Jacobi, ibid., pp. 107 f., and before him A. W. v. Schlegel and Monier Williams, also J. Jolly, *Recht und Sitte*, p. 68.

6. Cf. Winternitz, *Die Frau in den indischen Religionen*, I, 1920, pp. 58 f.; J. J. Meyer, *Das Weib im altindischen Epos*, pp. 307 f.

7. Jacobi, p. 78, 81 ff. ibid.

This opinion, goes much further than what is vouchsafed by facts, indeed it is even contrary to some facts. In more than one respect the Rāmāyaṇa represents an improvement in epic poetry over the Mahābhārata. Let us not forget that the epic evolved out of a mixture of prose and verse. In the Mahābhārata we still have a clear remnant of this primitive epic-form in this that as a rule the speeches of the persons making their appearance are preceded by words in prose like, "Kuntī spoke, Duryodhana spoke", etc., whereas in the Rāmāyaṇa the speakers are straightaway introduced in verse.[1] It was also pointed out already how greatly the Rāmāyaṇa already shows the characteristics of the style of the Kāvya, the ornate poetry of the courts.[2] It is certainly difficult to say what of that is old and what are later additions. But still this peculiarity of the Rāmāyaṇa by which it is very much removed from the Mahābhārata and comes close to the epics of Kālidāsa must make us hesitate to assume that the Rāmāyaṇa is very old.[3]

In one more respect the Mahābhārata makes a more antiquarian impression than the Rāmāyaṇa. In the Mahābhārata—at least in the nucleus of the poem that treats the Pāṇḍava-legend and the Kuru-battle—we come across much ruder customs and a more war-like mind than in the Rāmāyaṇa. The battle scenes of the Mahābhārata are worked in a much different way than those described in the Rāmāyaṇa. Those of the Mahābhārata create the impression that the poet belonged to a war-like race and had himself witnessed bloody battlefields whereas those of the Rāmāyaṇa give rise more to the impression that a narrator of fairy tales gave reports of battles of which he knew something only from hearsay. Between Rāma and Rāvaṇa, Lakṣmaṇa and Indrajīt there is not that embittered hatred, that

1. See above p. 303 and E. Windisch, *Mara and Buddha*, p. 224 f. Also individual stories in prose with speeches in verse are still found in the Mahābhārata. The Purāṇas have always retained these prose-forms in order to maintain the show of antiquity.

2. See above pp. 454-55 and 468 Note 1, 469 and cf. p. 442.

3. E. W. Hopkins (*Cambridge History*, I, p. 251) says of the Rāmāyaṇa: "Whatever may have been the date of its germ as a story, as an art-product it is later than the Mahābhārata". Cf. also Oldenberg, *Das Mahābhārata*, pp. 53 ff., and H. Raychaudhury in *Calcutta Review*, March 1922, pp. 1 ff.

wild fury as we read in the stories of the fights in the Mahābhārata between Arjuna and Karṇa or Bhīṣma and Duryodhana. The Sītā of the Rāmāyaṇa, as she is abducted, kidnapped and harassed or as she is rejected by Rāma always maintains in her accusations and lamentations a certain calmness and softness and in her words we find no trace of the wild passion which we find so often in the Draupadī of the Mahābhārata. Also Kuntī and Gāndhārī are mothers of true heroes of a war-like race whereas in the Rāmāyaṇa Kauśalyā and Kaikeyī are more like the stereotyped queens of the classical dramas. Evidently this seems to indicate that the Mahābhārata belongs to a ruder and more war-like age whereas the Rāmāyaṇa shows traces of a more refined culture. In order to stress this sharply striking difference between the two epics we must therefore presume that the Mahābhārata reflects a ruder culture of western India whereas the Rāmāyaṇa reflects a refined culture of eastern India and that the two epics represent the poetries not of two different epoques but of two different regions of India. Yet, even from this viewpoint it is difficult to imagine that the Mahābhārata is said to have become an epic only under the influence of Vālmīki's art of poetry.

That the Mahābhārata belongs to the west of India and the Rāmāyaṇa to the east cannot be doubted. Western races play the chief role in the Mahābhārata while the main events of the Rāmāyaṇa take place in the country of Kosala, where according to tradition Vālmīki is said to have lived and in all probability has also really lived.[1] But it is also in the eastern part of India that Buddhism was born and it has first spread in the Magadha as in the neighbouring Kosala country. The question is therefore all the more important : What is the relationship of the Rāmāyaṇa to Buddhism ?

It was already pointed out above (p. 450) that in the oldest Buddhist literature we still find examples of the Ākhyāna-poetry in which we have recognised, as Windisch has done, an earlier phase of the epic. From this Rhys Davids[2] has inferred that the Rāmāyaṇa as an epic cannot have yet existed at the time when

1. Jacobi, p. 66 ff., 69.
2. *Buddhist India*, London, 1903, p. 183.

those Buddha ballads were born. Now against this we may say that perhaps the old Ākhyāna-or ballad-poetry could have continued to exist by the side of the new artistic forms of the epic that had been developed from it. However, it is remarkable, that we find nothing but Buddha-ballads throughout early Buddhist literature, whilst a Buddha epic was not written until centuries later. It is still more important that in the Tipiṭaka we find the Daśaratha-Jātaka,[1] which relates how Bharata brings the news of the death of Daśaratha, whereupon Rāma tells Lakṣmaṇa and Sītā to step into the water to offer the libations for the departed. This gives rise to a conversation, in which Bharata asks Rāma how it is that he shows no sign of sorrow,[2] and Rāma replies with a lengthy speech of consolation, explaining how futile it is to lament over the dead, as death comes to all mortals. The fact that only one of the twelve ancient gāthās of the Jātaka appears in our Rāmāyaṇa,[3] proves that our epic cannot be the source of these verses, but that the Jātaka is based upon an ancient Rāma-ballad. In the same Jātaka book there is

---

1. The Pāli text of this Jātaka (No. 461) was first published with an English translation by V. Fausböll, Copenhagen, 1871. It has been treated in detail by Weber, ibid., 1 ff.; Jacobi, 84 ff. E. Senart, *Essai sur la légende du Buddha*, 2nd ed., Paris, 1882, pp. 317 f.; Lüders, *NGGW*., 1897, 1, pp. 40 ff: D. Ch. Sen, *The Bengali Rāmāyaṇas*, pp. 9 ff.; G. A. Grierson, *JRAS*., 1922, 135 ff.; N. B. Utgikar in *Centenary Supplement to JRAS*., 1924 pp. 203 ff. Only the gāthās of the Jātaka belong to the Tipiṭaka. The prose narrative is the fabrication of the compilers of the commentary (about the fifth century A.D.), and all conclusions drawn from this story, such as those of D. Ch. Sen and others, are faulty.

2. Here we see that even the Jātaka-gāthās were remodelled with a Buddhist tendency. In the Rāmāyaṇa Rāma himself laments exceedingly at the news of his father's death, before making the speech of consolation, s. Rāma. II, 102-105, and the same thing probably holds good for the ancient ballad too.

3. Parallels to other verses in Rāma's speech of consolation (Rāma. II, 105, 21:22) have been traced by Lüders (*ZDMG*., 58, 1904, 713 f.) in Jātaka 328, gā. 2-4. In the commentary on the Daśaratha-Jātaka there is also a verse about the ten thousand years' reign of Rāma, which corresponds to Rāma. VI, 128; 104. An allusion to the Rāma-legend also occurs in Jātaka 513, gā. 17.

also the Sāma-Jātaka,[1] which we may probably consider as an older form of the tale about the hermit-boy killed in the chase, which is told by Daśaratha in Rāmāyaṇa II, 63 f. There are a few other Jātakas, too, in which we find passages reminding us of the Rāmāyaṇa, but only very seldom literal agreement.[2] It is striking, too, that in the whole of the Jātaka, which tells so many tales of demons and fabulous animals, we hear not a word of the Rākṣasa Rāvaṇa or of Hanumat and the monkeys. All this makes it seem likely that, at the time when the Tipiṭaka came into being (in the fourth and third centuries B.C.) there were ballads dealing with Rāma, perhaps a cycle of such ballads, but no Rāma-epic as yet.[3]

Another question is this whether in the Rāmāyaṇa traces of Buddhism can be proved; to this the answer is a clear "no". For the only place where the Buddha is mentioned (above p. 465, Note 2) is decidedly spurious. It is not at all clear where in the Rāmāyaṇa allusions can be expected to Buddha or to Buddhist teachings. However conspicuous the lack of an indication to the Rāmāyaṇa if it were known at all should appear in the Buddhistic Tipiṭaka, we can infer practically nothing from the absence of Buddhist traces in the epic. And still one relation — although a very remote one — to Buddhism perhaps exists. Weber had still believed that the Rāmāyaṇa is based on an "old Buddhist legend of the pious prince Rāma, in whom it glorified an ideal of Buddhist equanimity."[4] This is certainly not the case. But perhaps we cannot reject the thought that the

1. Jātaka 540, also in Mahāvastu II, 209 ff. Cf. Charpentier, *WZKM.*, 24, 1910, 397; 27, 1913, 94. Oldenberg, *NGGW.*, 1918, 456 ff.; D. Ch. Sen ibid., pp. 15 ff.

2. There are a few scenes and situations in the Vessantara-Jātaka which remind us of the Rāmāyaṇa, but there is not a single case of literal agreement between the Rāmāyaṇa and the Jātaka-gāthās. In Jātaka 519, however, there is a stanza in which a demon tries to persuade faithful Sambulā to desert her sick husband and to follow him, uttering the same threat as is used by Rāvaṇa to Sītā in Rām. V, 22, 9, namely, that if she is not willing, he will devour her for his breakfast. Cf. D. Ch. Sen, ibid., pp. 18 ff. The Jātaka-gāthās, too, contain earlier and later portions, and some parts may be later than the Rāmāyaṇa.

3. Cf. T. W. Rhys Davids, *Buddhist India*, p. 183.

4. *Über das Rāmāyaṇa*, pp. 6 ff.

extra-ordinary kindness, gentleness and calmness of the soul which are attributed to Rāma are to be explained from Buddhist undercurrents. At least this much is quite understandable, that in a country strongly, influenced by Buddhism a non-Buddhist too composed an epic whose hero, in spite of his splendid battles with demons is more a wise man as per the taste of the Buddha than a war-hero. If we consider further that according to Oldenberg[1] even the prosody of the Rāmāyaṇa represents a later stage of development than that of the Pāli-poetry, then everything indicates that our epic was composed only after the appearance of the Buddha and of the birth of the oldest Pāli-literature i.e., after the 5th century B.C.

But from the language of the epic it was thought that we can draw conclusions about its pre-Buddhistic time of origin. This epic-language is a popular Sanskrit. But by about 260 B.C. King Aśoka employs for his inscriptions addressed to the folk not Sanskrit but dialects similar to Pāli, Buddha too preached as early as in the 6th and 5th centuries B.C. not in Sanskrit but in the language of the people. Popular epics however it is said[2] cannot be composed in the living language of the folks. But now because at Aśoka's and even at Buddha's time Sanskrit was not the language of the folk any more, the popular epics (in their original form) must belong to an earlier, pre-Buddhist time, in which Sanskrit was still a living language. But against this it can be argued that Sanskrit has always "lived" in India as a literary language by the side of popular dialects and has been understood also in large circles where it was not spoken. There is nothing strange in this that at the same time as Buddhist and Jain monks composed poetry and preached in popular dialects, also Sanskrit epics were composed and heard. Till the present day it is not at all unusual in India that in one and the same region two or more languages are in use side by side. And in a large portion of northern India even today they use a modern Indian literary language (besides Sanskrit) which is

1. Cf. H. Oldenberg in *Gurupūjākaumudī*, pp. 9 ff., and E. W. Hopkins, *Great Epic*, pp. 236 ff. Jacobi, ibid., p. 93, and Keith, *JRAS.*, 1915, pp. 321, 324 ff., contest the soundness of this argument.

2. Jacobi, p. 116 ff.

much different from the colloquial language.[1] Therefore if we find here and there in Pāli or Prākṛt in the Buddhist or Jain texts the same texts as we find in the Rāmāyaṇa or the Mahābhārata then it does not at all always follow that these Sanskrit verses must have been translated from the popular languages. There is still less justification for the view of some excellent scholars that originally all epics were composed in the popular dialects and were only later translated into Sanskrit. It is highly questionable in itself that such a translation should have taken place without their being the slightest information about it anywhere. How unacceptable this hypothesis is even otherwise has been convincingly shown by Jacobi.[2] If, with respect to the view that "a popular epic must be told in the language of the people" he reminds us here that even the songs of the Ilias and Odyssee were composed in the Homeric language although the language of the audience was much different from it", and if he emphasises that the term "Folk" (or people) can never have in India the same meaning that we associate with it (in Europe), then he is contradicting thereby his own view that the Rāmāyaṇa must have been composed at a time when Sanskrit was still a "popular language" and that before it is pre-Buddhistic.[3]

1. Cf. above p. 37, Note 1 Grierson in *JRAS.*, 1906, p. 441 f.

2. *ZDMG* 48. 1894, p. 407 ff. The view that the epics were originally composed in Prākṛt was first expressed by A. Barth (*Revue Critique*, 5 avril 1886) and later thoroughly defended in (*Revue de l'histoire des religions*, t 27, 1893, p. 288 ff. and t. 45, 1902, p. 195 f.) cf. also Grierson in the *Ind. Ant.* xxiii, 1894. p. 55.

3. The question, whether and how far Sanskrit was a "living language" has been discussed at length in recent years in connection with the question of the age of the epics. R. Otto Franke in *Pāli and Sanskrit* (Strassburg, 1902) has collected a large amount of factual material which shows that all our old inscriptions (beginning with approximately 300 B.C.) are written in popular dialects and only the inscriptions from the post-Christian era in Sanskrit also. T. W. Rhys Davids in his *Buddhist India*, London, 1903 draws from this fact (independent of Franke) far reaching conclusions of importance to the History of Literature. But the inscriptions prove only that in those pre-Christian centuries Sanskrit was not yet used as Court-language, they do not prove anything against its use as a literary language. We can only agree with the elaborations of E. J. Rapson and F. W. Thomas (*JRAS.*, 1904, p. 435 ff and 460 ff). The objections of Rhys Davids (ib. 457 ff), Grierson (ib. 471 ff) and Fleet (ib. 481 ff) simply mean what everyone admits, namely

The Buddhists too have made use of Sanskrit in later times and one of the oldest of the Buddhist Sanskrit works, the Buddha-Carita of Aśvaghoṣa in particular is of special significance for determining the age of the Rāmāyaṇa. The Buddha-Carita is an ornate poem (Kāvya) which the poetry of Vālmīki has certainly served as model.[1] On the other hand we find in a spurious piece of the Rāmāyaṇa one scene[2] which is most probably an imitation of a scene of the Buddha-Carita. Now as Aśvaghoṣa is a contemporary of Kaniṣka, we may infer that in the beginning of the 2nd century A.D. if not earlier[3] the Rāmāyaṇa was already considered as a model epic, that it was however not completed to such an extent that no more interpolations took place. But towards the end of the 2nd century it must have been already completed as can be deduced from the relationship of the Rāmāyaṇa to the Mahābhārata described above.

A public recitation of the Rāmāyaṇa is already mentioned in Kumāralāta's Kalpanāmaṇḍitika,[4] which was probably written towards the close of the second century A.D. In Chinese translations of Buddhist tales, which are said to date back to the

---

that Sanskrit was not a spoken popular dialect when the epics were composed, but they prove nothing against this, that it was used as a literary language, spoken in parts and largely understood. cf. also A. B. Keith and Grierson in the *JRAS*, 1906, pp. 1 ff and 441 ff.

The topic of "Archaic elements in the language of Rāmāyaṇa" is treated by T. Michelson in the *Journal of the American Oriental Society*, vol. xxv, 1904, 89 ff. That the Sūtas speak only Sanskrit in the dramas indicates clearly in a similar manner that the Sūta-poetry, i.e., the epic was composed in Sanskrit. On archaisms in the language of the Rāmāyaṇa, see T. Michelson, *JAOS.*, 25, 1904, 89 ff. and *Transactions and Proceed. American Philol. Assoc.* 34, pp. xl f.; M. A. Roussel, *JA.*, 1910, s. 10, t. xv, pp. 1 ff.; Keith, *JRAS.*, 1910, pp. 1321 ff.

1. Cf. A. Gawronski, *Studies about the Sanskrit Buddhist Literature*, W. Krakowie, 1919 (Prace Komiji Orj. Pol. Akad. Um. No. 2), pp. 27 ff.

2. The seraglio-scene above, pp. 470 f, Note 3.

3. Much as has been written about the period of Kaniṣka, it is not yet definitely settled. However, there is ever increasing evidence for the theory that he reigned during the first half of the second century A.D. Cf. Smith, *Early History*, pp. 271 ff., 276 n.

4. Translated from the Chinese as *Aśvaghoṣa's Sūtrālaṅkāra* by Ed. Huber, Paris, 1908, p. 126.

third century A. D., the Rāma legend is related in a form prepared to suit Buddhist, purposes.[1] We glean from Chinese sources, too, that, at the time of the Buddhist philosopher Vasubandhu (fourth century A.D.) the Rāmāyaṇa was a well-known and popular poem also among the Buddhists in India.[2] As early as in the second half of the first century A.D. the Jain monk Vimala Sūri recast the Rāma legend in his Prākṛt poem Paumacariyu (Padmacarita), bringing it into line with the religion and philosophy of the Jains.[3] It was obviously his intention to offer his co-religionists a substitute for the poem of Vālmīki which was already famous at that time. In about 600 A.D. the Rāmāyaṇa was already famous in far-off Cambodia as a sacred book of Hinduism, for an inscription reports that a certain Somaśarman presented "the Rāmāyaṇa, the Purāṇa, and the complete Bhārata" to a temple.[4]

1. Cf. S. Lévi in *Album Kern*, pp. 279, ff.; Ed. Chavannes, *Cinq cents contes*, III, p. f.; Ed. Huber in *BEFEO*., 4, 1904, 698 ff.

2. See K. Watanabe, *JRAS*., 1907, pp. 99 ff.

3. According to the concluding verses belonging to the poem itself, it was written in the year 530 after Mahāvīra (i.e. about 62 A.D.). E. Leumann (to whom we are indebted for valuable information about the Paumacariyu) considers this date as unassailable. H. Jacobi (*ERE*., VII, p. 467) assumes that it was written in the third century A.D. The later Jain recensions of the Rāma legend (in the 68th Parvan of Guṇāḍhya's Uttarapurāṇa and in the 7th Parvan of Hemacandra's Ṣaṣṭiśalākāpuruṣacaritra) are based on the Paumacariyu. On Hemacandra's "Jain Rāmāyaṇa" see D. Ch. Sen, *Bengali Rāmāyaṇas*, pp. 26 ff. (The Jain Rāmāyaṇa influenced the Bengali versions of the Rāmāyaṇa, as is shown by D. Ch. Sen, ibid., pp. 204 ff.). However, the appearance of Rāvaṇa as a great sage and ascetic, and of Sītā as Rāvaṇa's daughter in Buddhist and Jain versions of the poem of Rāma, should not be looked upon as traits pointing to ancient traditions, as is done by D. Ch. Sen. In the Adbhutottarakhaṇḍa, too, Sītā appears as the daughter of Maṇdodarī, Rāvaṇa's queen. This, however, is a late appendix to the Rāmāyaṇa, written in praise of Sītā as Śakti, and is popular among the Śāktas in Kashmir. Cf. Weber, *HSS. Verz*. I, pp. 123 f., Eggeling, *Ind. Off. Cat.* VI, p. 1183; D. Ch. Sen, ibid., pp. 35, 59, 227 f,; Grierson, *JRAS*, 1921, pp. 422 ff.

4. See A. Barth, *Inscriptions Sanscrites du Cambodge* (Notices et extraits des MSS. de la bibliotheque nationale, t. xxvii, 1, Paris 1885), pp. 29 ff. On the Old Javanic Rāmāyaṇa, see R. Friedrich, *JRAS* 1876., pp. 172 ff. and H. Kern, *Verspreide Geschriften*, Vol. 9, pp. 251 ff., 297.

That the old poem already served as a model for Aśvaghoṣa and therefore must have been composed long before his time agrees very well with the fact that we do not find any traces of Greek influence or of an acquaintance with the Greeks in the old and genuine Rāmāyaṇa. For, two places where the Yavanas (Ionians, Greeks) are mentioned are indisputably spurious. But that the Homeric poems should have had any kind of influence on Vālmīki's poetry, as Weber thinks, can be really ruled out completely. Between the abduction of Sītā and that of Helen, between the march on Laṅkā and that on Troy there is not even a remote similarity of motif, between the bending of the bow by Rāma and that by Odysseus there is only a very remote resemblance.[1]

The Rāmāyaṇa as an epic is very far from the Veda and even the Rāma-legend is connected with the Vedic literature only through very thin threads. Whether the king Janaka of Videha mentioned very often in the Upaniṣads[2] is the same as the father of Sītā must be left undecided. Weber has pointed out some weak connections between Rāmāyaṇa and the Yajurveda.[3] Sītā the heroine of the Rāma-legend belongs to the oldest contents of the Rāma-legend. Her name means "ploughshare", she is born out of the earth and Mother earth admits her into her womb again. Although the last feature of the legend occurs only in the late Book VII, still it might be very old. In any case the idea of an agricultural goddess Sītā who is invoked in a field benediction of the Ṛgveda (iv, 57, 6) is of hoary past and reaches back into the Vedic times. The Gṛhyasūtras have preserved to us prayer-formulas in which she appears in an unusually lively personification—"lotus-wreathed, radiating in all parts, black-eyed" etc.[4] But Weber is certainly

1. See Jacobi, p. 94 ff.

2. Rāma does not appear in the old Upaniṣads. The Rāmapūrvatāpanīya-upaniṣad and the Rāmottaratāpanīya-upaniṣad (Deussen, *Sechzig Upaniṣads*, p. 802 ff.) are only later works of inferior quality, which bear only the name "Upaniṣad", in them Rāma is praised as an incarnation of god Viṣṇu. (See also: *The Vaiṣṇava-Upaniṣads. . . .*, ed. by Mahādeva Śāstrī, Adyar, 1923, pp. 305 ff., 326 ff.)

3. *Über das Rāmāyaṇa*, pp. 8 f.

4. *Kauśikasūtra* 106, see A. Weber, "*Omina and Portenta*" *ABA.*, 1858 p. 368 ff.

right[1] when he remarks that this Vedic notion of Sītā as the Goddess of the ploughshare "is separated from her portrait in the Rāma-legend by the wide gulf". And there is no indication to show that there have been epic songs of Rāma and Sītā already in the Vedic time.[2] Even if we, like Jacobi, would find the old myth of Indra's battle with Vṛtra again in the battle of Rāma with Rāvaṇa,[3] the wide gulf that separates the Veda from the epic still continues to exist.

If we now sum up the results of our investigations on the age of the Rāmāyaṇa, we can say the following:

1. The more recent portions of the Rāmāyaṇa, especially Books I and VII are separated from the genuine Rāmāyaṇa of Books II to VI by a long space of time.

2. The whole Rāmāyaṇa together with the more recent portions was already a very famous work when the Mahābhārata had not yet received its present shape.

3. It is probable that the Rāmāyaṇa had already in the 2nd century A.D. its present extent and content.

4. But the oldest nucleus of the Mahābhārata is presumably older than the old Rāmāyaṇa.

5. In the Veda we do not find any trace of a Rāma-epic and only very poor traces of a Rāma-legend.

6. The ancient Buddhistic texts of the Tipiṭaka do not exhibit any knowledge of the Rāmāyaṇa but they contain traces of Ākhyānas, in which the Rāma-legend was sung.

7. Clear traces of Buddhism are not found in the Rāmāyaṇa, it is however possible to trace the characterisation of Rāma back to remote Buddhistic influences.

8. There can be no questioning of Greek influences in the Rāmāyaṇa and the genuine Rāmāyaṇa exhibits also no acquaintance with the Greeks.

9. It is possible that the Rāmāyaṇa was composed by Vālmīki in the 4th or 3rd century B.C. by making use of Ākhyānas.

---

1. *Episches im vedischen Ritual* (*SBA*, 1891, p. 818).

2. It is not possible to follow the fanciful elaborations of Julius V. Negelein who believes he can find the basic feature of the Rāma Sitā-legend in the Veda. (*WZKM* XVI, 1902, p. 226 ff.)

3. Jacobi, ibid., p. 131.

The Purāṇas and their Position in Indian Literature[1]

It is difficult to classify the Purāṇas in the History of Indian Literature both with respect to their contents and with respect to their times. They belong actually to religious literature, and for the later Indian religion which is some times called "Hinduism"[2] and which culminates in the worship of Viṣṇu and Śiva they are approximately what the Veda is for the oldest religion, the Brahmanism. But how closely the Purāṇas on the other hand are connected with epical poetry is sufficiently clear even from the fact that in the preceding chapters we had to speak of them again and again. Indeed the Mahābhārata is to a great extent a Purāṇa and even the later books and chapters of the Rāmāyaṇa partake of the character of the Purāṇas. Further, the Purāṇas go back undoubtedly to a very distant past and have their roots in the Vedic literature; many a legend, already familiar from Ṛgvedic hymns and from the Brāhmaṇas, reappears in the Purāṇas.[3] But equally certain are

1. The first to make a thorough study of the Purāṇas was H. H. Wilson, in his *Essays on Sanskrit Literature* which first appeared in 1832 ff. and in the introduction and Notes to his translation of the Viṣṇu-Purāṇa (see Works by the late H. H. Wilson, ed. by R. Rost and Fitzedward Hall, Vol. III, pp. 1-155, and Vol. VI, Preface). He had a predecessor in Vans Kennedy, *Researches into the Nature and Affinity of Ancient and Hindu Mythology*, London, 1831. Valuable services have also been rendered to the investigation of the Purāṇa literature by Eugène Burnouf (Preface to his edition and translation of the Bhāgavata-Purāṇa) and by the compilers of the great Catalogues of Manuscripts, especially Th. Aufrecht (*Bodl. Cat.*, pp. 7 ff.) and Julius Eggeling (*Ind. Off. Cat.*, Part VI, London, 1899). For Wilson's services in the investigation of the Purāṇas, cf. Windisch, *Geschichte der Sanskrit-Philologie*, pp. 41 ff. For more recent researches on the Purāṇas see R. G. Bhandarkar, *A Peep into the Early History of India*, *JBRAS.*, 20, 1900, 403 f., new ed. 1920, pp. 66 ff.; W. Jahn *Festschrift Kuhn*, pp. 305 ff.; F. E. Pargiter, *ERE.*, X, 1918, 448 ff.; *Ancient Indian Historical Tradition*, London, 1922, pp. 15 ff. 136 ff.; E. J. Rapson, *Cambridge History*, I, pp. 296 ff.

2. On this religion cf. A. Barth, *Religions of India*, 2nd ed., London, 1889, pp. 153 ff.; M. Monier Williams, *Brahmanism and Hinduism*, London, 1891; E. W. Hopkins, *Religions of India*, Boston, 1895, pp. 434 ff.; Sir Charles Eliot, *Hinduism and Buddhism*, London, 1921, Vols. II; H. v. Glasenapp, *Der Hinduismus*, Munich, 1922.

3. Instances are the myths of Purūravas and Urvaśī (cf. T. Michelson, *JAOS* 28, 284 f.), of Śaraṇyu (see A. Blau, *ZDMG.*, 62, 1908, pp. 337 ff.). of Mudgala (see Pargiter, *JRAS.*, 1910, pp. 1328 ff.) of Vṛṣākapi (see Pargiter, *JRAS.*, 1911, 803 ff.).

also the works of later origin preserved to us under the title of "Purāṇas" and even upto our present day books are fabricated which assume the proud title of "Purāṇa" or call themselves constituents of old Purāṇas. Of these works in particular it is true what has been said in the introduction (above, p. 26) about "new wine in old bottles". Even the latest products of this literature have the external form and the antiquarian garb of the oldest Purāṇas.

The word "Purāṇa" meant originally nothing but "Purāṇam-ākhyānam" i.e., "old story."[1] In older literature, in the Brāhmaṇas, Upaniṣads and ancient Buddhist texts we come across this word generally in connection with Itihāsa. We have already remarked however (above pp. 293-94) that by the "Itihāsas and Purāṇas" or Itihāsapurāṇa mentioned so aften in olden times not the actual books were meant, and still less the epics or Purāṇas preserved to our present day. As against this it is certainly possible that certain works were meant when in the Atharvaveda[2] beside the four Vedas also the "Purāṇa" is enumerated. But only the Sūtra-literature testify the existence of real Purāṇas i.e., of works, whose contents approximately agree with those of the Purāṇa-texts preserved to our present day.

In the Gautama-Dharmasūtra[3] which is considered as the oldest of the law books that have come down to us, it is taught

---

1. The Kauṭilya-Arthaśāstra I, 5 (p. 10) in its definition of *itihāsa* enumerates *purāṇa* and *itivṛtta* as belonging to the content of *itihāsa*. As *itivṛtta* can only mean a "historical event", *purāṇa* probably means "mythological and legendary lore."

2. XI, 7, 24. In verse Athv. 19, 9 Ṛṣi Nārada is addressed in such a way that one could think that the verse was taken from a Purāṇa-dialogue. Cf. G. M. Bloomfield, *SBE*, Vol. 42, p. 435

3. XI, 19. Similarly also in the law books of Bṛhaspati (*SBE.*, Vol. 33, p. 2807) and Yājñavalkya I. 3 which are posterior to it by many centuries. In still later law books the Purāṇas are not only counted among the sources of law in general, but they are also quoted as such in innumerable places. Cf. Jolly, *Recht und Sitte* (Grundriss II, 8), p. 30 f. Kulluka the Jurist (on Manu I, 1) quotes "from the Mahābhārata" the verse, "The Purāṇas, Manu's law book, the Vedas with the Vedāṅgas and the Science of healing are four things which stand fixed by order; they are not to be disproved by grounds." However, this verse does not occur in our Mahābhārata editions.

that while dispensing law the king should be guided in his decisions by the Veda, the law books, the Vedāṅgas and "the Purāṇa". Here the expression "The Purāṇa like the Veda" can describe only a type of literature. It is still more important that another law book, the Āpastambīya Dharmasūtra that belongs probably to the 4th or 5th century B.C. contains not only two quotations from "the Purāṇa" but also one more, a third one, from a Bhaviṣyat-Purāṇa. Although the last quotation is not found in the Purāṇa that has come down to us under this name and also the two other quotations cannot be shown in our Purāṇas verbatim, yet similar texts are found in our books.[1] As there are good grounds for assigning the above-mentioned Dharma sūtras to the fifth fourth century B.C., there must have been even at that early period works resembling our Purāṇas.[2] And it is more than probable that our Purāṇas are only recensions of older works of the same literary genre, i.e., of works of religious-didactic contents in which old transmission on the creation of the world, on the deeds of the gods, on heroes, holy-men and founder-fathers of the human race, the beginnings of the royal houses and similar things were collected.

Even the relationship of the Mahābhārata to the Purāṇas[3] indicates that the latter can be traced to an early age and that similarly even a long time before the completion of the Mahābhārata the Purāṇas have existed. Our Mahābhārata does not only call itself a Purāṇa but it even begins just in the same way

1. Cf G. Bühler, *Ind. Ant.* 25, 1896, pp, 323 ff. and *SBE,* Vol 2, 2nd ed., 1897, pp. xxix ff., and Pargiter, *Anc. Ind. Hist. Trad.*, pp. 43 ff.

2. It does not, however, follow from these quotations that the Purāṇas contained separate sections on *dharma* at that time, as is the case with our present Purāṇas; we need only assume, that, in connection with the "ancient lore" they also handed down all kinds of ancient legal principles and maxims. Cf. Pargiter, Anc. Ind. His. Trad., pp. 48 f. The Kauṭilya-Arthaśāstra recommends that misguided princes be instructed by means of Purāṇas (V, 6, p. 257), and counts Paurāṇikas, i.e. "Purāṇa-specialists," among the court officials (V, 3, p. 247). However, we cannot agree with Pargiter (ibid. pp. 54 f.) in regarding this as a proof of the existence of definite Purāṇas in the fourth century B.C., as the Kauṭilya is considered to be a work of the 3rd or 4th century A.D.

3. Cf. A. Holtzmann, *Das Mahābhārata* iv p. 29 ff and E. W. Hopkins, *The Great Epic of India*, p. 47 ff.

as Purāṇa texts begin in general, while Ugraśravas, the son of Sūta Lomaharṣaṇa appears as narrator. This Ugraśravas is described as "well-versed in the Purāṇas" and Śaunaka while exhorting him to narrate, tells him, "your father once learnt the Purāṇa; ... in the Purāṇa the stories of gods and the genealogies of the sages are told, and we have heard them once upon a time from your father". ... In the Mahābhārata legends are introduced most often with the words, "It is heard in the Purāṇa"; Gāthās and ślokas, especially genealogical verses, "sung by those well-versed in the Purāṇa" are quoted; a creation story composed in Prose (Mahābh. xii, 342) is described as "a Purāṇa"; "the serpent sacrifice of Janamejaya is taught in the Purāṇa" and the Purāṇa-knowers recommend it; "in the memory of the Purāṇa" proclaimed by Vāyu[1] the past and future epoques of the world are described, and the Harivaṃśa quotes not only one Vāyu-Purāṇa, but in many places it concurs verbatim with the Vāyu-Purāṇa. Many sagas, legends and didactic pieces are common for the Purāṇas and the epics. Of the Ṛṣya-Śṛṇga-legend, Lüders[2] has proved that it has a more ancient form in the Padma-Purāṇa than in our Mahābhārata. In a verse of the Mahābhārata[3] which is however an interpolation, the 18 Purāṇas are mentioned. It follows from all this that long before the completion of the Mahābhārata there have been the Purāṇas as a literary genre and that in the Purāṇas also which have been preserved to our present day there is much that is older than our present day Mahābhārata.

But it is only paradoxical if we say that the Mahābhārata is older than the Purāṇas and the Purāṇas are older than the Mahābhārata. For, the Purāṇas are, just as little as the epic, unitary works, but even in them old things and new things are found side by side. And in the numerous cases in which the Purāṇas concur with one another or with the Mahābhārata more

1. Mahābh. III, 191, 16. According to Hopkins, ibid., p. 48 f., the description in our Vāyu-Purāṇa is more ancient than that given in the Mahābhārata.

2. *NGGW.*, 1897, No. 1, p. 8 ff.

3. XVIII, 695. Another verse, XVIII, 5, 46, is not found in all editions.

or less verbatim. It is more probable that they all can be traced back to the same very old source than that one work is dependent on another.[1] This old source was, on the one hand, oral tradition, comprising Brahmanic traditions reaching back to Vedic times, as well as the bard poetry handed down in the circles of the Kṣatriyas,[2] and on the other hand, it was certain definite texts, probably far less in bulk than our present Purāṇas. The number of these was probably not exactly eighteen from the outset. Perhaps there were only four, as indicated by the legendary report in the Viṣṇu-Purāṇa.[3] It is, however, most unlikely indeed that, as is assumed by some scholars[4] all the Purāṇas originated in a single original Purāṇa. There was never one original Purāṇa, any more than there was one original Brāhmaṇa whence all the Brāhmaṇas sprang. When, as we have seen above, ancient works here and there mention "the Purāṇa," they only mean "the old tradition" or "Purāṇa literature", in the same way as the expression "Veda" or "Śruti" or Smṛti" are used in the singular. That our present Purāṇas are not the old works themselves which bore these titles, follows naturally from the fact that none of them satisfies the definition of the concept of Purāṇa which is given in the Purāṇas themselves with respect to its content. According to this definition,[5] which is certainly very old, every Purāṇa shall have five characteristics (Pañcalakṣaṇa) i.e. it shall treat five subjects : (i) Sarga. "the creation", (ii) Pratisarga, the "recreation", i.e. the periodical destruction

1. Of course, it might not be denied that, in isolated cases, one Purāṇa may have copied from another.

2. It is doubtful, however, whether we are justified in drawing the line between the Kṣatriya tradition and the brahmanical tradition as definitely as is assumed by Pargiter.

3. III, 6. According to this, the Sūta Romaharṣana and three of his pupils wrote the four fundamental Purāṇasaṃhitās (mūlasaṃhitās). Similarly Bhāgavata-Pur. XII, 7. Cf. Burnouf, *Bhāgavata-Purāṇa*, I, Preface, pp. xxxvii, ff. However, we should not place much reliance on these legends.

4. A. M. T. Jackson, *JBRAS.*, 21, 1905, Extra-Number, pp. 67 ff.; A. Blau, *ZDMG.*, 62, 1908, 337; Pargiter, *Anc. Ind. Hist. Trad.* 35 ff., 49 ff.

5. It is found in all Purāṇas and is also vouchsafed by the most esteemed ancient Indian dictionary, Amarakośa, and by the other dictionaries also.

and renewal of the worlds, (iii) (Vaṃśa, "the order of the generations" i.e., the genealogy of gods and ṛṣis, (iv) Manvantaram, "the Manu-periods", i.e., the great epoques each of which has a Manu or fore-father of the human race and (v) Vaṃśānucarita, "the history of the generation," namely of the old and later royal families whose origin is traced back to the Sun (solar dynasty) and the moon (lunar dynasty). These five things constitute only in part the contents of the Purāṇas preserved to our day; some of these Purāṇas contain more than what is included in the "five characteristics" whereas the others do not at all treat these subjects, but to compensate for this they treat quite different things. But what is specially typical of almost all our Purāṇas is their sectarian character, that is, the fact that they are devoted to the cult of some god, of Viṣṇu or Śiva, of which the old definition does not say anything.[1] In most of these works there are also bigger chapters on the rights and duties of the castes and of the Āśramas, on the general Brahmanical rites, especially offerings to the dead (Śrāddhas)[2] as well as on special ceremonies and festivals (Vratas) in honour of Viṣṇu or Śiva and often also on chapters on the Sāṅkhya-and the Yoga-philosophies.

In such Purāṇas as have preserved an old nucleus, we find sections on cosmogony and history of primeval times, corresponding to the "five characteristics." We find, too, genealogical lists of the ancient royal houses, continued from the first kings, whose origin is traced back to the sun and moon, down to the heroes of the great war of the Mahābhārata. As our Purāṇas are ascribed to Vyāsa, who is said to have lived at the beginning of the Kaliyuga contemporaneously with the heroes

1. However, it is said in the Brahmavaivarta-Purāṇa that the "five characteristics" are applicable only to the Upapurāṇas, whereas the Mahāpurāṇas (the great Purāṇas) have ten characteristics, including "praise of Viṣṇu and of the individual gods". The Bhāgavata-Purāṇa likewise states in two places (II, 10, 1 and XII, 7, 8 ff) "ten characteristics of the Purāṇa". (Cf. E. Burnouf, *le Bhāgavata-Purāṇa*, t 1, I, Pref. p. xlvi ff.). But these definitions also correspond only to some extent to the contents of the actually available Purāṇas.

2. Here the Purāṇas often concur verbatim with later law books. Cf. W. Caland, *Altindischer Ahneukult*, p. 68, 79, 112.

of the Bhārata battle, the history of "the past" ends with the death of the Pāṇḍavas or shortly afterwards.[1] In several of these Purāṇas,[2] however, the royal dynasties of the "past" are followed by lists of the kings of the "future" in the form of prophecies[3]. In these lists of kings we come across the dynasties known to us from history the Śiśunāgas, the Nandas, the Mauryas, the Śuṅgas, the Āndhras and the Guptas. Among the Śiśunāgas are Bimbisāra and Ajātaśatru, who are mentioned in Jain and Buddhist writings as contemporaries of Mahāvīra and Gautama Buddha (6th to 5th century B.C.); and with the Maurya Chandragupta, who came to the throne in 322 B.C. we emerge into the clear daylight of history. Though these lists of kings of the Kali-Yuga can be utilised as historical sources only with caution and discrimination[4], V. A. Smith[5] has shown that

1. When the Kaliyuga-era had become current the Indians felt the need for assoeiating the starting point of the era with some important "historical" event, and they used the Bhārata battle for this purpose. There was, however, a school of astronomers, thus Varāhamihira (died A.D. 587) with whom the historian Kalhaṇa agrees, which does not date the beginning of the Kaliyuga from the battle of the Mahābhārata, but regards this battle as having been fought in the 653rd year of the Kaliyuga (2449 B.C.). In the Aihole inscription (634 A.D.) the date "after the Bhārata battle" is already mentioned. Cf. J. F. Fleet, *JRAS.*, 1911, 675 ff. Indian kings were just as fond of tracing their ancestry back to those who fought in the Bhārata battle as European princes wese anxious to prove their descent from the heroes of the Trojan war. Cf. Rapson, *Cambridge History,* I, p. 307. But it is entirely contrary to historical criticism to draw chronological conclusions as is done by Pargiter (*Anc. Ind. Hist. Trad.*, pp. 175 ff.) from this fiction of the coincidence of the Bharata battle with the beginning of the Kaliyuga.

2. Matsya-, Vāyu-, Brahmāṇḍa-, Bhaviṣya-, Viṣṇu-, Bhāgavata-, and Garuḍa-Purāṇas.

3. In Rāmāyaṇa, IV,62,3 *purāṇa* means a prophecy made in olden times.

4. F. E. Pargiter has rendered valuable services to the criticism of these lists of kings, by his book: The Purāṇa Text of the Dynasties of the Kali-Age, London, 1913. It is probable that the sources of these prophecies are ancient annals and chronicles; for this reason we find occasional expressions such as "abhavat", "smṛta" in our texts, in spite of the prophetical future tense (cf. Pargiter, ibid., p. ix) Patgiter gives good reasons for the hypothesis that these sources were written in Prākrit; but we should not therefore jump to the conclusion that the Purāṇas as a whole were translated from the Prākrit. Pargiter's views have been contested by A. B. Keith, *JRAS.*, 1914, 1021 ff.; 1915, 328 ff. Cf. the discussion ib. 141 ff., 516 ff., 799 ff.

5. *Early History,* Oxford, 1904, p. 11, and *ZDMG.*, 56, 1902, p. 654, 672; 57, 1903, p. 607 f.; Cf. D. R. Bhandarkar, *JBRAS.*, 22, 155 f.

the Viṣṇu-Purāṇa is the best source for the Maurya-dynasty (326-184 B.C.) and the Matsya-Purāṇa for the Āndhra-dynasty (ending with 236 A.D.), while the Vāyu-Purāṇa describes the reign of the Guptas as it was under Chandragupta I (about 320-330 A.D.). At the end of these lists of kings, these Purāṇas enumerate a series of dynasties of low and barbarian descent (Śūdras and Mlecchas), such as Abhīras, Gardabhas, Śakas, Yavanas, Tuṣāras, Hūṇas and so on, which were contemporary with the former, and then follows a dreary description of the Kali-age. This prophecy reminds us of the account given by the Chinese pilgrim Sung-yun[1] of the barbarian invasions in the northern Punjab in about 465 A.D., and of Kalhaṇa's vivid description of the rule of the Hun-chieftains. About 500 A.D. Toramāṇa the Hun-chieftain was reigning in Central India; he was succeeded by his son Mihirakula in 515, who—in the words of Kalhaṇa,[2] the historian—reigned "like the god of death in the kingdom flooded with barbarian tribes, was surrounded by thousands of murderers day and night and himself knew no pity even towards women and children." It can be easily presumed that the descriptions of the Kaliyuga in the Purāṇas have been prompted by the cruel reign of the Huns. The data are, however, too confused to serve as a basis for safe conclusions as to the date of origin of the Purāṇas. All that we can safely conclude is that the earlier Purāṇas must have come into being before the 7th century, for neither later dynasties nor later famous rulers such as for instance Harṣa, occur in the lists of kings.

Another point which would seem to bear out the theory that the earlier Purāṇas had come into being, with, to all intents and purposes, their present form, as early as in the first centuries of the Christian era, is the striking resemblance between the Buddhist Mahāyāna texts of the first centuries of the Christian era, and the Purāṇas. The Lalitavistara not only calls itself a "Purāṇa" but really has much in common with the Purāṇas. Texts like Saddharmapuṇḍarīka, Karaṇḍavyūha and even some passages of the Mahāvastu, remind us of the sectarian Purāṇas

---

1. Cf. S. Beal, *Buddhist Records of the Western World*, I; Smith, *Early History*, p. 328.
2. Rājataraṅgiṇī I, 289 ff. Cf. Smith, *Early History*, 328 ff., 333 ff.

not only by reason of the boundless exaggerations but also on account of the extravagance in the praise of Bhakti. The Digambara Jainas, too, composed Purāṇas from the 7th century onwards.[1]

But the view which was previously generally accepted and which is even today widely spread and according to which all our Purāṇas belong to the most recent products of Sanskrit literature and would have originated only in the last thousand years is in no way maintainable.[2] For even poet Bāṇa (about 625 A.D.) knows the Purāṇas exactly and narrates in his historical novel Harṣacarita how he attended a Vāyu-Purāṇa reading in his native village. Kumārila, the philosopher (about 750 A.D.) takes the support of the Purāṇas as sources of law, whereas Śaṅkara (9th century) and Rāmānuja (12th century) quote them as holy texts in support of their philosophical teachings. It is also important that the Arabian traveller Alberuni (about 1030 A.D.) who is quite conversant with the Purāṇas, gives a list of the "18 Purāṇas" and quotes not only Āditya-, Vāyu-, Matsya-, and Viṣṇu-Purāṇa but has also studied very precisely one of the decidedly later Purāṇa-texts, the Viṣṇudharmottara.[3] The erroneous opinion that the

1. Raviṣeṇa wrote the Padmapurāṇa in 600 A.D. See also Pargiter. *Mārkaṇḍeya Purāṇa Transl.*, p. xiv.

2. This opinion was first expressed by H. H. Wilson and often repeated after him. He thought that in the descriptions of the Kaliyuga there are allusions to the Mohammedan conquest. Vans Kennedy has already (see, Wilson, *Works*, v, 257 ff,) pleaded very energetically for a greater antiquity of the Purāṇas.

3. Cf. G. Bühler, *Ind. Ant.*, 19, 1890, 382 ff.; 25, 1896, 328 ff.; P. Deussen, *System des Vedānta* Leipzig, 1883, p. 36; Smith Early history, pp. 22 ff. A manuscript of the Skanda-Purāṇa in Gupta script is assigned by Haraprasāda Śāstri (*JASB.*, 1893, p. 250) to the middle of the 7th century. In records of land-grants of the 5th century B.C. verses are quoted, which according to Pargiter (*JRAS.*, 1912, 248 ff., *Anc. Ind. Hiit. Trad.*, p. 49), occur only in the Padma-, Bhaviṣya- and Brahma-Purāṇa, and hence he concludes that these particular Purāṇas are earlier. It is more probable, however, that these verses both in the inscriptions and in the Purāṇas were taken from earlier Dharmaśāstras. Cf. Keith, *JRAS.*, 1912, 248 ff., 756 and Fleet, ib., 1046 ff. Fleet himself believes that chronological deductions could be made from the fact that in some of the Purāṇas the planets, beginning

"Purāṇas" must be very modern is also connected with the wrong belief in the past that the Purāṇa religion, the worship of Viṣṇu and Śiva is of later origin. Later researches have proved however that the sects of the Viṣṇu and the Śiva worshippers can be traced back in any case to the pre-Christian and perhaps to pre-Buddhist times.[1]

Orthodox Hindus themselves consider the Purāṇas to be very old. They believe that the same Vyāsa who classified the Vedas and composed the Mahābhārata was also the author of the 18 Purāṇas in the beginning of the Kaliyuga,[2] the present world-epoque. But this Vyāsa is one form of the exalted god Viṣṇu himself, "for" (says the Viṣṇu-Purāṇa), "who else could have composed the Mahābhārata?" His pupil was the Sūta Lomaharṣaṇa and to him he told the Purāṇas.[3] Thus the Purāṇas have a divine origin. And the Vedānta-Philosopher Śaṅkara takes the support of the Itihāsas, and the Purāṇas for proving the personal existence of the gods because these Itihāsas and Purāṇas, as he says are based not only on the Veda but also on sense-perceptions, namely on observations of people like Vyāsa who have personally spoken with the gods.[4] We cannot however compare the authority of the Purāṇas with that of the Veda. The Itihāsa and the Purāṇa are in a certain way only a complement to the Veda mainly intended for teaching women and Śūdras who are not entitled

with the sun, are enumerated in the same order in which they appear in the days of the week, which points to the period after 600 A.D. However, any arguments of this nature are conclusive merely for isolated chapters, and not for complete Purāṇa texts.

1. Cf. G. Bühler, *Epigraphia Indica*, II, 1894. p. 95. Kadphises II (about 78 A.D.) was such an ardent Śiva-worshipper that on his coins he got Śiva's-image stamped. (V.A. Smith, ibid. p. 318).

2. This according to Mahābhārata XII, 349 and Śaṅkara in his commentary to the Vedānta Sūtras III, 3, 32.

3. Viṣṇu-Purāṇa III, 4 and 6. The name Lomaharṣaṇa (or Romaharṣaṇa) is explained in the Vāyu-Purāṇa I, 16 etymologically as "one who through his beautiful stories, causes the hair (loman) on the body of the audience stand erect out of joy (harṣaṇa)."

4. Ved Su I, 3,33, *SBE* Vol. 34, p. 222. Śaṅkara adds: That men do not speak with gods today does not at all mean that in olden times too they did not speak with them.

to the study of the Veda. Thus even an old verse says, "Through Itihāsas and Purāṇas the Veda shall be strengthened, for the Veda is afraid of an uneducated one that he could harm it."[1] For obtaining the highest knowledge, the knowledge of the Brahman, only veda is of help, says Rāmānuja[2] whereas Itihāsa and Purāṇa lead only to the purification from sins. The Purāṇas are therefore sacred books of second class.[3] And this is also easy to explain. For originally the Purāṇas were no priestly literature at all. The Sūtas or bards were doubtless the authors and carriers of the oldest Purāṇa-poetry just as that of the epic.[4] This is indicated by one more circumstance namely that in almost all Purāṇas the Sūta Lomaharṣaṇa or his son Ugraśravas, the "Sauti", i.e. "the son of the Sūta" appears as the narrator, so much is this the case that Sūta and Sauti are used in the Purāṇas almost like proper names. But the Sūta was certainly no Brahmin and he had nothing to do with the Veda.[5] But when the old institution of the bards ceased—we do not know when—this literature went over not into the hands of the learned Brahmins, the Veda-Scholars, but to the lower class of priests who gathered in temples and pilgrim centres and took possession of this literature and these rather uneducated temple-priests used it for glorifying the deities whom they served and in later times more

1. The verse is quoted by Rāmānuja (*SBE*, Vol. 48, p. 91) as "Purāṇa text". It is found in the Vāyu Pur. I, 201; Mahābhār. I, 1, 267 and Vasiṣṭha-Dharmas, 27,6.

2. *SBE*, Vol. 48, p. 238 f.

3. This is expressed most clearly by Rāmānuja (*Ved. Su* II, 1, 3, *SBE*, Vol. 48, p. 413) when he says that although the Purāṇas are proclaimed by the creator Hiraṇyagarbha, still they are (just like Hiraṇyagarbha) as little free from the properties of passion (rajas) and darkness (tamas) and hence subject to errors.

4. According to the Vāyu—and the Padma-Purāṇa, the preservation of the genealogies of the gods, Ṛṣis and famous kings, is the duty of the Sūtas. Cf. Pargiter, *Anc. Ind. Hist. Trad.*, pp. 15 ff. Thus even at the present day the Bhāṭas preserve the genealogies of the Kṣatriyas; see C. V. Vaidya, *History of Mediaeval Hindu India*, II, Poona, 1924, pp. 260 ff.

5. "The Sūta has no claim to the Veda at all," says the Vāyu-Purāṇa I, 33, and also according to Bhāg-Pur. I, 4,13 the Sūta is well versed "with the whole area of speeches", that is conversant with the whole literature "with the exception of Veda" Cf. E. Burnouf, *Le Bhāgavata-Purāṇa* I, p. xxix and liii ff.

and more for praising the temples and pilgrim-centres in which they found accommodation and usually enriched themselves.[1] But how much the Indians even today believe in the sacredness of the Purāṇas is shown best by a speech delivered by Manilal N. Dvivedi at the Congress of Orientalists in Stockholm (1889)[2] As a man with European education he speaks of anthropology and geology, of Darwin, Haeckel, Spencer and Quatrefages, but only to prove that the world-view of the Purāṇas and their teachings on the creation of the world are scientific truth, as he perceives in them in general everywhere only highest truth and deepest wisdom—when one takes everything only rightly that is, symbolically.

The Purāṇas are valuable to the historian and to the antiquarian as sources of political history by reason of their genealogies, even though they can only be used with great caution and careful discrimination.[3] At all events they are of inestimable value from the point of view of the history of religion, and on this head alone deserve far more careful study than has hitherto been devoted to them. They afford us far greater insight into all aspects and phases of Hinduism—its mythology, its idol-worship, its theism and pantheism, its love of God, its philosophy and its superstitions, its festivals and ceremonies and its ethics, than any other works.[4] As literary products they are no pleasant phenomenon. They are in every respect without shape

1. According to Manu, 152, temple-priests (devaloka) cannot be invited to sacrifices (as also physicians and meat-vendors). Kalhaṇa the historian speaks with unconcealed contempt of these priests. Cf. M. A. Stein Kalhaṇa's Rājataraṅgiṇī... translated.... (Westminister 1900) Vol. I. Introduction p. 19f. Both the epics as well as the Purāṇas are recited nowadays by Recitators (Pāṭhakas) or Narrators (Kāṭhakas) belonging to the Brahmin caste specially for this purpose.

2. Cf. *Actes du Śéme Congres Internat des Orientalistes* (Leiden 1893) II, p. 199 ff.

3. As historical sources they surely do not deserve such confidence as is placed in them by F. E. Pargiter (*JRAS* 1914, 267 ff.; *Bhandarkar Com. Vol.*, p. 107 ff., and *Anc. Ind. Hist. Trad.* 77., 119 ff. and passim).

4. Cf. Pargiter, *ERE* X, pp. 451 ff. and J. N. Farquhar, *Outline of the Religious Literature of India*, p. 136 ff. and passim.

and mass. The sloppy language and the inartistic verses in which for the sake of metre the grammar is often violated are for these works just as characteristic as the wild confusion of the content and the measureless exaggerations. Here are only a few examples for the latter features; whereas in the Ṛgveda Urvaśī stays with Purūravas for four years, in the Viṣṇu-Purāṇa the two lovers indulge in pleasures and joys for 61000 years. Whereas even the earlier Purāṇas know only seven hells, the Bhāgavata-Purāṇa speaks of "hundreds and thousands" of hells, and the Garuḍa-Purāṇa enumerates not less than 8,400,000[1] of them. The younger the Purāṇa—this can be considered as the rule—the more measureless are the exaggerations. This too indicates that it was an inferior class of literates, belonging to the lower, uneducated priesthood, who were concerned with transmitting the Purāṇas. Still many old sagas of kings and many very late genealogical verses (anuvaṃśaślokas) and song-stanzas (gāthās) of the original bard-poetry have been preserved to us in the later texts which we have received. And fortunately the compilers of the Purāṇas who worked haphazardly did not disdain what was good and have included in their texts some dialogues reminiscent of the Upaniṣads in form and content as well as individual legends and texts of profound thought-content taken from the ancient ascetic poetry. Thus the following short survey of the most important Purāṇas and their contents will show that even in the desert of the Purāṇa-literature there is no lack of oases.

Survey of The Purāṇa-Literature

In the Purāṇas themselves which have been handed down to us, the number of the existing Purāṇas "composed by Vyāsa" is unanimously stated as 18; and in respect of their titles there is almost complete concurrence. Most of the Purāṇas also agree in the order in which they enumerate the eighteen Purāṇas, viz.:

1. Scherman, *Visionslitteratur*, p. 32 f.

1. Brahma
2. Padma
3. Vaiṣṇava
4. Śaiva or Vāyavīya
5. Bhāgavata
6. Nāradīya
7. Mārkaṇḍeya
8. Āgneya
9. Bhaviṣya or Bhaviṣyat
10. Brahmavaivarta
11. Laiṅga
12. Varāha
13. Skanda
14. Vāmana
15. Kaurma
16. Matsya
17. Garuḍa
18. Brahmāṇḍa[1]

It is peculiar that this list of "eighteen Pūrāṇas" is given in each one of them, as though none was the first and none the last, but all had already existed when each separate one was composed. All these Purāṇas point out in extravagant terms the advantages to be attained both in this world and in the world beyond, by reading and hearing these works. In some places[2] the length (number of ślokas) of the various Purāṇas is mentioned, but the texts which have come down to us are mostly shorter. In one passage of the Padma-Purāṇa (I,62) all of the eighteen

---

1. The list is given thus in Viṣṇu-P. III, 6; Bhāgavata-P. XII, 13 (varying only slightly XII, 7, 23 f.); Padma-P. I, 62; Varāha-P. 112; Matsya-P. 53; Agni-P. 272 and at the end of the Mārkaṇḍeya-P. Padma-P. IV, III; VI, 219; and Kūrma-P. I, 1 only diverge by putting 6 after 9. Padma-P. IV, iii has also the order 16, 13, 12, 15, 14 instead of 12-16, and Padma-P. VI, 263 has the order 17, 13, 14, 15, 16 instead of 13-17. Saura-P. IX, 6 f. has the order 5,8, 7,9,6 instead of 5-9. The Liṅga-P. (see Aufrecht, *Bodl. Cat.*, p. 44) has the order 1-5, 9, 6, 7, 8, 10, 11, 12, 14-17, 13, 18. A list in which the order is quite different, is that of the Vāyu-P. 104, 1 ff. Matsya, Bhaviṣya, Mārkaṇḍeya, Brahmavaivarta, Brahmāṇḍa, Bhāgavata, Brahma, Vāmana, Ādika, Anila (i.e., Vāyu), Nāradīya, Vainateya (i.e. Garuḍa), Padma, Kūrma, Saukara (Śaṅkara? Varāha?) Skanda,. (These are only 16. though "18 Purāṇas" are spoken about.) A verse has probably been omitted. For a similar list in the Purāṇasamhitāsiddhāntasāra, see F. R. Gambier-Parry, *Catalogue of Sanskrit MSS. purchased for the Max Mueller Memorial Fund*, Oxford, 1922, p.43.) The list in the Devibhāgavata-P. (quoted by Burnouf, *Bhāgavata-Pur.*, Preface, I, p. lxxxvi) also begins with the Matsya, but otherwise diverges. Alberuni (Sachau, I, p. 130) gives a list of the 18 Purāṇas, which was read to him from the Viṣṇu-Purāṇa, and which agrees with our list, and also a second, widely diverging list, which was dictated to him. A list which is very different from the usual one is given in the Bṛhaddharma-Purāṇa 25, 18 ff.

2. Matsya-P. 53, 13, ff.; Bhāgavata-P. XII, 13; Vāyu-P. 104, 1-10; Agni-P. 272.

Purāṇas are enumerated as parts of Viṣṇu's body (the Brahma-Purāṇa is his head, the Padma-Purāṇa is his heart, etc.), and are thus all stamped as sacred books. In another text of the same work,[1] on the other hand, we find the Purāṇas classified according to the three Guṇas[2] from the standpoint of Viṣṇuism. According to this classification, only the Viṣṇuite Purāṇas (Viṣṇu, Nārada, Bhāgavata, Garuḍa, Padma, Varāha) are of the quality of "goodness" (sāttvika) and lead to salvation; the Purāṇas dedicated to Brahman (Brahmāṇḍa, Brahmavaivarta, Mārkaṇḍeya, Bhaviṣya, Vāmana, Brahma) are of the quality of "passion" (rājasa) and only serve to attain heaven; whilst the Purāṇas in praise of Śiva (Matsya, Kūrma, Liṅga, Śiva, Skanda, Agni) are described as charged with "darkness" and as leading to hell. The texts which have come down to us, only partially agree with this artificial classification.[3] All this is additional confirmation of the fact that none of the Purāṇas has come down to us in its original form.

Besides the eighteen Purāṇas, which are often called the "great Purāṇas" (mahāpurāṇa), some of the Purāṇas themselves make mention of so-called Upapurāṇas or "secondary Purāṇas," whose number also is occasionally given as eighteen.[4] While, however, in the enumerations of the Purāṇas there is almost complete agreement with regard to the titles, this is by no means the case with the titles of the Upapurāṇas. Obviously there was a definite tradition about the existence of eighteen Purāṇas, while any modern religious text could assume the

---

1. In the Uttarādhyāya of the Padma-P. 263, 81 ff.

2. See above, p. 412.

3. For instance, the Matsya-P., which is condemned as a tāmasa, has both Viṣṇuite and Śivite chapters in our text; the Brahmavaivarta-Purāṇa is dedicated rather to Kṛṣṇa than to Brahman, the Brahma-P. teaches sun-worship as well as Viṣṇu and Śiva worship, the Mārkaṇḍeya-P. and the Bhaviṣya-P. are not sectarian at all, and so on. The above classification of the Purāṇas also shows that we can hardly talk of a "canon of eighteen Purāṇas" (see Farquhar, *Outline*, p. 225); for the Purāṇas are not the books of one religion, neither do they form a unified whole in any respect. For the religious views of the Purāṇas, cf. Pargiter, *ERE* X, 451 ff.

4. But the Matsya-Purāṇa mentions only four Upapurāṇas. The Brahmavaivarta-P., without enumerating them, says that eighteen Upapur. exist. The Kūrma.P. enumerates them.

title of an "Upapurāṇa," if the author did not prefer to declare his work as a part of one of the "eighteen Purāṇas." The latter is the case especially with the exceedingly numerous Māhātmyas, i.e. "glorifications" of sacred places (places of pilgrimage, tīrthas).[1] But also many stotras, i.e. "songs of praise" (usually to Viṣṇu or Śiva, but also to other deities), Kalpas, i.e. "rituals" and Ākhyānas or Upākhyānas. i.e. "legends," give themselves out as belonging to one or the other of the ancient Purāṇas.

We shall now give a short survey of the contents of the 18 Purāṇas and in doing so we shall spend a bit longer time with the most important ones. The order is the one that is given in the Viṣṇu- and the Bhāgavata-Purāṇa.

1. The Brahma or Brāhma-Purāṇa:[2] This is enumerated in all lists as the first and is hence called sometimes Ādi-Purāṇa, that means the "first Purāṇa"[3]. In the introduction it is said that the Ṛṣis in the Naimiṣa-forest are visited by Lomaharṣaṇa, the Śūta, and they ask him to tell them of the origin and the end of the world. Then the Sūta says he is ready to tell them the Purāṇa which once the creator Brahman told Dakṣa one of the primeval fathers of the human race. Then follow the legends of world-creation, the birth of Manu, the first man and his descendants, the birth of the gods, demi-gods and other beings, all of these legends being common to all the Purāṇas. Then we have a description of the earth with its different sections, of the hells and the heavens. This is followed by an enumeration of individual holy places of pilgrimage (Tīrthas). This culminates in the glorification of the holy place of Utkala (the present day Orissa), which fills a great part of

1. The "Māhātmyas" of sacred texts or of rites and festivals are not so numerous.

2. i.e. "The Brahmaic Purāṇa of Brahman" or "The Purāṇa of Brahman" all the other double titles, e.g. Vaiṣṇava- ("the Viṣṇuite") or Viṣṇu-Purāṇa (" the Purāṇa of Viṣṇu") are similarly explained. The Brahma-Purāṇa has been published in *ĀnSS* No. 28.

3. But there are other Purāṇas also which occasionally call themselves "Ādi-Purāṇa." Eggeling, Ind. Off. Cat., VI, p. 1184 f., describes, for instance, an Upapurāṇa which calls itself Ādi-Purāṇa and is devoted to the praise of Kṛṣṇa and Rādhā.

the whole work. As Utkala owes its holiness to sun-worship, we find here also myths on the birth of the Ādityas (the light-gods) and of Sūrya the sun-god. The description of a holy forest in Utkala sacred to Śiva is the occasion for stories on the birth of Umā, the daughter of the Himālaya, and her marriage with Śiva and other Śiva-myths. A hymn to Śiva (Ch. 37) is also inserted here. Nevertheless the Purāṇa is by no means, Śivaite, for the Mārkaṇḍeyākhyāna (Ch. 52 ff.) contains numerous Viṣṇu legends, and rituals and stotras of the Viṣṇu cult. Here too we find the charming story of Kaṇḍu[1] the penitent, who spends many hundred years in erotic dallyings and, at last, waking up from his ecstasy of his love, thinks that only a few hours of a single day have passed by. A short report on the incarnations (Avatāras) of Viṣṇu is followed by the usual legends of Kṛṣṇa in exact concurrence with and often verbatim reproduction of the Viṣṇu-Purāṇa. This is followed by a number of chapters on Śrāddhas (offerings to the manes) and others especially Vaiṣṇavite ceremonies, elaborate descriptions of the divisions of time, the world-epoques (Yugas), the degeneration of humanity in the Kali-Yuga and the periodical destruction of the world and in the end a description of the Yoga and the Sāṅkhya philosophies.

The Gautamīmāhātmya, the glorification of the sacred places on the Ganges (Chapt. 70-175), frequently appears in manuscripts as an independent text. The Uttara-khaṇḍa (i.e. "last section") of the Brahma-Purāṇa, which occurs in some manuscripts, is nothing but a māhātmya of a sacred river Balajā (Banas in Marwar ?).

Surely only a small portion of what has come down to us as the Brahma-Purāṇa can lay claim to be an ancient and genuine Purāṇa. About the middle of the 7th century A.D. Hsuan-Tsang still found over a hundred Buddhist monasteries with a myriad monks, but he also already found 50 Deva temples in Orissa. Śivaism was introduced in Orissa in the 6th century,

1. Printed in Ch. Lassen's *Anthologia Sanscritica*, translated into German by A. W. v. Schlegel, *Indische Bibliothek*, I, 1822, p. 257 ff., and into French by A. L. Chezy in *JAI*, 1822, p. 1 ff. The legend is also related in the Viṣṇu-P., I. 15.

and Viṣṇuism still later.[1] As the sun-temple of Koṇārka, which is mentioned in our Purāṇa, was not built until 1241, at least the large section on the sacred places of Orissa cannot be earlier than the 13th century.[2] It is probable, however, that the Māhātmyas do not belong to the original Purāṇa.

The Saura-Purāṇa,[3] which claims to be a supplement (khila) of the Brahma-Purāṇa, but which is quoted as an authority by Hemādri as early as in the 13th century, proves that there must have been an earlier Brahma-Purāṇa. The Saura-Purāṇa (the "Purāṇa of the sun-god") which is mentioned in the lists of the Upapurāṇas, is of great value as regards our knowledge of Śivaism, especially of the Liṅga cult. Its main purpose is to glorify god Śiva. In many places however, Śiva is identified with the sun-god who reveals the Purāṇa, or else the sun-god recommends Śiva worship. The advantages of Śiva worship are praised in the most extravagant terms, instructions are given for the worship of the god and the Liṅga and many Śiva-legends are told. A few chapters also deal with the genealogies; in Chapter 31 on the descent of Yadu there is a version of the Urvaśī legend.[4] In the philosophical sections the work takes up an intermediate position between the orthodox systems. On the one hand Śiva is explained as the Ātman, in accordance with the Vedānta, and on the other hand the creation from the primal matter (prakṛti) is explained, as in the Sāṃkhya. Three chapters (38-40) are devoted to polemics against the system of Madhva (1197-1276), which is important from the point of view of chronology.[5]

---

1. See Th. Watters, *On Yuan Chwang's Travels in India* (London, 1905), II, p. 193; W. Crooke, *ERE*, Vol. 9, p. 566.

2. See Wilson, *Works* III, p. 18.

3. Text published in *ĀnSS* No. 18, 1889. An analysis with extracts and partial translation of the work has been given by W. Jahn, *Das Saurapurāṇam*, Strassburg, 1908. The Saura-P. is sometimes also called Āditya-P. However, there is another Āditya-Purāṇa, which is different from, though related to the Saura-P. See Jahn, ibid., pp. ix, xiv and *Festschrift Kuhn*, p. 308. The Brahma-P., too, is sometimes called "Saura-P." Cf. Eggeling, *Ind. Off. Cat.* VI, p. 1185 ff.

4. See P. E. Pavolini, *GSAI* 21, 1908, p. 291 ff, and Jahn, *Das Saurapurāṇam* p. 81.

5. See A. Barth in *Melanges Charles de Harlez*, Leyden, 1896, p. 12 ff. As Madhva lived from 1197-1276 and Hemādri wrote between 1260 and 1309, the

II. The Pādma or Padma-Purāṇa. There are two different recensions of this voluminous work.[1] The printed edition,[2] consisting of the six books Ādi, Bhūmi, Brahma, Pātāla, Sṛṣṭi and Uttara-Khaṇḍa, is a later recension. The earlier one, which has come down to us only in Bengali manuscripts, consists of the following books or Khaṇḍas.[3]

Book I, Sṛṣṭikhaṇḍa, i.e. "section of the creation," commences with the usual introduction:[4] Lomaharṣaṇa sends his son, the Sūta Ugraśravas, to the Naimiśa forest to recite the Purāṇas to the Ṛṣis assembled there. At the request of Śaunaka he tells them the Padma-Purāṇa, so-called after the lotus (padma) in which the god Brahman appears at the creation. The Sūta then reproduces the account of the creation as he has heard it from Brahmā's son Pulastya. The cosmological and cosmogonic myths are here too related similarly as in other Purāṇas. But in this book, it is not Viṣṇu who is assumed as the first cause, but the highest Brahman in the form of the personal god Brahman.

Saura-Purāṇa would have been compiled approximately between 1230 and 1250. However, as Chapters 38-40 do not occur in all the MSS. (see Edition, p. 125 note, and Eggeling, *Ind. Off. Cat.* VI, p. 1188), it is more probable that they have been interpolated, and that the work is earlier, Cf. Jahn, ibid., p. xiv.

1. In the Purāṇa itself (V, 1, 54; VI, 219, 28) and in the lists, the number of Ślokas is said to be 55,000. However, according to Wilson, the Bengali recension only contains nearly 45,000 ślokas, whilst the Ānss edition contains 48,452.

2. Edited by V. N. Mandlick in *ĀnSS* No. 28, 1894. 4 vols. At the end of the Bhūmi-Khaṇḍa in this edition there is a verse which enumerates the Khaṇḍas with the same titles and in the same order as in the Bengali MSS. The printed recension thus itself proves that the Bengali recension is the earlier one. Cf. Lüders, *NGGW* 1897, 1, p. 8. In the Sṛṣṭi-Khaṇḍa 1, 53-60, the Padma-Purāṇa is described as consisting of five Parvans: (1) Pauṣkaram, treating of the creation, (2) Tirthaparvan, about mountains, islands and oceans, (3) a chapter on the kings who offered rich sacrificial gifts, (4) a chapter on the genealogies of the kings, and (5) a chapter on salvation. This, too corresponds to the arrangement in the Bengali recension in all essentials.

3. This account of the Bengali recension is based on the Oxford manuscripts, which was inspected in 1898, and on the descriptions by Aufrecht, *Bodl. Cat.* I, p. 11 ff. and Wilson, *Works* III, p. 21 ff.; VI, p. xxix ff.

4. In the *ĀnSS* edition, too, the Sṛṣṭi-Khaṇḍa begins as though it were the beginning of the Purāṇa, but it has 82 Adhyāyas here, whilst in the Bengali recension, it only consists of 46 (Wilson) or 45 (Aufrecht).

Nevertheless, even this book is Viṣṇuite in character, and contains myths and legends for the glorification of the god Viṣṇu. After the account of the creation come the usual genealogies of the solar dynasty, into which a section about the Pitṛs, the 'fathers' of the human race and their cult by means of Śrāddhas has been interwoven,[1] and of the lunar dynasty down to the time of Kṛṣṇa. Myths are then told of the conflicts between gods and demons, followed by a chapter which is of interest from the point of view of the history of religion,[2] and from which we give here a short extract:

At first the gods were defeated by the demons. However, Bṛhaspati, the teacher of the gods, finally caused the gods to triumph in the following manner. In the guise of Śukra, the teacher of the Asuras, he goes to the Asuras, and by means of heretical speeches, lures them from their pious faith in the Vedas. He tells them that the Veda and the tenets of the Vaiṣṇavas and the Śaivas are full of violence (hiṁsā), and that they are preached by married teachers. How then can there be any good in them ? How can Śiva, the god in the form of a semi-female[3] (ardhanārī-īśvaraḥ), surrounded by hosts of evil spirits and even adorned with bones,)[3] tread the path of salvation? How can Viṣṇu, who uses violence, attain to salvation? If the path to heaven consists of felling a tree to make a sacrificial stake out of it, of killing a sacrificial animal and causing slaughter, what is the path to hell? How is it possible to attain heaven by sexual intercourse, or purity by earth and ashes ? Soma seduced Tārā, the wife of Bṛhaspati; Budha, the son whom she bore, violated her; Indra committed adultery with Ahalyā, the wife of the Ṛṣi Gautama. Then the demons beg him to tell them to which god they can fly for safety. Bṛhaspati considers in what way he can demoralise them. Viṣṇu now comes to his aid, by causing the phantom figures of a nude Jain monk (digambara) and a Buddhist monk

1. Chapt. 9-11 in *ĀnSS* edition.
2. V. 13, 316 ff. in *ĀnSS* edition. Cf. Viṣṇu-Purāṇa III, 17, 41-18, 33.
3. One of Śiva's forms is that of the half-female. His adornment is wreath of human skulls, and his retinue is formed by the Bhūtas or ghosts.

(raktāmbara, "red-mantle") to appear, to initiate the demons into Jain and Buddhist doctrines. After thus giving up their old (brahmanical) way of life, they yield dominion to god Indra.

One of the principal parts of the book consists of the description of the lake Puṣkara (Pokher in Ajmer)[1], sacred to Brahman, which is recommended and glorified as a place of pilgrimage. Numerous myths and legends, many of which occur in different connections in other Purāṇas, are told in praise of Puṣkara. Moreover, various feasts and vows (vrata) in honour of the goddess Durgā are mentioned here. Thereupon the theme of the creation is resumed. The book concludes with myths of Viṣṇu as the destroyer of demons, and the birth and marriage of Skanda.[2]

Book II, Bhūmikhaṇḍa[3] i.e. "section of the earth" begins with legends of Somaśarman, who in a later rebirth became the famous worshipper Prahlāda.[4] The aim of the legends is to explain why on the one hand he was born among the demons, and yet, on the other hand, was able to become so great a devotee of Viṣṇu. Besides a description of the earth this book contains many legends which are supposed to prove the sacredness of the several Tīrthas or holy places. As Tīrthas are considered not only sacred places, but also persons like the teacher, the father or the wife. To prove that a wife can be a "Tīrtha", for example, the story is told of Sukalā[5] whose husband undertakes a pilgrimage and leaves her back in misery and suffering; although Kāma the love-god and Indra the king of the gods try to seduce her she remains faithful to her husband,

1. The Sṛṣṭi-Khaṇḍa is therefore also called Pauṣkara-Khaṇḍa.

2. The contents of the Sṛṣṭi-Khaṇḍa are still more variegated in the *ĀnSS* edition, where among other things, Chapt. 61-63 are devoted to the cult of Gaṇeśa and the final chapters to the cult of Durgā. The Ādi-Khaṇḍa, with which the edition begins, consists almost entirely of Māhātmyas of various Tīrthas. Only the last chapters (50-60) deal with Viṣṇu-bhakti and the duties of the castes and āśramas.

3. On the whole, it corresponds to the Bhūmikhaṇḍa in the *ĀnSS* edition.

4. It is here taken for granted that the actual legend of Prahlāda, as told in the Viṣṇu-Purāṇa (see below) is known.

5. Sukalācarita in *ĀnSS* edition Adhy. 41-60.

and when he comes back from the pilgrimage he (!) receives heavenly reward for the virtues of his wife. For proving that a son can be a 'Tīrtha', we are also told here the story of Yayāti and his son Puru which is already known to us from the Mahābhārata.

The third book, called Svargakhaṇḍa,[1] i.e. "Section on the heavens' gives a description of the various worlds of gods, of the worlds of Sūrya, Indra, Agni, Yama, etc. into which numerous myths and legends are woven. A mention of King Bharata gives rise to the narration of the story of Śakuntalā, which is told here not like in the Mahābhārata, but in concurrence with the drama of Kālidāsa. A comparison of Kālidāsa's drama with the versions of the Mahābhārata and of the Padma-Purāṇa shows that in all probability Kālidāsa used the last-mentioned as a source.[2] A description of the world of the Apsaras occasions the narration of the legends of Purūravas and Urvaśī. Many other legends also, which are known to us from the epics, recur here. Further, it contains teachings on the duties of the castes and the Āśramas, on the kinds of Viṣṇu-worship and all sorts of things on rituals and morals.

The fourth book, 'Pātālakhaṇḍa', i.e. "Section on the nether world" describes at first the underground regions, especially the abodes of the Nāgas or serpent-deities. A mention of Rāvaṇa is the occasion for narrating the entire Rāma-legend, which is given here partly in concurrence with the Rāmāyaṇa and partly also often in verbatim concurrence with Kālidāsa's epic Raghuvaṃśa.[3] Here we also find the Ṛṣya-Śṛṅga legend in a version

1. There is an English translation of the Svargakhaṇḍa by Panchānan Tarkaratna, Calcutta, 1906.

2. This has been shown by Śarmā, Padmapurāṇa and Kālidāsa, Calcutta, 1925 (Calcutta Oriental Series, No. 17 E. 10). Professor Śarma here also gives the text of the Śakuntalā episode according to the Bengali MSS. Wilson (*Works* III, p. 40) had maintained that the Purāṇa utilised Kālidāsa's drama.

3. H. Śarma, ibid. has made it appear probable that, in this case also, the Padma-Purāṇa was Kālidāsa's source, and not, as Wilson (Works III, p. 47) assumed, that the compiler of the Purāṇa drew from the Raghuvaṁśa. H. Śarma, ibid. has published a critical edition of the text of this chapter (which is missing in the *ĀnSS* edition.)

that is more archaic than in our Mahābhārata.[1] The actual Rāma-legend is preceded by a story of the forefathers of Rāma which begins wit Manu, the son of the sun-god and his rescue from the deluge. The slaying of Rāvaṇa, who was a Brahmin, has laid the guilt of the murder of a Brahmin on Rāma. By way of expiation he arranges a horse-sacrifice. In accordance with the prescribed rules, the horse destined for the sacrifice is let loose to roam at will for the space of one year, accompanied by a host of warriors with Śatrughna at their head. The adventures of the steed and his followers on their wanderings over the whole of India take up a considerable portion of the book; many sacred places are described, and legends attached to them are told. At length the horse reaches Vālmīki's hermitage, which is an occasion for narrating that part of the Rāma-legend which concerns Sītā.[2] An extensive teaching on the 18 Purāṇas constitutes the end of the Pātālakhaṇḍa. Here it is said that Vyāsa proclaimed the Padma-Purāṇa at first, and then 16 others, and finally the Bhāgavata-Purāṇa, which is glorified as the most sacred book of the Viṣṇu-worshippers. The book ends with a few chapters, probably added at a very late date, on Kṛṣṇa and the cowherdesses, with mention of Rādhā, on the duties of Viṣṇu worshippers, the sanctity of the Śālagrāma stone and other details of the Viṣṇu-cult.[3]

Book V. Uttarakhaṇḍa, i.e. "last section," is a very long book expounding the Viṣṇu cult and the feasts and ceremoines

1. This has been proved by Lüders, *NGGW* 1897, 1, p. 8 ff. This circumstance is further proof of the greater antiquity of the Bengali recension of the Padma-Purāṇa.

2. Wilson (*Works*, III, p. 51) says: "This part of the work agrees in some respects with the Uttara-Rama-Charitra, but has several gossiping and legendary additions."

3. The Pātālakhaṇḍa in the *ĀnSS* edition only partly agrees with that of the Bengali recension. The sequence of the chapters is different, and it also contains a few chapters devoted to the Siva-cult (105-111). In the edition the Pātālakhaṇḍa is preceded by the short Brahmakhaṇḍa, which consists mainly of descriptions of Viṣṇuite feast days. Chapt. 7, treating of the birthday feast of Rādhā (Rādhājanmāṣṭamī), indicates late origin. The cult of Rādhā is mentioned neither in the Mahābhārata and the Harivaṃśa nor in the Rāmāyaṇa or the earlier Purāṇas. See below (Brahmavaivarta Purāṇa).

connected with it, in the most impressive manner. A large portion is devoted to the glorification of the month of Māgha, which is especially sacred to Viṣṇu. The silliest of legends are related as evidence of the great merit of bathing during this month. Another section glorifies the month of Kārttikeya, in which the giving away of lamps is especially meritorious. In order to give special prominence to the Viṣṇuite standpoint, the author causes Śiva himself, in a conversation with his wife Pārvatī, to declare the glory of Viṣṇu and to recite a long account of Viṣṇu's avatāras, which involves a repetition of the entire Rāma-legend in summary and the Kṛṣṇa legend with a fair amount of detail. In reply to Pārvatī's question who the heretics are, it is Śiva himself who declares that the Śivaite teachers and the adherents of the Śivaite Pāśupata sect are among the heretics. In another passage we find, curiously enough, the cruel goddess Durgā holding forth upon Ahimsā. Śiva also explains what Viṣṇu-Bhakti is, and the various forms of the Viṣṇu cult. This book also contains a glorification of the Bhagavadgītā.[1] In fact there are legends to illustrate the merit of reading each single canto. One chapter contains the enumeration of the thousand names of Viṣṇu, in another Rādhā is identified with the great goddess Lakṣmi, and the celebration of her birthday is described. The sectarian bias of this book cannot be better illustrated, however, than by the following legend:

A quarrel once arose among the Ṛṣis as to which of the three great gods, Brahman, Viṣṇu or Śiva, was deserving of greatest worship. In order to dissolve their doubts, they request the great ascetic Bhṛgu to go to the gods and convince himself personally which of them is the best. Accordingly Bhṛgu at first repairs to the mountain Kailāsa to visit Śiva, and is announced by Śiva's janitor Nandin. But Śiva is just enjoying the love of his wife, and does not admit the Ṛṣi at all. Thus insulted,

1. Gītāmāhātmya, Adhy. 171-188 in *ĀnSS* edition, where a glorification of the Bhāgavatapurāṇa (Adhy. 189-194) follows after it. This Bhāgavatamāhātmya also appears as an independent work in MSS. as well as in printed editions. The Māghamāhātmya and other parts of the Uttara-khaṇḍa also occur as independent works.

the Ṛṣi pronounces a curse on Śiva, condemning him to take on the shape of the generative organs,[1] and to be worshipped not by the Brahmins, but only by heretics. Thereupon Bhṛgu goes to the world of Brahmā. The god is seated upon his lotus-throne, surrounded by the gods. The Ṛṣi bows before him in reverential silence, but filled with pride, Brahman does not even rise to greet him and to honour him as a guest. Spurred to anger, Bhṛgu pronounces a curse whereby Brahman is to enjoy no worship at all from the human race.[2] The saint now goes to the mountain Mandara in Viṣṇu's world. There he sees the god reposing upon the world-snake, while Lakṣmi caresses his feet. He awakens the god roughly by a kick on his chest. Viṣṇu awakens, gently strokes the sage's foot, and declares that he feels highly gratified and honoured by the touch of his foot. He and his wife hasten to rise, and do honour the Ṛṣi with divine garlands, sandalwood oil, etc. Then the great ascetic bursts into tears of joy, bows before "the treasury of mercy," and praises Viṣṇu as the highest god, when he exclaims: "Thou alone shalt be worshipped by the Brahmins, none other of the gods is worthy of worship. They shall not be worshipped, Brahman, Śiva and other gods, for they are charged with passion (rajas) and darkness (tamas) : thou alone, endowed with the quality of goodness (sattva), shalt be worshipped by the first-born (i.e. the Brahmins). Let him who honours other gods, be counted among the heretics." Then Bhṛgu returns to the assembly of the Ṛṣis and tells them the result of this visit to the gods.[3]

A kind of appendix to the Uttarakhaṇḍa is formed by the Kriyāyogasāra,[4] i.e. "the essence of Yoga by works," which

1. This refers to the worship of the Yoni and the Liṅga as symbols of the god Śiva.

2. This is an allusion to the fact that there is scarcely any cult of Brahman in India.

3. In the Bengali recension this legend is found in the middle, in the *ĀnSS* edition at the end of the Uttara-khaṇḍa, which contains only 174 adhyāyas in the Bengali recension, but 282 in the Ānss edition.

4. Many extracts from this book which is mentioned in the list of Upapurāṇas, Bṛhaddharma-P. 25, 24, have been translated into German by A. E. Wollheim da Fonseca, *Mythologie des alten Indien*, Berlin, s.a. The same scholar has given an analysis of the book in the *Jahresbericht der deutschen morgenländischen Gesellschaft*, 1846, p. 153 ff.

teaches that Viṣṇu should be worshipped not by meditation (dhyānayoga), but by pious acts, above all by pilgrimages to the Ganges and the celebration of the festivals dedicated to Viṣṇu. In evidence of the fact that the fulfilment of all possible desires can be attained by worshipping Viṣṇu on the bank of the Ganges, many silly legends are told, but also the beautiful love story of Mādhava and Sulocanā.[1]

It is quite impossible to say anything definite as to the date of the Padma-Purāṇa. It is obviously a rather loose compilation, the parts of which belong to totally different periods, and are probably many centuries apart. The common characteristic of the five or six books is merely their rigidly sectarian character, for all of them inculcate the cult of Viṣṇu.[2] Moreover, all these books contain references to fairly modern aspects of the Viṣṇu cult, such as the adoration of Rādhā as a goddess, the sanctity of the Sālagrāma stone, of the Tulsi plant, and the like. The latest portions are certainly later than the Bhāgavata-Purāṇa, which belongs to the latest works of Purāṇa literature. Nevertheless there is sure to be an ancient nucleus at least in the Sṛṣṭi-, Bhūmi-, Svarga- and Pātāla-Khaṇḍas. It remains the task of future research to extract this ancient nucleus.[3]

The Vaiṣṇava or Viṣṇu Purāṇa.[4] This is the main work of the Vaiṣṇavas or Viṣṇu worshippers and is quoted by Rāmānuja, the philosopher, the founder of the Vaiṣṇavite sect of the Rāmānujas, in his commentary to the Vedānta-sūtras as an important authority. In this work Viṣṇu is praised and glorified as the supreme Being, as the one and only one god with whom also Brahmā and Śiva are identical. He is also the creator and protector of the world. Still it is precisely in this Purāṇa that we

1. Freely rendered into German verse by A. F. Graf von Schack, *Stimmen vom Ganges*, p. 156 ff.

2. The Sṛṣṭi-khaṇḍa, where Brahman is in the foreground, is an exception.

3. An essential preliminary for this would be a critical edition of the Padma-Purāṇa on the basis of the Bengali manuscripts.

4. Edited, with Ratnagarbha's commentary, Bombay Śaka 1824. An older commentary is that of Śrīdhara, from which Ratnagarbha has copied, see Eggeling, *Ind. Off. Cat.* VI, p. 1310. Translated by H. H. Wilson, London, 1840 (and *Works*, Vols. VI-X) and by Manmatha Nath Dutt, Calcutta, 1894.

do not find any directions regarding the festivals, sacrifices and ceremonies dedicated to Viṣṇu in particular; not even Viṣṇu-temples are mentioned, nor even places sacred to Viṣṇu. Even this makes us infer that this work is of great antiquity. Even to the old definition of the concept of the Purāṇa (see p. 499 above) the Viṣṇu Purāṇa comes closest by containing little that is not included in the "five characteristics". That the title Viṣṇu-Purāṇa has not been claimed for later works, Māhātmyas[1] etc. indicates similarly that it is a work of older Purāṇa literature which has preserved at least to a large extent its original form[2].

A somewhat more elaborate survey of the contents of this Purāṇa will also give the reader the best idea of the contents and the significance of the Purāṇas in general.

This work consisting of six chapters, begins with a dialogue between Parāśara, the grandson of Vasiṣṭha and his pupil Maitreya.

The latter asks his teacher about the origin and nature of the universe. Thereupon Parāśara replies that this question reminds him of what he once heard from Vasiṣṭha his grandfather; and he commences to repeat what he had heard. Contrary to tradition (also found in the Viṣṇu-Purāṇa) which attributes all Purāṇas to Vyāsa, here Parāśara is mentioned in particular as the author of the work. After glorifying Viṣṇu in a hymn at first, he gives a report on the creation of the world, as it appears

1. Aufrecht *CC.* I, 591; II, 140; III, 124, mentions only a few stotras and minor texts which claim to be parts of the Viṣṇupurāṇa. Nevertheless it is noteworthy that Matsya- and Bhāgavata-Purāṇa give the number of ślokas of the Viṣṇu-Purāṇa as 23.000, while in reality it has not quite 7,000 verses, and that also a "Great Viṣṇu-Purāṇa" (Bṛhadviṣṇupurāṇa, Aufrecht, *CC.* I, 591) is quoted.

2. It is no more possible to assign any definite date to the Viṣṇu-Purāṇa than it is for any other Purāṇa. Pargiter (*Anc. Ind. Hist. Trad.*, p. 80) may be right in thinking that it cannot be earlier than the 5th century A.D. However, I do not think that it is much later. Cf. Farquhar, *Outline*, p. 143. C. V. Vaidya (*History of Mediaeval Hindu India*, I, Poona 1921, p. 350 ff.; *JBRAS* 1925, 1, p. 155 f.) endeavours to prove that the Viṣṇu-P. is not earlier than the 9th century for he assumes that the Kailakila or Kaiṅkila Yavanas mentioned in IV, 24 reigned in Andhras between 575 and 900 A.D. and were at the height of their power about 782 A.D. This assumption is, however, purely hypothetical and not proven.

again and again in a rather identical form in most of the Purāṇas.[1] In a remarkable way philosophic views—mainly of the Sāṅkhya philosophy are mixed with mythical ideas for which we can find many parallels among the primitive folks.

The report on the creation of gods and demons, of heroes and forefathers of the human race is followed by numerous mythological stories, allegories and legends of Kings and Wise men of prehistoric times. Many of these stories we have already seen in the Mahābhārata; for example that of the churning of the ocean.[2] It is vividly described how the goddess of fortune Śrī rises in resplendent beauty from the churned ocean of milk, and throws herself into the arms of Viṣṇu. In a splendid hymn Indra addresses her as the mother of all beings and praises her as the source of all that is good and beautiful and the bestower of all happiness. Just as this piece mainly serves to glorify Viṣṇu, whose consort is Śrī, so also in all other stories it is always Viṣṇu, whose praise is sung in a very exuberent manner. While describing the power which one can acquire by worshipping Viṣṇu, the phantasy of the Indian knows no limits. An example of this is the myth of Prince Dhruva, who, mortified at the preferential treatment shown to his brother, dedicates himself even as a boy entirely to penance and Viṣṇu-worship, so that Viṣṇu feels obliged to grant him his wish to become something higher than his brother and even his father—he makes him the pole-star; which is of a higher and more everlasting duration, than all other stars of the heaven.[3] However, the power of Viṣṇu-worship is sung in the most splendid manner in the legend of the boy Prahlāda (I, 17-20) whom his father, the proud demon king tries in vain to divert from his Viṣṇu-worship. No weapon can kill him, neither serpents nor wild elephants, neither fire nor

1. A survey of the creation-reports in the Purāṇas is furnished by Wilhelm Jahn in *Über die Kosmogonische Grundanschauungen in Mānava-Dharma-Śāstra*." Inaug, —Diss. Leipzig 1904.

2. P. 374 above. A compilation of all passages common to both Viṣṇu-Purāṇa and the Mahābhārata is made by A. Holtzmann in his *Mahābhārata*. IV. 36 ff.

3. I, 11 f. An exhaustive version of the myth is found in the Bhāgavata-Purāṇa (IV, 8 f.); this is the basis for the poem of Schack, *Stimmen vom Ganges*, p. 189 ff.

poison nor magic-curses can do him any harm. Hurled down from the balcony of the palace, he falls gently on to the lap of the earth. Bound in fetters he is thrown into the ocean and mountains heaped on him—but in the bottom of the sea he sings a hymn to Viṣṇu, his fetters fall off, and he hurls the powerful mountains away from himself. Questioned by his father whence his marvellous powers are derived, Prahlāda replies:

"Whatever power I possess, father, is neither the result of magic rites, nor is it inseparable from my nature; it is no more than that which is possessed by all in whose hearts Acyuta[1] abides. He who meditates not of wrong to others, but considers them as himself, is free from the effects of sin, inasmuch as the cause does not exist; but he who inflicts pain upon others, in act, thought, or speech, sows the seed of future birth, and the fruit that awaits him after birth is pain. I wish no evil to any, and do and speak no offence; for I behold Keśava[1] in all beings, as in my own soul. Whence should corporeal or mental suffering or pain, inflicted by elements or the gods, affect me, whose heart is thoroughly purified by him? Love, then, for all creatures will be assiduously cherished by all those who are wise in the knowledge that Hari[1] is in all things."[2]

The second book of the Viṣṇu-Purāṇa gives at first (Chap. 1-12) a fantastic description of the world. The seven continents and the seven oceans are described, in the midst of which Jambūdvīpa is found with the golden mountain of Meru—the abode of the gods. In Jambūdvīpa lies Bhāratavarṣa i.e. 'India' whose countries, mountains and rivers are enumerated. This description of the earth is followed by a description of Pātāla, the nether world, in which the serpent gods live and then an enumeration and a description of the Narakas or hells lying still further deep under the earth. As a counterpart follows then a description of the celestial spheres, of the sun, of the sun's chariot and of the sun's horses together with astronomical discussions on the sun's course, the planetary system and the sun

1. Names of Viṣṇu.

2. I, 19, 1-9. Translated by H. H. Wilson. A version of the same legend is found in the Bhāgavata-P. VII, 4-6, on which the poetical rendering by Schack, *Stimmen vom Ganges*, p. 1 ff. is based.

as rain-giver and life-protector. Then follows a description of the moon, of her chariot, of her horses, of her orbit and her relation to the sun and the planets. The chapter closes with the explanation that the whole world is only Viṣṇu and he alone is the only real one.

In connection with the name of Bhāratavarṣa then (Chap. 13 to 16) a legend is told of the ancient King Bharata[1] which (legend) serves only to introduce a philosophical dialogue in which the old unitary doctrine is taught from the Vaiṣṇavite point of view. The style of the whole chapter reminds one in many ways of the Upaniṣads. The story of the legend is as follows:

King Bharata was a pious devotee of Viṣṇu. One day he went to bathe in the river. When he was bathing a pregnant antilope came from the forest to drink water. In the same moment the loud roar of a lion is heard in the vicinity. The antilope is frightened and runs away from there with a mighty leap. As a result of the leap her young one is born and she herself dies. Bharata took the young animal with him and brought it up in his hermitage. From then on he did not care for anything but the antilope. That was his only thought, that was his only worry. And as he finally died, always thinking only of the antilope, he was reborn soon after as an antilope;[2] however he had the remiscences of his previous birth. In his antilope existence also he worshipped Viṣṇu and devoted himself to expiatory exercises, so that in the next birth he was born again as the son of a pious Brahmin. Although he acquired knowledge of the unitary doctrine as a Brahmin, yet he did not care for any study of the Vedas, he performed no Brahminical rites, spoke incoherently and ungrammatically, went about in dirty and tattered clothes — in short he behaved entirely like an idiot. People called him simply "Jaḍa Bharata," the stupid Bharata[3]

1. Cf. E. Leumann, "Die Bharata—sage", *ZDMG* 48, 1894, P. 65 ff and "August Blau, Das Bharatopākhyāna des Viṣṇu-Purāṇas" (*Beitrage zur Bücherkunde und Philologie August Wilmanns zum* 25. Mar 1903 gewidmet, Leipzig 1903. p. 205 ff).

2. Till here the legend is adapted (according to the version of the Bhāg. Pur. V, 8 in the poem of Schack, *Stimmen vom Ganges*, p. 56 ff.

3. The corresponding story in the Bhāgavata-P. V, 9; 10 has the title "Jaḍabharatacarita." Life of Bharata the Stupid, in the colophons.

he was generally despised and employed for the menial duties of a slave. So it happened that once he was also employed for carrying the palanquin of the king of Sauvīra. On this occasion a conversation evolves between the apparent idiot and the king. In the course of this conversation Bharata is soon revealed as a great sage and proclaims to the great joy of the king the unitary doctrine. In explanation of this he tells him the story of Ṛbhu and Nidāgha.

The wise and holy Ṛbhu, the son of Brahmā the creator had been the teacher of Nidāgha. After a thousand years he visited his pupil once, was hospitably hosted by him and was asked where he lived, wherefrom he came and where he went to. Ṛbhu answered that these were foolish questions, for man, (i.e. the Ātman) is everywhere, for him there is no coming and no going, and he makes the doctrine of the unity so clear to him that Nidāgha falls enchanted at his feet and asks who he is. Only now he learns that it is his old teacher Ṛbhu who had come to teach him once again the true wisdom. After another thousand years Ṛbhu comes once again to the town where Nidāgha lives. There he sees a large crowd of people and a king who enters the town with a great following. Far away from the crowd his former pupil Nidāgha is standing, Ṛbhu approaches him and asks him why he is standing aside. Thereupon Nidāgha replies, "A king is coming to the town, there is a large crowd, therefore I am standing aloof." Ṛbhu asks, "who is then the king?" Nidāgha: "The king is the one who is seated on the big stately elephant." "Well" says Ṛbhu, "but who is the elephant and who is the King? Nidāgha: "Below is the elephant and above the King", Ṛbhu: What is meant by below and what is meant

Jaḍabharata is mentioned, along with Durvāsas, Ṛbhu, Nidāgha and other Paramahaṃsa ascetics, who "though not mad, behave like madmen," in the Jābāla-Upaniṣad 6. In Viṣṇu-P. I, 9 a legend is related of the ascetic Durvāsas (i.e. "Badly-Clad") "who observed the vow of a madman." Cf. also A. Barth, Religions of India, p. 83. Similarly there were in the Middle Ages certain Christian saints, like St. Symeon Salos and St. Andreas, who wandered about like fools or idiots, exposing themselves to mockery and insults as a kind of asceticism. Cf. H. Reich, *Der Mimus.* Berlin, 1903, I, 2, p. 822 f., and J. Horovitz, *Spuren griechischer Mimen im Orient*, Berlin, 1905, p. 34 ff.

by above?" Then Nidāgha springs on to the back of Ṛbhu and says, "I am above like the king, you are below like the elephant". "Very Well" says Ṛbhu, but just tell me my dear, who of us both is then you and who am I?" Only now Nidāgha recognises his old teacher Ṛbhu because nobody is permeated with the unitary doctrine like him. Then the doctrine of the unity of the universe got impressed on Nidāgha so well that from now on he considered all beings as one with himself and attained complete satisfaction.

The third book of the Viṣṇu-Purāṇa begins with a report on the Manus (forefathers of the human race) and the epoques (Manvantaras)[1] governed by them. Then follows a discussion on the four Vedas, on the division of the same through Vyāsa and his pupils and on the origin of various Vedic schools. An enumeration of the 18 Purāṇas and a list of all the sciences follow.

Then the question is raised and discussed, as to how one can attain salvation as a pious worshipper of Viṣṇu. In a beautiful dialogue (Chapter 7) between Yama, the god of death and one of his servants it is elaborated that he who is pure of heart and leads a virtuous life and has directed his mind to Viṣṇu is a real Viṣṇu-worshipper and therefore free from the bonds of the god of death. This is followed by a discourse on the duties of the castes and the Āśramas, on birth and marriage ceremonies, ritual baths, the daily sacrifices, the duties of hospitality, the conduct at the time of taking food etc. A long treatise (chap. 13-17) on the offerings to the dead and other ceremonies for worshiping the spirits of the manes (Śrāddhas) closes this chapter in which the Vedic-Brahminic religious practices are presented as the right kind of Viṣṇu-worship. The last two chapters of this book describe the birth of the heretic sects opposed to the Vedas whose followers, especially the Jainas, called Digambaras, and the Buddhists known as Raktāmbaras,[2] (i.e., Redmantles) are represented as the worst evil-doers. In order to show how

1. On the epoques of the World according to the Purāṇas, see Jacobi, *ERE*, I, 200 ff.

2. The rise of the heretical sects is here (III, 17 f.) explained by the legend according to which Viṣṇu sent a phantom figure to the demons in order to alienate them from the Veda religion, whereupon they can be defeated by the gods. Cf. Padma-Purāṇa, above p. 514

sinful it is even to maintain contact with such heretics, the story of the old King Śatadhanu is told (chapter 18), who was a pious worshipper of Viṣṇu but for exchanging a few words with a heretic merely out of politeness and in consequence was born as a dog, a jackal, a wolf, a vulture, a crow and a peacock one after another, until at last, — due to the everlasting faithfulness and piety of his wife Śaibyā —he was again born as a king.

The fourth book of the Viṣṇu-Purāṇa contains mainly genealogical lists of ancient royal houses, of the solar dynasty which traces its origin to the Sun-god and of the lunar dynasty which traces it to the Moon-god. Long lists of ancient kings many of them purely mythical, some perhaps also historical are interrupted only occasionally in order to tell some legend about one or the other of them. In all these legends the element of wonder plays a big role. There is Dakṣa who is born out of Brahmā's right thumb; Manu's daughter Ilā, who is transformed into a man; Ikṣvāku, who owes his existence to the sneezing of Manu; King Raivata who goes to heaven with his daughter Revatī in order to make god Brahmā recommend a husband for his daughter[1] or even King Yuvanāśva, who becomes pregnant and gives birth to a son, whom Indra suckles with the drink of immortality by making the child put its finger in the mouth of the god and suck it. Because Indra says, "He will be suckled by me" (Māṃ dhāsyati) the child receives the name Māndhātṛ. He became a powerful king and father of three sons and fifty daughters. How he obtained a son-in-law is narrated with that peculiar humour which sometimes pleasantly interrupts the seriousness which is generally predominant in the legends of Indian holymen, in the legend of the pious penitent Saubharī who practises asceticism for twelve years in water until the sight of the fish king enjoying the company of his young ones rouses in him the desire for parental pleasures.[2]

Many of the legends known to us from the epics are found again in this book, for example that of Purūravas and Urvaśī,[3]

1. Adapted by Schack, *Stimmen vom Ganges*, p. 120 ff.
2. IV, 2 Treated beautifully by Schack, *Stimmen vom Ganges*, p. 87 ff.
3. Translated by Geldner, *Vedische Studien* I, p. 253 ff.

of Yayāti, etc. A short summary of the Rāma-legend is also found here. On the birth of the Pāṇḍavas and of Kṛṣṇa also there is a report here and the legend of the Mahābhārata is shortly touched upon. This voluminous genealogical book closes with the prophecies on the "future" Kings of Magadha, the Śaiśunāgas, Nandas, Mauryas, Śuṅgas, Kaṇvāyanas and Āndhrabhṛtyas (See above p. 501 f), on the barbarian foreign kings following them and the terrible epoque brought about by them — an age without religion and without morals — to which only Viṣṇu in his incarnation as Kalki will put an end.

The fifth book forms a book complete in itself. It contains only an exclusive description of the life of the divine Cowherd Kṛṣṇa in which the same adventures are told in the same sequence as in the Harivaṃśa.[1]

The sixth book is very short. Once again the four world epoques (Yugas) — Kṛta, Tretā, Dvāpara and Kali—are thought of and in the form of a prophecy the evil Kaliyuga is described which is then followed by a description of the various kinds of the dissolution (Pralaya) of the Universe. In a pessimistic manner then (Chap. 5) the evils of existence, the pain of rebirth, of childhood, of adult life and of old age and death, the torture of the hell and the imperfection of the bliss in heaven are described, and from this it is concluded that only salvation from existence, freedom from rebirth is the greatest fortune. For this it is however necessary to recognise the essence of God, for only that wisdom is perfect, by which God is seen, everything else is ignorance. The means for attaining this wisdom is however Yoga, the meditation on Viṣṇu. The two penultimate chapters of the book give information on this means. The last chapter contains one more short repetition of the whole Purāṇa and ends with a praise of Viṣṇu and a closing prayer.

IV The Vāyava or Vāyu-Purāṇa.[2] This appears in some lists under the name of Śaiva or Śiva-Purāṇa,[3] a title that

---

1. This chapter is translated into German by A. Paul, *Krischnas Weltengang, ein indischer Mythos ... aus dem Vischnupurāṇam* München 1905.

2. Editions in *Bibl. Ind.* 1880-1889 and in ĀnSS No. 49, 1905.

3. So in the Viṣṇu and Bhāgavata-Purāṇa. But there is also a Śiva-Purāṇa which is a completely different work and belongs to the Upapurāṇas.

the Purāṇa gets because it is devoted to the worship of God Śiva. A Purāṇa preached by the Wind-God, i.e. a Vāyu-Purāṇa is quoted in the Mahābhārata as well as in the Harivaṃśa, and the Harivaṃśa concurs verbatim in many respects with our Vāyu-Purāṇa.[1] It was already mentioned (p. 503 above), that poet Bāṇa (about 625 A.D.) had a Vāyu-Purāṇa read out to him and that in this Purāṇa the Gupta reign is described as it existed in the 4th century A.D. Certainly there has been an old Purāṇa with this name and doubtless even in our texts there is still much of the ancient work, which is probably not later than the 5th century A.D.[2] In this work also the same topics—characteristic of the old Purāṇas – world creation, genealogies etc. — are treated as in the Viṣṇu-Purāṇa. Only the legends told here serve to glorify Śiva, not Viṣṇu. Like the Viṣṇu-Purāṇa the Vāyu-Purāṇa also gives in its concluding part a description of the end of the world and treats the efficiency of Yoga, but ends with a description of the splendour of Śivapura, "the town of Śiva," whither the Yogin goes who is totally engrossed in the meditation of Śiva. There are also many Māhātmyas.[3] Stotras and ritual texts which claim to be parts of the Vāyu-Purāṇa. We cannot unhesitatingly call the whole Vāyu-Purāṇa as we find it 'old.'

This Purāṇa treats very elaborately the spirits of manes (Pitṛs) and their cult (Śrāddhas).[4] One chapter is devoted to

---

cf. Eggeling, *Catalogue of Sanskrit MSS. in the India office library* p. 1311 ff. The Brahmāṇḍa-P. is also called "Vāyavīya", i.e. "proclaimed by Vāyu." Pargiter (*ERE* X, 448) believes that Vāyu and Brahmāṇḍa were originally one Purāṇa and only got separated later.

1. Cf. Hopkins, *Great Epic*, p. 49. Holtzmann, *Das Mahābhārata* IV, p. 40 f. and above p. 498 f.

2. Cf. Bhandarkar, *Vaiṣṇavism* etc., p. 47; Farquhar, p. 145. C. V. Vaidya's argument (*JBRAS* 1925, 1, p. 155 f.) for ascribing the Vāyu-P. to the 8th century is not convincing.

3. Thus a Gayāmāhātmya is found in the editions which is missing in some manuscripts. On the other hand it appears in manuscripts as an independent work. Cf. Eggeling ibid., p. 1299 ff., 1301 ff. Editions of the Vāyu-Purāṇa appeared in the *Bibliotheca Indica*, Calcutta, 1880-89 and in the AnSS, Poona. 1905. This last-mentioned edition contains besides the usual division into four Pādas or "quarters", also one into 112 Adhyāyas or "lessons." The Adhyāyas 104-112 are in any case later interpolations.

4. Śrāddhaprakriyārambha and Śrāddhakalpa, Adhy. 71-86.

the art of song.[1] However, even in this Śaivite work we find two chapters on Viṣṇu.[2]

V. The Bhāgavata-Purāṇa: This is indisputably the most famous work of the Purāṇa-literature in India. Even today it exercises a tremendous influence on the life and the thinking of innumerable followers of the sect of the Bhāgavatas (worshippers of Viṣṇu under the name of 'Bhāgavat'). The unusually numerous manuscripts and imprints of the text itself as well as of many commentaries to the whole work and of individual explanatory works on parts of it[3] in addition to the various translations into Indian vernaculars[4] bear testimony to the great popularity and the high esteem of this work in India. In accordance with this great significance, the work has found at first an editor and translator in Europe.[5] Yet it is one of the later products of the Purāṇa-literature. In the matter of its contents it is closely connected with the Viṣṇu-Purāṇa with which it often concurs verbatim and is certainly dependent on it. Doubts have already been expressed even in India on the "genuineness" of the Bhāgavata as one of the ancient eighteen Purāṇas "composed by Vyāsa" and there are polemic writings[6] in which the question is discussed, whether the Bhāgavata or the Devī

1. Adhy. 87: Gitālaṁkāranirdeśaḥ.

2. Adhyāyas 96, 97.

3. See Eggeling, *Ind. Off. Cat.* VI, p. 1259 ff., and Aufrecht, *CC.* I, p. 401 ff.

4. In Bengali alone there are 40 translations, especially of the Kṛṣṇa-book. See D. Ch. Sen, *History of Bengali Language and Literature*, Calcutta, 1911, p. 220 ff.

5. *Le Bhāgavata-Purāṇa ou histoire poetique de Krichna*, traduit et publie par M. Eugene Burnouf, t, I-III, Paris 1840-47. T. IV et V publieś par M. Hauvette-Besnault et P. Roussel. Paris 1884 et 1898. A few legends from the Bhāg -P. have been translated into French by A. Roussel, *Legendes Morales de l'inde*, Paris 1900, I, 1 ff. and II, 215 ff. English translation by Manmatha Nath Dutt, Calcutta, 1895. A French translation of the Tamil version of the Bhāgavata was published as early as 1788 at Paris, and this was rendered into German, Zürich 1791 (see Windisch, *Geschichte der Sanskrit-philologie*, p. 47 f.).

6. Thus the "box on the ear for villains" (durjanamukhacapeṭikā), the "big box on the ear for villains" (durjanamukhamahācapeṭikā) and the "slipper in the face of villains" (durjanamukhapadmapāduka). They are translated by Burnouf, ib. I, Preface p. lix ff. These are quite modern writings.

Bhāgavata-Purāṇa,[1] a Śaivite work, belongs to the "eighteen Purāṇas." In this context the question is also raised and discussed, whether the grammarian Vopadeva is the author of the Bhāgavata-Purāṇa.[2] Colebrooke, Burnouf and Wilson have concluded from this (too hastily) that Vopadeva is really the author of the Purāṇa and hence this has originated only in the 13th century.[3] We cannot consider the work as of so late an origin as it already passed as a sacred book in the 13th century.[4] There are good grounds for assigning it to the 10th century A.D.[5] Rāmānuja, the philosopher (12th century) who is so closely connected with the Bhāgavatas, does not mention this work but quotes only the Viṣṇu-Purāṇa. But though it may have originated at a comparatively late date, it certainly utilised very ancient materials. Moreover, it is the one Purāṇa which, more than any of the others, bears the stamp of

---

1. This is also called simply Śrībhāgavatamahāpurāṇa in the MSS. Editions have been published in Bombay, and an English translation in the *SBH.* Cf. Aufrecht, *Bodl. Cat.* p. 79 ff.; Eggeling, *Ind. Off. Cat.* VI, p. 1207 f. There is also a Mahā-Bhāgavata-Purāṇa differing from it, which is described by Eggeling (ib. p. 1280 ff.) as "an apocryphal Purāṇa recounting the story and exploits of Devī and urging her claims to being worshipped as the supreme deity."

2. This supposition seems to rest only on the fact that Vopadeva is the author of the Muktāphala, a work dependent on the Bhāgavata, and of the Harilīlā, an Anukramaṇī (index) to the Bhāgavata.

3. Vopadeva was a contemporary of Hemādri, who lived between 1260 and 1309.

4. Anandatīrtha Madhva (1199-1278), who himself wrote a commentary on the Bhāg.-Pur. places it on a level with the Mahābhārata.

5. C. V. Vaidya (*JBRAS* 1925, 1, 144 ff.) makes it seem probable that it is later than Śaṅkara (beginning of the 9th century) and earlier than Jayadeva's Gītagovinda (12th century). Bhandarkar (*Vaisnavism* etc., p. 49) says that it "must have been composed at least two centuries before Ānandatīrtha." Pargiter (*Anc. Ind. Hist. Trad.*, p. 80) places it "about the ninth century A.D." Farquhar (*Outline*, p. 229 ff.) about 900 A.D., C. Eliot (*Hinduism and Buddhism*, II, p. 188 note) remarks that "it does not belong to the latest class of Purāṇas, for it seems to contemplate the performance of Smārta-rites, not temple ceremonial." Vaidya (ib., p. 157 f.) adduces arguments for the hypothesis that the author of the Bhāg.-Pur. lived in the land of the Draviḍas. Cf. Grierson, *JRAS* 1911, p. 800 f.

a unified composition. and deserves to be appreciated as a literary production on account of its language, style and metre.[1]

The incarnations of Viṣṇu[2], especially that as a boar are described exhaustively. It is noteworthy that also Kapila, the founder of the Sāṅkhya school is mentioned as an incarnation of Viṣṇu, and (at the end of the third book) delivers a long discourse on Yoga. Buddha, too, already appears among the incarnations of Viṣṇu.[3] Numerous are the legends that are told for glorifying Viṣṇu. Most of them like that of Dhruva, Prahlāda etc. are known to us already from the Viṣṇu-Purāṇa. Even with the Mahābhārata the work has much in common, some verses from the Bhagavadgītā are quoted verbatim.[4] The short narrative of the Śākuntala-episode (IX, 20) is taken probably from a very ancient source.[5] The tenth book is the most popular and most widely read of all. It contains the description of Kṛṣṇa's life, which is given here much more elaborately than in the Viṣṇu-Purāṇa and in the Harivaṁśa. The love-scenes with the cowherdesses (Gopīs) in particular occupy much more space.[6] This book is translated into almost all popular languages of India and is a favourite book of all classes of the Indian folk. The eleventh book narrates the destruction of the Yādavas

---

1. Side by side with the śloka, metres of ornate poetry also appear. Cf. Burnouf, I, Preface, p. cv f.

2. Fr. Majer has already narrated about "the incarnation of Viṣṇu" according to the Bhāgavata in J. I. Klaproth's *Asiatisches Magazin* I and II (Weimar 1802).

3. Though he appears, "to delude the foes of the gods" (I, 3, 24), he is among the avatāras, and as such (in the Nārāyaṇavarman, VI, 8, 17) he is invoked, whilst in the Viṣṇu-P. (III, 17 f.,). Viṣṇu in order to delude the Daityas, causes a phantom form to issue forth from himself, which comes into the world as Buddha.

4. See Holtzmann, *Das Mahabharata*, IV, 41-49. and J. E. Abbott, Ind. Ant. 21, 1892, p. 94.

5. In IX, 20, 16, *om* is used in the sense of 'yes', which is very archaic. Cf. Ait.-Br. VII. 18; Chānd.-Up. I, 1, 8 and above p. 173 Note. In Kūrma-P.I, 23 (p. 48) and I, 27 (p. 294) *om* is also used in the sense of 'yes' in the style of the old legends, though the Kūrma itself is a late work.

6. Rādhā, however, does not appear, from which Vaidya, ibid. rightly concludes that the Bhāg-Pur. is earlier than the Gitagovinda.

and the death of Kṛṣṇa while the last book contains the usual prophecies on the Kaliyuga and the world-destruction.

VI. The Bṛhannāradīya-Purāṇa ("the Great Purāṇa of Nārada").[1] It is generally so called to distinguish it from the Nārada — or Nāradīya-Upapurāṇa. It is doubtful, however, whether even the Bṛhannāradīya-Purāṇa deserves to be counted among the ancient Purāṇas; for it is a purely sectarian text, wherein the Sūta repeats a conversation between Nārada and Sanatkumāra, and the sage Nārada appears in the character of a teacher of Viṣṇu-bhakti—the pious adoration of Viṣṇu. The real themes of the Purāṇas, the creation of the world, etc., are not touched upon; the main themes are descriptions of the feasts and ceremonies of the Viṣṇu-cult, illustrated by all kinds of legends. Inserted in the legends we also find didactic sections upholding a rather intolerant brahmanical standpoint. Chapter XIV, a lengthy chapter containing a catalogue of the principal sins and the corresponding punishments of hell, is characteristic. By way of example, the following are included among the sinners for whom there is no atonement, and who must irrevocably be condemned to hell:

He who venerates a Liṅga or an image of Viṣṇu which is worshipped by a Śūdra or a woman; he who bows down before a Liṅga worshipped by a heretic, or who himself becomes a heretic, Śūdras, unintiated persons, women, outcastes, who touch an image of Viṣṇu or Śiva, go to hell. He who hates a Brahmin, can in no wise hope for atonement. There is no expiation for the Brahmin, who enters a Buddhist temple, even though he did so in a great emergency; even hundreds of expiation ceremonies are of no avail. The Buddhists are despisers of the Vedas, and therefore, a Brahmin shall not look at them, if he is truly devoted to the Vedas.[2] These sinners for whom there is no

1. Edited by Pandit Hrishikesa Sastri, *Bibl. Ind.* 1891, who calls the work an "Upapurāṇa." Cf. Wilson *Works*, VI, p. li ff., Eggeling, Ind. Off. Cat. VI, p. 1208 ff. In the Bṛhaddharma-P. I, 25, 23 both the Bṛhannāradiya and the Nāradīya are enumerated among the Upapurāṇas.

2. Pandit Hrishikesa concludes from this passage that the work was compiled when Buddhism "was rooted out and was universally despised." On the contrary, such violent outbreaks against the Buddhists could only have a meaning at a time when Buddhism was still a living power in India.

expiation, are not only condemned to roast in hell in hundreds and thousands of years — the author actually revels in the enumeration of the tortures of hell— but they are subsequently reborn again and again as worms and other animals, as Caṇḍālas, Śūdras and Mlecchas. Dreadful torments of hell await him who recites the Veda in the presence of women or Śūdras. Nevertheless, in contradiction to all these damnations, the same chapter teaches that Viṣṇu-bhakti annihilates all sins and that Ganges water, too, washes away the blackest sins.

Several chapters (22-28) deal in detail with the duties of the castes and āśramas and with Śrāddhas and the ceremonies of expiation (prāyaścitta). The last chapters deal with the misery of transmigration (saṁsāra) and with salvation (mokṣa) by means of Yoga and Bhakti. Devotion to Viṣṇu is again and again declared to be the only means of salvation. Thus we read (28,116): "Of what avail are the Vedas, the Śāstras, ablutions in sacred bathing-places, or austerities and sacrifices to those who are without the worship of Viṣṇu (Viṣṇubhakti)?"

The Nāradīya-Upapurāṇa includes the Rukmāṅgadacarita, which also occurs as an independent book. The "edifying" legend of King Rukmāṅgada is here told in 40 chapters. King Rukmāṅgada has promised his daughter Mohinī that he will grant her a wish, whatsoever it may be. She demands that he shall either break his fast on the Ekādaśī (the eleventh day of the half-month sacred to Viṣṇu) or slay his son; the king decides upon the latter, this being the lesser of the two sins.

VII. The Mārkaṇḍeya-Purāṇa:[1] This is one of the most important, interesting and probably also the oldest work of the whole Purāṇa-literature. But even this Purāṇa is no unitary work but it consists of parts which are not all of the same value and also belong certainly to the various times.

The work gets its name from the ancient Sage-Mārkaṇḍeya enjoying eternal youth who also appears as narrator in a big chapter in the Mahābhārata. (See Note on p. 382 and 408 above). And we may consider as the oldest constituent those chapters[2] in

1. Edited by K. M. Banerjea, *Bibli Ind.* 1862 and translated into English by F. Eden Pargiter, *Bibli Ind.* 1888-1905.

2. These are chapters 45-81 and 93-136 (conclusion). Cf. Pargiter, Introd. p. iv, Verse 45, 64 is quoted twice by Śaṅkara (Vedānta-Sūtras

which Mārkaṇḍeya is actually the speaker and enlightens his pupil Krauṣṭuki on the creation of the world, the epoques of the world, the genealogies and the other topics characteristic of the Purāṇas. Especially the fact that in these chapters neither Viṣṇu nor Śiva occupies a prominent place but that rather Indra and Brahman gain prominence and the primeval deities of the Veda, Agni (fire) and Sūrya (Sun) are glorified through hymns in some cantos and that a large number of sun-myths are told[1] — all this speaks in favour of the great antiquity of the chapters containing the old Purāṇa. This oldest part of the Purāṇa may, as Pargiter thinks, have originated in the third century A.D., but it can be also older. Moral and edifying tales also form a big chunk in this part.

It is more so in the earlier chapters of the work which follow most closely the Mahābhārata and have very much in common with the 12th book of the epic. The Purāṇa begins in particular with this, that Jaimini, a pupil of Vyāsa approaches Mārkaṇḍeya and after some praising of the Mahābhārata [2] requests him to answer four questions which the great epic leaves unanswered. The first question is, how Draupadī could become the common wife of the five Pāṇḍavas, the last why the children of Draupadī were killed at a tender age. Mārkaṇḍeya does not answer these questions himself but directs him to four wise birds—actually Brahmins who were born as birds as a result of a curse.[3] These

I, 2, 23, and III, 3, 16, see P. Deussen, *Die Sūtras des Vedānta aus dem Sanskrit übersetzt*, Leipzig 1887, p. 119 and 570) ; but it is by no means certain that Śaṅkara knew the verse from the Mārkaṇḍeya-Purāṇa, for he does not mention it, but only says, "It is said in the Smṛti."

1. Chapters 99-110. A very antiquarian impression is also made by the story of Dama, who, to avenge the death of his father, kills Vapuṣmat cruelly and makes an offer of his flesh and blood to the departed spirit of his father together with the other cakes of the funeral sacrifice (136). That in the Bengalee manuscripts the story comes to an abrupt end without there being any mention of the cannibal-offering is precisely a proof of the great antiquity of those traditions which were not acceptable any more to the notions of a later epoque (cf. Pargiter, p. VII).

2. These concur partly verbatim with the glorifications at the beginning and at the close of the Mahābhārata itself (cf. above p. 304 f and 388).

3. This again is a copy of a legend occurring in the Mahābhārata also (I, 229 ff.) where however one of the birds is called Droṇa whereas in the Mārk. Pur. the four birds are sons of Droṇa.

birds tell Jaimini a series of legends for answering the questions put to them. In reply to the last question it is said that five angels (Viśve Devas) once dared blame the great holy man Viśvāmitra when he treated Hariścandra cruelly for which they were cursed by the holy man to be born again as human beings, which curse he himself mitigated by saying that they would die young and unmarried. The five sons of Draupadī were precisely those angels. Connected with this the pathetic but genuinely Brahminic legend of King Hariścandra is told, who, out of fear from the anger and curse of Viśvāmitra undergoes sufferings and humiliations, until at last he is led into heaven by Indra himself.[1]

After the replies to the four questions a new chapter begins (ch. 10-44) in which we have a conversation between a father and his son. This is an extensive dilation of the conversation between father and son that we have seen in the Mahābhārata (p. 403 ff above). It is characteristic that in the Mahābhārata the son is called "intelligent" (Medhāvin) whereas in the Purāṇa he bears the epithet Jaḍa, "the stupid".[2]

Like in the Mahābhārata, here too the son scorns the way of life of the pious Brahmins as idealised by the father; he recalls to his mind all his earlier births and sees redemption only in escaping from the Saṃsāra. Then the "stupid one" gives a description of the Sāṃsāra and the results of the sins in various rebirths, especially of the hells and the punishments in the hells which are awaiting the sinners. In the midst of the description

1. Chapter 7 and 8. This famous legend has been translated into English by J. Muir, *Original Sanskrit Texts*, I, 3rd ed., p. 379 ff. and by B. H. Wortham, *JRAS* 1881, p. 355 ff., into German by F. Rückert (*ZDMG* 13, 1859, 103 ff.; *Ruckert-Nachlese* II, 489 ff.). The legend was a favourite theme for later dramatists, thus it forms the subject of the Caṇḍakauśika by the poet Kṣemīśvara (10th or 11th century A.D.). It is also told in a ballad that is still popular in the Punjab, see R. C. Temple : *The Legends of the Panjab* No. 42 (Vol. III, p. 53 ff.). The Śunaḥśepa legend, the Buddhist Vessantara-Jātaka, and the Hebrew Book of Job have been compared with the Hariścandra legend. Cf. Weber *SBA* 1891. p. 779 f. *Ind. Stud.* 15, p. 413 ff. On the legends of Viśvāmitra, Vasiṣṭha, Hariścandra and Śunaḥśepa in the Brāhmaṇas, Purāṇas and Epics, see F. E. Pargiter, *JRAS* 1917. p. 37 ff.

2. Even this "wise stupid-man" is like Jaḍabharata (p. 524 above) a proclaimer of Yoga.

of the hells,[1] splendid in its own way, although far from comforting, we find one of the best pearls of Indian legend-poetry, the story of the noble king Vipaścit ('the wise')[2] that really deserves to be reproduced here in short:

King Vipaścit who is extremely pious and virtuous, is taken to hell after his death by a servant of Yama. When he questions in surprise why he was taken there, Yama's servant replies to him, he once failed to cohabit with his wife at a time propitious for conception, for this small violation of religious injunctions he must make amends at least by a short stay in the hell. Then he enlightens the king in respect of good and bad deeds (karman) which must necessarily have their consequences and the punishments in the hell which are prescribed for every individual sin. After these explanations the servant of the god of death wants to lead him out of the hell. The king turns to go,—then horrifying cries of lamentation reach his ear and the inhabitants of the hell pester him to stay back just for one more moment, for an immensely pleasant odour was emanating from him which was alleviating the tortures of hell. To his astonished question Yama's servant gives the explanation that from the good works of a pious man a refreshing breeze blows and mitigates the tortures of the inhabitants of the hell. Then the king speaks:

> "Neither in the heaven nor in the world of Brahmā—so I think—
> Does a man find such a bliss, as when he
> On beings who are tortured can bestow comfort
> If through my presence becomes milder
> These poor beings' torture then will I remain here, my friend,

---

1. It is this which is the most exhaustive hell-description in the Purāṇa-literature, but similar descriptions occur also in the other Purāṇas. They are discussed by L. Scherman, *Visionsliteratur*, p. 23 ff. 45 ff.

2. Chapter 15. The Verses 47-79 have been translated into German by Fr. Ruckert in the 12th vol. of the *ZDMG* (1858), p. 336 ff. A Buddhist version of the legend is the basis for the beautiful poem of Betty Paoli, Der gute König in der Hölle (*Gedichte, Auswahl und Nachlass*, Stuttgart 1895, p. 217 ff.)

Like a pillar I don't move away from here".
Yama's servant spoke:
"Come O king, let us go, enjoy the fruits
Of your good deeds and let the tortures
To those who deserve them because of evil deeds"
The King spoke:
"No, from here I will not go, as long as these
Poor hell-inhabitants through my company are lucky.
Disgraceful and shameful is the life of a man
Who does not sympathise with the tortured, the down-trodden,
Who beg him for help—even with bitter enemies
Sacrifice, gift and penance serve neither now nor after death
The man who has no heart to protect the tortured ones
Whose heart is hardened towards children, aged and weak,
A man he is not, I think, a devil is he
Even if through the company of these hell-inhabitants
Purgatory torture suffer, the stinking hell
And the pangs of hunger and thirst rob me
Of my senses,—I do feel it sweeter than heavenly bliss
To them, the tortured ones help and protection to grant.
If through my suffering many poor people become happy
What more do I want ?—Don't hesitate, go away and leave me !
Yama's servant spoke:
"Look here, Dharma comes[1] and Śakra, to take you
You must indeed go, O king; up then, off from here !"
Dharma spoke:
"Let me accompany you to the heaven, which you well deserve,
Mounted in this divine chariot readily—off from here !"

---

1. Regarding Dharma as a name of the god of death see p. 381 above. Śakra is a name of Indra, the king of gods. In the real ancient Ākhyāna-style we are not told that the two gods came, but this arrival is made known by means of a dialogue and they immediately appear talking.

The King spoke:
"Here in this hell, Dharma, are men thousandfold tortured;
Protect us! they cry out to me in agony; I move not from this spot",

Śakra spoke:
"The wages for their acts these wicked ones get in the hell;
You must, O king, for your good deeds move upward to heaven".

For the king however the inhabitants of the hell are not the sinners but only the sufferers. And as upon his questioning how big are his good deeds, Dharma himself gives the answer that they are as numerous "as the water drops in the sea, the stars in the sky,... the grains of sand in the Gaṅga", then he has only this one wish, namely that through his good acts the inhabitants of the hell may be set free from their tortures. The king of the gods grants him this wish, and while he rises to heaven all those living in the hell are redeemed of their sufferings.[1]

In language and style this splendid dialogue reminds us in many respects of the Sāvitrī-poem of the Mahābhārata. But just as in the case of the great epic so also in our Purāṇa side by side with the most beautiful pieces of poetry we find the most insipid products of priestly literature. Immediately following the legend narrated above we find that of Anasūya that stands out as a caricature from the Sāvitrī-legend.

---

1. The story of Yudhiṣṭhira's visit to hell and journey to heaven in the 18th book of the Mahābhārata (page 359 f. above) is a copy and is, perhaps, only a weak and poor imitation of the Vipaścit-legend. Even that Yudhiṣṭhira has only a vision (māyā) of hell is an essential weakening. In the Padma-Purāṇa as penalty for having killed a cow king Janaka comes into hell for the sake of keeping the form and he then redeems similarly the condemned people there. (Wilson, *Works* III. p. 49 f not in the *AnSS* edition). King Janaka goes to hell as a matter of form, because he has struck a cow, and he releases the damned souls in a similar fashion. A Jewish fairy-tale tells of a selfless man who spent his whole life in succouring the distressed, and after his death refused to go to Paradise because there was nobody there in need of aid; he prefers to go to hell, where there are creatures with whom he can feel sympathy and whom he can help. (I. L. Perez, *Volkstümliche Erzahlungen*, p. 24 ff.). The original source of all these legends is probably to be found in a Buddhist Mahāyāna legend of the Bodhisattva Avalokiteśvara.

Anasūya is[1] the extremely faithful wife of a disgusting, crude and mean-minded Brahmin afflicted with leprosy. Following the Brahminic principle "The husband is the wife's deity", the woman serves him with utmost love and care and suffers his abuses with patience. One day this good man, who is also a libertine, expresses his urgent desire to visit a courtesan, to whom he has taken a liking. As he is himself too ill to go, his faithful wife carries him on her back to take him to the courtesan. On the way he unwillingly kicks with his foot a holyman and his holyman curses him to die before the sun rises. Then says Anasūyā: "The sun shall not rise". As a result of her piety actually the sun does not rise and consequently the gods are very much embarassed because they do not get any offerings. They are then forced to see that the gracious husband of Anasūyā remains alive.

Exactly like in the Mahābhārata we find here also further in addition to legends purely didactic dialogues on the duties of the house-holder, on Śrāddhas, on one's conduct in everyday life, on the regular offerings, festivals and ceremonies[2] as well as a treatise on the Yoga (chap. 36-43).

A work, complete in itself, which in any case was interpolated in the Mārkaṇḍeya-Purāṇa later on, is the Devī-Māhātmya[3] a glorification of goddess Durgā worshipped till most recent times. In the temples of this terrible goddess the Devīmāhātmya is read everyday and at the time of the great festival of Durgā (Durgāpūjā[4] in Bengal) it is recited with utmost ceremoniousness.

1. The name means "the Non-jealous."

2. Chapters 29-35. The chapter on Śrāddhas concurs partly verbatim with the Gautamasmṛti, according to W. Caland, *Altindische Ahnenkult*, Leiden 1893. p, 112.

3. Chapters 81-93. It occurs also under the titles Caṇḍī, Caṇḍimāhātmya, Durgāmāhātmya and Saptaśatī and exists in innumerable manuscripts as an independent work. There are also many commentaries to the text. A manuscript of Devīmāhātmya is dated 998 A.D. It has been translated in excerpts into French by Burnouf (*Journal Asiatique* IV, 1824, p. 24 ff) and completely into English by Wortham (*JRAS* XIII, 1881, p. 355 ff). Bāṇa's poem "Caṇḍīśataka", and Bhavabhūti's drama "Mālatīmādhava presuppose probably the Devīmāhātmya, so that this late interpolation into the Mārkaṇḍeya-Purāṇa must have existed already before the 7th century (Cf. Pargiter p. xii and xx).

4. Regarding this most popular of all religious festivals in Bengal compare Shib Chunder Bose. *The Hindoos as they are*, p, 92 ff.

VIII. The Āgneya or Agni-Purāṇa[1] so called because it is supposed to have been disclosed to Vasiṣṭha by Agni. It describes the incarnations (Avatāras) of Viṣṇu, among them also those of Rāma and Kṛṣṇa, where it admittedly follows the Rāmāyaṇa, the Mahābhārata and the Harivaṃśa. But although it begins with Viṣṇu, still it is in essence a Śaivite work and treats exhaustively the mystic cult of the liṅga (phallus) and of Durgā. Still chapters are not wanting on cosmology, genealogy and geography which are all so characteristic of the Purāṇas. But what characterises this Purāṇa especially is its encyclopaedic character. It actually deals with each and everything. In it we find chapters on astronomy and astrology, on marriage and funeral rites, on omens and portents, house-construction and other customs of everyday life, and also on politics (nīti) and the art of warfare, on law (whereby it closely follows the law-book of Yājñavalkya), on medicine, prosody, poetics and even on grammar.

To which age this remarkable encyclopaedia or its individual parts belong, it is impossible to say. However, although the work itself contains such varied things, there are many other Māhātmyas and similar texts, which give themselves out as belonging to the Agni-Purāṇa, but are not found in the manuscripts of the work itself.

IX. The Bhaviṣya- or Bhaviṣyat-Purāṇa. The title denotes a work which contains prophesies about the future (bhaviṣya). But the text preserved to us in manuscript-form under this title is certainly not the old work, which is quoted in the Āpastambīya-Dharmasūtra.[2] The report on creation which it contains is taken from the law book of Manu that is put to many other uses as well.[3] The greatest part of the work deals

---

1. Pub. in the *Bibl. Ind.* Calcutta 1873-79. A work occurring under the title Vahni-Purāṇa is also called Agni or Āgneya-Purāṇa, but it is different from the work described above. (Eggeling, *Catalogue*, p. 1294 ff).

2. See p, 497 f above. Still less claim to genuineness has the edition of the Bhaviṣya-Purāṇa that appeared in Bombay, which Th. Aufrecht (*ZDMG* Bd 57, 1903, p. 276 ff) has exposed as a "literary fraud."

3. Cf. G. Bühler, *SBE*, vol. 25, p. ix f and 78 note. Wilhelm Jahn ibid. 38 ff and also Wilson, works VI, p. lxiii.

with Brahminical ceremonies and festivals, the duties of the castes and similar things. Only few legends are narrated. A description of the festival of Nāgapañcamī consecrated to serpent-worship provides the occasion for an enumeration of snake-demons and for narrating snake-myths. A fairly big chapter concerning the worship of sun in "Śakadvīpa" (Land of the Scythians?) is also noteworthy. In this there is mention of sun-priests called Bhojaka and Maga, which doubtless relates to Zoroastrian sun and fire-cult.[1]

This Purāṇa is in a certain way continued in the Bhaviṣyottara-Purāṇa which, although containing some old myths and legends, is yet a more of a hand-book of religious rites.

Very many are the Māhātmyas and other modern texts which claim to be parts of the Bhaviṣya—and in particular of the Bhaviṣyottara-Purāṇa.

X. The Brahmavaivarta or Brahmavaivarta-Purāṇa.[2] The latter is the name in use in South India. This elaborate work is divided into four books. The first book, the Brahmakhaṇḍa, deals with creation by Brahman, the first-being who is none other than God Kṛṣṇa.[3] The second book, the Prakṛti-khaṇḍa, deals with Prakṛti, the original matter, which however appears to be understood here as fully mythologically, by getting dissolved into five goddesses (Durgā, Lakṣmi, Sarasvatī, Sāvitrī and Rādhā) on being ordered by Kṛṣṇa. The third book, the Gaṇeśa-khaṇḍa, tells legends of the elephant-headed god

---

1. Cf. Aufrecht, *Catalogues codd. MSS. Sanscrit. Bibl. Bodl*, p. 31 ff, Wilson, *Works* X, p. 381 ff. We learn from an inscription written in 861 A.D. by one Maga Mātṛrava, that the Magas lived in Rajputana as early as in the 9th century. "Maga" is a name for the Śākadvīpa Brahmins, who at the present day are still living in the district of Jodhpur, and trace their history back to the Sūrya-Purāṇa and the Bhaviṣya-Purāṇa, See D. R. Bhandarkar, *Ep. Ind.* IX, p. 279.

2. Editions published at Calcutta 1887 and 1888. English translation in *SBH.*, Brahmavaivarta-purāṇa specimen ed. by A. F. Stenzler, Berolini, 1829. A detailed analysis of the work by Wilson, *Works*, III, p. 91 ff.

3. The title Brahmavaivarta-P., which can be translated "Purāṇa of the transformations of Brahman,". However, the Southern Indian title is not intelligible.

Gaṇeśa, who is missing in the oldest pantheon, but belongs to the most popular modern Indian deities.[1] The last and most voluminous book, the Kṛṣṇajanma-khaṇḍa, "chapter on the birth of Kṛṣṇa", deals not only with the birth but also with the whole life of Kṛṣṇa, especially his battles and his amorous adventures with his cowherdesses (Gopīs). It is the main portion of the whole Purāṇa which does not pursue any other aim than to glorify God Kṛṣṇa and his favourite wife Rādhā through myths, legends and hymns. Rādhā is here Kṛṣṇa's Śakti. According to this Purāṇa Kṛṣṇa is so much the god above all gods that legends are narrated in which not only Brahmā and Śiva but even Viṣṇu himself is humiliated by Kṛṣṇa. A large number of Māhātmyas claim to belong to this Purāṇa.

XI. The Laiṅga-or Liṅga-Purāṇa.[3] The work has its name from the Liṅga that appears here as a mystic symbol of god Śiva in the creation-legend.[4] There is a somewhat confused account of the legend of the origin of the Liṅga-cult: on the occasion of Śiva's visit to the *Devadāru* forest, the hermits' wives fall in love with the god, who is cursed by Munis.[5] In

1. B. C. Mazumdar says that he has proved in the Bengali journal Vaṅgadarśana, "that the worship of Gaṇeśa as an affiliated son of Pārvatī was wholly unknown to the Hindus previous to the 6th century A.D." (*JBRAS* 23, 1909, p. 82).

2. Nimbārka, probably in the 12th century, regards Rādhā as the eternal consort of Kṛṣṇa, who, in his view, is not merely an incarnation of Viṣṇu, but the eternal Brahman (Cf. Farquhar, Outline, p. 237 ff.). It was not until the 16th century that the sect of the Rādhāvallabhis, who attach great importance to the worship of Rādhā as Śakti, arose. See, Grierson, *ERE* X, p. 559 f.; Farquhar, iqid., p. 318.

3. Editions have been published in Calcutta, Bombay, Poona and Madras, also with a commentary.

4. The Liṅga (the phallus), generally in the form of a small stone column, is for the worshippers of Śiva only a symbol of the productive and creative principle of Nature as embodied in Śiva; and it is worshipped by simple offerings of leaves and flowers and the pouring of water. The Liṅga cult certainly bears no trace of any phallic cult of an obscene nature. Cf. H. H. Wilson, *Works*, vol. VI, p. lxix; Monier-Williams, *Brahmanism and Hinduism*, 4th Ed., London, 1891, pp. 83, 90 f.; Eliot, *Hinduism and Buddhism*, II, 142 ff. The Liṅga-cult can be traced in Cambodia and Champa as early as about 550 A.D.; see, Eliot, ibid., p. 143, note 3.

5. I, 28-33, translated into German by W. Jahn, *ZDMG*. 69, 1915, pp. 539 ff. The same legend also occurs in other Purāṇas; see, Jahn, ibid., pp. 529 ff.; 70, 1916, p. 301 ff. and 71, 1917, 167 ff.

the account of the creation, Śiva takes the role which is otherwise allotted to Viṣṇu, so also legends are told on the 28 incarnations (Avatāras) of Śiva. Some passages show the influence of the Tantras.[1] This work is after all nothing but a religious book of Śiva-worshippers.

XII. The Vārāha or Varāha-Purāṇa: This too is not a Purāṇa in the original sense of the word. It contains only texts with alliterations and play of words on the creation, on genealogies, etc. strewn all over the work. Actually it is nothing but a hand-book of prayers and rules for Viṣṇu-worshippers. Of the few legends interspersed, some relate to Śiva and Durgā—in spite of the Vaiṣṇavite character of the work. A large portion of this containing 20 chapters (193-212) tells the legend of Naciketas[2] in which the descriptions of heaven and hell form the main theme. This Purāṇa gets its title from the fact that it is narrated to goddess earth (Pṛthvī) by Viṣṇu in his incarnation as a boar (Varāha).[3]

XIII. The Skānda- or Skanda-Purāṇa. This Purāṇa is named after Skanda, son of Śiva and commander of the celestial armies, who is said to have related it and proclaimed Śaivite doctrines in it.[4] The ancient Purāṇa of this name, however, is probably entirely lost, for though there is a considerable number of more or less extensive works claiming to be Saṃhitās and Khaṇḍas of the Skanda-Purāṇa, and an almost overwhelming mass of Māhātmyas which give themselves out as portions of

1. Cf. Farquhar, *Outline*, p. 195 f.

2. See p. 242 f. above. Cf. L. Scherman, *Visionsliteratur*, p. 11 f.; here the name is Naciketa.

3. An edition of the Varāha-Purāṇa by Hṛṣikeśa Śāstri has appeared in the *Bibliotheca Indica*, Calcutta, 1893. According to the first verse of the last chapter (218) in this edition the Purāṇa has been "written" by Mādhava Bhaṭṭa and Viśveśvara in Benares in the year 1621 of the Vikrama-era (1564 A.D.). However, this cannot be the date of the work itself, but only of a copy of it.

4. Matsya-P. 53,42 f. The length of the Skanda-P. is here, as elsewhere, stated as 81, 100 Ślokas. In Padma-P., VI, 363,81 f., too, the Skanda-P. is counted among the "tāmasa", i.e. the Śaivite Purāṇas.

this Purāṇa,[1] only one, very ancient, manuscript contains a text which calls itself simply "Skanda-Purāṇa."[2] Even this text, however, is scarcely identical with the ancient Purāṇa: for, though it contains all manner of legends of Śiva, especially of his battles with Andhaka and other demons, a few chapters on the hells and Saṃsāra, and a section on Yoga, there is hardly anything in it that corresponds to the "five characteristics" of a Purāṇa.[3] Texts which are considered as belonging to the Skanda-Purāṇa inform us[4] that there are six Saṃhitās, namely Sanatkumārīya, Sūta, Brāhmī, Vaiṣṇavī, Śāṅkarī and Saurī Saṃhitā, and fifty Khaṇḍas of the Skanda-Purāṇa. The Sūta-Saṃhitā, is a work of some bulk.[5] It consists of four Khaṇḍas, the first of which is devoted wholly to the worship of Śiva. The second section (jñānayogakhaṇḍa) deals not only with Yoga, but also with the duties of the castes and Āśramas. The third section teaches ways and means of attaining salvation; and the fourth section begins with rules about Vedic-brahmanical ceremonies, and then deals with "the sacrifice of meditation" and the "sacrifice of knowledge," as well as with devotion to Śiva (Śiva-bhakti). A second part contains a Śaivite Brahmagītā and a Vedāntist Sūtagītā. The Sanatkumāra-Saṃhitā, too, contains Śaivite legends, more especially relating to the sacred places of Benares.[6] The Saura-Saṃhitā, which is supposed to

1. Cf. Eggeling, *Ind. Off. Cat.* VI, pp. 1319-1389.

2. This is the old manuscript in Gupta script, which was discovered in Nepal by Haraprasad Śāstri, and has been assigned to the 7th century A.D. by him and C. Bendall on palaeographical grounds. See Haraprasād Śāstri, *Catalogue of Palm Leaf and Selected Paper MSS. belonging to the Durbar Library, Nepal*, Calcutta, 1905, pp. lii, 141 ff.

3. According to the short table of contents given by Haraprasad, ibid. As no khaṇḍa is named in the colophons of the Ms., Haraprasad considers the text to be the original Skanda-P. The supposition that it might be the Ambikā-Khaṇḍa (Haraprasad, *Report* I, p. 4), turned out to be erroneous. The Ambikā-Khaṇḍa (Eggeling, ibid., p. 1321 ff.) contains a collection of legends about Śiva and Durgā, told by Sanatkumāra to Vyāsa.

4. Eggeling, ibid., pp. 1321, 1362.

5. Ed. with commentary of Mādhavācārya in *ĀnSS* No. 25, 1893 in 3 vols.

6. The Sahyādri-khaṇḍa (publ. by J. G. da Cunha, Bombay 1877) belongs to the Sanatkumāra-saṃhitā. Cf. Eggeling, ibid., p. 1369 ff. The

have been revealed to Yājñavalkya by the sun-god, contains chiefly cosmogonic theories. The Śaṅkara-Saṃhitā is also called Agastya-Saṃhitā, because Skanda is supposed to have communicated it to Agastya. It is doubtful, however, whether this is the Agastya-Saṃhitā which teaches the cult of Viṣṇu especially in his incarnation as Rāma.[1] There is a Kāśī-Khaṇḍa,[2] dealing with the Śiva-temples in the neighbourhood of Benares and with the sanctity of this city itself. A Gaṅgāsahasranāman, a litany of the "thousand names of the Ganges" belongs to the same section. The above-mentioned are only a few of the many texts which are said to belong to this Purāṇa.

XIV. The Vāmana-Purāṇa.[3] This Purāṇa, too, has not come down to us in its original form, for the five themes of the Purāṇas, i.e. creation, etc., are scarcely mentioned, and the information given in the Matsya-Purāṇa[4] as to the contents and length of the work does not tally with our text. The text begins with an account of the incarnation of Viṣṇu as a dwarf (Vāmana), whence it takes its name. Several chapters deal with the Avatāras of Viṣṇu in general.[5] On the other hand, a considerable section deals with Liṅga-worship, and in connection with the glorification of sacred places, the Śaivite legends of the

---

Veṅkateśa-Māhātmya of the Sahyādri-khaṇḍa, a glorification of the temple of Mañjguni, is translated by G. K. Betham, *Ind. Ant.* 24, 1895, pp. 231 ff. The same khaṇḍa probably also includes the Ṛṣyaśṛṅga-legend, which was transformed into a local legend, and which has been translated by V. N. Narasimmiyengar (*Ind. Ant.* 2, 1873, pp. 140 ff.).

1. Cf. Eggeling, ibid., p. 1319 ff.; 1321. In the Śivarahasya-khaṇḍa of the Śaṅkara-saṃhitā (Eggeling. ib. p. 1363 f.) the 18 Purāṇas are enumerated of which ten (Śaiva, Bhaviṣya, Mārkaṇḍeya, Laiṅga, Varāha, Skanda, Matsya, Kaurma, Vāmana, Brahmāṇḍa) are declared to be Śaivite, four (Vaiṣṇava, Bhāgavata, Nāradīya, Garuḍa) Visnuite, whilst Brāhma and Pādma are said to be dedicated to Brahman, Āgneya to Agni, Brahmavaivarta to Savitṛ. It is added, however, that the Viṣṇuite Purāṇas teach the identity of Śiva and Viṣṇu, and the Brahma-P., the identity of Brahman, Viṣṇu and Śiva.

2. Pub. (with commentaries) in Benares, 1868. Calcutta 1873-80, and Bombay, 1881.

3. Pub. with Bengali translation, Calcutta, 1885.

4. 53, 45 f. Cf., Wilson, *Works*, Vol. VI, p. lxxiv f.

5. According to Aufrecht (*Bodl. Cat.* p. 46) these chapters (24-32) are mainly taken from the Matsya-P.

marriage of Śiva and Umā, the origin of Gaṇeśa and the birth of Kārttikeya are related.

XV. The Kaurma- or Kūrma-Purāṇa. In the work itself we read that it consists of four Saṃhitās, namely Brāhmī, Bhāgavatī, Saurī and Vaiṣṇavī; but the Brāhmī-Saṃhitā is the only one which has come down under the title "Kūrma-Purāṇa."[1] This work begins with a hymn to the incarnation of Viṣṇu as a tortoise (kūrma) on which the mountain Mandara rested when the ocean was twirled. At that time Lakṣmī arose from the ocean and became Viṣṇu's consort. When the Ṛṣis ask him who this goddess is, Viṣṇu replies that she is his highest Śakti. The Introduction then relates further how Indradyumna, who in a former birth had been a king, but was born again as a Brahmin by reason of his devotion to Viṣṇu, desired to gain knowledge of the glory of Śiva. Lakṣmī refers him to Viṣṇu. Then he worships Viṣṇu as the Universal God, the Creator and Preserver of the universe, but also as "Mahādeva," "Śiva" and as "father and mother of all beings." At length Viṣṇu, in his incarnation as the tortoise, imparts the Purāṇa to him. As in this Introduction Śiva is the Highest Being throughout the work, but it is emphasized over and over again that in reality Brahman, Viṣṇu and Śiva are one.[2] The worship of Śakti, i.e., "Energy" or "Creative force" conceived as a female deity, is also emphasized. Devī, the "Highest Goddess" (Parameśvarī), the consort and Śakti of Śiva, is praised under 8,000 names.[3] Just as Viṣṇu is none other than Śiva, Lakṣmī, Viṣṇu's śakti, is in reality not apart from the Devī.[4] When the sons of Kārttavīrya, some of whom worshipped Viṣṇu and the others Śiva, could not agree as to which god was the more worthy of worship, the

1. Published by Nīlamaṇi Mukhopādhyāya in *Bibl. Ind.* 1890. It contains 6,000 ślokas. According to the statements made in the Bhāgavata-, Vāyu-, and Matsya-P., the Kūrma-P. contains 17,000 or 18,000 ślokas.

2. In I, 6 (p. 56) Brahman is worshipped as Trimūrti. I, 9 especially inculcates the unity of the three gods. Cf. also I, 26.

3. I, 11 and 12. Śiva divides himself into two parts, a male and a female, the former gives rise to the Rudras, and the latter to the Śaktis. Cf. Farquhar, *Outline*, p. 195 f.

4. I, 17 (p, 206 f.) Prahlāda praises Viṣṇu and Lakṣmī as Viṣṇu's Śakti.

seven Ṛṣis decided the dispute by declaring that the deity worshipped by any man is that man's deity, and that all the gods deserve the worship of at least some beings.[1] Notwithstanding, Śiva is the god above all gods to such a degree that, though Kṛṣṇa is praised as Viṣṇu Nārāyaṇa, he obtains a son for his wife Jāmbavatī only after strenuous asceticism and by the mercy of Śiva.[2] Moreover, in spite of the tolerance as regards the recognition of all the gods, there are allusions in several places to the false doctrines which have been sent into the world to deceive mankind, and to false manuals which will come into existence during the Kaliyuga.[3]

The five themes of the Purāṇas, namely the Creation, the genealogies, etc., are also treated in the Kūrma-Purāṇa, and in this connection a few of Viṣṇu's Avatāras are touched upon. However, an entire chapter (I, 53) is devoted to the incarnations of Śiva. A considerable section of the first part consists of a description and glorification of the holy places of Benares (Kāśīmāhātmya) and Allahabad (Prayāgamāhātmya). The second part begins with an Īśvaragītā (a counterpart to the Bhagavadgītā), teaching the knowledge of God, i.e. Śiva, through meditation. This piece is followed by a Vyāsagītā, a larger section in which Vyāsa teaches the attainment of the highest knowledge through pious works and ceremonies, and therefore delivers a lecture on the duties of the householder, the forest-hermit and the ascetic. A few chapters deal with expiatory ceremonies for all sorts of crimes, where there is also a mention of chastity. This gives rise to the narration of a story of Sītā (not occurring in

1. I, 22 (p. 239 ff.)

2. I, 25-27. Here (p. 269) there is also a referenee to a Yogaśāstra written by the great Yogin Yājñavalkya, which is perhaps an allusion to the Yājñavalkyagītā, where Yoga is taught. Cf. F. E. Hall, *A contribution towards an Index to the Bibliography of the Indian Philosophical Systems*, Calcutta, 1859, p. 14, In I, 26, Kṛṣṇa recommends the Liṅga cult and explains its origin.

3. This appellation is given to the Śaivite sects and Śāstras of the Kāpālas, Bhairavas, Yāmalas, Vāmas, Arhatas, Nakulas (i.e. Lākulīśa-Pāśupata, cf. Bhandarkar, Vaiṣnavism, etc., p. 116 f.). Pāśupatas and the Viṣṇuite Pañcarātra: I, 12; 16; 30 (pp. 137, 184, 305). The Vāmas or "left-hand-ones", are those Śakti worshippers whose cult is connected with orgiastic rites. See below in the chapter on the Tantras.

the Rāmāyaṇa), how she is rescued from the hands of Rāvaṇa by the fire-god.

XVI. The Mātsya or Matsya-Purāṇa.[1] This, again, is one of the older works of the Purāṇa literature, or at least one of those which have preserved most of the ancient text, and do fair justice to the definition of a "Purāṇa." It commences with the story of the great flood out of which Viṣṇu, in the form of a fish (matsya) saves only Manu alone. While the ship in which Manu is sailing along is being drowned through the flood by the fish, there takes place between him and Viṣṇu, incarnated as a fish, the conversation which forms the substance of the Purāṇa. Creation is treated in detail, then follow the genealogies, into which is inserted a section about the Fathers and their cult (Chapters 14-22). Neither are the usual geographical, astronomical and chronological sections absent, and, according to V. A. Smith (see above p. 501) the lists of kings in this Purāṇa are particularly reliable for the Āndhra dynasty. It has very much in common with the Mahābhārata and the Harivaṃśa: thus the legends of Yayāti (Chapters 24-43), Sāvitrī (Chapters 208-214), the incarnations of Viṣṇu (Chapters 161-179, 244-248); and there is often literal agreement. There are, however, very numerous later additions and interpolations. For instance, we find a considerable section about all manners of festivals and rites (Vratas, Chapters 54-102), a glorification of the sacred places of Allahabad (Prayāgamāhātmya, Chapters 103-112, Benares (Vārāṇasī—and Avimuktamāhātmya, Chapters 180-185), and of the river Narmadā (Chapters 186-194); then sections on the duties of a king Chapters 215-227), on omina and portenta (Chapters 228-238), ceremonies at the building of a house (Chapters 252-257), the erection and dedication of statues of deities, temples and palaces (Chapters 258-270), the sixteen kinds of pious donations (Chapters 274-289), etc. As far as the religious content is concerned, the Matsya-Purāṇa might be called Śaivite with just as much reason as it is classed as Viṣṇuite. Religious festivals

---

1. Published in *ĀnSS* No. 54. (The quotations are given according to this edition.) Translated into English in *SBH.*, Vol. 17. The edition has 291 Adhyāyas, but the Ms. described by Aufrecht, *Bodl. Cat.*, p. 38 ff. has only 728.

of the Vaiṣṇavas are described side by side with those of the Śaivas, and both Viṣṇu and Śiva-legends are related. In Chapter 13 Devī (the Goddess, Śiva's wife Gaurī) enumerates to Dakṣa the one hundred and eight names by which she wishes to be glorified. It is obvious that both sects used the work as a sacred book.

XVII. The Gāruḍa-or Garuḍa-Purāṇa.[1] This is a Viṣṇuite Purāṇa. It takes its name from the mythical bird Garuḍa, to whom it was revealed by Viṣṇu himself, and who then imparted it to Kaśyapa. It treats some of the five themes, viz., creation, the ages of the world, the genealogies of the solar and lunar dynasties; but far more attention is given to the worship of Viṣṇu, to descriptions of Viṣṇuite rites and festivals (Vratas), to expiatory ceremonies (Prāyaścittas) and glorifications of sacred places. It is also cognizant of Śakti-worship, and gives rules for the worship of the "five gods" (Viṣṇu, Śiva, Durgā, Sūrya and Gaṇeśa).[2] Moreover, like the Agni-Purāṇa, it is a kind of encyclopaedia, in which the most diversified subjects are dealt with: thus, the contents of the Rāmāyaṇa, the Mahābhārata and the Harivaṃśa are retold, and there are sections on cosmography, astronomy and astrology, omina and portenta, chiromancy, medicine, metrics, grammar, knowledge of precious stones (ratnaparīkṣā) and politics (nīti). A considerable portion of the Yājnāvalkya-Dharmaśāstra has been included in the Garuḍa-Purāṇa.

What is counted as the Uttarakhaṇḍa or "second part" of the Garuḍa-Purāṇa is the Pretakalpa, a voluminous though entirely unsystematic work, which treats of everything connected with death, the dead and the beyond. In motley confusion and with many repetitions, we find doctrines on the fate of the soul after death, Karman, rebirth and release from rebirth, on desire as the cause of Saṃsāra, on omens of death, the path to Yama, the fate of the Pretas (i.e., the departed who still hover about the earth as spirits, and have not as yet found the way to the world beyond), the torments of the hells, and the Pretas as

1. Published by Jibānanda Vidyāsāgara. Calcutta 1890. English translation by Manmatha Nāth Dutt, Calcutta 1908 (*Wealth of India*, Vol. VIII).

2. Cf. Farquhar, *Outline*, p. 178 f.

causing evil omens and dreams. Interspersed we find rules of all kinds about rites to be performed at the approach of death, the treatment of the dying and of the corpse, funeral rites and the ancestor-worship, the especial funeral sacrifices for a Satī, i.e., woman who enters the funeral pyrē with her husband. Here and there we also find legends recalling the Buddhist Petavatthu, telling of encounters with Pretas who relate the cause of their wretched existence (sins which they committed during their lifetime).[1] An "extract" (Sāroddhāra) of this work was made by Naunidhirāma.[2] In spite of its title, this work is not a mere extract from the Pretakalpa, for the author also utilised material from other Purāṇas, and treated the subject more systematically. Among other works he drew on the Bhāgavata-Purāṇa, whence it follows that he was later than this Purāṇa.

Among the Māhātmyas which claim to be parts of the Garuḍa-Purāṇa, especial mention should be made of a Gayā-Māhātmya in praise of Gayā, the place of pilgrimage, where it is particularly meritorious to perform Śrāddhas.

XVIII. The Brahmāṇḍa-Purāṇa.[3] In the list in the Kūrma-Purāṇa the eighteenth Purāṇa is called "Vāyavīya Brahmāṇḍa," the "Purāṇa of the Brahman-egg proclaimed by Vāyu," and it is possible that the original Brahmāṇḍa was but an earlier version of the Vāyu-Purāṇa.[4] According to the Matsya-Purāṇa

---

1. A detailed analysis of the contents of the Pretakalpa is given by E. Abegg, *Der pretakalpa des Garuḍa-Purāṇa* (Naunidhirāma's Sāroddhāra). Eine Darstellung des hinduistischen Totenkultes und Jenseitsglaubens .... übersetzt .... Berlin und Leipzig 1921, p. 8 ff.; Chapters X-XII translated p. 229 ff.

2. This Sāroddhāra was published under the title "Garuḍa-Purāṇa" in Bombay *NSP* in 1903 and with an English translation by E. Wood and S. V. Subrahmaṇyam in *SBH*, Vol. IX, 1911. There is a good German translation by Abegg, *Pretakalpa* etc. (see Note 1 above).

3. Published in Bombay, Sri-Venkatesvara Press, 1906.

4. Cf. Pargiter, *Anc. Ind. Hist. Trad.*, p. 77 f. H. H. Wilson (*Works*, Vol. VI, p. lxxxv f.) mentions a MS. of the Brahmāṇḍa-P., the first part of which agrees almost entirely with the Vāyu-P., whilst the second part is dedicated to Lalitā Devī, a form of Durgā, and teaches her worship by Tāntric rites. On the island of Bali a Brahmāṇḍa-P. is the only sacred book of the local Śiva-worshippers. Cf. R. Friedrich, *JRAS* 1876, p. 170 f., Weber, Ind. Stud. II, p. 131 f.

(53, 55f.) it is said to have been proclaimed by Brahman, and to contain a glorification of the Brahman-egg[1] as well as a detailed account of the future kalpas in 12, 200 ślokas. It appears, however, that the original work of this name is lost, because our manuscripts for the most part contain only Māhātmyas, Stotras and Upākhyānas which claim to be parts of the Brahmāṇḍa.

The Adhyātma-Rāmāyaṇa, i.e.,[2] the "Rāmāyaṇa in which Rāma is the Supreme Ātman," in which Advaita (the monism of the Vedānta) and Rāma-Bhakti are taught as paths to salvation, is a very well known book, which is considered as a part of the Brahmāṇḍa-Purāṇa. As in the case of Vālmīki's poem, the work is divided into seven books, bearing the same titles as in the ancient epic; but it is only an epic in its external form—in reality it is a manual of devotion, Tāntric in character. Like the Tantras it is in the form of a dialogue between Śiva and his wife Umā. Throughout the work Rāma is essentially the god Viṣṇu, and Sītā who is abducted by Rāvaṇa is only an illusion, whilst the real Sītā, who is identical with Lakṣmī and Prakṛti, does not appear until after the fire ordeal at the end of the book. Rāmahṛdaya (I, 1) and the Rāmagītā (VII, 5) are texts which are memorised by the devotees of Rāma. The fact that the Marāṭhī poet-saint Ekanātha, who lived in the 16th century, calls it a modern work, proves that the work cannot be very ancient.[3]

The Nāciketopākhyāna, which also claims to be a part of the Brahmāṇḍa Purāṇa, is nothing but a most insipid, amplified and corrupted version of the beautiful old legend of Naciketas.[4]

1. Even the Brāhmaṇas and Upaniṣads already tell of the golden egg out of which the universe was created. Cf. Śatapatha-Br. XI, 1, 6 (above, p. 206 f.) and the Chāndogya-Upaniṣad III, 9, 1. According to the cosmogony of the Purāṇas Brahman (or Viṣṇu in the form of Brahman) dwells in the egg in which the whole of the universe is locked up, and out of which it unfolds itself by the will of the Creator. Cf. Viṣṇu-P. I, 2; Vāyu-P. 4, 76 ff.; Manu I, 9 ff.

2. There are numerous Indian editions (the Bombay NSP 1891 edition is recommended) and several commentaries, among them one by Śaṅkara. English translation by Lala Baij Nath in *SBH* 1913.

3. Cf. Bhandarkar, *Vaiṣṇavism* etc., p. 48; Farquhar. *Outline*, p. 250 f.

4. Cf. F. Belloni-Filippi in *GSAI* 16, 1903 and 17, 1904 : Eggeling, *Ind. Off. Cat.* VI, p. 1252 ff.

As regards the Upapurāṇas, they do not in general differ essentially from the Purāṇas, except inasmuch as they are even more exclusively adapted to suit the purposes of local cult and the religious needs of separate sects. Those of the Upapurāṇas which claim to be supplements to one or other of the great Purāṇas have already received mention. We shall now only refer to a few of the more important among the other Upapurāṇas.

The Viṣṇudharmottara is occasionally given out as a part of a Purāṇa, namely the Garuḍa-Purāṇa, but generally it is counted as an independent Upapurāṇa. It is repeatedly quoted by Alberuni as the "Viṣṇudharma"[1] It is a Kashmīrī Vaiṣṇava book of encyclopaedic character in three sections. Section I deals with the usual themes of the Purāṇas: the Creation of the world, cosmology, geography, astronomy, division of time, genealogies, stotras, rules about Vratas and Śrāddhas.[2] Among the genealogical legends, that of Purūravas and Urvaśī is also related more or less in agreement with Kālidāsa's drama. Section II deals with law and politics, but also with medicine, science of war, astronomy and astrology. There is here a prose section with the special title "Paitāmaha-Siddhānta". If, as is probable, this is an extract from the Brahma-Sphuṭa-Siddhānta written by Brahmagupta in 628 A.D., the Viṣṇudharmottara must have been compiled between 628 and 1000 A.D.[3] Section III too, is of a very miscellaneous character treating of grammar, lexicography, metrics and poetics, dancing, singing and

1. Edition of the text in Bombay, Sri-Venktesvara Press 1912. Analysis of the contents according to Kashmiri MSS and a comparison with the quotations of Alberuni by G. Buhler, *Ind. Ant.* 19, 1890 p. 382 ff. According to Buhler Alberuni used two separate works with the same title and mixed them together. Eggeling, *Ind. Off. Cat.* VI p. 1308 f. describes a MS which contains six chapters more than the edition. In the MS the title of the work is "Viṣṇudharmāḥ."

2. As regards the Śrāddhas W. Caland, *Altindischer Ahnenkult*, Leyden 1893, pp. 68, 112, has traced connection with the Viṣṇu-Smṛti. Cf. Abegg, *Der Pretakalpa*, p. 5 f.

3. Cf. G. Thibaut Astronomie, etc. (*Grundriss* III, 9) p. 58. The commentators of Brahmagupta's work maintain that this author drew upon the Viṣṇudharmottara. MSS of the "Viṣṇudharma" are dated 1047 and 1090 see Haraprasād, *Report* I p. 5.

music, sculpture and painting (the making of images of gods)[1] and architecture (construction of temples).

The Bṛhad-Dharma Purāṇa,[2] "the Great Purāṇa of the Duties," which appears as the eighteenth in a list of the Upapurāṇas,[3] only devotes the beginning of its section, and its last section to Dharma, with the glorification of which it begins. The greater portion of the first section is in the form of a conversation between the Devī and her two friends Jayā and Vijayā, which gives it a Tantric stamp. In the second section, too, the Devī appears as the great Goddess, to whom Brahman, Viṣṇu and Śiva come singing her praises, and II, 60 teaches that the universe and all the gods have their existence in Śiva and Śakti. The fact that it is not a Tantra is, however, shown by the contents of the work, which by reason of its relations with the epic and the legal literature, is deserving of some interest, though the work cannot be a very ancient one.

In the opening chapters the duties towards one's parents especially the mother, and the Gurus in general are inculcated in great detail. By way of illustrating the importance of these duties, a legend of a "hunter Tulādhāra" is told, which though having some reference to the Mahābhārata stories[4] of Dharmavyādha and Tulādhāra, has little in common with them except the name. Then some sections on the Tīrthas, the incarnation of Viṣṇu as Rāma, the story of Sītā and the origin of the Rāmāyaṇa The latter work is called the root of all kāvyas, Itihāsas, Purāṇas and Saṃhitās. It was only after Vālmīki had completed this poem at the command of the god Brahman and had declined to write the Mahābhārata also that the Vyāsa set to work to compile both the Mahābhārata and the Purāṇas[5] Vālmīki in his hermitage converses with Vyāsa on the composition

1. On this extremely interesting section see Dr. Stella Kramrisch *Calcutta Review*, Feb. 1924, p. 331ff and *Journal of Letters*, Calcutta University, Vol. XI, 1924.

2. Edited by Haraprasād Sastri in *Bibl. Ind.* 1897. The work consists of a "first," middle and "last" khaṇḍa.

3. In the Bṛhad-Dharma itself (I, 25, 26).

4. See above.

5. There is here a list of the 18 Purāṇas and the 18 Upapurāṇas (i, 25, 18 ff, and also an enumeration of the Dharmaśāstras (I. 29, 24f.).

of the Mahābhārata, which is then praised extravagantly. A prayer which also contains the titles of the most important Parvans of the Mahābhārata, is recomemnded as an amulet (I,30, 41-ff.) The second section consists mainly of legends of the origin of Gaṅgā, but all manner of other myths and legends are interwoven with them. Among the Avatāras of Viṣṇu, mention is made of those as Kapila, Vālmīki, Vyāsa and Buddha. Śiva sings a song in praise of Viṣṇu[1] A section of considerable length (II, 54-58) contains rules for the cult of the Ganges (Gaṅgādharmāḥ). The legend of the miraculous origin of Gaṇeśa is told in the last chapter (II,60). The last section deals with the duties of castes and Āśramas, the duties of women, the adoration of various gods, the festivals of the year, the worship of the sun, the moon and the planets, with the Yugas, the origin of evil and wickedness in the world (III, 12) and with the inter-mixture of castes (III, 13-14).

The Śiva-Purāṇa, which is said to consist of no less than twelve Saṃhitās, is one of the most voluminous Upapurāṇas.[2] The Gaṇeśa-Purāṇa[3] and the Caṇḍī or Caṇḍikā-Purāṇa[4] are also Śaivite Upapurāṇas. The Sāmba-Purāṇa[5] is dedicated to the cult of the sun. The deeds of Viṣṇu in the future age at the close of the Kali-Yuga are described in the Kalki-Purāṇa.[6] The Kālikā-Purāṇa[7] treats of the deeds of the goddess Kāli in her numerous forms and of the worship dedicated to her. One chapter[8] deals in detail with the animal and human sacrifices which

1. Śivagānam (II, 44). Previously Nārada delivers a lecture to Viṣṇu on the significance of the Rāgas and Rāgiṇis in the art of singing.

2. Eggeling *Ind. Off. Cat.* VI p. 1311 ff. Editions of a Śiva-Purāṇa appeared in Bombay (1878, 1880, 1884).

3. Aufrecht, *Bodl. Cat.* p. 78f Eggeling ib. p 1199. An edition appeared in Poona in 1876. In the Maudgala too (Eggeling, ib. p. 1289 ff.) Gaṇeśa is worshipped as the highest deity.

4. Eggeling ib. p. 1202 ff.

5. Eggeling ib. p. 1316 ff. A Sāmba Purāṇa was published in Bombay in 1885.

6. Eggeling ib. p. 1188 f. Editions have appeared in Calcutta.

7. Eggeling ib. p. 1189 ff. Edition in Bombay 1891.

8. The chapter of blood (Rudhirādhyāya) translated into English by W. C. Blaquiere in *Asiatick Researches*, Vol. 5 (4th ed. London 1807) p. 371ff.

should be offered to her. Curiously enough, it also contains a chapter on politics.

The majority of the Māhātmyas which are connected with or included in the Purāṇas and the Upapurāṇas, is, on the whole, inferior literature. They arose as hand-books for the Purohitas of the Tīrthas praised in them and tell legends which in part belong to tradition and in part are inventions with the purpose of proving the holiness of these places of pilgrimage. They describe too, the ceremonies which the pilgrims are to perform and the route they are to follow. For this reason they are not unimportant from the point of view of the topography of India. Thus in particular, the Nīlamata[1] the Kāśmīra-māhātmya, is an important work from the point of view of the history, legendary lore and topography of Kashmir.[2] The Nāga king Nīla is a kind of cultural hero of Kashmir and the work contains "the doctrines of Nīla" which he imparted to the Brahmin Candradeva.[3] It tells the legend of the primeval history of Kashmir (verses 1-481), whereupon there is a description of the ceremonies and festivals prescribed by Nīla. Many of these are the usual Brahmanical and Purānic rites, but we find some which are peculiar to Kashmir. Thus joyous festivals are celebrated with singing, music and drinking bouts at the New Year, on the first of the month Kārttika, on which Kashmir is said to have arisen (v 561 ff.) and then again on the occasion of the first fall of snow (v 579 ff.). On the fifteenth day of the bright half of the month Vaiśākha, the birthday of Buddha as an incarnation of Viṣṇu is solemnly celebrated by the Brahmins; a statue of Buddha is erected, Buddhist speeches are made and Buddhist monks are honoured (v 809 ff). The historian Kalhaṇa (about 1148 A.D.) drew on the Nīlamata in his Rājataraṅgiṇī for the ancient history of

1. *Nīlamatapurāṇam* (Sanskrit Text) edited with Introduction etc. by Ramlal Kanjilal and Pandit Jagaddhar Zadoo, Lahore 1924 (Punjab Sanskrit series)

2. Cf. *Buhler report* p. 37 ff LV ff M. A. Stein Kalhaṇa's *Rājataraṅgiṇī* Translated I p. 76 f; II p. 376ff; Pandit Anand Kaul, JASB 6 1910, p. 195 ff,

3. Cf. Nilamata verses 424 ff Rājataraṅgiṇī I. 182-184.

Kashmir; and he regarded it as a venerable Purāṇa.[1] It must therefore be several centuries earlier than Kalhaṇa's work.

Among the offshoots of the Purāṇa literature mention should also be made of the Nepalese Vaṁśāvalīs ("Genealogies") which are partly Brahmanical and partly Buddhist, the Nepāla-Māhātmya and the Vāgvatī-Māhātmya, which claims to be part of a Paśupati-Purāṇa.[2]

Finally we mention here another work, which, though an epic and not a Purāṇa, nevertheless has the sectarian character of the Purāṇas: this is the Aśvamedhikaparvan of the Jaimini-Bhārata[3] i.e. of the Mahābhārata Saṃhitā ascribed to Jaimini.[4] This poem, written in the ornate style, describes the combats and the adventures of the heroes Arjuna, Kṛṣṇa, etc., who accompanied the sacrificial steed destined for Yudhiṣṭhira's horse sacrifice, but it diverges greatly from the Mahābhārata story. Besides the narrative of the horse-sacrifice merely provides a welcome opportunity to insert numerous legends and tales of which there is not the slightest trace in the Mahābhārata. A considerable section (Kuśalavopākhyāna, "the episode of Kuśa and Lava") contains a brief reproduction of the entire Rāmāyaṇa. Among other lands the heroes go to the realm of the Amazons (Strīrājya) and we hear of the adventures which happened to them there. The story of Candrahāsa and Viṣayā (Candrahāsopākhyāna)[5] is of importance in the literature of the world.

---

1. Kalhaṇa calls the work Nīlamata (Rājataraṅgiṇī I, 14 16) or "Nīlapurāṇa" (ib. I, 178) Bhandarkar, Report 1883-84, p. 44 mentions a MS in which the work is described as a Kāśmiramāhātmya with the title Nīlamata. The pandits of Kashmir usually call it "Nīlamata-Purāṇa."

2. See S. Levi, *Le Nepal*, *AMG*, Paris 1905 I, 193 ff 201 ff 205 ff.

3. Editions published in Bombay, Poona and Calcutta. There are numerous MSS. Cf. Holtzmann *Das Mahābhārata* III. p. 37 ff Weber *Hss Verz.* I, p. 111 ff Aufrecht *Bodl. Cat*, I, p 4 Eggeling *Ind. Off. Cat*. VI. p, 1159.

4. In the Mahābhārata (I, 63, 89 f.) it is related that Vyāsa taught the Mahābhārata to his five pupils Sumantu, Jaimini, Paila, Śuka and Vaiśampāyana and that each one of these published a Saṃhitā of it. It is open to doubt, however, whether there was actually a complete Mahābhārata Saṃhitā by Jaimini and whether this Aśvamedhikaparvan is the sole remnant of it. Talboys Wheeler (*The History of India* London 1867, 1, 377) has unwittingly reproduced the contents of the Jaimini-Aśvamedhikapurāṇa in the chapter on "The Horse sacrifice of Rājā Yudhiṣṭhira."

5. Told by T. Wheeler ib. p 522 ff Text and German translations by a Weber (*Monatsberichte der preuss, Akademie der Wissenschaften* 1869 pp. 10 ff 377ff) who was the first to call attention to the western parallels and more

It is a version of the story recurring so frequently in Indian (Buddhist and Jain) and in Western narrative literature, of a youth who has been born under a lucky star and always escapes the infamous machinations of the wicked adversary who seeks his destruction. Finally the persecuted young man is made to deliver a letter ordering his own death; when a maiden alters or exchanges the fatal letter and becomes the bride of the youth, who attains to wealth or power, whilst the fate which had been destined for him befalls the adversary or the adversary's son. Now the youth Candrahāsa, in the Jaimini-Bhārata was immune from all dangers solely because, from his childhood onwards, he was a devout worshipper of Viṣṇu and always carried a Śālagrāma-stone (the sacred symbol of Viṣṇu) about with him.[1] The conclusion of the legend takes the form

recently by J. Schick *Corpus Hamleticum* I, 1, *Das Gluckskind mit dem Todesbrief, Orientalische Fassungen*, Berlin 1912 p. 167 ff. In this book Schick deals in detail with the Buddhist and Jain versions of this story (which will be dealt with in Vol II) the popular modern Indian versions and the western Asiatic adaptations through the medium of which the story reached Europe. In Europe we find the story among other places in Chapter XX of the Latin *Gesta Romanorum* (cf. M. Gaster *JRAS* 1910, p. 449 ff) in Dasents Norse tales (cf. Tawney in *Ind. Ant.* 10, 1881, p. 190 f) in the French romance of the Emperor Constantine after whom Constantinople is named (cf. Joseph Jacobs in his introduction to *Old French Romances done into English* by William Morris London, 1896, p. viii ff) and in the story of Ahmleth by Saxo Grammaticus. Only the motif of the altered fatal letter has been adopted in Shakespeare's Hamlet. In German the narrative is best known through Schillers poem "Der Gang nach dem Eisemhammer." Cf. Th. Benfey *Pantschatantra* I, 321, 340 E Kuhn in *Byzantinische Zeitschrift* IV 242 ff., E. Cosquin *La Legende du page de sainte Elisabeth de Portugal.* Paris 1912 (*Extrait de la Revue des questions historiques.* The earliest of all versions hitherto known is that in the Chinese Tripiṭaka (Ed. Chavannes *cinq cents contes et apologues extraits du Tripiṭaka Chinois* I No. 45) which was translated into Chinese by Seng-houei who died in 280 A.D

1. Among the Bhāgavatas, Candrahāsa became a Vaiṣṇava saint and in Nabhādāsa's Bhakt-māla his story is narrated as in the Jaimini-Bhārata as that of the thirty-first of the forty-two beloved ones of the Lord; s. Grierson *JRAS* 1910, p. 292 ff. Cf. NB Godabole, *Ind. Ant.* 11. 1882, p. 84f. The story also occurs in Kasiram's Bengali version of the Mahābhārata (see *Calcutta Review* December 1924, p. 480 ff) The motif of the changed letter of death alone occurs in *Folk tales from Bengal*, *Punjab and Kashmir*. Cf. Hatim's *Tales Kashmiri Stories and Songs* by Sir Aurel Stein and Sir G.A. Grierson, London 1923, p. 97 with Notes by W. Crooke ib p xliv ff.

of a glorification of the sacred stone and the tulasi plant, which is also sacred to Viṣṇu, in the extravagant style of the later Purāṇas. In the whole poem Kṛṣṇa is not only a hero, but is honoured as the God Viṣṇu. He appears as a helper, to all who appeal to him with love (bhakti). He works all manner of miracles, he restores a dead child to life, he feeds multitudes of munis with a single leaf of a vegetable, and so on and whosoever beholds Kṛṣṇa's countenance is freed from all his sins. Nothing definite can be said regarding the date of the Jaimini-Bhārata, resp. its Aśvamedhikaparvan. Judging by the nature of the Viṣṇu worship appearing in the work, it is probably not earlier than the later works and sections of the Purāṇa literature. At any rate it is later than the Bhāgavata-Purāṇa quoted at the end of the Candrahāsa legend.[1]

The Tantra-Literature

Saṃhitās, Āgamas, Tantras

"Tantric" influences have already been noticed in several of the later Purāṇas, namely isolated allusions to the cult of the Śaktis, the female deities, considerable sections in the form of dialogues between Śiva and Pārvatī and the occasional use oi mystic syllables and formulas (mantras) and diagrams (yantras). Whereas, however, the Purāṇas always maintain a certain connection with epic poetry, and are as it were, a repertory of Indian legend poetry, the Tantras and the Saṃhitās and Āgamas which differ from them but slightly, rather bear the stamp of purely theological works teaching the technicalities of the cult of certain sects together with their metaphysical and mystical principles Strictly speaking, the "Saṃhitās" are the sacred books of the Vaiṣṇavas, the "Āgamas" those of the Śaivas and the "Tantras" those of the Śāktas. However, there is no

1. The astrologer Varāhamihara (6th century A.D.) is mentioned in 55, 8, the scene of the story of Candrahāsa is laid in the South in the land of the Keralas. A Canarese version of the Jaimini-Aśvamedhikaparvan by the Brahmin Lakṣmīśa is the most popular work in Canarese literature. Lakṣmīśa lived after 1585 and before 1724 Cf. E. P. Rice Kanarese literature (*Heritage of India Series*), 1921 and H.F. Mogling *ZDMG* 24 1870, 309 ff; 2529 ff; 27;1879; 364 ff.

clear line of demarcation between the terms, and the expression "Tantra" is frequently used as a general term for this class of works[1].

As a matter of fact all these works really have characteristic features in common. Though they are not positively hostile to the Veda, they propound that the precepts of the Veda are too difficult for our age, and that for this reason, an easier cult and an easier doctrine have been revealed in them. Moreover these sacred books are accessible not only to the higher castes but to the Śūdras and women too. On the other hand, it is true that they contain Secret Doctrines which can be only obtained from a teacher (guru) after a ceremonial initiation (dīkṣā) and which must not be communicated to any uninitiated person.[2] A complete Tantra (Saṃhitā, Āgama) should consist of four parts according to the four main themes treated viz., (1) Jñāna, "knowledge," comprising actual philosophical doctrines, sometimes with a monotheistic bias, and sometimes leaning towards monism, but also a confused occultism including the "knowing" of the secret powers of the letters, syllables, formulas and figures (mantraśāstra, yantraśāstra); (2) *Yoga*, i.e. "meditation, concentration" also more especially with a view of acquiring magic powers, hence also "magic" (māyāyoga); (3) "Kriya," action" i.e. instructions for the making of idols and the construction and consecration of

1. Thus the Viṣṇuite Padma Saṃhitā is also called Padma-Tantra. The "Sāttvataṁ tantram" mentioned in the Bhāgavata-P. 1, 3, 8 is probably the Sātvata-Saṃhitā. Lakṣmī-Tantra is a Viṣṇuite work and Pañcarātra-Āgama is spoken of as well as Pañcarātra-Saṃhitās, Cf. Eliot, *Hinduism and Buddhism* II p. 188 f. Tantra means "a system of doctrines," "a book," i.e. Bible; Āgama means "tradition" and Saṃhitā a "collection of sacred works."

2. "The Vedas, Śāstras and Purāṇas are like harlots accessible to all but the Śaivite science is well concealed like a woman of good family." (Avalon. *Principles of Tantra* I p. ix) In the Kulacūḍāmaṇi-Tantra, Chapter I we read that the doctrine is not to be communicated to any uninitiated person, not even to Viṣṇu or to Brahman. The Kulārṇava Tantra III 4 says: Vedas, Purāṇas and Śāstras may be propagated but the Śaiva and Śākta Āgamas are declared to be secret doctrines.

temples; (4) Caryā, "conduct," i.e. rules regarding rites and festivals, and social duties. Though in reality all these four branches are not treated in every single one of these works they all contain a medley of philosophy and occultism, mysticism and magic and ritual and ethics.

Hitherto little is known about the Śaiva-Āgamas.[1] There are 28 Āgamas which are said to have been proclaimed by Śiva himself after the creation of the world, and each Āgama has a number of Upāgamas. As we know scarcely anything of the contents of these works, we are not in a position to determine their date.[2]

We have little more information about the Saṃhitās of the Viṣṇuite Pañcarātra sect.[3] Though the traditional list enumerates 108 Pāñcarātra Saṃhitās, there is actually mention of more than 215, of which, however, only twelve have been published.[4] One of the earlier Saṃhitās is the Ahirbudhnya-Saṃhitā,[5]

1. Cf. H. W. Schomerus, *Der Śaiva Siddhānta*, Leipzig 1912, p. 7ff. a list of the 28 Āgamas ib p. 14. Only fragments of 20 Āgamas have been preserved. Portions of 2 Upāgamas, Mṛgendra and Pauṣkara are printed. Cf. Eliot, *Hinduism and Buddhism* II p. 204 f.

2. According to Schomerus (ib. p. 11f) the Āgamas were used by Tirumulār and other Tamil poets as far back as the first or second century A.D. and would therefore originate in pre-Christian times. However it is more likely that these poets should be assinged to the 9th century and the Āgamas to the 7th or 8th century A.D. Cf. Farquhar, *Outline*, p. 193 ff.

3. Especially by the researches of F. O. Schrader, *Introduction to the Pāñcarātra and the Ahirbudhnya Saṃhitā*, Adyar, Madras 1916. Cf. A Govindācarya-Svāmin *JRAS* 1911, p. 935 ff. Bhandarkar; *Vaiṣṇavism*, etc. p. 39 ff; Eliot, *Hinduism and Buddhism* II p. 194 ff; Farquhar, *Outline*, p. 182 ff. There are various explanations of the name Pañcarātra; it is probably connected with the Pañcarātra-Sattra, a sacrifice lasting five days which is taught in the Śatapatha-Brāhmaṇa. Cf. Schrader, p 28 ff Govindācārya ib. p 940 f.

4. See the lists in Schrader ib pp. 4-13. A list of 24 Pāñcarātra "Tantras" is enumerated in the Agni Purāṇa, Chapt. 39. Most of the published texts are difficult of access. A few extracts from the Sāttvata-Saṃhitā are given by Schrader ib. p. 149. ff. in translation. On the Padma-Saṃhitā cf. Eggeling, *Ind. Off. Cat.* IV p. 847, on the Lakṣhmī-Tantra in which Lakṣmī is worshipped as Śakti of Viṣṇu Nārāyaṇa and the final cause of the world, cf. Eggeling ib p. 850 f.

5. Edited for the Adyar library by M. D. Rāmānujācārya under the supervision of F. Otto Schrader, Adyar, Madras S., 1916. This is the only critical edition of the Saṃhitā.

a Kashmīri work which probably originated not long after the fourth century A.D.[1]

The work takes the form of a conversation between Ahirbudhnya, i.e. Śiva and Nārada. The smaller portion of the work is philosophical in content and the greater portion occult.[2] Several chapters deal with the Creation.[3] When Nārada asks how it is that men hold such varied opinions regarding the Creation, Ahirbudhnya replies (Chapt. 8) that it is due to various causes, (1), it is impossible to express the truth about the Absolute in the language of human beings, (2) human beings often take various names to be various objects, (3) human beings vary in intelligence and (4) the deity has endless number of forms of which the philosophers usually comprehend only one or another. In connection with the Creation, Chapts. 12 and 13 give a very interesting survey of the "sciences," i.e. the various systems of religion and philosophy. Then come the rules for the castes and Āśramas. The paterfamilias and the forest hermit attain to heaven of Brahman but the ascetic (sannyâsin) "is extinguished like a lamp" 15, 26ff) Chapters 16-19 deal with the mysterious significance of the letters of the alphabets. Chapt 20 on Dīkṣā begins with a fine description of the ideal Vaiṣṇava teacher. He is not only to know the truth of the Veda and Vedānta and to be ever mindful of the ceremonies due to the Gods and the fathers but also he should be "a non speaker of evil speech" and a non-doer of evil deeds, free from the envy of the good fortunes of the others, pitying all creatures, rejoicing at the joy of his neighbour full of admiration of the good man, forbearing towards the wicked, rich in asceticism, contentment

1. As it is aquainted with the three great schools of Buddhism and as the astrological term horā occurs (XI, 28) it cannot have possibly originated before the fourth century A.D. From its presentation of the Sāṃkhya system as the Śaṣṭitantra (XII, 18 ff) Schrader (*ZDMG* 68, 1914, 102ff. Introduction p. 98 ff concludes that it is earlier than Īśvarakṛṣṇa's Sāṁkhyakārikā. As Īśvakṛṣṇa himself describes the Sāṃkhya as a Śaṣṭitantra we might be justified in assuming that the Ahirbudhnya Saṃhitā and the Sāṃkhykārikā belong to the same period.

2. Cf. the table of contents in Schrader, *Introduction*, p. 94 ff.

3. On the philosophy of the Pāñcarātras as connected with the theory of the Creation, s. Schrader ib, p. 26 ff.

and uprightness, devoted to Yoga and study" and he is not only to possess a detailed knowledge of the Pāñcarātra, the Tantras, Mantras and Yantras but also the knowledge of the Highest soul, and must be calm, passionless, having control over his senses, and born of a good family. Chapts. 21-27 then describe diagrams which are also to be used as amulets. Further chapters deal with the cult, the theory and practice of Yoga, "the hundred and two magic weapons" i.e. secret powers by which might can be attained. A few chapters deal with ceremonies to be performed by a king when in danger during times of war, in order to ensure victory. Sorcery forms the subject matter of several chapters. An appendix (Pariśiṣṭa) contains a hymn of the thousand names of the Divine Sudarśana.

Though the Pāñcarātra-Saṃhitās probably originated in the North, the earliest of them perhaps dating from the 5th to the 9th century A.D.[1] it is mainly in the South that they were circulated. One of the earlier of these Southern Saṃhitās is the Īśvara Saṃhitā, quoted by Rāmānuja's teacher Yāmuna who died in about 1040 A.D. Rāmānuja himself quotes the Pauṣkara,[2] Parama and Sāttvata Saṃhitās. On the other hand the Bṛhadbrāhmasaṃhitā[3] which is supposed to belong to the Nārada-Pāñcarātra, already contains prophecies regarding Rāmānuja, and cannot, therefore, be earlier than the 12th century. The Jñānāmṛtasārasaṃhitā, which is published with the title "Nārada-Pāñcarātra"[4] and is entirely devoted to the glorification of Kṛṣṇa and Rādhā, is quite a modern and apocryphal work. As the cult taught in this book agrees most with that of the Vallabhācārya sect, it appears to have been written a little before Vallabha at the beginning of the 16th century.[5]

---

1. The Viṣṇuite Upaniṣads of these sects which worship Viṣṇu as Nṛsiṃha or Rāma in Mantras and Yantras as the Nṛsiṁhatāpanīya Upaniṣad (already commented by Gauḍapāda) and the Rāmatāpanīya Upaniṣad possibly belong to the same period. Cf. Farquhar Outline, p. 188 ff.

2. On the Pauṣkara Saṃhitā cf. Eggeling, *Ind. Off. Cat.* IV, p. 864 f.

3. Published in *Ānss* No. 68.

4. Ed. by K. M. Bannerjea, *Bibl. Ind.* 1865. Translated in *SBH* Vol 23 1921. Cf. A Roussel *Etude du Pāñcarātra in Melanges Charles de Harlez Leyde* 1896 p. 251 ff.

5. See Bhandarkar, *Vaiṣṇavism* etc. p. 40 ff.

However, when we speak of "Tantras" we think primarily of the sacred books of the Śāktas, i.e. the worshippers of the Śaktis or "energies" conceived as female deities, or of the "Great Śakti" the "Great Mother" the "Goddess" (Devī) who in spite of her countless names (Durgā, Kālī, Caṇḍī) is only one, the one "Highest Queen" (Parameśvarī). To an even greater degree than is the case with other forms of Hinduism, Śāktism, the religion of the Śāktas, presents a curious medley of the highest and lowest, the sublimest and the basest conceptions ever thought out by the mind of man. In Śāktism and its sacred books the Tantras we find the loftiest ideas and profound philosophical speculations side by side with the wildest superstition and the most confused occultism; and side by side with a faultless social code of morality and rigid asceticism, we see a cult disfigured by wild orgies inculcating extremely reprehensible morals. In former years people laid stress only on the worst aspects of this religion or else deemed it best to enshroud this episode in the development of Indian religion in the charitable veil of oblivion.[1] It is John Woodroffe (under the pseudonym of Arthur Avalon) who, by a series of essays and the publication of the most important Tantra texts, has enabled us to form a just judgement and an objective historical idea of this religion and its literature.[2]

A few of the Tantras themselves say that there are 64 Tantras or 64 Tantras each in three different parts of the world.[3] However the number of the Tantras existing in the manuscripts is far larger.[4] Their original home seems to have been Bengal,

1. Cf. H.H. Wilson *Works* Vol I 240-265 M. Monier Williams, *Brāhmanism and Hinduism* 4th Ed. London 1891 p. 180 ff. A Barth, *The Religions of India* 2nd Edition London 1889 p. 199 ff.; Bhandarkar, *Vaiṣṇavism* etc. p. 142 ff.

2. A. Avalon, *Principles of Tantra* Part I London 1914; Part II 1916 Sir John Woodroffe, *Shakti and Shākta* 2nd. Ed. Madras and London 1920 and the Introductions to the translations of the Mahānirvāṇa Tantra and to the *Tāntrik texts* edited by him. Cf. also N. Macnicol, *Indian Theism* 1915, p. 180 ff; Eliot, *Hinduism and Buddhism* II, 274 ff; and Farquhar, *Outline*, pp. 199 ff 265 ff.

3. Avalon, *Tantrik texts* Vol. I, Introduction.

4. Numerous Tantras have been catalogued and described by Haraprasād Śastri, *Notices of Sanskrit MSS., Second Series* I, Calcutta 1900, pp. xxiv-xxxvii *Catalogue of Palm leaf and Selected Paper MSS. belonging to the Durbar*

whence they spread throughout Assam and Nepal and even beyond India to Tibet and China through the agency of Buddhism. In reality they are known throughout the length and breadth of India even in Kashmir and the South. As a rule the Tantras take the form of dialogues between Śiva and Pārvatī. When the Goddess asks the questions like a pupil and Śiva replies like a teacher they are called Āgamas; when the goddess is the teacher and answers Śiva's questions they are called "Nigamas".

The class of Āgamas includes the very popular and widely known Mahānirvāṇa tantra[1] in which we see the best aspect of Śaktism. Though it is not an ancient work it is an example of the superior Tantras and as such we may accord somewhat more detailed treatment to it, because the same thought may also occur in the earlier works of this nature and much has been taken literally from earlier Tantras.

This Tantra speaks of the Brahman the highest divine principle in the same expressions as the Upaniṣads. Now according to the doctrines of the Śākta philosophers the Brahman is nothing but the eternal and the primeval force (Śakti), out of which all things have been created. Śakti, "Energy", is not only feminine as far as grammar is concerned, for all human experience

---

Library, Nepal, Calcutta, 1905. pp. lvii-lxxxi. *Report* II 7ff 11f. M. Rangacharya, *Descriptive catalogue of the Sanskrit MSS in the Government Oriental MSS Library*, Madras, Vols XII and XIII. On the Tantras in Malabar S. K. Ramavarma Raja, 1910, p. 636. Cf. also Wilson, *Works* II 77 ff, Aufrecht *Bodl. Cat.* I, p. 88ff., Eggeling, *Ind. Off. Cat.* IV, p. 844, Bhandarkar, *Report*, 1883-84, p. 87 ff

1. "The great work which enjoys a popularity next perhaps to the Bhagavadgītā" says Haraprasād, notices I, p. xxxiv. Several editions have appeared in Calcutta the first being in 1876 by the Ādi Brahma Samāj. A Prose English Translation by M. N. Dutt, Calcutta 1900. Tantra of the Great Liberation (Mahānirvāṇa Tantra), a translation from the Sanskrit with Introduction and Commentary by A. Avalon London 1913. The work seems to have been written in Bengal, because in VI, 7,3 it recommends three species of fish for the sacrifice which are found especially in Bengal (s. Elliot, *Hinduism and Buddhism* II, 278 Note 4. Farquhar (*Outline* p. 254 f.) regards it as quite a modern work not earlier than the eighteenth century? The Nirvāṇa Tantra in which Rādhā is glorified as the wife of Viṣṇu is an entirely different work, Haraprasād ib.

teaches that all life is born from the womb of woman, from the mother. Hence, these Indian thinkers believe that the conception of the highest Deity, the loftiest creative principle, must be made comprehensible to the human mind not by the word "Father" but by the word "Mother". Just as every human being calls upon this mother in his sorest distress, the great mother of the universe is the sole being who can remove the great misery of the existence.[1] All the philosophical conceptions to which language has assigned the feminine gender-first and foremost prakṛti, primeval matter, which is identical with Śakti—as well as all the mythological figures which popular belief imagined as being female—Pārvatī, Śiva's consort, also called Umā, Durgā, Kālī, etc., and Lakṣmī, Viṣṇu's consort, or Rādhā; the beloved of Kṛṣṇa—became divine mothers. In reality all these are but different names for the one great universal mother, Jaganmātā, "the mother of all living creatures." The Indian mind had long been accustomed to recognise the unity of what appears in manifold forms. Just as one moon is reflected in innumerable waters, thus Devī "the Goddess," by whatever other name she may be described, is the embodiment of all the gods and all the "energies" (śaktis) of the gods. In her are Brahman, the Creator, and his Śakti, in her are Viṣṇu, the Preserver, and his Śakti, in her too, is Śiva as Mahākāla, "the great Father, Time," the great Destroyer; as she herself devours the latter, she is also Ādyā Kālikā, "the primeval Kālī," and as a "great sorceress," Mahāyoginī, she is at the same time the female Creator, Preserver and Destroyer of the world. She is also the mother of Mahākāla, who, drunk with wine pressed from the Madhūka blossoms, dances before her.[2] Since the Highest Deity is a woman, every woman is regarded as an incarnation of this Deity. Devī, "the Goddess," is in every female creature. This conception it was which led to a cult of women, which, though in some circles it assumed the form of wild orgies, could, and no doubt did appear also in a purer and ennobled form.

The cult of Devī, the Goddess, who is the joyous creative principle of nature, includes the "Five Essentials" (Pañcatattva)

1. Avalon, *Principles of Tantra* I, p. 8.
2. Mahānirvāṇa-T., IV, 29-31; V., 141.

by which man enjoys his existence, preserves his life and obtains issue: Intoxicating drink (madya) which is "the great medicine for humanity, helping it to forget deep sorrows, and is the cause of joy"; meat (māṃsa) of the beasts bred in villages, in the air, of forest, which is nourishing, and increases intelligence, energy and strength; fish (matsya) which is "pleasing and of good taste, and increases the generative power of man"; delicacies of parched food (mudrâ) which is "easily obtainable, grown in the earth, and is the root of the life of the three worlds"; and fifthly sexual union (maithuna)[1] which is "the cause of intense pleasure to all living things, is the origin of all creatures, and the root of the world which is without either beginning or end."[2] However, these "five essentials" may only be used in the circle (cakra) of the initiated, and even then only after they have been "purified" by sacred formulas and ceremonies. In these "circles" of initiated men and women, in which each man has his "Śakti" on his left hand,[3] there are no distinctions of caste, but evil and unbelieving persons cannot be admitted into the "circle." Neither is there to be any abuse of the "five essentials." He who drinks immoderately, is no true devotee of the Devī. In the sinful Kalī age a man is to enjoy only his own wife as a "Śakti". If a householder is unable to control his senses, sweet things (milk, sugar, honey) shall be used instead of intoxicating drink, and the worship of the lotus feet of the goddess shall take the place of sexual union.[4] It is true that the "hero" (vīra), i.e., he who has secret powers and is suited to be a Sādhaka or "sorcerer" is entitled to unite himself in the "circles" to a "Śakti" who is not his wife. He has only to make her his "wife" by a ceremony prescribed

1. As all the "five essentials" begin with an "m", they are also called "the five m's".

2. Mahānirvāṇa-T. VII, 103 ff. (Avalon's Transl., p. 156). Detailed description of the "five essentials," VI, 1 ff.

3. Even in the Śatapatha-Brāhmaṇa (VIII, 4,4,11) we already read that "the woman's place is on the left" of the man. Hence most probably comes the term vāmācāra, "left-hand ritual," for this kind of "cult in the circle" (cakrapūjā.

4. Mahānirvāṇa-T., VI, 14 ff.; 186 ff., VIII, 171 ff., 190 ff.

especially for this purpose. It is only in the highest "heavenly state" (divyabhāva), i.e., in the case of the saint who has completely overcome earthly things, that purely symbolical acts take the place of the "five essentials."[1]

The cult of the Devī attaches especial importance to Mantras, i.e., prayers and formulas, and Bījas, i.e., syllables of mysterious significance, such as "aim," "klīm," "hrīm", etc.; as well as Yantras, i.e., diagrams of mysterious significance, drawn on metal, paper or other material, Mudrās, i.e., especial positions of the fingers and movements of the hands, and Nyāsas. The last-named consist of placing the finger tips and the palm of the right hand on the various parts of the body, whilst reciting certain mantras, in order thus to imbue one's body with the life of the "Devī."[2] By using all these means, the worshipper causes the deity to show goodwill towards him, he compels the deity into his service, and becomes a Sādhaka, a sorcerer; for Sādhana, "sorcery," is one of the principal aims, though not the final goal of the worship of the Devī.

This final goal is that of all Indian sects and systems of religion, namely, Mokṣa or salvation, the becoming one with the deity in Mahānirvāṇa, the "great extinction." The perfect saint, the Kaula, who sees everything in the Brahman and the Brahman in everything, whether he fulfil the rites laid down in the Tantras or not, attains this state even in this life, and is "released through living" (Jīvanmukta).[3] However, the path

1. The distinction of the three classes of mankind: *paśu.* "the animal", "the brutish man," *vīra*, "the hero" and *divya*, "the heavenly one," occurs very frequently in all the Tantras. It is not quite clear what *paśu* means; for a *paśu* is not necessarily a stupid or bad man. The term appears to be applicable to a person who is not suited to comprehend occult matters. Cf. Avalon, *Tantra of the Great Liberation*, Introduction, p. lxv. ff.

2. Eliot, *Hinduism and Buddhism* II, p. 275, compares the Nyāsa with the Christian sign of the Cross, and points out further analogies between the Tāntric and the Christian ritual.

3. Mahānirvāṇa-T., X, 209 ff. *Kaula* or *Kaulika* is "one who belongs to the family ((*kula*) of the goddess Kālī." Cf. Haraprasāda Śāstrī, *Notices of Sanskrit MSS.* I, pp. xxvi, xxxiii. For a different interpretation see, *Avalon, Tāntrik Texts*, Vol. IV, Introduction, where *Kaula* is derived from *Kula* in the sense of "community" or "combination of soul, knowledge and universe." The Tantras speak of the Kaula someimes as the loftiest sage and sometimes as a

of salvation can only be found through the Tantras; for the Veda, the Smṛti, the Purāṇas and the Itihāsas, all these were the sacred books of bygone periods of the world's existence, whereas the Tantras were revealed by Śiva for the welfare of humanity, for our present evil age, the Kali period (I, 20 ff.). In this way the Tantras describe themselves as comparatively modern works. In this age Vedic and other rites and prayers are of no avail, but only the mantras and ceremonies taught in the Tantras are of value (II, 1 ff.). Just as the cult of the Devī leads to the grossest material issues by means of sorcery, as well as to the loftiest ideal of Nirvāṇa, even so the sensual and spiritual elements are well mixed in the cult itself.

There is a meditation on the Devī, which is characteristic of the above. It is taught in the following manner: The devotee first offers Devī spiritual adoration by bestowing the lotus of his heart as her throne, the nectar which trickles from the petals of this lotus-flower as water wherein to wash her feet, his mind as a gift of honour, the restlessness of his senses and his thoughts as a dance, selflessness, passionlessness, etc., as flowers, but afterwards sacrifices to the Devī an ocean of intoxicating drink, a mountain of meat and fried fishes, a heap of parched dainties in milk with sugar and butter, the nectar of the "woman flower" (strīpuṣpa) and the water which has been used for washing the Śakti.[1] Besides the "five essentials" and other elements of a most sensual cult and one based upon the intoxication of the senses, from which even bells, incense, flowers, candles and rosaries are not missing, there is also calm meditation on the deity (dhyāna). In like manner, beside mantras which are devoid of all meaning and insipid, we find such beautiful lines as for instance V; 156; "O Ādyā Kālī thou who dwellest in the inmost soul of all, who art the inmost light, O Mother! Accept this the prayer of my heart. I bow down before thee."

Along with the Tāntric ritual, the Mahānirvāṇa-Tantra also teaches a philosophy which is little different from the orthodox

---

person to whom all is permitted as regards the "five essentials". The last verse of Ch. X of the Jñānatantra teaches that only Brahmins of the fourth Āśrama may fulfil "the left-hand cult," whilst householders may perform only the "righthand cult." (Haraprasāda Śāstri, ibid. pp. xxxi, 126).

1. Mahānirvāṇa-T., V. 139-151.

systems of the Vedânta and Sâṃkhya,[1] and which is at times recognizable even in that chaos of non-sensical incantations. As regards the ethics, the doctrine of the duties in the Chapter VIII of the Mahânirvāṇa-Tantra reminds us at every turn of Manu's Lawbook, the Bhagavadgītā and the Buddhist sermons. Though there are no caste distinctions in the actual Śākta ritual, all castes and sexes being accounted equal, the castes are nevertheless recognised in agreement with Brahmanism, except that in addition to the usual four castes a fifth one is added, namely that of the Sâmânyas, which arose through the mingling of the four older castes. Whilst Manu has four Āśramas or stages of life, our Tantra teaches that in the Kali epoch there are only two Āśramas, the state of the householder and that of the ascetic. For the rest, all which is taught here about duties to one's parents, to wife and child, to relatives and to one's fellow men in general, might be found exactly the same in any other religious book of even in a secular manual of morality. We quote only a few verses from this Chapter VIII by way of example:

A householder should be devoted to the contemplation of Brahman and possessed of the knowledge of Brahman, and should consign whatever he does to Brahman (23)

He should not tell an untruth, or practise deceit, and, should ever be engaged in the worship of the Devatās and guests. (24)

Regarding his father and mother as two visible incarnate deities, he should ever and by every means in his power serve them. (25)

Even if the vital breath were to reach his throat,[2] the householder should not eat without first feeding his mother, father, son, wife, guest and brother. (33)

The householder should never punish his wife, but should cherish her like a mother. If she is virtuous and devoted to her husband, he should never forsake her even in times of greatest misfortune. (39)

---

1. On the philosophy of the Tantras see S. Das Gupta in *Sir Asutosh Mookerjee Silver Jubilee* Vol. III, 1, 1922, p. 253 ff.

2. i.e., even if he were about to die of hunger.

A father should fondle and nurture his sons until their fourth year, and then until their sixteenth they should be taught learning and their duties. (45) Upto their twentieth year they should be kept engaged in household duties, and thenceforward, considering them as equals, he should ever show affection towards them. (46) In the same manner a daughter should be cherished and educated with great care, and then given away with money and jewels to a wise husband. (47)

The man who has dedicated tanks, planted trees, built rest-houses on the roadside, or bridges, has conquered the three worlds. (63) That man who is the happiness of his mother and father, to whom his friends are devoted, and whose fame is sung by men, is the conqueror of the three worlds (64). He whose aim is truth, whose charity is ever for the poor, who has mastered lust and anger, by him are the three worlds conquered. (65)

The duties of the separate castes as well as the duties of the king, as prescribed here, do not greatly differ from those laid down by Manu. The value of family life is put very high. Thus there is a strict injunction that no man who has children, wives or other near relatives to support, shall devote himself to the ascetic life.[2] In complete agreement with the regulations in the brahmanical texts, Chapter IX describes the "sacraments" (saṁskāras) from conception till marriage, and Chapter X similarly gives instructions for the burial of the dead and the cult of the departed (śrāddhas). A peculiarity of the Śāktas as regards marriage is that, in addition to the Brāhma-marriage, for which the brahmanical rules provide, there is also a Śaiva-marriage, i.e., a kind of marriage for a certain time, which is only permitted to members of the circle (cakra) of the initiated.[3] However, the children of such marriages are not legitimate and cannot inherit. This shows to how great an extent brahmanical law is valid for the Śāktas too. Thus also the section on civil and criminal law in Chapters XI and XII agrees in essentials with Manu.

1. Translated by Avalon, pp. 161 f., 163, 165 f.

2. In the Kauṭiliya-Arthaśāstra II, 1, 19 (p. 48) a fine is prescribed for him who becomes an ascetic without first having provided his wife and children.

3. See p. 568 above.

Nevertheless the Kaula dharma which is recited in Tantra, is declared in extravagant terms to be the best of all religions, and the adoration of the Kula saint is praised as supremely meritorious. In words similar to those of a famous Buddhist text we read in our Tantra: "As the footmarks of all animals disappear in the footmark of the elephant, so do all other Dharmas disappear in the Kula-Dharma.[1]

One of the principal works of the Kaulas, i.e., the most advanced of the Sāktas, is the Kulārṇava-Tantra,[2] which teaches that there are six forms of life (ācāra),[3] which are but an introduction to the Kulācāra, and that release from suffering, and the highest salvation can only be attained through the Kulācāra or Kula-Dharma.

When the Devī asks: "Whereby is release from suffering to be attained?" Śiva replies: Only through the knowledge of the Unity; for the creatures, surrounded by Māyā, are but as sparks emanating from the fire of Brahman. There are people who boast of their knowledge of Brahman, smear their bodies with ashes, and practise asceticism, but are yet only devoted to the pleasures of their senses. "Asses and other animals, go about naked without shame, whether they dwell in the house or in the forest: does this make them Yogins?" (I, 79). In order to become a Kaula a man should avoid all external things and strive only for true knowledge. Ritual and asceticism are of value only as long as a man has not yet recognised the truth. Kula-Dharma is Yoga (meditation) as well as Bhoga (enjoyment), but only for the man who has purified his mind and has control over his senses. We can well understand, the statement, so often repeated in the Tantras, that it is easier to ride on a drawn sword than to be a true Kaula, when in one and the same book we find, not only doctrines on the true knowledge of the Brahman and Yoga, but also the minutest details

1. Mahānirv-T., XIV, 180, transl. Avalon, p. 356; Cf. Majjhimanikāya, 28 (at the beginning).

2. Ed. by Tāranāth Vidyāratna in *Tāntrik Texts*, Vol. V., 1917.

3. These are Vedācāra. Vaiṣṇavācāra, Śaivācāra, Dakṣiṇācāra, Vāmācāra, Siddhāntācāra (or Yogācāra). Cf. Avalon, Tantra of the Great Liberation, Introduction, p. lxxviii ff.

concerning the preparation of twelve kinds of intoxicating drinks and everything connected with the "five essentials," which bestow bhukti (enjoyment) and mukti (salvation) at the same time.[1] "The Brahmin", we read, "should drink at all times, the warrior at the beginning of the battle, the Vaiśya when purchasing cows, the Śūdra when performing the funeral sacrifices." (V, 84). On the other hand, when these and similar rules have been formulated, we again read that true drinking is the union of Kuṇḍalinī Śakti with Ciccandra ("moon of thought"), others being merely imbibers of intoxicants, that the true "flesh-eater" is he who merges his thought in the highest Being, and a true 'fish-eater" is he who curbs his senses and unites them with the Ātman—"others merely kill animals"; and that true maithuna is the union of the highest Śakti or Kuṇḍalinī with the Ātman—"others are merely slaves to women. This comes at the close of Chapter V. In Chapter VII, however, the necessity of drink in the cult of Śakti is again emphasized. Ii is true that one should only drink in moderation, but this moderation is reckoned very liberally. "As long as the eye, the understanding, speech and the body do not become unsteady, a man may continue drinking, but drink taken in excess of this is the drinking of a brute beast" (VII 97). Though it is true that only the initiated are allowed to drink, it is to them that the oft-quoted maxim is addressed: "He is to drink, drink and drink again, till he falls to the ground, and when he has arisen, he is to drink yet again—then there will be no rebirth" (VII, 100).[2]

Another oft-quoted work of the Kaula School of the Śāktas is the "Head jewel of the Kula, " Kulacūḍāmani,[3] an example

1. Though the *surā* drink is extolled in the most extravagant fashion (V, 38 f.) the others are also recommended (V, 30). The eating of meat at the Kulapūjā is a permissible exception to the rule of non-killing (ahiṃsā).

2. The saying occurs frequently in the Tantras. According to Avalon these and similar verses do not refer to actual drinking, but to the symbolical "drinking" of the Yoga. This, however, is difficult to believe.

3. Ed. by Girisha Chandra Vedāntatīrtha, with an Introduction by A. K. Maitra in *Tāntrik Texts*, Vol. IV, 1915. The ritual of the Kaulas is also treated in the Nityaṣoḍaśi-Tantra, which is a part of the Vāmakeśvara-Tantra (publi. in *ĀnSS* Vol. 56, 1908) and the Ādiśvaracaritra, an analysis of which is given by L. Suali (*SIFI* Vol. 7).

of a Nigama in which Devī proclaims the doctrine and Śiva listens in the character of a pupil. In reality Śiva and Devī are one, and the latter says at the end of the book:

"Thou appearest now as the father, now in the form of the teacher, then thou becomest the son, then again a pupil. . . . Everything whatever exists in the world, consists of Śiva and Śakti. Thou, O God of gods, art all, and I, too, am all to all eternity. Thou art the teacher when I am the pupil, but then there shall be no distinction. Therefore, be thou the teacher, O Lord, and I shall be thy pupil, O Highest Lord!"

One of the more important texts of the Tantras is the Prapañcasāra-Tantra,[1] which is ascribed to the philosopher Śaṅkara or the god Śiva in his incarnation as Śaṅkara. Though the name Śaṅkara appears not infrequently in the Tantra literature, it is by no means certain that the texts attributed to him were really his work. Prapañca means "the expansion" the expanded universe," hence Prapañcasāra, "the Essence of the Universe."

The work begins with an account of the Creation.[2] This is followed by treatises on chronology, embryology, anatomy, physiology and psychology, which are no more "scientific" than the succeeding chapters on the occult doctrines of Kuṇḍalinī and the secret significance of the Sanskrit alphabet and the Bījas. According to the general teaching of the Tantras the human organism is a microcosm, a miniature copy of the universe, and contains countless canals (nāḍī) through which some secret power flows through the body. Connected with these canals there are six great centres (cakra) lying one above the other, which are also furnished with occult powers. The lowest and most important of these centres contains the Brahman in the form of a Liṅga and coiled round this Liṅga

---

1. Ed. by Tāranātha Vidyāratna in Tāntrik Texts, Vol. III, 1914. The author Śaṅkara is supposed to be identical with the commentator of the Nṛsiṃha-pūrvatāpanīya-Upaniṣad. Cf. Vidhusekhara Bhattacharya, *Ind. Hist. Qu.* I. 1925, p. 120.

2. On the Creation theories of the Tantras, see J. G. Woodroffe *Creation as explained in the Tantra* (read at the Silver Jubilee of the Chaitanya Library, Calcutta, 1915).

like a serpent, lies the Śakti called Kuṇḍalinī.[1] This Kuṇḍalinī is forced up into the highest centre by Sādhanā and Yoga, and then salvation is attained. The Bījas and Mantras,[2] that is, the letters and syllables and the formulas composed from them in all of which, according to an ancient doctrine already foreshadowed in the Brāhmaṇas and Upaniṣads,[3] a potent influence on the human organism and the universe lies concealed, are means to the attainment of the highest perfections (siddhi).

The chapters on the ritual for the consecration (dīkṣā), the worship of the mothers and the meditations on the Devī are of considerable significance from the point of view of the history of religion. The very prominent part played in the whole of this cult by the erotic element is exemplified in IX, 23 ff., where it is described how the wives of the gods, demons and demigods, compelled by Mantras, come to the sorcerer "scattering their ornaments in the intoxication of love, letting their silken draperies slip down, enveloping their forms in the net of their flying tresses, their every limb quivering with intolerable torments of love, the drops of sweat falling like pearls over the thighs, bosom and armpits, ... torn by the arrows of the love-god, their bodies immersed in the ocean of the passion of love, their lips tossed by the tempest of their deep-drawn breath" etc. Chapter XVIII teaches the Mantras and Dhyānas (meditations) for the worship of the love-god and his Śaktis, and the union of man and woman is presented as a mystical union of the ego (ahaṃkāra) with knowledge (Buddhi) and as a holy act of sacrifice. If the man honours

1. Kuṇḍalinī, "the coiled one." The theory of the Nāḍīs and Cakras is also to be found in the Varāha-Upaniṣad V, 22 ff. and in the Śāṇḍilya-Upaniṣad (Yoga Upanishads, ed. Mahādeva Śāstri, pp. 505 f., 518 ff.).

2. The monosyllabic meaningless sounds such as "hrīṃ," "śrīṃ," "krīm," "phaṭ," etc., are Bīja, "seeds." because they are the seed from which the fruit of magic powers (siddhi) is produced, and because they are the "seed" of the Mantras. Cf. Avalon, *The Tantra of the Great Liberation*, *Introd.* p. lxxxiii ff.

3. There is considerable truth in the contention of B. L. Mukherji (in Woodroffe, *Shakti and Shāktas*, p. 441 f.) that the occultism of the Tantras is already foreshadowed in the Brāhmaṇas, and that allusions to sexual intercourse play a prominent part in the symbolism of the Brāhmaṇas as well as in the Tantras.

his beloved wife in this manner, then, wounded by the arrows of the love-god, she will follow him as a shadow even into the other world (XVIII , 33). Chapter XXVIII is dedicated to Ardhanārīśvara, the god, who is half female — the right half of his body is in the form of Śiva who is represented as a wild-looking man, and the left half is his Śakti, represented as a voluptuous, woman,. Chapter XXXIII, with which the work originality seems to have closed, devotes its first part to a description of ceremonies to prevent childlessness, which is the result of carelessness in the worship of the gods and of scorning the wife. The second part deals with the relationship between teacher and pupil, which is of paramount importance in the Śakti religion.

The ritual and the Mantras described in this Tantra are not limited to the worship of the various forms of Devī and Śiva, but frequently also Viṣṇu and his avatāras are referred to. Chapter XXXVI contains a reflection on Viṣṇu Trailokyamohana ("the confounder of the triple world"). This description is replete with sensual fire: "Viṣṇu shines like millions of suns and is of supreme beauty. Full of kindness his glance rests upon Śrī, his consort, who embraces him lovingly. She, too, is incomparably beautiful. All the gods and demons and their wives do honour to the lofty, divine couple; but the divine women press around Viṣṇu full of the fiery longing of love, and exclaim: "Be our consort, our refuge, O Highest Lord !"[1]

The first part[2] of the Tantrarāja-Tantra bearing the proud title "King of Tantras" treats of the Śrīyantra, the "famous diagram," which consists of nine triangles and nine circles cleverly drawn one within the other and each one of which has a special mystical significance. By meditation with the aid of this Śrīyantra one attains knowledge of the Unity, i.e., the knowledge that everything in the world is one with the

1. XXXVI, 35-47, translated by Avalon in the Introduction, p. 61 ff.

2. This one alone (Part I, Chapters I-XVIII) has been published by M. Laksmana Shastri in *Tāntrik Texts*, Vol. VIII, 1918.

Devī. The Kālīvilāsa Tantra,[1] which belongs to the "prohibited" Tantras, i.e., those which are valid not for our age but only for a bygone period, is a later text. The attitude adopted towards the Pañcatattva ritual is very ambiguous indeed. All that we can glean clearly from the text is that there were two different schools of Śāktas, one of which condemned this ritual, while the other considered it as compulsory. A few chapters deal with Kṛṣṇa as the lover of Rādhā, who is identical with the goddess Kālī. The Jñānārṇava-Tantra[2] deals with the various kinds of Tantra ritual and the meditations on the various forms of Devī. The Kumārīpūjana, the worship of young maidens, is described as the highest sacrifice. The Śāradātilaka-Tantra,[3] written by Lakṣmaṇa Deśika in the 11th century, begins with a theory of the Creation and the origin of human speech, but treats chiefly of Mantras, Yantras, and magic.

In addition to the actual "revealed" Tantras there are innumerable manuals on separate branches of Tāntric ritual[4] and great collections compiled from the various Tantras.[5]

---

1. Ed. by Pārvatī Charana Tarkatirtha in *Tāntrik Texts*, Vol. VI, 1917. One chapter contains a Mantra in a dialect which is a mixture of Assamese and East Bengali, another contains Mantras with the words written backwards.

2. Published in *ĀnSS* No. 69, 1912.

3. An analysis of its contents by A. H. Ewing, *JAOS*, 23, 1902, p. 65 ff. Cf. Farquhar, *Outline*, p. 267.

4. Thus there are glossaries and dictionaries to explain the mysterious significance of the letters, Bijas and Mantras, as well as the Mudrās or positions of the fingers to be observed with the Yoga. A few of these texts (Mantrābhidhāna from the Rudrayāmala, Ekākṣurakośa by Puruṣottamadeva, Bījanighaṇṭu by Bhairava, Mātṛkānighaṇṭus by Mahīdhara and by Mādhava, Mudrānighaṇṭu from the Vāmakeśvara-Tantra) are published by A. Avalon, *Tāntrik Texts*, Vol. I, 1913. Cf. also Th. Zachariae, *Die indischen Wörterbucher* (Grundriss, I, 3 B, 1897) para. 27, and Leumann, *OC* VI, Leyden, Vol. III, p. 589 ff. The six centres (cakra) and the Kuṇḍalinī are treated in the Ṣaṭcakranirūpaṇa from the Śrītattvacintāmaṇi by Pūrṇānanda svāmi and the Pādukāpañcaka, both published by Tārānātha Vidyāratna in *Tāntrik Texts*, Vol. II, 1913 and translated into English by A. Avalon, *The Serpent Power*, 2nd ed., Madras 1924.

5. Thus the Tantrasamuccaya, very popular in Malabar, written by Nārāyaṇa of the Jayanta-maṅgala family of N. Travancore about 1426 A.D., published by T. Gaṇapati Śāstrī in *TSS* Nos. 67 and 71.

The earliest Nepalese manuscripts of Tantras date from the seventh to the ninth century,[1] and it is not very likely that this literature originated further back than the fifth or sixth century. Even in the latest portions of the Mahābhārata, with their frequent allusions to Itihāsas and Purāṇas, there is no mention of Tantras, and the Amarakośa, among the meanings of the word "tantra" does not give that of a religious book.[2] Neither do the Chinese pilgrims as yet mention the Tantras. In the seventh and eighth centuries they began to penetrate into Buddhism, and in the second half of the eighth century Buddhist Tantras were translated into Chinese[3] and in the ninth century into Tibetan also. The fact that the worship of Durgā, which plays so great a part in the Tantras, harks back to the later Vedic period,[4] does not prove that Tantrism and the Tantras are of an equally venerable age. There is no doubt that this goddess and her cult do unite traits of very different deities, Āryan as well as non-Āryan. It is probable, too, that the system of the Tantras adopted many characteristics

1. A Kubjikāmata-Tantra is said to date from the 7th century, and a Niśvāsatattva-Saṃhitā from the 8th century. A Parameśvaramata-Tantra was written in 858 A.D. Cf. Haraprasad, *Report*, I, p. 4.

2. Amarakośa, III, 182, gives for tantra the meaning siddhānta, which is really "a system of doctrines" in general, and not a particular class of texts. Cf. Wilson, *Works*, I, 250. The other Kośas, too, give all kinds of meanings for tantra, but not that of the sacred books of a sect. When mantra and tantra are mentioned side by side (Ahirbudhnya Saṃhitā XX, 5; Pañcatantra, text, simpl., ed. F. Kielhorn I, v, 70; Daśakumāracarita II, NSP edition, p. 81; mudrātantramantra-dhyānādibhiḥ) tantra means "magic rite," and mantra "incantation." The passage in the Daśakum, probably presupposes a knowledge of Tantras. Daṇḍin, however, did not live earlier than the 7th century A.D. The Bhāgavata-Purāṇa (IV, 24, 62; XI, 3, 47f., 5, 28; 31) is the first work to mention the Tantras as a class of works apart from the Veda.

3. According to L. Wieger, *Histoire des croyances religiouses et des opinions philosophiques en Chine*, Paris, 1917 (quoted by Woodroffe, *Shakti and Shākta*, p. 119 ff.), as early as in the 7th century. It is not likely that the nigamas mentioned side by side with the nighaṇṭu in Lalitavistara XII (ed. Lefmann, p. 156) are identical with the Tantras known as "nigama", as is the view of Avalon (Principles of Tantra, p. xli). As in Manu IV, 14; IX, 14, texts of Veda-exegesis are no doubt meant.

4. Jacobi in *ERE* V, 117 ff.

from non-Āryan and non-brahmanical cults.[1] On the other hand, some essential traits of the Tantras can be found as far back as in the Atharvaveda, as well as in the Brāhmaṇas and Upaniṣads. Śāktism was prevalent from the twelfth to the sixteenth century in Bengal especially among the aristocracy, and even at the present day its adherents are to be found not in the lower castes but among the educated.[2] On the whole the Tantras and the curious excrescences and degenerations of religion described in them, are not drawn from popular belief or from popular traditions either of the aboriginal inhabitants or of the Āryan immigrants, but they are the pseudo-scientific productions of theologians, in which the practice and theory of Yoga and doctrines of the monist (advaita) philosophy are seen mingled with the most extravagant symbolism and occultism.

Neither the Purāṇas nor the Tantras make enjoyable reading, and this is much more applicable to the latter. They are the work of inferior writers, and are often written in barbarous and ungrammatical Sanskrit. On the other hand neither the literary historian nor the student of religion can afford to pass them by in silence; for during centuries and even at the present time these writings are the spiritual food of millions of Indians. "The Purāṇas," says a learned Hindu,[3] "form an important portion of the religious literature of the Hindus, and, together with the Dharmaśāstras and Tantras, govern their conduct and regulate their religious observances at the present day. The Vedas are studied by the antiquarian, the Upaniṣads by the Philosopher; but every orthodox Hindu must have some knowledge of the Purāṇas, directly or vicariously, to shape

1. In the Jayadrathayāmala it is said that Parameśvari is to be worshipped in the house of a potter or oil-presser (who belong to the lowest classes). Cf. Haraprasād, *Report*, I, p. 16; *Catalogue of the Durbar Library, Nepal*, p. lxi.

2. The present-day Śāktas are probably for the most part such as will have none of the Pañcatattva ritual. At any rate, in Kashmir all the Śāktas abhor rites of this nature.

3. N. Mukhopadhyaya in the Introduction to his edition of the Kūrma-Purāṇa (*Bibl. Ind.*), p. xv.

his conduct and to perform the duties essential to his worldly and spiritual welfare." Whatever also may be our opinion of the literary, religious and moral value of the Tantras, the historian of Indian religion and culture cannot afford to neglect them, and from the point of view of comparative religion, too, they contain valuable material.

o o o

INDEX

PRONUNCIATION OF INDIAN WORDS AND NAMES WRITTEN IN ROMAN SCRIPT

Vowels :

(1) Pronounce r like a vowel as er in Scottish bak*er*

(2) In Sanskrit (not in Prākṛt) e and o are always long like m*a*ke and sp*o*ke without diphthongal influence.

Palatals :

(1) Pronounce c like *ch* in *ch*ild and j like *j* in *j*ust.

(2) Pronounce ṭ , ḍ , ṇ like t, d, n in English by rolling the tip of the tongue up and backward against the palate.

(3) Pronounce t, d, n as in French.

Sibilants :

Pronounce s palatal and s cerebral.

Nasals :

(1) Pronounce ṅ (guttural) like ng in English si*ng*.

(2) Pronounce ñ (palatal) like gn in French monta*gne*

(3) Pronounce ṃ (Anusvara) like n in French Jea*n*.

Aspirates :

h is written after k, g, c, j, ṭ, t, ḍ, and d to make them aspirate.

h is written after a vowel to produce a surd-effect, for example, pronounce devaḥ like devaḥ(a).